Anthropology
of
Religion

ANTHROPOLOGY OF RELIGION

A Handbook

Edited by
Stephen D. Glazier

Westport, Connecticut
London

The Library of Congress has cataloged the hardcover edition as follows:

Anthropology of religion : a handbook / edited by Stephen D. Glazier.
    p. cm.
    Includes bibliographical references and index.
    ISBN 0-313-28351-6 (alk. paper)
    1. Religion. I. Glazier, Stephen D.
  GN470.A55 1997
    306.6—dc20   96-10742

British Library Cataloguing in Publication Data is available.

A hardcover edition of *Anthropology of Religion* is available from
Greenwood Press, an imprint of Greenwood Publishing Group, Inc.
(ISBN 0-313-28351-6)

Library of Congress Catalog Card Number: 96-10742
ISBN: 0-275-96560-0 (pbk.)

First published in 1997

Praeger Publishers, 88 Post Road West, Westport, CT 06881
An imprint of Greenwood Publishing Group, Inc.

Printed in the United States of America

The paper used in this book complies with the
Permanent Paper Standard issued by the National
Information Standards Organization (Z39.48-1984).

10 9 8 7 6 5 4 3 2 1

CONTENTS

Introduction

Stephen D. Glazier

[Meyer Fortes] once invited a rainmaker to perform the ceremony for him for an attractive fee, and the officiant in question replied, "Don't be a fool, whoever makes a rain-making ceremony in the dry season?"

Stanley J. Tambiah (1990)

If a major goal of anthropology is—to borrow James W. Fernandez's (1985: 2) felicitous phrase—"to find the strange in the familiar" and "to find the familiar in the strange," then the anthropology of religion should be at the center of the anthropological enterprise. We are not there, or at least many anthropologists don't think that we are there. The valiant efforts of Morton Klass and others to establish a section within the American Anthropological Association have been highly contested, and many anthropologists of religion express concern that their subject area has become "marginalized" within the anthropology curriculum. With the notable exceptions of the programs at Princeton, Drew, Rice, California, and Michigan, a prospective Ph.D. student might experience considerable difficulty in putting together a plan of study that focuses on the anthropology of religion.

Some might say that the anthropology of religion is in the doldrums. Others might say it is at a crossroads. Still others may feel we are—like Meyer Fortes's informant—asked to be rainmakers in the dry season. Fewer new textbooks in the anthropology of religion are published each year, and much of what is available for classroom use is ten, twenty, and sometimes seventy years old (e.g., Robert H. Lowie [1924]; W. W. Howells [1948]; E. E. Evans-Pritchard

[1965]; Annemarie de Waal Malefijt [1968]; Paul Radin [1937]; Anthony F. C. Wallace [1966]; William Lessa and Evon Z. Vogt [1979]; Sam Gill [1982]; Edward Norbeck [1961, 1974]; John Middleton [1967a, 1967b, 1967c]).

Still, interest in the anthropological study of religion remains strong. As Reynolds and Tanner (1995: 3) boldly proclaim: "Against expectations, religion has, in the 1990s, become a topic of everyday conversation and concern." Scholars from many fields read anthropology of religion texts with great interest, and anthropologists of religion are cited frequently in books and journals in a variety of disciplines—perhaps more so by scholars outside anthropology than within it. To some, the anthropology of religion may be in the midst of a golden age, but—to appropriate a quote that Clifford Geertz (1985: 624) attributes to Randall Jarrell—"the problem with Golden Ages is that people in them go about complaining that everything looks yellow." Perhaps this *is* the anthropology of religion's golden age, and anthropologists of religion simply have failed to recognize it as such.

It is encouraging that many of the aforementioned textbooks (Lowie, Howells, de Waal Malefijt, Radin, Wallace, among others), while dated, continue to earn a place on publishers' lists, which, given the current realities of academic publishing, indicates that they continue to sell adequate copies. Contrary to Morton Klass (1995: xi) who finds these earlier texts not only outdated but "based on theoretical perceptions and assumptions that have long since been jettisoned in most other areas of anthropological concern and activity," I believe that these older texts may serve as valuable starting points for anyone wishing to learn something about the anthropological study of religion. Robert H. Lowie's *Primitive Religion* (1924), for example, remains the model for all modern textbooks in the anthropology of religion, while Paul Radin (1937) provides an unusually sensitive introduction to Amerindian religions; Edward Norbeck's 1974 text—at a mere seventy-four pages—contains all the essentials; and Annemarie de Waal Malefijt (1968)—probably the most thorough introduction to the anthropology of religion ever published—was reissued in paperback by Waveland Press in 1989.

In addition, there are notable exceptions to the aforementioned trend of reprinting old texts in the recent and welcome publications of Klass (1995), Firth (1995), Jacob Pandian (1991), Child and Child (1993), Lehmann and Myers (1985, 1993), Reynolds and Tanner (1995), and Brian Morris (1987), which may serve as competent, updated assessments of the field. All of the above texts are appropriate for undergraduate use, although Brian Morris may assume too much background in philosophy and the history of social science.

As Mark Kline Taylor (1986: 77–78) and Brian Morris (1987: 28) have pointed out, in the nineteenth century every would-be theorist—and especially theorists of an evolutionary bent—provided his or her own theory of religion. For many nineteenth-century theorists, religion was considered to be little more than an archaic mode of thinking from which modern science, law, and political forms emerged but now was to be safely discarded. For twentieth-century scholars, however, religion is seldom seen as a throwback to earlier modes of thought, interpreted as evidence for what Lucien Levy-Bruhl (1966) termed ''pre-logical mentality,'' or understood primarily as science manqué. Religion in the twentieth century is understood in its own terms as—in Talal Asad's (1993: 27) words— ''a distinctive space of human practice and belief which cannot be reduced to any other.'' This cannot help but have profound ramifications for religious people, both ''civilized'' and ''primitive''; and of course it has implications for those who would study those religions as well.

It has never been difficult to make a case for the significance of religion in human life. Religion is a universal. It has been found in all societies studied by anthropologists and is one of the hallmarks of human creativity as well as a tribute to humankind's nearly infinite resourcefulness and adaptability in coping with the problems of daily existence. As William White Howells (1948: 16) so aptly put it: ''Man's life is hard, very hard. And he knows it, poor soul; that is the vital thing. He knows that he is forever confronted with the Four Horsemen—death, famine, disease, and the malice of other men.''

As in past generations, most of the leading anthropologists of the day (e.g., Clifford Geertz, Claude Lévi-Strauss, Weston La Barre, James Clifford, Vincent Crapanzano, James W. Fernandez, Victor Turner, Mary Douglas, Sherry B. Ortner, Jim Boon, Roy Rappaport, Richard and Sally Price, Benson Saler, Melford Spiro, and Barbara and Dennis Tedlock) continue to devote more than passing attention to the subject of religion. For each of these eminent anthropologists, religion has been central to their respective research and writing, and in fields such as religious studies, performance studies, drama, and comparative literature—where theories of ritual developed by the late Victor Turner have been prominent—there is a renewed interest in the anthropology of religion.

Major shifts in the subject matter of the anthropology of religion are reflected in the content of this handbook. Had such a reference work been commissioned twenty years ago, a majority of the contributions (as in Lessa and Vogt 1979; Leslie 1960; Middleton, 1967a, 1967b, 1967c) would have dealt with tribal religions in Africa, Asia, and Oceania. For example, of the fifty-six essays contained in Lessa and Vogt, thirty-one deal with tribal religions. Such would no longer be the case. A majority of chapters in this volume are—to again borrow Jim Fernandez's (1985) felicitous phrase—more about finding the ''strange in the familiar'' than about finding the ''familiar in the strange.'' Jim Birckhead, whose research now focuses on the spiritual life of Australian Aborigines, has chosen instead to focus on his equally ''exotic'' American fieldwork among snake handlers. A majority of the chapters in this handbook examine religion from a metropolitan (''Great Tradition'') context, occasionally touching upon religions in tribal settings but usually for comparative purposes. The content of this handbook, thus, reflects a shifting focus within the anthropology of religion itself.

Another major change is that even in tribal settings anthropologists increasingly find themselves in competition with other social scientists. In many cases, the groups studied by anthropologists are no different from the groups that have traditionally been studied by political scientists, economists, sociologists, and others; and participant observation—once seen as unique to the anthropological enterprise—is no longer exclusively the domain of anthropologists. Indeed, some of anthropology of religion's leading practitioners such as Clifford Geertz, Vincent Crapanzano, and Melford Spiro have devoted almost all of their respective careers to studying religion within the context of developing nations such as Indonesia, Morocco, and Burma.

In "Waddling In," Geertz (1985) openly laments—with his usual perspicacity and style—the passing of the anthropological monopoly on the interpretation of isolated tribal peoples. He acknowledges that anthropology—particularly ethnography—has changed dramatically over the past twenty years and that it is highly unlikely that future generations of anthropologists will have the opportunity to study a previously uncharted tribal religion, publish the definitive interpretation of that religion, and—as in the cases of E. E. Evans-Pritchard's masterful work on the Azande (1937) and the Nuer (1956) or Bronislaw Malinowski's (1935) classic studies of Trobriand garden magic—remain *the* "authority" on that religion for the remainder of his or her life. Challengers abound. For the current generation of fieldworkers, there is a strong possibility that no matter how remote the group, another anthropologist will have "just left" or be "on the way" to study them and that ethnographers will find themselves conducting their research in the midst of anthropologists and alongside other social scientists. Natives, too, are getting into the act and may even write their own books, sometimes beating the ethnographers to the punch. While increased competition may be disturbing to some anthropologists, this increased competition and the resulting "accountability" cannot but represent a healthy state of affairs and is a vast improvement over the imperial stance that sometimes informed earlier ethnographic research.

Such an imperial stance was assumed in the works of Edward B. Tylor (1873: 11) who, in the first volume of *Primitive Culture*, envisioned the anthropologist as sitting high on a hill looking down on a vast array of human activities. Today Tylor's stance is no longer seen as possible or desirable. Perhaps no hills were found that are high enough to afford such a view? More likely, anthropologists of the 1990s lack the confidence in their own positions to make such sweeping pronouncements. Contemporary anthropologists of religion—like all contemporary ethnographers—have been forced into the position of either "saying more with considerably less authority" or "saying less with considerably more authority." Social scientists have long struggled with this dilemma, but their deliberations have largely been left unstated. Now it is necessary for anthropologists to make their deliberations more explicit, and the latter policy ("saying less with more authority") has become the accepted policy. The anthropology of religion will be the beneficiary. This is not to detract from the accomplishments of an earlier generation of fieldworkers like E. E. Evans-Pritchard but simply to acknowledge that contemporary ethnographers among the same

groups—like John W. Burton's (1981) research on the religions of Nilotic pastoralists—have of necessity couched their findings in more modest terms.

But I digress. This volume is not primarily a textbook, nor is it an exposition
on the state of the art in contemporary anthropology, although the reader may
find elements of both within its pages. This is first and foremost a reference
book intended as a practical guide for professional anthropologists and graduate
students preparing to undertake primary research in the anthropology of religion.
While it may appear that greater attention is given to methods than to theory,
seldom can one effectively separate the two. In the anthropological study of
religion, it has often been the case that method flowed from theory rather than
theory from method. But this, too, is changing.

A secondary goal has been to assemble in one place many of the key findings
and methods in the anthropology of religion. It is hoped that this volume may
also prove useful to others who are not specialists in anthropology but have
collected, or plan to collect, data on religious rituals and beliefs that may require
systematic analysis from an anthropological point of view. As is to be expected
in a reference book, references are extensive.

A third—and no less important—goal is to build bridges between anthropologists studying religion and theologians, psychologists, psychiatrists,
economists, neurophysiologists, philosophers, political scientists, historians, sociologists, and scholars in the history of religions.

Anthropology of Religion: A Handbook is comparable in style and format to
John J. Honingmann's seminal *Handbook of Social and Cultural Anthropology*
(1973) and Tim Ingold's *Companion Encyclopedia of Anthropology* (1994). But
while Honingmann's and Ingold's volumes attempt to deal with *all* major topics
within the field of anthropology, this handbook deals *only* with the anthropology
of religion and topics that are directly related to the anthropology of religion.
Currently, there are no handbooks and/or guides dealing exclusively with religion. In reviewing the literature, it is apparent that few books of this nature
have been published and that there is great need for a volume such as this
offering in-depth and ''up-to-date'' surveys of major theoretical and methodological issues.

While most contributors to this volume have drawn from their previous
publications, all chapters are original works and were written especially for this
handbook. This is not a reader in the tradition of Leslie (1960), Lessa and Vogt
(1979), Middleton (1967a, 1967b, 1967c), or Lehmann and Myers (1985, 1993).
While considerable ethnographic data are included in each chapter, these are not
specialized ethnographic reports.

Serendipity played no small part in gathering the work now before you. Chapters were both commissioned and volunteered. I am pleased to have been able
to include here the work of both junior and well-established scholars. Although
chapters were written to stand alone and were composed independently, even
contributors addressing vastly disparate topics cite one another's works and raise
common concerns. In light of the fact that many contributors have never met

face-to-face, I continue to be impressed at how well these chapters flow together. All have undergone multiple updates and revisions. It has been my good fortune to have attracted such a diligent and gifted group of scholars united by a common and abiding interest in furthering the anthropological study of religion in all of its aspects. Credit for the quality of this volume rests squarely with them.

This reference book is not intended to be an exhaustive survey. It is not, and never was intended to be, an encyclopedic treatment. It is, however, intended to adequately reflect dominant concerns within the subdiscipline of the anthropology of religion. Authors were encouraged to provide overviews of their respective topics but were also allowed the freedom to present their own points of view. This makes for more interesting essays and, I believe, keeps the book's material at the "cutting edge." While not every topic in the anthropology of religion has received full coverage here, a second book will be published by Greenwood Press in 1998. Between these two books, we hope to have touched on all major issues in the anthropological study of religion and to have given considerable attention to a number of "side issues" not usually covered in edited works such as this.

The volume begins, appropriately enough, with Jim Birckhead's masterful "Reading 'Snake Handling': Critical Reflections," a highly personal account of Birckhead's research experiences in Appalachia. A sensitive and down-to-earth appraisal of the research process, Birckhead deftly chronicles his reactions to his informants and other researchers as well as their reactions to him. His chapter explores the increasingly blurred boundaries between scientific and popular discourse that challenge all ethnographic enterprises. This chapter was chosen to be the first as Birckhead's contribution so artfully encompasses many of the major difficulties encountered and demands peculiar to research in the anthropology of religion and touches on many of the theoretical and methodological issues raised by other contributors to this volume. Birckhead's work is notable for its breadth, unusual candor, and keen artistic and ethical sensibilities.

Birckhead traces the various—and often undocumented—influences on his research: predecessors (Weston La Barre); other researchers (Steven Kane, T. G. Burton, Loring M. Danforth); the media (movies like *Cape Fear*); personal relationships and their psychological consequences for both researchers and informants (Wengle 1988); compiling, reading, and rereading field notes (Sanjek 1990); going over lists of appointments; and the unanticipated complications that arise when informants read what we write about them (Brettell 1993). He even reproduces sections from his own field notes and letters from the field to give the reader insight into the "nuts and bolts" and daily activities of his research agenda.

Special problems of doing research at home are raised by Melinda Bollar Wagner in her "The Study of Religion in American Society." Wagner has conducted two field studies "at home" among metaphysical movements in the United States and, most recently, among members of the home school movement. The second project is even closer to home for Wagner who lives and works in the midst of the "Bible Belt." Traditionally, ethnographers have struggled to overcome "distance" between themselves and their informants and sought to establish and maintain rapport with informants perceived to be fundamentally different from themselves. In conducting anthropological fieldwork at home, however, obvious differences are no longer apparent, and it is sometimes necessary to reestablish a degree of distance in order to successfully complete one's research agenda. This can also lead to problems after the work is completed and the results are published. Wagner's chapter addresses a common difficulty—one she shares with an increasing number of anthropologists and sociologists of religion: being perceived as a potential convert while simultaneously attempting to conduct one's research.

The issue is not only one of objectivity. As Jim Birckhead astutely points out in his chapter, there are pluses and minuses inherent in any research situation, and the issue of belief itself is a thorny one in the history of anthropology and religion (cf. Needham 1972; Taylor 1986; Saler 1993; Clarke and Byrne 1993: 79–97—see especially their treatment of theologian John Hicks). In *The Elementary Forms of Religious Life*, Émile Durkheim ultimately concluded that belief is more pivotal than reason in the determination of human affairs. Science, he suggested, always lags behind belief because belief "is before all else an impetus to action, while science, no matter how far it may be pushed, always remains at a distance from this" (Durkheim 1912/1995: 479). According to Durkheim, science is always unsatisfactory because it advances too slowly, while life events are demanding and cannot wait for scientific conclusions.

Belief also enters into the discussion in James Lett's provocative "Science, Religion, and Anthropology." Lett forcefully argues that anthropologists have ignored or ingeniously skirted the impact and implications of their own personal beliefs and/or disbeliefs on the research process itself. In this, he moves considerably beyond Roy Clouser's (1991) analysis of the hidden role of religious beliefs in the formation of various social theories. Lett's argument is considerably more subtle than it might appear at first reading. Ultimately, he chides anthropologists for being unable or unwilling to take a position on whether or not religion is a "good thing." Of course, whether understood in terms of behaviors, beliefs, sentiments, or symbols, religion is truly not a "thing" like a pencil, a desk, or a chair. It is—as psychoanalyst Jacque Lacan so convincingly argued (cf. Crapanzano 1978)—the very articulation of the concept "religion" itself that plays a major determining role in its manufacture and subsequent significance. Indeed, it is but rarely when anthropologists step back to examine the concept religion itself as Lett has done.

In *Imagining Religion*, Jonathan Z. Smith (1982: ix) goes to the heart of the matter when he argues that "while there is a staggering amount of data, of phenomena, of human experiences and expressions that might be characterized in one culture or another, by one criteria or another, as religious—*there is no data for religion*." Anthropologist Paul Radin (1937: 58) reached a similar conclusion when he admonished potential religious researchers to keep in mind that religion "comes from life and is directed towards life. In itself it is nothing."

What is true for the study of religion is also true for the study of magic. In his final publication, Gregory Bateson (Bateson and Bateson 1987: 55) elegantly summarized the modern psychological perspective regarding the efficacy of magic: "I believe that all spells, mediations, incantations, procedures of sympathetic and contagious magic, and the like, do indeed work—but they work upon the practitioner." Bateson further qualified his position by emphasizing that none of these procedures has any effect on any other person at all unless that other participates in the spell or suggestion. Magic, for Bateson, follows its own logic.

Michael F. Brown's chapter "Thinking about Magic" explores the logic of magic and bridges the increasingly narrow gap between tribal consciousness and the dominant, skeptical worldview of modern psychology and the cognitive sciences. Entering into the ongoing "Rationality Debate" first outlined by Sir James G. Frazer (1890/1935), elaborated by Bronislaw Malinowski (1935), refined by Bryan R. Wilson (1970), and continued to the present in the writings of Robin Horton (1993: 122–123) and Gilbert Lewis (1994: 563–590), Brown makes a careful, detailed analysis of magic and its logic among the Arguaruna of Peru as well as providing a lucid discussion of the approaches of Malinowski, Tambiah (1990), and Mauss (1972). Whatever the ultimate outcome of this ongoing scholarly debate, it is apparent that whether magic is to be seen as rational or obsessive, logical or—following Levy-Bruhl (1966)—"prelogical," there is general agreement that magic is "culture specific" and that outsiders cannot fully comprehend magic without reference to its underlying cultural assumptions. A more detailed discussion of Brown's ideas can be found in his *Tsewa's Gift: Magic and Meaning in an Amazonian Society* (1985).

The anthropology of religion and the study of ritual are very much interrelated. The connections, of course, are obvious, and as Ronald Grimes (1990: 1) points out: "Whoever first exclaimed that religion is not thought but danced echoed a scholarly as well as a popular attitude." The next part—under the skilled editorship of Bobby C. Alexander—looks at religious ritual from an anthropological perspective. Alexander took sole responsibility for this part and has provided his own informative introduction. It is of interest that while anthropologists have had a long-standing interest in ritual forms within tribal settings, many recent advances in ritual studies (e.g., Smith 1982; Bell 1992; Grimes 1990) have come not from anthropology but from the discipline of religious studies. Therefore, it is not surprising that the majority of Alexander's contributors—including Alexander himself—have been employed in Departments of Religious Studies and that most are active in the "Ritual Studies" section of the American Academy of Religion. This is an accurate reflection of the field itself. One would be hard-pressed to imagine a group of topical chapters that more accurately represent the excitement, the varied perspectives, and the multitude of approaches that encompasses contemporary ritual studies.

Part III, "Little and Great Traditions," deals with major world religions (Islam, Hinduism, Buddhism, and Christianity) and their impact and interaction with local religious traditions (Leslie 1960). Robert Redfield (1953) is usually credited with bringing the distinction between Little and Great Traditions to the forefront of anthropological theory, but there is ample evidence that nineteenth-century theorists such as E. B. Tylor (1873) and Sir James G. Frazer (1890/1935) also struggled with these same distinctions but reached very different conclusions (Ackerman 1987; Asad 1993: 59).

Not all researchers have been comfortable with the Little/Great dichotomy. As anthropologists became more committed to a "community studies" approach in the 1930s and 1940s, old solutions seemed less satisfactory. Benson Saler (1993) correctly points out that the distinction between Little and Great Traditions is a highly malleable one, and many so-called Great Traditions have themselves evolved over many centuries out of Little Traditions and are highly heterogeneous. It could be argued effectively that no individual has ever fully participated in a Great Tradition. Even the pope lives and acts within the Little Tradition of Vatican City, which bears a less-than-perfect resemblance to world Catholicism or even to the brands of Catholicism practiced in much of the Italian countryside (Kertzer 1988). Many Great Traditions and Little Traditions share a common origin. A further complicating factor is that all Great Traditions begin as Little Traditions, and all Little Traditions are affected and effected by Great Traditions; for example, the *umbilicus urbis* of Rome is essentially the *poteau metan* (center pole) of Haitian vodun, and vice versa (cf. Eliade 1959). While I knew this to be true intellectually (I am a specialist in African-American religions), it was brought home to me personally when I happened to visit the Roman Forum at the same time as a tour group from Haiti. Several women pointed at the *umbilicus urbis*, exclaiming, "*Poteau metan, poteau metan!*"

In "The Anthropology of Islam," Gregory Starrett provides an unusually comprehensive survey and assessment of ethnographic research on Islamic societies. As has been frequently noted, anthropology's treatment of Islam often reflects Western biases toward the supposedly inscrutable "East" (Asad 1993). Since the typical American view of Islam is that it is monolithic, one is struck by the tremendous religious diversity so systematically recorded by generations of anthropologists. Monolithic Islam, Starrett's chapter suggests, may only exist in the eye of the beholder and not in the mind of the believer.

Cynthia Keppley Mahmood's "Hinduism in Context" raises a number of related, yet largely unresolved, issues in the anthropological study of Hinduism: What does it mean to talk about "Hinduism" as if it were a uniform religious tradition? What does it mean to speak of "Hindus" as if they were a readily definable social group? And what has been the role of religion in the creation of ethnic and cultural identities in India? Mahmood introduces frequently ignored data on the historical connections between Hinduism and Buddhism in India and—in so doing—sheds new light on hitherto unexplored relationships between two Great Traditions (Hinduism and Buddhism) and various Little

Traditions in Asia. Most significantly, she calls into question the prevailing notion of Hindu tolerance of other religions as presented in the literature. The issues she raises will doubtless inform future scholarship in the region.

Todd T. Lewis's "Buddhist Communities: Historical Precedents and Ethnographic Paradigms" provides both a comprehensive bibliographic survey and a methodological statement addressing special problems associated with the anthropological study of Buddhism. The connection between so-called true Buddhism and "village" Buddhism is a thorny one (Southwold 1982: 137–138). Lewis's exceptional grasp of the literature as well as firsthand fieldwork experience provide him with extraordinary breadth and refreshing "common sense" in his assessment of the works of his predecessors and contemporaries.

Mary I. O'Connor's "The Pilgrimage to Magdalena" argues convincingly that the distinction between Little and Great Traditions remains useful in some Latin American contexts, especially with respect to anthropological studies of pilgrimages (see Morinis 1992). As N. Ross Crumrine and Alan Morinis point out in their introduction to *Pilgrimage in Latin America*, Latin American pilgrimages combine sources rooted in a diversity of religious traditions and represent a coming together (and/or juxtaposition) of Roman Catholicism and pre-Columbian religious thought. Researchers, like O'Connor, who examine any facet of any Latin American pilgrimage—whether from the perspectives of ritual, belief, or personnel—are "immediately struck by the multiple influences that have shaped the ideas, roles, structures, and performances of these ceremonies" (Crumrine and Morinis 1991: 4).

The final section, Part IV, emphasizes cognitive and symbolic approaches to religion, focusing on the various types of religious consciousness and the relationship between forms of religious consciousness and spiritual healing. Michael Winkelman's "Altered States of Consciousness and Religious Behavior" draws on the extensive cross-cultural data available in the Human Area Relations Files, while Joan B. Townsend's "Shamanism" draws on a vast ethnographic literature as well as her own fieldwork among Tibetan shamans, Amerindian shamans, and neoshamans in North America. It is doubtful, however, that Townsend would be willing to accept the distinction Jacob Pandian draws in Chapter 19 between the "shamanistic-sacred self" and the "priestly sacred self." She might also take issue with Pandian's assertion that shamans lack potential for sociopolitical and economic authority. The ethnographic record is replete with examples of shamans who accumulated vast wealth and political power. In the Lesser Antilles, for example, Island-Carib shamans were among the wealthiest members of their respective societies and successfully challenged Island-Carib chiefs (Glazier 1980).

Winkelman and Townsend deal explicitly with trance, spirit possession, and altered states of consciousness as highly significant manifestations within a multitude of cultural and religious contexts. However, their definitions of shamanism differ. Both authors' works exemplify what Janice Boddy (1994: 427) has identified as the "increased attention to local contexts, cultural logics, human imagination and creativity in recent anthropological studies of consciousness."

In what may well be her only unprophetic statement concerning the future direction of anthropology of religion, the late Annemarie de Waal Malefijt (1968: 103) wrote: "The greatest accomplishment of twentieth century anthropology is the establishment of a clear distinction between man as a biological organism and man as a creator and bearer of culture and thus also of religion. The importance of this distinction cannot be overestimated." Since 1968, however, this once-clear distinction—if indeed it was ever truly established—has again become blurred and spawned a myriad of theoretical and methodological trends. The final three chapters address some of these recent theoretical and methodological advances.

Charles D. Laughlin, Stewart Guthrie, and Jacob Pandian focus on interconnections among religious forms, cognitive processes, and the fabrication of meaning. In "The Cycle of Meaning: Some Methodological Implications of Biogenetic Structural Theory," Laughlin provides a promising new synthesis of anthropological and neurophenomenological theories of consciousness that will have widespread implications for the anthropological study of religion. His primary achievement is in suggesting ways in which symbols operate neurocognitively to channel meanings within cultural and religious systems.

Stewart Guthrie's "The Origin of an Illusion" updates major arguments contained in his 1993 book *Faces in the Clouds: A New Theory of Religion* and could profitably be read in conjunction with James Lett's contribution. While Guthrie's main thesis is simple, elegant, and far from new, few anthropologists have taken his argument to its logical and forceful conclusion: that *all* religions are essentially anthropomorphic because they postulate deities in or behind natural phenomena and credit nature with the human capacity for symbolic action. In this assertion, Guthrie joins in a welcome—and in this century unprecedented—resurgence of interest in naturalistic explanations of religion (Boyer 1993, 1994; Horton 1993). Guthrie, however, argues that earlier theorists did not take the thesis of anthropomorphism far enough and that modern theorists (Boyer and Horton) fail to recognize its full espistemic status and implications (cf. Yonan 1995: 31–34). Perhaps Guthrie's greatest insights flow from his keen recognition that human beings never just "see" things but always "see as." Everything is seen in terms of something else.

Guthrie, who began his anthropological career studying new religious movements in Japan (Guthrie 1988), takes issue with the classical position of Emile Durkheim (1912/1995: 45) who—in *The Elementary Forms of Religious Life*—adamantly asserted that Buddhism was *not* anthropomorphic. Guthrie (1993: 191) emphasizes to the contrary—and in agreement with Todd T. Lewis—that "Buddhism in fact has many gods from local *bodisattvas* to the Buddha himself."

Jacob Pandian's "The Sacred Integration of the Cultural Self: An Anthropological Approach to the Study of Religion" provides a fitting final chapter for this volume. While Guthrie and Laughlin focus on cognitive processes, Pandian examines the special qualities inherent in symbols. He argues—paralleling Laughlin and Guthrie—that the foundation of all religions is in symbolizing human identity in terms of what he calls "super-natural characteristics" or whenever humans posit qualities or attributes that go beyond the physical and/or natural world. Pandian's chapter—like his textbook *Culture, Religion, and the Sacred Self* (1991)—ably explores complex connections between cultural representations or "projective systems" of the supernatural (à la Guthrie) and cultural representations of human identity. Religion, Pandian argues, does not so much eliminate suffering and death as it eliminates blatant contradictions between cultural formulations of suffering and the "symbolic self."

In closing, I would like to thank George Butler, acquisitions editor at Greenwood Press, for suggesting this volume and allowing me to serve as its editor. Most of all, however, I thank him for his faith in me and his extraordinary patience in awaiting the completed product. Reference books such as this always take longer to complete than anticipated. This is a longer work than originally planned; there are more authors than projected; reference sections are quite extensive; and I have attempted, whenever possible, to keep all chapters at the "cutting edge." As noted, a second volume of related topics will appear in 1998.

Finally, I wish to thank my teachers in anthropology of religion for giving me the background and confidence to undertake a project such as this. Were it not for the dedicated efforts of Stan Mumford, Sam Blizzard, Leslie G. Desmangles, Carl Saalbach, Vincent Crapanzano, Hildred Geertz, Jim Fernandez, James Loder, Albert J. Raboteau, Seth Leacock, Jim Faris, Bob Bee, and Ron Wintrob, I would know much less of the anthropology of religion than I now do. My wife, Rosemary C. Glazier, and my daughter, Katie, have both been extremely supportive of this project. I am also grateful to Professor Murray L. Wax of Washington University at St. Louis (whose own work will appear in the next volume) for his valuable suggestions concerning a number of the chapters and to my student assistant, Gayle Smith, who read and commented on a number of the chapters. Dr. Ken Nikels, graduate dean at the University of Nebraska, and the University of Nebraska Research Services Council provided much-needed financial support to help cover editorial expenses.

REFERENCES

Ackerman, Robert. 1987. *J. G. Frazer: His Life and Work.* New York: Cambridge University Press.

Asad, Talal. 1993. *Genealogies of Religion: Discipline and Reasons of Power in Christianity and Islam.* Baltimore: Johns Hopkins University Press.

Bateson, Gregory, and Mary Catherine Bateson. 1987. *Angels Fear: Toward an Epistemology of the Sacred.* New York: Macmillan Publishing Company.

Bell, Catherine. 1992. *Ritual Theory, Ritual Practice.* New York: Oxford.

Boddy, Janice. 1994. "Spirit Possession Revisited: Beyond Instrumentality." *Annual Review of Anthropology* 23: 407–434.

Boyer, Pascal, editor. 1993. *Cognitive Aspects of Religious Symbolism*. New York: Cambridge University Press.

Boyer, Pascal. 1994. *The Naturalness of Religious Ideas: A Cognitive Theory of Religion*. Berkeley: University of California Press.

Brettell, Caroline B., editor. 1993. *When They Read What We Write: The Politics of Ethnography*. Westport, CT: Bergin and Garvey.

Brown, Michael F. 1985. *Tsewa's Gift: Magic and Meaning in an Amazonian Society*. Washington, D.C.: Smithsonian Institution Press.

Burton, John W. 1981. *God's Ants: A Study of Atuot Religion*. St. Augustin, West Germany: Anthropos Institute.

Child, Alice B., and Irvin L. Child. 1993. *Religion and Magic in the Life of Traditional Peoples*. Englewood Cliffs, NJ: Prentice-Hall.

Clarke, Peter B., and Peter Byrne. 1993. *Religion Defined and Explained*. New York: St. Martin's Press.

Clouser, Roy A. 1991. *The Myth of Religious Neutrality: An Essay on the Hidden Role of Religious Belief in Theories*. Notre Dame: University of Notre Dame Press.

Crapanzano, Vincent. 1978. "Reading Lacan's *Ecrits*." *Canto* 2: 283–291.

Crumrine, N. Ross, and Alan Morinis, editors. 1991. *Pilgrimage in Latin America*. Westport, CT: Greenwood Press.

de Waal Malefijt, Annemarie. 1968. *Religion and Culture: An Introduction to Anthropology of Religion*. New York: Macmillan. (Reprinted by Waveland Press in 1989)

Durkheim, Emile. 1912/1995. *The Elementary Forms of Religious Life*. A New Translation by Karen E. Fields. New York: Free Press.

Eliade, Mircea. 1959. *The Sacred and the Profane: The Nature of Religion*. New York: Harcourt, Brace.

Evans-Pritchard, E. E. 1937. *Witchcraft, Oracles and Magic among the Azande*. Oxford: Clarendon Press.

Evans-Pritchard, E. E. 1956. *Nuer Religion*. Oxford: Clarendon Press.

Evans-Pritchard, E. E. 1965. *Theories of Primitive Religion*. Oxford: Clarendon Press.

Fernandez, James W. 1985. Foreword to *Magic, Witchcraft, and Religion: An Anthropological Study of the Supernatural*. Palo Alto: Mayfield Publishing Company.

Firth, Raymond. 1995. *Religion: A Humanist Interpretation*. New York: Routledge.

Frazer, Sir James G. 1890/1935. *The Golden Bough: A Study of Magic and Religion*. New York: Macmillan.

Geertz, Clifford. 1985. "Waddling In." *Times Literary Supplement* (June 7): 623–624.

Geertz, Clifford. 1995. *After the Fact: Two Countries, Four Decades, One Anthropologist*. Cambridge, MA: Harvard University Press.

Gill, Sam D. 1982. *Beyond the Primitive: The Religion of Nonliterate Peoples*. Englewood Cliffs, NJ: Prentice-Hall.

Glazier, Stephen D. 1980. "The Boye in Island-Carib Culture." *La antropología americanista en al actualidad: Homenaje al Raphael Girard*. Francis Polo Sifontes, Jorge Luis Vallacorta, and Horacio Figueroa, editors. Mexico City: Editores Mexicanas Unidos.

Grimes, Ronald L. 1990. *Ritual Criticism: Case Studies in Its Practice, Essays on Its Theory*. Columbia: University of South Carolina Press.

Guthrie, Stewart E. 1988. *A Japanese New Religion: Rishho Kosei-kai in a Mountain Hamlet*. Ann Arbor: University of Michigan Center for Japanese Studies.

Guthrie, Stewart E. 1993. *Faces in the Clouds: A New Theory of Religion*. New York: Oxford University Press.

Honingmann, John J., editor. 1973. *Handbook of Social and Cultural Anthropology*. Chicago: Rand McNally and Company.

Horton, Robin. 1993. *Patterns of Thought in Africa and the West*. New York: Cambridge University Press.

Howells, William White. 1948. *The Heathens: Primitive Man and His Religion*. Garden City, NY: Doubleday. (Reprinted by Sheffield Publishing)

Ingold, Tim, editor. 1994. *Companion Encyclopedia of Anthropology: Humanity, Culture and Social Life*. London: Routledge Reference.

Kertzer, David. 1988. *Ritual, Politics, and Power*. New Haven: Yale University Press.

Klass, Morton. 1995. *Ordered Universes: Approaches to the Anthropology of Religion*. Boulder, CO: Westview Press.

Laughlin, Charles D.; John McManus; and Eugene G. d'Aquili. 1993. *Brain, Symbol and Experience: Toward a Neurophenomenology of Human Consciousness*. New York: Columbia University Press.

Lehmann, Arthur C., and James E. Myers, editors. 1985. *Magic, Witchcraft, and Religion: An Anthropological Study of the Supernatural*. Palo Alto: Mayfield Publishing Company.

Lehmann, Arthur C., and James E. Myers, editors. 1993. *Magic, Witchcraft, and Religion: An Anthropological Approach to the Supernatural*. 3rd edition. Mountain View: Mayfield.

Leslie, Charles M., editor. 1960. *Anthropology and Folk Religion*. New York: Vintage Books.

Lessa, William A., and Evon Z. Vogt. 1979. *Reader in Comparative Religion: An Anthropological Approach*. 4th edition. New York: Harper and Row.

Levy-Bruhl, Lucien. 1966. *Primitive Mentality*. Boston: Beacon Press.

Lewis, Gilbert. 1994. "Magic, Religion and Rationality of Belief." *Companion Encyclopedia of Anthropology: Humanity, Culture, and Social Life*. T. Ingold, editor. New York: Routledge Reference.

Lowie, Robert H. 1924. *Primitive Religion*. New York: Liveright. (Reprinted in 1948 and 1970)

Malinowski, Bronislaw. 1935. *Coral Gardens and Their Magic*. 2 vols. New York: American Book Company.

Mauss, Marcel. 1972. *A General Theory of Magic*. Boston: Routledge and Keegan Paul.

Middleton, John J., editor. 1967a. *Gods and Rituals: Readings in Religious Beliefs and Practices*. New York: Natural History Press. (Reprinted by University of Texas Press)

Middleton, John J., editor. 1967b. *Magic, Witchcraft and Curing*. New York: Natural History Press. (Reprinted by University of Texas Press)

Middleton, John J., editor. 1967c. *Myth and Cosmos: Readings in Mythology and Symbolism*. New York: Natural History Press. (Reprinted by University of Texas Press)

Morinis, Alan, editor. 1992. *Sacred Journeys: The Anthropology of Pilgrimage*. Westport, CT: Greenwood Press.

Morris, Brian. 1987. *Anthropological Studies of Religion: An Introductory Text*. New York: Cambridge University Press.

Needham, Rodney. 1972. *Belief, Language, and Experience*. Oxford: Basil Blackwell.

Norbeck, Edward. 1961. *Religion in Primitive Society*. New York: Harper.

Norbeck, Edward. 1974. *Religion in Human Life: Anthropological Views*. New York: Holt, Rinehart and Winston. (Reprinted by Waveland)

Pandian, Jacob. 1991. *Culture, Religion, and the Sacred Self: A Critical Introduction to the Anthropological Study of Religion*. Englewood Cliffs, NJ: Prentice-Hall.

Radin, Paul. 1937. *Primitive Religion: Its Nature and Origin*. New York: Viking. (Reprinted by E. P. Dutton)

Redfield, Robert. 1953. *The Primitive World and Its Transformations*. Chicago: University of Chicago Press.

Reynolds, Vernon, and Ralph Tanner. 1995. *The Social Ecology of Religion*. New York: Oxford University Press.

Saler, Benson. 1993. *Conceptualizing Religion: Immanent Anthropologists, Transcendent Natives, and Unbound Categories*. Leiden: E. J. Brill.

Sanjek, Roger. 1990. *Fieldnotes: The Making of Anthropology*. Ithaca, NY: Cornell University Press.

Smith, Jonathan Z. 1982. *Imagining Religion: From Babylon to Jonestown*. Chicago: University of Chicago Press.

Southwold, Martin. 1982. "True Buddhism and Village Buddhism in Sri Lanka." *Religious Organization and Religious Experience*. J. Davis, editor. New York: Academic Press.

Spiro, Melford E. 1994. *Culture and Human Nature*. New Edition edited by Benjamin Killborne and L. L. Langness. New Brunswick, NJ: Transaction Publishers.

Tambiah, Stanley J. 1990. *Magic, Science, Religion and the Scope of Rationality*. New York: Cambridge University Press.

Taylor, Mark Kline. 1986. *Beyond Explanation: Religious Dimensions in Cultural Anthropology*. Macon, GA: Mercer University Press.

Tylor, Edward B. 1873. *Primitive Culture*. 2 vols. London: John Murray.

Wallace, Anthony F. C. 1966. *Religion: An Anthropological View*. New York: Random House.

Wengle, John L. 1988. *Ethnographers in the Field: The Psychology of Research*. Tuscaloosa: University of Alabama Press.

Wilson, Bryan R., editor. 1970. *Rationality*. Oxford: Blackwell.

Yonan, Edward A. 1995. "Religion as Anthropomorphism: A New Theory that Invites Definitional and Epistemic Scrutiny." *Religion* 25: 31–34.

Part I

LOOKING AT RELIGION ANTHROPOLOGICALLY

Reading "Snake Handling": Critical Reflections

Jim Birckhead

CAPE FEAR—READING THE "BIZARRE"

> "You see, granddaddy handled snakes in church. Granny drank strychnine.
> You could say I have a leg up, genetically speaking."
>
> Max Cady, *Cape Fear* (1992)

These lines from Martin Scorsese's internationally popular feature film *Cape Fear* invite us to ask, What kind of people handle snakes and drink strychnine in church? Max Cady—"from the hills, Pentecostal cracker(s)"; possibly "inbred," Bible quoting and exhorting, tongue speaking, flagrantly tattooed with biblical passages ("Vengeance is mine"); cigar chewing, "ugly, fat, hairy hillbilly," menacing and sinister; "some sort of Pentecostalist avenging angel" (Hayward 1992: 6); fire brandishing; seemingly immune to the effects of the boiling water thrown on him by his intended victim—provides one kind of "reading." A reading not inconsistent with popular views of Pentecostal-Holiness people as a "bunch of backwoods Holy Roller snake handlers" (Flagg 1992: 18), "the illiterate gun-happy, snake-handling Appalachian mutants of the Angles and the Saxons" (Seltzer 1978: 134).

Fiction is an appropriate entrée to the world of "snake handlers" as most of "us" encounter and know "them" through popular rather than ethnographic texts. And many of these texts because of their overt bias and prurient sensationalism occupy the space somewhere between fiction and realism. Tabloid press photo essays, television news magazine features, shocking newspaper headlines and stories about deaths by snakebite and poison, men's genre magazines (e.g., *Argosy*—Mink 1973; *Hustler*—Fortunato 1980, Grodsky 1990; *Playboy*—Watts 1973), human interest and women's magazines" (e.g., *US*—Taublieb 1983; *Woman's World*—Phillips 1990), popular science formats (e.g., *Science 83*—Watterlond 1983), regional reviews (e.g., *Foxfire* 1973), and media digests (e.g., *The Listener*, BBC—Esler 1983) all have helped to construct somewhat larger-than-life fictionalized representations of this newsworthy religion. Journalistic articles (e.g., Alther 1975, 1976), popular books (Carden and Pelton 1976; Collins 1947; Covington 1995; Day 1941; Holliday 1966; Pelton and Carden 1976), short stories (Fee 1989; W. Miller 1991), novels (Alther 1977; J. Barker 1985; Flagg 1992; Hankla 1988; Oates 1978; Sharpe 1979; Smith 1995), plays (Linney 1971; Martin 1983), photographic works and essays (Adams 1993; *Appalachian Heritage* 1978:29–32; Dickinson and Benziger 1974; Murray 1974), and documentary films (see Burton 1993:202–204; Clements 1977, 1979) have contributed to discourses about "snake handling" as well.

Taken as a whole—there are some exceptions (e.g., Alther 1976; Carden and Pelton 1976)—popular coverage of snake handling constructs these people as exotic, bizarre, and grotesque denizens of a southern nether world, as a trivial sideshow spectacle beyond the ken of humanity.

Selected headlines over the years tell the story of "our" gaze[1] and their position in popular discourse: "America's Strangest Religion" (*Saturday Evening Post*, September 28, 1957:25–30), "Holiness Splinter Sects: Reincarnation, Polygamy and Snakes" (*Los Angeles Times*, April 29, 1973), "Snake Handler Convention—Ecstasy with a Deadly Cobra" (*Atlanta Constitution*, July 2, 1973), "The Jaws of Death" (*Atlanta Constitution*, January 8, 1973), "Two Dead from Poison—Religious Cult to Add Test of Faith by Fire" (*Los Angeles Times*, April 14, 1973), "Snakes Handled at Two Burials" (*Knoxville News-Sentinel*, April 12, 1973), "The Gospel of Death" (*Globe*, July 26, 1983), " 'They Shall Take Up Serpents'—The Salvation of Suffering Technology Can't Stop" (*St. Louis Post-Dispatch*, March 18, 1987), "Mark of the Serpent: Southerners Cling to Deadly Practice" (*Atlanta Journal Constitution*, February 1992), and so forth. Such headlines and stories play on the commonsense understanding that "normal" people do not handle snakes and drink strychnine in church.

Similarly, in the televisual world, a recent episode of *The Extraordinary* (Prime Network, Australia, April 8, 1993) looked at "the fundamentalist church that follows the literal word of the Bible to defy deadly snake bites and the drinking of strychnine poison . . . where men and women held death itself in the palms of their hands." Just one of "the stories that lie beyond our normal understanding, tonight on the extraordinary."[2]

Indeed, "they" share the "lunatic fringe" slot in the headlines with Branch Davidians (King and Breault 1993), Jonestown (E. Barker 1986; Drummond 1983), Japanese and Korean suicide cults, "devil worship" and ritual torture, Good Friday crucifixions in the Philippines, voodoo,[3] and the myriad other improbable cults and sects that become newsworthy from time to time. The fact that "they" are, for the most part, white, Anglo-Saxon, Protestant Americans and not indigenous Americans, Haitian voodoo practitioners in Brooklyn (K. M. Brown 1991), or Yoruba Ibeji Temple devotees in Atlanta (Morales et al. 1991) only amplifies this construction and "our" perplexity.

As Heider (1993: 4) notes: "The Pentecostal handling of serpents . . . [is] one of the most exotic—no, we must say 'exotically constructed'—cultural patterns of the twentieth century South." One could argue in fact that serpent handling religion has been so excessively overrepresented by the media that " 'the snake handler' has emerged as an icon of Appalachian and Southern 'otherness' " (Birckhead 1993a: 173).

This, perhaps, is not surprising. The media spectacle of modern-day Americans suffering injury and death by snakebite and poison for the sake of a passage in the Bible is provocative indeed to people of a pragmatic, postmodern society. Snake handling, like the deaths at Jonestown, shocks and affronts us with images of irrationality and seemingly senseless suffering and death. Lurid tabloid photos of people "fondling" snakes or drinking strychnine, of snakebite victims with swollen, distorted hands and fingers, or of a dead saint in his or her casket or dramatic footage of plaintive graveside scenes as a handler or strychnine drinker is laid to rest test the limits of our commonsense understanding and cultural relativism. (See Freeman 1965.)

And like the deaths at Jonestown (Drummond 1983: 172), serpent handling has inspired relatively little in-depth published ethnographic analysis by anthropologists (see Birckhead 1978d, 1993, 1996; Kane 1974b, 1974c, 1978, 1982, 1987; La Barre 1962a, 1962b, 1964, 1970).[4] Jonestown, Drummond (1983: 172) argues, was structured largely as a "journalistic" and "media event" and because of its "sensationalism and its ugliness" was not of interest to ethnographers. Namely: "The Jonestown massacres/suicides are a specifically nonethnographic event for them [anthropologists] because they were so bizarre and so modern." Drummond (173) suggests that "[w]e begin and end our studies by asking the native to be beautiful and whole. But what if he is deformed and self-destructive? This is the question Jonestown poses."

Snake handling religion poses similar sorts of questions with respect to ethnography and cultural representation. What stance, voice, perspective do we assume with people such as "snake handlers" who are generally seen not as being "beautiful and whole" but as "deformed and self-destructive," ugly, and bizarre? The popular representations of this group have been so much structured by media and entertainment values that we tend to read these texts as fiction and parody, having little or nothing to do with real humans in a real world.

Alas, some scholarly texts in fact lapse into the same sort of commonsense, pejorative language and assumptions, and obsession with snakes, sexuality, and death (see Birckhead 1993a). Symptomatic of this type of writing in a social science context is the comment made by Menninger Foundation psychologist Paul W. Pruyser (1963: 136) in a review of Weston La Barre's *"They Shall Take Up Serpents"—Psychology of the Southern Snake-Handling Cult* (1962):

The lunatic fringe of a population is rarely interesting enough to be written about, but its manifestations in religion can usually count on considerable attention, positive or negative, from the rest of the citizenry. Snake-handling in the American South has been outlawed by State Legislatures, its practitioners have been persecuted by police author- ities, *Life* magazine has made reportages of live snake-handling sessions, and now we even have a scholarly study about it by a well-known anthropologist. Who are the men and women who engage in this weird and unsanitary activity?

Similarly, Pruyser in his psychology of religion textbook (1968: 187) reflects: "The snake-handlers about whom La Barre has reported not merely represent a cultic oddity at which one could look in bemusement but manifest an emo- tional condition to which the members of solemn assemblies would react with panic."

Eminent sociologist of religion J. Milton Yinger (1970: 278) writes, "Dealing with a more bizarre movement . . . like a snake-handling cult in the Southern United States," while La Barre (1962a: 113) poses the question, "What is the meaning of the strange and dangerous behavior of handling deadly serpents and drinking deadly poisons?"

La Barre writes elsewhere with respect to "crisis cults" (1970: 278): "Fur- ther, many minority systems are so bizarre—the snake-handling cult, for ex- ample—that one wonders 'How on earth can people believe such obvious nonsense!' "[5] Or Miles Richardson (1977: 321) states in a tongue-in-cheek comparison between "The Good Old Boy and the Redneck," "The Redneck is a foot-washing Pentecostalist who speaks in tongues, drinks strychnine, and handles snakes." He is "the nigger-hater, the lynch mob, the cross burning late at night on the high school grounds." (Perhaps Max Cady!)

These scattered snippets of scholarly writing reflect to varying degrees the blurred boundaries between scientific and popular discourses and our common- sense notions about the "strange" and the "bizarre." How do we read and represent these "weird and unsanitary practices"? At best, many scholarly texts (not all anthropological) represent selected aspects of the religion, but we mostly are not left with a nuanced and textured ethnographic reading of these people's lives that makes "them" reasonably comprehensible and accessible to "us" in everyday human terms.

Perhaps, as Edgerton and Langness (1974) so graphically portray, writing cannot adequately capture the full meaning and intensity of the religious behav- iors exhibited by such groups. Film may be a more evocative medium:

Other films do more than this because they show us something so foreign to our expe- rience that reading about it, especially in the standard monograph, is a wholly inadequate means of comprehension. Take Peter Adair's (1967) film, *The Holy Ghost People*, about a fundamentalist snake-handling cult in West Virginia. Weston La Barre (1969) has written a skillful account of these people; how they congregate to cure by beseeching God, how they dance and sing, go into trances, fall down in convulsions, speak in tongues, handle deadly rattlesnakes and copperheads, and drink strychnine. They are a dramatic people to read about and La Barre writes about them well, but actually seeing them is something altogether different. The fervor is visible—starkly so. Their convulsions appear to be stereotyped yet at the same time they are violent and frightening. The trances are impressive; and along with the accompanying music, are compellingly infectious. Speaking in tongues, when witnessed in this way, no longer seems grotesque or merely clinical; it is fascinating and serious. The snakes are terrifyingly real. When one snake eventually bites the minister, his fear and confusion are communicated to us in a shocked denouement. The strange is suddenly real, and frightening and puzzling in a way that few artists achieve in a book. (85–86)

Yet Clements (1977: 504) in a review article of this and another film on serpent handling argues that *The Holy Ghost People* "fail[s] adequately to put the snake-handlers' beliefs and practices into any sort of general cultural context." And without this context, their beliefs, practices, and lives remain fairly incomprehensible to most viewers of the film.

So what kind of people handle snakes and drink strychnine in church (not to mention apply fire to their unprotected skin and "tread" on serpents and scorpions)? How can "we" know "them"? Why do we want to? What kind of people bother to study such stigmatized groups, given the adage that "You are what you study" (Van Maanen 1988: 39)? How does an anthropologist select such a topic to study in the first place, connect with and become involved with such people, and maintain contact with "them" for many years? What are the ethical issues in witnessing and condoning illegal and potentially life-threatening behaviors? In concrete terms, what does one do day to day "in the field" with such a group? What are the personal consequences of prolonged, intense involvement in such an ecstatic, mercurial religious milieu?

I have been trying to make sense (and of my making sense) of this religion for the past twenty-six years (albeit at a distance much of the time); I have tried to interpret members' meanings and, more recently, how the religion has been constructed and represented by popular media as well as by scholarly, print, and visual texts (Birckhead 1986, 1993a, 1993c, 1994, 1996).

Although my most concentrated and in-depth "fieldwork" took place in the early 1970s, I have kept in touch with some of the people and have gone back for brief visits every couple of years. My last visit was in 1995. While my primary research area for the past number of years has been Australian Aboriginal cosmology as related to indigenous land management issues (Birckhead, De Lacy, and Smith 1992), many questions about serpent handling are still very much on my mind and unresolved.

This is in part because recent critiques of the "crisis of representation in Western science" (Marcus and Fischer 1986) have opened up new discursive spaces for "reading," rereading, and "writing" cultures (Brady 1991; Bruner 1990; Clifford 1988; Clifford and Marcus 1986; Geertz 1973; G. Marcus 1992; J. Marcus 1990; Rose 1990; Taylor 1992). My own ongoing quest for ways of knowing and textualizing people considered bizarre and exotic has taken me through almost every theoretical stance toward social life from psychoanalysis to postmodernism. Each of these has given me a partial vantage point (Bakhtin 1981: 25), a particular reading position. Yet, taken in the aggregate, the disparate written and visual texts do not add up to a comprehensive and clear picture of the meaning of this movement or of the existential contours of these people's lives.

Most of this work, in Appalachian author Wilma Dykeman's terms, is writing that puts us in a position of "looking at" rather than "allowing us" to "live with" people (in J. Miller 1977: 87). In this chapter, I critically reflect on my experience of "reading" and coming to terms with serpent handling religion— my attempts to "live with" people—against the background noise of popular media depiction, on the one hand, and the sometimes distanced and scientized representations of the scholarly literature, on the other.[6] This is part critique, part personal reflection on fieldwork and interpretation. Fieldwork, as Hastrup notes (1992: 117), "is situated between autobiography and anthropology. It connects an important personal experience with a general field of knowledge."

This chapter is not about "snake handling" per se but about how "we" make sense of and "read" a religion that has been so sensationalized and misrepresented. More generally, these reflections may have applicability to the study of fringe "cults" and "sects" that have become media events because of their seemingly insane beliefs and bizarre practices.

I develop this critique around a number of themes that reflect key aspects of the intersection of personal experience and theoretical "ways of seeing" (Berger 1972): "Snake Handlers Are in the Circus"—Situating a Practice; Appalachian Dreaming—Self-Reading; Setting—"The Snake Handling Capital of the World"; My People/My Church—Experiencing Serpent Handling; and "Zion, Oh Zion—What's the Matter Now?"

"SNAKE HANDLERS ARE IN THE CIRCUS"—SITUATING A PRACTICE

> And they don't pass bread and wine in the Church of the Lord Jesus. They pass snakes; deadly snakes. . . . They are called snake handlers. West Virginia is the last state in America where the ancient religious ceremony of snake handling is still legal.
>
> *The Extraordinary* (Prime Television Network, Australia, April 8, 1993)

> I may take up serpents, but I am not a snake handler. Snake handlers are in the circus.
>
> Reverend Alfred Ball (1973)

> Fortunately, neither Rhine nor myself (since there are—or used to be— tourist traps all over the South where for a dollar one could watch somebody handle rattlesnakes "with impunity," quite outside any context of religion

or PK) were ever so naive as to regard snake-handling with impunity as
being bizarre (or paranormal).

                                                              Joseph K. Long (1982: 75)

Pentecostal-Holiness serpent handling religion has persisted in its various theological traditions and subregional manifestations since its obscure and debated
origins in rural Grasshopper Valley, Tennessee, circa 1908–1913 (see Ambrose
1970; Birckhead 1976b; Burton 1993; Carter 1987; Collins 1947; Kane 1979;
Kimbrough 1992, 1995; La Barre 1962a; Vance 1975). St. Mark 16: 15–18 of
the King James Bible provides one rationale for serpent handling and for four
of the other ritual practices of this religion:

And he said unto them, Go ye into all the world, and preach the gospel to every creature.
He that believeth and is baptized shall be saved; but he that believeth not shall be
damned.
   And these signs shall follow them that believe; in my name shall they cast out devils;
they shall speak with new tongues; they shall take up serpents; and if they drink any
deadly thing, it shall not hurt them; they shall lay hands on the sick, and they shall
recover.

The five "signs," along with the "quenching through faith the violence of
fire" (Burton 1993: 98) and "treading" on "serpents and scorpions," are performed in some twenty-five to forty-five independent churches in the Appalachian and Deep South and, with the migration of southern folk to northern cities,
in such centers as Detroit, Cincinnatti, Cleveland, and Columbus. Because these
Free Pentecostal congregations, widely dispersed from Florida to Michigan, do
not keep or report comprehensive records of membership and are little studied
demographically, it is difficult to know for certain how many churches and
members exist today. Kane (1987: 118) estimates that this religion has some
2,000 followers, one half of whom live in the state of West Virginia (Daugherty,
in Watterlond 1983: 51).
   Members hold that "the five signs" (and other acts) "follow" true believers
as irrefutable demonstrations to sinners (and to the faithful) of the "reality" of
God's power as manifested through His modern-day "saints" and "apostles."
Only a church "with signs following the believers," they reason, can convincingly validate its claims to holiness and Apostolic descendancy.
   To "work" in a particular sign, a saint should have the "anointing" of the
Holy Ghost. Anointing is tangible and real. It is experienced in a variety of
physical ways: numbness in the hands, mouth, or tongue; palpitation of the heart;
involuntary movement of the arms, legs, or tongue; blurring of vision; or even
total collapse. From a physiological perspective, anointing is seen as "possession trance" (Kane 1974c; Sargant 1975; Schwarz 1960). Snakes and poisons
used in services are rarely doctored as demonstrated by the number of deaths
and injuries from these causes over the years. While firm figures of deaths by

serpent bite or poison are lacking, Burton (1993: 161) estimates some seventy-one people, a half dozen of whom died from drinking "the deadly thing" (164). It is difficult to know as well whether serpent handling per se is on the wane. Burton thinks that "their numbers are not nearly as great as they once were, even twenty years ago. . . . Currently, there are more oral reports of churches where serpents are no longer handled than those where that practice has been taken up" (168). Even so, Burton predicts that the practice will persist "probably for some time" (169), contrary to predictions of its imminent demise made by writers in the 1960s and early 1970s (e.g., La Barre 1962a: viii; personal communication 1971; and Nichol 1966: 157).

Having given a thumbnail sketch of serpent handling, I once again return to the question, What kind of people handle snakes and drink strychnine in church? What sense are "we" to make of these "strange" and "bizarre" behaviors of popular depiction? What accounts for the enduring popular interest in these often-represented practices of a very few individuals?

Or, we can ask, What kind of behavior or phenomenon is snake/serpent handling religion? How should it be classified, thought about, and hence interpreted, explained, and represented? Intertextually speaking, what do we read it as? What do we read it against? In other words, in what ethnographic and ethnological spaces do these "exoticized" practices fit?

Reading the Literature

Part of the answer to these questions can be found in a quick glance over the scholarly literature on serpent handling to see how the movement has been constructed and analyzed (placed and slotted in). What are the dominant themes, issues, and questions? Popular interest not withstanding, published academic interest in the religion has been less than one might expect. (And, as I mentioned before, even less work has been done on it by anthropologists.)

To my knowledge, besides Weston La Barre's (1962a) classic *"They Shall Take Up Serpents—Psychology of the Southern Snake-Handling Cult,* only two other full-length scholarly books have appeared: Thomas Burton's (1993) *Serpent Handling Believers* and David Kimbrough's (1995) *Taking up Serpents: Snake Handlers of Eastern Kentucky* (although Rowe's 1982 thesis was reprinted as a book in 1986, cited in Burton 1993).

Serpent handling to date largely has been textualized in master's theses and doctoral dissertations, representing a scattering of disciplines, topics, and approaches. Master's work by Ambrose (1970) and Kane (1973) provides general, overview surveys of the religion, while other students focus on specific aspects such as revitalization (K. Miller 1977a), church music (Moore 1976, cited in Burton 1993), spatial and cultural relations (Rowe 1982), deviancy (Tripp 1975), services as "rhetorical paradigms" (Van Hoorebeke 1980, cited in Burton 1993), and history of the practice in three southern states (Vance 1975).

Ph.D. dissertations by Ambrose (1978), Birckhead (1976b), Cobb (1965),

Kane (1979), and Kimbrough (1992) examine "commitment" in an urban mid-western congregation; identity and meaning creation through interaction; religious origins and community norms and identity; origins and diffusion, symbolic meanings of serpents, unconscious motives, and diversity of needs being met; and historical perspectives on serpent handling in eastern Kentucky, respectively.

Unpublished conference, seminar, and working papers, often derived from thesis or dissertation work, further delineate the variety of ways of viewing serpent handling: Birckhead (1970a, 1970b, 1971a, 1971b, 1972, 1974a, 1974b, 1975, 1976a, 1977, 1978a, 1978b, 1978c, 1978e, 1980, 1981, 1982, 1986, 1991, 1993b, 1993c), Carter and Ambrose (1982), Carter, Green, and Ambrose (1985), Elifson and Tripp (1975), Kane (1974a, 1976), K. Miller (1977b), Mullis (1988), Schwartz (1991, 1992, cited in Burton 1993), Sullivan and Elifson (1976), Tonks (1967), and Tripp/Sullivan and Elifson (1975).

Journal articles and book chapters make serpent handlers accessible with respect to popular media positioning (Birckhead 1993a, 1996); sociological correlates and general features of urban participants (Carter 1987); folkloric features (Clarke 1975); serpent handling as a "sacrament" (Daugherty 1976); reflections of author's experience of showing a film on serpent handling to a South Carolina African-American sea island community (Dunlap 1975, 1993); sociological functions (Gerrard 1968, 1971); general cultural and religious features, including trance and possession states (Kane 1974b, 1974c, 1984, 1987, 1989); psycho-physiological considerations of fire handling (Kane 1978, 1982); ethnographic and historic overviews (La Barre 1964); music as "socioeconomic double entendre" (Moore 1986); theology (Romero 1975, cited in K. Miller 1977b); comparison with Hellenistic Greece (Rousselle 1984); physiology of performance of rites (Schwarz 1960, 1989); preference for copperheads to rattlers (*Scientific American* 1940); impact on secular folk genres (Stekert 1963); and personality characteristics as derived from Minnesota Multiphasic Personality Inventory (MMPI) protocols (Tellegen et al. 1969).

Unpublished reports by Gerrard and Gerrard (1966) and Gerrard (1966) and manuscripts by Daugherty (n.d., cited in McCauley 1987) and Elifson and Tripp (1976) form a not-easily accessible but valuable resource base for understanding serpent handling.

Finally, a number of writers mention serpent handling in passing to illustrate or exemplify a particular point or position, for example, Finney (1969), personality change and mental health; Gerlach and Hine (1970), an example of a segmented polycephalous interaction network (SPIN) and with respect to paranoia; Hine (1969), glossolalia, religious conversion, and development of new mental and emotional patterning; Hughes (1992), cult/revitalization movements; La Barre (1962b), case of "acting out with very little discernible therapy"; La Barre (1970, 1971), as a crisis cult; Morland (1958), with respect to strikes and social class; Parker (1970), Appalachian folk religion; Pope (1942), religion as substitute for social status; and emotionalism and suggestibility; Pruyser (1968), risk taking, "phallic features," and psychopathology; Samarin (1972), glosso-lalia and personality; Sargant (1949, 1957, 1975), role in behavior change, as "cultural group abreactive technique," and trance and possession states; White (1972), ecstasy and unconscious phallic symbolism; Williams (1980), as "pop-ular religion"; Wilson (1970), "Thaumaturgical sect"; and Yinger (1970), "re-ligion, stratification and protest" and psychopathology.

Despite the apparent diversity of work shown here, the underlying problematic of most studies fairly singularly reflects concern with the psychosocial and phal-lic symbolic correlates and functions of "cult" participation, on the one hand, and the psychophysiological mechanisms of trance and possession states, on the other. Maintenance of belief, commitment, structure, and meaning over time concerns some writers as well.

In a sense, regardless of what specific focus one takes, the media, popular writing, common sense, and anthropological theory all structure explicitly or implicitly a reading derived from ideas of what is and is not rational behavior. Part of the stance one assumes almost automatically when writing about serpent handling is one of explaining and interpreting (see Lett 1991) as meaningful that which to most people seems mad and deranged. It is not surprising, then, that this invariably is construed in terms of social or psychological deprivation and pathology; and hence we look to see whether participation in this religion is functional or dysfunctional in these terms.

In this regard, when I started working on this topic in 1970–1971, two op-posing views were available; Weston La Barre's and Nathan Gerrard's.[7] La Barre (1962a, 1970, 1971), broadly speaking, saw snake handling as a "crisis cult," "a phenomenon of acculturation and a reaction to a new cultural and economic setting" (1962a: 163). Within this framework, and in terms of Freud-ian psychology, he saw snake handling as "a pathological response to stress," "a self-defeating mechanism, leading to a downward spiraling ever expanding, vicious circle, where the very attempts to cope with the problem on hand only exacerbates the stress and creates new difficulties" (1962a: 171). Yinger (1970: 308) aptly and succinctly characterizes La Barre's reading of snake handling cults:

He sees snake handling as the effort of a deeply deprived and sexually repressed group to deal with the "guilty terror" embedded in their repressions. By handling the snakes, they act out their unconscious, guilt laden but powerful sexual needs. He sees no therapy in the cult, but only a kind of bitter necessity . . . "because of the pressures of this sadly neurotic and archaic and unhappy culture, these people have to have what satisfactions they can without any psychological self-possession, knowledge of who they are, and what they are like, and what they are really doing."

Gerrard (1968, 1971) argued, on the other hand, based on ten years' fieldwork and MMPI results, that while these "stationary poor" people certainly suffered deprivations, they, nevertheless, found in their religion compensations and some mastery, allowing them to cope better than might otherwise be expected. He concludes:

Religious serpent handling, then—and all the other emotionalism of the Holiness churches that goes with it—serves a definite function in the lives of its adherents. It is a safety valve for many of the frustrations of life in present-day Appalachia. For the old, the serpent handling religion helps soften the inevitability of poor health, illness, and death. For the young with their poor educations and poor hopes of finding jobs, its promise of holiness is one of the few meaningful goals in a future dominated by the apparent inevitability of lifelong poverty and idleness. (1968: 28)

My goal prior to going to "the field" in 1971 was to resolve this "debate," a goal I abandoned for a more interpretive construction of meaning approach, once I had confronted the realities of serpent handling life. Namely, I found these terms of reference confining like a straitjacket and came to see that to focus on these exclusively would be at the expense of many other cultural and social processes that I felt better reflected the élan of serpent handling life. And, separating theory from "ethnographic fact," I did not find my church to be dominated by La Barre's (1962a) repressed, psychopathic, symbolic phallus handlers or by Kane's (1979: 272) snake/phallus-obsessed informants—" 'Hi, Brother Homer. How's your copperhead?' 'Just fine,' replied Homer. 'Do you want to take it out and play with it?' "

Snakes/Serpents and Boundaries

Having located serpent handling with respect to a substantial body of scholarly literature, we now need to sharpen our focus and situate it ethnologically with respect to other snake/serpent handling cultures and to explore the permeable boundaries between secular and sacred, snake and serpent handling.

Consideration of the quotations that open this section is a good starting point. Namely, although Pentecostal-Holiness serpent handling is neither a circus performance nor ethnographically an "ancient religious ceremony," it reflects features of both. Handling rattlesnakes, whether in a revival tent, roadside "tourist trap," or Texas rattlesnake roundup all share features of performance and danger, serpent lore and narrativity, and rely on "our innate wariness of snakes" (Mundkur 1983, in K. Brown 1991: 115) for maximum visceral effect. That snakes/serpents are involved taps into powerful physiological reactions and cultural meanings, suggesting comparisons with the numerous people who have throughout history and across cultures made much of serpents.

The snake from time immemorial has been a powerful multivocal symbol and feared primordial reptile presence of the "natural world"—"we are wired to react to it; it is an inherently potent symbol" (Mundkur 1983, in K. Brown 1991: 115–116). People are at once fascinated and horrified by snakes—their nature, movement, detachment, unpredictableness, sense of power, menace, and danger. As Mundkur (1983: 39) notes in his exhaustive and scholarly study of the sources of our contrasting responses to ophidians, ophiolatry and ophidi-ophobia: "[I]n a most fundamental way, the serpent's hold on human imagi-nation owes far less to its being good to think about [in Levi-Straussian terms] than to the intrinsic qualities—mere form of the body and undulant locomo-tion—which are its unique instruments of fascination. And ultimately it is its capacity to fascinate, to terrify and 'lay under a spell,' to hold 'mute and frozen,' that prompts man to adopt it as a symbol.''

Hardly a culture exists, including our own, in which snakes have not been "venerated" or "caluminiated" (Mundkur 1983: 41) and linked symbolically to cosmic meanings of life and death. "The snake," note Morris and Morris (1968: 9),

with its many and in some ways contradictory attributes, has been worshipped, feared, puzzled over, hated, loved, exploited, exterminated, studied and even petted. It has been used in magic, witchcraft, religion, medicine, war, torture, sport, science, commerce and entertainment. On the one hand, it has been a symbol of procreation, health, longevity, immortality and wisdom; on the other, it has represented death, disease, sin, lechery, duplicity, and temptation. It is a paradox: It is both sides of the coin, and mankind has seldom ignored it.

The link between snakes and religion is a long and enduring one. Burton notes (1993: 5): "Serpents have been associated with religion in some form since ancient, perhaps, prehistoric, times." La Barre (1962a) and Mundkur (1983) lavishly depict the scope and breadth of the use of serpent symbolism in many traditions as well as serpents themselves in various rites and rituals. Mundkur, in a section entitled "Serpent Handling Societies" (1983: 83–90), provides an exhaustive survey indeed. "The Free Pentecostal-Holiness Church in the rural southeastern United States" stands next to such people as Chinese followers of the mountain god Yùeh; Egyptian Gnostic Ophit sects of the "Christian era" (who "are known to have allowed their 'sacred snake . . . to crawl all over the consecrated bread, which the worshippers then ate and after-wards kissed the serpent on the mouth' "), "early third millennium, BC''; Su-merian " 'serpent-walkers' or 'serpent-charmers' ''; "cobra handlers and charmers of India, Burma, Egypt, and Southeast Asia''; "rattlesnake handlers of Aztec, Tahue, Tarahumara, and Hopi" New World societies; and so on. Dodds (1951) describes snake handling in the Dionysiac and Asllepius cults of classical Greece and compares these to serpent handling in Leslie and Perry Counties in Kentucky. (See also Rousselle 1984.) Many other examples of re-ligious serpent handling societies could be cited, not to mention the handling of snakes by secular specialists and entertainers (see Morris and Morris 1968).

Seen in this broad ethnological context—and against the literature of healing, trance, and possession states (Crapanzano and Garrison 1977; Lewis 1971; Sargant 1975); feats, ordeals, and use of fire (Danforth 1989; Leacock and Leacock 1972; Peterson 1977; Wijeyewardene 1979); eschatological rituals (Pandian 1991); vision quests and shamanic rites (Harner 1973; Siskind 1973); and "magical world view(s)" (Wax and Wax 1962)—modern-day Christian serpent handling is not particularly bizarre or noteworthy but only a particular manifestation in space and time of what humans have done in many other settings and times—part of an enduring human affinity with snakes/serpents and striving for ecstasy and transcendence (Goodman 1988; Norbeck 1974). The reasons for this are provocative and varied and much debated from a range of theoretical positions. Kane (1978), and La Barre (1962a), for example, place great emphasis on the phallic, sexual symbolism of the serpent in Pentecostal-Holiness and other serpent handling peoples.

Viewing serpent handling in this wide ethnological perspective is not meant to suggest that Pentecostal-Holiness people are descended from or related to these far-flung traditions (see Parker 1970: 196); only that serpents have been used extensively by many peoples (a most interesting ethnological question).

Mundkur (1983: 83) makes a number of pertinent points about serpent handling societies in general, the first being: "It is probable that the majority of ophiolatrus cultures that handled live animals in ceremonies favored nonpoisonous species." Similarly, when poisonous reptiles were handled "in religious ecstasy, the animals, more often than not, were defanged." He notes, finally:

It might seem that the awe that impels worship of a fully zoomorphic effigy of an ophidian deity could be strong enough to induce devotees to overcome inhibition and pay obeisance to an enshrined, live specimen. Serpent, after all, are easily procured, very convenient to maintain, and for the most part quite safe to handle. However, I know of no society whose members at large do this as nonchalantly as, say, a devout Hindu fondles a cow or an Ainu a captive bear—cult animals whose importance parallels the serpents in these cultures. In practically all serpent-handling societies, intimacy of this kind is the preserve of the priest, the medicine man, the shaman, or the professional charmer. For example, despite their strong traditions of ophiolatry, Brahman priests and most lay people never handle live serpents ritually but leave the task to specialists among the lower-caste Hindus.

Pentecostal-Holiness serpent handlers, in contrast, use only poisonous snakes, and ideally, any person who receives the appropriate "anointing" (not only ritual specialists) should be able to "take up serpents" and/or "work" in other "signs." But, in fact, in many congregations only a handful of members regularly handle serpents; in some others, the handling is more generalized within a fairly close knit congregation representing two to three generations of saints.

But perhaps we place too much emphasis on snakes and snake handling as a diagnostic cultural feature. There are congregations of serpent handlers in which serpents are taken up as infrequently as once a month, once a year, or even once in five years (and then by only one or two preachers or elders). Because "we" (people in general, the media, and social scientists) call "them" a "common denominator" (Van Maanen 1988: 49) "snake cult/snake religion" (Burton 1993: 10), we often fail to locate individual congregations (and the religion as a whole) within a continuum of the myriad of ecstatic religions in the southern United States.

Poison drinking and fire handling are practiced to varying degrees in these churches as well and within the same congregation over time. As this religion is quite free flowing and given to improvisation, the prominence given to a sign such as serpent handling waxes and wanes over time, depending on the specific individuals involved (visitors from other churches, new saints in a church, what messages the church's pastor receives from God, etc.) and other influences at any particular time. Most media people (e.g., Fortunato's [1980: 58] *Hustler* piece—"But I was in search of snake handlers") and some social scientists are interested in only seeing serpent and fire handling and poison drinking and, given these biases, have tended to select particular congregations that display these features to the fullest as sites of study. Generalizations taken from this skewed sample, then, misrepresent the importance of these particular signs for the widely scattered, highly varied, loose "federation" of religionists we have labeled "snake" or "serpent handlers."

Like studies of "traditional societies," serpent handling has been tarred with a uniformist brush. How "saints" ongoingly "reinvent" their culture and identities "in changing historical circumstances" (Marcus and Fischer 1986: 24) is rarely accounted for. Thus, even in this small corner of the world, distortion and misrepresentation are rife; studies of serpent handling religion have not yet been systematically subjected to the new anthropological criticism. (See Birck-head 1986, 1993a, 1993c, 1994, 1996.)

But, religiously speaking, remove the serpents, poison, and fire, and serpent handling is indistinguishable from the plethora of small, independent, Pentecostal and charismatic groups throughout the South, other parts of the United States, and around the world (see Abel 1974, 1982). Speaking in tongues, casting out devils, laying hands on the sick, foot washing, the Lord's Supper, personal access to the Holy Ghost, emphasis on personal salvation, noninfant baptism, spirited preaching, literalist reading of the Bible, a strict ascetic and moral code, an imminent end of the world, "second coming" eschatology, and the like, are features serpent handlers share with a large swath of fundamentalist Christianity. And without the snakes, poison, and fire, it loses its appeal as bizarre, exotic spectacle for the media and, no doubt, for many researchers.

Indeed, many serpent handlers belonged to such churches, as well as Southern and Old Regular Baptist congregations, prior to their involvement with serpent handling. Some, after years of attendance at a serpent handling congregation, in fact find their way back to such more mainline evangelical churches. As well, some serpent handling congregations have discontinued their newsworthy practices and thus have become indistinguishable from the small churches that so prolifically sprinkle roadsides across the South. Again, boundaries are fluid and permeable, eluding slice-of-time analysis.

The permeability of boundaries is also reflected in the distinction between "snake" and "serpent" (handler) made above by Brother Alfred Ball. Professional Australian snake handler George Cann says that "Showbiz' and snakes are in my blood and I love every minute of it" ("A Healthy Dose of Charm," *The Border Mail*, July 1, 1993: 9). Holiness people who "take up serpents" often aver: "We don't do this for no show; it's the Word of God." But the frequency with which this disclaimer is made suggests that it is a provocative and charged area of concern: "There's no self in this; it's the anointing power of the Holy Ghost." As writer Fortunato (1980: 54) observes, "there is a certain snake-handler's macho" in this religion.

Balaji Mundkur (1983: 40–41) recognizes as well the essential truth of "snake"/"serpent" handling: "Even when the serpent is harmless, its unpredictable, stealthy manner exacerbates the initial shock of seeing it at close quarters, thus prompting an awe of the entire ophidian family. On the other hand, shrewd possessors of knowledge of its behavioral traits often handle deadly poisonous serpents with impunity, *impressively filling the roles of shaman, priest, or entertainer*" (emphasis mine). Mundkur (2), like Brother Alfred, makes a distinction between "snake" and "serpent," arguing,[8] "A snake is merely the zoological entity, but 'serpent' . . . opens up vast metaphorical possibilities. The lexicographer Fowler aptly observes that 'we perhaps conceive serpents as terrible and powerful and beautiful things, snakes as insidious and cold and contemptible.' " It is perhaps because religious serpent handling is seen to occupy this highly charged symbolic and metaphorical space that "they" make "us" uncomfortable in a way that secular handlers do not.

My dad, Roy Birckhead, was known as "the snakeman" in his younger years because he kept, handled, and donated snakes (rattlesnakes, copperheads, and water moccasins) to Marlin Perkins of the St. Louis Zoo. A family friend, Chuck Bindner, a Native American, also handled snakes, eventually working at the Ross Allen's Reptile Institute at Silver Springs, Florida. Neither of these men nor the Australian handler George Cann (whose show I attended the other day) nor the dozens of roadside and shopping mall snake handlers I have watched over the years have been constructed as "bizarre," "weird," or "Manson-esque" (an appellation applied to my informant, Liston Pack, by a Canadian TV newsmagazine compere in 1973). Such people, on the contrary, often are seen as minor showbiz celebrities, colorful and interesting, even though they sometimes suffer snakebite and its sometimes fatal effects.

So why does the transformation from secular to sacred semantic space arouse such ire and attempts at stigmatization? While I am not able to fully explore this issue here, I believe that it taps into and resonates with intertextually dark and abiding cultural obsessions with cults, inbred and degenerate hill people, fanaticism, danger, sex, and death (see Birckhead 1993a). This heightened reading of serpent handling is especially interesting in the face of the degree to which the two practices, secular and sacred, intermingle and cohabit in everyday southern life. Stories of mean snakes, snakebites, "big snake(s)" (Taylor 1992), catching, keeping, and handling snakes, and so on, are valuable currency on both sides of (and often cross over) the "snake"/"serpent" handler divide[9] (see Stekert 1963).

Similarly, religious serpent handlers frequently interact with "sinners" who catch and bring their "wild ones" for "saints" to handle and with snake show people from whom they acquire exotic species such as cobras, Western Diamondback rattlesnakes, coral snakes, or "bamboo vipers." (See Kane [1979: 243–248] for a description of his informant's frequent interactions with snake shows, reptile farms, dealers, and a "rattlesnake roundup" in Georgia; also Ambrose [1970] and Birckhead [1976b, 1978d] for a discussion of the acquisition of snakes and interstate traffic through "serpent exchange networks.")

Finally, the permeability of boundaries between secular and sacred is quite consistent with the overall dynamics of southern salvation and deliverance, the fluid and permeable boundary between "sinners" and "saints." "Saints" were once "sinners" and can always "backslide" and again become "sinners." It is not as if the two, sinner/saint (secular/sacred) are hermetically sealed realms. Snake/serpent handling itself nicely reflects this dynamic interface—an act that is both secular and sacred, depending on context and always having the potential of reverting to secular modalities even in its sacred performance context.

APPALACHIAN DREAMING—SELF-READING

> The field project is shaped by our personality, our daydreams, the texts and field reports we read, our professors' theories and anecdotes and advice, budgets, families and friends: powerful images that move us long before we ever meet a native—and continue their effects to the end, as we make public our experience—ethnography.
>
> The field project designed at home is obviously based on selfhood, not just our theories or topical interests . . . [O]ne's imagination figures actively in selecting a field area and subject.
>
> Herdt and Stoller (1990: 34–35)

I have often wondered how personality, formative influences, specific experiences, and chance occurrences determine in a way the type of research one does (or if one does social research at all) and the way one conducts it. My work on serpent handling takes a somewhat different perspective than most other work on this religion, which I suspect is a matter of autobiography and personal style.

Students of serpent handling have been particularly unreflexive in their writing to date—"much of it . . . still in the old tradition of the objective outsider looking in" (Messerschmidt 1984: 374). They tell us very little about themselves as people or about the dialogue between "themselves" and serpent handling "others" that produced the interpretations of their respective texts. As Crick

(1982: 15–16) asserts: "Anthropological knowledge, after all, is not about 'the other,' it is generated by the mutual definition of 'us' and 'other' . . . and is therefore inherently autobiographical." Thus, the implicit "presence of 'us' in anthropological knowledge . . . should be made explicit" in order to provide a more informed reading of the interpretation of social life.

Without information of this kind, we are not fully informed of sources of bias emanating from the human observer. Herdt & Stoller (1990: 34–35) note: "It surprises us that even clinically-oriented anthropologists ignore awareness of prefield work. Long before the field, an ethnography is biased, however slightly. How aware of these influences are we; of our motives and preconception carried into our work? . . . of this earliest fieldwork in the head?"

Who I was to serpent handlers (see Dumont 1978) (and who they were to me) because of my background and personality greatly influenced, no doubt, my acceptance by key people, access to "back stage" scenes, friendships beyond field roles—in essence, what I chose, and was allowed, to "see" and ultimately the ways I have understood and represented this religion in print.

When I think about it, I sometimes am amazed that I became an anthropologist (the only one in my high school to do so) and even more amazed and bemused that my life ever became entangled with the lives of serpent handlers in east Tennessee. Colleagues, students, friends, and relatives often see me as strange for having taken this particular path to knowledge. I often feel that this has not really happened to me but to someone else, a character in a film or novel, perhaps, who I watch from a distance. Why does an anthropologist select this (and not many have) from all the cultures one could possibly study? How did this happen to me?

I recently have become increasingly aware of the early experiences and dreams that ultimately led me the 2,500 miles from Edmonton to "Snake Hollow" (not to mention from St. Louis via Virginia, Central America, Nebraska, Kentucky, and Tennessee to Edmonton, Alberta, to study anthropology) and how these experiences inevitably set the tone, style, and preoccupations of my studies of serpent handlers. My work is, in retrospect, a direct outgrowth of a multiplicity of background factors and influences that more or less predisposed me to find serpent handlers a congenial people with whom to live.

I will now sketch in some of these influences over a number of years to illuminate the wider issue of self and topic selection in anthropology of religion. To begin with, exposure to religion, ritual, death, and Appalachian people as a child and teenager aroused interests in me that were well reflected in serpent handling. Subsequent travel throughout the South and time spent living with a family in an eastern Kentucky hollow gave further definition and substance to my interests. In retrospect, though I did not see it at the time, I was attracted to serpent handling, like a moth to a flame, as an arena in which to confront and play out long-term existential obsessions and unresolved personality and identity themes and needs.

The first of these had to do with religion, ritual, and death—serpent handling of course being a site par excellence for the exploration of such issues. Religion, belief, ritual, and the possibility of miracles interested me greatly as a child. Given the choice between the dramatic and experientially rich, Irish folk Catholicism of my mother's family and the less exciting German "free thinking" skepticism of my father's family (and his inactive Baptist faith), I was drawn to the world of magic, miracles, ritual and mortification, and the promise of life eternal.

My experiences were eclectic. While in grade school, for example, I belonged to the YMHA (Young Men's Hebrew Association) in our neighborhood in order to use their swimming pool and gymnasium but sometimes found myself participating in Hanukkah and other ritual celebrations. Similarly, as our inner-city north St. Louis street changed from all "white" to almost all "black," the taverns at either end of the block closed down and reopened as African-American "Holy Roller" churches (a Church of God in Christ and a Temple of the Holy Ghost), which raged to the early hours of the morning.

My grandmother, expressing the opinion that the saloon hadn't been this noisy, sometimes phoned the police, but by the time they arrived, the watchers posted outside the front door had alerted the congregation and all was peace and quiet. But within minutes of their departing, the throbbing drumbeat, electric guitars, horns, tambourines, cymbals, spirited singing, shouting, and tongue speaking would once again dominate the night. These pounding sounds were etched in my brain, and stories of what "they did in there" grew to legendary proportions. Though I dared not venture into these frightening and forbidden realms of frenzied worship, I was fascinated and intrigued by the intensity of religious feeling manifested in the services and, unlike most of my family, was more curious about, than critical of, what "they" so noisily did "in there" across the street so many nights of the week.

Death always lurked nearby as old relatives passed on, and I spent many evenings in St. Louis funeral homes. As an altar boy in grade school, I eagerly plied the funeral trade and developed an unusual interest in the "culture" of funerals and funeral directors—the architecture and style of different mortuaries, types of hearses and limousines used, dress styles, ethnic differences in funerals (Irish, Italian, German, or African-American), types of caskets, and so on. I avidly read the death notices to see when funerals were scheduled for my church so I could "serve" them whenever possible. I knew the names of all the funeral homes in the city, the types of clientele they usually had, and how much of a tip I could expect from each (from $.50 to $5.00). My interest went beyond the attraction of missing a morning of school, riding in a limo to various cemeteries, or even the much-sought-after tips. It was, rather, the grim majesty of the event itself, a precise ritual performance in which I played a role as participant (and very much as observer). The plaintive death knell, funeral dirge, po-faced mortician, throngs of mourners, world-weary celebrants, gray pallbearers, hearse and funeral car drivers, aura of death, the coffin itself, collapse and breakdown of loved ones as the casket was placed in the grave, all became familiar parts of this drama, and I was engrossed and mesmerized by it.

The sudden death of my mother, aged thirty-five, not long after I turned thirteen, shattered the taken-for-grantedness of my life and catapulted me into personal chaos, depression, and early teenage rebelliousness. Not long after the funeral, my dad, brother, and I made a whirlwind trip to California and the Pacific Northwest, often driving all night and catching a bit of sleep in the car, before driving another 800–mile stretch of empty highway. It was on this trip that I discovered in bleak Wyoming truck stops the comforting pathos of jukeboxes blaring country and fifties rock and roll—two-minute musical melo-dramas about pain, tragedy, and death, usually sung by twangy, nasal voices from Alabama, Tennessee, or Texas.

Back from this trip, I passed sultry summer nights listening to the Grand Ole Opry on Station WSM from Nashville, as well as to local country and late-night blues stations from East St. Louis. From these musical idioms, I worked at fashioning a new identity for myself as an angry, hillbilly drifter and developed a romantic, escapist obsession with "Appalachia" and the South. I became increasingly aware of the many recently arrived migrants from Arkansas, Mis-sissippi, and Tennessee who were living in parts of St. Louis—black/"colored people" and white/"hoosiers" ("hillbillies"). These people looked and talked "different" and were certainly constructed as "other" by the dominant dis-courses in my milieu, as objects of humor and derision—"Hoosiers are worse than niggers!" I, naturally, was attracted to this tabooed and mythical zone of "hoosier" "otherness."

An article in the *St. Louis Post-Dispatch* in the late 1950s about "The Van-ishing Hillbilly" of southern Missouri, with its photos of teenage girls wearing "short shorts" and tight white cotton blouses, seductively languishing on the front porch swing with cigarettes hanging loosely from their mouths, plus feature films such as *Thunder Road, The Long Hot Summer, God's Little Acre, Cat on a Hot Tin Roof, Walk on the Wild Side, To Kill a Mockingbird*, and *Tobacco Road* added to the allure of my imaginary "South."

Time spent at my Great Uncle Chaunce's Ozark "farm" in the tiff mining country around Old Mines and Potosi, Missouri, contributed to the mystique of these folk with French surnames living in "shacks" and "cabins" up dirt tracks, with missing teeth and stubble on their faces, and their barefooted, long-haired wives wearing print dresses from the Sears, Roebuck catalogue—and always an abundance of free-living children and dogs.

In my wild imaginings, I pondered what it would be like to be such a person and leave the country for the factories of St. Louis. As a teenager, clad in patched jeans, black leather boots, a blue jean coat, floppy hat, all the stubble I could muster, and a piece of straw between my teeth, I often played out this fantasy on the trip back from the hills to the city (an early attempt at "a reci-procity of perspectives").

My dad, an auto mechanic who worked at a "hoosier" garage near Chuck

Berry's (now legendary rock and roller) house (and who sometimes repaired his Cadillac), worked with some men recently from the country with names like Dwight, Wayne, and Charlie. A couple of these men drove stock cars at the races we used to attend; they and the other drivers had the "look" and style of "down home boys" and served as powerful role models for me.

During my high school years, I frequently hitchhiked around the city and occasionally got rides with long-distance truckers passing through in furniture vans from Hickory, North Carolina, or Elizabethton, Tennessee. It was always a thrill to climb up into the cab of one of these big rigs and talk with the "colorful" driver, who conformed to type and whetted my appetite to go south.

Part-time jobs as a night watchman, municipal swimming pool attendant, golf course maintenance worker, truck loading dock hand, night shift driver and dispatch person at a large hospital, a stacker in the 7 Up bottling plant, and helper on 7 Up delivery routes also put me in contact with southern migrants to the city. One of my 7 Up delivery routes during a cold and dreary December serviced the dimly lit, smoke-filled, country music–playing "hillbilly" bars and brothels of South Broadway and Cherokee Street, complete with "Honky Tonk Angels" and "blues." The songs were sad, the patrons "down home" and "other," beat and tragic. Where did these tragic souls come from? How had they become caricatures of a country song, down on their luck in "blues city"?

I majored in geography at St. Louis University and often traveled *On the Road* style in a 1951 Ford with a couple of friends around the United States, Canada, Mexico, and Central America, sometimes traversing the upland and Deep South. The passing panorama of people and places on these hard-driving odysseys—from Pahokee, Florida, to Waterproof, Louisiana; Valdosta, Georgia, to Wheeling, West Virginia, and points beyond—left me with a yen to know more about southern "folk" and their lifeways.

Then during my senior year of university, I fortuitously took a graduate seminar from Dr. Gene Wilhelm, Jr., on "The Geography of the Blue Ridge Mountains." Because of my keen interest, he asked me to participate in a graduate field/research course in Shenandoah National Park and the Blue Ridge Parkway during the summer of 1965. This was part of a larger project to reconstruct aspects of "mountain culture" that had been all but obliterated when the park was established and residents forced to move elsewhere.

A chance detour through the eastern Kentucky coal fields on the way home led me to Pippa Passes, where I met an "authentic" local family in situ who later wrote to me and encouraged me to work in "Appalachia." (Ironically, the surviving members of this family now live in Vancouver, British Columbia, and Knopp-Labach, Germany.) This glimpse of "hard-core" "Appalachia" led me to apply to work with the Appalachian Volunteers during the summer of 1966, by which time I was a master's student in geography at the University of Nebraska.

Through this work, I finally fulfilled my dream of living in a televisionless rural hollow with a large mountain family of nine, in a rough timber shack, complete with washing machine on the front porch. The setting was Cutshin

Creek in rural Leslie County, near Pine Mountain, in an area in which some Holiness churches practiced snake handling. In fact, I first heard of snake handling while living in this community. Some of the people in the hollow had been involved in this religion in the past and recounted colorful stories of snake handling and feats with blow torches at the annual hillside graveyard "funeralizings" (see Cobb 1965).

While my adopted family did not attend church, I sometimes accompanied others in the hollow to services at the small, local extended family Holiness churches that they attended on Wolf Creek, the head of Persimmon Fork, and over the Mountain at Totz in Harlan County. The congregation at Totz believed in "following signs" (including serpent handling—"What about I got a box of venomous serpents outside"—but serpents, to my disappointment, were not "taken up" at any of these services.

The emotional intensity of these services and the sadness and tragedy recounted in people's testimonies spoke to me. Like Robert Coles (1972), I came to see these very dramatic services not as decontextualized pieces of exotica but as continuous and consistent with these people's lives. Indeed, some services had a political edge, in that speakers affirmed their God-given right "to stand up and be counted, especially in opposition to those who misuse power"; these were, in other words, "backtalking narratives" (Anglin 1992: 105).

I went to Totz with "a woman preacher," Sister Ethel Boggs, and her husband Boyd. They did not have a car, so I drove them there and at the time was shocked when she testified and spoke in tongues as we drove home through the night on the narrow, serpentine rutted roads.

Occasionally after church, Ethel, Boyd, and I would sit 'round the kitchen table at the home of the pastor, the Reverend Opre Simpson. As I was the best reader, they asked me to read specific passages that they would then discuss, especially about the biblical correctness of "woman preachers."

Although I was not very interested in religion per se at this time, mountain religion as it articulated with and reflected hollow life did become an interest— along with the challenges of living with a large family in close quarters and surviving the politics of attempting to be a "change agent" in this small, dispersed "community" (not to mention the Russian roulette of driving the narrow roads plied by thundering, overloaded coal trucks and drunken drivers from Perry County "beer joints").

Living on Cutshin Creek with the Williams family set the stage and gave me a rich experiential basis for later studying serpent handling. It certainly disabussed me of any romantic notions of exotic mountaineers living in a historical time warp. These people of hollow and coal camp were not the isolated, quaint bumpkins of popular (and my earlier) imagination but working people with a checkered and complex involvement with multinational corporations and the rise and fall of world coal prices.

The people with whom I lived—Bige, Lena, and children—were poor because of coal mining. He suffered from black lung, could no longer work for wages, and lived on a pension. He looked at life soberly and had no rosy illusions about "the American Dream." I lived in their house as a family member and fully participated in their round of life—ploughing, planting, weeding, harvesting, butchering a hog, hunting squirrel and groundhog, stringing beans to dry, "sanging" (collecting ginseng root for the export market to Korea), riding with the family to town or to visit relatives, going to the all-night drive-in movie in Hazard with the kids, helping the men on the "happy pappy" program patch the road, or dig a grave, and just passing time sitting on the front porch swing with the family, spitting watermelon seeds or drinking giant-sized bottles of Royal Crown Cola.

My trial by fire in eastern Kentucky gave me an in-depth knowledge of everyday life in a rural hollow and, with it, a certain ease or poise in interacting in this sometimes unpredictable and at times violent setting, and it very much set the stage for my work with serpent handlers. Because I knew this context so intimately, the snake handlers and other Pentecostal people whom I incidentally met as part of daily life did not seem bizarre or aberrant to me but were an understandable part of the fabric of life here. I, therefore, was never tempted to see snake handling as an entity unto itself but always as part of a much wider and somewhat fluid social context. My experiences here also set the tone of my later fieldwork in an Appalachian context—become immersed in people's everyday lives and meanings, take life as it comes, "roll with the flow."

By 1969, after months of cultural geography fieldwork in the hollow toward a master's in geography (which I eventually abandoned because it was seen as being "too anthropological" by geographers) and two years of teaching geography at Tennessee Technological University, where I as well worked with very poor hill people near Hanging Limb and Muddy Pond, I was ready for a change of scene and professional direction, so I moved to Edmonton, Alberta, Canada, to begin a qualifying year in a graduate program in anthropology with the idea of doing fieldwork with Native Canadians, Hutterites, or Dukhobors in northern or western Canada.

But I gave a number of guest lectures to classes on my work in eastern Kentucky, and students and staff expressed considerable interest. Then a chance viewing of the film *The Holy Ghost People* at an ethnographic film festival and a rereading of Nathan Gerrard's "The Serpent-Handling Religions of West Virginia" (1968) suggested the possibility of a research problem and general geographical area of "Appalachia." Why not, I reasoned, build on my existing knowledge and contacts in eastern Kentucky and Tennessee? Serpent handling churches were nicely bounded networks of believers who met regularly at a central place (like Liebow's *Talley's Corner* [1967]); they could be reached by road, and I even knew of one church in Harlan County that perhaps still practiced serpent handling. Little anthropological work (or scholarly work overall) had been done on this movement, and learning a language other than "downhome" English (which I already knew) was not required. As well, snake handling was sufficiently exotic as an anthropology "at-home" (Messerschmidt

1981) topic that it was anthropologically respectable (Caughey 1986; Hill 1977; Moffatt 1992) and lent itself well to comparative reading as it shared so many features with the "primitive and exotic" religions of textbook representation. With respect to access, being "white" was not a disadvantage, as it might have been working with indigenous people or African Americans; and politically, it was still possible, as far as I knew, to work with Holiness people, unlike other groups in the early 1970s that were becoming closed to anthropologists.

Underlying these rationales, however, was my "romance" with "Appalachia" and growing desire to go back, rekindled by distance and the dark frigid depths of an Edmonton winter. And for the personal and philosophical predispositions that I have revealed in this section, I was intrigued by the possibility of entering into this seemingly strange and highly charged realm of snake handlers to experience life, death, the human condition in this particular crucible, and like all good anthropologists, of finding a people of my own and interpreting their story more accurately than had been done previously by the press and by other scholars.

SETTING—"THE SNAKE HANDLING CAPITAL OF THE WORLD"

> This Homecoming was held in 1973 at a small church outside of Newport, Tennessee (once known as "the snake-handling capital of the world"), and attracted an international assortment of media.
>
> Frank Fortunato (1980: 52)

When I first "turned up" at the Holiness Church of God in Jesus Name in July 1971, it had not yet been dubbed "the snake handling capital of the world" by *Hustler*. In 1971, this recently formed (1969) church was a small congregation of some twenty-five to fifty participants. Yet it had already attracted some local, regional, and national attention in the press due to legal difficulties ensuing from their very open handling of serpents at service station parking lots (and, in one instance, in a non–serpent handling church).[10] In fact, I first learned of this church from the *Knoxville-News Sentinel* coverage of the serpent bite of Buford Pack on June 11 of that year (a story that was syndicated across the nation).

But I had no way of knowing at the time that this church would one day become for a time a newsworthy phenomenon, attracting hordes of media people, sightseers, writers, researchers, and filmmakers. Indeed, I was not looking for a publicity-attracting church to study in 1971 but, rather, for a somewhat isolated congregation in which I alone could observe and interpret the ebb and flow of serpent handling life.

I read widely before going "to the field" and wrote two seminar papers on serpent handling (1970a, 1971b) and two research proposals (1970b, 1971a), complete with models and hypotheses. As discussed before, I conceptualized my problem in terms of psychological and sociological functions and dsyfunctions—hence, "The Function of Serpent Handling Cults in Southern Appalachian Acculturation."

Having decided the "why" of ethnographic research, the next step was to decide "where" (Murphy 1989: 240); basically, a church or churches where people still took up serpents (the probability of which seemed somewhat dubious as Weston La Barre advised me in a letter in 1971 that to his "knowledge, serpent handling was still practiced in only two places, Big Stone Gap near Wise, Virginia, and perhaps near the Scrabble Creek area."

So in the spring of 1971 I headed south in my 1964 Pontiac Wagon with camera, tape recorder, and detailed research proposal and set of hypotheses (none of which I used that summer) to find a fieldwork site (if such churches still existed, and if so, to implement my research design). With respect to finding a field site, Cohen and Eames (1982: 22) correctly concluded: "For an anthropologist going into the field the most difficult and anxiety producing situation is the decision about the specific locale for research. Not only does the anthropologist experience anxiety in making the decision initially, but the anxiety may continue afterward. 'Is this the right place for research?' anthropologists ask themselves." My selection of a field site was fraught with difficulty and made me quite anxious. Because I assumed that such churches were rare, or no longer existed, and that such people would be secretive, and suspicious of my attempts to study them, I made a number of tactical errors that greatly affected my site selection and ultimately my approach to study.

Anthropologist Steven Kane and sociologist Kenneth Ambrose both did M.A. and Ph.D. theses on serpent handling. Both used their M.A. work as an opportunity to survey widely the range of serpent handling churches across a number of states or localities. Visiting a range of congregations before selecting a site has the advantage of making one aware of the diversity; having this information, one can select a site that is either representative or ideal in other regards with respect to the interests of the researchers. (For example, if one is interested in the psychophysiology of fire handling, it makes sense to select a congregation that regularly practices this rite, as many do not.) Similarly, congregations vary in their frequency of serpent handling and poison drinking, if these features happen to be of particular interest to the researcher.

My selection of site was neither systematic nor informed. It was serendipitous, somewhat analogous to Geertz's legendary Balinese cockfight scenario (Geertz 1973), the chance meeting of Liebow with "streetcorner men" (Liebow 1967), or Castaneda's apocryphal meeting with Don Juan Matus at an Arizona bus station (Castaneda 1971). Moreover, my effort to locate serpent handlers was not as effortless as those cited above appeared to have been. I had planned originally to conduct fieldwork in eastern Kentucky and to live in the community of Cutshin Creek, where I had worked in 1966, or to rent a room in Harlan, Kentucky. On the way to the field, however, I visited an old friend in Knoxville who lived across from the University of Tennessee. It turned out that the house in which he lived had a spare air-conditioned room that I could use for the summer. As I still had considerable library work to do, it made sense to use this as a base of operations. From Knoxville, I made a number of excursions into eastern Kentucky in search of a field site. I contacted Sister Boggs with whom I had attended Holiness services in 1966. She now had a small store and seemed interested in talking only about her business, not about religion, and hadn't been to a Holiness meeting since we drove to Totz in August of 1966. Other people in the hollow whom I visited seemed not to know or care about whether serpent handling was still practiced in this area or not.

I then visited universities in the region to speak with anthropologists, sociologists, and religious studies people. The consensus of these scholars was that such churches no longer existed, of if they did, they were very secretive and suspicious people who were difficult to contact. One professor of religious studies thought that the practice still occurred in the Newport-Covington area across from Cincinnati, Ohio. His impression was that it was like a floating crap game and one could not predict where or when it would occur again in the same area—there being a strong underground network of communication between serpent handlers to inform one another when services would occur so as to shield this information from "the law." He advised me against trying to work in Harlan County, where a colleague of his had recently been badly cut up and mutilated by locals, placed in a box, and dumped on the hospital steps.

An anthropologist who had done considerable research in the area also felt that serpent handlers were mobile and clandestine. She had heard of impromptu services being conducted on county lines to allow escape to the other side, should the sheriff appear. They also held meetings at remote off-the-road locations to avoid the gaze of the authorities. She wished me luck but felt that they would be a difficult group to locate and "break in to."

I then remembered the preacher who had conducted services in Totz in 1966 and drove there to see him. Sadly, I arrived just as the funeral party was returning from his burial. He had been hit by a coal train three days earlier. This was not an opportune time to ask questions about serpent handling.

During those initial weeks in the field, it seemed that I was on an endless quest of a mirage. This led to feelings of great frustration and deep depression. Rather than the rural nirvana I had imagined while still in Edmonton, some of my days in eastern Kentucky were nightmarish and horrible, plagued by heat, humidity, dust, loneliness, alienation, and car trouble. This also was due to the fact that many of the people who had taken me to visit churches in 1966 were no longer there: A number of old people had died; some families and most of the young people I had "hung around with" had all migrated to Ohio. I found that seeking out churches on my own to serve as a field site was a very different proposition from going along for the ride with people, and keeping a low profile as a removed spectator.

After long days on the road (the distances were sometimes great and the roads poor), my return to the air-conditioned room in Knoxville was a blessed escape. The attractiveness of (and rationalizations for) doing even more library work at the University of Tennessee (and in libraries in Chattanooga, Nashville, and even St. Louis) grew apace with my frustration at not finding serpent handlers (not to mention retreating to my room and the company of the group of students living in the house, as well as visiting friends in Cookeville, Nashville, and Richmond, Kentucky). I often feared in those days that the entire summer would pass in this way, and I would return to Edmonton without having found a single serpent-handling church. I was convinced as well that I did not want to study this religion after all and that I should find another topic, or even another profession.

My luck changed eventually, as I explained in a letter to my then–thesis adviser:

Around June 17, 1971, things started happening. That evening in the *Knoxville-News Sentinel* the enclosed article appeared (it tells of a case of serpent bite at an east Tennessee church). I contacted the reporter who covered the story, but he was at first reluctant to talk with me, as he was trying to sell a story on the church to a Chicago tabloid. He finally agreed to discuss it with me and agreed to take me to the church in a couple of weeks after he had more of a chance to finish his ''research'' at the church. His two weeks was more like four, as he went on vacation for two weeks. In the meantime, I made another concentrated effort in eastern Kentucky. This time, Bige, the man I stayed with in Cutshin Creek, remembered where serpent handling was conducted and a preacher who I might contact. Before when I visited him, he didn't remember or didn't want to talk about this. He is opposed to serpent handling.

Also, this time Sister Ethel was more interested in talking about religion. She admitted that she once had handled serpents and that even today, small, spontaneous services were conducted in her store. She also told me where a number of small Churches of God could be found which practiced serpent handling. To date, this has been the most exciting, rewarding part of the research—a sense of impending discovery.

The church that she directed me to was a classic, the Church of God at Pine Mountain where serpent handling had been conducted since 1931. The service lasted four hours and it was extremely emotional with about twenty minutes of serpent handling, much speaking in tongues and some faith healing. This group is very close knit and I felt awkward as people stared at me and whispered to one another as I entered the church house. This made me intensely uncomfortable and I had felt the need to flee the area forever and discontinue a study of serpent handling. But I returned for the Tuesday night service and had a better chance to talk with people before the church service and found them friendly in an understated way and they welcomed me to the service. I did not handle the field work role part very well, as, given my nervousness, I could only explain my presence in terms of my local ties on Cutshin Creek, rather that my hoped for research role.

Meanwhile in Tennessee, the reporter returned from vacation and directed me to the church that became my field site.

I recall that night in a piece called ''First Time'' (Birckhead 1993b: 50–51):

On a rainy summer night in July 1971 I nervously drove the 50 miles from my rented room in Knoxville to rural Carson Springs, Tennessee to make my first uncertain contact with the "snake handlers" of Smoky Mountain Holiness Church. A newspaper reporter reluctantly had given me sketchy directions over the phone and I was on my way to "Snake Hollow."

My palpitating heart, dry mouth and rational brain urged me to return to Knoxville and spend the evening at Brother Jack's (home of the famous Pig burger) with a side of barbecue ribs and a six pack of Budweiser. But a blind and callow dedication to anthropology pushed me onward through the mountain forests on sinuous, rutted tracks until I reached the "church house" in the clearing in an English Mountain Cove.

The loud, pulsating gospel rock music, shouting, hand-clapping and foot stomping told me that the service had already begun. I clumsily opened the door of the one-time hunting cabin, entered and slipped quickly (and very much noticed) into the back bench, feeling that I had just stepped off the planet. The place literally shook from the amplified music and foot-stomping. And these people looked alien and weird. Rattlesnakes and copperheads were being passed around by a number of men dancing about on a low platform in the front of the church, while a long-haired, bearded photographer clicked away frames of film. During the course of the evening I found out that these people walk barefooted on stinging scorpions and snakes, and applied flames of blow torches to their naked skin.

After considerable time when the service was drawing to a close, I quickly and quietly stole out of the church and returned to the security of my room across from the University in Knoxville. I did not want to speak to any of those "weirdos," at least not then and there.

Under the heading, "Everyday People," I go on to explain:

Two days later I was back in Snake Hollow, but this time before the service commenced. I met the very warm and friendly pastor of the church Jimmy Williams, and explained my research interests in a general way and was well on my way as an "ethnographer" of this cultural scene.

With the passage of time, and attendance at three, four-hour church services a week, I started putting names to faces, picking up biographical details of individuals, and learned to see church services as culturally patterned performances rather than as disorganized bedlam. And as even more time passed, my involvement in everyday serpent-handling life increased greatly, especially with people outside of formal services. And the more I experienced life with the "bizarre snake handlers," the less bizarre they became for me, lending support to the anthropological maxim "the exotic is everyday" (Condominas, in Chagnon 1974: viii).

Looking back now, the difficulties I had seem rather unnecessary. My misconceptions from the literature, from popular media, and from talking with a number of academics in the region colored my view of these people as secretive, clannish, suspicious of strangers, and even dangerous.[11] The way I approached serpent handlers and found a population no doubt affected my vantage point, stance, and the way I operated in the field. Because I was originally nervous and paranoid, I took a more low-keyed approach than I might otherwise have taken. Once there, I was more or less swept along with the action and ended up here and there as "my people" networked around the region. The emphasis and texture of my work no doubt reflect my somewhat unstructured approach. But what did I sacrifice by working this way? My slow to move, nonpushy approach was certainly well received by church members. Over the years, I have seen pushy, "Yankee" researchers attempt to work with these people but, one way or the other, be turned away. I tended not to force interaction, just to let things happen as they happen. This probably gave me a more organic picture of the religion and understanding less structured by my categories. But, no doubt, intense involvement in one group and with selected people[12] in that group limits one's overall perspective to some degree. So I have to be cautious not to generalize too widely from my experiences at one church and the half-dozen or so other churches that it linked into.

"MY PEOPLE/MY CHURCH"—EXPERIENCING SERPENT HANDLING

> After his father left, his mother really went off the deep end and got mixed up with a bunch of backwoods, Holy Roller snake handlers [in the Smoky Mountains of Tennessee]. One night, after an hour of ranting and beating the Bible, the red-faced, wild-haired preacher got his barefoot congregation all excited. They were all chanting and stomping their feet when suddenly he reached into a potato sack and pulled out two huge rattlesnakes and started waving them around in the air, lost in the Spirit.
>
> . . . The preacher was dancing around calling out for believers to take up the serpent and cleanse their souls in the faith of Abraham when all of a sudden his mother ran up, grabbed one of the snakes away from him, and looked it right in the face. She began babbling in the unknown tongue, the whole time staring into the snake's yellow eyes. Everybody . . . began to sway and moan. As she started to walk around the room with it, people began falling down on the floor, jerking and screaming . . .
>
> Still wild-eyed and in a trance, she glanced down at her child for one split second and in that second the rattler lunged and struck the woman in the side of her face. She looked back at the snake, stunned, and he struck again, fast and hard this time, striking her in the neck, the fangs puncturing her jugular vein. She dropped the angry serpent with a thud, and it crawled contemptuously away down the aisle.
>
> His mother looked around the room that was now as silent as death, with a surprised look on her face, and as her eyes glazed over, she sank slowly to the floor. She was dead in less than a minute.
>
> Fanny Flagg (1992: 18–29)

Fieldwork "usually means living with and living like those who are studied" (Van Maanen 1988: 2). "Living with" and "living like" the people being studied may cause tension for the observer—the tension of being both "stranger and friend'' (Powdermaker 1966). As Clifford and Marcus (1986: 13) note: "Since Malinowski's time, the 'method' of participant-observation has enacted a delicate balance of subjectivity and objectivity. The ethnographer's personal experiences, especially those of participation and empathy, are recognized as central to the research process, but they are firmly restrained by the impersonal standards of observation and 'objective' distance.''

While it is now fashionable to reveal the everyday details and trials of field-work (e.g., Crick 1982, 1989; Darnell 1991; Rose 1982, 1987, 1990; Van Maanen 1988; Wolf 1991), researchers of serpent handling, to date, have disclosed little of their experiences of working in this setting. And without this information, it is difficult for the reader to fully understand how knowledge about serpent handling "others" was constructed, how meanings were "imposed on experiences in the field so as to constitute the data of anthropology" (Crick 1982: 16).

How does one live "with" and "like" people such as serpent handlers? These churches are small and close-knit; an observer is very much visible at services of ten people in a saint's home. The larger services at church can become extremely emotional and intense, with people "dancing" wildly "in the Spirit" to a driving rock beat, punctuated by shrill screams and the eerie sounds of "unknown tongues." Sometimes, the "Spirit" causes the complete collapse and blackout of a saint onto the floor, a state that can last for minutes to hours. A "good Spirit" is palpable and contagious to "the observer" as well, affecting profoundly, if only subliminally, what he or she sees, feels, hears, and understands. A good Spirit ("anointing") also can lead to serpent and fire handling and poison drinking—acts potentially dangerous and sometimes fatal to participants (and possibly to the ethnographer). The possibility and immediacy of sudden death is real and gives a particular poignancy to living with and like saints. How should a city-born and-raised, university-educated person react when someone is bitten by a snake, appears to be dying, and refuses offers of medical attention? Or if one observes a member drink carbon tetrachloride, lye, battery acid, or strychnine and fears for the person's life, what ethical stance does one assume? (Two people in "my church" died of strychnine, and five others who sometimes attended, of "serpent-bite"). As Ambrose (1978: 27) reflects on his own fieldwork in Ohio and West Virginia: "The author became so involved with this group that he found it very difficult not to interfere and offer first aid to those who were bitten by serpents. It was painful to observe the suffering many of them experienced and especially hard to witness the deaths." (See Heider [1979: 17–18] for a discussion of similar concerns in a tribal setting.)

Similarly, as serpent handling is illegal in most states except West Virginia, what are the ethical and legal considerations of participating in and/or witnessing illegal acts or acts that can cause injury, suffering, and death? One can become easily implicated here, for example, by doing something as simple as carrying a serpent box into a church or by transporting serpents in one's car. And as an observer of illegal activity, the possibility of being called on to serve as a witness in court hearings is always present (as happened to me on one occasion when I appeared as a defense witness in an involuntary manslaughter case against two saints related to the strychnine deaths in the church in April 1973). Of course, as a defense witness, I could be accused (as I was by a Canadian Broadcasting Corporation TV newsmagazine program compere when I was interviewed on *Hourglass*, May 28 1973) "of helping to protect that environment" in which people die of strychnine and/or snakebite.

I do not offer clear answers to these questions, but my stance has been to come down firmly on the side of my hosts, the Holiness people. In essence, like most anthropologists, I was relativistic and guardedly pragmatic, with the aim of gaining knowledge and understanding of this subculture. (See Freeman [1965] for an argument against cultural relativism.)[13]

Other questions arise as well. How far does one actually participate as a "participant-observer"? The questions I am most frequently asked are: "Did I handle snakes and fire, or drink strychnine?" "Was I 'born again'?" "Was I baptized by total immersion in the French Broad River?" "Did I rely on spiritual healing, speak in tongues, or attempt to cast out (or have cast out of me) devils?"

The answer to these questions is, quite simply, no; I was not a full participant in this religion. Practically speaking, I was (and still am) afraid of poisonous snakes[14] and had no desire to drink poisons or subject my skin to fire. Theological, legal, and ethical considerations come in as well. Serpent handling requires "anointing" power from the Holy Ghost, and one usually needs to "be saved" (baptized, repentant of sins, born again, and "living right") to receive this power. As I hadn't "paid the price," my handling would have had to rely on faith or courage "in the carnal mind," either of which can "get you planted." And had I been bitten and sought medical help, the local authorities would have been notified and the church would have faced legal reprisals.

It would have been similarly infridig for me to have mimicked other manifestations of the Spirit such as speaking in tongues, shaking, shouting, or "being saved." Anyhow, people did not expect me to and more or less accepted me as I was. The people whom I knew well in the church did not exert pressure on me to convert to the faith. Occasionally, a visiting preacher would try to "get me to repent," but "my people" would simply say, "This is Brother Jimmy from Alberta, Canada. He is studying . . ." In one instance, the visitor replied: "But he still needs to be saved"—a retort that made people think and say, "Yes, I guess you're right." Yet I must emphasize that I was not pressured by the people I was close to in the church. They were very open and tolerant of our obvious differences. But I suspect that many felt because I so faithfully attended most church services, was so keenly interested in the religion, and was a friend and "brother" to many that I would probably "come into the faith" one day. And at least some people felt that my presence was of benefit to the church, as I could help to "publish the Word" in Canada and later in Australia;[15]

and as mentioned above, my testimony in the Cocke County Court as an informed outsider in the manslaughter trial contributed to a favorable outcome for the church.[16]

Comments about my "publishing the Word" usually made me uneasy, as I feared that saints did not really understand my work as an anthropologist and that perhaps in my early nervousness and tentative shyness I had explained my work in too general a way. Anxiety was a constant companion during the early phases of fieldwork. I often felt a tension between a duplicitous ethnographic self and an existential "true self." This sense of unease caused more grief and sleepless nights than any other part of this research (next to recurrent nightmares about being attacked by serpents) and, hence, profoundly affected how I behaved in the field and how and what I have written (and perhaps more important, what I have not written) about serpent handling.

I was inclined to overidentify with the saints, "my people," and to err on the side of "membership," involvement, and experience, as I had done in my previous work in eastern Kentucky hollows. When I began this work in 1971, I was twenty-seven years old, single, relatively new to anthropology, and doing my first real study as an anthropologist. Steeped in the literature on trance and possession states, ecstatic experience, transcendence, altered states of consciousness, the paranormal, and alternate and "separate" realities (Castaneda 1971), I was ripe for apprenticeship and experientially rich fieldwork.

My age, gender, and student and marital status all worked in my favor. This was a newly formed church, and some of its "elders" were my age or only slightly older (a couple were actually younger). I easily occupied the role of friend and student to the elders and as a peer to teenagers and young, unmarried adults in the church. But because I did not have the adult obligations of marriage, children, a job, and a mortgage and was a neophyte in my knowledge of the faith, I was socially younger than my years in this setting. And because I did not have such obligations, I could be fully open to the action, drama, excitement, and travel—the sometimes serendipitous rhythm of a serpent handling way of life.

This was fully consistent with the theoretical approaches that I had applied to this cultural scene. Specifically, readings of Berger and Luckmann (1966), Garfinkel (1967), Goffman (1959), and Murphy (1971) alerted me to the emergent, constructed, transitory, problematic, and fragile nature of all "social realities." Thus, my predilection was to read the small details of everyday interaction through which this "reality" was ongoingly constituted, created, and sustained "in the face of contradictions and competing definitions of reality" (Birckhead 1974a: 3).

Because members sought "personal dispensation from the normal laws of cause and effect and for miracles and oracles" (Wilson 1970: 167), this type of church served as a propitious site for interpreting questions of social order, meaning, reality construction, and the nature of minority belief systems and religious identity in the modern world.

Given my interest, personality, and terms of reference, I sometimes found it difficult to distance myself from interaction and immediate experience sufficiently to analyze and interpret this religion anthropologically. My dissertation adviser, Regna Darnell, used to remind me that I was an anthropologist, rather than a "member," and that when writing I must come back to an appropriate stance. Edward Norbeck, my external examiner, made a similar comment about how I positioned myself in the text with respect to "my people" and urged me to amplify my anthropological voice, lest my stated aim "to make sense of a religion that to outsiders seems bizarre, incomprehensible, or irrational" (Birckhead 1976b: vi) lapse into a defensive advocacy of "my church." He strongly urged me to qualify my claim that "I have tried to examine behavior from the perspective of the actors" with the following proviso:

For fear of overstatement I feel constrained to qualify my statement that this account describes the saints and their behavior from their own point of view. For brief periods I was sometimes able to shed my ordinary assumptions and views of the world but, of course, I did not become a saint in the sense of seeing the world through the "spiritual mind" or experiencing an infusion of power. From the perspective of saints, then, this study suffers from inherent limitations as I have no personal knowledge of certain experiences important to them. I am aware also that my account reflects the tension between my perspectives as a participant of community life and as an anthropologist who must make some theoretical sense of his subjects of study, and I trust that saints as well as fellow anthropologists will understand the problems of attempting to translate one conceptual system into the logic and terminology of another. (viii)

I must confess that at times the distinction between me and "they" became blurred. It was only with Norbeck's strong urgings that I was even able to textualize the idea of "my subjects of study." I felt some guilt in saying this, as it was similar to constructing my family as "subjects of study." The family analogy is apt here because some in the church became like brothers and sisters to me and/or respected elders and mentors (but subjects of study!). In this regard, Karl Heider's (1993: 4–5) introduction to my chapter in his book is more congenial with my sense of subject positioning: "Jim Birckhead tells how the media's prurient fascination with snake handling works against his attempts as an anthropologist to explain his Pentecostal friends."

At times I vacillated between an insider's identification with "my people" and a distanced outsider's "gut feeling" that "these are not my people." I often experienced transitions between, and juxtapositions of, my Holiness selves and my other selves as a strained and painful metamorphosis, which produced in the end a blurring of these boundaries in my head and hence my idea of "myself" (further explored in the concluding section). Such vacillating mental and personality gymnastics greatly affect the perspective or vantage point one assumes in a constantly shifting field world, making it difficult at times to find a solid position from which to view these unfolding realities. Burton (1993: 4–5) captures well aspects of the yin and yang of working with serpent handlers:

What we wished to provide was a perspective for understanding the people as well as the practice.

That perspective, however, is not easily attained. Since most of us tend to seek simple, concrete explanations for phenomena, it is easy to view one aspect of serpent handling rather than the whole and, consequently, either to romanticize or brutalize the people and the practice. One can feel after attending a service that it is completely irrational, wild—people running around, falling down, quivering, uttering strange sounds, drinking deadly poisons; taking venomous serpents (giant and tiny ones, coiled, extended limp, knotted together, rattlers, cottonmouths, copperheads, cobras) and staring at them nose to nose, wrapping them around their necks, wearing them on their heads, pitching them, carrying armloads of them, shaking them, petting them; displaying arms tattooed with snakes, hands atrophied by bites, fingers missing, clothing embroidered and etched with snakes—or feel the same sense of the bizarre after going into homes and seeing live deadly snakes in closets and adjoining rooms, pictures framed on the wall of people with handfuls of rattlers, photo albums of disfigured bodies from venom poisoning, or a huge frozen rattlesnake taken out of a freezer by a relative of a person whom the serpent killed during a funeral service for yet another snakebite victim. All of this can seem as abnormal as an episode from "The Twilight Zone."

On the other hand, one can leave a service or a home and feel completely awed by the faith, sincerity, and mysterious power manifested by these people—sensing that somehow they know, feel, have something in their lives that is redeeming amidst a lost world. As Lou Crabtree's persona in her poem "salvation" says, "jesus jesus this old body aint so important/i got holiness flirtin with death." The integrity of serpent handlers strikes one as something real in the omnipresence of appearances, an inspiring breath in the mists of "mouth honor."

Given this heightened and variegated environment of a serpent handling community, we can once again pose the question, How does one live with and like serpent handlers? The studies of serpent handling that I read prior to going there myself (and since) provided little or no explication of what the researchers actually did in the field day to day. I now present more grounded material—vignettes and fragments from my field notes, excerpts from letters to friends, working reports to my dissertation committee, and so forth—to better illustrate the concreteness of everyday experience in the field, from which my ethnographic "data" on serpent handling were constructed. The first is an outline of my field activities from July 12 to August 12, 1973 (from a progress report to my graduate committee):

Itinerary

1. Thursday, July 12, 1972, to Monday, July 16, 1973—enroute to Lexington, Kentucky (Edmonton to St. Louis by air; St. Louis to Lexington by road).

2. Monday, July 16, to Tuesday, July 17—discussed my research with fellow researcher Steven Kane in Lexington.

3. Wednesday, July 18—evening service at Newport; spent the night at home of church family.

4. Thursday, July 19—rode with Liston in truck to pick up load of canned vegetables at Tellico Plains, Tennessee.

5. Friday, July 20, to Saturday, July 21—visited and helped with farm chores at home of part-time tenant farmer. An interesting perspective from a man who some consider to be demon possessed, and who considers himself to be so.

6. Saturday, July 21—evening church service. Back to Al's for all-night discussion with Al, sociology student from a local university, two freelance writers, and a sociology instructor from Maryland.

7. Sunday, July 22—to WLIK radio broadcast studio for 12:15 P.M. weekly, live radio broadcast. During afternoon visited church people. Then, attended evening service. After service, 11:00 to 11:45 P.M., went to a baptism in French Broad River. After baptism rode with church people to Greenville, South Carolina, to pray for sister who had been seriously serpent-bit.

8. Monday, July 23—arrived at Greenville, at 4:00 A.M. At 5:00 A.M. I went to the church with brothers for an impromptu prayer service and rehash session of why sister had been bitten. At 9:00 A.M. we went to the hospital to pray for bitten sister. 10:00 A.M. to 2:00 P.M., returned to Newport and on way released vicious snake in a wooded area (a victim of rot root mouth). 4:00 P.M. to 9:00 P.M., visited with church family at farm, and returned to Knoxville for rest and work on field notes.

9. Wednesday, July 25—attended evening church service, then spent the night at home of church family.

10. Thursday, July 26—went shopping with some sisters and children. Took two boys to the barber shop. In afternoon a brother and I shot a vicious Western Diamondback named Rudolf that the brother had a dream about a year before it materialized. Rest of evening I discussed dreams and anointing with the brother. At 11:00 P.M., Liston picked me up in the semi that he drove and he and I headed out to Bowling Green, Kentucky, to pick up a load of green beans.

11. Friday, July 27—on the road with Liston.

12. Saturday, July 28—arrived at Tellico Plains cannery at 4:00 A.M. where we were met by Al and sociology student, who drove us back to Newport in time for 9:00 A.M. contempt of court hearing. After hearing, Al and I walked the hot, dirty streets of Newport wondering why it had turned out so badly. Went to evening church service followed by baptism in the French Broad River at 11:00 P.M., and then stayed overnight with church family.

13. Sunday, July 29—went to radio broadcast at 12:15 P.M.,then with family until evening service. People dropped in all afternoon, including two North Carolina boys with freshly caught, wild rattlesnake. Attended evening church service and drove back to Knoxville for rest and work on field notes.

14. Tuesday, July 31, to Friday, August 3—drove to Lexington, Kentucky, to see Steven Kane. Worked on field notes and returned to Knoxville via Harlan, Kentucky.

15. Saturday, August 4—attended evening church service. Tennessee Bureau of Investigation agents were present to see if serpents would be handled. Serpents were taken up by several brothers and sisters of the church. After service, went back to Al's for all-night discussion.

16. Sunday, August 5—attended 12:15 P.M. radio broadcast followed by afternoon with Al and family, visiting church people. Went to evening service and then back with Al and family.

17. Monday, August 6—7:00 A.M., a number of us drove to hospital in Asheville, North Carolina, to pray for a young brother who was about to undergo surgery. A minor hassle with his family ensued. From hospital we drove to Marshall, North Carolina, to home of church sister, and then returned to Newport. From Newport we drove to Knoxville to pick up freelance writer Robert Pelton and then on to Nashville to visit with gospel singing family, "The Singing Hemphills," at their home. They plan to write a book on the church. We stayed there until nearly midnight.

18. Tuesday, August 7—was on road all night, arriving back at Newport at 9:00 A.M. I returned to Knoxville for rest and field note work.

19. Wednesday, August 8—attended evening church service and back to Al's for late-night discussion.

20. Thursday, August 9—went fishing with teenagers in the church and visited members' homes on the way. In evening drove over to rural Rocky Top with a church family who wanted to show me the Sand Hill Church, where serpent handling had started in this area. We attended a service there. After service, went to Liston's house for a late-night visit and then back to Knoxville.

21. Friday, August 10—met Liston in Knoxville in morning to talk with the American Civil Liberties Union lawyer about the Supreme Court challenge to Tennessee anti–snake handling law. We then visited the Doc Walls traveling snake show. (Walls provided the cobra that was handled in July.) After that, I was interviewed by Bob Pelton for his book *The Persecuted Prophets*.

22. Saturday, August 11—took Al and family out to eat in Newport. Drove to Hot Springs, North Carolina, to pick up a brother and his wife so they could attend church service. At evening service a brother from Scrabble Creek, West Virginia, was present. After service back to Al's house where a group of serpent handlers from North Carolina were staying. Went joy-riding half of the night with a car load of teenagers, returning to Al's for late-night discussions.

23. Sunday, August 12—attended radio broadcast and afterwards two car loads of people from the church went on a picnic in Great Smoky Mountain National Park. After picnic went to evening service, during which a brother was nicked by a copperhead. After service at Al's, Al counseled the handler about why he had been bitten. After a farewell snack, I left for Knoxville to drive to St. Louis and then to fly back to Edmonton.

The following excerpt from a letter to a friend conveys the flavor of an ecstatic, but more relaxed, weeknight service, the type of service that produces good feelings, a sense of community, and fellowship and, I think, conveys why this religion appeals to people.

"A Wednesday Night Service"—August 16, 1972 (Excerpts from a Letter to a Friend)

I arrived earlier than usual and chatted with Brother Jimmy, Brother Burl and Brother Reuble. . . . Night was slowly coming on, and small groups of saints were scattered about the church yard, talking and resting after a day's work.

Brother Joe drove up in a new Cadillac with Ohio plates on it—local boy makes good up north. . . .

Some of the sisters were inside the weathered building, talking and joking with one another. Children ran in and out of the church house and around the parking lot, slipping and skidding on loose gravel.

At 7:20 P.M. we all shuffled into the close atmosphere of the converted hunting cabin church house. The night outside had a cool edge to it, and the creeping, crawling creatures of the rural South were just starting into their nightly orchestration.

Inside the somewhat clammy air of the church house, 'neath unshaded light bulbs, the musicians were tuning guitars while saints seated in the benches continued various conversations.

Jimmy stared off into space, no doubt in preparation for the coming of the Holy Ghost. The musty odor of human bodies permeated the air, and to my romantic nostrils it smelt down home and earthy. It was a familiar smell that I associate with being at church on sultry summer nights in east Tennessee.

The tuning of guitars imperceptibly drifted into music and spirited singing and the service began, with Brother Burlin playing drums, Brother Drew shaking the tambourine, two or three young teenagers playing electric guitars, and Sister Beulah (also playing a guitar) belting out the deep gospel number "I've Got a Right Thing Going with Jesus," followed without a break by the Holiness "anthem," "Holy, Holy, Holy"—"They call us serpent handlers, but it's alright. . . ."

As the song subsided, Brother Ed shouted a few words and called all Christians up to the "altar" to pray. Each person then recited aloud his or her own individual prayer, which formed a rising and falling cacophony of sound, punctuated only by Brother Drew's eerily high voice. The prayers ceased as abruptly as they commenced.

Sister Nellie and Sister Lola now joined the singers on the platform which supports the pulpit and performed an upbeat rendition of "This Little Light of Mine."

Brother Buford entered during the singing, carrying a box with a screen over one end. The box constrained two copperheads. Many saints gazed into the box as he placed it on the pulpit. He was wearing jeans, a plain, untucked long-sleeved shirt, and his longish hair was combed into a pompadour above his forehead. Three scruffy teenage "sinner boys" accompanied him into the church. They took places in the back bench next to the door.

As the spirited singing continued, one song merging into the next, Brother Jimmy untied the rope that secured the lid of the serpent box and peered in at the wriggling copperheads. He quickly closed the lid and testified that he was not ready to handle the serpents as he didn't have the "anointing."

Brother Buford didn't have the anointing either. Brother Joe, guitar hanging around his neck, moved into center stage and sang, Johnny Cash style, "Somewhere Down that Lonesome Road."

When the song finished, slight, frail Brother Robert mounted the platform and performed, as requested by Brother Bu, "Mansion in the Sky." He testified after the song finished, then got the spirit. He shouted, jumped up and down, ran around on the platform. Shouted some more, his face went a bright red, his protruding veins pulsating. He was animated, consumed with passion and ecstasy. His spirit was contagious, as if an electric current had passed through the throng of believers celebrating at the head of Snake Hollow.

The spirit fell off and Brother Robert stepped off the low platform and hugged and kissed Brother Bu on his way back to his seat.

Brother Buford testified about the "sinner boys" who brought a large, freshly caught rattlesnake to his house late last night; how he had gotten the "victory" over that serpent and stands as a testimony to the power of the Lord—"There's power in the blood . . . in the blood of the lamb."

The music regained control—the jangling tambourines, the clashing cymbals, the pounding drum beat, the amplified twangs of the electric guitars, foot stomping, and hand clapping.

At 9:15 P.M., Brother Ed had an altar call and invited anyone who wanted to, to come up front and pray and be "prayed over." A young sister of about seventeen years, wearing tennis shoes and a light cotton print dress, answered the call. She slipped out of her bench and made her way to the front of the brightly lit church house. She knelt down, her head resting on the "mourner's bench" just below the slightly raised pulpit. Brother Ed layed his hands on her head. Her hands whirled about and her head jerked. Her lip slipped into a rapid quiver. Sister Beulah prayed over her. As if given a shot of adrenaline, she "freaked out" and collapsed onto the floor, shaking and flailing arms and legs convulsively. Her mouth, which appeared to be in spasm, emitted an unearthly sound. Sister Beulah tapped her under the chin repeatedly until the spasm subsided. She attempted to stand up but lost her balance and fell into Beulah's arms. After regaining control, she rose to her feet and danced with abandon about the front of the church. Tambourine shaking, Brother Drew had to move out of her path. This lasted some fifteen minutes. Abruptly, she snapped out of the "spirit," dripping with perspiration and a dazed look in her eyes, and returned to her bench.

Sister Lola then came up to the mourner's bench, was anointed with oil, and had various hands "laid on" her. Her body vibrated and she spoke in tongues for a number of minutes, her outstretched arms and hands rhythmically in sync with her utterances. This eventually subsided and the music once again regained control.

Brother Ed attempted to dismiss the service but was interrupted by Brother Buford, who jumped up onto the platform and said, "You might think I'm crazy, but let's all come up front, shake everyone's hand, and tell them that you love them." We all shuffled out of our respective benches, moved up front, and I was hugged by many brothers. Brother Drew threw his arms around me and buried his head in my chest as he chanted about how much "we appreciate you in the church." Brother Bu hugged me and said he loved me. I lightly shook hands with some of the sisters. The feeling was high. . . . Illiamamamama, illiamamamama, . . . amen.

The service now over, we all poured out into the now very dark night at the head of Snake Hollow. A silver sliver of moon had risen just above the mountains but was barely visible through the tall, ancient trees. The gurgling of the creek could barely be heard above the loud crescendo of the night creatures in their brief struggle with life and death.

I talked to Brother Burlin and to a young guitar player. Bu brought out his copperheads and we looked into the box, commenting on their large size. Brothers and sisters talked in small groups, said their good-byes, and slowly moved to their cars. Bu placed his serpent box in the trunk of his beat-up car with a plate on the front announcing: "I'm a Jesus Man."

I wearily strolled to my 1964 black Pontiac Tempest wagon, got in, started the engine and drove slowly down the rutted, gravel road, and was soon at the gas station by the interstate entrance ramp. I bought my usual after-church carton of chocolate milk, got back into the car, turned on the radio, and was soon on the interstate for the hour's drive back. . . . My adrenaline continued to pump to "Voodoo Chile" on the radio as I approached the urban blues night of inner-city Knoxville's chemical plant air, rail yards, rows of decaying houses, and Brother Jack's Bar-B-Que and his locally famous "Pig Burger"—a different reality.

North Carolina Tent Revival—Snakebite and Fear (Exerpts from Notes, July 28, 1972)

During one of the more intense music sessions, Jimmy walked to the four serpent boxes and brought them center stage. He placed the boxes on the ground about two and a half feet from me. I started feeling fear in the pit of my stomach, as this seemed to be becoming too much like my recurring dreams from the early part of the summer. He first took up the large rattlesnake. It attempted to break free from him. The serpent hung in the air in front of my face with its head and body quite erect. My heart pounded and my stomach further sickened. (This was the first time that I was actually close enough to serpent handling to feel concern for my safety.)

After a couple of minutes, he attempted to put the struggling snake back into the box. He missed the box, and the snake was loose on the ground near my feet. He finally regained control over the serpent, placed it in the box, and quickly shut the lid but did not latch it. He then briefly took up the two copperheads and put them back in their cage. . . .

Brother Buford then brought his rattlesnake to center stage (in box) and Brother Dick a box of copperheads. The rattlesnake did not come out easily. After a few seconds of handling, the serpent struck one of his fingertips on his right hand. He momentarily let go of the snake, and it was free falling in the air in front of me. He then managed to grab it near its tail. (I was very frightened at this point, as he didn't seem to be in control of the situation and a couple of feet from me.) He then waved the serpent frantically and began jumping on and off of the platform, shouting, "It's all right." He screamed and moved about wildly. By this time, Jimmy was standing between Buford and the serpent and me, ready to take hold of the serpent if it should get loose again. After many minutes of this, orchestrated by pounding gospel music, it appeared as if the rattlesnake was trying to bite Buford a second time. He suddenly dropped it near the serpent box. Jimmy quickly grabbed it and placed it inside of the box. . . .

Buford continued moving about the platform area and shook hands with a number of brothers. . . . He eventually took the mike and wiped a small amount of blood onto his shirt. He held the mike with his right hand, which trembled as he spoke. "This snake had just been caught in the mountains today, and these brothers who were present had seen me bring it in; its fangs hadn't been pulled or anything done to it. It tried to bite me earlier in this afternoon, and I prayed to get a good victory over it." One of the brothers wanted to see its fangs, but the devil at that moment tried to tell him that his finger hurt, but he wouldn't listen. . . .

He testified repeatedly for the next while. He said that his hand didn't even swell up. He didn't care if he did die but that he had had a good victory over the serpent and that the bite wouldn't harm him. Would have been dead by now if he hadn't had the anointing. "You shouldn't reach into a serpent box unless you have the anointing; they will strike you dead. Serpents are filled with the evil of the devil, and they can really sock it to you. This may sound like hippie talk, but I don't know no other way to say it better. It is like a gun shooting poison darts."

He said finally that he couldn't handle serpents at that point as he had lost the anointing, except in the tip of his finger, which would last as long as necessary. He mentioned that he had been bitten many times before. . . . Brother Floyd said that we might as well stop waiting for Buford to die, as it would have happened by now. Buford then said that he knew he wasn't going to die this night. . . . He said that when a church has "signs following," there are usually multitudes following it, just as multitudes followed Christ. This is one of the reasons for working in the signs.

"Swapping Serpents" in Kentucky (From Field Notes, November 26, 1972)

Jimmy and Liston picked me up on this rainy and snowy morning at around 9:00 A.M. outside of Morristown at the Cherokee Lake bridge to drive up to London, Kentucky, to attend a late morning service at the Pentecostal Holiness Church there (a serpent handling church of the Trinitarian rather than Jesus-only tradition). I sat in the backseat of the VW Beetle with two rattlesnakes in a box on the seat next to me. The thought crossed my mind that if we were to have an accident, the serpents would get loose and bite me. . . .

As we were leaving this service, Jimmy suggested that we drive to Middlesboro, Kentucky, to see Brother Ben who had promised him two rattlesnakes sometime back. . . . We arrived at the church after nearly an hour's drive. Ben, his wife, mother, and a couple of young children were just leaving the church when we arrived. . . . The church house, which Jimmy and Liston had pointed out to me on the way up to London, was an unpainted, mountain shack perched on the hillside above the road, along with two others like it. Liston introduced me as Brother "Birchhead" from "Alberto," Canada, and said that I went around to a lot of different churches.

Brother Ben is a fairly tall, slim mountain man, with sharp features and a crop of wiry, unruly hair. Jimmy asked him if he had the serpents that he had promised him. Ben said, come up to the church house. The church house had no name written on it, and the inside was small with makeshift seats—a couple of car seats, wooden chairs, planks, and a few church benches.

Ben showed Jimmy the serpents and asked him how many did he want. Jimmy explained that we had been up to London and that he had already given a rattlesnake away to a brother there. Jimmy said that he would like two serpents. Ben said, "Pick you out one." He asked if Jimmy wanted the one back that he had given Ben awhile back. Jimmy said no (like, "Of course not"). He wanted the one that he had never taken up before and had only been handled a few times by anyone.

Jimmy then asked me to go to his car and bring him the cedar serpent box in the trunk. I had trouble opening the trunk, but a couple of kids did it for me. They kept asking me if there were any snakes in the car. I showed them the one rattlesnake. A woman sitting in a pickup truck (I think Ben's sister-in-law) asked if they were going to handle snakes up there. I answered that they were just swapping serpents. She seemed excited by this and walked up the hill with me and the box.

When we got to the front of the church a serpent was crawling on the floor, and Brother Ben had another outstretched in his hand. Ben handed the serpent to Jimmy, who handled it and then handed it back to Ben. He then handed it to me, but I declined, so he passed it to Liston. Ben's wife and sister's kids came in, and she held the kids back from getting too close. After a few minutes of the serpents being passed from person to person around a loosely formed circle, Jimmy put his rattlesnake into the box that I was holding flat in outstretched arms with its lid open. I thought that the snake felt awfully close to my fingers which were supporting the box.

After a couple of minutes, the other serpents were put back into their respective boxes. A brother then came in and wanted to look at one of the serpents. The box lid was opened and the serpent began to crawl out. Jimmy looked into his eyes and said that you can tell how much evil is in them by looking them in the eyes. Soon, the serpent was put back into its box, and we said good-bye to the people there, went to our car for the trip back to Tennessee, Jimmy with his new serpent in the cedar box on the seat next to me.

Midnight Tennessee Trucking (Excerpts from a Letter to a Friend, July 1973)

Liston's[17] big rig came screeching to a stop in front of Al's house on this quiet Newport street at 11:00 P.M. on a sticky, hot night in July 1973. He had come to pick me up for an overnight run to Bowling Green, Kentucky, to pick up a load of greenbeans from the bean fields. We waved good-bye to Al and his wife and were soon pounding through the hot night on Interstate 40. Between Knoxville and Nashville the highway was aglow from the eerie amber and red lights of semis.

The heat in the cab was oppressive, and the engine noise reduced conversation to shouting back and forth. We occasionally stopped along the interstate to kick the tires and to relieve ourselves, but for this we pushed on through the gritty night. Liston passed the time singing church songs and by occasionally speaking in tongues.

Dawn found us red-eyed, parked in the dew-covered bean fields, waiting for the army of mechanical pickers to load the trailer for the run to the cannery at Tellico Plains, Tennessee, not far from Chattanooga. The machines finally started to roll but broke down frequently. We threw a tarp under the trailer and attempted to sleep while the loading proceeded, but to little avail as the trailer shook and showered us with dust each time a load was dumped into it. By midday the heat was intense with an unmerciful sun bearing down. I felt lightheaded, grimy, sweaty, and slightly nauseated from lack of sleep and food. Liston looked like I felt.

To pass the time, he taught me gear-shifting patterns on this Diamond-T rig by drawing in the dust with his finger. (He often suggested that he and I should drive trucks together in the future.) When I mastered gear jamming in the dust, a discussion of the taxonomy of types of anointing and healing powers just worked its way into our conversation, as in a way, both domains, gears and "administrations of powers," follow somewhat similar general principles. He drew in the dust again, this time depicting the differences between anointing, faith, fruits, and gifts of the spirit and which applied to serpent handling, poison drinking, tongues, healing, casting out devils, prophecy, and so forth.

Drifting in and out of sleep under the trailer, Liston developed for me an intricate scheme which explained variable strengths and pragmatics of anointing; of why some people suffer and die from serpent bite and poison and others don't. Of how the devil interferes and of his personal experiences "working in the signs."

He was an excellent teacher and I a very willing learner, in spite of this harsh setting and my weariness from hunger and lack of sleep. (This reading of the quirky realm of spiritual power and its limitations was no doubt one of the more valuable insights into the religion in all of my fieldwork.)

We eventually saw another trucker who had disconnected his tractor from the trailer, and we drove with him to a nearby general store for chocolate milk, Mars bars, and Cokes.

By midafternoon, in the now-scorching one hundred-degree-plus temperature, our trailer was finally overflowing with green beans. After climbing on top of the load and raking it out, we were at last ready to hit the road again.

Just before nightfall we stopped in Nashville to visit the Hemphill family (gospel group, Joel Hemphill and the Singing Hemphills) and ended up having supper with them and visiting into the night. The coolness of the air-conditioning, their comfortable chairs, a tasty meal followed by Cokes, was almost too much to bear. Before leaving, we checked out their touring bus.

It was hard leaving this mecca and heading once again into the night in the hot, noisy Diamond-T. The truck strained and lumbered up some of the grades on I-24 heading to Chattanooga. At one point after we reached a rise and headed down the other side, Liston shifted into neutral and we went freewheeling down the incline at ninety mph. The air blowing in the open window felt refreshing on my sticky face. Liston leaned over, put his arm around my shoulder, and said, "Brother Jimmy, don't do this when you drive, 'cause this is dangerous, if you don't have the anointing. If a tire were to blow, that's all she wrote." I was reassured that the saint driving this rig in fact had the anointing.

In northern Alabama we stopped to refuel and to get a Coke and piece of apple pie. Liston pointed out a large, elegant rig from California driven by long-haired "hippie truckers." We laughed our heads off at the thought. Just after midnight we were heading into Chattanooga past a steamy love scene on an all-night drive-in movie screen. I gazed at these distant images and felt lonely and forlorn.

North of Chattanooga we turned off the interstate at about 2:00 A.M. onto the last, seemingly interminable, stretch on narrow, snaking road to the cannery. As a joke on Brother Al, who met us at the cannery, Liston and I swapped places and I drove the rig the last stretch into the cannery parking lot, at 4:00 A.M.

Leaving the truck and beans behind, we drove back to Newport so as to be ready for a 9:00 A.M. court appearance. We arrived back with time for a hot bath, change of clothes, and quick breakfast before going to the courthouse.

Dogwood Winter Mountain Funeral (From Various Sources, April 11, 1973)

The awful news of death in Tennessee reached me through a long-distance phone call to the Anthropology Department during the brief hilarity of an afternoon birthday celebration for an honors student in the department.

Liston Pack related an account of the event. Buford Pack and Jimmy Williams had died during an extremely ecstatic, highly charged Saturday night service at Carson Springs. [See Carden and Pelton (1976: 81–101) for an evocative portrayal of "The Night Jimmy Ray and Buford Drank Strychnine" and "The Strychnine Deaths in Carson Springs."]

Early the next morning I was on an Air Canada flight via Winnipeg to Chicago. At O'Hare I numbly shuffled through the crowds, past chanting Hare Krishnas, to the Delta flight to Lexington and Knoxville, arriving there at 10:50 P.M.

Friends from the University of Tennessee met me in a 1964 Chevy junker, which a professor of Religious Studies offered to sell to me for $150.00. Early the next morning I was en route in my ''new car'' to the mountains, but because it kept ''cutting out,'' I detoured to Morristown to borrow a friend's Volkswagen Beetle to drive to the funeral in North Carolina.

I arrived at Liston's house at 8:00 A.M. He and I then went to Jimmy's house, where a number of people had already gathered. I was warmly welcomed and filled in again on what had happened on Saturday night. It all had a dreamlike unreality to it; a bad dream from which I may awake. But it wasn't a dream and the ineluctable truth had to be faced; Buford and Jimmy were dead; had died of strychnine they drank in church during the Saturday night service. It did not seem possible. How could this have happened? They were good saints who often in the past had received a strong anointing for handling serpents and drinking ''deadly things.''

I felt incredibly sad and desolate, there at his house with his wife, children, and church people. This home had always had such a cheerful air about it. My thoughts raced back to times I spent there in the past—to visit recovering serpent-bit brothers when everyone stood around laughing, talking, swapping serpent-bite stories. I remembered having Thanksgiving dinner with Jimmy and his family and an old brother in the church, and the prayer service after which he showed me his scrapbook and photo album of his serpent handling life while we munched on apples in the kitchen, and the night we talked about the history of the church and ate chili and hot dogs when his family returned home, and the time on a cold winter's night we sat in his car talking while drinking hot chocolate at the local Dairy Queen. . . . I remembered also his joyful, exuberant style of preaching and enthusiastic ''working in the signs.''

It didn't seem the same without Brother Jimmy there. Such a loss. Such a waste. He was only thirty-three or thirty-four years old.

Liston and I walked up the hillside across from the church to Jimmy's grave, which was covered in floral displays, crosses, and wreaths proclaiming ''Jesus called him home.'' The empty church house now looked forlorn through the bare trees.

Gene, Lester, Clyde, and a box of serpents rode with me to western North Carolina for the funeral.

It was a brilliant dogwood winter day—clear turquoise sky highlighting the blossoms and emerging buds of green, flowing mountain streams; a bittersweet chill in the air. There was something incongruous about driving the winding mountain roads to a funeral against the backdrop of this lustily blossoming spring season; the irrevocability of life's thresholds; the suddenness with which life departs; and the stunned survivors in this Beckettesque existentialist play.

We arrived at Buford's wife's parents' house in a rural area near Marshall, North Carolina, where he was lying in state in an open casket with a Bible open on his chest to Mark 16: 15–18—''And these Signs Shall follow them that Believe . . .''—his large left hand draped over its lower corner. Polaroid shots were taken of our deceased brother and given to those present. Many flowers surrounded the white linen-lined coffin. Buford looked lugubrious and tired in his repose of death.

The funeral service itself was perfunctory and low-keyed. Brother Brown said that God ''called them home. . . . They are truly saints as they died in the Word, doing what they believed in. The Word is still the Word.'' Sister Nellie and Sister Eunice sang a poignant ''Precious Memories.''

The scene at the grave in the old family graveyard on the hillside above the church, on the other hand, was tense and chaotic. Liston and Clyde ''took up'' the serpents I had transported there. There were ructions among some non–serpent handling relatives. You could cut the tension with a knife, a feeling that something ominous and dreadful was about to happen. Violence lurked just beneath the surface. Whispers reached me that someone had a gun in his pocket and had threatened to kill Liston then and there. My license number had been taken down and phoned to the county sheriff. The three boys who rode over with me watchfully flanked me, ready for fight or flight.

Liston, on a razor's edge, urgency in his voice, told us to hit the road before the sheriff arrived. We slipped quickly through the throng of graveside mourners with the serpent box in hand, back to the waiting VW. With my nerves on edge and adrenaline pumping, I started the car and speedily negotiated the winding roads back to Tennessee. It was with great relief when we crossed the state line.

Aftermath 1 (From a Letter to Steven Kane)

The Saturday night after the funerals was like a circus at church. Reporters were every-where. Some university students and a couple of professors were present as well. All evening, there was an endless parade of onlookers and hecklers in and out of the small church house. People were standing on benches, sitting on the floor, peering through the windows—no doubt waiting to see another tragedy strike.

Brother Al gave the reporters present a severe tongue-lashing and suggested that they print the truth for a change. (During this time there were some amazingly inaccurate reports about the deaths. *Newsweek* and a number of newspapers said that the church would attempt to raise the two brothers from the dead on the Saturday following the funerals. It was said also that saints would test their faith by turning blowtorches on themselves. Other reports alleged that the deceased saints were buried vertically with snakes in the coffins. Another news media source claimed that Liston had said he would walk on water across Lake Douglas.)

Liston told me he was tired of all these people coming around and looking at them like they were a zoo. The hoopla continued for the next couple of services. My last Saturday night there, a UPI [United Press International] cameraman and reporter were present and filmed parts of the service for a syndicated news program to be shown across the United States and parts of Europe. During this service I sat in the "amen corner" with some of the brothers and felt affronted by the bright lights, intrusive cameras, students with notebooks, people with mini "spy" cameras, and the aggressiveness and hype of media people in general. I was glad in a way to be leaving behind the media freak show and to be returning to the peaceful tranquillity of Alberta in the spring but sad to leave "my people" in crisis.[18]

Aftermath 2 (From a Letter to a Friend)

So all the hoopla is over and I am back in Edmonton enjoying the splendid spring weather. But I have not been released or found deliverance from the happenings of those weeks. I have been having sad dreams about Jimmy and the church. The full impact has hit me back here as I have time to think about it and listen to tapes of Jimmy talking about taking up serpents and drinking deadly things. I guess his death has disturbed me a lot, as I was pretty close to him. When I first turned up at the church in 1971, it was Jimmy who I met and explained my interest in serpent handling to. Many times he went out of his way to explain things to me and include me in things like trips to Kentucky to visit other churches. When my girlfriend came down from Canada last December, he and Mary Kate made her feel very much at home. . . .

I often feared that someone in the church would die. I remember a tense Saturday night back in November when Jimmy drank carbon tetrachloride and at almost the same moment, Billy Jay was bitten by a serpent (all of which was recorded on film as part of the documentary "*They Shall Take Up Serpents,*" 1973, by filmmakers Thomas Burton and Jack Schrader.) I feared that both would surely die. . . . Billy Jay became quite ill and Jimmy perspired profusely. He told me later that his vision became blurred for awhile and that when he saw how the poison had eaten a hole in the plastic cup, he became worried about his fate. But he spent most of the night praying and pulled through.

The next night at Jimmy's house where Billy Jay was recovering, the atmosphere was jovial, with people exchanging stories about past incidents of serpent-bite, of those who had survived and some like the late Oscar Pelfrey who had died of serpent-bite. I guess I realized that Saturday night that sometime in the future death would befall someone in the church. I thought that Jimmy would be one of the most likely to perish, given his penchant for serpent handling and growing interest in drinking "deadly things."[19]

I also held fears for Buford as last summer he drank battery acid at a tent revival at Brevard, North Carolina. I didn't know Buford as well as I did Jimmy, but knew him fairly well. He had plans to build a church in Marshall, North Carolina, which would emphasize a gospel of Christian love. He often said that I would have to come up there someday soon.

In summary, the foregoing accounts represent the flow and texture of community life and my involvement in it during various periods between June 1971 and 1974. And, as depicted in the various sketches, my fieldwork was not all snake handling and mayhem but rather a balance between the intense, highly charged snake handling service of popular and scholarly depiction and the more laid-back everyday occurrence of people's lives outside formal ritual occasions. I valued especially, personally and intellectually, out-of-church participation with saints. Traveling with church people, for example, was thoroughly enjoyable for me—talk was relaxed; sense of humor and performance, keen. Such times yielded rich narratives of serpent lore, religious beliefs, and experiences. We sometimes visited people and churches in Kentucky, North Carolina, South Carolina, other parts of Tennessee, and Virginia to attend services, pray for bitten people, and attend funerals or revivals. Similarly, going on the road with Liston Pack, an interstate trucker, was always a learning experience, both in the culture of trucking and in seeing a serpent handler practicing his religion on the move—testifying at truck stops, speaking in tongues while jamming gears, relying on anointing power to keep his truck safely on the road under somewhat questionable driving conditions, and taking up serpents in the bean fields of southern Georgia.

Picnics in the Smoky Mountains, visiting saints at home, eating out at local cafes, visiting and praying for sick people, caring for and "playing with" snakes in people's homes (when I stayed with one family, I shared the spare bedroom with a couple of cages of rattlesnakes and copperheads), walking in the woods with church friends, going bowling in Newport, having Thanksgiving and other special dinners with saints, going to the radio studio with saints to present the weekly live broadcast (see Birckhead 1981), laughing with people at television documentaries on the church (not to mention the plethora of news stories and *Hustler* magazine galley proofs), and more recently, outings to Dollywood, Pigeon Forge, and Gatlinberg, breakfasts at Cracker Barrel, supper after church at "Western Sizzlin" discussing "reality" with long-term "informants," a visit with a couple to the University of Tennessee to view the video *The Jolo Serpent Handlers*—all pretty well reflect the tone of my extra church "fieldwork."

Also, seeing members interact with reporters, television crews, filmmakers, social scientists, writers, sightseers, and sinners gave me a view of "the community interface" (Harper 1982) of this religion and very much affected how I ended up seeing these people as being very much implicated in the wider world, rather than the isolated, out-of-touch hillbillies they are so often portrayed as. Indeed, this is Dolly Parton country, and the Nashville showbiz ethos interpenetrates the religious culture. A couple of saints went to school with Dolly, and Alfred and Jimmy once handled serpents at a revival at her grandpa's church. Going to Dollywood with saints is not a complete touristic experience, as they know so many people there behind the scenes, including some of the pickers and singers in the Parton family band. Saints, in other words, are not unaware of the "bright lights." As I mentioned before in one sketch, saints had contacts with a successful gospel-singing family and had dreams of a Nashville recording contract for their gospel group the "All for Jesus Singers." Similarly, because saints had been the subject of so much media attention—appearing as they did on talk shows; in films and television news digests; and newspapers and books—they as a group had much more exposure to and critical perspective on how media images are produced than most middle-class Americans. As well, in terms of wider outside experience, most saints have had to migrate out of the region at one time or another to find employment, living in places such as New Jersey or Florida. Long-distance truck drivers in the church regularly travel to Michigan and Florida, and some to Texas and California. As well, as this church is near the Great Smoky Mountain National Park, many in the church found employment in the tourist industry and were exposed to a wide diversity of people.

The above types of contacts with serpent handlers led me to appreciate their individuality, humanity, hospitality, and good humor in the face of adversity and outside intrusions, to appreciate how their religious commitment affects their everyday lives in small but powerful ways. And seeing people in their diverse and variegated everydayness made it impossible for me to construct the one-eyed, fanatical "snake charmers" and bizarre "cultists" of media (and some academic) depiction (see Birckhead 1993a; Burton 1993).

"ZION, OH ZION—WHAT'S THE MATTER NOW?"

Oh Zion, oh Zion
What's the matter now?
Oh Zion, oh Zion
What's the matter now?

We used to take up serpents
What's the matter now?
We used to take up serpents
What's the matter now?

Serpent handling song, author unknown

As country singer Bobby Bare laments in "500 Miles away from Home," "time changes everything." This is no less true for serpent handling communities, the ethnographer, and ethnographic styles and sensibilities. In this concluding section, I critically reflect on these changes and their respective effects on my twenty-six-year quest to understand, and represent in print, "my people." In critically considering self, other, and ethnography in this way, I hope to illuminate the practice of anthropology today in a complex, globalized world (see Appadurai 1991).

"My people" and "my church" have changed dramatically since I completed my main fieldwork in 1973. Some people who used to "take up serpents" no longer do so. Recent film documentaries, on the other hand (Burton and Headley 1983, 1987), show people handling serpents who did not do so in 1971. My main field site, the Holiness Church of God in Jesus Name at Carson Springs, has splintered into a number of other churches, each with its own special character; most serpent handling and "newsmaking"[20] now seem to be done at the offshoot congregation near Morristown, while a more mainline, non–serpent handling option now exists near Cosby. Sadly, the original converted hunting cabin "church house" at the head of Snake Hollow was recently destroyed by a fire.

The cast of characters has changed also. People have died, moved away, or "backslided" into lives of sin. Young children and babies I used to bounce on my knee in 1971 have grown up, married, have children, and perhaps are divorced and remarried and living in far-flung parts of the country. Divorce and remarriage, so much railed against from the pulpit in 1971, now seem to have touched many in the church community. A couple of spin-off churches now even have non-southern-born members who have moved in from "up North," the Midwest, or the far West. The strict dress codes, and prohibitions against TV and secular amusements of my day have given way to more pragmatic, relaxed attitudes to such "things of the world."

Alas, my life has changed, too. I am married with three children (a ten-year-old boy and twin seven-year-old girls), have a mortgage, and hold a tenured academic position at an Australian university, where I mostly study Aboriginal land management issues and spirituality. Yet serpent handling is still very much on my mind as an academic and a personal interest, especially in the last number of years when I have been able to apply new anthropological criticism to self/other relations in the construction of anthropological knowledge and to academic and popular representations of serpent handling religion. These issues, and the approaches they imply, more realistically reflect "my people" and my attempts to know and represent "them" than what was available anthropologically to me in 1970–1971. In 1971, I expected to be the "objective" observer looking in from an unsullied vantage point at a discretely bounded, isolated "cultural" community—a site where one could excavate and reveal core, essential "Appalachian" culture and values as the causative factor of serpent handling.

But this pristine image of anthropological practice was tested and shattered from my first tentative encounters with "my people," whom I first learned of from a newspaper article and my first contact with them, marred by the presence of a freelance photographer/filmmaker.

In 1971, I put on blinkers and hoped such "extraneous" influences would simply go away, leaving me alone, as the sole observer and representer of this scene. This was my turf, and I resented sharing it, as I often had to, with newspeople, filmmakers, researchers, and tourists; and I further resented them for coming in and "contaminating" this "culture" with mainstream styles and values. Sharing the viewing platform with such people was very much against my engrained expectations of what participant observation with one's "own people" should be like—which is perhaps why I so much liked small services in people's homes, nights at the bowling alley, walks in the woods, or going on the road with saints, times when "outsiders" were less likely to intrude. Yet, as I portray in a number of sketches, even such journeys involved touching bases with a Nashville gospel showbiz family and including a freelance writer and sociology student in a couple of these trips.

Being taken to lunch by New York– and Atlanta-based reporters and being pumped for information and contacts also did not conform to my idea of fieldwork. Ideas of "ethnographic modernity" (Clifford 1988: 3), "cosmopolitan scripts" (Appadurai 1991: 208) for even the most local of communities, how "many lives are now inextricably linked with representations" (Appadurai 1991: 208), or off/decenterdness (Clifford 1988) had not yet been fully realized or articulated in 1971. In reaction to this "predicament" (Clifford 1988), I defensively identified more strongly with "my people" and remember being especially pleased when media people and researchers mistook me for a member. For example, I appear inadvertently in the documentary film "*They Shall Take Up Serpents*" (Burton and Schrader 1973), and filmmaker Burton wrote in a letter to me dated March 12, 1986: "It's a pleasant surprise to hear from you again. Each time I have occasion to watch the original film made at Carson Springs I try to identify you, but I'm never sure. Would you tell me in what sequence you appear and how to identify you, please." While I am now wildly amused by the postmodern irony reflected in this incident, in 1971 such decenteredness was not my métier, as reflected in an angstful entry in my field notes of November 18, 1972, when the filming of the documentary took place:

Because of the "Big Orange" football game traffic in Knoxville, I arrived late for the service. The inside of the church house looked surreal as the small room was bathed in intense bright light emanating from a number of large bulbs installed around the room by the filmmakers. The church was full to overflowing, but I slipped into a back bench and found a place next to Brother Ralph, who was wearing bibbed overalls.

A bearded cameraman; a young female assistant, wearing slacks and an Indian buck-skin jacket with fringe on it, writing in a notebook and occasionally using the light meter; a short, older woman, also wearing slacks, who was constantly on the move with a tape recorder and a large, muffled microphone, following the action between the back benches and the "amen corner"; and the "professor"/director wearing a dress shirt, tie, sports jacket, and dress slacks, who worked from the "amen corner," comprised the film crew.

The combination of the unnaturally bright light, the strange intruders wandering about, and Brother Liston nowhere to be seen did not sit well with me. (I later learned that Liston had driven a last-minute load to Ashland, Kentucky, and did not return till 7 A.M. next morning.) During the collection, I self-consciously walked to the front to place my money on the bench, very much conscious of being watched by the "outsiders" through a camera lense.

The singing, and the service in general, seemed to be moving at an accelerated pace, in response to the presence of the filmmakers, or was this my imagination! The service had a quality of being staged for the camera; the filmmakers were getting what they wanted, a freak show. I am not saying the saints were consciously doing this, but they were, if they realized it or not, putting on a splendid performance. (My heart still pounds faster when I watch this footage today.)

An air of confusion and chaos hung over the service, as the crew moved in and out of the syncopated saints. The photographer was perspiring visibly as he strained to catch all the electric action as "the spirit" broke out here, there, and everywhere at once. He would film one scene, and "the professor" would tap him on the shoulder and point out another more filmicly interesting one, across the room.

The "alter" area was filled with dancing, singing, guitar- and drum-playing sisters and brothers. Sister B, at one point while belting out a spirited gospel number, broke out into tongues, jumping up and down with the microphone in her hand. Old, white-haired Sister S commenced bouncing up and down the aisle, while Sister G's shrill, discordant screams punctuated the din. Jimmy shook out a couple of rattlesnakes from his serpent box and took them up while speaking in tongues. Brother Al, and perhaps Lester, took them up as well. Billy J reached for the two rattlesnakes at once and grasped them in his hand. One slipped up his arm in slow motion. Jimmy in the meantime poured carbon tetrachloride into a glass and unceremoniously swigged most of it down in one gulp. The cameraman was focusing on the serpent handling until "the professor" pointed out the poison drinking to him.

The rattlesnake struck Brother Bill so quickly that I didn't realize it had happened until Brother Al asked all Christians to come up and pray for the "serpent-bit" brother. Jimmy or Al took the serpents from Bill and placed them back in the box. Jimmy looked red in the face and appeared to be perspiring heavily as a result of drinking the poison.

Billy J more or less collapsed onto the front bench with Al by his side, hugging and reassuring him. The faithful prayed feverishly over Bill and laid hands on him.

Brother Brown walked to the back of the church and had blood on his forehead, making me think that he had been bitten as well. But I heard later that he had fallen down and hit his head while praying over Billy J. The scene at this point was blurred and discordant, reminiscent for me of the frames in the film *Dead Birds* when the death of a boy was announced during the preparations for a feast. People in the church looked to be stunned and pallid. Sister B stood in shock, with tears streaming down her face at the front of the church. The cameraman shot some footage of her, but she seemed not to notice. The congregation stood mute as the camera rolled.

Billy J's head dropped forward, and I thought that he was going to vomit or die on the spot. In a few minutes as the praying subsided, Alfred and another brother helped him outside. He looked like living death as he passed me, supported with his arms around the two brothers' necks.

I felt ill, hostile towards the filmmakers, disillusioned with the church for letting these people come in. I felt a strong sense of identity with the congregation. Brother Ralph sat with his arm around my shoulders, and I felt good about this as this was filmed by the crew. It showed where I cast my allegiance. I felt strong hostility toward the academic world and felt that Brother Billy J wouldn't have been bitten if it were not for the lights, cameras, confusion, and artificial atmosphere of the event. This was rip-off social science; they hadn't done the groundwork or "paid the price." I felt that the footage they shot wasn't an accurate portrayal of the church in its total context. This service was quite atypical of what usually goes on. This made me question my own field procedures. I felt that maybe the way that they operated was, after all, the better way. Their way, they were in and out of people's lives and would soon be forgotten. In the long run, they were perhaps less intrusive that I was. My way, I hang around forever and, at least on one level, pretend to be what I am not.

But the "intrusions" of outsiders intensified rather than abated, especially after the strychnine deaths in 1973, and with the passage of time, I had no choice but to learn to live with this unforeseen feature of "fieldwork." Eventually, my ethnographic sensibilities changed to accommodate my field reality. I came to see as analytically useful the products and artifacts of news and documentary media in the "reading" of "my people's" lives—they recorded in print a wider range of narratives, in specific contexts, than I as a sole researcher could ever tap into; and in the case of TV and film materials, they provided an iconic record of slice-of-time action that I could rerun, slow down, speed up, or analyze frame by frame on an editing table. I was able to see, through such playing with frames, kinesic features in the constitution of the serpent handling ritual, for example, gain an insight into the socialization of young people into the practice of taking up serpents. Such analysis also deconstructed for me the codes and conventions throught which media "vérité" is constructed, an experience that moved my consciousness to the point that I was no longer studying serpent handling per se but was assuming the more decentered stance of reading popular and scholarly constructions of serpent handling and how these impinged upon the members' consciousness. I also came to see that media coverage, for example, is not an epiphenomenon in serpent handling communities but is integral to how people dialectically construct themselves within and against the reflections of popular commodified representations.[21] Some saints, for example, became media celebrities and lost their souls to show-biz values (see Birckhead 1982), while others through critically reading their parodically constructed selves in media became decentered serpent handlers, no longer able to continue the practice in a nonironic way or, in some cases, at all.

My growing "off centeredness" in the dynamic serpent handling world liberated me in ways and even further eroded the boundaries between self and ethnographic others (see Sanjek 1990: 407). That my main "informants" were virtually in the public domain, nonpseudonymous subjects of numerous documentary films, television news features, and tabloid press pieces; veterans of *Hustler, New York Times Magazine, New Scientist, The Listener*, BBC, and numerous talk shows and radio broadcasts; had their life histories included in popular and scholarly books (e.g., Burton 1993); and were interviewed by social scientists, including anthropologists (e.g., Steve Kane 1973),[22] in the end, became a resource rather than a liability. Namely, I was no longer the classic ethnographer, peering in at "my people." My informants became more like collaborators than "subjects of study." "They" had long been interested in "representation," and "fieldwork" increasingly consisted of our mutual "deconstructing" of popular and scholarly print and visual texts in which they were featured. This stance also helped to expiate my growing guilt of studying people, some of whom had become my long-term friends.

Brief trips back in 1974, 1979, 1981, 1983, 1987, 1991, and 1995 not only revealed a constantly changing community but, often as not, rewarded me with yet another film, videotape of a TV program, *Hustler* galley proof, or talk of a book or documentary film soon to be produced by someone or other. And in this expanded field, I sometimes found myself talking long-distance from Canada or Australia to authors, filmmakers, or BBC producers or faxing the BBC in London for permission to reproduce *The Listener* cover sketch of August 18, 1983, depicting an artist's conception of "my people" (under the title "Strange But True—Snakes In Church") (see Birckhead [1993a: 182–184] for a further discussion of this article and BBC-TV documentary.)

Indeed, I now do much of my "fieldwork" in front of a TV screen in my family room, as over the years a number of "documentaries" about snake handling have been screened on Australian television (see Birckhead 1993a). I have a sizable collection of off-air and commercially produced videos of "my people" and of other snake handlers. Although lives have changed dramatically, and the group I once studied no longer exists as such, these iconic moments, frozen in time, are always available for analysis and reanalysis.

There is something eerie and disturbing about working with images of long-dead people and a once-vital "community of saints" that is no longer there. One is reminded of the transciency of lives, including one's own, and the fragility of social realities. In this regard, "I recall watching television in my living room in 1984 when, to my amazement, I saw on the screen my deceased Holiness friend, Jimmy Williams, in the space of a few seconds drink carbon tetrachloride, dance around, and handle serpents" (Birckhead 1993a: 179). This few-second promo quite unexpectedly flashed on and off the screen, giving new meaning for me to notions of "ethnographic modernity/postmodernity."

I sometimes live uneasily with such images, the detailed descriptions in my field notes, and my strong and vivid memories of my time with Holiness people. These memories are bittersweet—at times, a fondly savored nostalgia of "good times in the spirit" and travels with larger-than-life popular culture celebrities who grew up with Dolly Parton but, at other times, a jumble of troubling images of dead friends and broken families and frightening flashes of striking serpents. Do I perhaps in a small way, as a witness, have these injuries and deaths on my hands?

Scarcely a day passes that thoughts of serpent handling do not tug at my consciousness. And in quiet moments of drifting in and out of sleep on planes, during long department meetings, or when insomnia strikes in the still of the night, I ponder the meaning of it all: Who are these people who I have spent so much of my life trying to comprehend? How much do I really know them, their meanings, their motivations? And, How did I ever become a student of this topic?[23]

Yet when I go "back home," I snap immediately back into that world and understand implicitly the meaning of serpent handling.[24]

But this is, in effect, "stigmatized" knowledge. It is coherent and sensible within certain subuniverses of meaning, but it does not translate well into "normal" parlance, as it appears to be so irrational, self-destructive, and incomprehensible to most people. Normal, rational people simply do not handle snakes and drink strychnine in church and then dance and jump around in the belief that in these ritual acts death is suspended. Even I know this, but at some submerged and ineffable level, I have a grasp of another underlying existential reality, an inchoate but fundamental truth about the human condition. It is this conflict between ways of knowing, of having witnessed and understood "the bizarre" at the edges of rationality, that has always weighed heavily on my mind—the illogic and irrationality of it yet its implicit, underlying intelligibility. I have spent many "dark nights of the soul" wondering what kind of person I am who is able to find this belief system intelligible, even alluring. I can't help but smile wryly when I watch and rewatch films on serpent handling. I know these people and what this means, but I can never really "explain" them adequately, given the logic and fixity of words and sentences and overarching theories that break up the flow and integrity of experience (see Ong 1982), not to mention the ethics of relating that which I was told in confidence.

Consequently, I have published few "straight" descriptions or theoretical explanations of serpent handling. I am only recently finding an appropriate critical voice and stance. Although I presented a number of conference papers (noted earlier) over the years on specific aspects of serpent handling (usually accompanied by film, audio- or videotape material), I ultimately found this to be an unsatisfying experience. Namely, it has always been difficult to present the significant theoretical features of this topic, as even anthropologists and sociologists are conditioned to read it as humorous, trivial, or mildly titillating. This is reflected in questions typically asked at conferences—questions and pre-occupations structured more by journalistic than by ethnographic discourses: "Are they inbred?" "How similar are they to the people in *Deliverance?*" "What kind of snakes do they use?"—even when this information was given in the paper (Birckhead 1993a: 172).[25]

Similarly, the fact that I have lived and worked with snake handlers does not always put me in good stead with colleagues, students, family, or people in general. A problem of working with marginal people is that some of it rubs off on the researcher. In other words, there are "few or no academic rewards in becoming a student of the stigmatized" (Rose 1982: 223). It seems not to be very fashionable to know about firsthand the rites of white serpent handlers and poison drinkers or the narratives of Protestant fundamentalists that support these behaviors. Although people are generally interested in the topic, in a voyeuristic way, my accounts of snake handling can inspire looks of incredulity, raised eyebrows, giggles, and sneers, whereas my accounts of Australian Aboriginal religion, rainbow serpents, Wanjinas, and Dreaming stories, and fieldwork with "traditional" people on Cape York, generally elicit reverential awe among students and colleagues alike. But when people learn that I lived with snake handlers and poison drinkers in "Appalachia," I sense that they see me as being bizarre as well. Snake handling in many respects is not seen to be a "politically correct" topic for one to study.

Ironically, I have not seen serpent handling in "my church" for the past thirteen years. My main informants no longer take up serpents or attend churches that do so. They have their own non-serpent handling church. So when I go back, these people host me, and I am swept along in a non-serpent handling, Holiness stream of events, practices, and meanings. (See Birckhead [1993a: 163–166] for a decentered reflection of "the last time I saw 'snake handling,' " performed on stage in western New South Wales, Australia, as part of the "Handler" sketch in Jane Martin's play *Talking With*, 1983.)

I often wonder what it is that I presently "study" when "in the field" with people who, at least for now, no longer handle serpents. Interestingly, as I suggested before, some of these decentered people have now become academic collaborators more than traditional informants. They are now once removed from the scene and offer more relativistic and detached insights.[26] Some of my deepest understandings have come from visiting these people and reflecting with them on filmic and printed texts on the church.

While I continue to be drawn back to this world (whatever one now calls it), I must admit that some of the thrill is gone without the serpents, strychnine, and fire. But I am consoled by the fact that at least now I won't read about the death of any of these serpent handling survivors in my local newspaper or receive an international phone call in the night.

NOTES

1. *Gaze* is an apt term here, as such stories reveal in print and/or visual images the most private details of serpent handlers' lives, including snakebite, suffering, and death, which "we" read or view as detached spectators from the comfort of our living rooms (see Birckhead 1993a, 1996).

2. Another story on the same program from Brazil: "It was the day real-life voodoo crept into a nation's favorite prime-time soap opera and left a beautiful young actress lying dead beside a road in tall grass." A similar positioning of "snake handling" as bizarre is reflected in its inclusion in the television program *Sightings: Snake Church* (Seven Network, Australia, April 26, 1996). This program mostly deals with flying saucer sightings and encounters with extraterrestrials.

3. John F. Day's 1941 (reprinted in 1987) book *Bloody Ground* begins with a chapter on snake handling called "Mountain Voodoo," while Dunlap (1975: 20; 1993: 198) refers to serpent handling as "a poor, white cargo cult."

4. I have included only published works and not theses, encyclopedic entries, or passing reference to or discussion of in books or articles. This, to my present knowledge, is the extent of published work by anthropologists on this religion. To emphasize this point, I have not included here the work of folklorists, historians, sociologists, psychologists, and so on.

5. In fairness to the late Weston La Barre, this statement taken in context serves a rhetorical function. His overall point is that "a salient feature of minority cults . . . is their striking cognitive dissonance with majority culture" (278). Given this dissonance, one may well wonder about how adherents continue to find such systems plausible. La Barre concludes this paragraph with the caution: "This is unfair to the faith. Believers do believe. . . . One's shock at the spectacle is merely the measure of one's own cognitive distance from the system being studied" (278). This, of course, mitigates the meaning of the quote taken out of context. I use the quote, nevertheless, for my own rhetorical purposes, as in my experience, this is how most educated people react to serpent handling religion, and La Barre said it so well.

6. I am not the only one who has difficulty representing serpent handling religion, given the overwhelming power of commonsense and popular constructions. Jerry W. Williamson, editor of the high-quality, long-established "Regional Studies Review," *Appalachian Journal*, recently wrote to me with regard to my review (see Birckhead 1994) of Burton's (1993) *Serpent Handling Believers*: "Snake-handling generally is a dicey topic for us, since it is so handy for blithering media types who always go for the exotic and who love huge cultural labels."

7. But La Barre cautioned me: "In my opinion, the functional/dysfunctional aspects of cult participation are not so much a difference of ethnographic fact between Durham and Nathan Gerrard's Scrabble Creek, as they are fundamental differences in theory about the nature and meaning of religion" (personal communication 1971).

8. Not all Holiness people necessarily make this distinction.

9. It is interesting as well that Holiness serpent handling has been written about two times in *Hustler*. An incongruous part of my "fieldwork" was tracking down back issues of *Hustler* and *Dude* in pornographic book shops in seedy sections of St. Louis, Vancouver, and Sydney.

10. And despite the fact that serpent handling is illegal in Tennessee, this church once ran this want ad in a local newspaper: "Wanted—Poison serpents for church services.

Rattlers and copperheads will do. Contact Jimmy R. Williams, Holiness Church of God in Jesus Name.''

11. My view in part came from the reputation of Newport and Cocke County, where the church is located, as a center of illegal cock fighting, bootlegging, prostitution, organized crime, and "snake handling"—a very violent place best avoided. (See biographical sketch on Liston Pack, "Liston Pack: Out of the World's Black Belly" [F. Brown 1993]). My friend Paul, who lived in the Knoxville house with me, worked as an orderly in the emergency room of a Knoxville hospital and frequently dealt with gunshot or stabbing victims brought in from Newport and the Del Rio area of Cocke Country, where Liston Pack used to live. Newport's reputation no doubt contributed greatly to my nervousness and wariness and hence to my preconceptions of this church before actually going there.

12. My "informants," at least in the beginning, tended to be the more active preachers who "took up serpents," drank poisons, and "cast out devils." Thus, I had less access to less active members of the congregation and no independent (of men) access to women's worlds, not surprising in this stereotyped sex-role culture.

13. I once presented a seminar on serpent handling at the Australian National University, chaired by Professor Derek Freeman, and was unprepared for the heated debate that ensued over the ethical responsibilities of an anthropologist in this type of setting. Freeman was critical of me, the presenter of the previous week who had worked on Sri Lankan firewalking, and anthropologists in general who specialized in studying "delusional systems" for not having the courage to expose these systems for what they are.

14. Yet at times I felt a desire to take up serpents, to be part of the group and for the full experience of participation. During serpent swapping meetings, for example, serpents are sometimes passed from person to person around a small circle, and at times like this, I would have felt comfortable handling the serpents.

I was not alone in feeling this desire. Sociologist Nathan Gerrard related to me in December 1971 how an anthropology graduate student attended a service at Scrabble Creek and had been so overcome by emotion that he in fact "took up serpents." This so disturbed him that he abandoned his plans to study this religion.

William Sargant (1975: 186) similarly describes snake handling by nonbelievers: "At both meetings I had a definite feeling that I would have been perfectly safe, even as an unbeliever, in handling the snakes, although I developed no belief that I would be protected by the Holy Ghost. At the Durham meeting I saw two sailors walk straight down the aisle, take the snakes into their hands, give them back, and then walk away. I felt very much like doing the same, but then began to wonder whether my judgement was not being impaired by the whole process. I remember feeling this quite strongly as Pastor Bunn came up to me and tried to make me take a snake myself, which I refused to do." Most recently, Dennis Covington (1995) and David Kimbrough (1995) "took up serpents" as part of their research. (See Birckhead 1996.)

15. Saints made much of the fact that I "was led" to the church all the way from Canada and, later, Australia. I visited the Pine Mountain Church of God in January 1982, and they emphasized in preaching and in testimonies that "this brother has come from Australia, a place where people don't take up serpents." Similarly, in July 1983, I was in the radio station studio with saints as they presented their live-to-air weekly "broadcast." It was mentioned that Brother Jim Birckhead was here "all the way from Australia, where there are some good Christians, but who don't work in all the signs."

16. It was somewhat harrowing appearing on the witness stand, trying to answer the questions of the aggressive prosecuting attorney, the judge, and afterward, the aggressive

media people. Needless to say, my court appearance greatly strengthened my rapport with church people.

17. Fred Brown (1993: 89) wrote of Liston: "There is about Liston Pack a certain uneasiness, a restlessness that feels like a wolf's breath on the back of the neck. In his presence there is a solid feeling of the known and yet a sense that the unknown is awaiting its turn to emerge, that something might tear loose at any minute. In geologic terms he would be labeled dichromatic, for there are many sides and many colors to this man of God, Holiness preacher unlike any other among the Holy Ghost people."

18. Steven Kane wrote to me in this regard (April 12, 1973): "I did not know Buford Pack, but Williams was exceedingly kind and generous to me during my visit, and his death is profoundly disturbing to me. I have made many dear friends among the serpent-handlers, and Williams' passing is a troubling reminder that any one of them could die in horrible agony from snakebite or poison."

19. As Steven Kane wrote in a letter to me, April 12, 1973, "A note of grim irony—last May when I was in Carson Springs, Jimmy Williams mentioned the difficulty he was having in obtaining strychnine for use in his church services."

20. While this church has been the subject of a number of media stories, including a short piece in our local paper here, about the snakebite death of Jimmy Williams's son in 1991 (see Burton 1993 for other references), this church would not be considered by media people to be "the snake handling capital of the world." The Church of the Lord Jesus at Jolo, West Virginia, now seems to have that distinction.

21. Even more remote churches in eastern Kentucky have not escaped their share of media attention. Ironically in this regard, the fiction is still maintained that it is difficult to gain access to serpent handling communities. For example, an issue of *Foxfire* (spring 1973: 21) on serpent handling recounted: "It started last August with an invitation to witness and record a series of religious services that few journalists have been allowed to see—much less record." But, later (13) in the same article, a member said: "This here paper (they did an article on us recently) called us mountain people and made like we was uncivilized." This church, in fact, has had a number of newspaper articles done on it, plus a couple of academic papers and a Ph.D. dissertation.

22. This at times seemed bizarre and banal to me. A *What's Up America* program titled "Holiness People" (August 1981) included spliced-in studio segments of Steven Kane presenting interpretations of serpent handling in general. These were juxtaposed with scenes from "my church." In one segment, Kane's point—that "these snake handlers are really, almost in a sense, the essence of Appalachia. We have here fundamentally normal people. This will sound somewhat paradoxical, but they're like other Appalachian people, but only more so. By that I mean, if Appalachia is an area in which people tend to be fundamentalist, then snake handlers are more fundamentalist. If Appalachia is a place where people court danger and seem to like being exposed to dangerous situations, the snake handlers seem to carry that a little further. . . . They are really very much the essence of Appalachia in many ways"—is illustrated visually by scenes of "my people" having a snack after church in the pastor's kitchen in the church's basement. The visuals that were used with Kane's talking head interpretation seemed not to relate much to what he was saying. To me, the effect was bizarre, as watching people eat sandwiches and drink Coca-Cola proves very little about normalcy or essential Appalachia predispositions to fundamentalism or risk taking, or "dependency needs," which Kane discussed as well.

23. This came back to me in a powerful way while writing the conclusions of this

chapter. Two of my distance education students in Darwin who are park rangers invited me to spotlight for them on a crocodile (croc)-catching expedition in Shoal Bay. We were out in the tropical night until 4 A.M. and caught twelve crocs. The visceral experience of my spotlight locking onto the red "eye shine" of a croc, the adrenaline-pumping pursuit through muddy mangroves, the wrestling and dragging aboard the small boat, and the sense of awe at having at your bare feet, dripping with mangrove ooze, a tangle of screaming, struggling crocs brought back, in an overwhelming flash, the sense of leaden fear I used to feel in the proximity of struggling rattlesnakes and copperheads in church. This crocodile's eyes reflection of my field experience brought me no great joy, as that very night my dreams alternated between being attacked by crocodiles and large Western Diamondbacks.

24. As I wrote in a letter after visiting east Tennessee in April 1991:

As always, Newport had a feeling of timeless chaos. I arrived at Alfred's church late afternoon and was snapped up immediately into another world. . . . I soon found myself driving the church bus into remote nooks and crannies of Cocke County, picking up people for the evening service, past fields of silent game cocks at dusk, each perched on its respective "house"—a rather bizarre sight. The hours melt away there, with church services, followed by drinking iced tea and Coke with people at fast food places, taking people to doctors and hospitals, and driving the roads with Alfred, talking, talking, talking. . . . I have experienced a lot of life with these people since 1971, from funerals, court cases, snakebites, marriage breakups, deaths, good times and bad. . . .

What amazes me about east Tennessee realities is how completely I snap (Billy Pilgram–like) into these discourses and ways of seeing the world, how commonsensical and taken-for-granted it all becomes. I roll with it, it flows over me, and that is that—a schizoid self. This could be an occupational hazard for the ethnographer!

25. In this regard, in 1978 I participated in a series of seminars entitled "Specialized Knowledge and Everyday Reality," chaired by Professor Thomas Luckmann. He was particularly interested in my presentation "The Social Construction of a Serpent-Handling Reality" (1978c) because of the way serpent handlers through anointing shifted into "finite provinces of meaning" (Berger and Luckmann 1966). Luckmann had to intervene in a rather authoritarian way to check the barrage of sensationalistic questions about types of snakes, what they eat, and so forth, reminding people that I didn't come to the seminar to answer these types of questions.

I similarly presented a paper in 1981, " 'To You Out There in Radioland'—Presenting 'the Broadcast' in an Appalachian Serpent-Handling Community," in an international symposium on "Language in Social and Cultural Context," chaired by the late Roger Keesing. It didn't take long for the questions to revert to snake lore and similar concerns. That this has been my experience on so many occasions suggests to me that even serious social scientists have difficulty relating to serpent handling in other than trivial ways.

26. I recently had a long telephone conversation with a long-term informant who no longer "takes up serpents." He feels too many young people have recently died in the faith. Many of these people did not "wait on the right anointing" or in some cases "were ruined by the media"—were caught up in a "showbiz" ethos and as a result acted carelessly for the cameras. People need a deep knowledge, wisdom, and spiritual understanding to "work in the signs."

REFERENCES

Abel, T. D. 1974. "The Holiness-Pentecostal Experience in Southern Appalachia." Ph.D. dissertation, Purdue University.

Abel, T. D. 1982. *Better Felt Than Said*. Waco: Markham Press.

Adams, S. L. 1993. *Appalachian Portraits*. (Narrative by Lee Smith.) Jackson: University of Mississippi Press.

Alther, L. 1975. "The Snake Handlers." *New Society* 34 (687) (December 4): 532–535.

Alther, L. 1976. "They Shall Take Up Serpents?" *New York Times Magazine* (June 6): 18–20, 28, 35.

Alther, L. 1977. *Kinflicks*. Penguin: New York.

Ambrose, K. P. 1970. "Survey of the Snake-Handling Cult of West Virginia." Master's thesis, Marshall University.

Ambrose, K. P. 1978. "A Serpent-Handling Church in a Midwestern City: A Study of Commitment." Ph.D. dissertation, Ohio State University.

Anglin, M. K. 1992. "A Question of Loyalty: National and Regional Identity in Narratives of Appalachia." *Anthropological Quarterly* 65 (3) (July): 105–116.

Appadurai, A. 1991. "Global Ethnoscapes: Notes and Queries for a Transnational Anthropology?" *Recapturing Anthropology: Working in the Present*. R. G. Fox, editor. Santa Fe, NM: School of American Research Press. 191–210.

Appalachian Heritage. 1978. [Serpent handling photos] *Appalachian Heritage* 6 (2) (spring): 29–32.

Bakhtin, M. 1981. *The Dialogic Imagination*. Austin: University of Texas Press.

Barker, E. 1986. "Religious Movements: Cult and Anticult since Jonestown." *Annual Review of Sociology* 12: 329–346.

Barker, J. 1985. *Copperhead Summer*. Berea: Kentucky Imprints.

Berger, J. 1972. *Ways of Seeing*. London: British Broadcasting Corporation/Penguin.

Berger, P. L. and T. Luckmann. 1966. *The Social Construction of Reality*. New York: Anchor Books.

Birckhead, (R.) J. 1970a. "A Critique of Weston La Barre's 'They Shall Take Up Serpents'—Psychology of the Southern Snake-Handling Cult." Unpublished paper, Department of Anthropology, University of Alberta.

Birckhead, (R.) J. 1970b. "Preliminary Research Proposal—The Function of the Serpent-Handling Cult in Southern Appalachian Acculturation." Unpublished paper, Department of Anthropology, University of Alberta.

Birckhead, (R.) J. 1971a. "Appalachian Serpent-Handling and Its Alternatives." Unpublished paper, Department of Anthropology, University of Alberta.

Birckhead, (R.) J. 1971b. "A Dissonance Approach to Appalachian Serpent-Handling Cults." Unpublished paper, Department of Anthropology, University of Alberta.

Birckhead, (R.) J. 1972. " 'Holy, Holy, Holy'—The Context and Structure of Religious Action in a Southern Appalachian Pentecostal-Holiness Church 'With Signs Following'—A Working Proposal." Unpublished paper, Department of Anthropology, University of Alberta.

Birckhead, (R.) J. 1974a. " 'God's Not Dead, He Is Still Alive'—A Study of 'Reality Management' in a Southern Appalachian Serpent Handling Church." Unpublished paper, Department of Anthropology, University of Alberta. (A Dissertation Proposal)

Birckhead, (R.) J. 1974b. " 'God's Not Dead, He Is Still Alive'—A Study of 'Reality Management' in a Southern Appalachian Serpent Handling Church." Paper, American Anthropological Association, annual conference, Mexico City.

Birckhead, (R.) J. 1975. " 'Sign' and Symbol in a Southern Appalachian Serpent Handling 'Community.' " Paper, American Anthropological Association, annual conference, San Francisco.

Birckhead, (R.) J. 1976a. " 'Power and Everyday Life in a Southern Appalachian Serpent-Handling 'Community.' '' Paper, Southern Anthropological Society annual meeting, Atlanta.

Birckhead, (R.) J. 1976b. "Toward the Creation of a Community of Saints." Ph.D. dissertation, University of Alberta.

Birckhead, (R.) J. 1977. " 'They've Gone Plum Crazy Up in Snake-Hollow'—The Social Reality of Appalachian Serpent-Handling." Paper presented to staff seminar, Kenmore Psychiatric Hospital, Goulburn, NSW, Australia.

Birckhead, (R.) J. 1978a. "Knowledge of 'Power' '' in an American Serpent-Handling Community." Symposium on "The Distribution of Knowledge in Society," Australian Anthropological Society meeting, Sydney.

Birckhead, (R.) J. 1978b. "The Negotiation of Meaning in an Southern Appalachian Serpent-Handling Community." Seminar, Department of Anthropology, Research School of Pacific Studies, The Australian National University, Canberra.

Birckhead, (R.) J. 1978c. "Religious Knowledge—The Social Construction of a Serpent-Handling Reality." Seminar series "The Nature of Knowledge," chaired by Thomas Luckmann, Department of Sociology, University of Wollongong.

Birckhead, (R.) J. 1978d. "Religious Serpent Handling Networks of the Eastern United States." Geography of Religion/Belief Systems Newsletter 2 (1) (January): 3–4.

Birckhead, (R.) J. 1978e. "Some Notes on 'Spiritual' vs 'Carnal' Knowledge in an American Serpent-Handling Community." Department of Sociology, University of Wollongong.

Birckhead, (R.) J. 1980. "Finite Provinces of Meaning: The Case of Holiness Serpent-Handlers." Paper, Australian Association for the Study of Religions, annual conference, Australian National University, Canberra.

Birckhead, (R.) J. 1981. " 'To You Out There in Radioland'—Presenting 'the Broadcast' in an Appalachian Serpent-Handling Community." Paper, International Symposium on "Language in Social and Cultural Context," Australian Anthropological Society annual meeting, Australian National University, Canberra.

Birckhead, (R.) J. 1982. " 'They Call Us Serpent-Handlers'—Minority Religious Identity and the Mass Media." Paper, Australian Association for the Study of Religions, annual conference, University of Melbourne.

Birckhead, (R.) J. 1986. "Tennessee Snake-Handlers and the Australian Aboriginality Debate." Seminar, School of Management, Technology, and the Arts, Riverina-Murray Institute, Albury.

Birckhead, (R.) J. 1991. " 'Bizarre Snakehandlers'—Popular Media and a Southern Stereotype." Paper, Southern Anthropological Society, Key Symposium, Colombia, South Carolina.

Birckhead, (R.) J. 1993a. "Bizarre Snakehandlers—Popular Media and a Southern Stereotype." Images of the South: Constructing a Regional Culture on Film and Video. K. G. Heider, editor. Athens: University of Georgia Press. 163–189.

Birckhead, (R.) J. 1993b. "First Time." Introduction to Anthropology. Wagga Wagga, Australia: Distance Education Package, Charles Sturt University. 50–53.

Birckhead, (R.) J. 1993c. " 'Snake Handlers' of Tennessee: The Presentation of American Exotica on Australian Television." Seminar, School of Social Sciences and Liberal Studies, Charles Sturt University, Bathurst.

Birckhead, (R.) J. 1994. "Review, Serpent Handling Believers, by Thomas Burton, 1993." Appalachian Journal 21 (3) (spring): 333–337.

Birckhead, (R.) J. 1996. "Snake Handlers—Heritage, Salvation, and Celebrity in the '90s." Appalachian Journal 23 (3) (spring): 260–274.

Birckhead, (R.) J.; T. De Lacy; and L. Smith, Editors. 1992. *Aboriginal Involvement in Parks and Protected Areas*. Canberra: Aboriginal Studies Press.

Brady, I., Editor. 1991. *Anthropological Poetics*. Savage, MD: Rowman & Littlefield.

Brown, D. E. 1991. *Human Universals*. New York: McGraw-Hill.

Brown, F. 1993. "Liston Pack: Out of the World's Black Belly." *Serpent Handling Believers* by T. Burton. Knoxville: University of Tennessee Press. 89–97.

Brown, K. M. 1991. *Mama Lola: A Vodou Priestess in Brooklyn*. Berkeley: University of California Press.

Bruner, E. M. 1990. "Introduction: Experiments in Ethnographic Writing." *Conversations in Anthropology: Anthropology and Literature*. P. J. Benson, editor. Urbana: *Journal of the Steward Anthropological Society* 17 (1–2). 1–19.

Burton, T. G. 1993. *Serpent Handling Believers*. Knoxville: University of Tennessee Press.

Burton, T. G., and T. F. Headley. 1983. *Carson Springs: A Decade Later*. Johnson City: East Tennessee State University. (Video)

Burton, T. G., and T. F. Headley. 1987. *Following the Signs: A Way of Conflict*. Johnson City: East Tennessee State University. (Video)

Burton, T. G., and J. Schrader. 1973. *"They Shall Take Up Serpents."* Johnson City: East Tennessee State University. (Film)

Carden, K. W., and R. W. Pelton. 1976. *The Persecuted Prophets*. South Brunswick, NJ: A. S. Barnes.

Carter, M. V. 1987. "From the 'Hollers' to High Street: A Brief Look at the Appalachian Serpent-Handlers' Presence in the Urban Midwest." *Faculty Studies*. R. M. Shurden, editor. Jefferson City, TN: Carson-Newman College. 12–22.

Carter, M. V., and K. P. Ambrose. 1982. "Appalachian Serpent-Handlers in the Urban Midwest: A Test of the Satisfaction Hypothesis." Paper, 5th Annual Appalachian Studies Conference, Boone, North Carolina.

Carter, M. V.; E. Green; and K. P. Ambrose. 1985. "A Case Approach to the Survival and Maintenance of the Appalachian Serpent Sect in the Urban Midwest: A Compensatory Hypothesis." Paper, Revisioning American: Religion-in American Life, Indiana University–Purdue University, Indianapolis.

Castaneda, C. 1971. *A Separate Reality*. New York: Simon & Schuster.

Caughey, J. L. 1986. "Epilogue: On the Anthropology of America." *Symbolizing America*. H. Varenne, editor. Lincoln: University of Nebraska Press. 229–250.

Chagnon, N. A. 1974. *Studying the Yanamamo*. New York: Holt, Rinehart and Winston.

Clarke, K. 1975. "Snake Handling and Plato: Identifying Academic Folklore." *Kentucky Folklore Record* 21: 100–104.

Clements, W. H. 1977. "Review Essay: Snake-Handlers on Film." *Journal of American Folklore* 90: 502–506.

Clements, W. H. 1979. "Film Review, *The Jolo Serpent Handlers*." *Journal of American Folklore* 92: 127–128.

Clifford, J. 1988. *The Predicament of Culture: 20th Century Ethnography, Literature and Art*. Cambridge, MA: Harvard University Press.

Clifford, J. and G. E. Marcus, editors. 1986. *Writing Culture: The Poetics and Politics of Ethnography*. Berkeley: University of California Press.

Cobb, A. L. 1965. "Sect Religion and Social Change in an Isolated Rural Community of Southern Appalachia—Case Story, Fruit of the Land." Ph.D. dissertation, Boston University.

Cohen, E. N., and E. Eames. 1982. *Cultural Anthropology*. Boston: Little, Brown and Company.

Coles R. 1972. "God and the Rural Poor." *Psychology Today* 5 (8) (January): 31–41.

Collins, J. B. 1947. *Tennessee Snake Handlers*. Chattanooga: Chattanooga News–Free Press.

Covington, D. 1995. *Salvation on Sand Mountain: Snake Handling and Redemption in Southern Appalachia*. Reading, MA: Addison-Wesley.

Crapanzano, V., and V. Garrison, editors. 1977. *Case Studies in Spirit Possession*. New York: John Wiley & Sons.

Crick, M. 1982. "Anthropological Field Research, Meaning Creation and Knowledge Construction." *Semantic Anthropology*. D. Parkin, editor. London: Academic Press. 15–37.

Crick, M. 1989. "Shifting Identities in the Research Process: An Essay in Personal Anthropology." *Doing Fieldwork—Eight Personal Accounts of Social Research*. J. Perry, editor. Geelong, Victoria: Deaken University Press. 24–40.

Danforth, L. M. 1989. *Firewalking and Religious Healing*. Princeton: Princeton University Press.

Darnell R. 1991. "Ethnographic Genre and Poetic Voice." *Anthropological Poetics*. I. Brady, editor. Savage, MD: Rowman & Littlefield. 267–277.

Daugherty, M. L. 1976. "Serpent-Handling as Sacrament." *Theology Today* (October): 232–243.

Daugherty, M. L. n.d. "Saga of the Serpent Handlers." Unpublished manuscript, Appalachian Ministries Educational Resource Center, Berea College, Berea, Kentucky.

Day, J. F. 1941. *Bloody Ground*. New York: Doubleday, Doran & Company.

Dickinson, E., and B. Benziger. 1974. *Revival*. New York: Harper & Row.

Dodds, E. R. 1951. *The Greeks and the Irrational*. Berkeley: University of California Press.

Drummond, L. 1983. "Jonestown: A Study in Ethnographic Discourse." *Semiotica* 46: 167–209.

Dumont, J. P. 1978. *The Headman and I*. Austin: University of Texas Press.

Dunlap, B. 1975. "Keepers of the Faith: The Worm and the Snake." *New Republic* (November 22): 19–22.

Dunlap, B. 1993. "The Worm and the Snake." *Images of the South—Constructing a Regional Culture on Film and Video*. K. G. Heider, editor. Athens: University of Georgia Press. 190–200.

Edgerton, R. B., and L. L. Langness. 1974. *Methods and Styles in the Study of Culture*. San Francisco: Chandler & Sharp.

Elifson, K. W., and P. S. Tripp. 1975. "The Belief System of Serpent Handlers: Ritual and Bites." Paper, Society for the Scientific Study of Religion Conference, Milwaukee.

Elifson, K. W., and P. S. Tripp. 1976. "Ultimate Faith: The Religion of Serpent Handlers." Unpublished manuscript, n.p.

Esler, G. 1983. "Snakes in Church." *The Listener* (August 18): 2–4.

Fee, J. R. 1989. "The Night I Lost My Religion at the 'Holy Roller' Church." *Appalachian Heritage* 17 (2) (spring): 41–47.

Finney, J. C., editor. 1969. *Culture Change, Mental Health, and Poverty*. Lexington: University of Kentucky Press.

Flagg, F. 1992. *Fried Green Tomatoes at the Whistle Stop Cafe*. London: Vintage.

Fortunato, F. 1980. "Snake Handlers—Risking Death as a Test of Faith." *Hustler* (April): 50–54, 58, 123–124.

Foxfire. 1973. [Special issue on serpent handling, untitled] *Foxfire* 7 (1) (spring): 2–75.

Freeman, D. 1965. "Anthropology, Psychiatry and the Doctrine of Cultural Relativism." *Man* 65: 65–67.

Garfinkel, H. 1967. *Studies in Ethnomethodology*. Englewood Cliffs, NJ: Prentice-Hall.

Geertz, C. 1973. *The Interpretation of Culture*. New York: Basic Books.

Gerlach, L. P., and V. Hine. 1970. *People, Power, Change: Movements of Social Transformation*. New York: Bobbs-Merrill.

Gerrard, N. L. 1966. "Scrabble Creek Folk: Part II, Mental Health." Unpublished report for the National Institute of Mental Health, Public Health Service/Department of Sociology, Morris Harvey College, Charleston, West Virginia.

Gerrard, N. L. 1968. "The Serpent-Handling Religions of West Virginia." *Transaction* 5: 22–28.

Gerrard, N. L. 1971. "Churches of the Stationary Poor in Southern Appalachia." *Change In Rural Appalachia—Implications for Action Programs*. J. D. Photiadis and H. K. Schwarzweller, editors. Philadelphia: University of Pennsylvania Press. 99–114.

Gerrard, N. L., and L. B. Gerrard. 1966. "Scrabble Creek Folk: Part I, Mental Health." Report for the Wenner-Gren Foundation, New York.

Goffman, E. 1959. *The Presentation of Self in Everyday Life*. Garden City, NY: Doubleday & Company.

Goodman, F. D. 1988. *Ecstasy, Ritual, and Alternate Reality*. Bloomington: Indiana University Press.

Grodsky, L. 1990. "The Saints and the Serpents." *Hustler* (July): 82–88, 98.

Hankla, C. 1988. *A Blue Moon in Poorwater*. New York: Ticknor & Fields.

Harner, M. J., editor. 1973. *Hallucinogens and Shamanism*. London: Oxford University Press.

Harper, C. L. 1982. "Cults and Communities: The Community Interfaces of Three Marginal Religious Communities." *Journal for the Scientific Study of Religion* 21 (1) (March): 26–38.

Hastrup, K. 1992. "Writing Ethnography: State of the Art." *Anthropology & Autobiography*. J. Okely and H. Callaway, editors. London: Routledge. 116–133.

Hayward, J. 1992. "The Dark Side of De Niro." *Weekend Australian* (January 4–5): 6.

Heider, K. G. 1979. *Grand, Valley Dani: Peaceful Warriors*. New York: Holt, Rinehart and Winston.

Heider, K. G. 1993. "Introduction." *Images of the South—Constructing a Regional Culture on Film and Video*. K. G. Heider, editor. Athens: University of Georgia Press. 106.

Herdt, G., and R. J. Stoller. 1990. *Intimate Communications: Erotics and the Study of Culture*. New York: Columbia University Press.

Hill, C. E. 1977. "Anthropological Studies in the American South: Review and Directions." *Current Anthropology* 18 (2) (June): 309–326.

Hine, V. H. 1969. "Pentecostal Glossolalia: Toward a Functional Interpretation." *Journal for the Scientific Study of Religion* 8 (2): 211–226.

Holliday, R. K. 1966. *Tests of Faith*. Oak Hill, WV: Fayette Tribune.

Hughes, J., ed. 1992. *Faces of Culture Film Notes*. Geelong, Victoria: Deakin University Press.

Kane, S. M. 1973. "Aspects of the Holy Ghost Religion: The Snake-Handling Sect of the American Southeast." Master's thesis, University of North Carolina.

Kane, S. M. 1974a. "Aspects of Spirit Possession in a Rural Southeastern Religious Sect: Some Preliminary Observations." Southern Anthropological Society Meeting.

Kane, S. M. 1974b. "Holy Ghost People: The Snake-Handlers of Southern Appalachia." *Appalachian Journal* 4 (spring): 255–262.

Kane, S. M. 1974c. "Ritual Possession in a Southern Appalachian Religious Sect." *Journal of American Folklore* 87 (October–December): 293–302.

Kane, S. M. 1976. "Holiness Fire Handling: A Psychophysiological Analysis." Unpublished paper, Department of Anthropology, Princeton University.

Kane, S. M. 1978. "Holiness Fire Handling in Southern Appalachia: A Psychophysiological Analysis." *Religion in Appalachia*. J. D. Photiadis, editor. Morgantown: West Virginia University Press. 113–124.

Kane, S. M. 1979. "Snake Handlers of Southern Appalachia." Ph.D. dissertation, Princeton University.

Kane, S. M. 1982. "Holiness Ritual Fire Handling: Ethnographic and Psychophysiological Considerations." *Ethos* 10 (4) (winter): 369–384.

Kane, S. M. 1984. "Snake Handlers." *Encyclopedia of Religion in the South*. S. S. Hill, editor. Macon, GA: Mercer University Press. 698–699.

Kane, S. M. 1987. "Appalachian Snake Handlers." *Perspectives on the American South*. Vol. 4. C. Cobb and C. R. Wilson, editors. New York: Gordon & Breach. 115–127.

Kane, S. M. 1989. "Snake Handlers." *Encyclopedia of Southern Culture*. C. R. Wilson and W. Ferris, editors. Chapel Hill: University of North Carolina Press. 1330.

Kimbrough, D. L. 1992. "Park Saylor and the Eastern Kentucky Snake-Handlers: A Religious History." Ph.D. dissertation, Indiana University.

Kimbrough, D. L. 1995. *Taking up Serpents: Snake Handlers of Eastern Kentucky*. Chapel Hill: University of North Carolina Press.

King, M., and M. Breault. 1993. *Preacher of Death*. Ringwood, Victoria: Signet Book/Penguin.

La Barre, W. 1962a. *"They Shall Take Up Serpents"—Psychology of the Southern Snake-Handling Cult*. Minneapolis: University of Minnesota Press.

La Barre, W. 1962b. "Transference Cures in Religious Cults and Social Groups." *Journal of Psychoanalysis in Group* 1 (1): 66–75.

La Barre, W. 1964. "The Snake-Handling Cult of the American Southeast." *Explorations in Cultural Anthropology*. W. H. Goodenough, editor. New York: McGraw-Hill. 309–333.

La Barre, W. 1970. *The Ghost Dance: The Origins of Religion*. Garden City, NY: Doubleday.

La Barre, W. 1971. "Materials for a History of Studies of Crisis Cults: A Bibliographic Essay." *Current Anthropology* 12 (1): 1–44.

Leacock, S., and R. Leacock. 1972. *Spirits of the Deep*. Garden City, NY: Doubleday/Natural History Press.

Lett, J. 1991. "Interpretive Anthropology, Metaphysics and the Paranormal." *Journal of Anthropological Research* 47 (3) (fall): 305–329.

Lewis, I. M. 1971. *Ecstatic Religion: An Anthropological Study of Spirit Possession and Shamanism*. Baltimore: Penguin.

Liebow, E. 1967. *Talley's Corner: A Study of Negro Streetcorner Men*. Boston: Little, Brown and Company.

Linney, R. 1971. *Holy Ghosts*. New York: Dramatists Play Service, Inc.

Long, J. K. 1982. "Psychoanalytic Anthropology: A Case of Aborted Critique." *Southern Anthropologist* 10 (1) (fall): 2, 6–9.

McCauley, D. V. 1987. "Mountain Preachers, Mountain Religion." *Appalachian Heritage* 15 (3) (summer): 40–48.

Marcus, G. E., editor. 1992. *Rereading Cultural Anthropology*. Durham: Duke University Press.

Marcus, G. E. and M. M. J. Fischer, editors. 1986. *Anthropology as Cultural Critique: An Experimental Moment in the Human Sciences*. Chicago: University of Chicago Press.

Marcus, J., editor. 1990. *Writing Australian Culture*. Adelaide: University of Adelaide, Department of Anthropology (Special issue, *Social Analysis* 27).

Martin, J. 1983. *Talking With*. New York: Samuel French, Inc.

Messerschmidt, D. A., editor. 1981. *Anthropologists at Home in North America*. Cambridge: Cambridge University Press.

Messerschmidt, D. A. 1984. "Review Article—Inside Looking Around: Studies of American Culture." *American Ethnologist* 11 (2) (May): 371–377.

Miller, J. W. 1977. "Appalachian Literature." *Appalachian Journal* 5 (1) (autumn): 82–91.

Miller, K. A. 1977a. "Religious Revitalization: The Serpent-Handlers of Appalachia." Master's thesis, University of Cincinnati.

Miller, K. A. 1977b. "The Serpent-Handlers and Communion with the Deity." Paper, Central States Anthropological Society, Cincinnati.

Miller, W. 1991. "Salvation Cocktail." *Habersham Review* 1 (1): 71–77.

Mink, K. 1973. "Tennessee Snake Cult." *Argosy* 377 (8) (August): 44–45, 86–87.

Moffatt, M. 1992. "Ethnographic Writing about American Culture." *Annual Review of Anthropology* 21: 205–229.

Moore, J. K. 1976. "The Music of the Snake Handlers of Southern West Virginia." Master's thesis, New York City University.

Moore, J. K. 1986. "Ethnic Hymnody Series: Socio-Economic Double Entendre in the Songs of the Snake-Handlers." *Hymn* 37 (2): 30–36.

Morales, B. S. D.; M. Arundar; D. Aubrey; and J. B. Morton. 1991. "The Ibeji Temple: A Yoruba Community in Atlanta." Paper, Southern Anthropological Society Meeting, Key Symposium, Columbia, South Carolina.

Morland, J. K. 1958. *Millways of Kent*. Chapel Hill: University of North Carolina Press.

Morris, R. & D. Morris. 1968. *Men and Snakes*. London: Sphere Books.

Mullis, H. T. 1988. "Psychological Aspects of Snake Handling in the Southern United States." Paper, Popular Culture Association, New Orleans.

Mundkur, B. 1983. *The Cult of the Serpent*. Albany: State University of New York Press.

Murphy, R. 1971. *The Dialectics of Social Life*. New York: Basic Books.

Murphy, R. 1989. *Cultural and Social Anthropology: An Overture*. Englewood Cliffs, NJ: Prentice-Hall.

Murray K. 1974. *Down to Earth—People of Appalachia*. Boone, NC: Appalachian Consortium Press.

Nichol, J. T. 1966. *The Pentecostals*. Plainfield, NJ: Logos International.

Norbeck, E. 1974. *Religion in Human Life: Anthropological Views*. New York: Holt, Rinehart & Winston.

Oates, J. C. 1978. *Son of the Morning*. New York: Fawcett Crest.

Ong, W. J. 1982. *Orality and Literacy.* London: Methuen.

Pandian, J. 1991. *Culture, Religion, and the Sacred Self.* Englewood Cliffs, NJ: Prentice-Hall.

Parker, G. K. 1970. "Folk Religion in Southern Appalachia." Ph.D. dissertation, Southern Baptist Theological Seminary.

Pelton, R. W. And K. W. Carden. 1974. *Snake Handlers: God Fearers? or Fanatics?* Nashville: Thomas Nelson.

Pelton, R. W., and K. W. Carden. 1976. *"In My Name Shall They Cast Out Devils?"* Brunswick, NJ: A. S. Barnes.

Peterson, N. 1977. *A Walbiri Fire Ceremony.* Canberra: Aboriginal Studies Press. Filmstrip.

Phillips, C. 1990. "God Told Me to Handle Snakes, So I've Got To." *Woman's World* (March 27): 26–27.

Pope, L. 1942. *Millhands and Preachers.* New Haven: Yale University Press.

Powdermaker, H. 1966. *Stranger and Friend: The Way of an Anthropologist.* New York: W. W. Norton.

Pruyser, P. W. 1963. "Review, 'They Shall Take Up Serpents: Psychology of the Southern Snake-Handling Cult.'" *Journal for the Scientific Study of Religion* 3 (1): 136–137.

Pruyser, P. W. 1968. *A Dynamic Psychology of Religion.* New York: Harper & Row.

Richardson, M. 1977. "Comments on C. E. Hill, 'Anthropological Studies in the American South: Review and Directions.'" *Current Anthropology* 18(2) (June): 321.

Romero, C. G. 1975. "Serpent-Handling as Act of Faith." *Diaspora* 7 (3): 1–2.

Rose, D. 1982. "Occasions and Forms of Anthropological Experience." *A Crack in the Mirror: Reflexive Perspectives in Anthropology.* J. Ruby, editor. Philadelphia: University of Pennsylvania Press. 219–274.

Rose, D. 1987. *Black American Street Life.* Philadelphia: University of Pennsylvania Press.

Rose, D. 1990. *Living the Ethnographic Life.* Newbury Park, CA: Sage.

Rousselle, R. 1984. "Comparative Psychohistory: Snake-Handling in Hellenistic Greece and the American South." *Journal of Psychohistory* 11 (spring):477–489.

Rowe, D. 1982. "Serpent Handling as a Cultural Phenomenon in Southern Appalachia." Master's thesis, East State Tennessee State University.

Rowe, D. 1986. *Serpent Handling as a Cultural Phenomenon in Southern Appalachia.* New York: Carlton Press.

Samarin, W. J. 1972. *Tongues of Men and Angels: The Religious Language of Pentecostalism.* New York: Macmillan Company.

Sanjek, R. S. 1990. "On Ethnographic Validity." *Fieldnotes: The Making of Anthropology.* R. S. Sanjek, editor. Ithaca: Cornell University Press. 385–418.

Sargant, W. 1949. "Same Cultural Group Abreactive Techniques and Their Relation to Modern Treatments." *Royal Society of Medicine Proceedings* 42 (5): 367–374.

Sargant, W. 1957. *Battle for the Mind.* Garden City, NY: Doubleday.

Sargant, W. 1975. *The Mind Possessed.* New York: Penguin.

Schwartz, S. W. 1991. "Sacred Fire Handlers: Music's Symbolic and Functional Relationship to the Appalachian Serpent-Handling Service." Paper, 14th Annual Meeting of Appalachian Studies Conference, Berea, Kentucky.

Schwartz, S. W. 1992. "Fire Handling in Appalachia: Myth, Magic or Just Good Old-

Fashioned Folklore?'' Paper, 15th Annual Meeting of Appalachian Studies Conference, Asheville.

Schwarz, B. E. 1960. ''Ordeal by Serpents, Fire, and Strychnine.'' *Psychiatric Quarterly* 34: 405–429.

Schwarz, B. E. 1989. ''Ordeal by Serpents, Fire, and Strychnine.'' *Appalachian Images in Folk and Popular Culture.* W. K. McNeil, Editor. Ann Arbor: UMI Research Press. 285–305.

Scientific American. 1940. ''Cult Snakes: Why Cultists Prefer Copperheads to Rattlers.'' *Scientific American* (October):215.

Seltzer, C. 1978. ''The Media vs Appalachia: A Case Study.'' *Teaching Mountain Children.* D. N. Mielke, editor. Boone, NC: Appalachian Consortium Press. 130–134.

Sharpe, T. 1979. *The Great Pursuit.* London: Pan Books.

Siskind, J. 1973. *To Hunt in the Morning.* London: Oxford University Press.

Smith, L. 1995. *Saving Grace.* New York: Putnam.

Stekert, E. J. 1963. ''The Snake-Handling Sect of Harlan County, Kentucky: Its Influence on Folk Tradition.'' *Southern Folklore Quarterly* 27: 316–322.

Sullivan, P. S., and K. W. Elifson. 1976. ''Death by Serpent Bite among a Religious Sect: A Sociological Interpretation.'' Paper, American Sociological Association meeting, New York.

Taublieb, P. 1983. ''Jesus Only—Snake Church.'' *US* 7(15) (July 18):34–36.

Taylor, E. M. 1992. ''The Taxidermy of Bioluminescence: Tracking Neighboring Practices in the Coal Camps of West Virginia.'' *Anthropological Quarterly* 65(3) (July):117–127.

Tellegen, A.; N. L. Gerrard; L. B. Gerrard; and J. N. Butcher. 1969. ''Personality Characteristics of Members of a Serpent-Handling Religious Cult.'' *MMPI Research Developments and Clinical Applications.* J. N. Butcher, editor. New York: McGraw-Hill. 221–242.

Tonks, R. 1967. ''Towards an Understanding of the Practice of Religious Snake-Handling as Evidenced in the Appalachian Area of the United States of America.'' Seminar paper, Southern Baptist Theological Seminary, Louisville.

Tripp, P. S. 1975. ''Serpent-Handlers: A Case Study in Deviances.'' Master's thesis, Georgia State University.

Tripp, P. S., and K. W. Elifson. 1975. ''Development and Analysis of Serpent Handling Ritual.'' Paper, Association for the Sociology of Religion, San Francisco.

Vance, P. 1975. ''A History of Serpent Handlers in Georgia, North Alabama, and Southeastern Tennessee.'' Master's thesis, Georgia State University.

Van Hoorebeke, K. 1980. ''The Rhetorical Paradigm in the Service of the Snake Handling Cult.'' Master's thesis, Western Illinois University.

Van Maanen, J. 1988. *Tales of the Field: On Writing Ethnography.* Chicago: University of Chicago Press.

Watterlond, M. 1983. ''The Holy Ghost People.'' *Science* 83 (30) (May):50–57.

Watts, A. 1973. ''The World's Most Dangerous Book.'' *Playboy* (July):120–122, 136, 278–280.

Wax, R., and M. Wax. 1962. ''The Magical World View.'' *Journal for the Scientific Study of Religion* 1 (2): 179–188.

White, J., editor. 1972. *The Highest State of Consciousness.* Garden City, NY: Anchor Books.

Wijeyewardene, G. 1979. ''Firewalking and the Scepticism of Varro.'' *Canberra Anthropology* 2(1) (April): 114–133.

Williams, P. W. 1980. *Popular Religion in America*. Englewood Cliffs, NJ: Prentice-Hall.

Wilson, B. 1970. *Religious Sects: A Sociological Study*. New York: World University Library, McGraw-Hill.

Wolf, D. R. 1991. "High-Risk Methodology: Reflections on Leaving an Outlaw Society." *Experiencing Fieldwork: An Inside View of Qualitative Research*. W. B. Shaffir and R. A. Stebbins, editors. Newbury Park, CA: Sage. 211–223.

Yinger, J. M. 1970. *The Scientific Study of Religion*. London: Macmillan.

2

The Study of Religion in American Society

Melinda Bollar Wagner

The ethnographic enterprise is the same, in many ways, wherever it is practiced. Yet ethnography inside religious groups, and within one's own culture, presents new problems while alleviating others.

Years ago, Evans-Pritchard (1962: 148) described "what the anthropologist does":

He goes to live for some months or years among a people. He lives among them as intimately as he can, and he learns to speak their language, to think in their concepts and to feel in their values. He then lives the experiences over again critically and interpretatively in the conceptual categories and values of his own culture and in terms of the general body of knowledge in his discipline. In other words, he translates from one culture into another.[1]

An ethnographic description presents the concepts that make up one culture in terms meaningful to readers in another (Spradley and McCurdy 1972). The anthropologist wants both to describe a culture and to explain why it has the form that it has. In order to write ethnographic descriptions, anthropologists must first acquire understanding of these "concepts that make up the culture" themselves. "The meaning system is presumed to have been acquired when the investigator can participate in the symbolism, ritual, and patterned interactions of the culture in a way that is deemed acceptable or 'correct' by its members" (Anthony and Robbins 1974: 481–482).

Acquiring this understanding proceeds in stages. Although we may label them differently, many ethnographers have noted a similar progression of stages, whether their fieldwork has taken them to traditional or modern settings. Those stages might be labeled (1) gaining entreé, (2) experiencing culture shock, (3) establishing rapport, (4) attaining an ever-increasing understanding of the culture, (5) leaving the field, and (6) analyzing and interpreting what has been learned.

STAGE: GAINING ENTREÉ

To gain entreé, ethnographers must somehow become acquainted with the groups they wish to learn about. As an example, Gertrude Enders Huntington's first Amish informants were her grandmother's neighbors. I made entreé into both the New Age metaphysical network and the conservative Christian schools by enrolling in various classes that metaphysical leaders or Christian school-teachers also attended (Wagner 1983a, 1983b, 1990, 1993).[2]

Gaining entreé brings with it some ethical questions. One of these questions—whether entreé should be covert—seems to bedevil participant observers from other fields but is a settled issue for the anthropologist (Richardson 1991). The American Anthropological Association's (1971) Statement of Ethics is clear on this point.

In research, an anthropologist's paramount responsibility is to those he studies. When there is a conflict of interest, these individuals must come first. The anthropologist must do everything within his power to protect their physical, social and psychological welfare and to honor their dignity and privacy. . . . The aims of the investigation should be communicated as well as possible to the informant. . . . Every effort should be exerted to cooperate with members of the host society in the planning and execution of research projects.

However, the role the ethnographer should take once entreé has been achieved is not nearly so clear-cut. Anthropological fieldwork brings with it a "triple bind," putting the fieldworker between a rock and two hard places. It is necessary to obtain good field data; anthropological ethics make it necessary to let the informants know what the ethnographer is doing; and it is necessary not to interrupt the ongoing flow and history of the society. (Although engagement and even advocacy are gaining proponents—especially in conflicts between the studied group and the larger society—it is still necessary to be aware of [if not beware of] the researcher's role in the group.) It is necessary to attend to these three goals simultaneously. The proper role of the ethnographer will be taken up again below, in a discussion of establishing rapport.

Once entreé has been made, it is customary in any ethnographic setting to stay in the field for at least one year. The reasoning behind this unwritten rule is threefold. First, one year will allow an annual round of seasons, holidays, and activities to unfold before the ethnographer. Even so, the ethnographer may miss events that do not happen annually. Second, staying in the field for an extended period of time will eventually give ethnographers the unnoticed "fly on the wall" or "mouse in the corner" status that they desire. Finally, the extended time in the field allows for sampling a wider variety of informants. Margaret Mead asserted that ethnographic sampling depends on knowing the various roles that informants carry; ethnographers use this knowledge as a substitute for the large numbers of anonymous respondents used by survey research to ensure that the sample represents the population.

STAGE: EXPERIENCING CULTURE SHOCK

After fieldwork is under way, even the professional student of culture is by no means insulated from culture shock. Generally, culture shock refers to the discomfort that accompanies perceiving phenomena that are surprising to the ethnographer, are misunderstood by the ethnographer, or are uncomfortable because they don't fit with the ethnographer's own cultural background. When fieldwork is undertaken in a subculture of the ethnographer's own society, the culture shock should not be as broad, nor last as long, as it would in a totally "foreign" culture. The problems associated with living day to day in a totally different environment are much mitigated. There is no new language to add to the struggle. Yet the vocabulary used in religious gatherings can seem nearly a new language (Zaretsky 1969, 1972). And its ring of familiarity can be shallow—leading ethnographers to mistakenly assume that they understand what they do not.

It is unfortunate that I have labeled culture shock a "stage" of fieldwork, as if it is to be gotten through and passed, never to be felt again. This is not the case; it waxes and wanes, taking its turn with rapport.

STAGE: ESTABLISHING RAPPORT

Anthropologists "break out" of culture shock (at least momentarily) and can begin to understand the meaning system of a culture when they have established rapport with people in the community. Establishing rapport generally occurs side by side with being given, or taking on, a role within the society. This occurrence does not necessarily follow from the ethnographer's own efforts; it is a give-and-take negotiation between the anthropologist and the informants.

Let us now deal with the dilemma of the ethnographer's proper role vis-à-vis informants—today's most controversial issue within the anthropological community. How much (or how little) "distance" should ethnographers keep from their "subjects"? Studying within one's own culture exacerbates the quandary.[3]

Scientifically detached, value-free, and *objective* are all different labels that have been variously applied to the social scientist's role, implying different degrees of distance. Some theorists say conscious reason, and language itself, inevitably separates us from the object of our thought (van Baal 1971). Durkheim (1895/1958) thought that the social facts that are the objects of study for sociologists and anthropologists are things to be known from the outside, rather than from within. He took it as a matter of principle that "the other" has no relation to the ethnographer; the ethnographer must learn about the other by observing. Levi-Strauss (1955/1969), on the other hand, took a different view of the ethnographic means of discernment. We all are human beings, he argued, and it was not necessary, nor desirable, for anthropologists to sacrifice their humanity and to become mere registering devices.[4]

The extreme distance of "scientific detachment" has not generally been pursued by anthropologists, whose methods include *participation* as well as observation. Being "value free" is no longer thought to be possible; a value-free social scientist has a fool for a philosopher. Postmodern science (in Toulmin's [1982] sense) "will be candid about its value dimension" and requires the same of its practitioners (Rappaport 1994).

Historically, ethnographers have sought to recognize their own values, thus not being caught in the value-free trap and delivering themselves from the culture blindness that might affect the objective nature of their studies. And to attain "objectivity" they have also striven to maintain some distance, wishing not to completely "go native." But some years ago, ethnographers began to question whether objectivity was possible. Today, some ethnographers are questioning whether objectivity is a worthy goal at all.

In mulling over the thorny points of this issue, let us begin with how active the ethnographer studying religion in American society should be. The degree of participation in "participant observation" can vary along a continuum from none at all ("nonparticipation" or "passive" participation, in Spradley's [1980a, 1980b] terms) to quite a lot ("active," or "complete" participation). For example, the degree of participation I undertook at the conservative Christian schools varied from school to school, from classroom to classroom, depending on how the teachers and I negotiated it. At some schools, my role was observer. At others I was observer and teacher's aide. Often, I was confidante. But I was always a "passive" observer in the sense that I wasn't in charge of or responsible for anything.

It would be very easy to take on roles of responsibility in groups within the researcher's own culture. Ethnographers come equipped with the academic credentials and skills that religious organizations are seeking. If the researcher is interested in learning about leadership in metaphysical groups, is it ethical to become a leader? If she is interested in learning about teaching in Christian schools, is it ethical to become a teacher? All anthropologists would not agree on the answers. I would say no. Both of these roles were offered to me, and I refused both. My reasoning is that these are roles of *responsibility* that put the ethnographer in the position of having an impact on the flow and direction of the group. Festinger, Riecken, and Schacter (1956) showed that the statements and actions of an active observer can assume much importance in groups that believe in the legitimacy of personal revelation.

Another reason for avoiding these roles is that an ethnographer has quite

enough to do to observe, maintain a balance between active and passive participation, keep informants apprised of what she means to be doing, and keep field
notes assiduously. How can totally active participants manage to record what
they and their informants are doing simultaneously? Fieldwork itself demands,
as Dorothy Lee (1986: 83, emphasis hers) says of motherhood, "full commitment to the situation, with all one's senses and other capacities *there*, alive and
straining and alert."

Reflexivity has become the label for some of the concerns contained within
the quandary of the ethnographer's proper role. Since this issue is a major one
for today's ethnographers, let me paint a broad-stroked portrait of its sources
and parameters.

In anthropology, there has long been a tension between those who see anthropology's goal as an emulator of the natural sciences, versus those who prefer
humanistic understanding. Eric Wolf (1990: 587):emphasized that anthropology
is the most scientific of the humanities, and the most humanistic of the sciences.
But in truth the two strains have often been at odds. The reflexivity—which
favors the humanistic side—could perhaps be seen in the context of that ongoing
tension. On the "scientific" "objective" margin of a continuum would be ethnographies that present data about a culture with the ethnographer removed from
the picture. As Stephen Tyler (1987) noted, this style of ethnography is a genre
that discredits or discourages narrative, subjectivity, confessional, personal an-
ecdote, or accounts of the ethnographer's experience. On the far other end is a
reflexive, personal, subjective account of the ethnographer's own experience in
the field. The rationale for this account is that ethnographers can only validly
report their own experience.[5] (See Ortner 1984 for a review article on anthropological theory; see Tedlock 1991 on reflexivity.)

A source of reflexivity is the questioning of epistemologies that began in the
1970s. Reflexivity, then, is akin to poststructuralism in general, and the New
Historicism in particular, in the literary world. An impetus for both was a similar
fear—that we are fooling ourselves and our readers to think that we can understand what the natives understand (Fabian 1983; Tedlock 1991; Veeser 1989).

Brandes (1991) noted application of literary techniques to ethnography as
another source of the turn toward reflexivity. In the days of anthropologist Franz
Boas and one of his many students, Paul Radin, the ethnographer was pencil,
recorder. Ethnographies were verbatim records of transactions with informants,
including however many versions of the origin story were collected, including
however many blueberry pie recipes were collected. In the new day, the ethnographer is storyteller. As Brandes (1991) noted, at the far end of the reflexive
continuum, stories about ourselves are being identified as the focus rather than
the background.

Closer to the center of our imaginary science/humanities continuum are reflexivists who think that the focus of the ethnography should be the dialogue
between the ethnographer and the natives. That is, the usual "what were they

to me'' information should be accompanied with "what was I to them" (Ted-lock 1991).

My critique of the controversy is signaled by the way I have organized this chapter, that is, by discussing the various stages of ethnographic fieldwork.[6] It seems to me that ethnographers in the field in the course of a year spend time being *both* the objective-at-a-distance "scientist" collecting data and the "gone-native" humanist. It seems, too, that the closeness and the distance are a constant back-and-forth movement of the mind. The feelings and thoughts one has during fieldwork—of friendship and loyalty, disjunctures with one's own value system, observation, understanding, and analysis—become a kind of dance of pulling in closer and pushing away. And it would be naive to think that we are the only ones pondering our relationship. Our informants, too, are coming close—then pushing away, distancing themselves—back and forth. We both are entrenched in an introspective pas de deux of "presentation of self."

I still think that it is possible and important, even and especially in the study of religion, to compartmentalize ethnographic activity and one's own reactions to the culture. Geertz (1973: 230) noted that "scientific studies of religion ought [not] to begin with unnecessary questions about the legitimacy of the substantive claims of their subject matter." It is possible to "dissociate" from concern for the truth or falsehood of religious doctrine; it is possible to "suspend belief or disbelief." Of course, ethnographers do not become unfeeling automatons upon entering the field. They react inside when hearing statements that don't match their own values. But "the promise of anthropology requires that the individual should agree to distinguish between his absolute convictions and his specialized activity as an anthropologist" (Dumont 1986: 205). Undergraduate methods students soon learn to distinguish empirical observations from their own judg-ments and feelings. They record the former in field notes and the latter in a diary. The diary is not unimportant. Indeed, it is the home of the information on the dialogue between informant and ethnographer that the best of the reflex-ivists desire. Indeed, it makes ethnographers' methods clear to themselves; it clarifies what they are and are not seeing, what they are and are not "looking for."

The controversy concerning reflexivity has brought to the ethnographer's awareness an important caution made by the philosopher Dilthey (1914/1976) long ago. There is a difference between life as lived (reality), life as experienced (experience), and life as told (expression). And ethnographers add still another level of abstraction to the story, as they interpret it for readers. The final product, it seems to me, should reflect a kind of biculturalism in which the ethnographer understands cultural phenomenon in both emic (native) and etic (outsider) ways. "Analogous experiences" can help to achieve emic understanding.[7] For ex-ample, Harding (1987: 169) describes nearly having a car accident after engag-ing in a long interview with a fundamentalist Baptist minister. As she slammed on the brakes, the thought came to her, " 'What is God trying to tell me?' " She reports, "It was my voice, but not my language. I had been invaded by the fundamental Baptist tongue I was investigating.'' Packing for a trip, I suddenly remember some seldom-worn shoes. I say to myself, ''[The conservative Christians would say] God showed me those shoes.'' These are analogous experiences. Evans-Pritchard (1962) would say that we have become successful in ''thinking in their concepts.''

As we noted earlier, the role of the ethnographer is a negotiated one. No matter how diligently the ethnographer tries to avoid certain roles, and to explain what she is and is not doing, no matter how she tries to maintain control over her presentation of self, informants will sometimes perceive the situation differently.

For example, in my fieldwork in the metaphysical fellowship, it was clear to me that there was a difference in my own conception of my role and the group's conception of it. To me, I was a member of the group because I was studying it. To the group, I was a member who was also studying it. Although the group leaders and most of the members knew I was a student of the group, they insisted from time to time that I was undergoing spiritual growth, just as they were. If I did not protest, I would be uncomfortable. If I protested too much, it would make the group uncomfortable, which would in turn make me uncomfortable.

Likewise, there were some roles that the conservative Christian schools held open for me that I could not take on. One of these was ''evaluator'' of their efforts at educating children. At each school I observed, it was necessary to explain that I was not evaluating the teachers and that I could not be seen as an ''educational consultant.'' I explained that I had no expertise that would allow me to take on those roles. Then it was necessary to follow through on this by not offering opinions, criticism, or even praise. It was necessary, of course, to thank the teachers for what they were teaching me but, at the same time, to avoid any kind of commentary. I tried to change their perceived ''evaluator/evaluatee'' statuses for us to the more appropriate ''collaborators in teaching me about Christian schools'' roles.

Another role that I had to avoid was ''spy'' of sorts. The Christian school administrators would ask me questions about the teachers, about what parents said, about other schools, and about what the students did when the teachers were out of the classroom—questions that I sidestepped as best I could.

It seems that the major epistemological difference in doing participant observation fieldwork in one's own culture and in an alien culture must be that when one crosses international cultural boundaries, one must constantly struggle to ''get close,'' to get in as far as he can, and to see as much as he can. He will never be all the way in because he is obviously foreign in some way. He is of a different color, taller or shorter, has a different native tongue, or at least a different background. Unlike anthropologists who do fieldwork in foreign lands and foreign languages, I had nothing to separate me from my informants. I was not different in age, sex, or background from many of my informants. When all the obvious cultural differences are obliterated, one must struggle to stay somewhat ''out'' of the group, to remember to observe and not just participate.

Rappaport (1994) has agreed that the anthropology of the strange and the anthropology of the familiar are different. In the anthropology of the strange, it is necessary to correct for being an observer by participating. In the anthropology of the familiar, the ethnographer corrects for being a participant and is more rigorous about observation.

STAGE: ATTAINING AN EVER-INCREASING UNDERSTANDING OF THE CULTURE

Once rapport is established (and it is a fragile thing, which waxes and wanes), the anthropologist can begin to understand the culture. Evans-Pritchard (1962: 148) said that ultimately the anthropologist lives the field "experiences over again critically and interpretatively in the conceptual categories and values of his own culture and in terms of the general body of knowledge in his discipline. In other words, he translates from one culture into another." He compares what he has observed in this culture to ethnographers' descriptions of other cultures.

Eventually, anthropologists take the specifics they have observed and generalize from them; they pin them to a theoretical backdrop. This is analogous to taking a photo and blowing it up to a larger size. If the original photo was taken with a sharp lens and fine-grained film, the blown-up image is still acute. If, however, the lens is out of focus or the film is coarse-grained, the blown-up picture is blurry. Just so, a record of human behavior must be clear and detailed if the analysis of it is to be valid.

To make this ethnographic record, I think most anthropologists use certain principles, perhaps not specifically labeling them as Spradley (1980a, 1980b) does; for example, "the language identification principle" requires that the ethnographer carefully record who said what so that various vocabularies used by different people, having various statuses, in different circumstances, can be learned. His "verbatim principle" requires that the record of what people say be exact and detailed. The "concrete principle" means that observations of what people do must be made, again, in exact, detailed language. Following these principles works to keep the "ethnographic film" fine-grained. If meanings, patterns, and generalizations are to be sought, the analysis cannot begin with field notes that are themselves already generalizations; it must start with what was seen, heard, tasted, smelled, and felt (in both the sensory and the emotional sense). Ethnographers use these principles in participant observation, ethnographic interviewing, collecting life histories, and recording time diaries. They may also utilize more structured interviews and questionnaires. These principles, Spradley (1980a, 1980b) notes, are meant to overcome the ethnographers' tendencies—be they students or professionals—to translate and simplify, to assume they understand what's going on. (See also Balch, Wagner, and Greil 1982 concerning principles for studying religion in the United States.)

A sign that some degree of understanding has been achieved is the ability to participate in the culture's activities with greater and greater ease—to be able to do things and say things correctly. Another sign of this understanding is the ability to explain cultural phenomena in both emic (native) and etic (outsider) terms. For example, Evans-Pritchard (1937) could understand that an Englishman and an Azande tribesman would derive different answers for the question, Why has this granary fallen and killed this man? The Englishman—with his penchant for such rationalized (in Weber's [1920–1921/1948, 1922/1963] sense) questions as, Why do the good die young and the evil flourish as the green bay tree?—would chalk the unfortunate incident up to carpenter ants, and to coincidence. The Azande, on the other hand, would be more likely to rephrase the question: Why has the granary fallen on my brother and not on someone else's brother? The answer: carpenter ants and witchcraft. A suicide that occurred in the metaphysical network during my fieldwork can also be explained in various idioms. To try to explain why a woman had ended her life, I could give the etic explanation—relying on sociological, psychological, and biological reasons. But I could also articulate and understand the emic reasons, which relied on overly long periods of meditation, opening of the chakras (psychic centers in the body), and possession.

A third signal that understanding has been reached is that the actions of the culture's actors become predictable to ethnographers. It is very much like learning a language. As long as you remain in the group, ability to use their concepts grows. As you move away, facility with use of the idiom lessens.

STAGE: LEAVING THE FIELD

Leaving the field is a stage that is seldom discussed by ethnographers. It is a stage of leaving behind those to whom one has become loyal, reentering the ethnographer's usual workaday world, and often encountering culture shock again in this world that has lost its familiar and taken-for-granted qualities. Leaving the field is made more complicated when studying within one's own country, because geographical distance as a signifier of the changed role is missing. After "leaving" the field, ethnographers may still see their erstwhile informants at the grocery store. They may take on new roles with them, which invites new ethical questions. For example, some of my informants later became students in my classes. By reading the journals my former informants wrote for my courses, I could gain insight into the conservative Christian way. Would it be unethical to treat these journals like field notes?

STAGE: ANALYZING AND INTERPRETING WHAT HAS BEEN LEARNED

In ethnography, like archaeology, the dig is the most fun, but then comes the lab work—the analysis—to see what has been learned. The ethnographic story must be based on empirical data and an analysis that seeks cultural patterns. Aids to seeing patterns are to look for repetition and to think about alternatives.

Imagining cultural alternatives shows what "might be"—and thus throws into relief "what is." What are all the *other* ways people could be doing this? Why, then, are they doing it *this* way? It helps, of course, if the ethnographer has a repertoire of cultural alternatives that she knows about or can imagine.

Another aid can be quantitative analysis of field data collected by qualitative means. This can act as a corrective for a "trust-me" impressionistic tone. For example, my *impression* of the sorts of solutions metaphysical devotees gave for personal problems was that they were all *spiritual* in nature ("Put it in the Light"; "Say the word 'God' "). My impression of the sorts of discipline used in Christian schools was that Christian symbols were often invoked ("What would Jesus say if you spit on him?" "If Jesus asked you to do your math page, what would you say?"). These made an impression on me, because they were new to me; they stood out in my mind. But in both cases, a quantitative analysis of field notes showed that my impressions were in error. Of course, a quantitative analysis is only as good as the field data on which it is based.

Some anthropologists take a much more deductive approach to ethnography than I am describing here, creating specific hypotheses before going into the field. I am partial to Spradley's (1980a, 1980b) image of the ethnographer as inductive "map-maker" charting unknown territory, saying "Let's see what's out there," unfettered by a *rigid*, preconceived research agenda. The ultimate question of this discovery-oriented research is, What are the cultural meanings people are using to build new cultural forms, to organize their behavior, and to interpret their experience? In this mode, after ethnographers have sought cultural patterns, they ask what explanations or theories best explain why these patterns are present in this culture and connect the data to the explanation. In a problem-oriented research method, these things occur the other way around, with the specific hypothesis or question following from the original theoretical perspective. Of course, these research decisions are linked to where the researcher stands on the matter of whether anthropology should pursue scientific or humanistic methods; the former would be more inclined to test hypotheses, and the latter to take an inductive approach.

ISSUE: LOYALTY—WHICH SIDE ARE YOU ON?

If a person embarks on ethnographic research inside religions in American society, she will face questions of loyalty.[8] This matter is intensified when the subjects are sophisticated about the dissemination of the ethnographer's findings. The apprehension such queries inevitably cause in the ethnographer has been called "audience anxiety" (Michalowski 1991). Loyalty questions arise at many stages along the way and from many quarters. Informants' concerns over loyalties are more prevalent in some religious entities than in others, and they rise and fall; ethnographers' academic colleagues question their loyalties; and in truth, ethnographers feel their own loyalties shift during the course of fieldwork.

Informants seldom questioned my loyalty in the New Age group because the metaphysicians were quite tolerant of views other than their own. However, seldom having loyalty questioned does not mean that informants are not making erroneous assumptions about it. In situations like these, it is well to remember that, at least within the United States, "silence signals assent."[9]

In the conservative Christian groups, loyalty is a more salient concern, since witnessing to nonbelievers is a requirement of evangelical religion. One of my informants doubted the anthropological enterprise in the same way that the reflexivists do. A college missionary, he thought that only a believer could understand Christian culture and that a neutral stance could never lead to understanding.

Another informant questioned my ability to be neutral, from the other side of the coin. She was a teacher in the Christian school where I spent the most time. In the first conversation I had with her, when I explained my mission, she asked, "How are you going to remain objective? Even captives eventually get to like their captors."

Colleagues, too, will question loyalties. These questions are particularly vexing when studying within one's own culture, when studying religion, and especially when studying a religion that is not acceptable to the societal mainstream (Harding 1991).

Although Robbins and Robertson (1991: 321) note that "many sociologists and other 'scientific students' of religion" in the early days of the scientific study of religion were clerics, a recent poll showed that when asked, "What is your present religion?" 65 percent of anthropologists claimed no religion. In this national survey of college faculty, anthropologists had the highest percentage of nonbelievers (ISAE 1991). (See also Kasnitz and Wagner [1972] and Reed [1974] for more discussion of the religious involvement of social scientists who study religion.) Most would answer this loyalty question as did Peacock (1986: 6–7) and for the same reasons. He reports that

once in a small-town mosque in Java, a congregation of several hundred prayed that I convert to Islam. What was the source of my resistance? For one thing, I had taken the stance of the "researcher," the fieldworker "studying" this tradition, rather than the stance of a believer in one thing open to something else. In fact, when the Muslim group once asked me, "What is your religion?" I replied, "My religion is anthropology"; I meant that I was a student of belief, rather than a believer. At a deeper level, to convert would have meant giving up a cultural identity as well as accepting a religious commitment.

These questions raised by the loyalty issue are queries for which, try as they might, researchers will not formulate answers that are satisfactory to interrogators. If, for example, researchers are admitted believers, their ethnographic work will be dismissed with, "They're too faith-committed." (Although good examples of believer-authored ethnographies are found in both the sociological and the anthropological literature on American religion.) If they are nonbelievers, questions and rumors regarding loyalties will never cease (see Harding 1991; Heller 1991; Schweitzer 1991a, 1991b; Wagner 1991a, 1991b). If they are successful in convincing the interlocutors that they are not believers, the ethnographers will be criticized for not being able to experience what believers do. If they refrain from "debunking" certain religious groups, they will be accused of being in league with unacceptable factions of American society.

These constant ambivalences of loyalty are unique to the study of religion in American society. Studying religion in other cultures produces no such ambiguity. No one thought that Evans-Pritchard had taken on the native Azande belief system. Although Peacock's (1986) informants were concerned about his beliefs, none of them thought that he *was* a Muslim. Studying other topics within American society produces no such concern and ambiguity. An economic anthropologist who studies contemporary economic manifestations in the United States may not be as persistently asked, "Did you grow up around flea markets?" "Are you a flea marketer yourself?"

Ethnographers' own loyalties do shift as the stages of fieldwork I have outlined here unfold. The words of the teacher who had allowed that even captives get to like their captors would echo back to me as I felt my own loyalties shift during and after my fieldwork in the Christian schools. I admit that I had seen the vans with "Faith Christian School" emblazoned on the side and had applied the usual stereotypes to them. The thought had crossed my mind, "Do I want to be associated with these people?" But as in any participant observation research, getting close to the people removes the cardboard cutout stereotypes held when first entering the field. After awhile, I gave no thought to being associated with these folks. During the time of my fieldwork, the teachers, administrators, parents, and students at these schools were my "peer group." I was away from my usual colleagues, and my loyalties did shift to the new peers.

During this stage, I had little problem with my own loyalties, as long as my efforts at compartmentalization worked: that is, if informants in the field remained informants (and friends and confidantes and teachers and collaborators— all the roles we ethnographer/informants allowed ourselves) and those outside the field did not become informants. (But people did not always cooperate with my neat categorizations.)

Culture shock reared its head again when I came out of the field and went back to teaching. I found that I had acquired a kind of pariah status for having spent time with the conservative Christians. (See Douglas [1982] and Marsden [1982] for the historical background to this vehemence of feeling against conservative Christians.)[10] Then I began to feel my loyalties shifting again. I was away from the conservative Christians now; my colleagues were again my peers, and I felt myself swaying to their "peer pressure." Nevertheless, questions of my loyalty have not ceased.

ISSUE: AVOIDING THE ANTI–POPULAR CULTURE BIAS

When studying subgroups within their own culture, obviously academics have to avoid being less than objective due to their own ideological convictions (they have to suspend belief/disbelief). In the case of some subgroups, they have to guard against intolerance of intolerance. But it seems to me that there is a more subtle threat to our neutrality—a bias against popular culture. We tend to presume that everyone is as concerned with ideology, language, and thought as we are. We expect that the discourse of religion, especially, takes place on a sophisticated and high plane—"different" from the everyday and common. When the Episcopalian Book of Common Prayer is "updated" so that "Save me, O God; for the waters are come in unto my soul" (Psalms 69:1, King James) becomes "Save me, O God! For the waters have come up to my neck" (Psalms 69:1, RSV), we wince, along with David Martin (1982). When Christmas becomes "Jesus is the reason for the season" and a sprig of holly printed on a "message button"; when children wear "God is awesome" T-shirts; when teachers can buy pop bottle–shaped stickers that say "God loves you and soda I"—we wince again. It offends our sensibilities; it upsets our epicurean natures. But these relatively naively pursued trends of the "common man" are important and worthy of study and understanding; popular culture is culture.

CONCLUSION

In my own work, I try to strike a balance between data gathering ("science") and understanding ("humanism"). I take careful field notes and quantify certain elements of them, because quantification has shown me that my *impressions* are colored by my own cultural experiences and by surprise stemming from my sometimes erroneous expectations—no matter how hard I have tried to rid myself of any expectations.

To me the most flattering comments about my work come from readers who say that they cannot tell whether I am a believer or not. This has been said about the ethnographies of New Age groups and conservative Christian groups alike. "Neutrality," meaning the ground that lies in the interstices between advocating, apologizing, and excoriating, is still my own goal in the study of religion in the United States. That ground may become shaky, however, and I may be called upon to reassess where I stand upon it; I may then find myself writing a different chapter on the anthropological study of religions in American society.

NOTES

1. Evans-Pritchard's work has garnered much criticism lately for discussing, as Tedlock (1991: 74) describes it, "highly abstract, non-empirical entities" presented in an "omniscient third-person authoritative voice," rather than a less-distanced, more subjec-

tive portrait of the people (Audience comments in session, "Self or Other?: Reflexive Anthropology in the European Context," American Anthropological Association meeting, Chicago, Illinois, November 20–24, 1991).

2. *Metaphysics* is defined by its adherents as a "practical religious philosophy." Devotees seek to use psychic phenomena in practical ways in everyday life and to experience "spiritual growth," defined as an ever-increasing awareness of the divine inner self. *Conservative Christians* refers to evangelical, fundamentalist, charismatic, Pentecostal, and Holiness believers.

3. There is no consensus on this issue; the commentary here must be seen as my own, based on several years of field research experience. I believe it to be a "middle ground" position.

4. The old and continuing argument within anthropology as to whether there is a psychic unity of humankind—whether thought processes of all human beings are the same—obviously plays a part in this debate.

5. Felicitas Goodman (1991: 339–340) says that studying religious *experience* is particularly problematic for Western anthropologists. On the one hand, when we "concern ourselves scientifically" with the "external accoutrements of a particular religious system"—the "history, the organizational form, the system of symbols, the dogma, the theology"—"little danger of attack accrues to us researchers." But when we "work on . . . the experiential contact with the alternative reality, that will for reasons deeply embedded in our history and psychological make-up touch a raw nerve. What appears in that case then is what we might term the discomfiture of religious experience."

6. I would like to add one other caution: It is not difficult to believe that American anthropologists could spend a good deal of time pondering them*selves*; perhaps we should keep this cultural context in mind. As Brandes (1991) noted, it is hoped that ultimately the ethnographer's reflexivity will reveal something about the other (and not, I would say, devolve into autobiographical angst).

7. I am grateful to Nancy Tatom Ammerman for giving situations similar to these this label, from the audience at the session on Qualitative Approaches to the Study of Religion at the Society for the Scientific Study of Religion meeting, Pittsburgh, Pennsylvania, November 8–10, 1991.

8. I owe a debt of thanks to Mary Schweitzer (1991a, 1991b) for helping me to clarify my thoughts on this issue, for giving me the nomenclature of "loyalty" to label it, and for organizing sessions at professional meetings that showed that the problem was by no means mine alone.

9. Gertrude Enders Huntington taught me this and many other necessary principles of doing fieldwork on religion in American society.

10. When anthropologists return from the field, they customarily display artifacts from their field sites in their offices. In my case, my colleagues would not have approved. My artifacts were paperweights from Jim Bakker's Heritage USA; Christmas message buttons that said "Jesus is the reason for the season"; seventh-grade essays critiquing the theory of evolution; and posters asking, "Where Will You Spend Eternity?" showing distressed people engulfed in the flames of hell.

REFERENCES

Anthony, Dick, and Thomas Robbins. 1974. "The Meher Baba Movement: Its Effect on Post-Adolescent Social Alienation." *Religious Movements in Contemporary*

America. Irving I. Zaretsky and Mark P. Leone, editors. Princeton, NJ: Princeton University Press.

Balch, Robert W.; Melinda Bollar Wagner; and Arthur L. Greil. 1982. Workshop on "Improving Field Studies of New Religious Movements," Society for the Scientific Study of Religion, Providence, Rhode Island, October 22–24.

Brandes, Stanley. 1991. Discussant's comments in session "Self or Other?: Reflexive Anthropology in the European Context." American Anthropological Association, Chicago, Illinois, November 20–24.

Dilthey, Wilhelm. 1914/1976. *Selected Writings*. New Edition edited by H. P. Rickman. Cambridge: Cambridge University Press.

Douglas, Mary. 1982. "The Effects of Modernization on Religious Change." *Religion and America*. Mary Douglas and Steven M. Tipton, editors. Boston: Beacon Press.

Dumont, Louis. 1986. *Essays on Individualism*. Chicago: University of Chicago Press.

Durkheim, Emile. 1895/1958. *The Rules of Sociological Method*. Translated by Sarah A. Solovay and John H. Mueller. New Edition edited by George E. G. Catlin. Glencoe, IL: Free Press.

Evans-Pritchard, Edward Evans. 1937. *Witchcraft, Oracles, and Magic among the Azande*. Oxford: Clarendon Press.

Evans-Pritchard, Edward Evans. 1962. *Social Anthropology and Other Essays*. New York: Free Press.

Fabian, Johannes. 1983. *Time and the Other: How Anthropology Makes Its Object*. New York: Columbia University Press.

Festinger, Leon; Henry W. Riecken; and Stanley Schacter. 1956. *When Prophecy Fails*. Minneapolis: University of Minnesota Press.

Geertz, Clifford. 1973. *The Interpretation of Cultures*. New York: Basic Books.

Goodman, Felicitas. 1991. "The Discomfiture of Religious Experience." *Religion* 21 (October): 339–344.

Harding, Susan F. 1987. "Convicted by the Holy Spirit: The Rhetoric of Fundamental Baptist Conversion." *American Ethnologist* 14 (1): 167–181.

Harding, Susan F. 1991. "Representing Fundamentalism: The Problem of the Repugnant Cultural Other." *Social Research* 58 (2): 373–393.

Heller, Scott. 1991. "Many Anthropologists Spurn Exotic Sites to Work the Territory Closer to Home." *Chronicle of Higher Education* (March 6): A5, A8.

ISAE (Institute for the Study of Evangelical Religion). 1991. "Thirty Percent of College Faculty Claim No Religious Belief." *Evangelical Studies Bulletin* 8 (2): 4.

Kasnitz, Devva, and Melinda Bollar Wagner. 1972. "Religion and the Anthropologist: Historical Traditions and Personal Beliefs." Graduate seminar for Anthropology 511 Ethnology, Anthropology Department, University of Michigan.

Lee, Dorothy. 1986. *Valuing the Self: What We Can Learn from Other Cultures*. Prospect Heights, IL: Waveland Press. (1st edition 1976)

Lévi-Strauss, Claude. 1955/1969. *Tristes tropiques*. Translated by John Russell. New York: Atheneum.

Marsden, George M. 1982. "The Religious New Right in Historical Perspective." *Religion and America*. Mary Douglas and Steven M. Tipton, editors. Boston: Beacon Press.

Martin, David. 1982. "Revived Dogma and New Cult." *Religion and America*. Mary Douglas and Steven M. Tipton, editors. Boston: Beacon Press.

Michalowski, Raymond J. 1991. "Who Can You Trust?: Ethnography in the Political

Vortex of U.S.-Cuban Relations.'' Paper, American Ethnological Society, Charleston, South Carolina, March 14–16.

Ortner, Sherry B. 1984. ''Theory in Anthropology since the Sixties.'' *Comparative Studies in Society and History* 26: 126–166.

Peacock, James L. 1986. *The Anthropological Lens: Harsh Light, Soft Focus.* New York: Cambridge University Press.

Rappaport, Roy A. 1994. ''The Anthropology of Trouble: A Conclusion.'' *Diagnosing America.* Shepard Forman, editor. Ann Arbor: University of Michigan Press.

Reed, Myer Stratton. 1974. ''The Sociology of the Sociology of Religion.'' *Review of Religious Research* 15: 20–24.

Richardson, James T. 1991. ''Reflexivity and Objectivity in the Study of Controversial New Religions.'' *Religion* 21 (October): 305–318.

Robbins, Thomas, and Roland Robertson. 1991. ''Studying Religion Today. Controversiality and 'Objectivity' in the Sociology of Religion.'' *Religion* 21 (October): 319–338.

Schweitzer, Mary. 1991a. Organizer/chair, session ''Fearing the Other: Anxiety and Suspicion in the Field.'' American Ethnological Society, Charleston, South Carolina, March 14–16.

Schweitzer, Mary. 1991b. Organizer/chair, session ''Dirty Little Secrets: Negotiating Loyalties in Anthropological Fieldwork.'' American Anthropological Association, Chicago, Illinois, November 20–24.

Spradley, James P. 1980a. *Ethnographic Interview.* New York: Holt, Rinehart and Winston.

Spradley, James P. 1980b. *Participant Observation.* New York: Holt, Rinehart and Winston.

Spradley, James P. and David W. McCurdy. 1972. *The Cultural Experience: Ethnography in Complex Society.* Chicago: Science Research Associates.

Tedlock, Barbara. 1991. ''From Participant Observation to the Observation of Participation: The Emergence of Narrative Ethnography.'' *Journal of Anthropological Research* 47 (1): 69–94.

Toulmin, Stephen E. 1982. *The Return to Cosmology: Postmodern Science and the Theology of Nature.* Berkeley: University of California Press.

Tyler, Stephen A. 1987. *The Unspeakable: Discourse, Dialogue, and Rhetoric in the Post-Modern World.* Madison: University of Wisconsin Press.

van Baal, Jan. 1971. *Symbols for Communication: An Introduction to the Anthropological Study of Religion.* Assen, The Netherlands: Koninklijke Van Gorcum.

Veeser, H. Aram, editor. 1989. *The New Historicism.* New York: Routledge.

Wagner, Melinda Bollar. 1983a. *Metaphysics in Midwestern America.* Columbus: Ohio State University Press.

Wagner, Melinda Bollar. 1983b. ''Spiritual Frontiers Fellowship.'' *Alternatives to American Mainline Churches.* Joseph H. Fichter, editor. New York: Rose of Sharon Press.

Wagner, Melinda Bollar. 1990. *God's Schools: Choice and Compromise in American Society.* New Brunswick, NJ: Rutgers University Press.

Wagner, Melinda Bollar. 1991a. ''Negotiating the Role of Ethnographer in Non-Mainstream Religious Groups.'' Paper, American Ethnological Society, Charleston, South Carolina, March 14–16.

Wagner, Melinda Bollar. 1991b. ''Which Side Are You On? Negotiating the Role of

Ethnographer in Controversial Groups." Paper, American Anthropological Association, Chicago, Illinois, November 20–24.

Wagner, Melinda Bollar. 1993. "Metaphysics: 'A Practical Religious Philosophy.'" *Religion and the Social Order*. Thomas Robbins and Arthur L. Greil, editors. Greenwich: JAI.

Weber, Max. 1920–1921/1948. *The Protestant Ethic and the Spirit of Capitalism*. Translated by Talcott Parsons. New York: Scribner.

Weber, Max. 1922/1963. *The Sociology of Religion*. Translated by Ephraim Fischoff. Boston: Beacon Press.

Wolf, Eric R. 1990. "Distinguished Lecture: Facing Power—Old Insights, New Questions." *American Anthropologist* 92 (3): 586–596.

Zaretsky, Irving I. 1969. "The Message Is the Medium: An Ethnosemantic Study of the Language of Spiritualist Churches." Ph.D. dissertation, University of California at Berkeley.

Zaretsky, Irving I. 1972. "The Language of Spiritualist Churches: A Study in Cognition and Social Organization." *Culture and Cognition: Rules, Maps, and Plans*. James P. Spradley, editor. San Francisco: Chandler.

3

Science, Religion, and Anthropology

James Lett

The anthropological literature on religion is diverse and voluminous, but there is one common perspective that pervades virtually that entire body of work, and that is the conviction that the epistemological principles of the scientific method cannot and/or should not be applied to the content of religious beliefs, on the grounds that nonempirical phenomena are necessarily beyond the purview of empirical science. Evans-Pritchard offers a familiar formulation of the position in *Theories of Primitive Religion*:

He [the anthropologist] is not concerned, *qua* anthropologist, with the truth or falsity of religious thought. As I understand the matter there is no possibility of his *knowing* whether the spiritual beings of primitive religions or of any others have any existence or not, and since that is the case he cannot take the question into consideration. (Evans-Pritchard 1965: 17)

Whatever personal convictions anthropologists may hold as individuals, the overwhelming majority have agreed with Evans-Pritchard that, as anthropologists, they either cannot or should not investigate the truth or falsity of religious beliefs. In virtually every major anthropological work on religion, and in most if not all introductory textbooks in cultural anthropology, the question of the truth or falsity of religious beliefs is evaded, ignored, or deemphasized in favor of questions concerning the social, psychological, ecological, symbolic, aesthetic, and/or ethical functions and dimensions of religion.[1]

Thus, for example, Anthony Wallace, who affirms that religion "is based on supernaturalistic beliefs about the nature of the world which are not only inconsistent with scientific knowledge but also difficult to relate even to naive human experience'' (Wallace 1966: vi), nevertheless chooses to ''ignore the extremes of fundamentalist piety and anticlerical iconoclasm'' and to regard religion as ''neither a path of truth nor a thicket of superstition, but simply [as] a kind of human behavior . . . which can be classified as belief and ritual concerned with supernatural beings, powers, and forces'' (5). Similarly, Edward Norbeck, who recognizes that ''religious beliefs and acts are created by man on the basis of his life'' (Norbeck 1974: 7), nevertheless explicitly restricts the anthropological study of religious beliefs to ''interpretations of their role in human life and of the factors that have molded the customs into their particular forms'' (3). Clifford Geertz (1973: 89), who defines religion as a system of ''sacred symbols'' that functions ''to synthesize a people's ethos . . . and their world view,'' is completely unconcerned with the question of whether any particular religiously supported worldview is true or false. And Marvin Harris, who has long been one of anthropology's most persistent critics of irrational modes of thought, nevertheless declares that he ''can readily subscribe to the popular belief that science and religion need not conflict,'' since science, he argues, ''does not dispute the doctrines of revealed religions as long as they are not used to cast doubt on the authenticity of the knowledge science itself has achieved'' (Harris 1979: 6).

In short, a common element of the anthropological perspective on religion can be summarized in a straightforward syllogism:

1. The essential defining feature of science is empiricism (i.e., the belief that the only reality that exists is the reality amenable to the five senses, implying that reliable knowledge of that reality can be obtained only through the five senses).

2. The essential defining feature of religion is supernaturalism (i.e., the belief that there is a reality that lies beyond or somehow transcends the reality amenable to the five senses, implying that reliable knowledge of that reality can be obtained by means other than the five senses).

3. Therefore, science cannot be used to determine whether religious beliefs are true or false, since empirical epistemological procedures cannot be applied to supernatural phenomena.

Despite its virtual ubiquity in anthropology, that argument is unsound, for the reason that both of its premises are false. The essential defining feature of science is *not* empiricism, and the essential defining feature of religion is *not* supernaturalism. The conclusion that religion is or should be immune from scientific scrutiny is thus wholly unwarranted; moreover, that conclusion is also ethically objectionable. Considerations of disciplinary integrity, public welfare, and human dignity demand that religious claims be subjected to anthropological evaluation.

My position, then, is that anthropological science can and should be applied to the content of religious beliefs. My goal here is to establish three points: first, that rationality rather than empiricism is the key element of science; second, that irrationality rather than supernaturalism is the key element of religion; and third, that anthropologists have an intellectual and ethical obligation to investigate the truth or falsity of religious beliefs. The first point concerns the nature of science; the second involves the nature of religion; and the third, obviously, is a question of value.

THE NATURE OF SCIENCE

In the most fundamental sense, science can be defined as a systematic and self-correcting method for acquiring reliable factual knowledge. "It is the desire for explanations which are at once systematic and controllable by factual evidence that generates science," the philosopher Ernest Nagel (1961: 4) observes, "and it is the organization and classification of knowledge on the basis of explanatory principles that is the distinctive goal of the sciences." The rules of the scientific method (which include testability, observer independence, replicability, and logical consistency) do not restrict science to the pursuit of *empirical* knowledge, however. Instead, they restrict science to the pursuit of *propositional* knowledge.

A proposition is an assertion of fact, a statement that makes a claim that is either true or false, depending on the evidence. The scientific method is simply a set of procedures for evaluating the evidence offered in support of any proposition. No proposition is ever rejected by science on an a priori basis (unless the proposition is self-contradictory); science is predicated upon the assumption that any factual assertion *could* be true. Nor does science demand that the evidence offered in support of any claim be empirical; science demands only that the evidence be objective.

As a set of guidelines for the acquisition of knowledge, scientific objectivity implies two things: first, that the truth or falsity of a given factual claim is independent of the claimant's hopes, fears, desires, or goals; and second, that no two conflicting accounts of a given phenomenon can both be correct (Cunningham 1973: 4). Critics of the scientific method commonly protest that objectivity in the first sense is unrealistic, because no individual scientist can ever be completely unbiased, and that objectivity in the second sense is unrealizable, because absolute certainty is unattainable. Both of those subordinate premises are correct (it is true that no individual can ever be completely unbiased, and it is true that absolute certainty about evidential questions can never be achieved), but neither of these points is relevant to the claim that science is objective, as Charles Frankel (1955: 138–139) explains:

There are two principal reasons why scientific ideas are objective, and neither has anything to do with the personal merits or social status of individual scientists. The first is that these ideas are the result of a cooperative process in which the individual has to submit his results to the test of public observations which others can perform. The second is that these ideas are the result of a process in which no ideas or assumptions are regarded as sacrosanct, and all inherited ideas are subject to the continuing correction of experience.

To be objective, then, in the scientific sense of the term, a statement must fulfill two criteria: First, it must be *publicly verifiable*, and second, it must be *testable*. In the words of the philosopher Carl Hempel (1965: 534), an "objective" statement is one that is "capable of test by reference to publicly ascertainable evidence." The scientific claim to objectivity is thus *not* a dogmatically positivistic claim to absolute certainty.[2] Scientific objectivity does not deny that perception is a process of active interpretation rather than passive reception, nor does it deny that the acquisition of reliable knowledge is a highly problematic undertaking. Instead, scientific objectivity merely denies that all claims to knowledge are equally valid, and it provides a set of standards by which to evaluate competing claims. To assert that science is objective, as Siegel (1987: 161) does, is to assert simply that all claims to knowledge should be "assessed in accordance with presently accepted criteria (e.g., of evidential warrant, explanatory power, perceptual reliability, etc.), which can in turn be critically assessed."

As a technique for acquiring reliable propositional knowledge, science necessarily demands objective evidence, which is to say evidence that is both publicly verifiable and testable. Evidence that was not publicly verifiable would not be reliable, and evidence that was not testable would not be propositional (since a proposition is, by definition, a statement that can be tested against the evidence). Objectivity, however, is *all* that science demands. As long as a propositional claim is both publicly verifiable and testable, it is scientific. There is nothing in the essential defining features of science that says that propositional claims must necessarily be empirical.

In practice, it is true, science has so far been restricted exclusively to empirical data and empirical data collection procedures, but that restriction is neither prejudicial nor arbitrary. Instead, it is a result of the fact that the empirical approach is the only approach to propositional knowledge that has ever passed the test of public verifiability. If publicly verifiable evidence of nonempirical reality were presented, the recognition of such reality would be incorporated into the scientific worldview. If nonempirical data collection procedures (e.g., faith, revelation, intuition) were publicly verifiable, they would be incorporated into the scientific method (Lett 1987: 18–22). It is not the fact that science is empirical that makes science objective; instead, it is the fact that science is objective that makes science empirical.

Thus, it is a mistake (although a common one)[3] to define science in terms of empiricism, as Bernard (1988: 12) does when he says that the scientific method is based on the assumption that "material explanations for observable phenomena are always sufficient, and that metaphysical explanations are never needed." Science, however, does not assume that material explanations are always sufficient; instead, science concludes, as an inductive generalization, that material explanations are always sufficient. (Further, under the epistemological principles of science, that conclusion would be subject to revision in the light of new evidence.) Bernard (11–12) offers a better definition of science when he quotes Lastrucci (1963: 6) to the effect that science is "an objective, logical, and systematic method of analysis of phenomena, devised to permit the accumulation of reliable knowledge." The term *empirical* is appropriately missing from that definition.

Scientific knowledge, then, means "objective knowledge," which means propositional knowledge that is both publicly verifiable and testable. In order to ensure the public verifiability of propositional claims, science relies upon the provisionally necessary rule of empiricism (while recognizing that empiricism is only a convenient means to an end—namely, intersubjectivity—and leaving open the possibility that some as-yet-unidentified nonempirical approach might satisfy the criterion of public verifiability). In order to ensure the testability of propositional claims, science relies upon the logically necessary rule of falsifiability, Karl Popper's (1959) indisputable sine qua non of the scientific approach to knowledge.

According to the rule of falsifiability, a claim or statement is to be considered propositional if and only if it is possible to conceive of evidence that would prove the claim false. The rule of falsifiability is simply a means of distinguishing propositional claims from nonpropositional ones. If the claim were to fail the test of falsifiability (if it were not possible, in other words, to even imagine falsifying evidence), then all possible evidence would be irrelevant, and the claim would be propositionally meaningless (it might, of course, be emotively meaningful, but it would be entirely devoid of any factual content whatsoever). If the claim were to pass the test of falsifiability, on the other hand (if it were possible to conceive of data that would disprove the assertion), then the evidence would be relevant, the claim would be propositionally meaningful, and the truth or falsity of the proposition could be tested against the evidence (in which case, of course, science would demand that the evidence be publicly verifiable).

The rule of falsifiability is the single most important rule of science. It is the one standard that guarantees that all genuine scientific statements are propositional (rather than emotive or tautological or nonsensical), and it is the salient feature that sharply distinguishes science from other ways of knowing. It is, further, the one standard by which all scientific explanations are judged, as Cohen (1970: 32) correctly observes: "Whether or not the theory is scientific depends ultimately on whether the ideas involved in the theory can be submitted to a test of their validity."

Thus, science is a technique for acquiring propositional knowledge that relies exclusively upon the publicly verifiable investigation of falsifiable claims, whatever those claims might be. In the insightful words of Richard Watson (1991: 276), "[S]cience in the most general sense is an attempt to learn as much as possible about the world in as many ways as possible *with the sole restriction* that what is claimed as knowledge be both testable and attainable by everyone'' (emphasis added). There is then no reason *not* to apply science to nonempirical claims. If the claim were a factual one, then it would be falsifiable, whatever the nature of its supporting evidence, and it would be the claimant's responsibility to identify reliable (i.e., publicly verifiable) evidence that would falsify the claim. As Lakatos (1970: 92) insists, ''[I]ntellectual honesty consists . . . in specifying precisely the conditions under which one is willing to give up one's position.''

Those who see empiricism as the defining element of science fail to recognize that the scientific method is a combination of both deduction and induction. Science, in other words, relies upon both logic and experience, both reason and observation, in the pursuit of knowledge. It would in fact be prejudicial to call science empirical; science demands only that the evidence collected through observation and experience be objective (i.e., publicly verifiable and testable), and it is at least logically possible that nonempirical evidence could be objective.

In sum, the essence of science lies in the exclusive commitment to rational beliefs, by which I mean beliefs that are both falsifiable and unfalsified. If a belief satisfies both criteria (if it is, in the first place, propositional, and it has, in the second place, survived unrelenting attempts at falsification in the light of publicly verifiable evidence), then it deserves to be called scientific knowledge. Scientific knowledge is thus provisional knowledge (it is always logically possible that evidence could be uncovered tomorrow that would falsify a previously unfalsified claim), but the scientific approach to propositional knowledge is nevertheless the only rational approach.[4] It would obviously be irrational to give factual credence to a purportedly propositional claim that was either nonfalsifiable (i.e., propositionally meaningless) or falsified (i.e., evidentially wrong). That brings us to religion.

THE NATURE OF RELIGION

In *Religion in Human Life*, Edward Norbeck (1974: 6) observes that ''religion is characteristically seen by anthropologists as a distinctive symbolic expression of human life that interprets man himself and his universe, providing motives for human action, and also a group of associated acts which have survival value for the human species.'' Various formulations could be subsumed under that general description, such as Lessa and Vogt's (1972: 1) notion that ''religion may be described as a system of beliefs and practices directed toward the 'ultimate concern' of a society'' or Geertz's (1973: 90) concept of religion as ''a system of symbols'' that integrates a culture's worldview and ethos. Those definitions, however, could logically embrace existentialism, communism, secular humanism, or other philosophies that most anthropologists would be reluctant to call religion. How, then, is religion distinguished from comparable sets of beliefs and behaviors that fulfill similar functions?

As Norbeck (1974: 6) explains, ''[T]he distinguishing trait commonly used is supernaturalism, ideas and acts centered on views of supernatural power.'' The concept of the supernatural has been firmly tied to the anthropological definition of religion since the origins of the discipline. Edward Tylor (1871/ 1958: 8), for example, argued that ''it seems best . . . to claim, as a minimum definition of Religion, the belief in Spiritual Beings.'' Frazer (1890/1963: 58) maintained that ''religion involves, first, a belief in superhuman beings who rule the world, and, second, an attempt to win their favour.'' Malinowski (1954: 17) observed that sacred ''acts and observances are always associated with beliefs in supernatural forces, especially those of magic, or with ideas about beings, spirits, ghosts, dead ancestors, or gods.'' The concept of the supernatural continues to dominate anthropological conceptions of religion today. Marvin Harris (1989: 399), for example, declares that ''the basis of all that is distinctly religious in human thought is animism, the belief that humans share the world with a population of extraordinary, extracorporeal, and mostly invisible beings.''

There is a fundamental problem with the term *supernatural*, however: It is so varyingly conceived in the different cultures of the world that it lacks a common, unambiguous definition. The Yanomamo, Roman Catholic, !Kung San, and Buddhist conceptions of the supernatural realm, for example, are widely divergent and even contradictory in some aspects. The problem is that the term *supernatural* is an *emic* concept—meaning that it is defined in terms of the categories and concepts regarded as meaningful and appropriate by the members of particular cultures; it is not an *etic* concept, one defined in terms of the categories and concepts regarded as meaningful and appropriate by the community of scientific observers (Lett 1990). As an emic concept, the term *supernatural* has as many definitions as there are cultures; as an etic concept, it has no recognized, agreed-upon definition.

Nor could any such objective, scientific definition be offered for the term *supernatural*, for the simple reason that the word is propositionally meaningless. The term *supernatural* is purportedly used to designate a reality that somehow transcends the natural universe of empirical reality, but what does it mean to ''transcend empirical reality''? If such a thing as nonempirical reality exists, how could we, as empirical beings, even know about it? (Revelation and intuition, after all, are demonstrably unreliable—witness the mutually exclusive claims to knowledge made by different people on revelatory grounds.) If such a thing as nonempirical reality exists, by what mechanism is it connected to empirical reality? (How, in other words, do supernatural beings and forces have an impact on the natural world?) Further, if such a thing as nonempirical reality exists, why is there not a single shred of objective evidence to indicate its existence? As the physicist Victor Stenger (1990: 33) points out, there is no rational reason whatsoever to even hypothesize the existence of the supernatural:

At this writing, neither the data gathered by our external senses, the instruments we have built to enhance those senses, nor our innermost thoughts require that we introduce a nonmaterial component to the universe. No human experience, measurement, or obser-

vation forces us to adopt fundamental hypotheses or explanatory principles beyond those
of the Standard Model of physics and the chance processes of evolution.

The term *supernatural* thus purports to describe a reality that we could not
know or recognize, one that could not have any impact on the reality we do
know and recognize, and one for which we have no evidence whatsoever; it is,
in short, unintelligible. The philosopher William Gray (1991: 39) eschews the
term *supernatural* and suggests instead that religious statements can be described
as *metaphysical*, by which he means statements that refer to facts that could not
possibly be observed. But what would an "unobservable fact" be? To substitute
metaphysical for *supernatural* is simply to play a semantic game. Terms such
as *supernatural, metaphysical,* and *nonempirical reality* are, in fact, oxymorons.
It would make just as much sense to talk about the "unreal real."

Connotatively, the term *supernatural* presents additional problems: It is not
sufficiently comprehensive to embrace beliefs and behaviors that are virtually
identical in form and function to so-called religious beliefs and behaviors but
that would not commonly be called supernatural. Gods, demons, angels, and
souls, for example, could easily be called supernatural, and so, too, perhaps,
could incubi, succubi, ghosts, goblins, fairies, sprites, trolls, and leprechauns.
But what about witches, clairvoyants, telepathists, psychokinetics, extraterrestrials, psychic surgeons, vampires, werewolves, spirit channelers, firewalkers,
astrologers, the Loch Ness Monster, and Sasquatch? Would those, too, be called
supernatural? Would anthropologists call beliefs in such beings and forces religious?

At least one recent anthropological text on religion recognizes this problem.
In *Magic, Witchcraft, and Religion*, Lehmann and Myers (1989: 3) argue that
it is time for anthropologists to abandon the restrictive connotations of the term
supernatural:

Expanding the definition of religion beyond spiritual and superhuman beings to include
the extraordinary, the mysterious, and unexplainable allows a more comprehensive view
of religious behaviors among the peoples of the world and permits the anthropological
investigation of phenomena such as magic, sorcery, curses, and other practices that hold
meaning for both pre-literate and literate societies.

Lehmann and Myers fail, however, to suggest an alternative term to replace
the word *supernatural*. Fortunately, there is an obvious alternative available,
one that is winning increasing acceptance both inside and outside anthropology,
namely, the word *paranormal*.[5] The term refers ostensibly to phenomena that
lie beyond the normal range of human perception and experience, although in
practice it does not denote simply anomalous phenomena. Instead, it describes
putative phenomena whose existence would in fact violate the rules of reality
revealed by science and common sense. From an etic point of view, therefore,
the notion of the paranormal, like the notion of the supernatural, is proposition-

ally meaningless. Unlike the term *supernatural*, however, the term *paranormal* is not restrictive in its connotations, and that is its principal advantage. *Paranormal* is a useful umbrella label for the complete set of emic beliefs concerning the unreal real. The term embraces the entire range of transcendental beliefs, covering at once everything that would otherwise be called magical, religious, supernatural, metaphysical, occult, or parapsychological.

Therein lies the real common denominator in all paranormal beliefs: not that they are all supernatural but that they are all *irrational*, by which I mean that every single paranormal belief in the world, whether labeled religious, magical, spiritual, metaphysical, occult, or parapsychological, is either nonfalsifiable or has been falsified. The vast majority of all paranormal propositions—such as the Judeo-Christian proposition that "God" exists—are nonfalsifiable and hence propositionally meaningless; a smaller percentage—such as the Judeo-Christian proposition that a universal flood covered the earth sometime within the past 10,000 years—are falsifiable but have invariably been falsified by objective evidence.

The simple fact of the matter is that every religious belief in every culture in the world is demonstrably untrue. Regardless of whether the religious practices are organized communally or ecclesiastically, regardless of whether they are mediated by shamans or priests, regardless of whether the intent is manipulative or supplicative, the one constant that runs through all religious practices all over the world is that all such practices are founded upon nonfalsifiable or falsified beliefs concerning the paranormal.

Irrationality is thus the defining element in religion. Religion and science are not at odds because religion wants to be "supernatural," while science wants to be "empirical"; instead, religion and science are at odds because religion wants to be irrational (relying ultimately upon beliefs that are either nonfalsifiable or falsified), while science wants to be rational (relying exclusively upon beliefs that are both falsifiable and unfalsified).

I am aware that many anthropologists are likely to react negatively to the pejorative connotations of the word *irrational*. The term, however, is simply descriptive and therefore entirely appropriate. It is unarguably irrational to maintain a belief in an allegedly propositional claim when that claim is either propositionally meaningless or has been decisively repudiated by objective evidence. Whether it is laudable or forgivable to do so is another question: It is not, of course, a factual question, but neither is it a question that scientists can entirely avoid.

A QUESTION OF VALUE

It seems to me that the obligation to expose religious beliefs as nonsensical is an ethical one incumbent upon every anthropological scientist for the simple reason that the essential ethos of science lies in an unwavering dedication to truth. As Frankel and Trend (1991: 182) put it, "[T]he basic demand of science is that we seek and tell the honest truth, insofar as we know it, without fear or favor.'' In the pursuit of scientific knowledge, the evidence is the only thing that matters. Emotional, aesthetic, or political considerations are never germane to the truth or falsity of any propositional claim. (There *are* moons around Jupiter, just as Galileo claimed, even though the Catholic Church and most Christians at the time did not like him for saying it.) In science, there is no room for compromise in the commitment to candor. Scientists cannot allow themselves to be propagandists or apologists touting convenient or comforting myths.

It is not simply our desires for intellectual honesty and disciplinary integrity that compel us to face the truth about religious beliefs; as anthropologists, we are specifically enjoined to do so by our code of ethics. According to the Revised Principles of Professional Responsibility adopted by the American Anthropological Association in 1990, anthropologists have an explicit obligation ''to contribute to the formation of informational grounds upon which public policy may be founded'' (Fluehr-Lobban 1991: 276). When anthropologists fail to publicly proclaim the falsity of religious beliefs, they fail to live up to their ethical responsibilities in this regard. In a debate concerning public policy on population control, for example, anthropologists have an ethical obligation to explain that God does not disapprove of the use of contraceptives because there is no such thing as God.

We also have an obligation not to pick and choose which truths we are willing to tell publicly. I think, for example, that the political threat from the oxymoronic ''scientific creationists'' would be better met if anthropologists were to debunk the entire range of creationist claims (including the belief that God exists as well as the belief that humans and dinosaurs were contemporaneous); otherwise, the creationists will continue to criticize us, with considerable justification, for our arbitrariness and inconsistency in choosing which paranormal claims we will accept or tolerate and which we will attack (see Toumey 1994).

I am convinced that our collective failure to stake out a firm anthropological position on paranormal phenomena has compromised our intellectual integrity, weakened our public credibility, and hampered our political effectiveness. Carlos Castaneda was able to use his anthropological credentials to buttress the credibility (and the sales) of his paranormal fantasies partly because, as far as the general public knew, the discipline of anthropology accepted the reality of hundred-foot gnats and astral projection (de Mille 1990). While it is true that most individual anthropologists rejected Castaneda's paranormal claims, few did so publicly or effectively (Murray 1990).

In fact, our discipline as a whole has a lamentable record when it comes to public responses to paranormal claims. There have been notable exceptions in archeology and biological anthropology, where a number of scholars have responded forcefully and well to the ancient astronaut and creationist myths (e.g., White 1974; Cole 1978; Rathje 1978; Cazeau and Scott 1979; Godfrey 1983; Stiebing 1984; Cole and Godfrey 1985; Harrold and Eve 1995; Feder 1980,

1984, 1990), but cultural anthropologists have been remarkably remiss in re-
sponding to the myriad paranormal claims that fall within their domain (see Lett
1991).

Margaret Mead, for example, maintained a lifelong interest in paranormal
phenomena and was an ardent champion of irrational beliefs (Gardner 1988).
She was apparently persuaded that "some individuals have capacities for certain
kinds of communications which we label telepathy and clairvoyance" (Mead
1977: 48), even though the most casual scholarship would have revealed that
that proposition has been decisively falsified (the evidence comes from more
than a century of intensive research that has been thoroughly documented and
widely disseminated—see Kurtz 1985; Druckman and Swets 1988; Hansel 1989;
Alcock 1990). In 1969, Mead was influential in persuading the American Association for the Advancement of Science to accept the habitually
pseudoscientific Parapsychological Association as a constituent member. In all
of this, Mead used her considerable talents for popularization to promulgate
nonsensical beliefs among the general public. However sincere and well inten-
tioned, her efforts were irresponsible, unprofessional, and unethical; worse still,
they were not atypical of cultural anthropology.[6]

Even those anthropologists who do not share Mead's gullibility have been
notably reluctant to confront the truth about paranormal beliefs. Anthony Wallace, for example, in all likelihood thought he was being purely objective when
he decided to avoid the "extremes of piety and iconoclasm" and to regard
religion as "neither a path of truth nor a thicket of superstition" (Wallace 1966:
5). In science, however, being objective does not entail being fair to everyone
involved; instead, being objective entails being fair to the truth. The simple truth
of the matter is that religion *is* a thicket of superstition, and if we have an ethical
obligation to tell the truth, we have an ethical obligation to say so.

I find Wallace's equivocation on the truth or falsity of religious beliefs to be
particularly regrettable because his *Religion: An Anthropological View* is one of
the justly celebrated classics in the anthropology of religion. Wallace, of course,
would not agree that his stance is anything less than fair and appropriate; indeed,
he is very forthright in declaring and defending his value position. In the opening
pages of his book, for example, he states that "although my own confidence
has been given to science rather than to religion, I retain a sympathetic respect
and even admiration for religious people and religious behavior" (vi).

I suspect that most anthropologists would be inclined to agree with Wallace.
Eric Gans (1990: 1), who has urged anthropologists to "demonstrate a far
greater concern and respect for the form and content of religious experience,"
is one who clearly shares Wallace's sympathy for the religious temperament.
Whether Wallace and Gans are justified in according religious people respect
and admiration is a debatable question, however. No reasonable person would
deny that religious people are entitled to their convictions, but an important
distinction must be made between an individual's *right* to his or her own opinion
(which is always inalienable) and the *rightness* of that opinion (which is never

unchallengeable). With that in mind, it could be argued that individuals who are led by ignorance or timidity to embrace incorrect opinions might deserve empathy and compassion, but they would hardly deserve respect and admiration. Respect and admiration, instead, should be reserved for individuals who exhibit dignity, courage, or nobility in response to the universal challenges of human life.

The philosopher Paul Kurtz (1983) articulates just such a position in a lengthy rebuttal to religious values entitled *In Defense of Secular Humanism*. From Kurtz's point of view, religious people live in a world of illusion, unwilling to accept and face reality as it is. In order to maintain their beliefs, they must prostitute their intellectual integrity, denying the abundant contradictory evidence that constantly surrounds them. They exhibit an "immature and unhealthy attitude" that is "out of touch with cognitive reality" and that "has all the hallmarks of pathology" (173). Religious people fail to exhibit the moral courage that is the foundation of a responsible approach to life.

The physicist Victor Stenger (1990) shares Kurtz's disdain for religious commitment, and he is one of many skeptical rationalists in a variety of fields who do so. Religious people, Stenger argues, fail to accept responsibility for defining the meaning and conduct of their own lives; instead, they lazily and thoughtlessly embrace an inherited set of illogical wish-fulfillment fantasies. By refusing to fully utilize their quintessentially human attributes—the abilities to think, to wonder, to discover, to learn—religious people deny themselves the possibility of human dignity or nobility. It is only those with the courage to reject religious commitment, Stenger (31–32) suggests, who deserve admiration; in his words, "Those who have no need to deny the reality they see with their own eyes willingly trade an eternity of slavery to supernatural forces for a lifetime of freedom to think, to create, to be themselves."

It would be disingenuous of me not to admit that I concur completely with Kurtz and Stenger. Nevertheless, my personal values regarding religion are entirely beside the point; I mention this only to point out the irony of our discipline's frequent sympathy for religious commitment. In Western culture, the concept of religious "faith" has a generally positive connotation, but there is nothing positive about the reality masked by that obfuscatory term. "Faith" is nothing more than the willingness to reach an unreasonable conclusion—that is, a conclusion that either lacks confirming evidence or contains disconfirming evidence. Willful ignorance, deliberate self-deception, and delusionary thinking are not admirable human attributes. Religion prejudicially regards faith as an exceptional virtue, but science properly recognizes it as a dangerous vice.

In the final analysis, however, it is irrelevant whether religious conviction deserves respect and admiration, as Wallace and Gans propose, or contempt and disdain, as I believe. My point instead is a very basic one: As scientists, we all have an ethical obligation to tell the truth, regardless of whether that truth is attractive or unattractive, diplomatic or undiplomatic, polite or impolite. As anthropologists, we have not been telling the truth about religion, and we should. The issue is just that simple.

CONCLUSION

As a diverse, multifunctional cultural universal, religion is unavoidably a phenomenon of surpassing anthropological interest. What the anthropology of religion has long ignored, however, is the fact that religion and anthropology are competitors in the attempt to fulfill many of the same functions. Much of the domain of inquiry that anthropology has recently claimed for itself is one that religion has long considered its own, including the fundamental questions of human origins, human nature, and human destiny. Elman Service (1985: 319) makes this point very tellingly in *A Century of Controversy*:

People, in the union of society, already know the answers to all of the questions they consider basic. . . . Unlike the natural sciences, which at first were called on simply to fill the dark void of ignorance with increasingly sure, or testable, knowledge (and which were likely to be the ones asking the question), the behavioral sciences faced questions that had already been asked *and* answered by the culture itself.

The conflict between religion and anthropology comes about because the answers that the two offer to the "basic questions" concerning humanity are in most cases fundamentally opposed. Religious and scientific perspectives on such questions are rarely complementary, as it is popularly supposed. More often, religious and scientific perspectives are mutually contradictory and ultimately incompatible. Anthropological science reveals, in addition, that the contradictory answers offered by religion are clearly, demonstrably, and unequivocally wrong. When it comes to the questions of human origins and human nature, for example, it is evident that the world's religions are mistaken. Consider the Judeo-Christian tradition as a single instance: The human species is *not* less than 10,000 years old, the present geographical distribution of human populations is *not* attributable to survivor dispersion following a universal flood, the origins of *Homo sapiens* are *not* distinct from the rest of the animal kingdom, the linguistic diversity of the human species is *not* the result of a historic event in southwest Asia 4,000 years ago, illness is *not* caused by the devil, and women are *not* intellectually inferior to men.

In my view, the goal of anthropology should be to give us the right answers to the questions that human beings have always asked. The exceptional value of our discipline does not lie in our subject matter, which is neither unique nor original. Instead, it is the anthropological approach (specifically, the scientific perspective) that makes our discipline worthwhile. No rational person can doubt the unequaled value of scientific investigation. "Since the eighteenth century," as Bernard (1988: 25) aptly observes, "every phenomenon, including human thought and behavior, to which the scientific method has been systematically applied over a sustained period of time, by a large number of researchers, has yielded its secrets, and the knowledge has been turned into more effective human control of events.''

The unfortunate truth is, however, that the scientific study of human thought and behavior has lagged behind the scientific study of the natural world, in part because social scientists, out of deference to the emotional sensitivities of their fellow humans, have been especially reticent about applying the scientific method to the entire range of anthropological phenomena. The study of religion is only the most obvious instance of that reticence. If we would like to achieve something comparable to the success that our colleagues in physics, chemistry, and biology have achieved, we will have to be equally consistent in our application of the scientific method (see Lett 1996).

To summarize briefly, we know that no religious belief is true because we know that all religious beliefs are either nonfalsifiable or falsified. In the interests of scientific integrity, we have an obligation to declare that knowledge. Doing so, of course, would not preclude other anthropological analyses of religion, and I would not want to be understood as having suggested that we should abandon the study of the social, psychological, ecological, symbolic, aesthetic, and ethical functions and dimensions of religion. It is precisely those areas where the anthropology of religion has made, and continues to make, its greatest contributions. Nevertheless, the scientific study of religion will never be fully legitimate until scientists recognize and proclaim the truth about religion.

NOTES

1. There have been exceptions, of course. Murdock (1980: 54), for example, makes this unambiguous observation: ''There are no such things as souls, or demons, and such mental constructs as Jehovah are as fictitious as those of Superman or Santa Claus.'' Similarly, Schneider (1965: 85) offers this forthright declaration: ''There is no supernatural. Ghosts do not exist.'' But these are the exceptions that prove the rule.

2. Scientific objectivity is, admittedly, founded upon a pair of ultimately unprovable assumptions: first, the assumption that ''reality is 'out there' to be discovered,'' as Bernard (1988: 12) says (or that ''there are things outside of the observer which no amount of merely logical manipulation can create or destroy,'' as Harris [1964: 169] puts it), and second, the assumption that reality is amenable to human inquiry (or that reliable knowledge is attainable, in other words). However, while it may not be possible to conclusively prove the truth of either assumption, neither is it possible to reasonably doubt the validity of either. Both assumptions are decisively validated by the overwhelming weight of human experience. Our lives are *not* mere illusions, and we have succeeded in understanding and predicting much of the world. To deny the first assumption is to engage in the worst sort of solipsism; ''it is quite true that facts do not speak for themselves,'' as Spaulding (1988: 264) astutely observes, ''but a conclusion that therefore there are no facts is a crashing *non sequitur*.'' To deny the second assumption is to claim to know that no knowledge is possible, and that, obviously, is self-contradictory.

3. It is a mistake that I myself have made. In the first edition of my textbook on anthropological theory (Lett 1987: 26), I suggested that science could be defined as "a systematic method of inquiry based upon empirical observation that seeks to provide coherent, reliable, and testable explanations of empirical phenomena and that rejects all accounts, descriptions, and analyses that are either not falsifiable or that have been decisively falsified." Of course, I was following some well-established anthropological precedents. Pelto and Pelto (1978: 22), for example, define science as "the structure and the processes of discovery and verification of systematic and reliable knowledge about any relatively enduring aspect of the universe, carried out by means of empirical observations, and the development of concepts and propositions for interrelating and explaining such observations." Harris (1979: 27) maintains that science "seeks to restrict fields of inquiry to events, entities, and relationships that are knowable by means of explicit, logico-empirical, inductive-deductive, quantifiable public procedures or 'operations' subject to replication by independent observers." I now recognize, however, that objectivity is the defining quality of science and that science is empirical as a consequence of objectivity, not as a condition of objectivity (see Lett 1996).

4. The fact that scientific knowledge is not absolutely certain knowledge in no way diminishes the unique value and demonstrable superiority of the scientific approach. As Watson (1991: 276) notes, "[P]ublic, objective knowledge of the world including human beings is not certain, but neither is it merely one interpretation out of many, each of which is no better than any other." When it comes to the acquisition of factual knowledge, the scientific method has a record of success that far outshines any other epistemological approach. The reliability, predictability, generalizability, and usefulness of scientific knowledge are simply unparalleled; the vindication of the scientific method on pragmatic grounds is decisive.

5. The term *paranormal* was first popularized by parapsychologists but is likely to be most familiar to anthropologists through the efforts of the Committee for the Scientific Investigation of Claims of the Paranormal (CSICOP). CSICOP, which was founded in 1976 by philosopher Paul Kurtz, is a national organization of philosophers, natural scientists, social scientists, physicians, engineers, attorneys, journalists, magicians, and other skeptical people committed to the rational analysis of paranormal claims. The organization includes a number of anthropologists among its fellows and contributors to its quarterly journal, *The Skeptical Inquirer*.

6. Joseph K. Long's (1977) edited volume *Extrasensory Ecology: Parapsychology and Anthropology* is perhaps one of the most regrettable examples of the irrational approach to the paranormal within cultural anthropology. Long's gullibility and flagrant disregard for rational principles of evidential reasoning are egregious. He baldly states, for example, that "ghosts, astral projections, and poltergeists are real" (viii), he describes levitation as "probable" (384–385), he claims that at least some so-called psychic surgeons (who are really sleight-of-hand artists) have successfully performed barehanded operations on human patients that involve "deep and random cutting, extraction of parts, and immediate healing of the wound leaving virtually no scar" (375), and he endorses the transparently fraudulent "psychokinetic" stunts of the Israeli showman Uri Geller as genuine (248).

REFERENCES

Alcock, James E. 1990. *Science and Supernature: A Critical Appraisal of Parapsychology*. Buffalo, NY: Prometheus Books.

Bernard, H. Russell. 1988. *Research Methods in Cultural Anthropology*. Newbury Park, CA: Sage Publications.

Cazeau, Charles J., and Stuart D. Scott, Jr. 1979. *Exploring the Unknown: Great Mysteries Reexamined*. New York: Plenum Press.

Cohen, Ronald. 1970. *Generalizations in Ethnology. A Handbook of Method in Cultural Anthropology*. Raoul Naroll and Ronald Cohen, editors. New York: Columbia University Press. 31–50.

Cole, John R. 1978. "Anthropology Beyond the Fringe." *Skeptical Inquirer* 2 (2): 62–71.

Cole, John R., and Laurie Godfrey, editors. 1985. "The Paluxy River Footprint Mystery—Solved." *Creation/Evolution* 5 (1) (special issue).

Cunningham, Frank. 1973. *Objectivity in Social Science*. Toronto: University of Toronto Press.

de Mille, Richard. 1990. *The Don Juan Papers: Further Castaneda Controversies*. Belmont, CA: Wadsworth Publishing Company.

Druckman, D., and J. A. Swets. 1988. *Enhancing Human Performance*. Washington, D.C.: National Academy Press.

Evans-Pritchard, E. E. 1965. *Theories of Primitive Religion*. London: Oxford University Press.

Feder, Kenneth L. 1980. "Psychic Archaeology: The Anatomy of Irrationalist Prehistoric Studies." *Skeptical Inquirer* 4 (4): 32–43.

Feder, Kenneth L. 1984. "Irrationality and Popular Archaeology." *American Antiquity* 49: 525–541.

Feder, Kenneth L. 1990. *Frauds, Myths, and Mysteries: Science and Pseudoscience in Archaeology*. Mountain View, CA: Mayfield.

Fluehr-Lobban, Carolyn, editor. 1991. *Ethics and the Profession of Anthropology: Dialogue for a New Era*. Philadelphia: University of Pennsylvania Press.

Frankel, Barbara, and M. G. Trend. 1991. "Principles, Pressures, and Paychecks: The Anthropologist as Employee." *Ethics and the Profession of Anthropology: Dialogue for a New Era*. Carolyn Fluehr-Lobban, editor. Philadelphia: University of Pennsylvania Press. 177–197.

Frankel, Charles. 1955. *The Case for Modern Man*. New York: HarperCollins.

Frazer, Sir James George. 1890/1963. *The Golden Bough: A Study in Magic and Religion*. New York: Macmillan.

Gans, Eric L. 1990. *Science and Faith: The Anthropology of Revelation*. Savage, MD: Rowman and Littlefield.

Gardner, Martin. 1988. *The New Age: Notes of a Fringe Watcher*. Buffalo, NY: Prometheus Books.

Geertz, Clifford. 1973. *The Interpretation of Cultures*. New York: Basic Books.

Godfrey, Laurie R. 1983. *Scientists Confront Creationism*. New York: W. W. Norton.

Gray, William D. 1991. *Thinking Critically about New Age Ideas*. Belmont, CA: Wadsworth Publishing Company.

Hansel, C.E.M. 1989. *The Search for Psychic Power: ESP and Parapsychology Revisited*. Buffalo, NY: Prometheus Books.

Harris, Marvin. 1964. *The Nature of Cultural Things*. New York: T. Y. Crowell.

Harris, Marvin. 1979. *Cultural Materialism: The Struggle for a Science of Culture*. New York: Random House.

Harris, Marvin. 1989. *Our Kind: Who We Are, Where We Came From, Where We Are Going*. New York: Harper and Row.

Harrold, Francis B., and Raymond A. Eve. 1987. *Cult Archaeology and Creationism: Understanding Pseudoscientific Beliefs about the Past*. Iowa City: University of Iowa Press.

Hempel, Carl. 1965. *Aspects of Scientific Explanation and Other Essays in the Philosophy of Science*. New York: Free Press.

Kurtz, Paul. 1983. *In Defense of Secular Humanism*. Buffalo, NY: Prometheus Books.

Kurtz, Paul, editor. 1985. *A Skeptic's Handbook of Parapsychology*. Buffalo, NY: Prometheus Books.

Lakatos, Imre. 1970. "Falsification and the Methodology of Scientific Research Programmes." *Criticism and the Growth of Knowledge*. Imre Lakatos and Alan Musgrave, editors. Aberdeen: Cambridge University Press. 91–196.

Lastrucci, Carlo L. 1963. *The Scientific Approach: Basic Principles of the Scientific Method*. Cambridge, MA: Schenkman.

Lehmann, Arthur C., and James E. Myers. 1989. "The Anthropological Study of Religion." *Magic, Witchcraft, and Religion: An Anthropological Study of the Supernatural*. 2nd edition. Arthur C. Lehmann and James E. Myers, editors. Mountain View, CA: Mayfield Publishing Company. 1–5.

Lessa, William A., and Evon Z. Vogt. 1972. "General Introduction." *Reader in Comparative Religion: An Anthropological Approach*. 3rd edition. William A. Less and Evon Z. Vogt, editors. New York: Harper and Row. 1–6.

Lett, James. 1987. *The Human Enterprise: A Critical Introduction to Anthropological Theory*. Boulder, CO: Westview Press.

Lett, James. 1990. "Emics and Etics: Notes on the Epistemology of Anthropology." *Emics and Etics: The Insider/Outsider Debate*. Thomas N. Headland, Kenneth L. Pike, and Marvin Harris, editors. Newbury Park, CA: Sage Publications. 127–142.

Lett, James. 1991. "Interpretive Anthropology, Metaphysics, and the Paranormal." *Journal of Anthropological Research* 47 (3): 305–329.

Lett, James. 1996. "Scientific Anthropology." *The Encyclopedia of Cultural Anthropology*. David Levinson and Melvin Ember, editors. New York: Henry Holt. 1141–1148.

Long, Joseph K., editor. 1977. *Extrasensory Ecology: Parapsychology and Anthropology*. Metuchen, NJ: Scarecrow Press.

Malinowski, Bronislaw. 1954. *Magic, Science and Religion and Other Essays*. Garden City, NY: Doubleday Anchor Books.

Mead, Margaret. 1977. "An Anthropological Approach to Different Types of Communication and the Importance of Differences in Human Temperaments." *Extrasensory Ecology: Parapsychology and Anthropology*. Joseph K. Long, editor. Metuchen, NJ: Scarecrow Press. 47–50.

Murdock, George Peter. 1980. *Theories of Illness: A World Survey*. Pittsburgh: University of Pittsburgh Press.

Murray, Stephen O. 1990. "The Invisibility of Scientific Scorn." *The Don Juan Papers: Further Castaneda Controversies*. Richard de Mille, editor. Belmont, CA: Wadsworth Publishing Company. 198–202.

Nagel, Ernest. 1961. *The Structure of Science*. New York: Harcourt, Brace and World.

Norbeck, Edward. 1974. *Religion in Human Life: Anthropological Views*. New York: Holt, Rinehart and Winston.

Pelto, Pertti J., and Gretel H. Pelto. 1978. *Anthropological Research: The Structure of Inquiry.* 2nd edition. New York: Cambridge University Press.

Popper, Karl R. 1959. *The Logic of Scientific Discovery.* London: Hutchinson.

Rathje, William L. 1978. "The Ancient Astronaut Myth." *Archaeology* 31 (1): 4–7.

Schneider, David M. 1965. "Kinship and Biology." *Aspects of the Analysis of Family Structure.* Ansley J. Coale, Marion J. Levy, and S. S. Tomkins, editors. Princeton: Princeton University Press.

Service, Elman R. 1985. *A Century of Controversy: Ethnological Issues from 1860 to 1960.* Orlando, FL: Academic Press.

Siegel, Harvey. 1987. *Relativism Refuted: A Critique of Contemporary Epistemological Relativism.* Dordrecht: D. Reidel Publishing Company.

Spaulding, Albert C. 1988. "Distinguished Lecture: Archeology and Anthropology." *American Anthropologist* 90 (2): 263–271.

Stenger, Victor J. 1990. *Physics and Psychics: The Search for a World beyond the Senses.* Buffalo, NY: Prometheus Books.

Stiebing, William H., Jr. 1984. *Ancient Astronauts, Cosmic Collisions and Other Popular Theories about Man's Past.* Buffalo, NY: Prometheus Books.

Toumey, Christopher P. 1994. *God's Own Scientists: Creationists in a Secular World.* New Brunswick, NJ: Rutgers University Press.

Tylor, Edward Burnett. 1871/1958. *Religion in Primitive Culture.* New York: Harper and Brothers Publishers.

Wallace, Anthony F. C. 1966. *Religion: An Anthropological View.* New York: Random House.

Watson, Richard A. 1991. "What the New Archaeology Has Accomplished." *Current Anthropology* 32 (3): 275–291.

White, Peter J. 1974. *The Past Is Human.* New York: Taplinger.

4

THINKING ABOUT MAGIC

Michael F. Brown

Why do people practice magic? If magic is so self-evidently false from an empirical perspective, why does it maintain such a tenacious hold on the human imagination? Does the persistence of magical thinking imply that there are radically different, even incommensurable, ways of experiencing the world—in other words, autonomous native epistemologies? Finally, is it the job of the anthropologist confronted with magical acts and utterances to explain those practices in terms of local understandings of cause and effect or is it to translate them into categories meaningful to social scientists?

These questions have vexed anthropology since the discipline's earliest days. The Western scientific tradition that spawned anthropology cultivated disdain for all that was "magical," for magic had become a symbol of the irrationality over which science had triumphed. Ironically, the persistence of magic outside the halls of empirical research helped to justify the existence of anthropology as a distinct branch of science devoted to the investigation of human cultural progress. In the late nineteenth century, magic was precisely the sort of outré phenomenon that anthropologists were expected to incorporate into their models of human behavior. On the cusp of the twenty-first century, anthropology has become a more nervous and self-conscious enterprise, but magic still provides grist for diverse analytical mills. Despite more than a century of scrutiny, the forms, aims, and meanings of magic—even its very definition—remain the subjects of vigorous debate.

My goal in this chapter is to review some issues at stake in the interpretation of magical beliefs, acts, and utterances. By reviewing critically the strategies by which anthropologists have tried to make sense of magic, I wish to suggest approaches that build on the insights and avoid the intellectual blind alleys of those who have preceded me. To gain some purchase on an extensive literature, I shall confine my discussion largely to magic in the narrow sense of ritual procedures intended to produce palpable effects in the physical world. Obvious examples include rites associated with fishing, farming, hunting, or canoe making. Although sorcery raises questions similar to those of magic, I have excluded it from the present discussion because its intimate links to social structure and patterns of social control demand a different approach than do rituals ostensibly intended to satisfy immediate practical needs.

One temptation that I have resisted—but only with great difficulty—is to argue that magic doesn't exist. Magic's terminological borders have been patrolled diligently for over a century, but anthropologists have been remarkably complacent about accepting the notion that the label is cross-culturally valid.[1] There are occasional dissident voices—among them J.D.Y. Peel (1969: 73), who contends that magic is merely a label for "those operations which the agents consider efficacious but which the scientific observer thinks deluded"—but they have thus far failed to dislodge magic from its important place in the display case of anthropological theory. The historical circumstances that shaped the concept of magic in the West are by no means universal, suggesting that the term should be applied to practices in other social settings only with the greatest care.[2] Anthropology awaits a bold reformulation that banishes "magic" from analysis altogether. Here I content myself with alerting the reader to the serious questions that have been raised about the term's utility.

MAGIC, MYSTICISM, AND THE ASSOCIATION OF IDEAS

In keeping with magic's obsession with the concrete, I present a brief case study of magical behavior that provides some solid ground from which we can survey the shifting currents of anthropological interpretation. The case is taken from my own fieldwork among a people of the Amazonian rain forest, the Aguaruna Indians of northeastern Peru.

Traditional Aguaruna subsistence is based on slash-and-burn agriculture, hunting, and fishing, but domesticated animals, especially poultry, have come to play an important role in the Aguarunas' twentieth-century household economy. The care of domestic fowl is mainly a responsibility of women. In addition to forms of attention that a Western expert in animal husbandry would recognize as useful and necessary, Aguaruna women tend their chickens by singing to them. More precisely, they perform *anen*, a term that encompasses a wide range of powerful songs said to produce real effects in the world. The words of one *anen* for poultry are as follows:

> A Nunkui woman cannot fail [Nunkui = a feminine earth spirit]
> Sparrow-hawk, sparrow-hawk
> The roosters call the sparrow-hawk

"*Tuntaya*," they say [i.e., they are so numerous and strong that they call the
    hawk in arrogant defiance of its power]
I feed my *puush*-birds [*puush* = a species of quail held to be prolific]
Make them grow rapidly, like the vines of the forest.

Besides strengthening their poultry with *anen*, Aguaruna women report feeding
them an aquatic herb, *Lemna* (specics), "because the fowl will reproduce rapidly
just as this plant does."

The song illustrates in microcosm certain features widely held to be typical
of magical thought and practice. The singer equates herself with Nunkui, a spirit
being who according to myth gave cultivated plants and pottery technology to
the ancestors of the Aguaruna. Nunkui, in other words, stands as an evocative
symbol of powerful femininity. The song marshals images of insolent roosters,
flourishing bird life, and fast-growing rain forest vines. Its language is impera-
tive ("Make them grow rapidly") rather than supplicative. The words of the
song may be complemented by the action of feeding a conspicuously productive
plant to the poultry.

This case epitomizes what E. B. Tylor (1871/1958) called the "association
of ideas" characteristic of magic. The song juxtaposes words and symbolic
objects with the poultry to induce a desired result. The allusion to Nunkui, for
example, implies that naming this powerful being will imbue the singer with
Nunkui's mythic prosperity. Feeding *Lemna* to the chickens is an attempt to
transfer the plant's fruitfulness to the fowl through a form of contact that mimics
empirical behavior.

According to Stanley J. Tambiah (1990), Tylor's insights about the association of ideas that characterizes magic were borrowed and further refined by Sir
James Frazer in his massive comparative work *The Golden Bough* (1890/1958).
Frazer divided the fallacious associations of magic into two general types or
"laws": sympathetic magic, based on similarity, and contagious magic, based
on contiguity. Following Frazer's system, the allusion to the quail called *puush*
in the Aguaruna song illustrates the law of sympathy, whereas the contact between poultry and the aquatic weed *Lemna* illustrates the law of contagion.[3]

The early taxonomic work of Tylor and Frazer laid the foundation for two
monumental studies of magic: Bronislaw Malinowski's *Coral Gardens and
Their Magic* (1935) and E. E. Evans-Pritchard's *Witchcraft, Oracles, and Magic
among the Azande* (1937). Both Malinowski and Evans-Pritchard contended that
practitioners of magic maintain a strict mental separation of the magical from
the practical. Evans-Pritchard (1937: 466) notes that his Azande informants were
never as confident in magic as in what he calls "routine empirical activities."
Malinowski's analysis is arguably more subtle. In Trobriand thought, he says,
magic and practical work are never conflated, yet they are so seamlessly linked
that they can be said to "form one continuous story" (Malinowski 1935: 1: 62).

If Evans-Pritchard were to analyze our case of Aguaruna poultry magic, I
suppose he would see it as an adjunct to the practical business of feeding the

chickens, shielding them from predators, and so forth—but an adjunct that draws on "mystical" concepts. The mystical principles underlying the magic are, to use Evans-Pritchard's language, "vaguely formulated" and therefore unlikely to be refuted by experience.[4] Malinowski, by contrast, would no doubt call attention to the psychological function of the ritual procedures. They reassure a woman that she is in control of the forces that can devastate her flock: epidemics, night raids by possums and vampire bats, the predation of hawks, and so forth. Malinowski would also focus on the figurative language that informs Aguaruna magical songs. Magical utterances differ from ordinary speech because of what Malinowski called their high "coefficient of weirdness." The strangeness of the language supports his view that words are the fundamental building blocks of magic. "From the very use of speech men develop the conviction that knowledge of a name, the correct use of a verb, the right application of a particle, have a mystical power which transcends . . . mere utilitarian convenience" (Malinowski 1935: 2:233). Malinowski's sensitivity to metaphor, rather than his theory of magic's psychological function, has been the most enduring legacy of his analysis of magic and his strongest influence on later work.[5]

MAGIC AS PERFORMATIVE ACT

Despite the insights that Evans-Pritchard and Malinowski brought to their ethnographic portraits, there is still something unsatisfactory about the appeal both make to the notion of "mystical thought," which leaves one with the impression that underneath indigenous canons of common sense there lies a massive substrate of irrationality. Attempts to reframe the argument in more productive ways have drawn largely on a distinction between acts that are "instrumental" in intent and those that are allegedly "expressive." Scholars such as Leach (1968), Beattie (1970), and Tambiah (1968, 1973) argue that not only do magicians distinguish between the *methods* of magic and practical work; they also perceive them as having different *goals*. John Beattie (1970: 245) makes the case in the strongest possible terms when he claims that the magician realizes that he is "performing a rite, not applying laws of nature, however dimly apprehended." Tambiah (1968: 202) argues that magic may "simulate" work but is never confused with it. In short, magic is intended to say something, practical work to do something.[6] This analysis rescues magic from the realm of flawed technology or irrational thought and redefines it as a form of self-expression, more aesthetic than operational in its ambitions.

Central to the analysis of Tambiah and those pursuing related lines of analysis is the concept of *performativity*, taken from the work of the philosopher John Austin (1962). Speech events are said to be performative when words have the power to constitute a new reality. Conventional examples of performative rituals include baptisms ("I baptize thee . . ."), weddings, and investiture ceremonies. If the officiating person is qualified to perform the ritual, participants emerge from the rite as baptized, married, or invested with a new title. In his reanalysis

of Trobriand garden magic, Tambiah (1973: 221) argues that the spells documented by Malinowski are performative because "by virtue of being enacted
. . . [they] achieve a change of state." The nature of this change remains murky
in his analysis, however. It would appear that the transformation is one of understanding, accomplished through a union of the "technical, aesthetic and ev-
aluative properties of [the magician's] activities, in a manner denied to us in
our segmented civilization" (Tambiah 1968: 200).

Although there is little doubt that a Trobriand spell or, for that matter, any
other ritual may change the internal state of its participants, Tambiah's formulation cannot withstand close scrutiny. First, it equates clearly performative rituals with rites whose transformative goal is far less specific.[7] Second, it ignores
the question of magicians' motives and goals as they weave their spells. The
Aguaruna woman who sings to her chickens certainly changes her internal
state—magical songs, I should add, are often performed after the singer has
consumed a small amount of tobacco water, inducing a mild intoxication—but
from the actor's point of view this change serves the practical goal of producing
healthy livestock. As Gilbert Lewis (1986: 415) has pointed out, if magicians
performed spells for explicitly symbolic or metaphorical purposes, then we
wouldn't consider them magic at all but instead a genre of poetry.

In fairness to Tambiah and others who subscribe to what has been called the
"symbolist" position, it should be noted that the Trobriand garden ritual central
to his analysis has a public and social aspect absent from the Aguaruna rite.
Trobriand ritual may thus perform an important social function (for instance,
vividly reminding participants of the moral implications of their horticultural
labors, thus motivating them to work harder) independent of a specific gardener's immediate intentions. One drawback of the concept of performativity is
that it works better when applied to group events than to those conducted pri-
vately in the service of specific practical ends. Since the power of language is
arbitrary and socially determined, performative rituals always partake of a con-
sensual character.[8]

In a later work, Tambiah (1990: 105–110) distances himself from the instru-
mental/expressive distinction in favor of a different set of complementary principles, which he calls "causality" and "participation." Causality is typified by
the "language of distancing and neutrality of action and reaction," whereas
participation denotes a sensibility in which a person is immersed in the natural
and social worlds, experiencing a primordial oneness of subject and object.
Tambiah finds these two principles operative in all societies but in different
proportions. Applying the distinction to our Aguaruna case, he might say that
the woman who sings to her chickens sees herself not as an autonomous person
connected to her flock only by utilitarian links (feeding them, protecting them
from harm) but as someone who literally shapes their world through her
thoughts, gestures, and songs. The Aguaruna magician therefore evinces a
stronger participatory sensibility than would her Anglo-American counterpart.

Although helpful in certain respects, Tambiah's framework still begs the difficult question, To what extent is magic *causal* in its intent?

Symbolist interpretations of magic, such as Tambiah's, typically privilege language over other aspects of ritual—for instance, sounds, smells, bodily movement, and material objects. This is consistent with a pervasive logocentrism in anthropological theory, most clearly manifest in approaches that see social life as text, to the apparent exclusion of such decidedly nontextual realities as physical coercion and the demands of subsistence. Where magic is concerned, language is an especially attractive focus because it is so self-evidently *symbolic*. Yet magic also draws on material objects or medicines for its power, forging undeniable links to practical activity. Consider, for example, the role of the plant *Lemna* in Aguaruna poultry magic. The use of a notably prolific species in magical procedures initially appears to illustrate the strategic use of metaphor by the Aguaruna magician. But the issue is more complex. Besides being one of the smallest species of flowering plants, *Lemna* produces leaves that are among the most nutritious in the plant kingdom. *Lemna*'s vernacular American name is "duckweed" in recognition of its value as a supplement to the diet of poultry. *Lemna*, in other words, is not only good to think; it's good for poultry to eat.[9] This knowledge forces us to move an element of Aguaruna practice from the category "magic" to that of "technology." But has anything changed for the Aguaruna magician? Has duckweed lost any of its power to evoke images of fecundity? One can only conclude that a convincing theory of magic must encompass both the role played by language and magic's strong ties to experimental process. Unfortunately, the cultural anthropologist who studies magic is likely to be more familiar with linguistics than with ethnobotany, ethnozoology, or other subspecialties that could lead ethnographic investigations of magic in new directions.

MAGIC AND CAUSAL MODELS

To move beyond the deficiencies of the instrumental/expressive dichotomy, one strategy is to return to a literalist perspective that takes the casual statements of interlocutors at face value and explores their full implications. If causal ideas are at work, however, they are likely to be more convoluted than the simple mechanical models traditionally thought to be magic's stock-in-trade. In his reinterpretation of the logic underlying headhunting in Southeast Asia, Needham (1983: 90) decries the tendency of ethnographers to propose mechanistic explanations for complex beliefs, a habit that "encourages a rigidity of outlook which is quite inappropriate to the subtle interplay of ideas" common to indigenous thought.

The Aguaruna woman who sings to her poultry operates within a causal framework in which poetics intertwines with pragmatics. Thoughtful Aguarunas assert that the world is a complicated place in which things are never quite as they seem. Ordinary practical knowledge is a necessary but not sufficient condition for success. One must also acquire *yachamu*, wisdom or visionary insight, that permits the manipulation of unseen forces lying beneath the surface of things. The words of magical songs evoke images that alter the world to conform more closely to the singer's desires. The Aguarunas with whom I discussed these matters felt that in theory one could clear fields and grow crops solely through magic, as did the powerful beings whose exploits are detailed in Aguaruna mythology. But people today lack such absolute knowledge. They work by the sweat of their brows and through the strategic use of sounds, images, and medicines. Aguarunas insist that their attitude toward the practices we call magic is skeptical, even experimental.[10] Power objects are put to the test when hunting or gardening; if found wanting, the charms are unceremoniously discarded. People eagerly seek new power objects when they travel to other Indian communities or to Peruvian towns. In sum, the expressive/instrumental fails to illuminate Aguaruna magical practices, which are at once profoundly expressive *and* (from the actor's point of view) decisively instrumental.

Despite the long history of anthropological interest in magic, there exist remarkably few ethnographic studies that explore indigenous ideas of causality in a systematic fashion. A recent exception is Alan Tormaid Campbell's *To Square with Genesis* (1989), an analysis of animism as it is practiced by the Wayãpí of Brazil. Instead of imposing terms such as *magic* or *shamanism* on events recorded in the field, Campbell's analytical strategy is to assess native statements that strike him as strange or inexplicable. Campbell deals with these phenomena in two ways: He tracks the language used to label moments of logical breakdown, and he systematically probes the indigenous thought that makes the statements meaningful.[11]

His conclusion is that for all its exotic elements (for instance, a belief that people's noisy horseplay in a river will cause heavy rains), Wayãpí ontology is not as different from its Western counterpart as is commonly supposed:

Causal reasoning discloses a continuum of intensities that varies through different degrees of vividness, conviction, and consistency of response to the animateness of what surrounds us. Just as it is inappropriate to make a terminal diagnosis of Wayãpí people as living within a carapace of animism, so it is misleading to assume that we live outside that. . . . These intensities [of Wayãpí causal reasoning] do seem extravagant to us, but they are so only in terms of extent and degree. They do not disclose a radically incompatible mode of being in the world. (Campbell 1989: 140–141)

With some justification, Campbell suggests that anthropologists are prone to fix their attention on the differences between an indigenous ontology and their own, while "avoiding the subtleties of more prosaic examples" (93).[12] To return to the Aguaruna example, an anthropologist who discovered that *Lemna* is nutritious poultry feed would typically reclassify its use as "technology," thus removing it from an account of Aguaruna magic. But for Aguarunas, leaves and songs form part of a unitary set of practices (to use Malinowski's language, "one continuous story"), most of which would be comfortably accommodated within a Western ontology. The application of the term *magic* brackets off the exotic and occludes its links to the ordinary.

ARE MAGICIANS RATIONAL?

Campbell's assertions would seem unremarkable if they did not speak so forcefully to anthropological arguments concerning the rationality of those who practice magic. The Rationality Debate, pursued vigorously in three volumes of essays published between 1970 and 1982,[13] is notable both for the high quality of the erudition brought to bear on the problem of magic and the distance between these concerns and those of anthropology only a decade later.

The participants in the Rationality Debate—notably, Robin Horton, Steven Lukes, Peter Winch, Martin Hollis, and Ernest Gellner—explored in detail the possibility that there are qualitative differences between what Gellner (1973) called the "savage and the modern mind." A key question in the assessment of these allegedly different "minds" was whether primitive social systems allowed and encouraged critiques of received knowledge in ways analogous to the experimental process of Western science. It was presumed that fallacious beliefs such as those underlying magic could only persist in the absence of a tradition of systematic skepticism. These reflections led naturally to the broader question of how anthropologists are to arrive at a cross-culturally valid notion of "rationality."

The conspicuous role played by philosophers in the Rationality Debate had the salutary effect of forcing anthropologists to be more precise in their use of key terms—for example, *belief system, rationality*, and *traditional thought*. Unfortunately, some of these same philosophers naively assumed that complex cultural systems should be reducible to an internally consistent set of logical propositions. This assumption was persuasively challenged by Dan Sperber (1982), who argued that people in all societies routinely traffic in abstract utterances that are "semi-propositional" in nature. Rather than providing evidence of our irrationality, semipropositional representations act as "sources of suggestion in creative thinking" (171).

The metaphorical and analogical thinking characteristic of magic has long been regarded as a potent source of creativity in technology, science, and cognition in general. What is surprising is how rarely this insight is applied to the study of innovation in preindustrial societies. A classic example drawn from Western history is the Doctrine of Signatures, the belief (essentially, an ontological assumption) that the healing powers of plants are signaled by their form, color, and smell. This provided a framework for experimentation that, while thoroughly "magical" in its underlying structure, eventually produced empirical advances. In an exploration of analogous symbolic principles in Aztec medical thought, Bernard Ortiz de Montellano (1986) has demonstrated that if we use *Aztec* etiological beliefs and expected outcomes to evaluate efficacy, most of their medicines were effective (124). When Aztec healers used medicines, they were enacting and expressing specific ontological principles, but they expected that enactment to produce practical results—and it did.

My point in exploring this line of analysis is not to rescue the old argument that magic is an embryonic form of science. I wish instead to underscore the problems of seeing magic solely as an inventory of exotic beliefs, to the exclusion of elements of magical practice that promote creative exploration of the natural world. The characteristic integration of magic with other kinds of activity—a feature of interest to Evans-Pritchard and Malinowski—suggests that magic can be separated analytically from those activities only with the greatest care. To do otherwise is to ride roughshod over the understandings of those whom we seek to comprehend (cf. de Sardan 1992).

The Rationality Debate drew attention to one indisputable difference between tribal societies and industrial ones: the means by which knowledge is produced, modified, and consumed, at least within some segments of society. The Enlightenment established the institutional arrangements and habits of mind that support Western science, which Tambiah (1990: 140) describes as a "labelled, self-conscious and reflexive activity of experimentation, measurement and verification." By implication, anthropologists should move beyond an essentialist concern with "modes of thought" to an analysis of how societies create and transmit knowledge—in short, the study of cognitive ecology. Yet there has been remarkably little research of this kind, aside from the studies of native classificatory systems that became popular in the 1970s and 1980s.[14]

The cognitive innovation that has thus far received the greatest attention is literacy. Jack Goody (1977) is prominent among those who have argued that literacy opens the door to qualitatively different understandings.[15] The essence of Goody's argument is that writing is a revolutionary cognitive technology that makes belief in magic impossible to sustain:

The magic of the spell is dependent, at least in part, upon the virtual identity of the speaker and spoken. How can one separate a man from his words? . . . Writing puts a distance between a man and his verbal acts. He can now examine what he says in a more objective manner. He can stand aside, comment upon, even correct his own creation. . . . [Writing] permits a different kind of scrutiny of current knowledge, a more deliberate sorting of *logos* from *doxa*, a more thorough probing into the "truth." (150)

Here Goody echoes the observation of Evans-Pritchard (1937: 475) that the Azande fail to perceive the contradictions in their magic "because the beliefs are not all present at the same time but function in different situations," a reality that would be transformed if Azande magic were codified in portable written documents.

Goody's thesis has received its share of criticism (for instance, Halverson 1992), largely because it exaggerates literacy's social impact and underestimates the degree to which skepticism, self-criticism, and syllogistic reasoning can be found among nonliterate peoples. It also perpetuates a key blunder of the Rationality Debate by assuming that scientific reasoning is the normal mode of thought employed by citizens of the developed world—or to amend a bon mot of Marshall Sahlins, that the science of the West contrasts with the magic of the Rest. But science has always been the methodology of an intellectual elite, not the practice of the masses. Aside from countless studies of "folkloric" forms of magic surviving in pockets of North American and European society, there is a small but growing literature on the persistence among highly educated adults of thinking that is magical in its form if not in its content.[16] Even more challenging to the pieties of scientific ascendancy is the appearance of extravagant forms of magic in such places as middle-class London (Luhrmann 1989) and the plantations and mines of working-class South America (Taussig 1980). The wage laborers studied by Taussig use magic to grapple with the logic of capitalism, which to them seems both irrational and devastatingly inhumane. In contrast, the middle-class witches studied by Luhrmann seek a reenchantment of their lives and are after mystery as much as meaning. (Ironically, Luhrmann's witches use literacy not to liberate themselves from magic but to educate themselves in its subtleties.) In both ethnographic cases, magic offers an implicit critique of the modernity toward which Evans-Pritchard and Malinowski assumed the human race inexorably to be moving.

CONCLUSIONS

By the mid-1980s, the Rationality Debate, which had invigorated the interpretation of magical acts and utterances, was displaced by other concerns considered more urgent within anthropology. The index to the volumes of the *American Ethnologist* published between 1985 and 1989 lists more references under "fisheries" (two) and "tattoos" (one) than under "magic" (none). Such a decline of interest in a classic problem could represent a mere shift in intellectual fashion, but it also reflects irreversible changes that have taken place within anthropology. It is no longer possible, for instance, to think of magic as an atavistic cultural trait doomed to eventual extinction; instead, it may be an enduring quality of the human imagination. Moreover, anthropologists are today less likely to see systems of thought as homogeneous and static than as historically contingent and internally contested, prompting different questions about how knowledge is created, controlled, used, and resisted. Even the doctrine of cultural relativism, which as recently as the 1980s seemed to offer a perspective from which one could undertake an impartial assessment of practices such as magic, is now being held up to critical scrutiny.[17]

It is by now clear that the traditional distinctions between magic, science, and religion have outlived their utility and, in fact, represent an obstacle to deeper understanding. Instead of conceptualizing magic as a discrete set of beliefs or practices, we might think of it as a *sensibility*—an intermediate point on a spectrum ranging from the purely instrumental to the purely expressive, or a state in which cause and effect are mediated by metaphor. Alternatively, we could reserve "magic" as a provisional label for moments of ethnographic breakdown, when our understanding is challenged by that of our interlocutors, a situation demanding deeper exploration of local ideas about how things come to pass in the world.

Another impediment to debate on the meaning of magic is that it has taken place in the long shadows cast by Malinowski and Evans-Pritchard. Few areas of contention in anthropology have been so thoroughly dominated by only two ethnographic accounts—albeit great ones. Surely it is time to declare a moratorium on reanalysis of the Trobriand and Azande material in favor of new case studies that explore the myriad lacunae in our understanding of the significance of magic from the actor's point of view.

If the links between magic and ritual have been investigated in great detail, the connections between magic and technology remain terra incognita. Research by scholars such as Ortiz de Montellano (1986) and Johns (1986) suggests how much we have yet to learn about the application of indigenous symbolic systems to the exigencies of survival—or, to use the formulation of Marcel Mauss (1902/ 1972: 141), the ways in which magic has "dealt with material things, carried out real experiments, and even made its own discoveries."[18]

Magic also merits the attention of scholars interested in the cultural construction and negotiation of gender.[19] Since men tend to find themselves drawn into the orbit of neocolonial economic relations and Western educational systems before women, women may become the principal repositories of all that is "traditional," including knowledge of magic—a development that can produce subtle, and still poorly understood, changes in relations between the sexes. In such cases, is magic a source of power for women, or does it become emblematic of their estrangement from new values and political realities? Are women covert guardians of ways of remembering (Connerton 1989) that play a key role in moments of cultural crisis or redefinition?

Finally, the revival of magic in unlikely places raises a host of questions about nostalgia, the search for authentic experience, and the dynamics of accommodation and resistance in mass society. When middle-class accountants and computer programmers take up magic, they act with a degree of self-consciousness that contrasts sharply with the taken-for-granted quality of magic in tribal societies. Yet the discontinuities between the two cases may be more apparent than real; the magical behavior of modern discontents may prove to be a source of new insights into the understandings of nonliterate peoples. At the very least, the persistence of magical practices in the late twentieth century offers compelling evidence that the anthropological casebook on magic is far from closed.

NOTES

I wish to thank David B. Edwards, Stephen D. Glazier, and Peter Just for their comments on an earlier version of this chapter.

1. I make no attempt to do justice to the vast literature on the proper definition of

magic. Significant contributions of which I am aware include Malinowski (1954), Rosengren (1976), and O'Keefe (1982). More recently, Tambiah (1990) has reviewed the definition question and analyzed the particular historical circumstances that determined the Western concept of magic.

2. Even classic studies of magic are marked by a disturbing vagueness about how the English term *magic* maps on to the beliefs and practices of the society under consideration. Evans-Pritchard (1937: 9), for instance, translates the Azande word *ngua* as "magic," yet he also notes that it is not applied to all the practices that a Western observer would consider magical but *is* applied to others—for example, leechcraft—that Westerners probably wouldn't consider magic at all. Malinowski's analysis of the definition question as it applies in the Trobriand Island case is more convoluted. Trobrianders classify garden ritual as *towosi*. "Magic and practical work are, in native ideas, inseparable from each other," says Malinowski (1935: 1:62), "though they are not confused." Nevertheless, what seems to separate *towosi* from ordinary work is not an intrinsic difference in the two activities or a marked divergence of goals but rather that expertise in *towosi* is invested in a ceremonial specialist rather than in the gardener himself (1: 77). When Malinowski insists that "magic is based on myth [and] practical work on empirical theory," he only displaces ambiguity to another level, as myth seems to be regarded as "really real" among the Trobrianders. When I studied the magical practices of the Aguaruna of Amazonian Peru (Brown 1986), I encountered no word that could be glossed as "magic," though there were broad terms that encompassed categories of magical songs or paraphernalia. Like the Trobrianders, the Aguaruna see magic as a set of procedures that are complementary to, and intertwined with, practices that we would call empirical. The Aguaruna think of magic as a challenging and esoteric form of action but nonetheless "real" for that.

The limitations of magic as a universal classificatory term are discussed with great clarity by John Skorupski, who asserts that "the traditional European conception of magic as a sacrilegious perversion of religious lore is probably responsible for a number of misconceptions in social anthropology" (Skorupski 1976: 159).

3. Although Frazer's work has virtually no place in modern anthropology except as a historical footnote, his system of classification has been resurrected—albeit in more recondite language—in the research of Hallpike (1979). Hallpike identifies forms of magic such as the Aguaruna song analyzed here as instances of "nominal realism" (mistaking words for things) and "hypostatization of process" (mistaking processes or recurrent events for things). The alleged frequency of these and other errors of thought in tribal societies leads Hallpike to conclude that preindustrial peoples are stuck in some "pre-operatory" stage of cognitive evolution analogous to that of Western children.

4. Jahoda (1982) provides an illuminating critique of the notion that there is a discrete form of thought that can be labeled "mystical" or "magical."

5. See, for example, Brown (1984, 1986), Endicott (1981), Rosaldo (1975), Rosaldo and Atkinson (1975), and Tambiah (1968). Malinowski's psychological theory of magic lives on in Gmelch's essay on baseball magic (Gmelch 1987), frequently reprinted in anthropology readers.

6. The definitive analysis of the distinction between what has come to be called the "intellectualist" and "symbolist" positions is Skorupski (1976).

7. More detailed critiques of this use of performativity will be found in Ahern (1979) and Gardner (1983).

8. Roy A. Rappaport, one of the few analysts of religious ritual who has paid atten-

tion to the implications of ritual events conducted in private, notes that "in solitary rituals various parts of the psyche may be brought in touch with each other," which leads him to identify ritual as "auto-communicative as well as allo-communicative" (Rappaport 1979: 178).

9. For details, see Swain (1981: 101–110). The relevance of *Lemna*'s nutritional content would obviously depend on whether Aguaruna poultry were fed the plant in a relatively systematic fashion, and in what quantities.

10. Even analysts who hold that magic has a primarily expressive intent acknowledge that practitioners may be more pragmatic in their attitude toward magical rites than they are toward public rituals of a conventionally liturgical character, which for Rappaport (1979: 196) exact an implicit "act of acceptance." In a recent essay, however, Grimes (1992) makes a persuasive case for the possibility of criticism from within a community of ritual participants.

11. I borrow the term *breakdown* from Michael Agar (1986: 20), who defines these moments as instances when "something does not make sense; one's assumption of perfect coherence is violated."

12. Campbell's assertions echo those of Dan Sperber (1982), who argues that anthropologists play fast and loose with the concept of cultural relativism. On the one hand, Sperber says, anthropologists have a vested interest in portraying other cultures as qualitatively different from our own. (Otherwise, why would anyone need an anthropologist to understand them?) On the other, the very work of anthropologists contradicts the alleged incommensurability of cultures: "[A]nthropologists transform into unfathomable gaps the shallow and irregular cultural boundaries that they have found not so difficult to cross, thereby protecting their own sense of identity, and providing their philosophical and lay audience with just what they want to hear" (Sperber 1982: 180).

13. Hollis and Lukes (1982), Horton and Finnegan (1973), and Wilson (1970).

14. Notable exceptions include Hallpike (1979), Scribner and Cole (1981), and the early groundbreaking studies of Mead (1932), Luria (1976), and Vygotsky (1962). See Harris et al. (1991) for research on "magical" thought among Western children, and Merrill (1988) for a study of the distribution and social negotiation of different concepts of the soul among the Rarámuri of northern Mexico.

15. Halverson (1992) provides a more complete bibliography of Goody's writings on literacy and other key works on this subject.

16. See, for instance, Nemeroff and Rozin (1992), Rozin and Nemeroff (1990), and Shweder (1977).

17. Aside from the works of Sperber (1982) and Campbell (1989) cited earlier, the debate between Geertz (1986) and Rorty (1991) about relativism and ethnocentrism attests to a growing uneasiness about the concept of cultural relativism.

18. Johns (1986) evaluates cultural selection for specific chemicals in two plants domesticated by prehistoric peoples of the Peruvian Highlands. His research suggests that indigenous Andean notions of male-female duality may have structured people's modification of these cultivars.

19. A provocative exception is Kane (1994).

REFERENCES

Agar, Michael H. 1986. *Speaking of Ethnography*. Sage University Paper Series on Qualitative Research Methods. Vol. 2. Beverly Hills, CA: Sage.

Ahern, Emily Martin. 1979. "The Problem of Efficacy: Strong and Weak Illocutionary Acts." *Man*, n.s., 14: 1–17.

Austin, John L. 1962. *How to Do Things with Words*. Oxford: Clarendon Press.

Beattie, J.H.M. 1970. "On Understanding Ritual." *Rationality*. Bryan R. Wilson, editor. New York: Harper & Row/Torchbooks. 240–268.

Brown, Michael F. 1984. "The Role of Words in Aguaruna Hunting Magic." *American Ethnologist* 11: 545–558.

Brown, Michael F. 1986. *Tsewa's Gift: Magic and Meaning in an Amazonian Society*. Smithsonian Series in Ethnographic Inquiry. Washington, D.C.: Smithsonian Institution Press.

Campbell, Alan Tormaid. 1989. *To Square with Genesis: Causal Statements and Shamanic Ideas in Wayãpí*. Iowa City: University of Iowa Press.

Connerton, Paul 1989. *How Societies Remember*. New York: Cambridge University Press.

de Sardan, Jean-Pierre Olivier. 1992. "Occultism and the Ethnographic ''I'': The Exoticizing of Magic from Durkheim to 'Postmodern' Anthropology." *Critique of Anthropology* 12: 5–25.

Endicott, Kirk M. 1981. *An Analysis of Malay Magic*. Oxford: Oxford University Press.

Evans-Pritchard, E. E. 1937. *Witchcraft, Oracles, and Magic among the Azande*. London: Oxford University Press.

Frazer, James G. 1890/1958. *The Golden Bough*. Abridged edition. New York: Macmillan Publishing Co.

Gardner, D. S. 1983. "Performativity in Ritual: The Mianmin Case." *Man*, n.s., 18: 346–360.

Geertz, Clifford. 1986. "The Uses of Diversity." *Michigan Quarterly Review* 25: 105–123.

Gellner, Ernest. 1973. "The Savage and the Modern Mind." *Modes of Thought: Essays on Thinking in Western and Non-Western Societies*. Robin Horton and Ruth Finnegan, editors. London: Faber & Faber. 162–181.

Gmelch, George. 1987. "Baseball Magic." *Conformity and Conflict*. 6th edition. James P. Spradley and David W. McCurdy, editors. Boston: Little, Brown, 344–354.

Goody, Jack. 1977. *The Domestication of the Savage Mind*. Cambridge: Cambridge University Press.

Grimes, Ronald L. 1992. "Reinventing Ritual." *Soundings* 75: 21–41.

Hallpike, C. R. 1979. *The Foundations of Primitive Thought*. New York: Oxford University Press.

Halverson, John. 1992. "Goody and the Implosion of the Literacy Thesis." *Man*, n.s., 27: 301–317.

Harris, Paul L.; E. Brown; C. Mariott; S. Whittal; and S. Harmer. 1991. "Monsters, Ghosts, and Witches: Testing the Limits of the Fantasy-Reality Distinction in Young Children." *British Journal of Developmental Psychology* 9: 105–123.

Hollis, Martin, and Steven Lukes, editors. 1982. *Rationality and Relativism*. Cambridge, MA: MIT Press.

Horton, Robin, and Ruth Finnegan, editors. 1973. *Modes of Thought*. London: Faber and Faber.

Jahoda, Gustav. 1982. *Psychology and Anthropology: A Psychological Perspective*. New York: Academic Press.

Johns, Timothy A. 1986. "Chemical Selection in Andean Domesticated Tubers as a

Model for the Acquisition of Empirical Plant Knowledge." *Plants in Indigenous Medicine and Diet.* Nina L. Etkin, editor. Bedford Hills, NY: Redgrave Publishing Co. 266–288.

Kane, Stephanie. 1994. *The Phantom Gringo Boat.* Smithsonian Series in Ethnographic Inquiry. Washington, D.C.: Smithsonian Institution Press.

Leach, Edmund, R., editor. 1968. *Dialectic in Practical Religion.* London: Cambridge University Press.

Lewis, Gilbert. 1986. "The Look of Magic." *Man*, n.s., 21: 414–437.

Luhrmann, T. M. 1989. *Persuasions of the Witch's Craft: Ritual Magic in Contemporary England.* Cambridge, MA: Harvard University Press.

Luria, A. R. 1976. *Cognitive Development.* Translated by M. Lopez-Morillas and L. Solotaroff. Cambridge, MA: Harvard University Press.

Malinowski, Bronislaw. 1935. *Coral Gardens and Their Magic.* 2 vols. New York: American Book Co.

Malinowski, Bronislaw. 1954. *Magic, Science, and Religion and Other Essays.* New York: Doubleday Anchor Books.

Mauss, Marcel. 1902/1972. *A General Theory of Magic.* New York: W. W. Norton.

Mead, Margaret. 1932. "An Investigation of the Thought of Primitive Children, with Special Reference to Animism." *Journal of the Royal Anthropological Institute* 62: 173–190.

Merrill, William L. 1988. *Rarámuri Souls: Knowledge and Social Process in Northern Mexico.* Smithsonian Series in Ethnographic Inquiry. Washington, D.C.: Smithsonian Institution Press.

Needham, Rodney. 1983. "Skulls and Causality." *Against the Tranquility of Axioms.* Berkeley: University of California Press. 66–92.

Nemeroff, Carol, and Paul Rozin. 1992. "Sympathetic Magical Beliefs and Kosher Dietary Practices: The Interaction of Rules and Feelings." *Ethos* 20: 96–115.

O'Keefe, Daniel L. 1982. *Stolen Lightning: The Social Theory of Magic.* New York: Random House/Vintage.

Ortiz de Montellano, Bernard R. 1986. "Aztec Medicinal Herbs: Evaluation of Therapeutic Effectiveness." *Plants in Indigenous Medicine and Diet.* Nina L. Etkin, editor. Bedford Hills, NY: Redgrave Publishing Co. 113–127.

Peel, J. D. Y. 1969. "Understanding Alien Belief Systems." *British Journal of Sociology* 20: 69–84.

Rappaport, Roy. 1979. "The Obvious Aspects of Ritual." *Ecology, Meaning, and Religion.* Richmond, CA: North Atlantic Books. 173–221.

Rorty, Richard. 1991. "On Ethnocentrism: A Reply to Geertz." *Objectivity, Relativism, and Truth: Philosophical Papers.* Cambridge: Cambridge University Press. 1: 203–210.

Rosaldo, Michelle Z. 1975. "It's All Uphill: The Creative Metaphors of Ilongot Magical Spells." *Sociocultural Dimensions of Language Use.* Mary Sanches and Ben Blount, editors. New York: Academic Press. 177–203.

Rosaldo, Michelle Z., and J. M. Atkinson. 1975. "Man the Hunter and Woman: Metaphors for the Sexes in Ilongot Magical Spells." *The Interpretation of Symbolism.* Roy Willis, editor. New York: John Wiley and Sons. 43–75.

Rosengren, Karl E. 1976. "Malinowski's Magic: The Riddle of the Empty Cell." *Current Anthropology* 17: 667–685.

Rozin, Paul, and Carol Nemeroff. 1990. "The Laws of Sympathetic Magic: A Psychological Analysis of Similarity and Contagion." *Cultural Psychology: Essays on Comparative Human Development.* J. Stigler, G. Herdt, and R. Shweder, editors. New York: Cambridge University Press. 205–232.

Scribner, Sylvia, and Michael Cole. 1981. *The Psychology of Literacy.* Cambridge, MA: Harvard University Press.

Shweder, Richard. 1977. "Likeness and Likelihood in Everyday Thought: Magical Thinking in Judgements about Personality." *Current Anthropology* 18: 637–658.

Skorupski, John. 1976. *Symbol and Theory.* Cambridge, MA: Cambridge University Press.

Sperber, Dan. 1982. "Apparently Irrational Beliefs." *Rationality and Relativism.* Martin Hollis and Steven Lukes, editors. Cambridge, MA: MIT Press. 149–180.

Swain, Roger B. 1981. *Earthly Pleasures: Tales from a Biologist's Garden.* New York: Charles Scribner's Sons.

Tambiah, Stanley J. 1968. "The Magical Power of Words." *Man,* n.s., 3: 175–208.

Tambiah, Stanley J. 1973. "Form and Meaning of Magical Acts: A Point of View." *Modes of Thought.* Robin Horton and Ruth Finnegan, editors. London: Faber and Faber. 199–229.

Tambiah, Stanley J. 1990. *Magic, Science, Religion, and the Scope of Rationality.* Cambridge: Cambridge University Press.

Taussig, Michael T. 1980. *The Devil and Commodity Fetishism in South America.* Chapel Hill: University of North Carolina Press.

Tylor, Edward B. 1871/1958. *Primitive Culture.* 2 vols. New York: Harper.

Vygotsky, L. S. 1962. *Thought and Language.* Translated by E. Hanfmann and G. Vakar. Cambridge, MA: MIT Press.

Weiner, Annette B. 1983. "From Words to Objects to Magic: Hard Words and the Boundaries of Social Interaction." *Man,* n.s., 18: 690–709.

Wilson, Bryan, editor. 1970. *Rationality.* New York: Harper and Row Publishers/Torchbooks.

Part II

THE STUDY OF RITUAL

5

Ritual and Current Studies of Ritual: Overview

Bobby C. Alexander

This chapter surveys some of the major developments that have taken place in the study of ritual over the past twenty-five or thirty years, highlighting their significance for the anthropology of religion. Major bibliographic sources on ritual and the study of ritual are identified along the way. These developments are offered as an overview of ritual's major features and roles. *Ritual* defined in the most general and basic terms is a performance, planned or improvised, that effects a transition from everyday life to an alternative context within which the everyday is transformed. Traditional religious rituals open up ordinary life to ultimate reality or some transcendent being or force in order to tap its transformative power. As we will come to see, ritual, including religious ritual, is grounded in the everyday, human world.

For a detailed discussion of shifts in interests, methods, and insights in the study of ritual, along with discussion of the contributions as well as the inadequacies of earlier, classical studies, and the strengths and weaknesses of newer studies that have built upon earlier studies and have attempted to correct them, see Bell's *Ritual Theory, Ritual Practice* (1992). While her book is given to theoretical discussion of ritual and to revision of classical theories, new and old (principally those of van Gennep, Durkheim, Geertz, and Turner), her study also offers a history of the study of ritual. Bell brings the reader up to date on current studies of ritual. She also offers an assessment of the status of the study of ritual and suggestions for further inquiry. For a succinct overview of newer studies of ritual as well as an extensive bibliography, over 1,600 entries, see Grimes's *Research in Ritual Studies: A Programmatic Essay and Bibliography* (1985).

For general overviews of ritual, see Zuesse (1987), Leach (1968), and Doty (1986).

The developments surveyed here have made the study of ritual more central to studies of the various religious traditions, societies, and cultures in which they are found. And they have made ritual more central to general studies of human society and culture, as well as general studies of human behavior and human experience. The developments have strengthened the assertion of earlier studies that ritual is fundamental to social and cultural life and to human experience itself. The variety of scholarly disciplines making the study of ritual more central has grown. Joining anthropology, sociology, the comparative study of religion, and religious studies—all of them engaged in the study of ritual earlier on—are historical studies, social psychology, theater studies and "performance theory," semiotics, and other disciplines. And as developments have increasingly cut across various aspects of society, culture, and human experience, the study of ritual has become more interdisciplinary. For general studies of ritual within these and other fields of study, see the bibliography found in Part 4 of Grimes (1985).

One of the most significant differences between earlier and newer studies is that the latter have called attention to the fact that ritual does not simply mirror society and culture. Following Clifford Geertz (1973), newer studies have shown that ritual helps shape the defining features of society and culture. And some of the newer studies, following Victor Turner, have shown that ritual gives birth to new views and social relations that redefine society and culture. Ritual is not a mere "epiphenomenon"; it has "ontological status" (Turner 1974). Ritual is generative of society and culture.

Durkheim had noted earlier on that ritual gives rise to new ideas. However, he treated these as compatible with existing views as well as the present social order, emphasizing ritual's role in maintaining the established order. Turner and others have shown that, given its capacity to generate ideas and social arrangements that challenge the existing order, ritual is also an agent of social change, even revolutionary political change (Turner 1974). We will return to ritual's role as social change.

Whether reinforcing the status quo or instigating social change, ritual is essentially a "showing *of a doing*" (Schechner 1977). Rituals are "performative acts." They do not simply dramatize society and culture; "they do something," enacting what they dramatize (Moore 1977). "In [ritual] performance we come upon something quite basic about human beings—that we constitute ourselves through our actions." "When we perform ourselves, we do not simply express what we already are. We perform our becoming, and become our performing" (Driver 1991).

Ritual's capacity to shape and shape anew is rooted in its capacity to create experiences of self, society, the world, and cosmos that reinforce tradition or generate new views and ways of living. Ritual is constitutive of human experience (see Geertz 1986), since it transforms the experiential base out of which people live their everyday lives. Ritual is part of "lived experience," and not merely symbolic (Turner 1986a), a mere replication of everyday experience (see Turner 1986b; see also chapters 8 and 9 in Turner 1985). Newer studies have overcome the tendency of earlier studies of ritual to oppose the symbolic and the real (Bell 1992).

RITUAL RECONCEPTUALIZED AS A HUMAN FUNDAMENTAL

Earlier definitions of ritual emphasized routine as the hallmark of ritual. The emphasis went hand in hand with an accent on keeping things in place or restoring things to their places as the goal of ritual. Routine was shown to serve the maintenance or reestablishment of the status quo. "This is the way it is done in ritual" set up the claim made in ritual that "this is the way things are done in life." Ritual was shown to bring daily life, interrupted or threatened by crises, conflicts, and other disruptions, in line with authoritative beliefs, values, courses of action, especially those provided by religion, which presented these as harmonious or convergent with the cosmic order.

More recent studies have called attention to less formalized forms of ritual, to ritual experimentation and newly emerging forms of ritual. They have also given attention to rituals that challenge the established order. And newer studies have extended the study of ritual beyond religion proper. Gluckman (1962) introduced the term "ritualization" in order to broaden the concept of ritual to include patterns of social interaction. Goody (1977) has argued that ritual is basic to all public activity. And Goffman has called attention to ritual as basic to human communication and interaction (see Goffman 1967, 1974). Ritual has also been said to be basic to all human behavior (see Rappaport 1979), both human interaction and negotiation with the larger ecosystem (see Rappaport 1979; for case studies, see Rappaport 1968/1984).

The interest in ritual's central role in human communication and interaction as well as interaction with the environment coincides with a growing interest in ritual's animal origins. There is a growing interest in ritualizing among animals in meeting basic communication, adaptation, and survival needs. Newer studies have drawn from studies of animal behavior (ethology) made by Huxley and others (see Huxley 1966; d'Aquili et al. 1979; see also Grimes 1982; Schechner 1977). There is also a growing interest in the biological and neurological bases of ritual. Newer studies have drawn linkages among the animal, the physiological and neurological—including operations of the human brain—the ecological, and the social dimensions and roles of ritual (see, for example, Turner 1983; and the essays in von Cranach 1979). These interests further distinguish newer studies from earlier ones.

The primacy given by early studies of ritual to the spoken word in the study of ritual's expressiveness, communicativeness, and mediating role in the world has been sharply rejected by the relatively new "ritual studies" approach. It focuses, among other interests, on the experiential and performative dimensions of ritual, on the physical, bodily, and gestural features of ritual. This approach no longer sees ritual as merely an enactment of myth or as pretext for myth, as the "myth and ritual" school had argued earlier in the century. 'Ritual studies" argues that the body and bodily experience help shape myth or worldviews of self, the world, and the cosmos (see Grimes 1982; see also Driver 1991; on the interplay of ritual and myth, see Doty 1986). These interests have led some to refer to ritual as "bodily knowing" (see Jennings 1982; see also Zuesse 1975).

"Ritual studies" began to emerge over fifteen years ago as a subfield of religious studies. For an overview of the ritual studies approach, see Grimes 1987. For a more developed discussion, see Grimes 1982 and Grimes 1990. For an assessment of the study of ritual, discussion of the contributions and weaknesses of classical and newer approaches, and suggested directions for future study as seen from the ritual studies perspective, see Grimes 1990. Grimes has been the principal shaper of the relatively new field.

For a contrasting view of the primacy of ritual, see Jonathan Z. Smith (J. Z. Smith 1987). He argues for the historical precedent of myth over ritual and for the importance of mythological precedent in the ritual sacralizing of time and space. But for Smith, of mythological significance in establishing time and space as sacred is not hierophany, the appearance of the gods or the sacred. This point was made earlier on by Eliade, whose theory Smith criticizes and revises, following Lévi-Strauss. The latter theorist had argued that space is made sacred by the semantics of ritual, assigning the various elements of the natural world a place, which is basically a social task. For Smith, space is made sacred by establishing its significance for a particular social system through myth. Critical to distinguishing the sacred is setting limits, putting everyone in her or his place, which a social hierarchy and hierarchically based relations of power accomplish. Space is made humanly meaningful through "emplacement." Smith argues that the success and attraction of ritual is that it simultaneously presents the possibility of establishing significance through the ordinary actions of everyday life while creating the perception that in reality this is not possible, thus setting off ritual from ordinary action, time, and space, and the ideal from the everyday. Ritual, for Smith, is "a means of performing the way things ought to be in conscious tension to the way things are." Smith emphasizes the conscious and cognitive dimension of ritual.

For other recent discussions of the ritual construction of the environment, see Goodman (1988), Paden (1988), and Sangren (1987). Sangren is interested in the organization of territory in China through religious ritual as a means of arranging and regulating village society. Like Smith, Goodman and Paden show the importance of ritually mediating the environment in the construction and integration of self, society, world, and cosmos.

Other recent schemes of the ritual construction of self, society, world, and cosmos have emphasized the role of the human body in ritually constructing and mediating all of these. The body, for example, plays a role in the formation of the social self as it is enscribed by the social body gathered together in ritual (see Douglas 1970/1973). For a recent case study of enscription of the body in ritual as formative of experiences of personhood distinctive to a particular culture, see Crapanzano's study of circumcision in Morocco (Crapanzano 1980). See also Kapferer's study of demonic ritual possession among Buddhists in Sri Lanka in the "construction, negation, and reconstruction of the Self" in relation to the "Other," or members of society represented by onlookers (Kapferer 1979; see also Kapferer's extended study: Kapferer 1983). For other recent studies of the mediation of self, society, and cosmos by the ritual use of the body, see B. Smith's study of Vedic Hindu ritual in India (B. Smith 1989) and Ortner's study of popular Buddhist ritual among the Sherpas of Nepal (Ortner 1978). Turner (1967) provides a classic study of the phenomenon by way of African ritual.

RITUAL AS ALL-ENCOMPASSING: THE CONVERGENCE OF THE SACRED AND SECULAR IN RITUAL

There is a growing interest among newer studies in the convergence of religious and secular interests in ritual, as ritual, including traditional religious ritual, society, and culture have increasingly come to be seen as intermeshed. And there is a growing interest in the overlap and even convergence between religious and secular ritual. These interests build upon and refine the observations made earlier on by Durkheim, Weber, and others that religion, society, and culture are mutually influential. Political ritual and public ritual, generally referred to as "civic ritual" or "ceremony," following Bellah (see Bellah 1974), have received special attention as instances of overlap and convergence (see Lukes 1975; and the essays in Moore and Myerhoff, editors, 1977). Civic rituals routinely make the case that existing social values and institutions, indeed the present political order, are authoritative by showing that they are given by the cosmic order or are in harmony with it. Ceremony is thus confirmatory; it is not transformative; this is the role of ritual, at least its fundamental role (see Turner 1982a). The ritual inauguration of the American president, for example, invokes the divine to give divine sanction to the new administration and to the American form of government (see Bellah 1974; Cherry 1970). By contrast, the Balinese court and state are made congruent with the cosmic order by presenting the king as divine (see Geertz 1980).

Or ritual is used by one faction to promote its ideology and rule as divinely sanctioned. For example, Ashura, the ritual dramatization of the martyrdom of Muhammad's grandson, helped to secure the power of the Shiite Muslim faction and to bring down the government of Shah Pahlavi and the Pahlavi dynasty during the revolution of 1979 in Iran. The ritual equates the Shiah party and those ruling in the name of Muhammad (see Hegland 1983). Establishing a political party or government as congruent with the divine or cosmic order can also be used to supplant the authority of a rival power.

Moore and Myerhoff show that religious and secular interests converge when secular ceremonies promote certain ideologies, values, and institutions as sacred. Political rituals, for example, often treat certain political ideas and ideals or social arrangements and forms of power as sacred when these are regarded and presented as absolutely unquestionable or sacrosanct. Paradoxically, they point out, asserting the fixedness and legitimacy of an existing political order calls attention to the alterability and arbitrariness of political power as well as the general disorder, indeterminacy, and "made-upness" of society, which this assertion is designed to mask (Moore and Myerhoff 1977).

See Alexander (1987) for an overview of treatments of the convergence of the religious and secular in ritual and of alternative expressions of the religious interest as it relates to political ceremony. See Moore and Meyerhoff (1977) for an in-depth discussion. For case studies of the convergence of religious and political interests in ritual, see the cross-cultural essays in Moore and Myerhoff (editors, 1977) and McMullen (1987) (on Confucian tradition in China); for extended case studies, see Lane (1981) (on secular rituals of state in the former Soviet Union), Bocock (1974) (on secular rituals of modern England), and Peacock (1968) (political performances in urban Indonesia). For more general discussion of the role of ritual in the establishment, display, and subversion of political power, see Kertzer (1988) and Lukes (1975). For case studies of ritual in the subversion of political authority, see Shaw (1981) (on the rituals of the American revolution), Davis (1975) (on rituals of sex-role reversal as social and political rebellion by women in early modern France), Babcock (1978) (on general forms of "ritual inversion" as protest), and Nash (1979). (Nash takes a Marxist-informed political economy view of a generalized ritual system of social solidarity among miners in the class politics of Bolivia.) For further discussion of ritual and power, see the issue on "Ritual and Power" of the *Journal of Ritual Studies* (1990) and Driver (1991).

Not all students of ritual accept that the boundaries between religious and secular ritual are distinct. Some distinguish purely secular ritual from religious ritual, or ritual focused on the sacred (see Goody 1961; Gluckman 1962).

The interest in the coming together of the sacred and secular in ritual takes a different form in the study of secular experimental theater and performance by some contemporary students of ritual. The ritualizing of experimental theater is interpreted as an interest in reintroducing a sense of the sacred in the modern, secular world. Actors use ritual preparation to strip off the roles and identities they play within the everyday world, which are more and more defined by narrow, technological interests and demands on human identity, in order to reveal to themselves, and then to the audience, their inner and more "authentic" selves, which are held as sacred. The audience undergoes this ritual transformation by participating along with the actors in the ritual activities undertaken during the course of the performance. To aid in this process, various forms of experimental theater have incorporated into actor training some of the techniques of yoga and other forms of meditation from Eastern religious traditions. Some have incorporated into the performance elements of religious ritual from non-Western cultures, for example, Haiti and Mexico (see Schechner 1987; Grimes 1982; Turner 1982a).

Standard religious drama is of interest to other scholars of ritual performance examining the convergence of more conventional religious concerns and secular, or social, and political interests. For an overview of religious drama as ritual, see Schechner's essay "Drama: Performance and Ritual" (1987). For discussion of the social and political roles of religious drama as ritual, see the essays on Indian Sanskrit theater, Indian Kathakali dance drama, Japanese Noh theater, Indonesian urban folk theater, and Purim performance among Orthodox Jews in Williamsburg and Boro Park, Brooklyn, in Schechner and Appel (1990). There is also a new interest in hybrid forms of ritual performance in popular culture (see the essays in Schechner and Appel 1990).

And there is a growing interest in the religious dimensions of rituals of leisure and entertainment that are predominant within secular society: play, sports, games, pastimes, television, theater, and the like (see Turner 1982a; Grimes 1982; for other sources, see the bibliography in Grimes 1985).

RITUAL AS DYNAMIC, FLUID ACTIVITY

Newer studies have increasingly shown the dynamic nature of ritual. They have placed the terms *ritualizing* and *ritualization* alongside *ritual* in order to call attention to ritual's responsiveness to the changing dynamics that make up actual life (see Bell 1992). There is a new emphasis on ritual as flowing and changing activity and greater attention to ritual's improvisatory and indeterminate or open-ended dimensions. Increasingly, these are understood to give ritual its exploratory capacity and its capacity to promote change (see Turner 1974) or to surprise and lead to the unforeseen (see Grimes 1982). There is a new interest in the reformulation of ritual (see Turner 1974, 1982a), as well as the reinterpretation and even uprooting of precedent and tradition in ritual (see J. Z. Smith 1982, 1987). And there is a new interest in newly emerging forms of ritual, especially within modern, secular society (see Grimes 1982). Earlier studies had tended to treat ritual as static routine.

In calling attention to the dynamic character of ritual, ritual studies rejects the rigid categorization of earlier studies (rites of passage, etc.) in favor of identifying various ritual "modes": ritualization, decorum, ceremony, liturgy, magic, and celebration. Grimes sees all of these modes as present in ritual, noting that one or another mode becomes dominant, depending upon the circumstances and the changing circumstances to which ritual responds. Ritual can be less and more formalized, less and more goal directed, and less and more creative and open. The ceremonious mode is more formalized and goal directed, and more directed to control, or power interests, for example (see "Modes of Ritual" in Grimes 1982). Nor does ritual studies treat the various "types" of ritual—for example, sacrifice, purification, healing, initiation, funerals, pilgrimage, and festival—as rigid classifications or compartmentalizations of ritual. For a discussion of types of ritual, see the introductory essay in Grimes 1985. For sources on types of ritual—sacrifice, initiation, pilgrimage, and so on—see the bibliography in Part 2 of Grimes 1985.

RITUAL AS CULTURAL PERFORMANCE AND SOCIAL DRAMA

Early sociologists engaged in the study of religion and ritual and those taking a sociological approach—W. Robertson Smith, Émile Durkheim, Marcel Mauss, and later, Marxist scholars—called attention to social interests and dynamics of society that underlie religion and ritual, principally social cohesion and social control. Anthropologists, Malinowski and Radcliffe-Brown chief among them, did the same. Durkheim's insights have been extended by Douglas (see Douglas 1970/1973). Early phenomenologists and historians of religion—including Max Muller, Edward Tylor, Herbert Spencer, James Frazer, E. O. James, and Rudolf Otto—focused on ritual as expressive of religious ideas about sacred beings and powers and on the influence of religious ideas on cohesion and control. Mircea Eliade is a more recent representative of this position (see, for example, Eliade 1958/1965). These studies tended to approach ritual as merely expressive of previously articulated religious, social, and cultural ideas, interests, and needs (principally those of cohesion and control) and as such as an instrument of regulating social life.

Newer studies of ritual as a "cultural system," Geertz's phrase, or as part of the "social drama," the phrase introduced by Turner, have emphasized the point that ritual is more than a symbolic expression of the outbreak of tension or conflict, and more than a mechanism for regulating a social and cultural system that exists independently of it. Turner has shown that the dramatizing of the breach of values and social arrangements along with the crisis that follows during a ritual performance serves to redress actual social conflict. Ritually recreating the breach and crisis extends the actual crisis into the ritual event. Ritual resolves the crisis as it dramatizes the advantages of the values and social arrangements under challenge, convincing those who have breached them of their advantages to them. Or ritual creates more communitarian, inclusive, and egalitarian values and social arrangements, the lack of which led to conflict in the first place (see Turner 1974).

Ritual is thus the social and cultural system regulating itself, the social drama bodied forth. It is in this basic sense that ritual is spoken of as a "cultural performance." For general discussions of ritual as cultural performance, see

Geertz (1973), Marcus and Fischer (1986), MacAloon (1984), Tambiah (1979), and Schechner (1977). For an extended case study of ritual as cultural performance, see Geertz (1980).

Newer studies also challenge the tendency of earlier theories to give ritual the exclusive role of restoring social cohesion and the established social order. Ritual does not always create agreement among rival social groups about which set of social values they wish to commit to or what social arrangements they want to live by (see Turner 1974). Or lack of correspondence between cultural values and ideas and a society's social arrangements and institutions will be so great, as in the case of social change, that ritual cannot bridge them (see "Ritual and Social Change: A Javanese Example" in Geertz 1973).

Bell has recently argued that ritual never resolves social tension and conflict; instead it presents schemes that imply and thereby defer resolution, allowing a temporary solution (Bell 1992). She further criticizes the cultural performance thesis as inadequate to uncovering the religious meaning of ritual for participants—ritual as intercession with deities, for example—even as it discloses the social interests and the ideas and ideals communicated and addressed in ritual (Bell 1992).

The nature of ritual as cultural performance or social drama has been established by two students of ritual, both cultural anthropologists: Clifford Geertz and Victor Turner. Their theories have been extremely influential and are worth elaborating.

GEERTZ

In "Religion as a Cultural System" (Geertz 1973), Geertz observes that ritual offers an intellectual argument in support of the credibility of a worldview and ethos, or style of life. The reasonableness of a certain worldview and lifestyle is important if these are to be accepted confidently as authoritative models for viewing and living in the world. Religious ritual underscores the reasonableness of a worldview and lifestyle by presenting them as congruent with the cosmic order. But, Geertz notes, intellectual argument alone does not have the power to create confidence in a view of the world or lifestyle or motivate people to live by them.

Conviction of the authority of a certain view of the world and lifestyle depends upon experiential evidence of their reasonableness and authority. Ritual convinces because it grounds a worldview and lifestyle in experiences that confirm both. The experiences created reinforce the view that the world is in accord with the way it is said to exist by a certain worldview. Ritual creates confirmatory experiences by making use of symbols and images in its dramatization of a worldview that is designed to elicit particular emotions, for example, anxiety and calm. Ritual thus makes a certain view of the world "actual," "make[s] it happen" (Geertz 1980).

Confirmation of a worldview in turn confirms a disposition to live in a certain way, when an ethos or style of living is shown to be in accord with the way the world is said to be put together and is therefore shown to be a reasonable strategy for negotiating the world as it is described by the religious view of things. The worldview is in turn reinforced, when the world is shown to be arranged in such a way as to accommodate a particular way of living in it. Worldview and ethos are made to go hand in hand, and even fused.

Once authenticated, worldview and lifestyle are presented as "models of" the world. And as authentic or ideal models, they then become "models for" thinking about and living in the world. The ritual modes thus "shape" the everyday world, bringing it in line with worldview and lifestyle. By highlighting the mutual reinforcement of worldview and ethos and the reinforcement of their authority, Geertz discloses the meaningfulness of ritual and its power to move.

Accepting the dynamic quality of social life, Geertz rejects the argument of earlier "functionalists" that society exists in a steady state. But he ends up assigning ritual the role assigned it by functionalists: keeping the present order in place. Geertz is concerned to show how ritual's "paradigmatic" or modeling feature reinforces the existing order. Ritual reasserts the authority of prior views, values, and actions (see "Religion as a Cultural System" in Geertz 1973). While ritual is part of a dynamic social life, it does not produce social change. Change, Geertz argues, results from discontinuity between cultural ideas and values and patterns of social interaction (see "Ritual and Social Change: A Javanese Example" in Geertz 1973). He does not specify how change comes about. Geertz shows how ritual occasionally instances incongruous cultural and social systems. When ritual cannot integrate culture and society, it breaks down. Any change that results only emerges out of the incongruity ritual occasions.

A radical objection to approaching ritual as a meaningful or symbolic social and cultural system has been raised by Fritz Staal. He argues that ritual is not composed of symbols that refer to meanings outside itself. For him, ritual is only meaningful as a system of actions and sounds governed by rules of action. This becomes apparent, he argues, when ritual is freed from a wider symbolic burden (see Staal 1989). The focus of Staal's "science" of ritual action and sound is Vedic and Indian ritual (see Staal 1983). Dan Sperber offers a different critique of the symbolic anthropology approach, objecting to the linguistic model it follows, which insists that ritual symbols refer to specific meanings (see Sperber 1975). Tambiah objects to the assumption of the symbolic approach that ritual symbols express intentional meanings (see Tambiah 1979). James Fernandez has proposed that the confusion surrounding ritual as meaningful can be cleared up by approaching it as metaphor rather than symbol. Metaphor allows for ambiguity and more accurately conveys diversity in the interpretations of ritual symbols for those involved in it. This approach also allows for the promotion of social solidarity by symbols that hold diverse cultural interpretations. Fernandez's approach distinguishes ritual belief and ritual action, showing that common actions create unity rather than agreement on belief or meaning (see Fernandez 1965; see also Fernandez 1977).

TURNER

Turner has gone beyond Geertz in illumining ritual's role in shaping human experience, society, and culture. He has called attention to ritual's capacity to bring into existence radically new, even unforeseen images, ideas, values, ideals, and social arrangements. And he has shown that ritual has the capacity through these innovations to challenge and even subvert existing cultural ideas and social arrangements, moving society and culture in a totally new direction. Turner has shown that ritual is primarily an agent of social change, especially in creating more communitarian social arrangements.

Turner rejects the argument of classical "functionalist" theorists (Malinowski and Radcliffe-Brown and others writing earlier in the century) that ritual is strictly an instrument of social cohesion and social continuity, or stasis. And he rejects the functionalist argument that ritual maintains cohesion by reaffirming the social-structural differentiation on which the existing social order is based.

Turner observes that ritual is put into play in response to the breakdown in human community during times of social conflict, in response to a threat to community, or is periodically put into play to rejuvenate community. He defines community as characterized by direct, or open, and egalitarian relationships, relationships that recognize common humanity and human equality and promote the common good. Turner views human community and the benefits of community within the everyday world as basic human needs.

Turner also views structured social relations as a basic human need. Women and men rely on structured relationships, social classifications, roles, and duties to organize themselves in order to meet their material needs. But for all of its positive benefits, social structure has its drawbacks. It defines people's identity, value, and worth too narrowly. It requires them to deny their full humanity for the sake of keeping to their places within the social system and fulfilling their social duties, and thus maintaining the existing social order. Social structure deprives them of direct and open human exchanges, which recognize their common humanity and equality and support the freedom to shape or determine their own lives. Social structure distances, alienates, and exploits people.

Given the equal need for human community and social structure, ritual's primary role, Turner argues, is that of creating more communitarian social arrangements within the everyday world, putting everyday social-structural arrangements in the service of community, human equality, and the common good.

Turner shows that ritual's capacity to create community and to promote social change in the direction of greater human community grows out of its "liminal" nature. Ritual puts the established world in limbo as it makes a transition away from the everyday world to an alternative context. Ritual transition relaxes the seemingly fixed assumptions about the way in which the world is put together as well as the rules and duties that regulate everyday routine: "role, status, reputation, class, caste, sex or other structural niche." Ritual is, "quintessentially, a time and place lodged between all times and spaces governed . . . by the rules of law, politics, and religion, and by economic necessity. Here the cognitive schemata that give sense to everyday life no longer apply, but are, as it were, suspended" (Turner 1982a: 84). People are "liberated" from social classification and social duty (Turner 1974).

Transition to an alternative context makes possible more spontaneous and immediate, more direct and open human encounters. Therein, people experience a directness and openness and, along with these, a sense of shared humanity and human equality not possible in encounters guided by obligation to social status or hierarchy, or by social categories or groupings that divide them. In the process, ritual permits and invites participants to experiment with new, more communitarian ways of conceiving society and their relationships to one another, including those that compete with the normative routines in place within the everyday world. Ritual liminality—freedom, spontaneity, and directness—give rise to the experience of human community.

Stepping back from everyday social structure also allows women and men to reflect on everyday social structure and assess the adequacy of the social arrangements in place as instruments of human community. Ritual invites experimentation with alternative social arrangements, ones that better promote community.

The use of ritual to restore the existing social order by reinvigorating or imposing established roles, duties, and social divisions is well known, Turner observes. Ritual is often used to step aside from conflict and to remind people of the advantages of sticking to their places within the social system. It is used to recount the benefits of keeping to one's social role, namely, a sense of stability or order. But these uses keep tight rein on ritual liminality and its radically transformative potential. When ritual is used to reinforce or legitimate an existing social structure, Turner argues, it has been "circumscribed, . . . pressed into the service of maintaining the existing order" as over against communitarian ends (Turner 1982a). Even though ritual may have been co-opted, it has the potential to subvert the existing social order, since ritual stands essentially opposed to social structure. Ritual, Turner argues, is inherently "anti-structure," given its liminal and communitarian features. Ritual's relation to social structure is dialectical. Ritual emerges in response to the limitations social structure places on human community; it then infuses everyday social relations with communitarian purpose.

In his criticism of Turner's presentation of his theory, Driver (1991) calls attention to inconsistencies in Turner's presentation that cloud his insight about ritual's transformative capacity. Driver argues that in earlier discussions of ritual Turner had not clearly established ritual's dialectical relation to social structure, on which depends social transformation and social change. The ritual dialectic was established only later.

These inconsistencies have led some of Turner's interpreters to understand him to say that the experience of ritual community is a form of catharsis. They understand Turner to argue that ritual is only a cathartic release from the burden of social structure. Ritual vents the tension or conflict created by the constraints placed upon community, or the lack of community, within everyday, social-structural life, and thereby keeps the existing social structure in place. For a discussion of these interpretations of Turner's theory, and a classification of his theory, see Alexander (1991) and Morris (1987). Turner's point is that the experience of community infuses or has the potential to infuse everyday social roles and duties with communitarian values and purpose, making everyday social-structural relations more communitarian, at least temporarily, until the demands of social structure erode community.

Late in his career, Turner turned his attention away from the traditional rituals of tribal Africa to the secular rituals of modern, technologically oriented Western society, which has its own burdens of social structure despite greater independence from traditional structures and greater freedoms (see Turner 1982a, 1985). Turner's influence on the study of ritual has extended beyond anthropology, making an impact upon a variety of fields engaged in the study of ritual, including religious studies, historical studies, communication theory, semiotics and hermeneutical studies, performance theory, and postmodern studies.

Turner's identification and treatment of ritual in modern, secular Western societies is also inconsistent, as Driver, Grimes (1982), Alexander (1991), and other observers of Turner have noted. A related problem, as these have observed, is that Turner's definition of ritual—"prescribed formal behavior for occasions not given over to technological routine, having reference to beliefs in invisible beings or powers regarded as the first and final causes of all effects" (Turner 1982a: 79)—conforms to more conventional definitions of ritual and does not suit or serve Turner's insights about ritual transformation and the inventiveness and subversiveness of ritual. For criticism of Turner's theory as ahistorical, and criticism of his portrayals of social structure and community as generalized and inaccurate, see Morris (1987).

OTHER TRENDS IN THE STUDY OF RITUAL

Newer studies of ritual have shied away from the grand theory making that characterized earlier studies. These tended to be ahistorical and highly speculative. They tended to approach ritual as autonomous activity that has universal, timeless, and set features and roles in religion, society, and culture. Case studies tended to support grand views of ritual as a regular, regulated, and regularizing event. Newer studies, which set ritual within the flux of daily social and cultural life and of human experience, emphasize the flexible, fluid, and open-ended qualities of ritual. Newer studies are interested in the immediacy and particulars of ritual. They are interested in the significance of ritual for participants, in the "native point of view" (Geertz 1973, 1983). Ritual studies especially has urged giving greater attention to the subjective side of ritual (see Grimes 1990), which was overlooked in earlier, grand views of ritual. Drewal (1992) has shown the critical importance of the subjective dimension for African ritual, which is minimized by the participant-observer methods favored by Western research. The problem has led to new methods of research and observation within ritual studies and other disciplines. These are identified below.

The new methods of study coincide with the recent emphasis within anthropological studies on the problems of observation and interpretation, problems also recently revisited by philosophical and hermeneutical studies (see Geertz's "Thick Description: Toward an Interpretive Theory of Culture" in 1973; Geertz 1983; Marcus and Fischer 1986; Marcus and Clifford 1986). Theory making is at once more qualified, resting upon careful ethnographic work, and, as a result, more potentially illumining. The methods of more recent studies of ritual reflect the interest within more general anthropological studies in more self-conscious reflection on ethnographic fieldwork. This includes more reflectiveness about the observer's own culture and about how cultural assumptions and biases come to bear on the interpretation of fieldwork. The new reflectiveness also encourages cross-cultural or comparative study in illumining fieldwork. These efforts are intended to allow greater participation in and understanding of the culture observed (see Geertz's "Thick Description" in 1973; Wagner 1981; Marcus and Fischer 1986; Marcus and Clifford 1986).

Students of ritual have become increasingly involved as participants in ritual, moving well beyond the limitations placed upon the observer by the old participant-observer model (see Turnbull 1990 and other essays in Schechner and Appel 1990; Grimes 1982, 1990). Scholars have even become ritual initiates in the attempt to push against the boundaries of knowledge available to the scholar-observer, exploring new approaches to knowledge of ritual. See Karen McCarthy Brown's discussion of the problem in the account of her initiation into a Haitian immigrant community in Brooklyn, New York (Brown 1991).

The interest in understanding better the significance of ritual for participants, and in cross-cultural and comparative studies of ritual, has led to additional new developments. There is growing interest in "performing ethnography," in recreating rituals observed in the field (see Turner 1982a, 1982b), and in engaging ritual specialists in recreating rituals outside the traditional ritual context (see Grimes 1982, 1990). And there is interest in the staging of rituals by different ritual traditions for one another (see Grimes 1990).

Also new among anthropologists, practitioners of ritual studies and performance theory, and other students of ritual as performance is an interest in the evaluation of ritual performance as " 'good' or 'bad.' " Of interest is whether or not there are any universal standards by which ritual can be judged and the extent to which standards unique to the culture in which the performance takes place must be used. The degree to which the perspectives of performers, audience members, critics, and scholars should enter into the evaluation is also of interest ("Introduction" by Schechner and Appel in Schechner and Appel 1990). Central to "ritual criticism," as practiced by ritual studies, is a new interest in how and why rituals fail and succeed (see Grimes 1990).

CHAPTERS TO FOLLOW

The chapters that follow illustrate how newer studies of ritual have been applied to the rituals of a variety of cultural groups from around the world to illumine their role in shaping social experience, in generating society and culture, and in social transformation or social change. The chapter on ritual in Africa sheds light on its role in social conflict and social change. The chapter on ritual in India calls attention to its role in shaping social experience. The role of ritual in balancing tradition and change is the focus of the chapter on Japan, as it is in the chapter on ritual among Native North Americans. Both chapters also discuss the role of ritual in the balance between social control and social change in these cultures. The chapter on ritual in the United States spotlights its role in shaping the social and cultural experiences of a wide variety of culture groups. The chapters that follow also provide sources for the study of ritual in the various cultures treated. For additional sources on ritual in these and other cultures, see Grimes (1985).

Mathias Guenther gives an overview of the history of scholarly studies of ritual in Africa and brings us up to date with a discussion of current studies in his chapter entitled "African Ritual." As he notes, some of the most influential theorists of ritual have been students of African ritual: Max Gluckman, E. E. Evans-Pritchard, and Victor Turner, to name a few. Guenther's focus is the development of the study of ritual in Africa, moving from the contributions of earlier studies on the role of religious ritual within African societies to more recent studies, which take a more comprehensive approach. While building on earlier studies, later studies avoid the narrow empirical and sociological interests of early studies, which had accentuated the social-structural dimensions of ritual. Later and current studies also give a great deal of attention to the symbolic dimensions of ritual, to the systems of cultural meanings, including religious belief, expressed in ritual. Guenther notes that later approaches have, however, abandoned the reductionism of earlier studies, which followed classical "functionalist" theory in seeing the sole role of ritual as that of creating social integration and social status. Later studies give greater attention to the role of African ritual in social conflict and in the ever-changing social process. Later studies also reject the tendency of earlier studies to treat participants in ritual as "puppets" of outside social forces rather than active agents engaged in ritual to shape their social experiences. Guenther also provides examples of rituals of spirit possession as well as examples from his own fieldwork.

In "Ritual Performances in India," Peter J. Claus shows how recent and current studies of ritual as performance and of performance as ritual have extended conventional understandings of performance. Linguists, folklorists, anthropologists, and others have extended studies in the philosophy of language, calling attention to the role of speech in human communication and social interaction, language having a social base or social context, ritual being one of these. Of interest are the effect and effectiveness of the performance of myths, tales, ballads, and the like, in everything from a curative sense to a political sense. Performance studies, ethno-theater studies, and other approaches have focused greater attention on transformations, brought about by performance, in the psychological state of the audience as well as the actors. Studies of ritual performance or ritual theater as cultural performance, including those of Geertz and Turner, have highlighted the role of performance as ritual transformation of social and cultural reality. Performance initiates a response or change, shaping history. Claus offers a caveat or qualification in the use of the theater paradigm. A ritual performance is often not just the reduplication of a received "score" but a mode of action taken by real and familiar people to affect the lives of other real and familiar people. Participants in ritual may be "acting," but they are not necessarily "just pretending." They are "enacting," which contradicts neither the notion of belief nor the practice of theatrical acting. The audience may be aware of the difference.

Noting that the main objective of current performance studies is to synthesize the insights of linguistic and theater approaches, he identifies elements of ritual performance that help link ritual, theater, language, belief, and society: the larger context, performance sequence, ritual configuration, and intent and achievement. Two very recent studies are offered as illustrative of current studies of ritual performance: Kuipers's study of the ritual performance of sacred oral texts centered on the "words of the ancestors" in ritual seances and divination to restore political and social order among the Weyewa of Indonesia, and Schieffelin's study of the effectiveness of the theatrical dimensions of ritual seances as a form of ritual curing among the Kaluli of Papua New Guinea. Claus then offers extended discussion of his study of the dramatic and performative, enactment dimensions of ritual possession as ritual curing within the Siri spirit rituals of southern India.

Mary Evelyn Tucker offers discussion of the religious roots of ritual in Japan, giving distinctiveness and coherence to the everyday life of modern Japanese society in her chapter "Ritual in East Asia: Japan." Behind the ritualized exchange ordering social interchange lie Confucian-based patterns of social ritual (rules of propriety or decorum and custom covering the domestic and political realms). Behind the communal festivals of national, seasonal, and local celebrations lie Shinto-based ritual traditions of communal release and renewal. The "Gion Matsuri," Japan's largest festival, held in Kyoto for over a thousand years, is offered as an illustrative example. Drawing from her own observations in the field, Tucker also offers extended discussion of the Hana Matsuri, one of Japan's most ancient rural festivals. Tucker highlights the dialectical relationship between these rituals of social control and communal celebration. The latter provide release from social control. The balance between control and release serves the persistence of tradition, as does the ritual presentation of tradition as part of a cosmic order. And in Japan, tradition helps promote a general order even as society adapts to the modern world and encounters the forces of change, including Westernization, that bring about the new and threaten the breakdown of Japanese society.

In his chapter "Rituals among Native North Americans," John A. Grim illustrates the role of a variety of religious rituals as lifeways organizing the societies and cultures of Native Americans living in the United States, as well as organizing their interaction with the environment. Grim observes that these rituals have enabled the various societies of Native Americans to respond to changing historical conditions, including the secularization of society in the United States. And he observes that while these rituals legitimate lifeways that stabilize the various societies, Native Americans are also engaged in ritual innovation, which allows them to adapt to their changing life circumstances. Noting that the various rituals cannot be understood independently of the religious or cosmological and cultural systems and worldviews of the various groups, Grim discusses the link between a variety of rituals and the religious and cultural systems in place, particularly as these relate to cosmic and earthly powers, as well as human power. Grim also notes that the various rituals cannot be understood apart from one another and the connections drawn by the various religious and cultural systems. To illustrate these points, he discusses various examples of current ritual practice among the Apsaaloke (Crow) of Montana: the sweat lodge ritual, tobacco ritual, the vision quest, and the *Ashkisshe*, or Sun Dance. Grim draws from his own fieldwork as active participant in various rituals. To illustrate the link between ritual and worldview, he then turns to *Midewiwin* among the Anishinabe (Ojibway); *Massaum* among the Tsistsistas (Cheyenne); the world renewal ritual, or Winter Dance, among the Okonogan (Kettle Falls); and the "Coming of the Kachina" among the Aashiwi (Zuni). A discussion of the adaptation by the Plains Lakota of the nineteenth-century Ghost Dance and the Southern Kiowas' adaption of the Peyote Way illustrate the role of ritual in promoting social control as well as social change.

Finally, Madeline Duntley's "Ritual in the United States" provides a bibliographic discussion of representative recent scholarly sources for studies of ritual in America—written by anthropologists, historians, scholars in religious studies, and sociologists—as well as popular sources—those of the religious traditions themselves as well as popular books. She also directs readers to sources for more general theoretical studies of ritual that have informed many studies of ritual in the United States. Many of the sources cited present community-based case studies as new models of fieldwork analysis. The sources cited treat ritual among various communities of Orthodox Jews, communities of non-Orthodox Jews, Italian-American Catholics, African-American Christians, nonmainline Christians of the American South, Native Americans, and new immigrant groups—Haitians and practitioners of Santeria. Duntley also presents

sources given to the historical, social, and cultural dimensions of a range of
religious and quasi-religious rituals, from the camp meetings of American revivalism and the magical rituals of colonial New England to Victorian rituals
of the hearth and modern reunions among southern Protestants. Public festivals,
ceremonies, and power are subjects of interest in other sources cited. Drama,
dance, music, language, and other elements of performance are of interest to
other sources, which range from Shaker performance and the Protestant camp
meeting to African-American and Native American worship. The reinvention of
ritual by feminist and men's movements is the subject of yet other sources.

REFERENCES

Alexander, Bobby C. 1987. "Ceremony." *The Encyclopedia of Religion*. Vol. 3. Mircea
    Eliade, editor. New York: Macmillan Publishing Company.
Alexander, Bobby C. 1991. *Victor Turner Revisited: Ritual as Social Change*. Atlanta:
    Scholars Press.
Babcock, Barbara A., editor. 1978. *The Reversible World: Symbolic Inversion in Art and
    Society*. Ithaca: Cornell University Press.
Bell, Catherine. 1992. *Ritual Theory, Ritual Practice*. New York: Oxford University
    Press.
Bellah, Robert. 1974. "Civil Religion in America." *American Civil Religion*. Russell E.
    Richey and Donald G. Jones, editors. New York: Harper & Row.
Bocock, Robert. 1974. *Ritual in Industrial Society: A Sociological Analysis of Ritualism
    in Modern England*. London: Allen & Unwin.
Brown, Karen McCarthy. 1991. *Mama Lola: A Vodou Priestess in Brooklyn*. Berkeley:
    University of California Press.
Cherry, Conrad. 1970. "American Sacred Ceremonies." *American Mosaic: Social Pat-
    terns of Religion in the United States*. Phillip E. Hammond and Benton Johnson,
    editors. New York: Random House.
Crapanzoano, Vincent. 1980. *Rite of Return: Circumcision in Morocco*. New York: Li-
    brary of Psychological Anthropology.
d'Aquili, Eugene G.; Charles D. Laughlin; John McManus; and Tom Burns. 1979. *The
    Spectrum of Ritual: A Biogenetic Structural Analysis*. New York: Columbia Uni-
    versity Press.
Davis, Natalie Z. 1975. *Society and Culture in Early Modern France*. Stanford: Stanford
    University Press.
De Cappet, Daniel, editor. 1992. *Understanding Rituals*. New York: Routledge.
Doty, William. 1986. *Mythography: The Study of Myth and Rituals*. Tuscaloosa: Uni-
    versity of Alabama Press.
Douglas, Mary. 1970/1973. *Natural Symbols: Explorations in Cosmology*. New York:
    Random House.
Drewal, Margaret. 1992. *Yoruba Ritual: Performers, Play, Agency*. Bloomington: Indiana
    University Press.
Driver, Tom F. 1991. *The Magic of Ritual: Our Need for Liberating Rites that Transform
    Our Lives and Our Communities*. San Francisco: Harper San Francisco.
Eliade, Mircea. 1958/1965. *Rites and Symbols of Initiation: The Mysteries of Birth and
    Rebirth*. New York: Harper & Row.

Fernandez, James W. 1965. "Symbolic Consensus in a Fan Reformative Cult." *American Anthropologist* 67: 902–929.

Fernandez, James W. 1977. "The Performance of Ritual Metaphors." *The Social Use of Metaphor: Essays on the Anthropology of Rhetoric.* J. David Sapir and J. Christopher Crocker, editors. Philadelphia: University of Pennsylvania Press.

Fernandez, James W. 1982. *Bwiti: An Ethnography of the Religious Imagination in Africa.* Princeton: Princeton University Press.

Fox, James J. 1979. "The Ceremonial System of Savu." *The Imagination of Reality: Essays in Southeast Asian Coherence Systems.* A. L. Becker and Aram A. Yengoyan, editors. Norwood, NJ: Ablex. (Indonesia)

Geertz, Clifford. 1973. *The Interpretation of Cultures.* New York: Basic Books.

Geertz, Clifford. 1980. *Negara: The Theatre State in Nineteenth-Century Bali.* Princeton: Princeton University Press.

Geertz, Clifford. 1983. *Local Knowledge: Further Essays in Interpretive Anthropology.* New York: Basic Books.

Geertz, Clifford. 1986. "Epilogue: Making Experiences, Authoring Selves." *The Anthropology of Experience.* Victor Turner and Edward M. Bruner, editors. Urbana: University of Illinois Press.

Gluckman, Max. 1962. "Les Rites de Passage." *Essays on the Rituals of Social Relations.* Max Gluckman, editor. Manchester: Manchester University Press.

Goffman, Erving. 1967. *Interaction Ritual: Essays on Face-to-Face Behavior.* Garden City, NY: Anchor Books.

Goffman, Erving. 1974. *Frame Analysis: An Essay on the Organization of Experience.* New York: Harper & Row.

Goodman, Felicitas D. 1988. *Ecstasy, Ritual, and Alternate Reality: Religion in a Pluralistic World.* Bloomington: Indiana University Press.

Goody, Jack. 1961. "Religion and Ritual: The Definitional Problem." *British Journal of Sociology* 12 (2): 142–164.

Goody, Jack. 1977. "Against 'Ritual': Loosely Structured Thoughts on a Loosely Defined Topic." *Secular Ritual.* Sally F. Moore and Barbara G. Meyerhoff, editors. Assen, the Netherlands: Van Gorcum & Company.

Grimes, Ronald L. 1982. *Beginnings in Ritual Studies.* Lanham, MD: University Press of America.

Grimes, Ronald L. 1985. *Research in Ritual Studies: A Programmatic Essay and Bibliography.* Metuchen, NJ: Scarecrow Press and American Theological Library Association.

Grimes, Ronald L. 1987. "Ritual Studies." *The Encyclopedia of Religion.* Vol. 12. Mircea Eliade, editor. New York: Macmillan.

Grimes, Ronald L. 1990. *Ritual Criticism: Case Studies in Its Practice, Essays on Its Theory.* Columbia: University of South Carolina Press.

Hegland, Mary. 1983. "Ritual and Revolution in Iran." *Political Anthropology.* Vol. 2, *Culture and Political Change.* Myron J. Aronoff, editor. New Brunswick, NJ: Transaction Books.

Holm, Jean and John Bowker, editors. 1994. *Rites of Passage: Themes in Religious Studies.* London: Printer Publishers, Inc.

Huxley, Sir Julian. 1966. "Introduction: A Discussion on Ritualization of Behaviour in Animals and Man." In "A Discussion on Ritualization of Behaviour in Animals and Man." Sir Julian Huxley, editor. *Philosophical Transactions of the Royal Society of London*, Series B, 251: 249–271.

Jennings, Theodore W. 1982. "On Ritual Knowledge." *Journal of Religion* 62 (2): 111–127.

Kapferer, Bruce. 1979. "Mind, Self, and Other in Demonic Illnesses: The Negation and Reconstruction of Self." *American Ethnologist* 6: 110–133.

Kapferer, Bruce. 1983. *A Celebration of Demons: Exorcism and the Aesthetics of Healing in Sri Lanka*. Bloomington: Indiana University Press.

Kertzer, David I. 1988. *Ritual, Politics, and Power*. New Haven: Yale University Press.

Lane, Christel. 1981. *The Rites of Rulers: Ritual in Industrial Society: The Soviet Case*. Cambridge: Cambridge University Press.

Leach, Edmund R. 1968. "Ritual." *International Encyclopaedia of the Social Sciences*. Vol. 13. David L. Sills, editor. New York: Macmillan.

Lessa, William A. and Evon Z. Vogt. 1972. *Reader in Comparative Religion: An Anthropological Approach*. 3rd edition. New York: Harper & Row.

Lincoln, Bruce. 1981. *Priests, Warriors and Cattle: A Study in the Ecology of Religions*. Berkeley: University of California Press.

Lukes, Steven. 1975. "Political Ritual and Social Integration." *Sociology* 9 (May): 289–308.

MacAloon, John J. 1984. *Rite, Drama, Festival, Spectacle: Rehearsals toward a Theory of Cultural Performance*. Philadelphia: Institute for the Study of Human Issues.

McMullen, David. 1987. "Bureaucrats and Cosmology: The Ritual Code of T'ang China." *Rituals of Royalty: Power and Ceremonial in Traditional Societies*. David Cannadine and Simon Price, editors. Cambridge: Cambridge University Press.

Marcus, George E. and James Clifford, editors. 1986. *Writing Culture: The Poetics and Politics of Ethnography*. Berkeley: University of California Press.

Marcus, George E. and Michael M. J. Fischer. 1986. *Anthropology as Cultural Critique: An Experimental Moment in the Human Sciences*. Chicago: University of Chicago Press.

Moore, Sally F. 1977. "Political Meetings and the Simulation of Unanimity: Kilimanjaro 1973." *Secular Ritual*. Sally F. Moore and Barbara G. Myerhoff, editors. Assen, the Netherlands: Van Gorcum & Company.

Moore, Sally F. and Barbara G. Myerhoff. 1977. "Secular Ritual: Forms and Meanings." *Secular Ritual*. Sally F. Moore and Barbara G. Myerhoff, editors. Assen, the Netherlands: Van Gorcum & Company.

Moore, Sally F. and Barbara G. Myerhoff, editors. 1977. *Secular Ritual*. Assen, the Netherlands: Van Gorcum & Company.

Morris, Brian. 1987. "Religion, Meaning and Function." *Anthropological Studies of Religion: An Introductory Text*. Brian Morris, author. Cambridge: Cambridge University Press.

Nash, June. 1979. *We Eat the Mines and the Mines Eat Us: Dependency and Exploitation in Bolivian Tin Mines*. New York: Columbia University Press.

Ortner, Sherry B. 1978. *Sherpas through Their Rituals*. Cambridge: Cambridge University Press.

Paden, William E. 1988. *Religious Worlds: The Comparative Study of Religion*. Boston: Beacon Press.

Peacock, James L. 1968. *Rites of Modernization: Symbolic and Social Aspects of Indonesian Proletarian Drama*. Chicago: University of Chicago Press.

Rappaport, Roy. 1968/1984. *Pigs for the Ancestors: Ritual in the Ecology of a New Guinea People*. New Haven: Yale University Press.

Rappaport, Roy. 1979. *Ecology, Meaning, and Religion*. Richmond, CA: North Atlantic Books.

"Ritual and Power." 1990. *Journal of Ritual Studies* 4 (2) (summer issue).

Sangren, P. Steven. 1987. *History and Magical Power in a Chinese Community*. Stanford: Stanford University Press.

Schechner, Richard. 1977. *Essays on Performance Theory, 1970–1976*. New York: Drama Book Specialists. (See also the revised and expanded edition published by Routledge, 1988).

Schechner, Richard. 1987. "Drama: Performance and Ritual." *The Encyclopedia of Religion*. Vol. 4. Mircea Eliade, editor. New York: Macmillan Company.

Schechner, Richard and Willa Appel, editors. 1990. *By Means of Performance: Intercultural Studies of Theatre and Ritual*. Cambridge: Cambridge University Press.

Shaw, Peter. 1981. *American Patriots and the Rituals of Revolution*. Cambridge, MA: Harvard University Press.

Smith, Brian K. 1989. *Relections on Resemblance, Ritual and Religion*. New York: Oxford University Press.

Smith, Jonathan Z. 1982. "The Bare Facts of Ritual." *Imagining Religion: From Babylon to Jamestown*. Chicago: University of Chicago Press.

Smith, Jonathan Z. 1987. *To Take Place: Toward Theory in Ritual*. Chicago: University of Chicago Press.

Sperber, Dan. 1975. *Rethinking Symbolism*. Translated by Alice L. Morton. Cambridge: Cambridge University Press.

Staal, Frits. 1983. *Agni: The Vedic Ritual of the Fire Altar*. 2 vols. Berkeley: Asian Humanities Press.

Staal, Frits. 1989. *Rules without Meaning: Ritual, Mantras, and the Human Sciences*. New York: Peter Lang.

Tambiah, Stanley J. 1979. "A Performative Approach to Ritual." *Proceedings of the British Academy* 65: 113–169.

Turnbull, Colin. 1990. "Liminality: A Synthesis of Subjective and Objective Experience." *By Means of Performance*. Richard Schechner and Willa Appel, editors. Cambridge: Cambridge University Press.

Turner, Victor. 1967. *The Forest of Symbols*. Ithaca: Cornell University Press.

Turner, Victor. 1969. *The Ritual Process: Structure and Anti-Structure*. Chicago: Aldine Publishers.

Turner, Victor. 1974. *Dramas, Fields, and Metaphors: Symbolic Action in Human Society*. Ithaca: Cornell University Press.

Turner, Victor. 1982a. *From Ritual to Theater and Back: The Human Seriousness of Play*. New York: PAJ Publications.

Turner, Victor. 1982b. "Performing Ethnography." *Drama Review* 26 (2): 33–50.

Turner, Victor. 1983. "Body, Brain, and Culture." *Zygon* 18 (3) (September): 221–245.

Turner, Victor. 1985. *On the Edge of the Bush: Anthropology as Experience*. Edited by Edith Turner. Tucson: University of Arizona Press.

Turner, Victor. 1986a. *The Anthropology of Performance*. New York: PAJ Publications.

Turner, Victor. 1986b. "Dewey, Dilthey, and Drama: An Essay in the Anthropology of Experience." *The Anthropology of Experience*. Victor Turner and Edward M. Bruner, editors. Urbana: University of Illinois Press.

von Cranach, Mario, editor. 1979. *Human Ethology: Claims and Limits of a New Discipline*. Cambridge: Cambridge University Press.

Wagner, Roy. 1981. *The Invention of Culture*. Review edition. Chicago: University of Chicago Press.

Zuesse, Evan M. 1975. ''Meditation on Ritual.'' *Journal of the American Academy of Religion* 43 (3): 517–530.

Zuesse, Evan M. 1987. ''Ritual.'' *Encyclopedia of Religion*. Vol. 12. Mircea Eliade, editor. New York: Macmillan Publishing.

6

AFRICAN RITUAL

Mathias Guenther

Encouraged by the colonial presence in Africa, the anthropological coverage of that continent has been extensive, especially on the part of British social anthropologists (see A. Kuper 1983: 106–107, 109–110, 140–141). While most of the work by the British social anthropologists focused on kinship, social organization, politics, and land tenure (see Turner 1969: 2–5), a considerable number of them turned their attention toward the cultural domain of religion. Indeed, some of the classic works in the anthropology of religion were written by the masters of that school within the context of Africa (and in the spirit of Durkheim).

Because the early, classic work on African religion tended to focus on ritual, the body of data and concepts on this aspect of African religion is very rich. While this is a fortunate state of affairs for academic scholarship focused on the social utility of religion, the fact that "too much emphasis" has been placed on religious rites has disconcerted some students of Africa (Ayisi 1972: 61). One of them, Nigerian anthropologist, Eric Ayisi, deems this emphasis "absurd," akin to trying to "draw a comparison between Roman Catholic and Protestant beliefs by witnessing their respective religious services" (67). Assigning a privileged analytical position to ritual not only fits the agenda of social anthropology (Evans-Pritchard 1965: 53; Saliba 1975, 1977) but, more generally, is consistent with the epistemology of social anthropology, which holds sense perception to be the basis of knowledge. As a cultural form that is socially enacted and visible, oftentimes saliently and dramatically so, ritual is, arguably, more amenable to empirical study than belief, the more elusive and symbolically dense component of religion (see Turner 1969: 1–2; Guenther 1979: 121–122). As this survey of the field of African ritual will show, functionalism, or the general study of social utility, has remained one of the basis paradigms for the anthropological study of the field; however, functionalism has been amended in a number of ways and has drawn the components of belief and meaning squarely within its analytical purview.

FUNCTIONALIST APPROACHES

Studies on African religion during the first half of the present century, the heyday of functionalism, were all given to the prominent patterns of ritual. These were treated in the static terms of classic "functionalist" theory, that is, as institutions within the wider context of social organization, the order and integration of which they help to maintain. There were monographs or papers on *divine/sacred kingship* (see Roscoe 1923; Krige and Krige 1943; Lloyd 1960; Beidelman 1966; H. Kuper 1947; Evans-Pritchard 1948/1962; see Feeley-Harnik 1985 for a comprehensive review of the studies and issues of early and later students of the topic); on *ancestor cults* (see Junod 1927; Colson 1954; Fortes 1959, 1965; Middleton 1960; Goody 1962; Bradbury 1966; Kopytoff 1971); on *cults* (Doutreloux 1965; Goody 1972); on *spirit possession* (see Beattie and Middleton 1969, an anthology of papers on the subject, most of them by the leading British anthropologists of the day; Fry 1976); on *communal ritual* (see Wilson 1959); on *sacrifice* (see Evans-Pritchard 1953, 1954, 1956: 197–286; Lienhardt 1961; Rigby 1968, 1971; Beidelman 1966, 1969 [the latter resulting in a spirited debate about one "female" element of Nuer sacrifice—the *gorot*—between Beidelman 1976 and Arens and Burton 1975; see also Burton 1976]); on *initiation rites* (see Richards 1956/1982; Turnbull 1957); on *divination* (see Park 1963; Beattie 1964, 1966, 1967; Bascom 1969; McLean and Solomon 1971/1972; Bohannan 1975); and on *witchcraft* (see Evans-Pritchard 1937; Reynolds 1963; Middleton and Winter 1963; Crawford 1967; Harwood 1970; Simmons 1971; Douglas 1970b; Marwick 1965, 1970, 1982).

From the 1950s onward, some of the leading writers in the African field started to amend the Durkheimian-influenced, classic "functionalist" paradigm in three significant ways, one sociological, one symbolic, and the third a combination of the other two. The first was a reappraisal of the element of conflict within social organization and ritual, resulting in a less static and more dialectical or processual, as well as transactional, model of society and religion. This approach is represented by Max Gluckman and his associates (Marwick, Colson, Mitchell, Epstein, Barnes, and van Velsen), who later came to be known as the "Manchester School," after the relocation to Manchester of the Zambia-based Rhodes-Livingstone Institute. The second approach, represented by E. E. Evans-Pritchard, emphasized the dimension of meaning that social actors attribute to the social actions they are involved in. The third approach, represented by Victor Turner, is a combination of the other two, synthesizing the processual with the symbolic, especially in the analysis of ritual.

Gluckman: Ritual and Conflict

Gluckman and his associates conducted extensive ethnographic work among African villagers whose societies contained structural contradictions and a high incidence of tension. This field situation may account for why these basically Durkheimian social anthropologists redefined the nature of social equilibrium and social conflict (along the lines of the sociologists Simmel and Coser). Conflict—between opposed values and principles and between interest groups—they saw as an integral part of social organization and, as a result of countervailing tendencies and cross-cutting loyalties among the elements of opposition, as capable of generating social integration (Gluckman 1955/1963). Instead of expressing the group's cohesion and solidarity (as Durkheim would have it), ritual expresses the conflicts of social life, indeed, exaggerates them. This is the "license of ritual" and, in "exaggerating real conflicts of social rules," ritual "affirms that there was unity despite these conflicts" (Gluckman 1963: 18; see also Gluckman 1955/1963: 118–119). "Rituals of rebellion," Gluckman's special interest (Gluckman 1963), clearly reflect this sociostructural ambivalence toward conflict.

This is shown within the context of two rites: a Zulu agricultural rite that involves women in a dramatic situation of gender reversal, in which they dominate and taunt men, and the royal ritual of *Incwala* of the Swazi, which includes an episode wherein the king degrades himself before his subjects and is derided by them. The latter is a classic African royal ritual, and having been witnessed three times by its ethnographer (H. Kuper 1947), it is one of the best-described rituals of its kind in African ethnology. As a ritual performance, the three-week-long *Incwala* is dramatic and varied; its rich and multiplex symbolism has led anthropologists to interpret and reinterpret the ceremony in a number of ways. One of them is Gluckman's treatment of the ceremony as a ritual of rebellion (Gluckman 1955/1963: 125; and Gluckman 1963: 110–137; for alternative views and critical evaluations thereof, see Norbeck 1963; Beidelman 1966; see also Mair 1977: 46–48; Morris 1987: 250–252).

The central figure of the *Incwala* is the king, representing the descendants of all previous Swazi kings. The other participants are the ranked representatives of all the sections of the Swazi nation. The people are represented also by their nonliving members; the ancestors are held to be present at every stage of the ceremony, and their praises are recited throughout. The timing of the ritual complex is based on lunar and solar coordinates, and cosmic considerations underlie its division into two phases, the short, two-day-long "little" and the week-long "big" *Incwala*. Respectively, they represent the old year and the past, and the new year and the future. The period in between presents the occasion for the performance of ritual song and dance, held at various key villages of the realm. The ceremony ends with a grand finale, as relics of the past are burned on a pyre inside the king's great kraal and rain is awaited. When it falls—through the benevolent offices of the ancestors—it extinguishes the fire and the past, and it drenches and revitalizes the king and his people as they enter the new year.

The *Incwala* brings the king in touch with cardinal elements of the Swazis' natural and social world: He is bathed, and revitalized, with seawater as well as with fresh water brought in from each of the main rivers of the land; mixed in his bathwater are a number of plant species, symbolizing toughness, evergreen freshness, and fastness of growth; he eats ritually prepared meat from a bull immolated by unmarried warriors; and he ritually "bites"—infuses with "medicine"—the year's new crops. In the latter act, he is followed by his mother (who holds elevated political and ritual rank in this society), the queen, princes, councillors, and commoners.

The *Incwala*'s function as a rite of solidarity between rulers and ruled becomes strikingly evident at this point in the ritual. This theme reappears again, near the end, when, at a climatic moment, ordinary loyal commoners express their support for the king, regarding him as both their child and father.

However, at a ritual moment prior to this expression of loyalty, commoners also deride their king, and his own deportment, in turn, is one of abjection. The rebellious aspect of the *Incwala* is manifest also in the ritual enactment of the basic faction and rivalries in this complex state society between the king and the princes of his own blood.

It is on this aspect of the ritual, rather than its solidarity-infusing force, that Gluckman's analysis of the *Incwala* is primarily focused; like the Zulu agricultural rite, it is a potent and poignant ritual of rebellion. The integrative force of such rituals lies in their forceful expression of conflict, especially the hostility of the oppressed (women, subjects) toward those in power (men, the king). Yet this conflict is also contained and kept within the bounds that are set by the ritual; moreover, as seen in the *Incwala*, the conflict is also held in balance by integrative forces and sentiments that are swept up by the ritual. There are also obvious psychological implications to such conflict rituals (which Gluckman mentions only in passing and refrains from elaborating, showing the disdain for psychological explanations typical for British social anthropologists of his time). Because of the intensity of the ritual performance, the participants are presented an occasion for cathartic release from the anger and frustration they may feel toward those who hold power over them. Throughout such ritual, the authority of the power holders—which must prevail—is expressed at the same time. In the case of the royal ritual, the opposition that is expressed by the subjects is directed to the incumbent of the throne, not to the throne itself; it is an act of rebellion gainst the officeholder, not revolution against the office.

Evans-Pritchard: Ritual and Meaning

Evans-Pritchard did not introduce the "social action" focus (on the meaning component of behavior) to replace the social-functional one, as did later American symbolic anthropologists working with what was to become a full-fledged paradigm of interpretive anthropology. His analysis of social and ritual behavior utilized both perspectives in complementary fashion. Describing his studies of Nuer religion—which includes ethnographically and analytically rich sections on sacrifice and possession rites—Evans-Pritchard (1956: 320) stated: "I have tried to show how some features of their religion can be presented more intelligently in relation to the social order described in earlier volumes but I have tried also to describe and interpret it as a system of ideas and practices in its own right."

The same dual agenda that shaped Evans-Pritchard's work on Nuer religion guided his analysis of Zande witchcraft, magic, and divination, undertaken some twenty years earlier. Explicitly stated in the introduction to the book (Evans-Pritchard 1937), he said the author's task was to show the way in which mystical beliefs and rites form an "ideational system" and how this system manifests itself in social action. While the Zande study of witchcraft and sorcery is best known for its then highly original concern with epistemological questions—witchcraft as a logically coherent explanatory device for misfortune—he was equally interested in the social and political effects of witchcraft accusations on intra- and intervillage conflict and on the exercise of princely power.

An exceptionally large number of studies on witchcraft followed Evans-Pritchard's paradigmatic work, reflecting both the seminal nature of his analysis of this ritual as well as the magical pattern and the ubiquitousness of witchcraft in African—especially central African—village society (see Mair 1969: 30). These studies were primarily sociological, treating witchcraft as a mechanism for handling moral nonconformity or social conflict, in the context of either internal or external contradictions or disequilibriums brought on, respectively, by the social structure or colonial setting. Witchcraft and sorcery were seen to be mechanisms for identifying social tensions and either resolving them or, by accusing one's rivals or enemies, providing the pretext and justification for "blasting apart" social relations that have become untenable, usually along chronic structural lines of cleavage (see, for example, Marwick 1982: 16–18). Witchcraft can also be a mechanism for advancing one's political interests and ambitions (see Crawford 1982: 316–317). These works have moved the study of African witchcraft beyond descriptions of quaint and sinister exotica into the sociological and symbolic analysis of social conflict and moral conformity, and of alternate styles of rationality.

Godfrey Lienhardt, Evans-Pritchard's colleague at Oxford University, wrote an account of the religion of the Dinka, who are closely similar in culture to the Nuer, their neighbors (Lienhardt 1961). Lienhardt's analysis of Dinka religion is similar to Evans-Pritchard's in that he gives consideration to both the social as well as the natural environment and the Dinkas' mythological and cosmological meanings and symbols. The work focuses primarily on Dinka cosmology and myth, especially the many divinities of Dinka supernaturalism and their priestly mediators (the spearmasters). Lienhardt's analysis stresses the existential, the pervasiveness of divinity within society and nature in the pantheistic view of the Dinka. Thus, the twitching in the thigh of the sacrificial ox is interpreted as divinity (Flesh) immanent within the animal, as it is within the dying spearmaster at his voluntary death and burial, one of the central rituals of Dinka religious life that brings together participants from all the tribal segments. Lienhardt's analysis of Dinka religion shows that it is rooted within the people's experience of nature and society. It is a somewhat more existential variant of Evans-Pritchard's social action approach to ritual, his notion that "religion is what religion does." As noted by Rosalind Shaw (1988: 256), Lienhardt's analysis of Dinka myth and ritual—as control of experience—contains, implicitly, also the element of individual agency. She sees Lienhardt as one of the first functionalists to treat participants in ritual "as active agents rather than functionalist puppets" (255). This notion was inherent also in the theoretical approach of Gluckman and the Manchester School in general, especially its most influential member, Victor Turner (A. Kuper 1983: 153).

Turner: Ritual Process and Symbols

The basic reason, perhaps, for Turner's seminal effect on the field of African ritual, as well as the study of ritual in general, is that he combined, on a firm ethnographic basis, the processual and the meaning approaches of Gluckman (his mentor) and Evans-Pritchard and showed, more convincingly yet than did the latter, that "ritual is not the dumb, silent cousin of myth" (Lessa and Vogt 1979: 220). One intellectual experience in Turner's early scholarly career was the Third International African Seminar held at Salisbury Harare in Zimbabwe (then Salisbury and Rhodesia) in 1960, at which Turner was one of the contributors (see Turner 1965). The seminar brought together the leading British and French students of African religion. Its co-organizers were Meyer Fortes and Germaine Dieterlen. This collaboration, between British and French anthropologists concerned, respectively, with social organization and systems of knowledge and beliefs, enjoined the two groups of contributors to consider one another's focus of analysis. In a lengthy introduction to the volume that arose out of the conference (Fortes and Dieterlen 1965), the complementarity of these two approaches was recognized, as were the salutary effects of combining them in the study of African religion (see also Richards 1967). In the introductory section on ritual and symbolism (contributed by Turner, in addition to his conference paper), Turner identified what the conference had revealed as the principal requirement for the study of African ritual: the development of "a theoretical frame which would take full account both of the structural-functional and logico-meaningful . . . modalities of religion and would reveal their hidden interconnexions [sic]" (Turner 1965: 15). Much of Turner's subsequent writing on African ritual would be guided by these theoretical objectives.

Turner's theoretical work was based on an extremely rich body of ethnographic data that he had gathered among the Ndembu of Zambia over a four-year period (1950–1954). This work yielded half a dozen monographs and books (Turner 1957, 1961, 1962, 1967, 1968, 1969, 1975) as well as numerous articles (see H. Barnard 1985). His method of fieldwork was an exemplar of what was to become one of the hallmarks of the Manchester School (with which Turner was associated for the early half of his career): the extended case method and situational analysis. As shown by van Velsen (1967), both of these methods are admirably suited for the analysis of social processes and conflicts. In Turner's hands the methodology was especially felicitous, because he analyzed the tension- and faction-torn village life of the Ndembu in terms of cycles (breach, crisis, redress, reintegration) and as "social dramas." The latter analysis follows the activities of individuals and groups as they, as active agents rather than as "functionalist puppets," set out to serve their own interests by exploiting the principles and values of their culture. The phases of such a social drama are structurally akin to the phases of a ritual process. These Turner analyzed in the terms of Van Gennep's tripartite scheme for rites of passage, focusing in particular on the transition phases. The "liminal," symbolic, and ontological makeup of the participants at this phase—creating *"communitas"* and "anti-structure"—became for Turner a general model for social organization that he applied not only to ritual but to such other social phenomena as pilgrimages, festivals, utopian movements, and social marginals.

Turner's early work was primarily concerned with social conflict and its resolution. One of the mechanisms serving that end in Ndembu society was ritual. The politically integrative effects of ritual—rather than Durkheimian moral consensus—was a theme of his first monograph: "[I]n the course of a ritual, symbols and verbal behaviour are manipulated so as to discharge tensions in the social system" (Turner 1957: 316). Here Turner echoes Gluckman's view that by expressing conflict, ritual resolves the same, allowing for a psychological discharge of tension. Turner explored the symbolic dimensions of ritual more thoroughly than any of his predecessors in the field of African ritual studies. He later identified different levels of symbolic analysis—operational, or a symbol's external form; positional, within the total symbolic context; and exegetical, the native interpretation (Turner 1964)—as well as the semiotic qualities of symbols (condensation, unification of disparate significata, polarization of meaning). The last of these sees the various meanings of a symbol spread out, fanlike, from a normative to an orectic (or sensory) pole and as connected, respectively, with the social and the physiological domains of human experience. This spectrum of meanings renders symbols multivocal. By conflating the moral, or normative, with the material and sensory, ritual symbols allow for

an exchange of qualities . . . in the psyches of the participants under the stimulating circumstances of the ritual performance, between orectic and normative poles; the former, through its association with the latter, becomes purged of its infantile and regressive character, while the normative pole becomes charged with the power of the grossly physiological. (Turner 1967: 54–55)

(For a summary and explication of Turner's more developed theory of ritual as agent for transforming the existing social order, creating a more communitarian order, as opposed to serving as a mere safety valve for easing social tension and maintaining the existing social order, see "Ritual and Current Studies of Ritual: Overview.")

STRUCTURALIST APPROACHES

Structuralism is the second broad theoretical paradigm for the study of ritual in Africa. This approach is associated principally with French anthropology, especially its grand master, Claude Lévi-Strauss. While Lévi-Strauss never worked in Africa, nor used African ethnographic material, he is represented by a "most faithful disciple" (Willis 1988, citing Vansina), namely, Luc de Heusch. This Belgian anthropologist brings the hallmark approach of structuralism—the analysis of the deep structures of a cultural institution in the terms of binary opposition—to bear on sacrifice (see de Heusch 1985) and on "divine kingship" (see de Heusch 1987). De Heusch offers a structuralist-semantic reworking of Hubert and Mauss's classic theoretical account of sacrifice in India and an application of it to sub-Saharan African data. He is also critical of Hubert and Mauss, for example, their two dichotomies, sacred-profane, and "sacralized" and "desacralized" sacrifice (referring, respectively, to the establishment of sacred communion between the sacrificer and divinity through the mediation of the consecrated victim and the reestablishment of ritual purity in the sacrificer, which had been jeopardized through taboo violation). On the basis of African ethnography, de Heusch shows these dichotomies to be either ethnocentric or lacking in universality. Holding sacrifice to be "a symbolic labour on living matter" (de Heusch 1985: 95), de Heusch sets out to find the axes of symbolic opposition that African sacrifice defines and mediates. In the process, he also castigates functionalist theorists (especially Evans-Pritchard) for the inherent reductionism of their analyses of sacrifice (as well as of religion in general, as in de Heusch 1988). A massive French work on sacrifice, taking off from Hubert and Mauss and structuralist in orientation, was released by the École Practique des Hautes Études of Paris in 1979.

One key theme in de Heusch's structural analysis of "sacred royalty" (as he prefers to call "divine kingship") is the nature-culture opposition that is the symbolic leitmotiv of classic structuralism. The divine king, as a supernatural and supercultural being,

signifies his integrated wholeness by ritually breaking the rules that constrain his merely human subjects, particularly in committing incest with a royal sister, and in cannibalism. Such acts relate him to the sorcerer and to black magic. But the sacred king is also a white magician or priest, again uniting opposites in his person, which is why his badge of office in Africa is often the skin of a dappled predator such as civet cat, genet or leopard. (Willis 1988: 268)

Earlier, de Heusch had analyzed the ritual and myths surrounding the Luba king and the founding of the Luba state in like terms (see de Heusch 1975; see

also Schneider 1981: 198–199). He argued that they are more than just Malinowskian charter myths that endorse royal power; they are metaphysical and
philosophical discourses on the historical and mythological origins of kingly
power. These are placed within the dialectical context of basic, elemental questions about the opposition between civilization and savagery, orderly state life
and disorderly barbarism, fertility and sterility.

Another highly formalist structuralist treatment of divine kingship among some
east African societies is by Serge Tcherkezoff (Tcherkezoff 1987), which is based
not on fieldwork but on secondary ethnographic sources. Highly polemical in tone
and based on the structuralist ideas not of Lévi-Strauss but of Louis Dumont,
Tcherkezoff is critical of other structuralists (especially British ones, particularly
Rodney Needham). He dismisses as overly mechanistic and metaphoric (rather
than metonymic) their much-used two-column, balance-sheet method of structuralist analysis. One of the main shortcomings of this structuralist method, so it is argued, is that it ignores the coincidence of opposites. A structuralist heuristic
underlies the Canadian anthropologist Jean-Claude Muller's study of sacral power
among the kingless Rukuba of Nigeria (see Muller 1980; see also Muller 1990, in
which chiefly power is examined in the context of initiation ritual). In his book on
African ethnology, American anthropologist, Harold Schneider employs the structuralist paradigm in his discussion not only of divine kingship and sacrifice but of
African ritual in general (Schneider 1981: 201–229).

Because of their materialist bent, structural-Marxist studies have had relatively
little to offer to the anthropological study of religion and even less to the study
of African ritual. The one exception where this approach has yielded interesting
analyses of ritual are studies on some of the hunting-gathering peoples of Africa,
especially the Pygmies and Bushmen (or San) of central and southern Africa.
The culture of such people is informed with nature; climate, seasons, topography, water, plants, and animals are all important influences on social organization and cultural patterns (including religion). The reason such societies have
such a strong ecological bent is primarily the foraging way of life—or "mode
of production"—of its members. As non–food producers who are dependent on
such wild plant and animal resources as are available in the marginal environments they inhabit, nomadic in lifestyle, and equipped with simple technology,
their societies become strongly and pervasively influenced by the environment.

Maurice Godelier explicated his concept of "symbolic labour" in the context
of the ritual of one of these societies, the Mbuti Pygmies (Godelier 1977: 9–10,
51–61). The specific case Godelier focuses on is the *molimo* rite, an intense rite
of solidarity, as well as of affliction (held on occasions of sickness, death, and
failed hunts), which involves the use of wooden trumpets representing the natural elements (water, earth, air, fire) that constitute the forest (see Turnbull 1965:
310). The trumpet is played and songs are sung (see Swada 1990) in order to
awaken the forest to the needs and afflictions of humans. In line with his general
thesis that its mode of production is a society's underlying structural blueprint,
Godelier treats the ritualized and mythologized forest of the Mbuti as a myth-

ological inversion of their hunting mode of production: Instead of the hunters chasing wary game away from themselves into the forest, the forest sends game away from itself, to come to the hunters. In the words of Brian Morris, who sees echoes of Durkheim in this cultural materialist notion, "the forest represents the totality of the material and social conditions for the reproduction of Mbuti society" (Morris 1987: 327). As presented by Godelier, the *molimo* is an instance of symbolic labor, and it serves not mystical or metaphysical purposes but material ones. In short, this rite is "an intensification of the process of production" (327). Recently Marion McCreedy (1994) described a similar ritual performed by the Biaka Pygmies, in the crisis event of the failed hunt. With its focus on the women, the vital players in the ritual, the analysis emphasizes the complementarity of the genders in hunting, the men operating at the instrumental level, the women at the symbolic one.

The ritual of the Bushmen, specifically their trance dance, lends itself to a similar analysis. Like the *molimo* rite of the Mbuti, the trance dance is a crisis ritual and, as such, addresses itself to critical events in the life situation of the people. Apart from disease, the other troubling existential problem of this hunting-gathering folk is the failed hunt. Given their simple and moderately efficient hunting tools, coupled with the small number of people that make up their band societies, technological and logistical constraints are placed on the hunters, such that the robust, fleet-footed, and furtive game they go after in the Kalahari frequently escape. In its cosmological notions, its symbols, and ritual performance, the shamanic religion of the Bushmen, as of other hunter-gatherers universally, is intimately tied up with game animals and with the hunt (Vinnicombe 1976; Lewis-Williams 1981. Guenther 1988, 1994). It is thus a classic instance of symbolic labor.

This applies especially to the trance dance, the central Bushman rite that is held with the greatest frequency during the dry winter season, the time of greatest scarcity. It includes the ritual and mystical acts of extrabody travel (during trance collapse) and therianthropic transformation into a game antelope (or a lion). With respect to the first, one of the purposes of extrabody travel is to scan the landscape for game so that, upon awakening from trance, the shaman might brief the hunters and provide them with clues for their next hunts. The second ritual act creates a mystical, as well as psychological, bond of sympathy between the shaman/hunter and the animal. In part, it is an element of curing as the shaman, qua powerful animal, is able to draw healing potency from this other creature (see Lewis-Williams 1981). Moreover, animal transformation allows a shaman, in trance, to enter the animal and draw it near the hunter. Because the shaman's ritual status tends not to be highly specialized among traditional Bushmen (for instance, among the !Kung, one out of three men might be a shaman), this sympathetic, intersubjective encounter with animals is more than a bit of ritual esoterica in this society of hunter-gatherers. It is an integral and explicitly recognized, semantically labeled component of hunting with which many a hunter has approached his quarry (see Guenther 1988).

Another area of Bushman culture that reveals a beguilement with animals, and an emotional closeness to animals and moral interaction with them, is rock art. Half of the painted images and about 90 percent of the engraved ones depict animals; a small number of them are therianthropes. The central motif of the art, according to Lewis-Williams and his students (Lewis-Williams 1981; Lewis-Williams and Dowson 1989), is, in fact, the trance dance rite. Thus, Bushman rock art is viewed as "shamanic art" and is treated as a key component of Bushman ritual (see also Guenther 1994). It is also possible, although difficult to prove and doubtful (see Lewis-Williams 1981: 5), that the painting of animals may have been a form of hunting magic; were this the painting's main function, it would be eminently appropriate to refer to this pattern of Bushman ritual and expressive culture as "symbolic labor."

In my fieldwork (in the 1960s and 1970s) among the acculturated, indigent, and oppressed farm Bushmen of the Ghanzi District of Botswana, for whom hunting had lost its economic importance and game animals had become scarce, I found that the trance dance had come to address different and new existential crises. Poverty, hunger, disease (much of it imported), and despair, as well as bitterness and resentment against the dominant white and black settler groups who were the owners of what had until a few generations been Bushman owned, were the existential issues of the day to be addressed by the trance dancers. Because of the prevalence of these problems, their performances became a great deal more frequent than they had been in traditional times and occurred year-round, sometimes several times a week. Trance dancing also became more complex and arcane with respect to the ritual skills they demanded of the shaman. While his role became more professionalized, he commanded the admiration of the Bushmen who saw in their dancers potential political leaders to take them away from the farms and the white bosses, to their "own place," with its own herds of cattle, houses, trucks, trade stores, schools, and hospitals. In my analysis of the ritual of the farm Bushmen (Guenther 1975/1976; 1986, chap. 8), I treated their trance dance as a classic Durkheimian rite of solidarity and, following Anthony Wallace, as an instance of cultural revitalization, as well as political opposition.

CONTEMPORARY STUDIES IN AFRICAN RITUAL

Quite a few of the contemporary anthropologists working in the field of African ritual studies continue to approach their field of study with what is basically a functionalist paradigm. This may either be of the classic, Durkheimian (or Marxian) stamp, or it may be derived from one of the three later social anthropologists discussed above, in particular Victor Turner. Some of these studies are synchronic (focused on a particular time or era), regional comparative, or psychological in orientation; others are diachronic, dealing with historical change or with diffusion.

Functionalism, of one sort or another, is the basic analytical modus operandi of most of the general ethnographic monographs on specific African tribes (for instance, in the American "Case Studies in Cultural Anthropology" series edited by George and Louise Spindler, or the equally prolific German "Studien zur Kulturkunde'' published by the Frobenius Institute). While these works are too numerous to list, let alone discuss individually, it should be noted that much of the ethnographic information on African ritual is contained in these volumes. In line with the holistic trope of ethnographic reportage, which covers all of the cultural domains of a society, these studies all include more or less detailed sections or chapters on ritual.

There are a number of classically functionalist studies on *African art*, mainly those that are concerned with the articulation of this prominent domain of African culture within ritual and politics especially West and central Africa, as well as southern Africa. The functionalist leanings of a scholar—toward Durkheim or Marx—are revealed by which of these two related institutional systems is emphasized. Thus, a particular study will make the point either that art in Africa is religious art and linked profoundly and extensively to ritual, or that is is ultimately political art, with ritual mediating the connection to politics.

Thus, Bushman rock paintings are treated as ''shamanic art'' by the most current interpretive paradigm for this expressive cultural form—the so-called trance hypothesis (see Lewis-Williams 1981; Lewis-Williams and Dowson 1989; Guenther 1988, and linked to the symbolism and ritual practices of the curing dance. Just as Bushman art was one of the sources of healing potency, art is also shown to be the locus of power in the Yoruba Gelede cult, which is devoted to the propitiation of spiritually powerful women, such as elders, ancestors, and gods (see Drewal and Drewal 1983). The power is female power; it pervades some of the cult's ritual paraphernalia (masks and costumes), as well as ritual performance. The recipients of power are men, the performers of the cult.

That most of West and central African plastic art is ritual art is obvious when considering its motifs and roles. As surveyed in a detailed study of the art of West and central Africa by Miklos Szalay (Szalay 1986), many of these figures—statuettes, heads, masks, as well as ancestral screens (see Barley 1988)—are depictions of ancestral or other types of spirits, for example, the Luba ancestral figures, the royal ancestor figures of the Bemba, or the masks of the powerful Forest Spirit of the secret Poro and Sande cults (see also Isichei 1988). The ritual intention of some figures (such as among the Baule of the Ivory Coast) is to propitiate vidictive ancestral spirits, or it may be to commemorate: for example, the Akan terra cotta heads placed on graves, or Benin commemorative relief plaques recalling early rulers, dignitaries, or war leaders. (For monographs on the relationship between art and ritual in specific West African societies, see Carroll [1967], Laude [1973], Biebuyck [1973], and Fardon [1991].) Other well-known specimens of ritual art are the wooden ''nail fetishes'' of Zaire (the *nkisi*), which have unclear, ''multi-functional'' ritual uses, including perhaps ratifying contracts or oaths, curing, or sorcery (see Szalay 1986: 104–105).

Another ritual objet d'art is the drum. Among the Yoruba, drums are also objects of veneration as they are informed with spirits (see Adjegbite 1988). That there is, universally, a symbolic, as well as physiological, connection between percussion music and certain ritual patterns (such as transition and altered stats) has been suggested by a number of anthropologists (see Needham 1967:

Neher 1962: Sturtevant 1968). As mentioned above, the connection between dancing and singing and ritual is intimate with respect to the Bushmen and Pygmies, providing, among the former people, the "active ingredients" for trance.

Like others before him (see Harley, 1950 and Fraser and Cole 1972), Szalay suggests that, notwithstanding its religious idiom and employment, in the final analysis, West African plastic art is political (Szalay 1986: 166–186; see also Szalay 1990). Like royal charter myths, the ultimate function of this West African art is to endorse political power holders. It was created for and used and owned by the political elite. Providing an illustration are the masks employed during Suku male initiation. The professionally made, aesthetically sophisticated, and mystically charged masks are worn by the old men. After the ceremonies, they are ritually handled and kept in storage. The masks of the young initiates are crude by comparison. They are carved by the young men themselves and are discarded after initiation. The appropriation and ownership of masks acts as a mechanism for both boundary maintenance and conspicuous consumption on the part of the powerful elders. They are designed to impress upon the young men an appreciation of the elders' might and glory (see also Crowley 1972).

b   In Szalay's view, art, ritual, and politics constitute a unit. The classic illustration of this point is provided by the well-known Golden Stool of the Ashanti, a piece of art and a ritual paraphernalia upon which converge the sacred, myth and royal power. Another well-known case to illustrate that same convergence is the Poro cult (Little 1965, 1966); indeed, it is treated by Keesing (1981: 296–298) as an instance par excellence of Marxist "celestialization of power" (see also d'Azevedo 1962; Murphy 1980). Here, the central spirit of the cult, represented by a two-meter-tall imposing mask, combines within himself the will of all other forest spirits and represents, cumulatively, the might of all supernatural beings. The Kpelle of Liberia refer to him as the "Great Masked Figure" or "Grand Master," *Namu*, in their language, or "Forest Thing" (Gibbs 1965: 219). He was deemed the most utterly real embodiment of divinity and the actual owner of the land. Only the highest Poro functionaries had access to the Forest Spirit, and in order to carry out their political decisions, they donned Poro masks, thereby "fusing secular and ritual roles" (220). The important Poro functionaries were also chiefs and other persons of authority; thus, "political power and Poro power tend to be lodged in the hands of the same individual" (221). Yet another example cited by Szalay is the ruler statues created by the Bangwa on the occasion of his enthronement. At that portentous political occasion, this statue is placed with the statues of all of the king's predecessors, side by side, inside a special ritual house. In this fashion the continuity of supremacy and dynasty is expressed, and by linking the incumbent ruler to ancestral predecessors, his power is celestialized.

Another sophisticated representative in African ritual studies of a *Marxist-inspired* variant of functionalism is the late British social anthropologist Maurice Bloch, who has conducted ethnographic work among the Merina of Madagascar (see Bloch 1986, 1989, 1992). Unlike classic functionalist theory, which is static and synchronic in orientation, Bloch's work is markedly diachronic as he diligently traces the connection between the ideological-ritual and the political-social domains through time. His historical and ethnohistorical data are rich, and his methodological approach is in this regard a continuation of what was practiced and advocated by Evans-Pritchard in his early career, namely, "historical sociology" (see Evans-Pritchard's monograph on the North African Sanusi, a militant, orthodox Islamic fraternity—Evans-Pritchard 1949; see also Evans-Pritchard 1962). In his study on Merina circumcision rituals, Bloch traces the social determinants and the contradictory meaning the ritual takes over time (as it shifts from blessing to violence), over a 200–year period (Bloch 1986). The symbolic stability of the ritual, as over against its sociopolitical plasticity, is the "historical paradox" revealed about the nature of this rite. The relationship between political power and ritual among a variety of African societies is one topic of a recent collection of essays on African ritual and ceremonialism (Arens and Karp 1989).

Regarding *historical approaches* to the anthropological study of ritual, one should note that these were in vogue as a theoretical approach during an earlier anthropological period and that today this field has, for the most part, moved out of the province of anthropology. A review of the work of the many excellent practitioners within this field thus lies beyond the scope of this chapter. Much of this work is on the impact of Christianity and Islam on native African religion and on the myriad syncretistic churches, sects, cults, or on the brotherhood that this contact has created.

Two diachronic approaches in the anthropological study of African ritual that deserve brief mention are studies of religious change and diffusion. Both are somewhat dated today, as acculturation theory and historical diffusionism are both theoretical directions of the past. The former is represented by the work of Herskovits (1958; see chapters 7 and 13) and that of Herskovits and Bascom (1959, which includes essays on religious change and acculturation). Examples of more recent work along the same lines are Swantz's monograph on the Zaramo that focuses on religious change as it affects women (Swantz 1970) and Stevens, detailed study of change to all of the diverse ritual patterns of a Haya village in Tanzania (Stevens 1991). In the field of African ritual the issue of diffusion is today restricted to virtually only one matter: the diffusion of ritual patterns from Africa to the Americas, such as spirit possession cults (see Walker 1972; Zaretsky and Shumbaugh 1978), African cults in general (Janzen 1982), the West African Ogun (Barnes 1988) and Shango (Bascom 1972, see also Simpson 1962), and divination among the Ifa (Bascom 1980). There are also works on the impact of African religion, cosmology, and art on North and South American religions (see Simpson 1960; Bastide 1971a, 1971b, 1978; Thompson 1983).

Another application of the functionalist paradigm can be found in the various *regional and/or structural comparisons* on African ritual that social anthropologists have undertaken over the years, for instance, Kilson's "comparative sociological" study of the degree of involvement of women with respect to supernatural agents, communal cults, and initiation rites (Kilson 1976). The study covered thirteen African societies varying in "level of social differentiation." The topic of gender and its manifestation in African ritual is the theme of a special issue of the *Journal of Religion in Africa* (1988). While not explicitly comparative in focus, all of the contributions are about Nigeria as well as mostly by Nigerians; thus, the papers of the issue lend themselves well to comparative analysis. The classic comparative studies on African ritual are the pieces by Wilson (1951) and Nadel (1952) on witchcraft, and Goody's paradigmatic monograph on West African funeral rites and ancestral cults (Goody 1962). Death and mortuary practices are the topics also of Woodburn's comparative piece on four African hunter-gatherer societies: the Hadza, Mbuti, Baka, and !Kung (Woodburn 1982). Given its institutional fluidity and flexibility, this societal type of Africa is especially suitable for the comparative analysis of structural variation. This is the case especially with regard to the nomadic Bushmen, who are, on the one hand, markedly varied with respect to social organization and cultural patterns and, on the other, uniform with respect to basic, underlying social and symbolic structures (see A. Barnard 1992). Systematic comparative analyses of Bushman religion in general and of witchcraft specifically have recently been undertaken by A. Barnard (1988) and Guenther (1992), respectively.

A seminal application of functionalist analysis—with Malinowskian, psychological overtones—is Ioan Lewis's treatment of spirit possession in terms of what he calls "peripheral (as against 'central') possession cults" (see Lewis 1969, 1971; see also Kilson 1971/1972). These provide marginal and oppressed members of a society with an emotional outlet for frustration and resentment, as well as a social mechanism for pressing their demands on, and gaining concession from, those who hold power over them. The most common and most studied exemplars of Lewis's concept are women living within a patriarchal society. The prime example in Africa is the Zar cult of Islamic Africa (as well as the Middle East), which Lewis (1986) and others (Lewis, Al-Safi, and Hurreiz 1991) have analyzed in terms of this social-psychological paradigm (as over against Boddy's hermeneutic analysis, to be discussed below). Mary Douglas (1970a) presents an opposite sociological explanation of spirit possession; it is not explained by social deprivation, frustration, and oppression of socially marginal members but by "anomie," that is, an overall looseness of social structure and diffuseness of its symbols. Lewis has engaged Douglas on this point with spirited polemic and has reasserted his own theoretical position, mainly that "the ecstatic style of religiosity is typically a response not to lack of structure, but to an oppressive excess of it" (Lewis 1977: 12).

"Central" possession cults, representing in the societies in which they are found the main form of ritual, are typical either for societies undergoing change and disruption or for societies with shamanic religions. African examples are offered in Colleyn's study of the Nya antisorcery cult of Mali (Colleyn 1988) and Heintze's historical study of central African possession cults (Heintze 1970). Katz's monograph on !Kung Bushman trance possession is another variant of a central (albeit spiritless) cult (Katz 1982); however, in this psychological study, trance is in no way connected to either oppression and deprivation or structural anomie but is seen to be a solidarity-inducing curing rite.

"Curing" is a central ingredient of African ritual and one of the key tasks of the African ritual expert, whether he is a diviner, priest, shaman, prophet, "witch doctor," or "witch finder." His central *materia magica* are "medicines," of which he may have a vast variety (see Schapera 1953: 61–63 for an inventory of Tswana medicines; also see Kiev 1964 for a cross-cultural study of ritual and healing that contains a number of cases from Africa). Disease is a prevalent threat for Africans (see Bohannan and Curtin 1995: 28–32), especially those living in the tropical regions. Explanations for it are couched in mystical terms—spirit (ancestors, ghosts, gods) or human agents (witches, sorcerers)—and they constitute an oftentimes complex element of ritual expertise (see Mitchell and Mitchell 1982; Zahan 1979: 92–119; Wyllie 1983). The study of African approaches to disease, the diagnosis and treatment of which operates within social, ritual, and cosmological domains of culture, is thus a component of the wide range of methodological and analytical approaches to ritual, especially the study of witchcraft and divination (see Ray 1976: 102–153). The effectiveness of the medical and "psychoanalytical" treatments provided by African healers for their patients has received the attention, as well as the admiration, especially of medically and psychologically trained observers (see Kiev 1964; Margetts 1965; Gelfand 1964; Edgerton 1971; Lehmann 1993).

Another ritual pattern that lends itself well to psychological or psychoanalytical study is *initiation rites*. A recent African example is Simon Ottenberg's study of Igbo boys' puberty rites (Ottenberg 1989). The worldwide, comparative study by the Frieds contains two African case studies, the !Kung Bushmen and the Muslim Hausa (Fried and Fried 1980). The authors had done ethnographic fieldwork on the latter group.

The Evans-Pritchardian relationship between social structure and systems of thought is the basic theme of Schloss's study of initiation rites among the Eling of Senegal (Schloss 1988), and Barton's study of the Atnot ancestor cult (Barton 1978). The African ritual pattern to have received the most attention from anthropologists working with a meaning-through-social-action approach to ritual is still divination (as it had been for Evans-Pritchard in his pioneering work on Zande oracles). Wendy James's work on the ebony oracle of the Uduk complements and expands Evans-Pritchard's and Lienhardt's work on the religion of two other Nilotic groups, specifically the latters' notion of religion as lived and grounded in experience (James 1988). Experience is taken by James beyond the domains of the social and natural, and beyond the consciously recalled past, to the Uduk's "archive" of culture, a notion she derived from Foucault that refers to the accumulated, unremembered, implicit events and ideas that have been deposited over time within the mental culture of a people. This "moral knowledge" is revealed through ritual practice, rather than religious doctrine. By taking into account also the colonial past and contemporary present, especially the impact of and resistance to Christianity, James moves her study of Uduk ritual beyond the static ethnographic present of her two predecessors. A study on divination, assembled by Peek (1991), views this ritual pattern as a combination of "logical-analytical" and "intuitive-synthetical" cognitive modes, a treatment that situates this recent work on divination within the epistemological discourse opened by Evans-Pritchard in 1937.

Others working on this key African ritual pattern since Evans-Pritchard have followed much the same analytical path, such as Turner (1961), Park (1963), Jackson (1978), Parkin (1982), Kirby (1986), and Whyte (1990). For a critique of the "structuralist-functionalist" and cognitive approaches to the topic, see Devisch (1985). As a novel alternative, there is David Zeitlyn's (1990) study of Nambila divination, along ethnomethodological lines, specifically "artificial oracles" of this Nigerian people, oracles, that is, that elicit binary questions. Zeitlyn sets out to demonstrate how meaning is negotiated through the contradictions contained in the oracle's answers. "Active negotiation of meanings" is the key process in another study of divination, among the Temne of Sierra Leone (Shaw 1985). The aim of such negotiations is to further the interests of the individuals involved in divination, by restructuring those dominant conceptions of reality that go against the persons' interests.

As one surveys the field of African ritual, one can find Victor Turner's stamp on many a study. On some, it is explicit and acknowledged by an author who employs one or another of Turner's concepts. In others, Turner's echo is more faint. Only a sample of Turnerian studies of African ritual is presented here.

German anthropologist Elisabeth Grohs's study of female initiation rites among the East African Zigua and Ngulu employs a processual (as well as regionally comparative) analysis, with a focus on the symbols and meaning of the various phases of the rite, explicated with rich vernacular song texts that accompany them (Grohs 1980). Andrew and Harriet Lyons employ Turner's "anti-structural" concepts of "liminality" and "*communitas*" in their perceptive analysis of ritual dramas as they are performed within the context of a popular Nigerian television series in Benin City. The analysis focuses on an episode that features ancestral ghosts and shades and contrasts its performance with ancestral rites as they are performed within the traditional village context (Lyons and Lyons 1985). Visser (1989) anchors his functionalist ethnographic account of Pokoot religion in a Gluckman- and Turner-like account of conflict and process, as does Spencer (1988) in his study of Maasai ritual rebellion. Turner's models of social and ritual process are employed by Janzen (1982) in his historical and comparative analysis of West African cults. Lewis-Williams's (1981) interpretation of the cosmological and ritual symbols of /Xam Bushman rock art employs Turner's tripartite levels-of-meaning scheme.

Two major studies on spirit possession strongly challenge the widely held

functionalist approach to this elusive ritual pattern of "oppressed women as
extortionists" and propose a performance and hermeneutical approach instead:
Lambek's study of the Mayotte of the Comoros (Lambek 1981) and Boddy's
study of the Zar cult in the northern Sudan (Boddy 1989). Lambek emphasizes
the normalcy of possession (echoing Walker 1972), pointing to the appearance,
as "distinct and credible actors," of spirits that are featured in the drama of
possession. His study looks at the performance context of possession ritual—
curing, drama, symbolic activity, myths—and probes its various levels of meaning. Lambek holds that trance is "mediated by thought structures" that are
"guided and constrained by cultural models" (5). They form a complex, conceptually coherent symbolic system as they are "of deep significance for the
generating, ordering and interpretation of social experience" (5). Employing the
analytical techniques of hermeneutics and discourse analysis, Boddy treats the
trance experience of the woman spirit medium as a text that, being phrased in
a "meta-cultural" language, is "unmediated" and thus "pure experience." It
allows the subject to look at the problems of her gender (which are acute in the
patriarchal society she is a part of) from that "outside" perspective and deal
with its tensions and strains. Possession is thus antihegemonic. As an ingenious,
if somewhat strained, aside, Boddy suggests that in this way the anthropological
experience of fieldwork can be seen to parallel possession.

  "Emic" or "phenomenological" ethnography is another methodological approach to African ritual that can be linked to Turner's work on ritual symbols,
especially his identification of the "exegetical" level of the meaning of symbols.
This approach to ethnography, often yielding "thick description" and dense and
complex strands or levels of symbolic meaning, deeply probes and mines the
"native point of view." It is associated with Clifford Geertz and has now taken
on a life of its own as one of the most current and productive paradigms in
American anthropology. The canonical work in the field (Clifford and Marcus
1986) contains pieces pertaining to Africa, primarily North Africa. Pratt's piece
(Pratt 1986) is on the Bushmen (San) of southern Africa; its focus is largely on
the late Marjorie Shostak's *Nisa: The Life and Words of a !Kung Woman* (1981),
an autobiographical account on !Kung society that includes Nisa'a perspectives
on the trance ritual. Katz's social-psychological study of the same ritual (Katz
1982)—which he treats as an instance of "community healing"—also has a
pervasively emic flavor to it as it attempts to convey the insider's perspective
on this elusive and ineffable event of altered states of consciousness. Such "phenomenological" studies can be especially revealing if they are written by Africans themselves ("in a way that is in line with and faithful to the ideas of the
people themselves"), for instance, J. K. Olupona's recent monograph on five
Yorutan festivals of the religious cycle of Oudo (Olupona 1991). Olupona was
driven to write this work—as have been a number of other African scholars
(see Ray 1976: 14–16; Ukpong 1982)—because of his dissatisfaction with the
heavily Christianized view other writers have brought to their work on African
religion. Welbourn (1968) provides a verbatim, ethnographically rich and moving account by a Keyo informant of the latter's own experience of puberty

initiation. Collections of religious texts—such as prayers (see Mbiti 1975; Lincoln 1990)—are another type of ethnographic reportage that attempt to reveal the African religious perspective directly and without mediation by the anthropologist.

A number of the classic studies on African ritual are the detailed, in-depth reports of just one informant whose testimony is presented by the anthropologist-editor either verbatim or in more or less edited form. Dogon cosmology and ritual are known through Marcel Griaule's "conversations" with just one Dogon, a wise blind man by the name of Ogotemmeli (Griaule 1965/1972). Griaule's record of these conversations appears to be "oversystematized" (Schneider 1981: 182); it would seem that in the retelling Griaule filtered Ogotemmeli's account through a Gallic structuralist filter. Bascom's masterly work on Ifa divination is also based on just one informant (Bascom 1969, 1980), as is Kilson's 1971 study of Kpele songs, symbols, and ritual (Kilson 1971).

A central question in the study of African ritual—as of all other African social and cultural institutions—which such emic studies have the potential of answering, is the extent to which anthropological categories and conceptualizations, forged by scholars, are overly formalist or altogether contrived or fabricated. This question is a basic problematic of cultural anthropology, especially the anthropology of religion, which explores a particularly elusive cultural domain (Evans-Pritchard 1965: 14–17). The participants at the aforementioned 1960 International African Seminar identified this issue as the lead question to guide their explorations of African religion. It remains a problem within the field of African ritual to this day. Three anthropologists who have tackled it in a formal and systematic fashion are Kilson (1970), Mendonsa (1978), and Burton (1980), the first in the contexts of Ga religion as a whole, the second and third with respect to Sisala divination and Atuot sacrifice. Burton applies Needham's notion of polythetic (or analogic) classification (i.e., by several or sporadic resemblances) to Atuot sacrifice. Looking at diverse types of Atuot sacrifice in terms of the various contexts that bring them about in Atuot life, Burton shows that, in the cognitive terms of the Atuot, sacrifice is not the monothetic category (i.e., one defined by a common attribute) that anthropologists would apply to this ritual pattern. Sisala divination is seen to emphasize the communicative nature of divination, and Mendonsa derives from certain Sisala divination patterns a cognitive theory on this ritual form. Divination is treated as the key institution in the "truth system" of the Sisala (the latter concept being derived from Geertz, who presents it as the meaningful link between ethos and worldview, or emotion and cognition). (See "Ritual and Current Studies of Ritual: Overview" in this handbook.)

ECLECTIC APPROACHES

This review of past and present methodological and theoretical approaches to the anthropological study of African ritual has revealed an exceptionally rich diversity of approaches (to a field of long-standing and accumulating work by anthropologists of religion). The salutary effect of this diversity on contemporary scholarship in the field is that it provides workers with an arsenal of concepts and paradigms with which to study their subject, or to restudy ritual patterns anew, with different and complementary approaches. As seen above, the major ritual complexes of Africa—spirit possession, divination, sacrifice, royal ritual, witchcraft—have all been subjected to multiparadigmatic analyses.

Today's theoretical challenge is to integrate these various parameters of African ritual—symbolic, social, psychological, historical—which the various theoretical approaches have identified and privileged into their respective analyses. Such a challenge is best met by scholars who combine several of these approaches and focus on several parameters. There are a number of such studies within the field today. One is Richard Werbner's (1989) book of essays on a variety of rituals in different regions of Africa (divination and possession among the Tswapong and Kalanga of Botswana, sacrifice among the Kalanga, regional cults among the Ashanti and Tale of Ghana, and three new churches in rural Zimbabwe). He employs an eclectic array of theoretical approaches, some of them derived from French structuralism, some from Turner and Gluckman (situational analysis), some from Pierce (semiotics), Bakhtin (dialogics), and Eliade (phenomenology). A strong theoretical presence in Werbner's book is James W. Fernandez. The latter's paradigm of rhetorical and cultural performance—"the play of metaphors ('tropes') in people's definition and redefinition of their experiences"—is the topic also of a substantial paper by Werbner (1990) on body imagery in the Bwiti cult of the Fang of Gabon. Looking specifically at the all-night vigil and the ascetic ordeal of the cult, Werbner analyzes the sequences of the rite and its key tropes. Following Fernandez (see Fernandez 1982, 1986), Werbner calls these "predicative metaphors"; akin to Turner's multivocal symbols, they are "a set of apt images and symbols and their multiple and evocative associations" (Werbner 1990: 68). Fernandez (1990) responded expansively to the paper in the same volume and provided additional ethnographic details on Bwiti body symbolism.

Rosalind Shaw identifies the eclecticism of a recent collection of theoretical essays by a variety of scholars (Binsbergen and Schoffeleers 1985) by referring to it as "a synthesis of symbolic analysis, socio-structural analysis and transactional approach" (Shaw 1988: 255–256). Another theoretically eclectic volume on African religion—dealing with diviners, seers, and prophets in eastern Africa—is the recent special issue of the journal *Africa*, published by the International African Institute ("Diviners, Seers and Prophets in Eastern Africa" 1991). With its focus primarily on history, the contributions are drawn from a wide theoretical spectrum.

Theoretical synthesis, frequently an elusive goal in anthologies, is achieved more readily in monographs. Two examples are Lan's work on spirit mediums and guerillas in Zimbabwe (Lan 1985) and Erlman and Magagi's study of a Hausa initiation ceremony (Erlman and Magagi 1989). Both are studies that combine social-structural with symbolic-structural modes of analysis and that focus equally on the social and political as well as on the cosmological and mythological cultural domains. Another monograph with a functional and explicitly de Heuschian structuralist theoretical focus is Fardon's book (1991) on the relationship between masks and cults and sociopolitical structure among the Chamba of Nigeria and Cameroon. Its focus is on three key ritual specialists: blacksmith, chief (rainmaker), and priest. Adding yet another methodological and theoretical dimension to this study is its systematic, comparative perspective on two Chamba villages, one hierarchical, the other acephalous.

The result of the theoretical eclecticism of scholarship in the anthropological study of African ritual today is that a "new synthesis" has now become possible which is more encompassing than ever before and which holds the promise of raising our understanding of this deep and complex feature of African culture beyond the limiting terms of classical functionalism. While still in action, as an analytical mode, the static, sociological-empirical, and social-structural elements of classic functionalism have been largely expunged, and more modern—symbolic, cosmological, hermeneutical, processual, transactional—branches have been grafted on the functionalist trunk.

REFERENCES

Adjegbite, A. 1988. "The Drum and Its Role in Yoruba Religion." *Journal of Religion in Africa* 18: 15–26.

Arens, W., and J. W. Burton. 1975. "Death by Suffocation." *Man*, n.s., 10: 313–315.

Arens, W., and Ivan Karp, editors. 1989. *Creativity of Power: Cosmology and Action in African Societies*. Washington, D.C.: Smithsonian Institution Press.

Ayisi, Eric O. 1972. *An Introduction to the Study of African Culture*. London: Heinemann.

Barley, N. 1988. *Foreheads of the Dead: An Anthropological View of Kalabari Ancestral Screens*. Washington, D.C.: Smithsonian Institution Press.

Barnard, A. 1988. "Structure and Fluidity in Khoisan Religious Belief." *Journal of Religion in Africa* 18: 216–236.

Barnard, A. 1992. *Hunters and Herders in Southern Africa*. Cambridge: Cambridge University Press.

Barnard, H. G. 1985. "Victor Witter Turner: A Bibliography (1952–1975)." *Anthropologica* 27: 207–234.

Barnes, Sandra T., editor. 1988. *Africa's Ogun: Old World and New*. Bloomington: Indiana University Press.

Bascom, William R. 1969. *Ifa Divination: Communication between Gods and Men in West Africa*. Bloomington: Indiana University Press.

Bascom, William R. 1972. *Shango in the New World*. Austin: African American Research Institute.

Bascom, William R. 1980. *Sixteen Cowries: Yoruba Divination from Africa to the New World*. Bloomington: Indiana University Press.

Bastide, Roger. 1971a. *African Civilisations in the New World*. New York: Harper & Row.

Bastide, Roger. 1971b. *African Religions in the New World*. New York: Harper & Row.

Bastide, Roger. 1978. *The African Religions of Brazil: Toward a Sociology of the Inter-penetration of Civilization.* Baltimore: Johns Hopkins University Press.

Beattie, John. 1964. "Divination in Bunyoro, Uganda." *Sociologus* 14: 44–61.

Beattie, John. 1966. "Consulting a Diviner in Bunyoro: A Text." *Ethnology* 5: 202–217.

Beattie, John. 1967. "Consulting a Nyoro Diviner: The Ethnologist as Client." *Ethnology* 6: 57–66.

Beattie, John, and John Middleton. 1969. *Spirit Mediumship and Society in Africa.* London: Routledge & Kegan Paul.

Beidelman, T. O. 1966. "Swazi Royal Ritual." *Africa* 36: 373–405.

Beidelman, T. O. 1969. "The Ox and Nuer Sacrifice." *Man*, n.s., 4: 209–211.

Beidelman, T. O. 1976. "Death by Suffocation." *Man*, n.s., 11: 116–121.

Biebuyck, Daniel. 1973. *Lega Culture: Art, Initiation and Moral Philosophy among a Central African People.* Berkeley: University of California Press.

Binsbergen, Wim van, and Matthew Schoffeleers, editors. 1985. *Theoretical Explorations in African Religion.* London: KPI Limited.

Bloch, Maurice. 1986. *From Blessing to Violence: History and Ideology in the Circumcision Ritual of the Merina of Madagascar.* Cambridge: Cambridge University Press.

Bloch, Maurice. 1989. *Ritual, History and Power: Selected Papers in Anthropology.* London: Athlone Press.

Bloch, Maurice. 1992. *Prey into Hunter: The Politics of Religious Experience.* Cambridge: Cambridge University Press.

Boddy, Janice. 1989. *Wombs and Alien Spirits: Women, Men, and the Zar Cult in Northern Sudan.* Madison: University of Wisconsin Press.

Bohannan, Paul. 1975. "Tiv Divination." *Studies in Social Anthropology.* J. Beattie and R. G. Lienhardt, editors. Oxford: Clarendon Press.

Bohannan, Paul, and Philip Curtin. 1994. *Africa and Africans.* 4th edition. Prospect Heights, IL: Waveland Press Inc.

Bouissac, Paul, editor. 1985. "Victor Turner: A Canadian Tribute." Special issue of *Anthropologica*, 27.

Bradbury, R. E. 1966. "Fathers, Elders and Ghosts in Edo Religion." *Anthropological Approaches to the Study of Religion.* Michael Banton, editor. New York: F. A. Praeger.

Burton, J. W. 1976. "Death by Suffocation." *Man*, n.s., 11: 388–391.

Burton, J. W. 1978. "Ghosts, Ancestors and Individuals among the Atuot of the Southern Sudan." *Man*, n.s., 13: 600–617.

Burton, J. W. 1980. "Sacrifice: A Polythetic Class of Atuot Religious Thought." *Journal of Religion in Africa* 9: 93–105.

Burton, J. W. and W. Arens. 1975. "Death by Suffocation." *Man*, n.s., 10: 313–315.

Carroll, K. 1967. *Yoruba Religious Carvings: Pagan and Christian Sculpture in Nigeria and Dahomey.* London: Geoffrey Chapman.

Clifford, James, and George E. Marcus, editors. 1986. *Writing Culture: The Poetics and Politics of Ethnography.* Berkeley: University of California Press.

Colleyn, J. P. 1988. *Les chemins de Nya: Cultes de possession au Mali.* Paris: École des Hautes Études des Sciences Sociales.

Colson, E. 1954. "Ancestral Spirits and Social Structure among the Plateau Tonga." *International Archives of Ethnography* 47: 21–68.

Crawford, J. R. 1967. *Witchcraft and Sorcery in Rhodesia*. London: Oxford University Press.

Crawford, J. R. 1982. "The Consequences of Allegation." *Witchcraft and Sorcery*. 2nd edition. M. G. Marwick, editor. Harmondsworth: Penguin Books.

Crowley, D. J. 1972. "Political Art in a Plebeian Society." *African Art & Leadership*. Douglas Fraser and Herbert M. Cole, editors. Madison: University of Wisconsin Press.

d'Azevedo, W. 1962. "Uses of the Past in Gola Discourse." *Journal of African History* 3: 11–34.

de Heusch, Luc. 1975. "What Shall We Do with the Drunken King?" *Africa* 45: 363–372.

de Heusch, Luc. 1985. *Sacrifice in Africa: A Structuralist Approach*. Bloomington: Indiana University Press.

de Heusch, Luc. 1987. *Ecrits sur la royauté sacrée*. Brussels: Editions de l'Université de Bruxelles.

de Heusch, Luc. 1988. "Myth as Reality." *Journal of Religion in Africa* 18: 200–215.

Devisch, R. 1985. "Perspectives on Divination in Contemporary Sub-Saharan Africa." *Theoretical Explorations in African Religion*. Wim van Binsbergen and Matthew Schoffeleers, editors. London: Kegan Paul International Limited.

"Diviners, Seers and Prophets in Eastern Africa." 1991. *Africa*, 61(3).

Douglas, Mary. 1970a. *Natural Symbols: Explorations in Cosmology*. New York: Pantheon Books.

Douglas, Mary, editor. 1970b. *Witchcraft, Confessions & Accusations*. London: Tavistock Publications.

Doutreloux, A. 1965. "Prophetisme et culture." *African Systems of Thought*. London: Oxford University Press.

Drewal, Henry J. and Margaret T. Drewal. 1983. *Gelede: Art and Female Power among the Yoruba*. Bloomington: Indiana University Press.

Ecole Practique des Hautes Etudes. 1979. *Système de pensée en Afrique noire*. Le sacrifice III. Ivry: CNRS.

Edgerton, R. B. 1971. "A Traditional African Psychiatrist." *Southwestern Journal of Anthropology* 17: 259–278.

Erlmann, Veit, and M. Magagi. 1989. *Girkaa: Une ceremonie d'initiation au culte de possession B'oorii des Hausa de la région de Maradi*. Berlin: Dietrich Reimer Verlag.

Evans-Pritchard, E. E. 1937. *Witchcraft, Oracles and Magic among the Azande*. Oxford: Clarendon Press.

Evans-Pritchard, E. E. 1948/1962. "The Divine Kingship of the Shilluk of the Nilotic Sudan." *Social Anthropology and Other Essays*. New York: Free Press.

Evans-Pritchard, E. E. 1949. *The Sanusi of Cyrenaica*. Oxford: Clarendon Press.

Evans-Pritchard, E. E. 1953. "The Sacrificial Role of Cattle among the Nuer." *Africa* 23: 181–198.

Evans-Pritchard, E. E. 1954. "The Meaning of Sacrifice among the Nuer." *Journal of the Royal Anthropological Institute* 84: 21–33.

Evans-Pritchard, E. E. 1956. *Nuer Religion*. Oxford: Clarendon Press.

Evans-Pritchard, E. E. 1962. "Anthropology and History." *Social Anthropology and Other Essays*. New York: Free Press.

Evans-Pritchard, E. E. 1965. *Theories of Primitive Religion*. Oxford: Clarendon Press.

Fardon, R. 1991. *Between God, the Dead and the Wild: Chamba Interpretations of Religion and Ritual*. Edinburgh: Edinburgh University Press.

Anthropology of Religion

Feeley-Harnik, G. 1985. "Issues in Divine Kingship." *Annual Review of Anthropology*
14: 273–313.

Fernandez, James W. 1982. *Bwiti: An Ethnography of the Religious Imagination in Africa.* Princeton: Princeton University Press.

Fernandez, James W. 1986. *Persuasions and Performances: The Play of Tropes in Culture.* Bloomington: Indiana University Press.

Fernandez, James W. 1990. "The Body of Bwiti: Variations on a Theme by Richard Werbner." *Journal of Religion in Africa* 21: 92–111.

Fortes, Meyer. 1959. *Oedipus and Job in West African Religion.* Cambridge: Cambridge University Press.

Fortes, Meyer. 1965. "Some Reflections on Ancestor Worship in Africa." *African Systems of Thought.* London: Oxford University Press.

Fortes, Meyer, and Germaine Dieterlen. 1965. "Preface." *African Systems of Thought.* London: Oxford University Press.

Fraser, Douglas, and Herbert M. Cole, editors. 1972. *African Art and Leadership.* Madison: University of Wisconsin Press.

Fried, Morton, and Martha Fried. 1980. *Transitions: Four Rituals in Eight Cultures.* New York: Norton & Co.

Fry, Peter. 1976. *Spirits of Protest: Spirit Mediums and the Articulation of Consensus among the Zezuru of Southern Rhodesia (Zimbabwe).* Cambridge: Cambridge University Press.

Gelfand, Michael. 1964. *Witch Doctor: Traditional Medicine Man of Rhodesia.* London: Harvill Press.

Gibbs, James L., Jr. 1965. "The Kpelle of Liberia." *Peoples of Africa.* James L. Gibbs, Jr., editor. New York: Holt, Rinehart & Winston.

Gluckman, Max. 1955/1963. *Custom and Conflict in Africa.* Oxford: Basil Blackwell.

Gluckman, Max. 1963. "Rituals of Rebellion in South East Africa." *Order and Rebellion in Tribal Africa.* London: Cohen & West.

Godelier, Maurice. 1977. *Perspectives in Marxist Anthropology.* Cambridge: Cambridge University Press.

Goody, Jack. 1962. *Death, Property and the Ancestors: A Study of the Mortuary Customs of the LoDagna of West Africa.* Stanford: Stanford University Press.

Goody, Jack. 1972. *The Myth of the Bagre.* Oxford: Clarendon Press.

Griaule, Marcel. 1965/1972. *Conversations with Ogotemmeli: An Introduction to Dogon Religious Ideas.* London: Oxford University Press.

Grohs, Elisabeth. 1980. *Kisazi: Reiferiten der Mädchen bei den Zigua und Ngulu Ost-Tanzanias.* Berlin: Dietrich Reimer Verlag.

Guenther, Mathias. 1975/1976. "The San Trance Dance: Ritual and Revitalization among the Farm Bushmen of the Ghanzi District, Republic of Botswana." *Journal of the South West African Scientific Society* 30: 45–53.

Guenther, Mathias. 1979. "Bushman Religion and the (Non)sense of Anthropological Theories of Religion." *Sociologus* 29: 102–132.

Guenther, Mathias. 1986. *The Nharo Bushmen of Botswana: Tradition and Change.* Hamburg: Helmut Buske Verlag.

Guenther, Mathias. 1988. "Animals in Bushman Thought, Myth and Art." *Property, Power and Ideology in Hunting-Gathering Societies.* T. Ingold, J. Woodburn, and D. Riches, editors. London: Berg.

Guenther, Mathias. 1992. "Not a Bushman Thing": Witchcraft among the Bushmen and Hunter-Gatherers." *Anthropos* 87: 83–107.

Guenther, Mathias. 1994. "The Relationship of Bushman Art to Ritual and Folklore." *Contested Images: Diversity in Khoisan Rock Art Research.* D. Lewis-Williams and T. Dowson, editors. Johannesburg: Witwatersrand University Press.

Harley, G. W. 1950. "Masks as Agents of Social Control." *Papers of the Peabody Museum of American Archaeology and Ethnology* 22.

Harwood, Alan. 1970. *Witchcraft, Sorcery and Social Categories among the Safwa.* London: Oxford University Press.

Heintze, Beatrix. 1970. *Besessenheits-phänomene im Mittleren Bantu-Gebiet.* Wiesbaden: Franz Steiner Verlag.

Herskovits, Melville. 1958. *The Human Factor in Changing Africa.* New York: Vintage Books.

Herskovits, Melville, and William R. Bascom. 1959. *Continuity and Change in African Cultures.* Chicago: University of Chicago Press.

Isichei, E. 1988. "On Masks and Audible Ghosts: Some Secret Male Cults in Central Nigeria." *Journal of Religion in Africa* 18: 42–70.

Jackson, M. 1978. "An Approach to Kuranko Divination." *Human Relations* 31: 117–138.

James, Wendy. 1988. *The Listening Ebony: Moral Knowledge, Religion and Power among the Uduk of Sudan.* Oxford: Clarendon Press.

Janzen, John M. 1982. *Lemba 1650–1930: A Drum of Affliction in Africa and the New World.* New York: Garland.

Journal of Religion in Africa. 1988. Vol. 18, no. 1.

Junod, Henri A. 1927. *The Life of a South African Tribe.* 2 vols. London: Macmillan.

Katz, Richard. 1982. *Boiling Energy: Community Healing among the Kalahari !Kung.* Cambridge: Harvard University Press.

Keesing, R. 1981. *Cultural Anthropology.* 2nd. edition. New York: Holt, Rinehart & Winston.

Kiev, Ari, editor. 1964. *Magic, Faith, and Healing.* New York: Free Press of Glencoe.

Kilson, M. 1970. "Taxonomy and Form in Ga Ritual." *Journal of Religion in Africa* 3: 45–66.

Kilson, M. 1971. *Kpele Lala: Ga Religious Songs and Symbols.* Cambridge: Harvard University Press.

Kilson, M. 1971/1972. "Ambivalence and Power: Mediums in Ga Traditional Religion." *Journal of Religion in Africa* 4: 171–177.

Kilson, M. 1976. "Women in African Traditional Religions." *Journal of Religion in Africa* 8: 133–143.

Kirby, J. P. 1986. *Gods, Shrines and Problem Solving among the Anufo of Northern Ghana.* Berlin: Dietrich Reimer Verlag.

Kopytoff, I. 1971. "Ancestors as Elders in Africa." *Africa* 41: 129–142.

Krige, E. J. and J. D. Krige. 1943. *The Realm of a Rain-Queen.* Oxford: Oxford University Press.

Kuper, Adam. 1983. *Anthropology and Anthropologists: The Modern British School.* London: Routledge & Kegan Paul.

Kuper, Hilda. 1947. *An African Aristocracy.* London: Oxford University Press.

Lambek, Michael. 1981. *Human Spirits: A Cultural Account of Trance in Mayotte.* Cambridge: Cambridge University Press.

Lan, David. 1985. *Guns and Rain: Guerillas & Spirit Mediums in Zimbabwe*. London: John Currey.

Laude, Joan. 1973. *African Art of the Dogon: The Myths of the Cliff Dwellers*. Translated by Joachim Neugroschel. New York: Viking Press.

Lehmann, A. C. 1993. "Eyes of the Ngangas: Ethnomedicine and Power in Central African Republic." *Magic, Witchcraft and Religion: An Anthropological Study of the Supernatural*. 3rd edition. Arthur C. Lehmann and James E. Myers, compilers. Mountain View: Mayfield Publishing Company.

Lessa, William A., and Evon Z. Vogt. 1979. *Reader in Comparative Religion: An Anthropological Approach*. 4th edition. New York: Harper & Row.

Lewis, Ioan M. 1969. "Spirit Possession in Northern Somaliland." *Spirit Mediumship and Society in Africa*. John Beattie and John Middleton, editors. London: Routledge & Kegan Paul.

Lewis, Ioan M. 1971. *Ecstatic Religion: An Anthropological Study of Spirit Possession and Shamanism*. Harmondsworth: Penguin Books.

Lewis, Ioan M., editor. 1977. *Symbols and Sentiments: Cross-Cultural Studies in Symbolism*. New York: Academic Press.

Lewis, Ioan M. 1986. *Religion in Context: Cults and Charisma*. Cambridge: Cambridge University Press.

Lewis, Ioan M., Ahmed Al-Safi, and Sayyid Hurreiz. editors. 1991. *Women's Medicine: The Zar-Bori Cult in Africa and Beyond*. Edinburgh: Edinburgh University Press.

Lewis-Williams, J. David. 1981. *Believing and Seeing: Symbolic Meanings in Southern San Rock Paintings*. New York: Academic Press.

Lewis-Williams, J. David, and T. Dowson. 1989. *Images of Power*. Johannesburg: Southern Book Publishers.

Lienhardt, R. Godfreu. 1961. *Divinity and Experience: The Religion of the Dinka*. Oxford: Clarendon Press.

Lincoln, T. 1990. "*Oriki Orisa*: The Yoruba Prayer of Praise." *Journal of Religion in Africa* 22: 205–224.

Little, K. 1965. "The Political Function of Poro, Part 1." *Africa* 35: 349–365.

Little, K. 1966. "The Political Function of Poro, Part 2." *Africa* 36: 62–73.

Lloyd, P. C. 1960. "Sacred Kingship and Government among the Yoruba." *Africa* 30: 221–237.

Lyons, A., and H. Lyons. 1985. "Return of the Ikoi-Koi: Manifestations of Liminality on Nigerian Television." *Anthropologica* 27: 55–78.

McLean, D. A., and T. J. Solomon. 1971/1972. "Divination among the Bena Lulua." *Journal of Religion in Africa* 4: 225–244.

Mair, Lucy. 1969. *Witchcraft*. New York: McGraw-Hill.

Mair, Lucy. 1977. *African Kingdoms*. Oxford: Clarendon Press.

Margetts, E. L. 1965. "Traditional Yoruba Healers in Nigeria." *Man*, n.s., 65: 115–118.

Marwick, Max G. 1965. *Sorcery in Its Social Setting: A Study of the Northern Rhodesia Cewa*. Manchester: Manchester University Press.

Marwich, Max G., editor. 1970. *Witchcraft and Sorcery: Selected Readings*. Harmondsworth: Penguin Books.

Marwick, Max G., editor. 1982. *Witchcraft and Sorcery*. 2nd edition. Harmondsworth: Penguin Books.

Mbiti, John. 1975. *The Prayers of African Religion*. London: SPCK.

Mendonsa, E. L. 1978. "Etiology and Divination among the Sisala of Northern Ghana." *Journal of Religion in Africa* 9: 33–50.

Middleton, John. 1960. *Lugbara Religion: Ritual and Authority among an East African People*. London: Oxford University Press.

Middleton, John, and E. H. Winter, editors. 1963. *Witchcraft and Sorcery in East Africa*. London: Routledge & Kegan Paul.

Mitchell, H. F., and J. C. Mitchell. 1982. "Social Factors in the Perception of the Causes of Disease." *Witchcraft and Sorcery*. 2nd edition. Max G. Marwick, editor. Harmondsworth: Penguin Books.

Morris, Brian. 1987. *Anthropological Studies of Religion: An Introductory Text*. Cambridge: Cambridge University Press.

Muller, J. C. 1980. *Le Roi bouc émissaire: Pouvoir et rituel chez les Rukuba du Nigeria central*. Quebec: Fleury.

Muller, J. C. 1990. *La Calabasse sacrée: Initiation Rukuba (Nigeria Central)*. Montreal: Editions La Pensee Sauvage PUM.

Murphy, W. P. 1980. "Secret Knowledge as Property and Power in Kpelle Society: Elders versus Youth." *Africa* 50: 193–297.

Nadel, S. F. 1952. "Witchcraft in Four African Societies: An Essay in Comparison." *American Anthropologist* 54: 18–29.

Needham, Rodney. 1967. "Percussion and Transition." *Man*, n.s., 2: 606–614.

Neher, A. 1962. "A Physiological Explanation of Unusual Behaviour in Ceremonies Involving Drums." *Human Biology* 44: 151–160.

Norbeck, E. 1963. "African Rituals of Conflict." *American Anthropologist* 65: 1254–1279.

Olupona, Jacob K. 1991. *Kinship, Religion and Rituals in a Nigerian Community: A Phenomenological Study of Oudo Yoruba Festivals*. Stockholm: Almquist & Wilsell.

Ottenberg, Simon. 1989. *Boyhood Rituals in an African Society*. Seattle: University of Washington Press.

Park, G. K. 1963. "Divination and Its Social Context." *Journal of the Royal Anthropological Institute* 93: 195–209.

Parkin, P. 1982. "Straightening the Paths from Wilderness: Simultaneity and Sequencing in Divinatory Speech." *Paideuma* 28: 71–88.

Peek, Philip M., editor. 1991. *African Divination Systems: Ways of Knowing*. Bloomington: Indiana University Press.

Pratt, Mary Louise. 1986. "Fieldwork in Common Places." *Writing Culture: The Poetics and Politics of Ethnography*. James Clifford and George Marcus, editors. Berkeley: University of California Press.

Ray, Benjamin C. 1976. *African Religions: Symbol, Ritual, and Community*. Englewood Cliffs, NJ: Prentice-Hall.

Reynolds, Barrie. 1963. *Magic, Divination and Witchcraft among the Barotse of Northern Rhodesia*. London: Chatto & Windus.

Richards, Audry I. 1956/1982. *Chisungu: A Girl's Initiation Ceremony among the Bemba of Zambia*. London: Tavistock.

Richards, A. 1967. "African Systems of Thought: An Anglo-French Dialogue." *Man*, n.s., 2: 286–298.

Rigby, P. 1968. "Some Gogo Rituals of 'Purification': An Essay on Social and Moral

Categories." *Dialectic in Practical Religion*. Edmund R. Leach, editor. London: Cambridge University Press.

Rigby, P. 1971. "The Symbolic Role of Cattle in Gogo Ritual." *The Translation of Culture: Essays of E. E. Evans-Pritchard*. T. O. Beidelman, editor. London: Tavistock Publications.

Roscoe, John. 1923. *The Bakitara or Banyoro*. Cambridge: Cambridge University Press.

Saliba, J. 1975. "Religion and the Anthropologists, 1960–76. Parts I." *Anthropologica* 18: 179–214.

Saliba, J. 1977. "Religion and the Anthropologists, 1960–76. Part II." *Anthropologica* 19: 177–208.

Schapera, Isaac. 1953. *The Tswana*. London: International African Institute.

Schloss, M. R. 1988. *The Hatchet's Blood: Separation, Power and Gender in Eling Social Life*. Tucson: University of Arizona Press.

Schneider, Harold K. 1981. *The Africans: An Ethnological Account*. Englewood Cliffs, NJ: Prentice-Hall.

Shaw, R. 1985. "Gender and the Structuring of Reality in Temne Divination: An Interactive Study." *Africa* 55: 286–303.

Shaw, R. 1988. "Agency, Meaning and Structure in African Religion." *Journal of Religion in Africa* 18: 255–266.

Shostak, Marjorie. 1981. *Nisa: The Life and Words of a !Kung Woman*. Cambridge: Harvard University Press.

Simmons, W. 1971. *Eyes in the Night*. Boston: Little, Brown.

Simpson, George E. 1960. *Black Religions in the New World*. New York: Columbia University Press.

Simpson, G. E. 1962. "The Shango Cult in Nigeria and Trinidad." *American Anthropologist* 64: 1204–1219.

Spencer, Paul. 1988. *The Maasai of Matapato: A Study of Rituals of Rebellion*. Manchester: Manchester University Press.

Stevens, L. 1991. "Religious Change in a Haya Village, Tanzania." *Journal of Religion in Africa* 21: 1–25.

Sturtevant, W. C. 1968. "Categories, Percussion and Physiology." *Man*, n.s., 3: 133–134.

Swada, M. 1990. "Two Patterns of Chorus among the Efe Forest Hunter-Gatherers in Northeastern Zaire. Why Do They Love to Sing?" *African Studies Monograph* 10: 160–172.

Swantz, Marja-Liisa. 1970. *Ritual and Symbol in Transitional Zaramo Society with Special Reference to Women*. Lund: Gleerup.

Systemi de Kensee en [Marique Noire]. 1979. Vol. 5 of *Le Sacrifice*. Jury: CNRS.

Szalay, Miklos. 1986. *Die Kunst Schwarzafrikas*. Part 1. Zurich: Volkerkundemuseum der Universität Zürich.

Szalay, Miklos, editor. 1990. *Der Sinn des Schönen: Ästhetik, Soziologie und Geschichte der Afrikanischen Kunst*. Munich: Trickster Verlag.

Tcherkezoff, S. 1987. *Dual Classification Reconsidered: Nyamwezi Sacred Kingship and Other Examples*. Cambridge: Cambridge University Press.

Thompson, Robert F. 1983. *Flash of the Spirit: African and Afro-American Art and Philosophy*. New York: Random House.

Turnbull, Colin. 1957. "Initiation among the Bambuti Pygmies of the Central Ituri." *Journal of the Royal Anthropological Institute* 87: 191–216.

Turnbull, Colin. 1965. "The Mbuti Pygmies of the Congo." *People of Africa*. J. L. Gibbs, Jr., editor. New York: Holt, Rinehart & Winston.

Turner, Victor. 1957. *Schism and Continuity in an African Society: A Study of Ndembu Village Life*. Manchester: Manchester University Press.

Turner, Victor. 1961. *Ndembu Divination: Its Symbols and Techniques*. Manchester: Manchester University Press.

Turner, Victor. 1962. *Chihamba, the White Spirit: A Ritual Drama of the Ndembu*. Manchester: Manchester University Press.

Turner, Victor. 1964. "Symbols in Ndembu Ritual." *Closed Systems and Open Minds*. M. Gluckman, editor. Chicago: Aldine.

Turner, Victor. 1965. "Ritual Symbolism, Morality and Social Structure among the Ndembu." *African Systems of Thought*. London: Oxford University Press.

Turner, Victor. 1967. *The Forest of Symbols: Aspects of Ndembu Ritual*. Ithaca: Cornell University Press.

Turner, Victor. 1968. *The Drums of Affliction: A Study of Religious Processes among the Ndembu of Zambia*. Oxford: Clarendon Press.

Turner, Victor. 1969. *The Ritual Process: Structure and Anti-Structure*. Chicago: Aldine.

Turner, Victor. 1975. *Revelation and Divination in Ndembu Ritual*. Ithaca: Cornell University Press.

Ukpong, J. S. 1982. "Sacrificial Worship in Ibibo Traditional Religion." *Journal of Religion in Africa* 13: 161–188.

van Velsen, J. 1967. "The Extended-Case Method and Situational Analysis." *The Craft of Social Anthropology*. A. L. Epstein, editor. London: Tavistock.

Vinnicombe, Patricia. 1976. *People of the Eland: Rock Paintings of the Drakensberg Bushmen as a Reflection of Their Life and Thought*. Pietermantzburg: University of Natal Press.

Visser, Johannes Jacobus. 1989. *Pokoot religie met een samenvatting in het Nederlands*. Oegstgeest: Hendrik Kraemer Instituut.

Walker, Sheila S. 1972. *Ceremonial Spirit Possession in Africa and Afro-America: Forms, Meanings, and Functional Significance for Individuals and Social Groups*. Leiden: E. J. Brill.

Welbourn, F. B. 1968. "Keyo Initiation." *Journal of Religion in Africa* 2: 212–232.

Werbner, Richard P. 1989. *Ritual Passage, Sacred Journey: The Process and Organization of Religious Movement*. Manchester: Manchester University Press.

Werbner, R. 1990. "Bwiti in Reflection: On the Fugue of Gender." *Journal of Religion in Africa* 21: 63–91.

Whyte, E. R. 1990. "Uncertain Persons in Nyole Divination." *Journal of Religion in Africa* 20: 41–62.

Willis, R. 1988. Review of *Ecrits sur la royaute sacree*, by Luc de Heusch. *Journal of Religion in Africa* 18: 267–268.

Wilson, M. Hunter. 1951. "Witch-Beliefs and Social Structure." *American Journal of Sociology* 56: 307–313.

Wilson, M. Hunter. 1959. *Communal Ritual of the Nyakyusa*. Oxford: Oxford University Press.

Woodburn, J. 1982. "Social Dimensions of Death in Four African Hunting and Gathering Societies." *Death and the Regeneration of Life*. Maurice Bloch and J. Parry, editors. Cambridge: Cambridge University Press.

Wyllie, R. W. 1983. "Ghanaian Spiritual and Traditional Healers' Explanations of Ill-
ness: A Preliminary Survey." *Journal of Religion in Africa* 14: 46–57.
Zahan, Dominique. 1979. *The Religion, Spirituality, and Thought of Traditional Africa.*
Chicago: University of Chicago Press.
Zaretsky, Irving I., and Cynthia Shumbaugh. 1978. *Spirit Possession and Spirit Medium-
ship in Africa and Afro-America: An Annotated Bibliography.* New York: Gar-
land.
Zeitlyn, D. 1990. "Professor Garfinkel Visits the Soothsayers: Ethnomethodology and
Nambila Divination." *Man,* n.s., 25: 654–666.

7

Ritual Performances in India

Peter J. Claus

When Muthu first came to the Siri festival, a hundred full moons ago, she
was desperate. Her husband's family had made her life a living death. But
once she came back from the annual ritual . . . she was a new woman. Her
in-laws started treating her with respect, even reverence. Now in her late
30's, Muthu says: "It's as if a strange force drags me here. When I return,
I feel peace within myself."

India Today (May 31, 1992: 74)[1]

Like Muthu, hundreds of women and men partake in the Siri ritual in South
India. They gather into groups of twenty to thirty individuals. In the open center
of each group stand two or three men, dressed in deep-red waistcloths, and four
or five women, wearing orange saris. Around the perimeter stand the remaining
women, wearing white saris. The men and women in the center are adepts, who
have been coming to the rituals for years; among the other women are novices,
coming for the first time. They all begin to chant a mythic narrative that depicts
the lives of a family of spirits, the Siri spirits. At the commencement of the
song, all show signs of being mildly possessed, their individual personalities
dissolved into the characters of the myth. In subsequent discourse, they address
one another in kin terms appropriate to the spirits that possess them: mother,
son, uncle, niece, sister. After some time one of the novices begins a decidedly
more violent form of possession. She shouts incoherent utterances, hisses, or
utters curses. The adepts come and speak to her, asking what term of address
they should use: "Are you my sister?" or "Mother, speak to me." Eventually,
she identifies herself as one of the spirits. The kinsmen who brought the novice

to the ceremonies may refute the claim, saying it is nothing more than a mischievous, evil spirit. Generally, the reason the novice is brought in the first place is that she has been suffering attacks of possession at home and a diviner has advised attending the Siri festival. At the ritual site, in a complex religious psychodrama, women are able to express themselves in personal family situations by identifying themselves with an alternative mythical family whose story of tragedy overcome by virtue is known by everyone.[2]

This is but one kind of ritual drama. We will return to it later for further discussion. Based in myth, the possessed take on the role of mythic characters and improvise a script. Rituals such as this contain a variety of performative acts that transform people into characters and direct action toward restorative goals. But if there is an audience, the performers seem not to be aware of it. Although very "dramatic," ritual performances often do not expect audiences. Made aware that they are being watched, the performers may be reluctant to perform.

There are many other kinds of ritual performances within Indian culture. The high, Brahmanical ritual offerings or a person's daily prayers and worship also contain performative acts but lack the drama and do not necessitate a dynamic transition from one reality to another. There are also many folk theatrical productions that narrate religious stories. They are dramatic, but normally they, too, lack the dynamic transition from one state to another. All of these performances have many things in common, but here we shall concentrate only on ritual performances that are dramatic and involve a transition from one "reality" to another. The history of anthropological thought has taught us that it is unwise to attempt narrow definitions of worldwide phenomena. Instead, I will only try to develop a paradigm for an adequate understanding of how ritual performance works in a particular dramatic religious setting.

THEORETICAL UNDERPINNINGS OF PERFORMANCE STUDIES

Ritual performances have drawn the interest and attention of ethnographers since the beginnings of anthropology. And ritual has long been conceived as "being performed" and frequently studied as "a performance." But the words *performed* and *performance* have taken new theoretical connotations over the past several decades. Before we can contemplate ways modern ethnographers study ritual performances as performances and focus on the performative aspects of ritual, we have to examine some of the ways they have extended the concept of performance.

For many researchers, *performance* refers to communicative behavior. During the 1960s, linguists, under the leadership of Noam Chomsky, began to distinguish between linguistic competence and linguistic performance. The former, the purview of "theoretical linguistics," has to do with grammar and syntax;

the latter has to do with actual speech in its utilitarian contexts. Performance, or "speech," has been disdained by the theoretical linguist as the messy side of language, because it is determined by the seemingly limitless possibilities of personal and contextual situations. Nevertheless, investigation of speech spawned a number of research subspecialties both within linguistics and at the disciplinary borders between linguistics and folklore, anthropology and literature: discourse analysis, sociolinguistics, ethnography of speaking, text linguistics, and several others, all engaged in recording language use in a multitude of different contexts from the world's cultures, trying to discern a paradigm with which to discover the regularities of speech acts and thus to understand not only what is being said, but how it is spoken and, more important, why. Philosophers of language—most notably J. L. Austin (1962), H. P. Grice (1989, 1975b) and M. M. Bakhtin (1981, 1986)—had independently come to the conclusion that this "messy" side of language was also the more "human," in the sense that humans are essentially social beings and language does not exist apart from particularly contextualized social interaction. While some linguists turned to the study of conversational and discourse analysis, folklorists began looking at more fixed-genre text traditions (epic, myths, tales, ballads, etc.) in their performance manifestations or tellings (see Hymes 1975, 1981; Bauman 1977; Briggs 1988). Ritual is one of these contexts, and it was not long before folklorists, along with anthropologists and students of religious literature, began looking at the important relationships contained in a "texts in contexts" paradigm.[3]

For other researchers, *performance* has meant *theater*, the two words being used almost interchangeably. Richard Schechner, a leading spokesperson in ethno-theater studies, defines performance as "an inclusive term meaning the activities of actors, dancers, musicians, and their spectators and audiences" (Schechner 1987: 436). Performance in this sense is not restricted to secular theater, and it is used not simply in a metaphorical sense in reference to ritual. Indeed, ritual and theater are not easily distinguished in many societies. Researchers in the field of ethno-theater often find that the neat Western categories of ritual, dance, and theater are difficult to maintain when trying to understand performance traditions in other cultures—or, for that matter, even within Western culture. In many of the world's cultures, ritual performances are not merely symbolic enactments of past religious events but live performances of the supernatural accomplished through theatrical means and dramatic interactions. Enactment lends special qualities to an action. It often requires training, costuming, staging, accompaniment, and deep psychological transformations. It affects not only, nor even especially, the actor but also the audience and, indeed, reality itself. Enactment not only changes present action but draws upon tradition, linking past events (mythical or otherwise) with the present and sets a course for the future. What performance is all about in this sense is "doing again," that is, "doing" in a legitimating way. (See "Ritual and Current Studies of Ritual: Overview.")

STUDIES IN RITUAL PERFORMANCE

One of the precursors of current ritual performance studies is Lévi-Strauss's "The Effectiveness of Symbols" (1963a).[4] In this article, Lévi-Strauss examines the perlocutionary side of a text, what the utterance of it in a certain context is able to accomplish, that is, what it performs. Specifically, Lévi-Strauss demonstrates how a South American magicoreligious text is used in a ritual drama by a shaman to ease a difficult childbirth. The text takes the shaman on an imaginary journey into the spiritual world, which is at the same time, by the double meaning of words, the cosmos of the woman's physical body. Delivery is effected when the shaman frees the fetus from obstructions in the mythic world. Lévi-Strauss likens the ritual session to a modern psychoanalytic cure during which the psychiatrist encourages the patient to create a narrative of his or her life's troubles and then, from within the narrative world, helps free the client from the imagined bonds of a repressive childhood.

Clifford Geertz sees in ritual performance a means by which sacred symbols and abstract concepts are given a concrete meaning accessible to both the anthropologist and the native. Many have likened Geertz's hermeneutical approach to the study of cultures to the discipline of literary criticism: For him, the drama of day-to-day social behavior is to be "read" like a novel. Particularly important in a culture—not only for the anthropologist but for its members themselves—are those performances that serve as models both *of* and *for* behaving. As models of behavior, ritual performances, a subset of what Milton Singer (1955) called "cultural performances," serve to "give meaning, that is, objective conceptual form, to social and psychological reality both by shaping themselves to it and by shaping it to themselves" (Geertz 1973: 93).[5] Ritual performance is thus a materialization of a culture's ethos and a fulfillment of it. "In these plastic dramas men attain their faith as they portray it" (114). Through a number of articles, Geertz demonstrates the usefulness of ritual performances within interpretive anthropology, reading cultural symbols contextualized in a variety of forms: cockfights, *wajang* shadow puppet plays, and ritualistic theater.

Another of the leading figures in anthropological thought, Victor Turner, developed links between drama and social change even further. A glance at the titles of his most influential books shows how important the notions of ritual and theater were to his studies: *Dramas, Fields, and Metaphors* (1974), *From Ritual to Theatre* (1982), and *The Anthropology of Performance* (1986). In one of his earliest works, *Schism and Continuity in an African Society* (1957), Turner had used the phrase "social drama" to incorporate a more dynamic element into his study of Ndembu kinship than was usual at the time. As he saw it, the fragile threads linking aggregates of matrilineal kin groups were frequently tested during times of quarreling. Quarrels, like drama, moved through regular stages, leading ultimately to either a reaffirmation of ties or separation of the quarreling parties, producing a schism in the group. Through his later studies of ritual, he developed a variety of techniques for analyzing ritual and its processual form, first drawing from van Gennep's earlier studies of transitional moments (rites of passage) and then, on a grander geographic scale, the transitions that take place at both a personal and a societal level, during pilgrimage and during the larger process of social change for society as a whole. Going beyond mere metaphor and analogy, he saw an essential relationship between social action and dramatic enactment:

[B]oth ritual and theatre crucially involve liminal events and processes and have an important aspect of social metacommentary. In many field situations I have observed in markedly different cultures, in my experience of Western social life, and in numerous historical documents, I have clearly seen a community's movement through time taking a shape which is obviously "dramatic." It has a proto-aesthetic form in its unfolding—a generic form like the general mammalian condition that we still have with us throughout all the global radiation of specific mammalian forms to fill special niches. (Turner 1990: 8)

Turner postulated a universal four-stage model of all performances, ritual or otherwise: *breach*—a person or a subgroup publicly breaks a rule of behavior; *crisis*—conflicts between factions reveal hidden clashes of interest, threatening the unity of the group unless redressive action is taken; *redressive action*— ritualized action is taken to seal off the conflict and publicly measure the participants' behavior against jural norms or religious morals; and *outcome*—the final stage may be either a restoration of peace and normality, or the social recognition of an irremediable schism within the larger community (see Turner 1974). (For further discussion of Turner, see "Ritual and Current Studies of Ritual: Overview.")

A number of more recent ethnographic studies have explored the usefulness of these ideas and elaborated on the ways ritual performances link language, society, theater, and religious belief into an emergent reality. By way of characterizing these developments, we might look at two studies that advance the study of ritual performance from the different intellectual roots of linguistics and theater. The major effort in ritual performance studies today is to bring together these two approaches and the skills and sensitivities they entail.

Few studies of ritual performances focus as clearly on the way words (sacred oral texts) are used to wield power than Joel C. Kuipers's *Power in Performance: The Creation of Textual Authority in Weyewa Ritual Speech* (1990). According to Kuipers, among the Weyewa of Indonesia, neither annual ceremonies nor rites of passage hold as much significance as rites of misfortune and change, the two concepts being closely related. Calamities of this sort are considered a result of someone neglecting the words and promises of the ancestors. The "words of the ancestors" are restored by means of ritual performances consisting of poetic dialogues, divination seances and recitation of migration narratives. Weyewa restore political and social order not only in the name of the ancestors but also in their recreated words and stories.

For Weyewa, authentic performances of the "words of the ancestors" are the ultimate expression of an indigenous system of religious and social authority. . . . For them, complete saturation in the words of the ancestors is an important goal guiding the stages of a prolonged ritual process of atonement and exchange between the ancestors and their descendants, between wife-givers and wife-takers, and ultimately between life and death. . . . They re-engage this ancient discourse . . . through a series of rites of divination, placation, and fulfillment. . . . It establishes a clear sociolinguistic trajectory. (Kuipers 1990: 1–2)

Although the authoritative "words of the ancestors" are manipulated and controlled by the living orator, the manner in which they are performed masks their situated character through a process Kuipers labels "entextualization," "in which a speech event (or series of speech events) is marked by increasing thoroughness from the immediate pragmatic context. The end result is a relatively coherent text conceived 'inter-textually' as an authoritative version of one that existed before, or elsewhere. It is not regarded as merely a novel, spontaneous creation by an individual performer in the 'here and now,' even though in may ways it is" (Kuipers 1990: 4). In this detailed examination of a specific ethnographic example of the flexible ways language is used to build and adapt meaning from the past in a ritual context, Kuipers sees the Weyewa political use of language as a specific instance of the ways language is used politically to wrest power and authority from others. Apparently, the Indonesian government does, too, for the rituals have been made illegal!

The importance of dramaturgy in understanding the effectiveness of ritual is emphasized in Edward L. Schieffelin's study of Kaluli (Papua New Guinea) curing seances (Schieffelin 1985). In function, Kaluli seances are not unlike the South American curing rituals Lévi-Strauss had written about, but in this case, the patient is either not present or asleep, and so the metaphorical reality established by the performance cannot directly affect the patient's problems. Instead, as Schieffelin points out, Kaluli ritual works to shape the community's expectations of the outcome of the illness, whether recovery or otherwise.

Kaluli seances employ a number of powerful theatrical devices. For a stage, the medium lies on a raised sleeping platform; the light of fires inside the already intimate hut is dimmed; and throughout the ritual the medium is surrounded by a supportive chorus of village men. The medium utilizes a variety of hissing and gasping sounds to indicate the coming of a spirit but then assumes multiple voices as different spirits pass into his body. Schieffelin argues that an understanding of belief, even as it is woven into a logically coherent and symbolically plausible form (structure) of resolution to the problem, is not sufficient to explain the ritual's effectiveness. For that, it is necessary to show "why the Kaluli accept what they see in the seance as a convincing, even compelling, reality" (712).

The effectiveness is rooted in the emotions that precede the performance: anxiety, anger, tension, and hope that the performance will resolve these. People enter the seance with a few general assumptions—reconfirmed with each successful performance—that there are spirits, that spirits can help discover the source of illness, and that seances can bring spirits to the people. "But," as Schieffelin notes, "if their assumptions are not sustained, they are perfectly capable of calling the medium a fraud, disrupting the performance, and leaving in anger and disgust" (713).

Although a seance resembles theater, there are important differences between the two. In the performance space of the seance, the "stage" does not separate a passive audience from the performer as it does in most Western theater. Instead, the performance emerges from the interaction of the medium and the active chorus of participants.

In the seance the imaginative space of the proscenium stage is exchanged for the liminal realm of the medium's trance, the actor (that is, the medium) is excluded from the performance (since his soul has left his body), and the characters (the spirits) then enter reality. This is accomplished by a double transfer across the break between the visible and invisible. The medium ascends to the invisible realm while the spirits descend to the human plane. Thus theater becomes reality, where spirits who are birds converse with men in human voices. (713)

A successful medium is one who can skillfully compose impromptu songs in response to the participant-audience mood and, through song, manipulate their emotions. The songs make reference to familiar scenes and sights that are associated in people's memories with those they know and love. The shaman assumes the voices of different spirits, each distinct not only from his own normal speaking voice but from one another. The spirits are, then, "the central characters of the seance and provide both its edifying and entertaining aspects. It is in the audience's engagement with the spirits that the spirits become living personalities, and the work of the seance gets done" (715).

LOOKING FOR AND LISTENING TO PERFORMANCE IN RITUAL

As our review of the literature has shown, in contemporary anthropology and folklore the study of ritual performance is not simply the study of a particular kind of cultural event but the focus of a new way of studying culture. Ritual performance studies have grown out of modern ethnographic movements that prioritize observation and experience over static theoretical paradigms. Ritual performance is regarded as a marked and heightened mode of communication utilizing a variety of verbal, visual, gestural, and spacial media. It requires sensitivity to the effects of an unfolding drama and skill in a variety of analytical techniques. In the paragraphs below, I shall try to identify some of the features of ritual that are critical in understanding them *as performance*.

Actual Events

For most contemporary theorists, performance means, in the words of Richard
Bauman, "the actual execution of an action as opposed to capacities, models or
other factors that represent the potential for such action or an abstraction from
it" (Bauman 1992: 41). The focus of their studies is, therefore, a series of actual
performances. Actual performances are seen less as a means to generalization
than they are as an arena in which the work of culture is done and as unique
contributions to a culture's emergent reality (see Hymes 1975; Bauman 1975;
Briggs and Bauman 1990). Rituals of a kind, of course, may have many commonalities and a regularity to them: a score, a script, a form, and various functions. If so, this will emerge during analysis. But one should be careful not to
jump too quickly to a level (or kind) of understanding of ritual that acknowledges only its normal or ideal form and not be attentive to the sometimes subtle,
but often significant, way it is conducted. A performance approach to ritual
usually implies attention to the way symbols and actions acquire meaning from
the specific context and conditions, rather than the abstract meaning they may
possess in themselves (Schieffelin 1985). In writing up one's research, it is often
not the ritual paradigms of a culture but the subtle differences between particular
ritual events that become significant. A culture (to say nothing about Culture)
is not merely a monolithic conceptual form but the result of a dynamic interaction between people and groups of people. Attention to ritual performance
implies attention to the dynamics of a culture. It is seen as a part of a culture's
dialogue with itself.

The Larger Context: Social, Physical, Temporal

While one sense of the idea of a performance is that it is "marked" or
"heightened," set apart from its contextual surroundings, it is also set up by
them and judged appropriate or not in terms of them. Indeed, ritual performances
can often be distinguished and classified according to their appropriate context.
The context may be temporal, in either an abstract cyclical time period (daily
prayer, weekly service, annual festival), or a moment in a person's life (the life
cycle ceremonies of puberty, marriage, death, etc.) or a combination of these
(annual celebrations such as a birthday, anniversary, or other commemorations
of a person's life cycle event). But the context may also be a particular physical
setting, such as a border crossing, or a particular place, such as a temple, a
shrine, or fair grounds. The context may be primarily social, the gathering of a
particular group of people, wherever or whenever they may gather or meet. The
focal context will usually determine not only a limited range of performances
but who is appropriately to perform and who may participate. Attention to context is one of the contributions anthropology has made to earlier, more text-
centered approaches to the study of ritual, but situating a ritual in its
"traditional" context is not sufficient. Many modern performance theorists

would like to see contextualization taken further, by showing that through performances people effect and display claims to identities, new statuses, and new
ideas, embedding a ritual's significance in a particular social space and historical
moment (see Claus 1989; Kuipers 1990).

Performance Sequence and Cues

An adequate description of ritual performances is often a major undertaking.
While daily or weekly rituals may become routine for participants and frequently
performed rituals may be highly formalized for professionals, all ritual performances entail a heightened sense of reality contrasted to "ordinary life." Often
the community of worship, the participants as well as the professional who
execute ritual acts, take days, weeks, and even months to build up to the core
events. Events taking place before the core event may include a process of
deciding to enact the performance, choosing the main participants, selecting a
date, contracting with performers, preparing costumes and ritual paraphernalia,
inviting guests, collecting money, and preparing the ritual grounds. All of these
activities may be governed by rights and may be carried out according to strictly
established rules and frequently entail small, formal ritual performances of their
own. Whether or not these activities are specified by written canon, all have an
evocative function and are to be regarded as part of the ritual performance, for
without them the ritual performance is neither set apart nor properly executed.
Too often the ethnographer focuses exclusively on the more dramatic and temporally condensed core event, leaving the reader with a distorted and incomplete
picture of the meaningful activities that go into the event. Schieffelin, in the
article cited above, however, carefully notes that Kaluli mediums may initially
refuse to perform and must be cajoled into doing so by the community. By the
time the performance actually begins, there is considerable tension and hope
that the performance will work, which, of course, adds to the probability that it
will.

The interaction between the contents of a performance and its dramatic unfolding contains cues—performance markers—that not only convey to the participants where in the structure of the performance they now are but serve to
increase or decrease the special heightened emotions a particular ritual entails
(see Blackburn 1981, 1986; Claus 1989). For the participant, it is in such quintessential moments that the verity of a ritual is founded. Needless to say, the
observer must fully comprehend the effects of performance markers within the
performance structure. But it is also important to be aware that performers themselves control and manipulate these dramatic moments for specific ends and, in
doing so, may meaningfully vary performances from time to time. Not only
does a realization of this emphasize the long-neglected role that individual performers play in ritual, but it should also indicate to us that any given ritual event
should be seen in relation to a culture's history.

Ritual Configuration

Ritual performances are long, complicated events combining oratory, song, dance, costuming, staging, sometimes requiring travel from one location to another, and so forth. All of this has to be coordinated. Individual ritual performers may have to enact their character through gesture, dance, dialogue. In the case of trance and possession, they even have to alter their state of consciousness. Performer training, the coordinating activities of a "director," and the cost born by the "producer" are all parts of the performance. Minimally, all dimensions of a performance must be adequately recorded. This itself, in the case of complex ritual performances, where sometimes many things are going on at once, means that the researcher has to attend not one but many performances in a ritual tradition. But beyond this, one may assume that the configuration of activities is a meaningful one and that sometimes alterations in the performance configuration have significance.[6] Ideally, the researcher should master analytical skills for a variety of presentational media and should be sensitive to subtle changes in modes of presentation and interaction. Performance of ritual, unlike talk about ritual or the "text" within the ritual, is a display of ritual, a communication of whatever it is the ritual is about.[7] Performance of a ritual is where its effectiveness is accomplished. Occasionally, when a ritual is criticized within the community, it is because it was configured improperly. A researcher can learn a great deal about a ritual by paying attention to such a critique and taking note of who is offering it.[8]

Intent and Achievement

Ritual is a conscious display of ideas and intentions. It has a purpose, and it purports to do something. Performance of ritual allows us to confirm or discover what of the vast materials of most religions is important to whom, when, and in what context. Although there may be multiple interpretations of why a ritual should be performed and what it is said to accomplish, analysts have been able to use it to understand individual, group and societal structures and processes. One aspect of performance that the analyst cannot fail to note is who controls the performance, who "holds the stage" or directs the performance from "behind the scenes." In an ordinary conversation the speaker momentarily "holds the stage," as it were, and then passes control to others. During conversation one is conscious of whom one is talking to and in what context. Unstated but deeply felt rules govern the content of speech, the mode of discourse, the meaning of utterances, and the length of time a given person is expected to speak (see Grice 1989; Goffman 1981). Similarly, in ritual, as control of the performance passes from one participant to another, rules limit what one may be expected to do or say. Other participants, or a critical audience, if there is one, are affected by the words and actions and will either enfold divergent expressions into what they had been expecting or demonstrably enforce the rules by bringing a performer in line. In most, if not all, of the world's ritual traditions, changes—sometimes tiny, sometimes great—occur at each performance. Trying to understand and account for these, and the reaction to them, is at the heart of modern ritual performance studies.

To be sure, a performance approach to ritual has its limitations. In the sense we have outlined it above, it is difficult to view performances comparatively. Performance studies are geared to look at changing events within a tradition and the relationships between traditions within a cultural context and system of belief. This explains why there are relatively few attempts at comparative performance structures and processes. It is difficult to see how elements of culturally and historically contextualized significance can easily be compared cross-culturally.

It probably goes without saying that the researcher should also not become too overpowered by the metaphorical analogy between theater and ritual. Looking at ritual as theater, "participants" as "actors," "playing" "roles," and the whole thing "staged" is useful only up to a point. The researcher may think she or he has uncovered something profound. But often participants, too, see the analogy—and see beyond it as well. Although society itself can in some ways be seen as a group of actors playing out allotted roles, it is not only that; a brief moment of self-reflection indicates that real people are not so simple and that social interaction is also based in unique individual experience and unique contributions to a culture. The roles that people play in ritual, too, are played by characters well known to the other participants. Often their role in a ritual performance is derived from their social role. But how they enact it is drawn from a wide variety of sources to which they have been exposed as people. It is probably rare that each performance is identical to ones before it, and although codes of audience interpretations serve to standardize most kinds of variation, the potential for the individual performer's contribution to the ongoing tradition is normally evidenced in temporal, local, and class variation.

Emphasis on the theatrical in ritual and curing can also lead researchers and theorists to a cynical attitude toward other people's beliefs. If we do not acknowledge the existence of other people's gods, we tend to view their rituals as doing something other than what they purport. To bolster our insistence that ritual cannot possibly do what a people say it does, it has become almost anthropological custom to quote the shaman who doesn't believe in the deities that others seem to assume possess him. However, it might be wise for the researcher to ask whether members of the "audience" believe he is possessed, too, and in what sense. In my own experience, a good part of the adult audience at public possession ceremonies at which a cast of professional performers enact possession by the deity is also doubtful that he is "really possessed" by the deity. Most feel that in the performance of the ritual, god is pleased and that god is present only in the sense shared with other rituals where god is worshiped in the form of an idol. "God is pleased when we remember him and when he is in our mind. We are pleased when we can see and talk to him in this way."

Further, it seems to me that if many performers and participants (particularly the younger ones) view the performances cynically, one must remember, too, that there is a great deal of disillusionment in the world today as Western materialism and rationalism sweep through every known culture. The generation gap and class differences one encounters all around the world also create problems in authenticating belief. Perhaps the best attitude is one of listening to many voices and establishing dialogues with a wide variety of participants.

AN EXAMPLE: DRAMA IN THE SIRI RITUALS OF SOUTHERN INDIA

A study of the performative dimensions of ritual performance does more than acknowledge the theatricality of a particular ritual. It analyzes the components of ritual to see what is done, by whom, how, and in what context. While it may not get us any closer to the ultimate question of why people perform ritual, it does lead us to a more detailed understanding of the dynamics of ritual. Let us return to the Siri rituals briefly described in the opening paragraphs, which, as I have already noted, are a set of highly dramatic ritual performances themselves.

At one of the locations where the cult holds its annual ceremonies, the head priest has added an even more "theatrical" act dramatizing the ending portion of the myth, where two sisters quarrel over a game and the elder kills the younger. A platform (*katte*) has been added to the ritual grounds, which serves as a stage. The head priest (called Kumar) and two girls—in reality, adult women, but in the myth, girls, called Abbaga and Daraga—sit at opposite sides of the game board, with Kumar between them. All three are mildly possessed, their persona being that of the spirits. The girls wear white saris. Kumar wears a red silk waistcloth. They commence singing.

What they sing is drawn from a text in an oral tradition genre called *paddana*, normally sung by women in the fields during paddy transplantation. The song is regarded as a sacred narrative, a myth, not a merely historical account of the Siris' lives.[9] But in this context the traditional manner of singing has been changed. The recited text is a product of Kumar's questions put to the girls. "Who are you? Where were you born? Who were your mother and father?" The recitation is thus presented as a discourse, a dialogue, or rather an interrogation, a speech form that puts the questioner, Kumar, in control of the text. Although still sung in *paddana* style, the text in this context is recited by the girls in the form of a first-person narrative, a narrative genre quite different from myth, which, necessarily, is told in the third person. Myth, in relation to this ritual performance recitation, becomes hearsay. This is the real thing, an account from those who were there. It engages us differently. We listen more sympathetically.

The dramatization is not initially a recreation of a scene from the myth. Nowhere in the traditional myth do the girls meet Kumar, their uncle, for he had already died before they were born. The initial scene, we must imagine, is an encounter after death, in the other world, the realm of *maya*. Although the dramatization thus extends the text, in presenting it in this way, we, the audience, as well as the "actors" are drawn gradually into the myth. The psychological distance between audience, narrators, and narrative is drastically reduced. Not only does this alter the experiential time frame (beyond the tenses used in the sentences), but it opens out the paradigmatic structure of myth into the syntagmatic uncertainty of discourse. Although we (the audience) know the outcome of the myth, we are not certain about the outcome of *this* verbal interaction.

Kumar, the head priest, is intermediary between the drama's discourse and the text of the myth. Kumar is also our intermediary, asking the questions we in the audience have. He intercedes between us, in this world, and the girls, Abbaga and Daraga, who are beings from the other world. In interceding for us, he (through the girls) is also explaining to us. He not only brings the myth to the ritual but the ritual to the myth. Indeed, in bringing about the performance and acting as its master of ceremonies, he brings the worlds themselves together. He is a priest and a medium, the nexus of two realities.

The girls yield their identity to the claims they make to Kumar. In the relationship between myth and performance, however, we are still in an intermediate stage in which both text and performance coexist, somewhat at odds with one another. But at a certain point in the recitation the speech genres once again shift, this time from narration of life history to direct speech as Kumar commands the girls to play the game. In doing so, he assumes the character of a deity, Bermerü, who in the myth appeared before the girls to induce them to play, knowing they would quarrel. The drama now recreates the tragic final scene from the myth. The myth is no longer recounted as life history but propelled by the talk associated with a current activity, the play of a game. As audience, we are transformed from listeners of a narrative to witnesses of live action. The girls, however, in this new speech act are now more vulnerable. If they are no longer themselves (as their use of "I" convinces them) reciting the myth, but participants in the story as they relate it, then they will die—unless the story changes. Will the drama follow the narrative paradigm of the myth, or will it generate some new text to follow?

To heighten the sense of danger and suspense, musicians begin to play loud music. As the girls play the game, their emotions are so heightened that their movements are distorted and uncoordinated. They speak to each other in phrases directly drawn from the myth. Their speech is now conversation, the specialized conversational exchanges associated with the game, *cenne*, competitive, taunting, of winning and losing, address and response.

The performance leads—in reality—from this point to its fated end. The girl who is Abbaga really *does* pick up the board and really *would* smash the other girl's head, were it not that Kumar (the priest-medium) physically restrains her. We, the audience, are convinced the myth is true and real. The game's play, the girl's speech, Bermerü's commands, reality, myth, and the sounds of possession are inseparable. Ordinarily discrete realities lose focus and become jumbled with one another. But when, in the confusion of identity and time frames, Abbaga picks up the board to kill her sister, Daraga is only Daraga. There is no confusion in her panicked fear: "Sister! It is I, sister! It is!" She is, for us as well as for herself, a spirit.

Kumar-Bermerü-human-medium, however, traverses the realities, matching various commands with possible identities: "Drop the board, mother. Drop it, child! By my order, drop it, child. Come down to earth. Stand on the ground. You go too fast. Descend to Urmbitota [the place of the ritual]. Let go of the board." But he does so from the sudden perspective of the ritual grounds where the activity is entirely under his control.

When we (the audience) accept these transformations of the original myth, we accept the placement of the dramatic interaction in a mythological time zone. And we are there. The transitional situation—the meeting between uncle and nieces, which never happens in the *paddana* the women sing in the fields—supersedes whatever the women may sing, since the girls now speak for themselves. We are already in the myth; the women's field song thus becomes merely recorded history, replaced by the girl's personal experience narrative. Having changed the narrative mood from myth to mythological real life and from the genre myth (inherently third person) to personal historical narrative, the ritual text supersedes the myth. When, then, the discourse changes to active dialogue, not narrative, we become witnesses to the actual mythological events. At this point, for us, ritual itself supersedes narrative.

In reflecting upon the relationship between myth and drama, it might be supposed that the myth is the direct antecedent for the drama; that though it gets transformed, it provides the script for the drama; that it is a straightforward transformation of its story into a dramatic form. In some ways it is; verbal portions of the drama are certainly borrowed directly into the dramatized plot. In very important other ways, the ritual itself, although it is preceded by the drama, can be shown to be its actual source. It is upon the existence of previous ritual that the drama draws its form and operative functions. Previous ritual establishes the drama's alterations of the myth and legitimates its personifications. The myth serves as a referential text (not script, here).

The discrepancies (transformations) between myth and drama can be best explained by the drama's relation to the activities of the ritual tradition. The most obvious similarity between drama and ritual is the central role the men play in both. While the myth is traditionally a women's genre (performed by women, thematically woman-centered), men dominate the ritual sphere and control its discourse. Kumar's role in both drama and ritual is far out of proportion to Kumar's place in the Siri myth. Kumar occupies only a small part of the myth, perhaps a dozen lines.

Kumar, who is in ordinary life a man called Monappa Moily, is not, after all, perceived as their *real* uncle. The mythic relationship of these people was, we presume, established ritually, at an earlier time. Those who have attended the cult know that it is through cases of spirit identification that Kumar calls to the spirit possessing the novice, asking it to identify itself as his mother, sister, or niece. Their use of the term *uncle* in the drama is predicated on an earlier event of this sort. The audience need not actually have been there when this particular relationship was established, since it is known that much of the Siri ritual consists of the establishment of reciprocal identities.

So while the discourse of the drama has no precedence in myth, it closely resembles the countless scenes of ritual cases where Kumar calls out to the spirit possessing the novice, asking it to identify itself. There, too, the dialogue is in the form of an interrogation, asking who the spirit is and what is its "story." There, too, the response is a form of personal narrative that eventually gets projected into mythical form. He uses kin terms, alternatively pleading with the spirit, and commanding it, identifying himself as brother, son, uncle, all supportive male roles. It is when the spirit addresses him by a kin term that the spirit can be identified. The Siri myth here, too, is a reference text: Although he borrows passages from the myth to suggest a form for the spirit's identity, the myth is not a script for the ritual. Once the spirit is assimilated to the story of the myth and the novice is able to affirm her spiritual identity by reciting, along with other adepts, the discourse of the possession, she becomes an adept herself. At subsequent rituals she retains the acquired spiritual identity.[10] It is from among these women that the girls of the drama were once chosen.

The ritual's innumerable cases of spirit identification are, like the drama, transformations of the myth in the women's field song tradition. Just as the dramatization transforms the outcome of the myth—the girls are prevented from reenacting their earthly deaths—the operating function of the ritual cases, too, brings about change in the real-life conditions of the women participants.[11] The ritual tradition co-opts the story of the mythic tradition and replaces it with a narration that necessarily contradicts the myth's static nature and fateful finality. The drama initiates the ensuing ritual mood, reestablishing the participants' identities, and legitimates the ritual's intent and authority. The ritual must move from real-life ambiguity to mythological clarity but then back to real life, which is its dominant end. The development of the drama as an event within the ritual tradition is only a small step from what has gone on in the ritual tradition for as far back as we can confidently reconstruct it. It serves here to connect one event in the ritual tradition with the next, to charter ritual on previous ritual.

NOTES

1. *India Today* is a popular English-language national news magazine modeled after *Time* and *Newsweek*. Text and accompanying photographs respond to the readers' interest in the huge variety of dramatic ritual performances practiced around the country by a regionally diverse, "traditional" rural population. Modern, urban, English-educated, middle-class readers presumably have a fascination for such spectacles, much as Americans might have for Mardi Gras or the snake handling cults of Appalachian evangelists.

2. For further description and analysis of this ritual, see Claus (1975, 1986).

3. One of the first anthropologists to explicitly adopt a performative approach to the study of ritual was Stanley Tambiah (1979).

4. Another of Lévi-Strauss's early papers is also often cited in connection with performance studies, "The Sorcerer and His Magic" (1963b). In this, Lévi-Strauss discusses the theatrical techniques and training of native North American shamans.

5. Theater often, or maybe always, has a strongly reflexive characteristic, but many researchers are skeptical about this self-conscious relective quality of ritual. The "language" by which the cultural axioms are conveyed in ritual is complex and indirect. While theater is usually meant to communicate a social message, a ritual drama often tries to communicate mystical and mysterious ideas, often interpreted differently by different participants. There is no guarantee that an outside observer can correctly interpret the social message of a ritual performance and then be able to directly construct the culture's axiomatic principles from them. The general use of ritual as reflexive cultural performances often amounts to little more than a heuristic expository device to assume an authoritative, insider's stance toward cultural interpretation.

6. There may be, as Peacock (1990) has found, tension between the different elements of a performance configuration.

7. See Fabian (1990: 11) for a discussion of the difference between informing and performing as objects of ethnographic study, that is, eliciting information from an informant and observing a cultural performance.

8. Cf. Grimes 1990, *Ritual Criticism*, passim. In folklore the importance of "folk literary criticism" was introduced by Alan Dundes (1979).

9. The discussion and analysis contained in this example are abstracted from Claus (1991).

10. Other characteristics that would place this narrative in the category myth are that the beings are sacred and the account is regarded as true. Numerous customs are said to have arisen from events in the story. In other respects, it might be regarded as a legend, since it takes place in historical time. Since it is sung, it could also be regarded as an epic. The term *paddana* is derived from the root for "song" and so gives little indication of either its authenticity or historicity.

11. At home she is respected as a medium associated with a protected spirit.

REFERENCES

Austin, J. L. 1962. *How to Do Things with Words*. Oxford: Clarendon Press.

Bakhtin, M. M. 1981. *The Dialogic Imagination*. Austin: University of Texas Press.

Bakhtin, M. M. 1986. *Speech Genres and Other Late Essays*. Translated by Vern W. McGee. Austin: University of Texas Press.

Basso, Ellen B. 1985. *A Musical View of the Universe: Kalapalo Myth and Ritual Performances*. Philadelphia: University of Pennsylvania.

Bauman, Richard. 1975. "Verbal Art as Performance." *American Anthropologist* 77 (2) (June): 290–311.

Bauman, Richard, editor. 1977. *Verbal Art as Performance*. Prospect Heights, IL: Waveland Press.

Bauman, Richard, editor. 1992. *Folklore, Cultural Performances, and Popular Entertainments: A Communication-Centered Handbook*. New York: Oxford University Press.

Bauman, Richard, and Joel Sherzer, editors. 1974. *Explorations in the Ethnography of Speaking*. London: Cambridge University Press.

Ben-Amos, Dan. 1976. "Analytical Categories and Ethnic Genres." *Folklore Genres*. Dan Ben-Amos, editor. Austin: University of Texas.

Blackburn, Stuart H. 1981. "Oral Performance: Narrative and Ritual in a Tamil Tradition." *Journal of American Folklore* 94: 207–227.

Blackburn, Stuart. 1986. "Performance Markers in the Interpretation of an Indian Story Type." *Another Harmony: New Essays on the Folklore of India*. Stuart Blackburn and A. K. Ramanujan, editors. Berkeley: University of California Press. 167–194.

Briggs, Charles L. 1988. *Competence in Performance: The Creativity of Tradition in Mexicano Verbal Art*. Philadelphia: University of Pennsylvania Press.

Briggs, Charles L., and Richard Bauman. 1990. "Poetics and Performance as Critical Perspectives on Language and Society." *Annual Review of Anthropology* 19: 59–88.

Claus, Peter J. 1975. "The Siri Myth and Ritual: A Mass Possession Ritual of South India." *Ethnology* 14 (1): 47–58.

Claus, Peter J. 1986. "Playing Cenne: The Meanings of a Folk Game." *Another Harmony: New Essays on the Folklore of India*. Stuart Blackburn and A. K. Ramanujan, editors. Berkeley: University of California Press.

Claus, Peter J. 1989. "Behind the Text: Performance and Ideology in a Tulu Oral Tradition." *Indian Oral Epics*. Stuart Blackburn, Peter J. Claus, S. Wadley, and J. Flueckiger, editors. Berkeley: University of California Press.

Claus, Peter J. 1991. "Ritual Transforms a Myth." Paper, Conference on South Asia, Madison, Wisconsin.

Dundes, Alan. 1979. "Metafolklore and Oral Literary Criticism." *Readings in American Folklore*. Jan H. Brunvand, editor. New York: W. W. Norton.

Fabian, Johannes. 1990. *Power and Performance: Ethnographic Explorations through Proverbial Wisdom and Theater in Shaba, Zaire*. Madison: University of Wisconsin Press.

Frisbie, Charlotte J., editor. 1980. *Southwestern Indian Ritual Drama*. Albuquerque: University of New Mexico Press.

Geertz, Clifford. 1973. *The Interpretation of Cultures*. New York: Basic Books.

Gill, Sam D. 1987. *Native American Religious Action: A Performance Approach to Religion*. Columbia: University of South Carolina Press.

Goffman, Erving. 1981. *Forms of Talk*. Philadelphia: University of Pennsylvania Press.

Grice, H. P. 1975a. "Logic and Conversation." *Syntax and Semantics 3: Speech Acts*. P. Cole and J. L. Morgan, editors. New York: Academic Press.

Grice, H. P. 1975b. "Utterer's Meaning and Intentions." *Philosophical Review* (April): 147–177.

Grice, H. Paul. 1989. *Studies in the Way of Words*. Cambridge, MA: Harvard University Press.

Grimes, Ronald L. 1976. *Symbol and Conquest: Public Ritual and Drama in Santa Fe, New Mexico*. Ithaca, NY: Cornell University Press.

Grimes, Ronald. 1990. *Ritual Criticism: Case Studies in Its Practice, Essays on Its Theory*. Columbia: University of South Carolina Press.

Hymes, Dell. 1975. "Breakthrough into Performance." *Folklore: Performance and Communications*. Dan Ben-Amos and K. S. Goldstein, editors. The Hague: Mouton.

Hymes, Dell. 1981. *"In Vain I Tried to Tell You"*: Essays in Native American Ethnopoetics. Philadelphia: University of Pennsylvania Press.

Jenkins, L. W. and E. Wapp, Jr. 1976. "Native American Performance." *Drama Review*
20: 5–12.

Kirby, E. T. 1974. "Indigenous African Theatre." *Drama Review* 18 (4): 22–35.

Kuipers, J. C. 1990. *Power in Performance: The Creation of Textual Authority in Weyewa Ritual Speech.* Philadelphia: University of Pennsylvania Press.

Lee, Du-Hyun. 1990. "Korean Shamans: Role Playing through Trance Possession." *By
Means of Performance: Intercultural Studies of Theatre and Ritual.* Richard
Schechner and Willa Appel, editors. Cambridge: Cambridge University Press.

Lévi-Strauss, C. 1963a. "The Effectiveness of Symbols." *Structural Anthropology.*
Claire Jacobson and Brooke Grundfest Schoepf, translators. New York: Basic
Books.

Lévi-Strauss, C. 1963b. "The Sorcerer and His Magic." *Structural Anthropology.* Claire
Jacobson and Brooke Grundfest Schoepf, translators. New York: Basic Books.

Obeyesekere, Gananath. 1969. "The Ritual Drama of the Sanni Demons: Collective
Representations of Disease in Ceylon." *Comparative Studies in Society and History* 11 (2): 175–216.

Obeyesekere, Ranjini. 1990. "The Significance of Performance of Its Audience: An Analysis of Three Sri Lankan Rituals." *By Means of Performance: Intercultural Studies of Theatre and Ritual.* Richard Schechner and Willa Appel, editors.
Cambridge: Cambridge University Press.

Peacock, James L. 1990. "Ethnographic Notes on Sacred and Profane Performance." *By
Means of Performance: Intercultural Studies of Theatre and Ritual.* Richard
Schechner and Willa Appel, editors. Cambridge: Cambridge University Press.

Schechner, Richard. 1987. "Drama: Performance and Ritual." *Encyclopedia of Religion.*
Vol. 4. Marcia Eliade, editor. New York: Macmillan.

Schechner, Richard and Willa Appel. 1990. *By Means of Performance: Intercultural
Studies of Theatre and Ritual.* Cambridge: Cambridge University Press.

Schieffelin, Edward L. 1985. "Performance and the Cultural Construction of Reality."
American Ethnologist 12 (4): 707–724.

Singer, Milton. 1955. "The Cultural Pattern of Indian Civilization." *Far Eastern Quarterly* 15: 23–26.

Singer, Milton. 1958. "The Great Tradition in a Metropolitan Center: Madras." *Traditional India.* M. Singer, editor. Philadelphia: American Folklore Society.

Tambiah, Stanley J. 1979. "A Performative Approach to Ritual." *Proceedings of the
British Academy* 65: 113–169.

Turner, Victor. 1957. *Schism and Continuity in an African Society: A Study of Ndembu
Village Life.* Manchester: Manchester University Press.

Turner, Victor. 1968. *The Drums of Affliction: A Study of Religious Processes among
the Ndembu of Zambia.* Oxford: Clarendon Press; London: International African
Institute.

Turner, Victor. 1974. *Dramas, Fields, and Metaphors: Symbolic Action in Human Society.* Ithaca, NY: Cornell University Press.

Turner, Victor. 1982. *From Ritual to Theatre: The Human Seriousness of Play.* New
York: Performing Arts Journal Publications.

Turner, Victor. 1986. *The Anthropology of Performance.* New York: PAJ Publications.

Turner, Victor. 1990. "Are There Universals of Performance in Myth, Ritual, and

Drama?'' *By Means of Performance: Intercultural Studies of Theatre and Ritual*. R. Schechner and W. Appel, editors. Cambridge: Cambridge University Press.

Zarrilli, Phillip. 1990. ''What Does It Mean to 'Become the Character': Power, Presence, and Transcendence in Asian In-body Disciplines of Practice.'' *By Means of Performance: Intercultural Studies of Theatre and Ritual*. Richard Schechner and Willa Appel, editors. Cambridge: Cambridge University Press.

8

Ritual in East Asia: Japan

Mary Evelyn Tucker

Everyday life in Tokyo, one of the world's most modern, bustling and prosperous cities, is made up of a maze of elaborate rituals. To a visitor, some of these rituals are readily apparent while others lie deep below the surface. Although not completely visible or fully comprehensible to an outsider, without these rituals the city would probably not function as efficiently as it does. This is true not only in Tokyo but throughout Japan as well. From the cities of Kyoto and Osaka to the rural areas of Kyushu and Hokkaido, a web of local and national rituals lends conformity, and distinctiveness, to Japanese society. Similar patterns of intricate social interactions have created coherent structures for ordering family life, educating children, carrying on business, and even conducting government. Moreover, these patterns are punctuated by a rich and varied festival life involving national, seasonal, and local rituals. Thus, the formalities of social exchanges are balanced by the color, exuberance, and play of festivals. The combination of intricate social rituals circumscribing daily life, together with the ritual release provided by various communal festivals during the year, make Japanese life distinctive, demanding, and enriching. The roots of ritual in Japan draw on religious thought and practice from Confucianism, Buddhism, and Shinto, the indigenous religion. This chapter will discuss these two important dimensions of ritual life in Japan, namely, the Confucian-based patterns of ritualized social interchange and the Shinto-based traditions of festival rituals. They represent a dialectic in Japanese society of rituals of social control and rituals of communal release that serve the ordering of Japanese society.

Rituals in Japan are based on both custom and necessity. Decades and even centuries of agreed-upon patterns of behavior have been embedded in Japanese consciousness, giving rise to a meticulous attention to form embodying various levels of meaning. Moreover, the realities of a crowded island country have made rituals even more necessary as a means of survival. With over 10 million people in Tokyo and 110 million in all of Japan (a space the size of California), rituals have become widely accepted guidelines for social behavior. The combination of historical habit and current necessity have allowed many ritual patterns to continue to exist and to be adapted to new circumstances in contemporary Japan. In addition, the homogeneous nature of Japanese society has reinforced traditional behavior patterns.

Thus, forces of tradition and adaptability, historical precedents and modern pragmatism have kept alive social rites and festival rituals alongside the latest fashions and trends from the West. Old and new coexist in Japan in a surprisingly uncomplicated manner. The old is not devalued or destroyed; rather, it is preserved and often nurtured alongside the new. For example, the traditional arts such as the tea ceremony and flower arrangement, as well as the various martial arts, continue to be appreciated and studied. At the same time, traditional social customs and festival rituals have not disappeared beneath the facade of modernity. This has been part of the success of the Japanese in allowing tradition and modernity to grow together. It has been an uneasy coexistence at times and one where no definitive resolution may be possible. However, this lends to Japanese society a certain dynamism, tension, and creativity.

It is true that many Japanese are beginning to echo their counterparts in Western countries as they lament the breakdown of social structures, ritual patterns, and traditional values. Moreover, as in many traditional societies, there is inevitably a negative side of ritual as a means of social control. Nonetheless, the fact that Japan continues to function on a high level of efficiency is partially a reflection of the coexistence of many traditional ritual patterns along with imported modern ways. The endurance and transmission of those rituals form an indispensable dimension of Japanese culture.

While Japanese social rituals may appear to be extremely formalistic, the spirit behind the ritual gestures is not to be ignored. At the same time, Japanese festivals may seem to be unrestrained displays of emotion, and yet their formal structures are not forgotten. This blending of form and feeling helps give Japanese ritual processes their potential effectiveness in promoting a harmonious, ordered society. The patterns of formal daily social rituals are balanced by the renewal and release provided by festivals. Perhaps no other country has preserved such an intricate web of rituals of propriety and decorum as well as such numerous and varied festivals.

While rituals are clearly present in all societies, the extent to which they constitute and support the social fabric of Japanese life accounts, in part, for the cohesiveness of the society. Combined with the homogeneity of the society, it helps to explain the difficulty faced by outsiders in becoming full participants in Japanese life. To know one's role in the scheme of things means recognizing and practicing correct ritual behavior. To offend is to break the established codes of human interaction. Moreover, in the Japanese language itself there are embedded ritual forms that must be carefully followed. The Japanese spoken by men and women is quite different, and various levels of politeness used even in daily conversations reflect the importance of hierarchical relationships in the society. Thus, Japan is a culture distinguished by innumerable ritual processes that form patterns which connect individuals and groups, weaving them into coherent units of meaning.

How to read these ritual processes becomes a key to understanding the significance of living out the patterns of membership in such a community. To see the complex ritual life of Japan is to begin to understand the symbolic language of communication, where meaning is often conveyed by gesture and where silence may be pregnant with communicative meaning. It requires a different way of seeing, one that calls our attention to body language, to group processes, to historical precedents, including the religious traditions of Japan, and to distinctions of hierarchical relationships.

THE MEANING OF *LI*

The comprehensiveness of the Chinese and Japanese character for ritual (*li*) makes it difficult to limit the discussion of its meanings. While originally associated with the idea of religious sacrifice, it later came to mean "ceremony," "ritual," "decorum," "rules of propriety," "good form," "good custom," and even natural law. Etymologically it is generally agreed that the character for *li* originally was associated with religious sacrifices. It consisted of two parts, one of which means showing or manifesting, the other represents a sacrificial vessel. *Li* implies "treading" or "following," namely, the activity of serving gods or spirits so as to obtain happiness and blessing. By the time of Confucius, it was closely associated with the activities and conduct of the nobility but gradually came to imply general rules of behavior necessary for an orderly society and government.

Li has been translated to include both rules of social propriety and ceremonial or festival usages. Ritual in this broad sense is something that gives texture and balance to individual human lives. It provides rhythm and punctuation for space and time, thus helping to harmonize emotions and validate action. In the Japanese context, as in East Asia at large, ritual is indispensable for giving orientation and meaning for individuals as part of a larger societal and cosmological order. These ideas on the function of ritual will be developed further, but let us begin by describing certain ritual patterns present in contemporary Japanese life.

RITUALS IN CONTEMPORARY JAPAN

The day of a typical family in Tokyo is organized around ritual. A businessman's morning begins with his commute from his home to his office. As he stands on the platform, waiting for the train, a white-gloved attendant blows his whistle and waves the train in with his flag. Trains are rarely late, and the gloved attendant is more formality than functional. The commuters line up on the platform in spaces designated for waiting. The train pulls into the specified space, people file out, and others move in, often directed by platform attendants. While this procedure is frequently accompanied by some aggressive shoving and pushing on the part of the passengers, without these unwritten ritual rules of commuting, chaos would rapidly ensue. Approximately 2 to 3 million people must commute to Tokyo each day on public transportation, many for two hours or more each way. This would be impossible without some generally accepted rules of decorum, along with an efficient transportation system.

In his office, the businessman meets his clients with elaborate bows, polite phrases, and an exchange of name cards before they settle down to discuss business over green tea poured by young office ladies. A perusal of one another's name cards is not merely to learn the other person's name but also to know his or her rank within another company. Then the proper level of linguistic politeness may be utilized, and correct hierarchical and gender relations are more easily established. When they conclude their discussions, a similar ritual of leave-taking will occur with carefully orchestrated bowing accompanied by standard polite phrases and responses.

In the evening after work, and yet also as a continuation of work, a period of fraternizing with one's colleagues is encouraged. Seen as part obligation and part relaxation, these evening rounds of dinner and drinking involve intricate social rituals that cement friendships and smooth over the tensions of human relations from the workplace.

Meanwhile, at home his wife has carried out her daily tasks with another appropriate set of rituals. She begins her day, like her neighbors, by hanging out the sleeping mattresses (*futons*) on the balcony of the apartment to air. She carefully fixes elaborate lunch boxes (*obento*) for her two children and sees that their uniforms and hats are in order for school inspection. As a mother deeply involved in the educational activities of her children (*kyoiku mama*), she reads through the latest list of detailed instructions that the children have brought home from school to make sure they are fully equipped for the day's activities.

Later in the morning, she sets out to the nearby department store on her bicycle. She is greeted at the entrance by two white-gloved young women in spotless uniforms with identical round white hats. They bow discreetly and welcome her in honorific-style Japanese. She is then ushered up the escalator and later taken down the elevator by similarly polite, uniformed white-gloved young women. As she selects what she needs, the saleswomen make every effort to assist her. Her purchases are wrapped with ritualistic grace and elegance.

In the afternoon before her children return home from after-school lessons (*juku*), she attends a flower arrangement (*ikebana*) lesson at a neighborhood school devoted to the practice of the art for four decades. She enjoys watching the skillful ritual movements of the teacher and is quietly attentive as he explains the subtle integration of heaven, earth, and human in the arrangement he has created. She hopes one day her daughter will likewise take flower arrangement lessons at the same school.

On her way home, she meets a neighbor who asks if she will be attending the festival at the local shrine this weekend. She replies that she will, as her son will be helping to carry one of the small portable altars (*mikoshi*), and the family is eager to watch. The neighborhood association has been preparing for the festival for weeks, and almost every family has been involved in some way. With several polite bows, they take leave of one another, exchanging hopes of seeing each other at the festival.

How did these patterns of repetitive ritualized behavior for social interaction come to play such an important part in Japanese life and in East Asia as a whole? In what way do these various rituals function? How do daily social rituals relate to seasonal rituals and local festivals? To answer these questions, we will first examine some of the principal ritual texts of East Asia to show that ritual has had a long and varied history in these Confucian-influenced societies. These will reveal the philosophical sources of East Asian ritual as linking the individual, the community, and the cosmos.

THE THEORY OF RITUAL IN THE CONFUCIAN RITUAL TEXTS

Many social rituals in Japan can be traced to some of the broader sources of East Asian ritual life, such as the Confucian *Analects*, the *Hsun Tzu*, and the *Book of Rites*. Each of these books provides a record and a philosophy of ritual behavior that has significantly influenced East Asian societies. Just as the *Dharmasastras* and the *Laws of Manu* were important records for shaping Indian society and customs, and the books of Torah served as sacred compilations of law and customs for the Jewish community, so were the ideas expounded in the *Analects*, the *Hsun Tzu*, and the *Book of Rites* regarded as vital sources of behavior and of ceremony in East Asia. The *Analects* are the selected sayings of Confucius, who lived from 551 to 479 B.C.E. It is uncertain when they were recorded, but most likely before the *Hsun Tzu* and the *Book of Rites*. Hsun Tzu himself lived during the third century B.C.E. and was the most important early Confucian after Confucius and Mencius. The *Book of Rites* was a Han Confucian compilation written down during the first century B.C.E., but it recorded much earlier practices, especially from the first part of the Chou period.

With the arrival of Confucianism in Japan in the seventh century, rituals came to play an increasingly important role in the life of the Japanese court and the nobility and, gradually, in the larger society as well. An examination of the principles and practices of ritual as found in these texts will thus give us some insight into the way social rituals have functioned in Japanese life, even down to the present. While these texts represent the written scriptures of a tradition recorded over two millennia ago, it is nonetheless striking that many aspects of the philosophy of ritual that they embody have endured to the present century in East Asia.

The *Analects* of Confucius

One of the most important goals of Confucius was to restore the ritual system of the early Chou dynasty (1115–722 B.C.E.), which to him represented an ideal social order. He saw Chou society as being held together by all-embracing rituals of kinship relations and by ritual sacrifices of the nobility. Confucius's overriding ideal was to establish harmony or concord (*ho* in Chinese and *wa* in Japanese) through the practice of ritual. Indeed, for Confucius, ritual was an alternative to law and had broad implications for government, for society, for families, and for individuals. Confucius felt people should be led by ritual practices as a means of government rather than by strictly imposed laws, as was later advocated by the Legalists. ''Lead the people by governmental orders and govern them by punishment, they will avoid wrong-doing but have no sense of shame. Lead the people by virtue and govern them by ritual, they will have a sense of shame and, moreover, will become upright'' (*Analects* 2.3). In other words, for Confucius, internal restraints on behavior were more effective than external constraints.

Thus, through reverent observance of decorum, correct human relations could be fostered. If individuals cultivated themselves through ritual, they would be in right relation with other human beings, beginning with their family and extending out into the larger society. Without appropriate rituals a person would not be able to achieve satisfactory balance. ''Courtesy not bounded by the prescriptions of ritual becomes tiresome. Caution not bounded by the prescriptions of ritual becomes timidity, daring becomes turbulence, inflexibility becomes harshness'' (*Analects* 8.2).

Moreover, these rituals were intended not simply as empty formalities but as actions carried out with reverence, respect, and love. Thus, the component of feeling was as important to correct ritual behavior as the form itself. Ultimately, for Confucius the practice of self-cultivation and proper ritual conduct was the basis for an empathetic identity with all human beings. ''If a gentleman attends to business and does not idle away his time, if he behaves with courtesy to others and observes the rules of ritual, then all within the Four Seas are his brothers'' (*Analects* 12.5).

Hsun Tzu

For Hsun Tzu (born ca. 312 B.C.E.) ritual is also central to his program of education, learning, and self-cultivation. Rituals are a means of establishing patterns of order that govern life and society. They help to clarify distinctions and encourage reciprocity so that human relations can be the basis of a humane society and benevolent government. Hsun Tzu felt that ritual had three bases:

"Heaven and Earth are the basis of life, the ancestors are the basis of the family, and rulers and teachers are the basis of order" (*Hsun Tzu* 1963: 91).

The personal and the cosmic dimensions of ritual are especially emphasized by Hsun Tzu. On a personal level, rituals serve to help regulate and express human feelings. They are a means to cultivate and preserve emotions, not to suppress them. Hsun Tzu recognizes that desires are a natural part of human life and rituals are a means by which desires and things can be mutually supported and regulated. Thus, rather than let desires or feelings run rampant, through ritual they can be satisfied and elevated. In short, by means of rituals people's "likes and dislikes are regulated and their joys and hates made appropriate" (94). This channeling of emotions through ritual is a key element in cultivating and educating oneself.

In a broader sense, for Hsun Tzu rituals also serve to bind the human to the cosmos. They reflect the larger rhythms of nature and of the seasons and ultimately form a harmonious link between heaven and earth. The cosmic implications of ritual are evident in the following passage: "Through rites Heaven and Earth join in harmony, the sun and moon shine, the four seasons proceed in order, the stars and constellations march, the rivers flow, and all things flourish" (94). This sense of correspondences and relational resonance between the microcosm and the macrocosm is explored more fully by the Han Confucians in their study of rituals.

Book of Rites

The *Book of Rites* (*Li Chi*) was reportedly compiled in the first century B.C.E. by the Han Confucians. It represents a synthesis of earlier practices and customs and derives some of its ideas on ritual from the *Hsun Tzu*. It was essentially one of the three books on ritual that made up the last of the five Confucian Classics. The other ritual texts were the *Book of Etiquette and Ceremonials* (*I Li*) and the *Rites of Chou* (*Chou Li*).

The *Book of Rites* is a compilation of discussions on the philosophical basis and functional aspects of ritual. It illustrates these discussions with numerous examples of ritual and ceremonial customs. It also provides exemplary models of the actions of earlier sages. It is a rich combination of theory and practice that has had a significant influence in East Asian societies for nearly two millennia. Its importance as a historical record of the past and as a manual for use over many centuries cannot be underestimated.

One of the most celebrated sections of the *Book of Rites* is the "Li Yun" chapter, which opens with a description of the Great Commonality (*Ta t'ung*) that once prevailed in human society. The ideal time of primordial harmony and unity became a touchstone for many later Confucians, including the Maoists in twentieth-century China.

To maintain something of this ideal of order and harmony, it was necessary to observe ritual rules of propriety. In this same "Li Yun" chapter, Confucius

observes, "Those rules [of propriety] are rooted in heaven, have their correspondences in earth, and are applicable to spiritual beings. They extend to funeral rites, sacrifices, archery, chariot-driving, capping, marriage, audiences and
friendly missions. Thus the sages made known these rules, and it became possible for the kingdom, with its states and clans, to reach its correct condition"
(*Book of Rites* 1967: 367). There follows a detailed description of the origin,
development, and intention of rituals. The *Book of Rites* reflects the attempt at
synthesis that distinguished Han Confucianism. Han Confucianism and the Chinese ritual texts were imported into Korea and Japan during the fourth and fifth
centuries. These became the basis for the interconnected ritualization of the
social, political, and cosmological orders in East Asia. Because of its significance in creating the philosophical and practical foundation of ritual life in East
Asia, a brief summary of Han Confucianism follows.

THE HAN CONFUCIAN SYNTHESIS: A RITUALLY
ORDERED COSMOS AND SOCIETY

The Han (202 B.C.E.–C.E. 220) was a period of tremendous synthesis when
Confucian orthodoxy was being established and the unification of the state that
had been achieved earlier by the Legalists was being given a metaphysical basis.
The Han Confucians were the heir to the Legalists' institutions and bureaucracy,
and some scholars have felt they were likewise heirs to their stricter methods
of legal coercion and punishment.

However, it would appear that the conflict faced by the Confucians of this
period was one of combining Legalist methods of government by law and pun-
ishments with Confucian principles of government by moral exhortation and
rituals. In so doing, Confucianism itself was changed, and many Confucians
were caught in the dilemma of participating in a government that in its severity
seemed contrary to the more humane ideals of their tradition. Nonetheless, it
was perhaps this combination of realism and idealism that made Han thought
so distinctive and established Confucianism as the state orthodoxy for future
generations.

This might be best seen in the ideas of Tung Chung Shu (179?–104? B.C.E.)
who attempted to synthesize the cosmic, political, social, and personal orders in
his commentary *The Deep Significance of the Spring and Autumn Annals*. For
Tung, it was the emperor who was the axis mundi of heaven, earth, and the
human. This is seen even in the Chinese character for emperor, he points out.
Tung reconstituted the kingly way articulated by Mencius and the earlier Confucians. He expanded it to include the efficacy of moral virtue and rituals along
with laws and institutions. Power, however, was seen not as autocratic or un-
limited but as a shared responsibility in relationship to the whole cosmic order.

Tung provided a cosmological scheme in which to set his political theories
and humanistic philosophy. These ideas reflect an understanding of the cosmos
itself as participating in macrocosmic seasonal rituals that are mirrored in the

human order. This required an elaborate system of theoretical correspondences and practical rituals between the macrocosm and microcosm. For example, he used the five elements and the principles of yin and yang—the paired feminine and masculine principles of ordered change—to describe the ritual operations of the natural order as well as the human order. Thus, he saw corresponding relationships between the elements, the seasons, and the directions that helped to regulate and harmonize human ritual behaviors.

These corresponding relationships are influenced by the operation of the yin and yang, which cause the transformation and regeneration of things in their waxing and waning. Cosmic changes have their counterpart in the political and human orders. In the political sphere, for example, the king must regulate his emotions according to the seasons and must cooperate with the pattern of changes that can be discerned in the cosmos. Likewise, he must encourage his people to develop virtue, to practice ritual, and to cooperate with the ways of heaven and earth.

The creative participation of human beings with heaven and earth extends especially to the process of self-cultivation. By rituals and music, a person cultivates his or her inner self and regulates his or her desires. In so doing, one establishes a relational resonance with other humans and with the natural world as a whole.

Tung saw the yin and yang of the exterior order as having corresponding parts in human beings themselves. The yang was human nature, while the yin was human desires. The yang must be cultivated, while the yin must be regulated and restrained. Thus, he combined a recognition of the rational and intuitive nature of human beings as being potentially good, providing these dimensions were cultivated, disciplined, and brought to full development through rituals.

For Tung and the Han Confucians, ritual was a means of educating individuals to live harmoniously without external, regulating authorities. In this sense, it was seen as a vehicle of individual self-cultivation as well as social regulation. It helped establish appropriate distinctions in the society and relieved the burden of autonomous choice for every action by providing well-defined patterns of appropriate behavior. Even more, rituals were the aesthetic expression of the moral nature of human beings and as such were the beautifiers of human life by fostering refinement and decorum. Tung and the other Han Confucians used the ritual texts to establish a basis for fostering this process of self-cultivation. For them it was rituals, not law, that could regulate the society and encourage a harmonious social and political balance.

Tung Chung Shu, in particular, provided a synthesis for the Han Confucians in which the macrocosm and microcosm could be seen in active relationship and correspondence. This was not simply a political view; it was also an insight into the power of relational resonance between humans and the cosmos. This capacity for relational reciprocity through ritual practices distinguished human beings and became the source of energy for one's creative participation in the Confucian triad of heaven, earth, and the human order. This model became an important cosmological basis of ritual relations for individuals and groups in East Asia.

CONFUCIAN RITUAL AS THE BASIS OF EAST ASIAN SOCIETIES

Confucian rituals in East Asia reflect an underlying assumption that the structure of reality has a complex cosmological order. Thus, as the Han Confucians described it, the microcosm and the macrocosm were inextricably linked to one another by a series of correspondences. In their ultimate sense, rituals are a means for humans to relate to the very sources of their existence, namely, heaven and earth, as well as their ancestors and families. Rituals are a vehicle for participation in this network of correspondences that ultimately connect the human to the cosmos. Thus, the practice of ritual is seen as a means of establishing harmony not merely between humans themselves but also between the seen and unseen worlds, between humans and ancestors, and between the human order and the cosmic order. Indeed, as the *Book of Rites* tells us, "Rituals constitute the great methods by which we nourish the living, bury the dead and serve the spirits of the departed. They supply the channels by which we can apprehend the ways of Heaven and act as the feelings of human beings require" (*Book of Rites* 1967:388–389).

To effectively join the human and cosmic orders, a constant spirit of reverence is required for the proper performance of ritual. Indeed, in *Mencius* it is said, "The feeling of respect and reverence is what we call ritual" (*Mencius* VI A: 6). Moreover, the opening sentence of the *Book of Rites* (1967) states: "The summary of the Rules of Propriety says, 'Always and in everything let there be reverence' " and " 'a superior person is said to convey the feeling of reverence and respect' " (II. 64; II. 329).

Thus, in East Asian society there are significant ritual patterns of social interaction that provide the social glue or cohesion of these societies. The case of Japan is especially interesting to observe, for the strength of that society is in part due to the unusual blend of traditional social ritual patterns along with highly sophisticated modern industry and technology. Whether the social glue of ritual exchanges will continue to endure in the face of increasing materialization and Westernization remains to be seen.

SHINTO: RITUALS AND FESTIVALS

There are, however, in Japan also means of ritual release from intricate social rituals. These are the Shinto rituals and festivals that occur throughout Japan in local regions, both in cities and in the countryside. Perhaps nowhere in Asia are as many festivals preserved and performed by local communities as in Japan. These provide a means of communal identity and local celebration that is both structured and spontaneous. These festivals combine ancient ritual patterns with free-form release in eating, drinking, laughter, song, and dance. As a counterpoint to the formalized Confucian rituals of daily interaction, Shinto festivals are a colorful means for a display of emotions and a cathartic vehicle for renewing a community. We will examine this phenomenon using the example of Japan's largest festival, Gion Matsuri, held in Kyoto each July for over 1,000 years. With its roots in Shinto, this festival has become a paradigm of other local festivals. A few comments on Shinto and Shinto festivals are in order.

Shinto is a religion without a specific founder and without a body of dogma. It is the indigenous religion of Japan, and the name *Shinto* means "the way of the gods" (*kami*). This was in contrast to Buddhism or the way of the Buddha, which came to Japan in the sixth century. Shinto's origins are closely connected with mythology and with the earliest chronicles of Japanese history, the *Kojiki* and the *Nihongi*. *Kami* means god, but cannot be exactly translated in the Western sense of personal deity removed from nature. Praying to the *kami* is thought to bring about blessings for the faithful and protection from harm. A festival is the principal form of ritual worship for the community—thus, the relative frequency of festivals in Japan. The same general goals are sought in a festival as in individual prayer, namely, blessing and protection. More specific goals depend on the origin of the celebration.

In terms of individual or communal practices the four essential elements of Shinto ritual worship are purification (*harai*), offering (*shinsen*), prayer (*norito*), and a symbolic feast (*naorai*). These elements of ritual can be seen in the simple gestures of an individual before a shrine. The practitioner symbolically cleanses his mouth and fingers with water and then makes a small offering or donation to the shrine. Then one claps one's hands before the shrine entrance to summon the *kami* and to make one's prayer heard. In a larger ceremony or festival, purification is much more elaborate. It includes fasting, ritual bathing, abstinence from sex, and thorough cleansing of the shrine and its premises. Similarly, in addition to money, offerings consist of food and drink and various other objects of value to the participant. Frequently, sprigs of the sacred sakaki tree are placed before the temple. Prayers read by the priest take on a variety of forms, namely, praise, petition, or thanksgiving to the *kami*. Finally, in a group ceremony or festival, the act of worship is completed by a sacred feast in which the participants are thought to eat together with the *kami*.

Perhaps the most colorful ritual events of Shintoism are the numerous local and seasonal festivals (*matsuri*). The festivals are elaborate events that usually involve the whole community. They often celebrate a historic event as, for example, the Gion Matsuri in Kyoto, which commemorates a similar procession held in C.E. 876 to ward off a plague. This festival originated as a redressive ritual action against any potential disease. In contemporary Japan, it is an important rite of purification and renewal for the community.

Gion Matsuri arose in a time when a serious breach had occurred in the normal patterns of things. In 869 C.E. a plague in Kyoto, the capital city, threatened to destroy the people and the land. Some immediate redressive action was requested by Emperor Seiwa. He sent a messenger to convey this to Urabe, the head priest of Yasaka Shrine in Kyoto. Urabe responded to the emperor's request by setting up sixty-six halberds on platforms throughout the city. The number sixty-six corresponded to the number of provinces in Japan at the time. The halberd was called a *hoko* in Japanese ("ho" meaning strength, and "ko" meaning something made of wood). This swordlike structure was about twenty-five feet in height and was intended to drive off the evil spirits creating the plague. Today the *hoko* are still being reproduced in the huge halberd floats used in the procession.

After establishing the halberds throughout the city, Urabe led a group of the faithful from the shrine to the Imperial garden. As they proceeded through the city, they played flutes and drums, shouting to scare off the evil spirits. In the Imperial garden a purification ceremony was held, and the gods were called upon to intervene. The plague did indeed abate a short time afterward, and in thanksgiving the emperor decreed that the ceremony should be repeated annually. Thus, the festival became a health-insuring rite, celebrated for over 1,000 years.

The major symbols of most Shinto festivals are the *mikoshi* (sacred palanquin) and the *dashi* (floats). The *mikoshi* symbolically houses the *kami* and is usually kept in a special place within the shrine. During the festival it is taken out of the shrine and processed among the people. It is allowed to remain in a temporary shrine (*Otabisho*) in the middle of a community or city. It is then returned to its original dwelling place in the shrine. To mark this procession on a larger, more secular scale, there is usually a float procession through the city streets. Colorfully decorated floats parade through the city as a sign of welcome to the *kami* who will dwell in the midst of the people during the festival.

The principal symbolic behavior of Gion Matsuri follows this pattern of purification and procession. It consists of a purification and prayer service held at Yasaka Shrine, the site of the original festival. On July 10, the *mikoshi* are ritually purified in the nearby Kamo river. The following week (July 17) a huge float procession welcomes the *kami* and the *mikoshi* into the city. Later that same afternoon, the *mikoshi* is carried from the shrine to its place of temporary sojourn. It remains there for a week, after which it is returned to the shrine (July 24). This is also preceded by a float procession but on a smaller scale than that on July 17. Finally, on July 28, the *mikoshi* is once again symbolically purified in the river and returned to its place within the shrine.

The ritual, then, involves a threefold pattern of separation, transition, and reincorporation. In the case of Gion Matsuri, a breach occurred at one point in history, namely, at the time of the plague. In subsequent years, to prevent a recurrence of such a disaster, a ritual separation takes place. This involves the preliminary or pretransition ceremonies of purification for the shrine, the *mikoshi*, and the priests. The shrine is thoroughly cleansed, while the *mikoshi* is ritually cleaned. It is carried to the Kamo river, where the head priest, using a special branch of a sakaki tree, sprinkles water over it. After saying some prayers, it is carried back to the shrine to await the important processional day. The priests themselves undergo strict fasting and cleansing rituals before the festival. These vary in length, depending on the festival.

The rite of transition comes when the *mikoshi* remains for a week in its place of sojourn (*Otabisho*). During this time the principal part of the festival takes place. This is a large float procession throughout the main streets of Kyoto. Huge wooden floats with colorful tapestries, figures, and decorations are carried or pulled through the streets. The floats parallel, on a larger scale, the *mikoshi* procession. They mark the beginning and end of the transition period—welcoming the *kami* into the midst of the people and ushering the *kami* back to the shrine.

In fact, the origin of the floats has a similar function to that of the *mikoshi*. In ancient harvest rituals, two huge ''marking mountains'' (*shimeshi-no-yama*) were made from mounds of earth. This was to guide the *kami* to a safe place so he would not alight on an unholy spot. The mounds were decorated with banners for the sun and moon. Later the decorations became more elaborate and lost some of their specifically religious significance.

Today the floats used in Gion Matsuri symbolize these original marking mountains. The *kami* can ride safely on them. Thus, the night before the procession, large offerings of food and sake are placed before the floats for the *kami*. The morning of the festival, a sacred festoon (*shimenawa*) stretched across the main street is cut. This signifies that the floats are ready to receive the *kami*. The floats can now pass from the world of the profane to that of the sacred.

This entrance of the floats into the world of the sacred is the most significant feature of the transitional period of the festival. The Shinto priests purify the floats as a sign of this. Humans now have more direct recourse to the *kami* who dwells in their midst. It is an auspicious time for interaction between the two distinct forces of gods and humans. When the *mikoshi* is returned to the shrine, a reintegration occurs. The community has been regenerated and purified as a result of the direct contact with the sacred.

This, then, is Japan's largest festival—one that reenacts the rites of separation, transition, and incorporation. Although the original impetus of the festival (the plague) is no longer an actual threat, the symbolic potential of pollution remains in the community. Consequently, the community must purify itself, rid itself of evil spirits, and regenerate itself once again. The effectiveness of this symbolic ritual is seen in the fact that Gion festivals have spread to various parts of the country. Although smaller in scale, they retain the same features of the ritual process. The ritual objects of the *mikoshi* and the floats remain prominent in all these festivals, as does the symbolic action of carrying them through the streets.

Another example of a communal festival ritual is the Hana Matsuri in Shimoawashiro, a rural area of northern Aichi Prefecture. This celebration consists of a three-day festival of religious rites and *kagura* dances that dates back to the Muromachi period (1392–1573). It was originally performed at harvest time but is now held during the New Year holidays when people return home. Until

1980 it was conducted in private homes in the village on a rotating basis but, due to the expense and time for preparation, it is now held in the village hall.

Like so many festivals in Japan, the Hana Matsuri brings together both this-worldly and other-worldly concerns. It is a ritual designed to ensure the perpetuation of the life of the ancestors while also assisting to maintain the health of crops and of villagers. The festival is thus marked by rituals of purification and of petition. There is a desire to purify the ancestors and their living descendants in the village. It is believed that through this ritual contact with the ancestors the health and prosperity of the village are fostered.

Outside the village hall, a wooden shrine is set up to receive the local *kami*. This temporary shrine is the focus of the opening ceremonies of the festival when the *kami* are carried here in a *mikoshi* from the local Shinto shrine. The *kami* are then moved inside to the *kanza* (*kami* seat) near the dance floor, and when the festival is over, they are carried back in the *mikoshi* to the local shrine. This procedure is central to all Shinto festivals where the *kami* are processed from the sacred vicinity of the shrine into the secular community to bring blessings to the people.

The main activities of the festival occur on the concrete dance floor inside the village hall. In the center is a specially constructed clay stove shaped like a mountain with a flat top. Underneath is a fire heating a pot of boiling water. The fire, known as *saito*, is intended to purify the *matsuri* area and to drive away evil spirits. The water is used in one of the most important rituals of the entire festival, namely, the *Yudate*, or boiling water purification. In this opening ritual the dance floor is purified by elaborate prayers, by invocations to the *kami*, and by sprinkling water in the four directions.

Before the festival actually begins, a communal meal is held. Afterward, the ritual instruments are refurbished, and paper cuttings and other decorations are prepared. A waterfall ceremony (*Takibarai*) is held in which the participants purify themselves. Pure water is also collected for the cauldron that is to be placed on the stove at the center of the dance floor. Sacred paper cuttings (*gohei*) are hung at selected mountain and field sites, thereby inviting blessings from the local gods and protection from evil spirits.

Before the first public ceremony, the participants (singers, dancers, and assistants) are served a large meal to fortify them for the twenty-four-hour performance. The chief Shinto priest (*daiyu*) performs various ritual invocations to welcome the gods and to purify the room with rice, water, and salt.

These solemn rituals of purification and invocation are in marked contrast to the series of lively dances that follow throughout the night, culminating in the appearance of the masked dancers in the early morning hours. The dancers are encouraged by an audience of about one hundred people who are enjoying periodic sips of sake (rice wine). These dances are begun by a single dancer who circles the central clay stove with ecstatic whirls and leaps. The tempo is taken up by the successive dancers, accompanied by drum, flute, and bells. Occasionally, the spectators join in the dancing, adding to the raucous, festive atmosphere.

Around 11 P.M. a charming series of dances is performed by young children assisted by adults. While the children dance, the audience is served stew and sake. More dances follow late into the night with the dancers using fans, bells, and ritual instruments.

Finally, about 4:30 A.M., several masked dancers appear. They are long-nosed *oni* (devils) dressed in red with a white skull cap under their masks. They carry axelike halberds which they wave as they leap about the cauldron to the sound of the flute and drums. There soon appears a fourth figure also dressed in red and with a huge reddish-brown mask. This is the *Yamawari oni*, the devil of the mountain. He, along with the other *oni*, performs a dramatic dance of symbolically cutting the mountain (the clay stove) to release the purifying and transforming boiling water within. Another dance follows with spectacular sword manipulation by several young boys.

In the early morning hours, while it is still dark, the most respected and feared masked figure appears, the *Sakaki oni*. Like the *Yamawari oni*, he is led in the dance movements by a lighted candle because his mask is so huge. Again, he symbolically releases the purifying water in the cauldron in his dance. One of the male shrine attendants (*negi*) approaches the *Sakaki oni* with a sacred sakaki branch and strikes him on the shoulder. This sets in motion a dialogue (*mondo*) while holding the sakaki branch between them. Finally, the shrine attendant throws the sakaki branch toward the *kami* altar. At the same time, the *Sakaki oni* stomps twice in unison with the drums, symbolizing the driving out of evil forces in the earth that might threaten the local crops.

As the first signs of dawn become evident, a group of masked clowns appear who chase people with paddles covered with bean paste and sticky rice. To catch someone and smear them with the paste or rice is believed to ensure blessings for abundant food. Two more masked dances follow, one by a female shrine attendant (*miko*) and one by a male shrine attendant (*Hino negi*). Near noontime the celebrated mask of an old wise man (*Okina*) appears. This is an auspicious figure believed to bring good fortune to the community.

Finally, a *Yubashi* dance takes place that culminates in purification by the hot, boiling water. The dancers perform an energetic dance for nearly an hour. Then suddenly, without warning, they dip their straw bundles into the steaming cauldron and throw hot water randomly on the audience. This is clearly a numinous moment, as the water is both attractive as a blessing and fearful due to its heat.

One more *oni* appears who strikes open the large paper decoration over the dance floor. Inside there are numerous symbols of prosperity that are showered down on the participants. The last dance is that of a lion (*shishi*) manipulated by two people, one for the mask and one for the cloth body. The lion takes a straw bundle to the cauldron and again distributes the hot waters of blessing over the crowd, much to their delight and amusement.

While this signals the end of the public dances, several religious rituals are performed to complete the festival. The most significant of these is the sending of the *kami* back to the local shrine. This marks the end of an elaborate three-day festival that involves both purification and petition. There appears to be a desire on the part of the villagers to purify and be purified by the *oni*, whom some interpreters suggest may represent the ancestors. At the same time, there is a consciousness of the need to pray for a good harvest—for the health of crops and that of the crop caretakers. The intricacy and care with which this ritual has been maintained and performed over the centuries constitutes another indication of the remarkable vitality of communal rituals in Japan. Just as Gion Matsuri represents one of the oldest urban festivals in Japan, so Hana Matsuri represents one of Japan's most ancient rural festivals.

CONCLUSION

Each of these festivals of purification and regeneration is an important example of communal rites of renewal that are both colorful and cathartic amidst the more customary Confucian-based rituals of daily social exchange. The balance of these two—daily social rituals and communal festival rituals—provides both orderly pattern and celebratory release, thus helping to reinforce values of harmony and consensus. Whether or not this balance will continue to function in Japan in the face of increasing modernization is an open-ended question that merits further study.

REFERENCES

Akiyama, Aisaburo. 1929. *The Gion Festival.* Kyoto: Miyakoa Hotel.
Analects (Lun yu). 1979. Translated by D. C. Lau. New York: Penguin.
Bauer, Helen, and Sherwin Carlquist. 1965. *Japanese Festivals.* Garden City, NY: Doubleday and Co.
Befu, Harumi. 1964. "Ritual Kinship in Japan: Its Variability and Resiliency." *Sociologus* 14 (2): 150–168.
Bell, Catherine. 1988. "Ritualization of Texts and Textualization of Ritual in the Codification of Taoist Liturgy." *History of Religions* 27 (4): 366–392.
Benedict, Ruth. 1946. *The Chrysanthemum and the Sword: Patterns of Japanese Culture.* Boston: Houghton Mifflin Company.
Book of Rites. 1967. Vol. 1. Translated by James Legge. New Hyde Park, NY: University Books.
Chapin, Helen. 1934. "The Gion Shrine and the Gion Festival." *Journal of the American Oriental Society* 54: 282–289.
Earhart, H. Bryon. 1970. *A Religious Study of the Mount Haguro Sect of Shugendo.* Tokyo: Sophia University Press.
Ellwood, R. S. 1968. "Harvest and Renewal at the Grand Shrine of Ise." *Numen* 15: 165–190.
Ellwood, Robert S. 1973. *The Feast of Kingship: Accession Ceremonies in Ancient Japan.* Tokyo: Sophia University Press.

Epstein, Sam, and Beryl Epstein. 1974. *A Year of Japanese Festivals*. Champaign, IL: Garrad Publishing Co.

Grim, John, and Mary Evelyn Tucker. 1982. "Viewing the Hana Matsuri at Shimoa-washiro, Aichi Prefecture." *Asian Folklore Studies* 41: 2.

Haga, Hideo. 1970. *Japanese Folk Festivals Illustrated*. Translated by Fanny Hagin Mayer. Tokyo: Miura Printing Co.

Haga, Hideo. 1977. *Hanamatsuri*. Tokyo: Kokusho Kankokai.

Haga, Hideo, and G. Warner. 1968. *Japanese Festivals*. Osaka: Hoikusha Publishing Co.

Herbert, Jean. 1967. *Shinto: At the Fountainhead of Japan*. London: George Allen and Unwin Ltd.

Holtom, Daniel C. 1940–1941. "The Meaning of Kami." *Monumenta Nipponica* 3: 27, 32–35; 4: 25–68.

Holtom, Daniel C. 1972. *The Japanese Enthronement Ceremonies: With an Account of the Imperial Regalia*. Tokyo: Sophia University.

Hori, Ichiro. 1975. "Shamanism in Japan." *Japanese Journal of Religious Studies* 2: 231–287.

Hsun Tzu. 1963. Translated by Burton Watson. New York: Columbia University Press.

Kobayashi, Kazushige. 1981. "On the Meaning of Masked Dances in Kagura." *Asian Folklore Studies* 40 (1): 1–22.

Ludwing, Theodore M. 1974. "The Way of Tea: A Religio-Aesthetic Mode of Life." *History of Religions* 14 (1): 28–50.

McMullen, David. 1987. "Bureaucrats and Cosmology: The Ritual Code of T'ang China." *Rituals of Royalty: Power and Ceremonial in Traditional Societies*. David Cannadine and Simon Price, editors. Cambridge: Cambridge University Press.

Ono, Montonori. 1962. *Shinto: The Kami Way*. Rutland, VT: Charles E. Tuttle Co.

Sakurai, Tokutaro. 1970. *Japanese Festivals: Annual Rites and Observances*. Entire issue of *Understanding Japan*. Tokyo: International Society for Educational Information Inc.

Satow, Sir Ernest, and Karl Florenz. 1927. "Ancient Japanese Rituals." *Transactions of the Asiatic Society*. Reprints, Vol. 2.

Swanson, Paul L. 1964. "Shugendo and the Yoshino-Kumano Pilgrimage." *Monumenta Nipponica* 36: 55–79.

Tung, Chung-shu. 1966. *Tung-tze wen chi*. Tai-Pei: I wen, min Kuo. 55.

Watson, James L., and Evelyn S. Rawski, editors. 1988. *Death Ritual in Late Imperial and Early Modern China*. Berkeley: University of California Press.

Wechsler, Howard J. 1985. *Offerings of Jade and Silk: Ritual and Symbol in the Legitimation of the T'ang Dynasty*. New Haven: Yale University Press.

Wolf, Arthur P., editor. 1974. *Religion and Ritual in Chinese Society*. Stanford: Stanford University Press.

Yanagita, Kunio. 1988. *About Our Ancestors*. Translated by Fanny Hagin Mayer and Ishiwara Yasuyo. New York: Greenwood Press.

9

Rituals among Native North Americans

John A. Grim

In the beginning we were one people. Then we divided into Summer people and Winter people; in the end we came together again as we are today.[1]

When Tewa Pueblo elders recite this proverb, they summarize their whole ritual system as well as the lifeway in which their ritual calendar is elaborated. They recapitulate their mythic reflection upon themselves and describe deep-seated movements from emergent unity, through the diversity they have experienced as a people, to the participatory presence they create by means of ritual life. Ritual happenings, oral narratives, and seasonal subsistence activities intertwine in Native North American religious paths through life, or lifeways, themselves mirroring the tensions and struggles that constitute these diverse peoples in all their complexity, contemporaneity, and vitality.

The traditional thought of this Pueblo elder serves to remind us also of the limitations of a literate text, such as this, in penetrating the subjective and semantic meanings of rituals in an oral tradition. Native North American rituals spring from oral narrative traditions that are subtly amplified and legitimated by the rituals themselves. That is, rituals generate structured systems of thought and affirm hierarchies that fit the real world of experience to categories of meaningful order. By fixing the structure and taxonomies of order, rituals serve to legitimize traditions and to privilege the power generated in the rituals themselves.

This chapter will explore this relationship between ritual and tradition among particular ethnic nations often called "Native Americans," "American Indians,'' and "First Peoples." However, in exploring a range of different rituals among Native North American peoples, it should be underscored that much of this analysis constitutes limited descriptions of ritual situations, strategies, symbols, and processes. The vital character of rituals as happenings often helps the participants to transcend the very ritual structures that guide them and, thus, enables practitioners to "play" in the liminal fields of a deeper sense of community.[2] Situating the rituals discussed in their cultural context helps us to understand the trajectories of function and purpose that dynamize these ceremonial activities. But interpretive trajectories themselves constitute a strategy in the secularized "place" of articles that cannot communicate the experiential or meaning of the rituals discussed for the actual participants.

AN OVERVIEW OF THE DISCUSSION

The intention of this chapter is to explore organized ritual activity as well as more spontaneous ritualization among Native North Americans.[3] Using investigative themes drawn from studies of ritual, this work will draw attention to inherent features of rituals such as display and performance as well as intentional acts by individuals and communities to effect transformation or to establish order through ritual. This overview also seeks to illuminate the cultural particularity of specific Native North American rituals as well as to situate that diversity in selected ritual histories, calendars, and organizations of indigenous communities. No attempt at an exhaustive survey is undertaken here; rather, selective rituals are discussed in order to introduce a general reader to the importance of ritual among Native North American peoples. The geographical boundary of North America has been set by this writer as an aid in defining the scope of the discussion and should not be taken as a cultural boundary across which influences or ritual practices did not cross.

Indeed, the importance of Mesoamerican rituals and mythic narratives in early Pueblo settlements and Mississippi riverine mound cultures from the first millennium before the current era is becoming clearer with increased archaeological study. Thus, the Pueblo communities of the North American Southwest can correctly be shown to relate to Mesoamerican urban cultures in ritual structures, mythic themes, agricultural cycles, and social organizations. Similar relations can be drawn from the emerging archaeological information and limited ethnographical data on the Mississippian Mound cultures that were intact into the eighteenth and early nineteenth centuries of the current era. Funerary and tobacco ceremonialism evident in these early sites continues to be found in the last phase of monumental mound developments at Cahokia near St. Louis, Missouri. Sites, such as those associated with the Natchez peoples, are dated into the late Woodland period of the sixteenth century and overlap with documented encounters between southeastern Native North American peoples and Mediterranean-Atlantic cultures.[4] The questions engendered by these historical diffusions are not taken up in this chapter, but they are acknowledged as fundamental issues in any developed investigation of Native North American ritual.

In order to explore a set of rituals, the opening discussion focuses on one upper Plains people, the Apsaaloke/Crow of contemporary Montana. This opening project emphasizes four themes that are proposed as strategies for understanding rituals in diverse Native North American settings. First, ritual practices in small-scale, noncapitalist societies need to be understood in terms of the whole religious system, or lifeway. Second, there are meaningful relationships between rituals too often presented as separate entities. Third, familiar and structured rituals often obscure the significant role of spontaneous ritualization. Finally, rituals respond to changing historical conditions. The Apsaaloke rituals discussed below are the sweat lodge, tobacco ceremonialism, the vision quest, and the *Ashkisshe*, or, as it is more popularly known, the Sun Dance.

Following the opening discussion, two sections will explore different questions in the study of rituals. In the first, the relation of ritual systems to their particular cultural logic, or worldview, will be briefly discussed. Ritual examples will be drawn from the Anishinabe/Ojibway ritual and society of *Midewiwin*; the Tsistsistas/Cheyenne ritual of *Massaum*; the Okonogan/Kettle Falls world renewal ceremony known in English as the Winter Dance; and the Aashiwi/ Zuni "Coming of the Kachina" ceremony during which the *kokko*, or kachinas, return to the pueblo.

The second section will investigate the manner in which rituals relate to power in promoting social control and social change. These issues will be considered in terms of Plains Lakota adaptation of the nineteenth-century Ghost Dance and in light of the southern Kiowa people's adaptation of the Peyote Way.

INTERRELATEDNESS OF RITUALS IN THE APSAALOKE/ CROW CONTEXT

Once, after an Apsaaloke ceremony, the following teasing remarks were made. They sum up this people's view of the interrelationship of distinct rituals, the expectation that changes are always occurring, and that life itself is a spiritual path. An Apsaaloke elder mused about a particularly industrious and ritually active bachelor who had survived a terrific explosion at the plant where he worked, though he had been knocked unconscious and had momentarily "died." The elder commented that this man had from an early age endured the grueling heat of the sweat lodge, he had "died" of fasting when he "went up on the hill" to undergo his vision quest, he had sponsored an *Ashkisshe*/Sun Dance, and he had even died and lived again after the accident in the plant. "Now," the elder continued, "all he has to do is get married!" The force of the joking plays on the ritually evoked experiences of life and death as compared with marriage, which is not a major occasion for ritual among the Apsaaloke. Joking itself, however, is a ritualization that suddenly reverses thought so as to reflect upon a deeper interpretation of such a life event as marriage.[5] The joking de-

scribed here suggests that the major rituals of the Apsaaloke lifeway are both
social-performative strategies for ordering and transforming life as well as
self-reflective disciplines whereby one undergoes "death" in order to live more
deeply.

Among the Apsaaloke the sweat lodge ritual (*awusua*) is considered one of
the oldest ceremonials, originating in the primal time of the mythic beings.[6] The
Apsaaloke practice this ritual using a small, domed lodge built from saplings,
usually of willow, bent over and tied to one another. The lodge is covered now
with canvas and blankets rather than the buffalo robes of earlier days. The
number of saplings, the construction of the lodge itself, and the rite of pouring
water over the heated stones must all be transferred to a person by one who has
received these privileges. The ones who sweat will take off their clothes before
entering the lodge, signaling their humility, wholeness, and original condition
before the Creator. Men always sweat together and generally prepare the lodge
after their ceremony for the women to sweat later.

The participants enter the lodge in the "clockwise" direction of the sun, being
careful not to cross the path that the heated stones will travel. The stones will
be carried from the fire, some twenty or so feet east of the sweat lodge entrance,
to a pit in the sweat lodge. If it is a social sweat, the pit for holding the heated
stones will be off to the right of the eastern facing entrance. If the sweat is for
a healing ritual, the pit will be in the center. An assistant outside the lodge, or
a participant entering last, will carry first a single stone heated in the fire. Guiding the stone toward the pit, the leader addresses the stone and prays for the
desires of the group assembled. After this the practitioners say "*Aho.*" This is
a broad statement of thanks to the collective mysterious presence of creation,
or "First Maker."

The next three stones are treated with respect as evoking the four places of
orientation, the four guardians who make present the fullness of power (*baxpe*),
the four seasons, and the four components of the world: fire, rock, water, and
air.[7] Following these first four stones, as many stones as the leader desires for
the sweat, in concert with the practitioners, will be placed in the pit. The leader
might then place "bear root," cedar, or an herb that he or she has spiritual
permission to place on the stones and pray for the group as the smoke pervades
the small lodge. Now the water bucket and switches for stimulating the body
during the sweat are passed into the lodge before the flap is lowered.

After the assistant drops the flap covering the entrance, the leader may invite
the ones sweating to wet their hair and heads, making more manageable the
intense steam heat that will rise up from the stones.[8] The leader will also wet
the switches of sage, chockcherry, or willow branches in the bucket of water,
sprinkling the water on the stones and gradually raising the temperature in the
confined space. Talking to the participants, the leader might speak about the
purpose of this sweat ceremony, using appropriate circumlocutions so that names
and specific intentions might be suggested but not explicitly mentioned.

The sweat ritual itself has four segments, or "quarters," that correspond to the broad, symbolic categories of the fourfold presence of power. After warming the lodge with initial pourings of water, four dippers of water will be gradually ladled over the stones. Each of the quarters ends with a prayer by the leader or a participant, and after each quarter, the flap is raised. Following the first round, there are seven pourings for the seven stars of the "Big Dipper." Then follow ten pourings for the number of moons during which a mother carries a child in her womb. Finally, a countless "infinity" of pourings, spontaneously determined by the leader and participants, ends the ceremony. Typically, water is passed around, and the participants drink after the third and fourth rounds when the flap is up. It is also customary to rinse one's body with water after the sweat or to enter into a nearby river or stream and completely immerse and wash oneself.

On occasion the leader of the sweat lodge may pray with tobacco rolled in corn husk paper or with the sacred pipe. The role of tobacco ceremonialism in the Apsaaloke lifeway is also ancient and finds unique expression among the Apsaaloke in the Tobacco Society. One student of this ritual complex has written that the "Plains tribes shared a conceptual understanding of the mediating power of tobacco which was the sole agent that enabled their political, social and ceremonial transactions within an otherwise volatile, competitive and divisive ecological arena."[9] Unlike many Plains Native peoples who have strict protocols regarding the use of tobacco, the Apsaaloke retain a fierce sense of individual ritualization in their tobacco ceremonialism. Thus, the central points to be emphasized are not descriptions of consistent actions but, rather, the understanding of ritual reciprocity that the Apsaaloke transmit in their tradition of more spontaneous tobacco ritualization.

The primordial presence of tobacco on the earth is placed before the creation of the human, according to some Apsaaloke creation accounts. In this version the interchangeable mythic personalities of Sun and Old-Man Coyote create the solid earth from mud retrieved by the earth-diver animal, or ducks. Stretching out the dry earth, Coyote came upon another person and said:

"Look, yonder is a human being. There are more of them. That one is one of the Stars above. He is down here now and standing on the ground. Come on, let us look at him." They approached, but he had transformed himself into a plant. When they got to the weed, they found that it was the Tobacco; no other plant was growing as yet. "From now on all the people shall have this, take it in the spring and raise it. It is the stars above that have assumed this form, and they will take care of you. This is the Tobacco plant. Take care of it and it will be the means of your living. Use it in dancing. When you plant it in the spring sing this song: Female comrade, the earth where shall I plant it?"[10]

The Apsaaloke oral tradition narrated here is the genre of origin myth linked to the Apsaaloke Tobacco Society in which tobacco is associated with the stars. Other ritual occasions may evoke alternative genres describing the meaning and origin of tobacco as well as the spiritual forces associated with its origin. Regardless of the genre, however, such ritual narrations detail tobacco as the means for establishing reciprocity with supernatural powers. Kinship with that power is emphasized by means of spontaneous ritualization rather than through a strict set of ritual actions.

The Apsaaloke often recall the mythic dimension of tobacco in their ritualization and couple it with the conception of *dasshuussuua*, or "breaking with the mouth," that is, making the sound of words. Breath and words are understood in the Apsaaloke tradition as having immediate effect on the world. Thus, performative word-as-prayer joined with tobacco usage establishes an intimate and indissoluble bonding between the participating humans and the spiritual powers. Both performative prayer and tobacco ceremonialism are, as the Apsaaloke say, "up to you," namely, dependent upon personal motivation and spontaneous expression. Ritualization, then, is the context in which prayer and tobacco ceremonialism mediate between the Apsaaloke rituals discussed here. The interaction of formal rituals and unrehearsed ritualization enables this people to transact within the human-to-human, the human-to-earth, and the human-to-divine spheres.[11]

As with tobacco ritualization, the vision quest among the Apsaaloke is highly individualized. Rather than a formal repertoire of established actions, the Apsaaloke have a developed process with a consistent structure.[12] The questing process begins with a felt need to fast apart from other humans in an effort to receive something that might relieve a painful need. A sense of ritual process, rather than more random or spontaneous ritualization, engendered in the vision quest is strongly affirmed in the oral narrative tradition. Time and time again the myths compare the one questing to an orphan, or as the Apsaaloke say, *akeeleete*, "one with no possessions, one who has nothing."[13] Thus, a sense of need is valorized in Apsaaloke thought as the traditional ritual place from which to seek medicine (*xapaaliia*) from the world of the cosmic powers (*baxpe*). This need may not be exclusively felt by the faster. The clan or immediate family may have needs that prompt the parents or grandparents to encourage the young to go out alone to the high ridges and "thirst" so that they might be adopted by the cosmic powers for the good of the family or larger group.

Acknowledging one's need, a potential faster will seek out the help of a shaman (*akbaalia*) to guide her or him. The shaman will lead the one seeking assistance through a preparatory sweat lodge and tobacco prayer. Then the shaman will take the faster to a remote site. Here the faster abstains from food and water and attempts to cultivate the attitude of *diakaashe*, "doing something with sincerity, pride, and determination." If successful the vision quester will receive an experience from the Creator (*Akbaatatdia*) through the agency of the spiritual powers associated with animals, plants, places, or cosmic presences such as the stars. United with the Creator, the faster is separated from his or her community. Thus, the faster becomes ritually "orphaned," or liminal, and the experience may establish contact with a "spiritual guide" (*ilaxpe*).

The vision experienced may be ritualized and brought back to the community along with the faster's changed attitudes. The relationship established during the vision quest is that of parent to child and is often discussed as "adoption." The personal transformation may be articulated and the vision experience interpreted during another sweat lodge ceremony with a shaman or elders after the faster returns. Often, discussions within the family will find parallels between the faster's experiences and the stories of past heros who also went from "orphaned status" to the acquisition of efficacious power. In many instances, power objects (*xapaaliia*) may be authorized by the spiritual guide-as-parent. These "tokens" may be gathered into a "bundle" after the questing and become a central focus during the power-bestowing ritual of the successful vision quester. Now the community looks upon this individual in a different manner.

It may happen that a mature individual who has a sense of need will vow to enter the Big Lodge, the *Ashkisshe*, the ritual structure that symbolically makes present the universe.[14] In this ceremonial, self-selected Apsaaloke gather together to fast and to dance under the leadership of a sponsor of the ritual and with one or more shamans. These individuals fast (*bilisshiissannee*) as a sacrifice to draw power into the ceremonial pole of the Big Lodge for all the community rather than for themselves exclusively. The preparations for the building of the lodge and for conducting the Sun Dance ritual begin with the sponsor and a Sun Dance "chief," a shaman, who has the privilege of guiding dancers and overseeing their contact with power. The individual who sponsors the ritual begins preparations with the shaman and with his clan a year or more in advance. In the months ahead of the dance during the full moons, four "outside dances" are held at the site where the lodge will be built. Not only do these outside dances instill in the sponsor and his relatives an actual sense of the performative character of the ritual, but these preliminary rites set the architectural boundaries of the lodge itself. Alignment of the fire at these outside dances with the rising sun, along with the dance place of the sponsor and his relatives, will eventually be used to determine the location of the center tree around which the Big Lodge will be built.

The Big Lodge is centered on a cottonwood tree, trimmed clean except for two large upper branches, which are left intact on the tree trunk with their shining green leaves. The cottonwood tree will have been selected by the officiating "Sun Dance chief" before the last outside dance. After the ritual cutting of the tree, it is brought to the Sun Dance site and set up with twelve notched trees at a measured distance of ten to fifteen paces in a circle around the center tree. From the outer notched trees, rafter poles span to the center tree. A buffalo head and an eagle or feathers along with willow branches, tobacco, and two flags, one blue and one white, will be installed on the cottonwood tree. The buffalo head is at the level of the dancers' gaze, whereas an eagle body or feathers are set among the fir needles of the rafter pine trees lying in the notch of the two limbs of the center tree. Surrounded by shade trees for the dancers, the Big Lodge is ready for the entry of the male and female dancers who will fast from food and water. The number of fast days is determined by the sponsor and Sun Dance chief and indicated by charcoal-painted circles on the bottom of the center tree.

As the dancers enter the lodge on the evening of the first day, their families gather from the camps located in a horseshoe arrangement around the Big Lodge at a distance of several hundred yards. The families and visitors watch as the dancers charge toward the center tree and slowly dance back to their places around the lodge. The repetitive dance is a prayer (*chiwakiia*, "to pray, to ask repeatedly") addressed to the center tree, which acts as a vehicle for the exchange with the Creator. The dancers move to the Sun Dance songs of drummers and singers who perform for hours in order that the dancers might carry on their prayerful dialogue.

Occasionally, during the days of the *Ashkisshe*, outsiders will request of the announcers at the entrance to the Big Lodge that they be allowed to enter and receive a healing from a shaman at the center pole. Taking their shoes off as a sign of respect, these individuals stand at the center pole and wait for a shaman to fan them with his medicine fan. At the same time, the dancers will be charging the pole all around them or coming to the center tree with a tobacco cigarette so as to pray for their desires and the needs that prompt them to dance and to fast. It is understood that dancers undertake their sacrifice at the center pole, the cosmic axis, imbued with the powers of Buffalo, Eagle, and Willow and with its roots in the Earth and its branches reaching up to the Creator, so as to assist someone other than themselves.

At times a dancer who is especially moved by sincere determination (*diakaashe*) will have the experience that she or he is being accompanied by the spiritual Eagle or chased by the symbolic Buffalo. Eventually, that person might take a "hard fall," that is, become unconscious on the dance ground. No one disturbs such a person. A shaman may pray over the unconsious person, but she or he is thought to be in a visionary state. After rising, the dancer may be refreshed by gifts brought by her or his family, such as mint, sage, or cattails. Vision experiences are sought by determined dancers, encouraged by the increasingly vigorous chanting of the singers, and deeply appreciated by all of those attending. The dancers come out of the Big Lodge after their days of fasting and dancing, greeted by the Apsaaloke community. The people believe that the benefits of all the dancers and especially those who have displayed sincerity serve to renew all the people, all the animals and plants, all the lands of the Apsaaloke.

The sequence of rituals among the Apsaaloke discussed here—namely, the sweat lodge, tobacco ceremonialism, vision questing, and the Sun Dance—are obviously not separate rituals. Rather, they constitute a significant component of what can be called the lifeway or "religion" of the Apsaaloke people. These rituals are joined by meaningful acts and values that serve to order life for the Apsaaloke and provide legitimation for that way of living that is called Apsaaloke tradition. All of these actions—tobacco ceremonialism, endurance of painful situations, such as intense heat and fasting, or repetitive prayer in dance or chant—effect the transactions sought between the Apsaaloke individual and the source of sustaining power, the Creator (*Akbaatatdia*). Thus, it can be said that the rituals both display the heritage of the Apsaaloke people and make possible the ritualization that manifests individual commitment to that heritage.

The rituals acknowledge the human "orphaned state" known in the Apsaaloke tradition, and these same rituals embody values that can transform that existential condition. The rituals transact relations between many types of groups during the *Ashkisshe*, such as powerful shamans and determined practitioners, between drum groups and the sponsor/Sun Dance chief group in the back of the Big Lodge. Most important for the Apsaaloke is the transaction between the cosmic powers and humans by means of efficacious ritualizations such as word-prayer and tobacco ceremonialism. Through reenactment of the oral narrative traditions in ritual actions, and by undertaking sacrificial activity with determination, pride, and sincerity, the seemingly disparate rituals of the Apsaaloke are brought into coherent, meaningful relation to one another.

The four rituals discussed here obviously serve to bond the people together. The immediate family and the extended clan assist a sponsor in gathering and assembling materials for the lodge and for feeding those who work to build the *Ashkisshe* lodge. So also the rituals themselves draw together individuals' diverse desires, expectations, and experiences into a coherent order. The rituals channel disparate energies into a focused social agenda, provide a release for individual aggression, and define a symbolic universe. These rituals as models for individual behavior promote a deepened sense of community, and as models of larger realities, such as the local bioregion and the cosmos, the rituals provide taxonomies for organizing thought and space.

All four rituals mentioned above also demonstrate historical change as well as traditional continuity over the period, from earliest contact, through the inception of the reservation era, to the present. The *Ashkisshe*, or Sun Dance, provides the most striking example of historical change in a ritual. The Sun Dance ritual described above actually returned to the Apsaaloke in 1941 after the traditional piercing Sun Dance of these people had been prohibited and lost in 1875. The traditional piercing Sun Dance had been a warrior's questing for a vision of revenge against an enemy. The Sun Dance that returned to the Apsaaloke in 1941, however, came from the Shoshone of Wyoming and had been transformed into a world-renewal ceremony.[15]

Not only had the motivation for sponsoring the Sun Dance changed in 1941, but the position in relation to attendant rituals discussed here also changed from the early reservation period. The older traditional Sun Dance was more marginal in relation to the tobacco ceremonialism of the Tobacco Society. The recently returned Sun Dance (from the Shoshone) has become more central to the Apsaaloke lifeway. Yet both the traditional and the more recent Sun Dance have retained a complex of relations with basic tobacco ceremonialism, vision questing, and the sweat lodge. Significant features of rituals in Native North America, then, are their integral relations with other elements of the ethnic lifeway and their complex interweaving of formal ritual structure and spontaneous ritualization that may, to some extent, account for their resilience. These configurations have changed in response to historical pressures and opportunities. Yet many ancient Native American rituals continue to transmit cultural values and to affirm the cultural worldview in which they are embedded, despite the pressures of secularizing modernity. The close relationship of rituals to cultural worldview brings us to the following considerations.

RITUALS, WORLDVIEW SYSTEMS, AND TRADITION

Anishinabe/Ojibway *Midewiwin*

Among the Woodland cultures of the Great Lakes Native peoples, a major ritual that continues to be practiced is the *Midewiwin*.[16] The very term *Midewiwin* carries a multivalent charge referring to a shamanic society, to an eight-day ceremony, and to the lore that has been transmitted by that shamanic society. Believed to have developed among the Anishinabe/Ojibway of the Michillimackinac region where Lakes Superior and Huron meet, this ritual complex brought together systems of cultural logic that expressed Anishinabe group identity during extensive seventeenth- and eighteenth-century migrations.[17] The ritual of *Midewiwin* drew on cultural worldview values to mark this particular historical event of migration. *Midewiwin* also coordinated ancient calendrical systems of village life with movement into new territorial areas west of the Anishinabe homeland. Finally, ritual *Midewiwin* demonstrated a remarkably creative organizational system whereby ancient shamanic vocations were integrated into both the mythic dimension and the performative display of the ceremony. These complex developments wove innovative elements into *Midewiwin*, effectively establishing the basis for a new tribal polity as well as affirming traditional Anishinabe identity.

Beginning with the ancient shamanic vocations, the *Midewiwin* ceremony elaborated both a healing ritual and an initiation rite into a new collective shamanic vocation. *Midewiwin* continues to be performed among the Anishinabe/Ojibway and other Great Lakes peoples by a prescribed number of ritual officers who are selected from among the shamanic personalities within the tribe.[18] The Mide Society hierarchy comprises four earth and four sky degrees that are achieved by learning the *Midewiwin* lore and undergoing the ritual cure. The ancient shamanic vocations, such as *tcisaki* (shaking-tent diviner), *nanandawi* (tube-sucking curer), *wabeno* (fire manipulator), and *meda* (family healer) were incorporated into *Midewiwin* status terminology.

The word *midewiwin* derives from *mide*, meaning "sound of the drum," and *wiwin*, meaning "doings."[19] The healing power of the ceremony comes from the dramatic reenactment of the primordial *Midewiwin* by the assembled cosmic spirits (*manitou*). Eight ritual days are set aside for specific actions and recitations that involve both the patient to be cured (or a proxy) and the Mide Society shamans, who represent the mythic *manitou*. *Midewiwin* was traditionally celebrated during the late spring maple sugar harvest when separated extended-family villages drew together for seasonal fishing. It was also proper for a *Midewiwin* ritual to be performed at any time for those in urgent need. The ritual prescriptions regarding the number of Mide shamans and instruction periods could be curtailed by taking up the pipe, smoking it, and engaging in "mystic talk" (*manitou kazo*) with the *manitou* spirits.

The *Midewiwin* tradition is considered sacred and secret by its Ojibway practitioners. It is believed to be sacred by virtue of its origin among the *manitou*. Indeed, the ceremonial talk, or "mystic doings," of *Midewiwin* is the narration of the tribal cosmology and the story of the ritual's formation during the sacred time of mythic narratives. *Midewiwin* is secret because of the tribal prohibition against profane mention of sacred matters. The holistic connections engendered by the society and ceremonial of *Midewiwin* serve to reflect and to maintain the order of the Ojibway worldview.

In giving order and meaning to the potential chaos of events, the Ojibway worldview articulates a cosmic structure that is at once highly differentiated and centrally oriented. Differentiation in the Ojibway cosmology is evident in the multilayered universe, the plurality of *manitou* spirits, and the ongoing elaborations and alterations of the cosmological stories themselves. Yet this differentiation is not simply diffused. There is also a central understanding of *manitou* power unifying the Ojibway cosmology, which finds theoretical and devotional expression, for example, in the phrase *Kitche Manitou*, the creative, mysterious presence of power. Profound encounters with this personalistic power (*manitou*) are the special province of the Ojibway shaman. These experiences became the ritual field of *Midewiwin*, which was capable of adapting to the seventeenth- and eighteenth-century, westward migrations of the Ojibway and the ongoing contact with dominant Canadian and U.S. cultures. The *Midewiwin* society drew on cosmological values, then, to culturally construct their history.

Ojibway shamanic personalities transcended their highly individualistic and family-oriented ethos to systematically organize and fix *Midewiwin* as central to Ojibway tradition. The ritual creativity of *Midewiwin*, charged with cosmological symbolism, brought together the ancient calendrical system tied to village subsistence practices and the challenges of migration into new areas. *Midewiwin* provided the context for negotiating between new territories west of Lake Superior and the olden cosmological system tied to hunting, fishing, and gathering villages at Michillimackinac. Finally, *Midewiwin*, in its expansion and alteration of ancient mythic materials, provided the historical consciousness needed for meaningfull reflection on potentially chaotic moves into western regions. An Algonquian language cousin of the Ojibway, namely, the Tsistsistas/Cheyenne of the northern plains, also developed a complex ritual during their many migrations, the *Massaum* ceremony. However, the Cheyenne were not able to sustain this important ritual, which was known to ethnographers before it was lost.

Tsistsistas/Cheyenne *Massaum*

The *Massaum* ceremony of the Tsistsistas/Cheyenne peoples was an event that drew together ancient shamanistic capacities to call animals into a hunter's entrapment with the Tsistsistas memory of seeking ritual validation for their entrance onto the Missouri River drift plains. This ancient ceremony was last performed in the early twentieth century according to ethnographic accounts.[20] The *Massaum* was a complex of rituals that involved specially prepared lodges, masked animal dancers, and sacred earth altars. Each of these ritual practices embodied a cultural logic in which systematic oppositions enabled deeper reflection upon self and society.

The lodges reenacted mythic narratives of the achievements of the culture hero Motseyoef, thus making present cosmic powers that generated vertical oppositions between the human and the supernatural. During *Massaum*, animal-masked dancers also reenacted ancient shamanic powers associated with the hunt in which horizontal oppositions between humans and animals were evoked. The earth altars provided the place for ritual experience of these oppositions in which cosmic powers of the worldview were brought into relationship with local animal powers in order to valorize Cheyenne self- and social identity. The *Massaum* ceremonial was a complex, multilayered symbolic process performed over several days in which the Tsistsistas celebrated their mythic remembrance of themselves as a people. Most important, the *Massaum* contained ritual actions undertaken by the Tsistsistas people to legitimate their entry onto the Plains. They evoked the numinous relationships between themselves and their culture hero, their animal relatives on the Plains, and their worldview values embedded in the cosmic powers in order to sanction their presence in this country.[21]

The central symbolic axis of the *Massaum* ceremony, as an "earth-giving" ceremony, was grounded in the "Earth-mound altars." These altars were prepared from layers dug out of the surface soil where humans walk and from the "deep earth" where the spiritual powers that sustain human life are believed to reside. The mound altars symbolically make present the interior forces of the mythic cave in which Motseyoef, the Tsistsistas culture hero, encountered the powers of the earth. Thus, the ritual of the "Earth-mound" altars incorporated the oppositions in the Motseyoef mythology and in the Tsistsistas cosmology. The ritual performance of the shamans building the altars as well as the placement of these deep-earth altars on the top layer of Plains earth also made present the oppositions associated with the ancient hunting powers. *Massaum* as ritual control dominated these systems of cultural logic located in the cosmic powers (*exhastoz*) in the visible earth and sky and the deeper, unseen regions of both earth and sky.

These powers were evoked during *Massaum* as an act of renewing the primordial tie of the Tsistsistas people with the primal order (*vonoom*) in the cosmos. In the manifold ritual acts of *Massaum* a cosmic and eco-consciousness served to construct group identity by distinguishing powers within ritual *Mas-*

saum and by logically ordering these powers in relationship to the people themselves. In *Massaum*, then, the Tsistsistas people validated their habitation on the northern grasslands of the continent by displaying and controlling meaningful cultural systems.

Among the Aashiwi/Zuni of the southwestern United States, the return of the kachina-masked dancers each year marks the beginning of a ritual calendar that firmly establishes the lifeway of these peoples in their cosmological values.

Aashwi/Zuni "Coming of the Kachinas" Ceremony

After the Winter Solstice ceremony, initiated by astronomical observances in mid-December, the kachinas, the masked dancers who make present the spiritual forces of Zuni cosmology, return to the pueblo. The Kachina Society (*kotikane*), which still performs the masked dances in the New Mexico pueblo of Zuni, is composed of all adult males. It is one of six major cults among the Zuni, but it is said to be the dominant ritual association and activity. This complex religious society stages a series of dances throughout the ceremonial calendar in which large numbers of masked dancers impersonate the kachinas (Zuni, *kokko*, or "raw people"). Zuni cosmology describes people as "raw" (spiritual) or "cooked" (ordinary).[22] The kachinas are "raw people" who are capable of transformations and are identified with the dead, with clouds, and with rain. According to Zuni mythology, the dancing of the adult males serves as a substitute for the real kachinas, who no longer come in person. The Zuni believe that the coming of the mythic kachinas caused the death of children because of too intimate a contact with these numinous presences. The Zuni myths say, "When they left, someone always went with them [*kokko*]." Gradually, according to Zuni myth, the dancing celebrations, which formerly eased the suffering of parents who had lost their children, became a rainmaking ceremony.

Foremost among the kachinas are the six Shalako masks that play a major role in the solstice ceremony. The sequence of Shalako rituals at the Winter Solstice initiates the great annual ceremonial cycle among the Zuni kachina priests. The term *Shalako* refers both to the giant masked figures and to the initiation of this annual ceremonial cycle. This ritual, which sets in motion the annual ceremonial cycle, not only regulates attendant social and political systems; it is also a self-regulatory system. This regulatory hierarchy, manifest in the Shalako and "Council" kachina activities, serves to determine who the ritual officiants will be throughout the year and invests them with the ritual authority to fulfill their roles. This ritual hierarchy is set in motion by the return of the Shalako kachinas.

Under the light of the moon at the Winter Solstice the Shalakos cross the river dividing the pueblo. The mask of each Shalako is ten feet tall and is set on top of a pole, which a dancer carries in his hands. This impersonator looks out through an opening in the blankets. On the Shalako's head are macaw and downy feathers and a crest of eagle feathers. A red feather hangs from each horn. The bill projecting from his turquoise face opens and shuts with a terrific clatter. He is the only Zuni kachina with a mouth like this. There are six Shalako masks, one for each kiva, the underground ceremonial sites in the Zuni pueblo. These six Shalako masks perform at separate Shalako houses. In each Shalako's house a dancer carries the tall mask while dancing in a center trench. Another dancer who will periodically relieve, and consequently become, the Shalako handler rests at a side bench. In the house are an altar, blankets, and other hangings on the wall for a giveaway ceremony.

Each of the six Shalako masked dancers has a group of singers who accompany him. Each of the masked figures and singers goes to his respective new house for an all-night dance. During the blessing ceremonies at their house, the Shalako singers chant these verses:

> This night the ones who are our fathers
> Masked *kokko* priests
> All the masked *kokko*,
> At their precious mountain, their precious lake,
> Perpetuating what has been since the first
> Beginning, have assumed human form.
> Carrying your waters,
> Carrying your seeds,
> Making your roads come forth.
> You have passed us on our roads
> This night.[23]

In this chant recited at the house of the Shalako, cosmological themes are announced that hearken back to the time of origin, when, according to Zuni cosmology, the ancestors (*alacina we*) emerged from the depths of the earth. The ritual cycle, or ''roads,'' established and renewed by the Winter Solstice ceremonies knits together the subsistence, governance, and ritual systems of the Zuni in terms of the ancestors-as-kachinas. The kachinas come from their mountain home and from their place in the lake to revitalize life through agriculture, through governance, and by means of all of the lifeway cults known to the Zuni. As anthropologist Ruth Bunzel has noted in her studies of the ritual activity of the Zuni, ''Between all of these independent cults is the binding element of calendrical observances. Each cult has ceremonies extending through an annual cycle, starting from the winter solstice, and returning again into the winter solstice. Their [Zuni] solstice ceremonies are all neatly synchronized.''[24] With the rituals associated with the Winter Solstice and the ''Coming of the Kachinas'' there is a ''fit'' established for the Zuni between self, society, and cosmology. This fit is evoked and renewed by the coming of the ancestors as kachinas. And the arrival of the kachinas is a beautiful moment.

Bunzel, who collected these verses, observed that the kachina dances manifest the aesthetic character of the Winter Solstice ceremonies. She wrote:

The public rituals constitute the most important aesthetic expression of the people. Not only are they "artistic" in the superficial sense, in that they embrace the types of behavior which we arbitrarily lump together as the "arts"—ornament, poetry, music, the dance—but they provide the satisfaction of the deeper aesthetic drive. . . . Zuni rituals have a style of their own that belongs to ritual as an art. They are ordered and formal; they are well-designed; they begin in quietness and in serenity. Their quality is gracious and benign.[25]

This valorization of harmony pervades the Zuni worldview, is a central ideal of social ethics, and identifies the sense of ritual that is inculcated in Zuni inhabitants. In this period of the Winter Solstice when the kachinas return to the pueblo, an elaborate ritual cycle is initiated that not only regulates the social, political, and ecosystemic relations of these Pueblo peoples but also organizes and represents a hierarchy of understandings of the rituals themselves. A ritual style is articulated among the Zuni that provides insight not only into their annual ceremonial cycle but into their very lifeway. As Bunzel has expressed it, "If Zuni civilization can be said to have a style, that style is essentially the style of its rituals."[26] Along with the Shalako at this Winter Solstice ceremony come various kachinas associated with the "Council of the Kachinas."

The interpretive patterns established in the ritual of the Coming of the Kachinas begins eight days before the kachinas arrive when the sacred clowns (*koyemsi*) announce their arrival in garbled, obscene speeches. The chaos, which these sacred clowns creatively perform, ushers in the middle period (*itiwanna*) of the ritual calendar in the middle place (*itiwanna*), namely, the ceremonial name for Zuni Pueblo itself. Arriving in this time-out-of-time and on the day legitimated by calendrical observation, the six Shalako masked dancers cross the river toward their specially prepared houses. These ten-foot-tall masked figures require care and dexterity in their handling as the Zuni watch anxiously, lest they trip or fall while performing extended and demanding dancing. In another part of the pueblo the Council of the Kachinas appear.

On the day that the Shalako come, the "Fire Spirit" (*Cula'witsi*) kindles the new fire. Thus, the Zuni renew their ritual calendar with the arrival of the kachina and the extinguishing of all extant fires in the pueblo. With the young boy who dances the incredibly demanding steps of the *Cula'witsi* kachina, there come the kachinas of the Council. First, there is the leader of the gods, *Saiyataca*, whose impersonator occupies a position of power and prestige in the pueblo. This dignified kachina leads the other masked dancers with ponderous walk and grave speech. His deputy (*Hu'tutu*) moves more rapidly and gives a deep call, from which he receives his name. The kachina *Yamuhaktu* also comes with the Council, bringing prosperity. The *Salimopiya* kachinas accompany the *Saiyataca* group. They are whippers, who keep the people away from the kachina, but they are believed to impart good fortune through their yucca whips. The complex character of the Winter Solstice ceremonies and the return of the kachinas to Zuni pueblo underscore the organizational content of this ritual calendar. Embedded within the Shalako and Council of the Kachinas is a ritual process derived from the regard the Zuni hold for their mythic ancestors (*alacina we*), which authorizes and interprets the rituals themselves.

The structured character of this ritual is vastly different from the highly individualized and ecstatic ritual of the Winter Dance among the Columbia River Salish people of eastern Washington state.

Okonogan/Kettle Falls Winter Dance

The Winter Dance ritual complex is especially focused on the singing of guardian-spirit songs over the four days of the ceremonial.[27] Singing begins in the evening of each day and continues until dawn. *Ceremonial* also refers to the accompanying ritual activity that occurs during the day, such as feasting, sweat lodge rituals, giveaways, stick-game gambling, and storytelling. At the heart of the Winter Dance as ritual, however, is the individual guardian-spirit relationship. Most important, this spirit-human exchange is established in cosmogonic symbolism that is believed to renew community life and to regenerate plants and animals. The individual guardian-spirit relationship also forms the core of the Kettle Falls synthetic ethics in which stories, songs, and symbolic sickness bind individual and community together to generate cohesiveness and empathy. This Native American ritual, then, provides an excellent example of the close relationship between ritual, cosmology, and ethics. In this sense the Winter Dance is a ritual in which individual decision making is affirmed and moral behavior is emphasized.

Among the Kettle Falls people the Winter Dance begins the annual ritual calendar. Rituals performed during the calendar year include individual activities such as sweat lodge ceremonies, vision questing, menstrual hut seclusion, and community rituals, such as first fruits and harvest festivals for deer, salmon, and root crops, as well as stick gambling and curing rituals. However, the major ritual that draws together all of the old subsistence and healing rituals is the Winter Dance. This dance is a complex renewal ritual convened by individual sponsors from late December through February. An abbreviated form of the ceremony can also be performed at any time for someone in need. Simply by ritually establishing the center pole, the most significant symbol during the Winter Dance ceremonial, the curative and transformative powers of the ritual can be evoked.

Prior to the contact with dominant America and into the early reservation period, the Winter Dance also provided the major impetus for independent villages, such as Nchaliam, to undertake ritual diplomacy with other village settlements. The ritual was the locus of interaction that smoothed individual conflicts and encouraged group cohesion. Thus, the multifaceted Winter Dance diminished aggressive rivalry between villages and brought the villages together for the shared task of world renewal. Just as the Winter Dance was the locus for negotiation between fiercely egalitarian villages, so also this ritual continues to be the central place for negotiation between the human and spirit realms.

As a world-renewal ceremony, then, the Winter Dance calls the spirit powers of the bioregion into reciprocal relationship with the human communities. This ceremonial makes explicit the interdependence of minerals, plants, animals, and humans through the songs that are sung by singers who have had visionary experiences of that mineral, plant, animal, or place. There is no explicit recitation of a cosmogony during the Winter Dance; however, during the days between the evening and all-night ritual activity, individuals are encouraged to tell stories. Coyote stories are especially popular on these occasions. While there is no single cosmogony among the Kettle Falls people, the cycle of Coyote stories has cosmogonic features that describe the formative activities in the time of mythic beginnings.[28]

Three dimensions of Kettle Falls cosmogony can be isolated that have special significance in the Winter Dance symbol system. First, the communication of a guardian spirit is an act of sacred power (*sumix*). Second, the ability of a human to communicate with a guardian spirit implies, in Kettle Falls understanding, that the person has passed through the experience of spirit sickness. This spirit sickness is an empathetic experience of kinship with the primal sacrifice of the animal-plant-and-mineral persons who gave of their bodies and of their spirit songs so that humans might live. Finally, the center pole, namely, a lodgepole pine of ninety or so inches, is the most significant place for communication with and communication from guardian spirits. The center pole, symbolic of the world, is set up in the middle of the dance hall. The singers and participants go to that center pole to sing and speak in moral exhortation to the assembled community. While dancing around the pole to the songs of the visionaries, the participants are said to be like the animals who "are moving around" during the snows of the Winter Dance season. These features are presented as having moral force in Kettle Falls thought. More than isolated ritual acts or symbolic gestures, they are understood as bringing a person and a community into the moral order established during the time of the cosmogonic events.

In the traditional Winter Dance, singers renewed themselves in the centering experience of the Winter Dance and by doing so recreated their village communities. Much has been lost due to the intrusion of the dominant American worldview that has devalued the sacredness of the community of all life forms and has often misunderstood the visionary experiences of guardian spirits. Still, the Kettle Falls Winter Dance retains striking continuity with a traditional ethic of giving, evident in the giveaway features of the ritual, and of empathy, apparent in the spirit sickness. This is the result of the evocation in the Winter Dance ritual of the ancient cosmogonic knowledge transmitted in the sacred power of the mineral-plant-and-animal persons, in the spirit sickness of the singers, and in the cosmic symbolism of the centering tree. This relationship between ritual and ethics in this system can be labeled "synthetic" to signal its holistic character in the traditional lifeway of these people.

The symbolic integration of this ethics enables any one part of the ritual Winter Dance complex—vision song, spirit sickness, or center pole—to engage the individual participant and village groups in the reciprocal whole of the cosmos. The Kettle Falls synthetic ethics enabled egalitarian village groups, before loss of traditional governance to the United States, to maintain their distinctive riverine character without falling prey to power-based aggrandizement. The particular ethical aspect associated with giving enabled Kettle Falls people to use the resources available to them without any one group asserting authority over either fishing grounds or hunting areas. The ethical aspect of empathy emerged from a profound reflection upon the biological, botanical, and seasonal cycles of life giving and life taking. The complementarity of these ethical aspects within the one ethical system, or synthetic ethics, constituted a ritual path that drew together maturity, economics, and politics.

Ritual Power in the Ghost Dance and Peyote Way

Among the rituals associated with "revitalization" and "relative deprivation," two pan–Native American rituals stand out, namely, the Ghost Dance of the Paiute holy man, Wovoka, and the "Peyote Way," or as it is known by its incorporated and legal name, the Native American Church.[29] These two ritual activities, which demonstrate significant differences in local expressions as well as historical changes over the years of their performance, are clear examples of the manner in which the cognitive materials within rituals can model ideal worlds of power that influence actual communities. The following section will briefly consider, first, how the Ghost Dance, and second, the Peyote Way, embody and exercise power in social change.

The Ghost Dance stems from Wovoka (1856/8–1932), the Paiute religious prophet and self-proclaimed messiah of the late 1880s and 1890s. Traditional Paiute beliefs and ritual practices of earlier prophetic-shamanic movements of the Pacific Northwest region informed the Ghost Dance of Wovoka, especially the prediction of the return of the ancestral dead. The return of the Paiute ancestors was linked to the reversal of devastating experiences at the hands of mainstream America as well as a rolling back of the altered bioregion to reveal animals, plants, and places changed or absent since the coming of dominant America. The return was to be effected by the practice of a round dance that would bring the participants into trance state encounters with their ancestors. Such a powerful encounter would purify the practitioner and result in an earthly cataclysm, which would bring about both restoration of the old ways and transformation of the intrusive ways of mainstream America.

Wovoka's power appears to have derived from his trance experiences, beginning in 1888, in which he contacted his dead ancestors. These trance journeys were also cosmological in that they were articulated in terms of a syncretic reflection upon established Paiute ritual and mythology. Wovoka ritually dramatized his understanding of his experiences by means of personal shamanic power symbols, such as his sombero, eagle, magpie, and crow feathers and red ocher paint from the traditional Paiute holy mountain, now called Mount Grant.

The rapid rise and spread of the Ghost Dance from Nevada throughout many Indian nations recently contained on reservations was related both to the deprived state of the Native peoples and to the shared experience of shamanic power among traditional Native American peoples. The local expressions of the Ghost Dance, such as among the Lakota, derived from the adaptation of the Ghost Dance ceremony to particular indigenous traditions. For example, the emergence of warrior Ghost Dance shirts among the Lakota may relate to the warrior ethos of the Lakota peoples often symbolically expressed in the warrior's buckskin shirt. So also it is conjectured that the Ghost Dance shirt was developed in Nevada from the Mormon practice of baptismal coverings.[30] Regardless of the actual etiology of the Ghost Dance shirt, its use by the Lakota in their Ghost Dance exemplifies a power symbol that identified a member of the new cult who was in continuity with traditional Lakota culture. Thus, ritual in the Ghost Dance was oriented toward effecting social change, but it also augmented traditional social control by modeling power relationships well known to the people. This selective focus in renewing traditional ritual elements is what Wallace referred to as "revitalization" (see no. 29).

In the following descriptions from James Mooney's (1965) study of the Ghost Dance among the Sioux [sic], typical Plains Lakota features predominate alongside innovative ritual techniques:

Before going into the dance the men, or at least the leaders fasted for twenty-four hours, and then at sunrise entered the sweat-house for the religious rite of purification preliminary to painting themselves for the dance. . . . After the sweating ceremony the dancer was painted by medicine-men who acted as leaders, of whom Sitting Bull was accounted the greatest among the Sioux. The design and color varied with the individual, being frequently determined by a previous trance vision of the subject, but circles, crescents, and crosses, representing respectively the sun, the moon, and the morning star, were always favorite figures upon forehead, face, and cheeks.

At the beginning the performers, men and women, sat on the ground in a large circle around the tree. A plaintive chant was then sung, after which a vessel of some sacred food was passed around the circle until everyone had partaken, when at a signal by the priests, the dancers rose to their feet, joined hands, and began to chant the opening song and move slowly around the circle from right to left. The rest of the performance, with its frenzies, trances, and recitals of visions, was the same as with the southern tribes. . . . Like these tribes also, the Sioux usually selected Sunday, the great medicine day of the white man, for the ceremony.[31]

The adaptation of the Paiute Ghost Dance to Lakota ritual forms is exemplified in the preliminary sweat, the body painting, and the individuated symbols. Moreover, ritual specialists in the Ghost Dance among the Lakota were not restricted to those original Lakota pilgrims who rode trains west to visit Wovoka but, in customary Lakota ritual understanding, developed among both the established power personalities and those who demonstrated a capacity to lead in trance experience.[32]

The adaptation of the Ghost Dance by the Lakota exemplifies a major concern of ritual in social life, namely, effecting social change through ritual processes of transformation. Obviously, the Ghost Dance was not brought into Lakota or other Native traditional societies simply to establish social order or deepen community life. Though weakened by contact with dominant America, Native North American societies still maintained cohesive ritual systems in the late nineteenth century. One clear feature, then, of the transformative power of the Ghost Dance understood by the Lakota was religious resistance. Thus, the performance took place typically on Sunday as a counter to the American Christian power performance. Perhaps the more correct term for describing the ritual force of the Ghost Dance is "transformance."[33] This elision of the term *transformative performance* signals a condition found in the Ghost Dance as ritual, namely, the attempt to reorder the world through performance. This reordering in the Ghost Dance made present the ancestors, those traditional guardians of ethical behavior, to disclose the injustices and contradictions that the living community suffered. Another innovative ritual that reawakened Native American social and religious power was the Peyote Way or Native American Church.

The Native American Church is the contemporary legal name taken by practitioners from a wide variety of Native North American peoples for the ancient ritual practice of eating the peyote cactus. This rite focuses primarily on the peyote cactus itself and the sacramental eating of the cactus as a power substance that has a therapeutic healing capacity. The ritual spread from northern Mexico into Oklahoma and among the Indian nations during the twentieth century. The ritual practice of eating peyote has assumed a number of syncretic expressions. These can be summarized under two broad headings associated with the form of altar used during the peyote meeting, namely, the traditional half-moon altar and the Christianized cross altar.

The acculturation of the Peyote Way into varied Native American lifeways emphasizes again the multidimensional pathways for experience and expression of power among these First Peoples. Often, Peyote Way practitioners participate in Christian services as well as keep the seasonal calendar of traditional rituals indigenous to their ethnic group. While the rationale for the spread and success of the Peyote Way is the subject of a large and growing literature, one experiential feature of eating peyote that is often mentioned by participants is the ritual healing it provides.

Peyote meetings are always undertaken for a specific purpose, whether to celebrate, to mourn, or to heal. The ritual healing in Peyote Way underscores another interpretive position, relative deprivation, used to understand this ritual. Often deprived of both traditional healing practices as well as the means or inclination to enter into scientific healing, the Peyote Way provides an acceptable expectation for healing as well as control of healing techniques among many Native peoples. In a contemporary setting the Peyote Way is often used as a symbolic sacred healing practice in conjunction with scientific medical healing.

Curing in this ritual, as with all aspects of the Native American Church, revolves around the peyote cactus itself. The ritual system is highly structured, with ritual officers leading sessions of singing and prayer. The officers themselves are often from the ranks of the cured. The ritual caregivers, led by the Road Man, as well as specialists for the fire, the drum, the cedar incense, and the entry through the door, exhibit a special aesthetic concern in their formal actions. The beauty of the ritual is not only experiential, that is, a function of the hallucinogenic quality of the peyote; it is also set in a cosmological frame whereby the peyote is understood as cosmic power. In the half-moon tradition, peyote is believed to be the creative, sustaining, and healing power long known to traditional Native North American peoples, whereas in the cross altar form, the peyote is understood as the embodiment of Jesus.

In the following account, the ritual healing draws on the cross altar tradition as well as familiar symbols in the Plains Native American lifeways. This Kiowa ceremony describes the actions of a Road Man and his Fire Man who work in tandem to develop a therapeutic field during this segment of the ritual:

Leaving his place shortly after the ritual of the Midnight Water [the ritual begins in the evening and goes over night into the morning], the leader walked to the patient, lying at the side of the tipi. The fire-man handed the leader a cup of water, and the leader offered several prayers in which the words Jesus Christ were frequently used. He handed the patient fourteen mescal buttons [that is, pieces of peyote] which he himself had partly masticated before the treatment. While the patient was swallowing them, the leader waved the cup of water in cedar incense produced by throwing dried juniper needles (*Juniperus viriginiana*) into the altar fire. He also wafted this incense to the patient's bare chest with an eagle feather fan. Following this, he chewed several more buttons, expectorated them into his cupped hands, and anointed the patient's head with the saliva while praying. Then he picked up a glowing ember from the altar fire and placing it almost in his mouth, blew its heat over the patient's chest. The ritual ended with a long prayer.[34]

A ritual such as the Peyote Way is important both for what it symbolically says as well as for what is not said. Obviously, in the ritual described above, the mix of Peyote Way ceremonialism with traditional Plains shamanic healing triggers the perception in the patient and practitioners that this ritual engenders transformative healing. In this sense the ritual creates agents of transformation in the practitioners by symbolically working on their bodies the "transformance" of power. The practitioners themselves maintain and transmit the ritual schemes, manipulations, and techniques associated with power in their own bodies. The ritual openly expresses ancient healing techniques, but it also transmits a way of dealing with the cultural gap caused by an alienated life in mainstream American society. The healing process of the ritual that creates a new person is overtly stated; what is not stated is the use of acculturated Christianity to structure a new hegemonic order and a new redemptive process in the Peyote Way.

In this sense, a strategic misrecognition embedded in the Peyote Way rituals masks the privileges of power exercised by Christian Americans as well as the relationships of ends and means in the use of Christian symbols.

NOTES

1. Alfonso Ortiz, *The Tewa World: Space, Time, Being and Becoming in a Pueblo Society* (Chicago: University of Chicago Press, 1969), 27.

2. This sense of ritual play, liminality, and community (*"communitas"*) is drawn from Victor Turner, *The Ritual Process: Structure and Anti-Structure* (Chicago: Aldine, 1969), 6. (For additional discussion of Turner, see "Ritual and Current Studies of Ritual: Overview.")

3. Tom Driver has distinguished the terms *ritual* and *ritualization* in the following manner:

> The difference between ritualization and ritual is not, however, categorical. A single event may be viewed under either aspect. We deal with a continuum, extending from the most inchoate and random behaviors imaginable to those with the greatest degree of formality and achieved cultural meaning. Throughout the gradient, differences are of degree more than kind. Without its ritualizing (new-making) component, ritual would be entirely repetitious and static. Without aiming at the condition of ritual, ritualizing would lack purpose and avoid form; it would fall back into that realm of informal, noncommunicative behavior from which it arose.

See Tom F. Driver, *The Magic of Ritual: Our Need for Liberating Rites that Transform Our Lives and Our Communities* (San Francisco: Harper San Francisco, 1991), 19–20.

4. For Mesoamerican influences in North America, see Friederich Katz, *The Ancient American Civilizations* (New York: Praeger, 1972). Regarding the widespread Mississippian riverine mound civilization, see Lynda Shaffer, *Native Americans before 1492: The Moundbuilding Centers of the Eastern Woodlands* (Armonk, NY: M. E. Sharpe, 1992). On the Cahokia finds, see Melvin L. Fowler, "A Pre-Columbian Urban Center on the Mississippi," *Scientific American* 233, no. 2 (August 1975): 92–101.

5. Keith H. Basso, *Portraits of "The Whiteman": Linguistic Play and Cultural Symbols among the Western Apache* (New York: Cambridge University Press, 1979); and Joseph Medicine Horse, *From the Heart of the Crow Country* (New York: Orion, 1992).

6. See the mythic narrative of the "Seven Bulls" in Michael O. Fitzgerald's *Yellowtail: Crow Medicine Man and Sun Dance Chief* (Norman: University of Oklahoma Press, 1991), 110–113.

7. See Rodney Frey, *The World of the Crow Indians: As Driftedwood Lodges* (Norman: University of Oklahoma, 1987).

8. Robert Lowie mentions the stifling heat in a 1910 sweat with Medicine-crow and One-star in which "I clandestinely raised the flap of one blanket under cover of the darkness and thrust my nose into the air." See Robert H. Lowie, *The Crow Indians* (Lincoln: University of Nebraska Press, 1983), 257–258. (Originally published in 1935)

9. See Peter Nabokov, "Cultivating Themselves: The Inter-play of Crow Indian Religion and History" (Ph.D. diss., University of California at Berkeley, 1988), 11.

10. Robert H. Lowie, "Myths and Traditions of the Crow Indians," *Anthropological Papers* (American Museum of Natural History) 25 (1918): 14–15.

11. For a fuller discussion of the "transactional paradigm," see Nabokov, "Cultivating Themselves," 136.

12. The structure discussed as vision questing is more fully described in Frey, *The World of the Crow Indians*, 77–97.

13. Ibid. Frey states, "One of the most commonly used expressions in prayer during a sweat, before a meal, or during a Sun Dance is, 'I am poor, pitiful, in need' " (81).

14. A visual presentation of the Apsaaloke/Crow Sun Dance can be found in the video *Crow/Shoshone Sun Dance: A Traditional Ceremony*, from Thunderous Productions, New York, 1990.

15. See Fred Voget, *The Shoshoni-Crow Sun Dance* (Norman: University of Oklahoma Press, 1984).

16. For a detailed study of the *Midewiwin*, see Ruth Landes, *Ojibwa Religion and the Midewiwin* (Madison: University of Wisconsin Press, 1968); and John A. Grim, *The Shaman: Patterns of Siberian and Ojibway Healing* (Norman: University of Oklahoma Press, 1983).

17. Harold Hickerson, "Notes on the Post-Contact Origin of the Midewiwin," *Ethnohistory* 9 (1962–1963): 404–423.

18. See Basil Johnston, *Ojibway Ceremonies* (Lincoln: University of Nebraska Press, 1990); and Landes, *Ojibwa Religion*, 71–72.

19. Landes, *Ojibwa Religion*, 3–4; and Basil Johnston, *Ojibway Heritage* (New York: Columbia University Press, 1976), 84.

20. See George Bird Grinnell, *The Cheyenne Indians*, 2 vols. (New Haven: Yale University Press, 1923), 2: 285–336.

21. Karl H. Schlesier, *The Wolves of Heaven: Cheyenne Shamanism, Ceremonies, and Prehistoric Origins* (Norman: University of Oklahoma Press, 1987), 79.

22. For a parallel discussion of Tewa pueblo cosmology involving distinctions between cosmologically different types of persons in one society, see Ortiz's *The Tewa World*.

23. Ruth Bunzel, "Introduction to Zuni Ceremonialism" (Smithsonian Institution, Bureau of American Ethnology, 47th Annual Report, Washington, D.C., 1929), 762.

24. Ibid., 534.

25. Ruth Bunzel, "Zuni Katcinas, an Analytical Study" (Smithsonian Institution, Bureau of American Ethnology, 47th Annual Report, Washington, D.C., 1929), 509.

26. Bunzel, "Introduction to Zuni Ceremonialism," 509.

27. For a discussion of this ritual, see John A. Grim, "Cosmogony and the Winter Dance: Native American Ethics in Transition," *Journal of Religious Ethics* (fall 1992): 389–413.

28. In the Coyote cycle, two myths relate specific cosmogonic features. These are the "Earth Diver" myth, which discusses producing the dry land, and the "Naming" myth, which describes the naming of the animals. For a discussion of this lack of a specific cosmogony among the So Okanagon, see Walter Cline, "Religion and World View," in *The Sinkaietk or Southern Okanagon of Washington*, General Series in Anthropology, ed. Leslie Spier, no. 6 (Menasha, WI: George Banta Publishing Co., 1938); for the Kettle Falls specifically, see Mourning Dove, *Mourning Dove: A Salishan Autobiography*, ed. with introduction by Jay Miller (Lincoln: University of Nebraska Press, 1933).

29. For "revitalization" movements, see Anthony Wallace, "Revitalization Movements," *American Anthropologist* 58 (1956): 260–282; for "relative deprivation," see David F. Aberle, *The Peyote Religion among the Navajo* (Chicago: University of Chicago Press, 1982).

30. See Paul Dayton Bailey, *Wovoka: The Indian Messiah* (Los Angeles, CA: Westernlore Press, 1957).

31. James Mooney, *The Ghost-Dance Religion and the Sioux Outbreak of 1890*, ed., abridg., and intro. Anthony Wallace (Chicago: University of Chicago Press, 1965), 66, 68–69. (Originally part 2 of the 14th Annual Report of the Bureau of Ethnology, 1892–1893)

32. As an individual visionary known by his people as a healer-shaman (*wicasa wakan*), Black Elk described his reactions to the Lakota version of the Ghost Dance to John Neihardt in this manner:

"It seemed that I could recall all my vision in it [Lakota Ghost Dance near his home in Manderson, South Dakota]. The more I thought about it, the stronger it got in my mind. Furthermore, the sacred articles that had been represented were scarlet relics and their faces were painted red. Furthermore, they had that pipe and the eagle feathers. It was all from my vision. So I sat there and felt sad. Then happiness overcame me all at once and it got ahold of me right there. I was to be intercessor for my people and yet I was not doing my duty. Perhaps it was this Messiah that had pointed me out and he might have set this to remind me to get to work again to bring my people back into the hoop and the old religion.

From *The Sixth Grandfather: Black Elk's Teachings Given to John G. Neihardt*, ed. Raymond J. DeMallie (Lincoln: University of Nebraska Press, 1984), 258.

33. See Richard Schechner, *Essays on Performance Theory, 1970–1976* (New York: Drama Book Specialists, 1977).

34. Richard E. Schultes, "The Appeal of Peyote (*Lophophora williamsii*) as a Medicine," *American Anthropologist* 40 (1938): 709.

REFERENCES

Axtell, James. 1981. *The European and the Indian: Essays in the Ethnohistory of Colonial North America*. New York: Oxford University Press.

Axtell, James. 1985. *The Invasion Within: The Contest of Cultures in Colonial North America*. New York: Oxford.

Berkhofer, Robert, Jr. 1979. *The White Man's Indian Images of the American Indian from Columbus to the Present*. New York: Vintage.

Bierhorst, John, editor. 1974/1984. *Four Masterworks of American Indian Literature*. Tucson: University of Arizona Press.

Bierhorst, John, editor. 1976. *The Red Swan: Myths and Tales of the American Indian*. New York: Farrar, Straus & Giroux.

Brown, Jennifer S. H., and Robert Brightman. 1988. *"The Orders of the Dreamed": George Nelson on Cree and Northern Ojibwa Religion and Myth, 1823*. Winnipeg: University of Manitoba Press.

Brown, Joseph E. 1953. *The Sacred Pipe: Black Elk's Account of the Seven Rites of the Ogala Sioux*. Norman: University of Oklahoma Press.

Brown, Joseph E. 1964/1982. *The Spiritual Legacy of the American Indian*. New York: Crossroad.

Bullchild, Percy. 1985. *The Sun Came Down*. San Francisco: Harper & Row.

Capps, Walter H., editor. 1976. *Seeing with a Native Eye: Essays on Native American Religion*. New York: Harper & Row.

Cronon, William. 1983. *Changes in the Land: Indians, Colonists, and the Ecology of New England*. New York: Hill and Wang.

Crosby, Alfred W., Jr. 1972. *The Columbian Exchange: Biological and Cultural Consequences of 1492*. Westport, CT: Greenwood.

Deloria, Vine, Jr. 1969. *Custer Died for Your Sins: An Indian Manifesto*. New York: Macmillan.

Deloria, Vine, Jr. 1973. *God Is Red*. New York: Grosset & Dunlap.

DeMallie, Raymond J. 1984. *The Sixth Grandfather*. Lincoln: University of Nebraska Press.

Edmunds, R. David. 1983. *The Shawnee Prophet*. Lincoln: University of Nebraska Press.

Gill, Sam. 1982. *Native American Religions*. Belmont, CA: Wadsworth.

Gill, Sam. 1983. *Native American Traditions: Sources and Interpretations*. Belmont, CA: Wadsworth.

Gill, Sam. 1987. *Native American Religious Action: A Performance Approach to Religion*. Columbia: University of South Carolina Press.

Hultkrantz, Ake. 1979. *The Religions of the American Indians*. Berkeley: University of California Press.

Hultkrantz, Ake. 1983. *The Study of American Indian Religions*. New York: Crossroad.

Hultkrantz, Ake. 1987. *Native Religions of North America: The Power of Visions and Fertility*. New York: Harper & Row.

Hultkrantz, Ake. 1992. *Shamanic Healing and Ritual Drama*. New York: Crossroad.

Hymes, Dell. 1981. *"In Vain I Tried to Tell You": Essays in Native American Ethnopoetics*. Philadelphia: University of Pennsylvania Press.

Jilek, Wolfgang G. 1982. *Indian Healing: Shamanic Ceremonialism in the Pacific Northwest Today*. Surrey, British Columbia: Hancock House.

Jorgensen, Joseph G. 1972. *The Sun Dance Religion*. Chicago: University of Chicago Press.

Kohl, Johann G. 1956/1975. *Kitchi-Gami*. St. Paul: Minnesota Historical Society.

Kroeber, Karl. 1981. *Traditional Literatures of the American Indian: Texts and Interpretations*. Lincoln: University of Nebraska Press.

Kupperman, Karen. 1980. *Settling with the Indians: The Meetings of English and Indian Cultures in America, 1580–1640*. Totowa, NJ: Rowman and Littlefield.

La Barre, Weston. 1938/1969. *The Peyote Cult*. Enlarged edition. New York: Schocken.

La Barre, Weston. 1972/1979. *The Ghost Dance: Origins of Religion*. New York: Dell.

Lame Deer (John Fire), and Richard Erdoes. 1976. *Lame Deer: Seeker of Visions*. New York: Pocket.

Linderman, Frank. 1962. *Plenty-coups*. Lincoln: University of Nebraska Press.

Linderman, Frank. 1974. *Pretty-shield: Medicine Woman of the Crows*. Lincoln: University of Nebraska Press.

Loftin, John D. 1991. *Religion and Hopi Life in the Twentieth Century*. Bloomington: Indiana University Press.

Marquis, Thomas. 1957. *Wooden Leg: A Warrior Who Fought Custer*. Lincoln: University of Nebraska Press.

Momaday, N. Scott. 1976. *The Names: A Memoir*. New York: Harper & Row.

Murie, James R. 1989. *Ceremonies of the Pawnee*. Lincoln: University of Nebraska Press. (Originally Smithsonian Contributions to Anthropology, 1981)

Myerhoff, Barbara G. 1974. *Peyote Hunt: The Sacred Journey of the Huichol Indians*. Ithaca, NY: Cornell University Press.

Nabokov, Peter. 1967. *Two Leggings*. New York: Crowell.

Neihardt, John. 1932/1988. *Black Elk Speaks: Being the Life Story of a Holy Man of the Oglala Sioux*. Lincoln: University of Nebraska Press.

Nelson, Richard. 1983. *Make Prayers to the Raven: A Koyukon View of the Northern Forest*. Chicago: University of Chicago Press.

Niethammer, Carolyn. 1977. *Daughters of the Earth: The Lives and Legends of Indian Women*. New York: Collier Books.

Parsons, Elsie Worthington Clews. 1933. *Hopi and Zuni Ceremonialism*. Menasha, WI: American Anthropological Association.

Powell, Peter J. 1969. *Sweet Medicine: The Continuing Role of the Sacred Arrows in the Sun Dance, and the Sacred Buffalo Hat in Northern Cheyenne History*. Norman: University of Oklahoma.

Powers, William K. 1977. *Oglala Religion*. Lincoln: University of Nebraska Press.

Powers, William K. 1982. *Yuwipi: Vision and Experience in Oglala Ritual*. Lincoln: University of Nebraska Press.

Powers, William K. 1986. *Sacred Language: The Nature of Supernatural Discourse in Lakota*. Norman: University of Oklahoma Press.

Radin, Paul. 1920/1963. *The Autobiography of a Winnebago Indian*. New York: Dover.

Radin, Paul. 1945/1973. *The Road of Life and Death: A Ritual Drama of the American Indians*. Princeton: Bollingen.

Ramsey Jarold. 1977/1984. *Coyote Was Going There: Indian Literature of the Oregon Country*. Seattle: University of Washington Press.

Reichard, Gladys. 1950/1974. *Navaho Religion: A Study of Symbolism*. Princeton: Bollingen.

Ridington, Robin. 1990. *Little Bit Know Something: Stories in a Language of Anthropology*. Iowa City: University of Iowa Press.

Rothenberg, Jerome. 1972. *Shaking the Pumpkin: Traditional Stories of the Indian North Americas*. Garden City, NY: Doubleday.

Sandner, Donald. 1979. *Navaho Symbols of Healing*. New York: Harcourt Brace & Jovanovich.

Schwartz, Warren E. 1988/1989. *The Last Contrary: The Story of Wesley Whiteman*. Sioux Falls, SD: Center for Western Studies, Augustana College.

Silko, Leslie. 1977. *Ceremony*. New York: Viking Press.

Simmons, Leo. 1942. *Sun Chief: The Autobiography of a Hopi Indian*. New Haven: Yale University Press.

Siskin, Edgar E. 1983. *Washo Shamans and Peyotists: Religious Conflict in an American Indian Tribe*. Salt Lake City: University of Utah Press.

Sturtevant, William C., Jr., editor. 1978. *Handbook of North American Indians*. 20 vols. Washington, D.C.: Smithsonian Institution.

Swann, Brian. 1983. *Smoothing the Ground: Essays on Native American Oral Literature*. Berkeley: University of California Press.

Tanner, Adrian. 1979. *Bringing Home Animals: Religious Ideology and Mode of Production of the Mistassini Tree Hunters*. New York: St. Martin's Press.

Tedlock, Dennis and Barbara Tedlock. 1975. *Teachings from the American Earth: Indian Religion and Philosophy*. New York: Liveright.

Todorov, Tzvetan. 1984. *The Conquest of America: The Question of the Other*. New York: Harper & Row.

Tooker, Elisabeth, editor. 1979. *Native North American Spirituality of the Eastern Wood-*

lands: Sacred Myths, Dreams, Visions, Speeches, Healing Formulas, Rituals, and Ceremonials. New York: Paulist.

Turner, Frederick W., editor. 1974. *The Portable North American Indian Reader*. New York: Viking Press.

Underhill, Ruth. 1965. *Red Man's Religion: Beliefs and Practices of the Indians North of Mexico*. Chicago: University of Chicago Press.

Walker, James R. 1980. *Lakota Belief and Ritual*. Ed. Raymond J. DeMallie and Elaine A. Jahner. Lincoln: University of Nebraska Press.

Weltfish, Gene. 1965. *The Lost Universe*. New York: Basic Books.

Witherspoon, Gary. 1977. *Language and Art in the Navajo Universe*. Ann Arbor: University of Michigan Press.

Wyman, Leland Clifton. 1970. *Blessingway*. Tucson: University of Arizona Press.

Zolbrod, Paul G. 1984. *Dine bahane: The Navajo Creation Story*. Albuquerque: University of New Mexico Press.

10

RITUAL IN THE UNITED STATES

Madeline Duntley

Presenting ritual in the United States as a taxonomy merely serves to organize the many disparate sources available for the study of ritual. While monographs and articles on ritual are usually case studies or broad-based theoretical works produced by scholars in anthropology, history, religious studies, and sociology, writing about ritual is not the sole province of the academician. Scholars interested in so-called popular religion must not overlook the array of ritual sourcebooks and mainstream and revisionist guides produced by nonacademics— works that can provide valuable insights into current religious practice. Because of the vast number of books available on ritual in the United States, this chapter can only provide a survey of selected texts organized by subject, goal, and purpose. An introduction to recent general theoretical works precedes a section illustrating the types of sources available. Next, this chapter outlines scholars' use of community case studies as a way to present new models of fieldwork analysis; then it considers works concerned with the historical and sociocultural dimensions of ritual in America. Studies of ritual power, healing, performance, display, music, and language are the focus of the middle section, followed by a discussion of books by academics and practitioners on the subject of popular religion and the "invention and reinvention" of ritual. Lastly, there is a list of academic journals that regularly publish articles and reviews of interest to students of ritual in the United States.

GENERAL THEORETICAL WORKS

To begin a study of ritual in the United States, one must begin with theory. For a thorough account of the past and present use of the term *ritual* in scholarship, consult Catherine Bell, *Ritual Theory, Ritual Practice* (Bell 1992). Bell's work provides a critical background to the cross-disciplinary study of ritual by sketching the history of academic approaches to ritual. In the past, most scholars based their work on the theoretical presumptions and assumptions of the "classic" approaches of Arnold van Gennep, Clifford Geertz, Victor Turner, and Émile Durkheim—theorists too well known to require mention here. Yet lesser-known general works on theory produced within the past fifteen years are becoming increasingly influential in the field.

Ronald L. Grimes has produced several works of note to ritual theorists and fieldworkers. *Beginnings in Ritual Studies* (Grimes 1982/1995) is a text on "ritual studies" intended for classroom use. See Chapter 2, "Mapping the Field of Ritual," for an insightful essay directing students how to view a ritual in participant observation through the careful observation of ritual space, time, action, objects, identity, language, and gestures. Grimes's *Research in Ritual Studies: A Programmatic Essay and Bibliography* (1985) is a thematic bibliography of over 1,600 works on ritual published between 1960 and 1983. His *Ritual Criticism: Case Studies in Its Practice, Essays on Its Theory* (1990) uses the concept of "ritual criticism" to redirect field observers, challenging them to explore the subjectivity, idiosyncracies, and creativity of ritual. This study demonstrates how rituals are critiqued, assessed, and performed differently by ritual participants, ritual creators, and observing scholars, respectively. Chapter 9 is of special interest, for it proposes ways to determine how and why a ritual "fails" or "succeeds."

Roy Rappaport also focuses on the format as well as the function of religious ritual in *Ecology, Meaning, and Religion* (1979). He establishes a set of criteria for determining what is a religious ritual and how it is uniquely efficacious. By extending the possible functions of ritual (i.e., existential, psychological, social) to include "ecology," he shows how religious ritual helps human beings adapt to the physical world.

Tom F. Driver's *The Magic of Ritual: Our Need for Liberating Rites that Transform Our Lives and Our Communities* (1991) is a corrective to the idea that ritual is a backdrop or prop of myth or theology. Ritual is more than static, text oriented, and tradition enforcing; it also shapes and transmits theological meaning and reflection. Driver uses insights ranging from ethology to performance studies to offer an alternative to Jungian and Campbellian explanations for ritual's enduring attraction to human beings. Using a variety of examples from theory and field observation, Driver outlines the complex relation between belief and ritual and highlights ritual's potential for human "transformation" and "liberation."

William G. Doty examines the interplay of myth and ritual by reviewing and historically contextualizing current theories in *Mythography: The Study of Myths and Rituals* (1986). Jonathan Z. Smith also considers the connection of myth and ritual—how the historical privileging of myth over ritual affects ritual's relation to sacred space, place, and time. In *To Take Place: Toward Theory in*

Ritual (1987), Smith uses a wide array of examples to show how "place" is an essential component of ritual and that "sacrality is, above all, a category of emplacement." His earlier volume, *Imagining Religion: From Babylon to Jonestown* (1982), contains the essay "The Bare Facts of Ritual," where Smith defines ritual as "a means of performing the way things ought to be in conscious tension to the way things are" and compares ritual action to both ordinary and ideal action.

One who disclaims all discussion of meaning and context in preference for a "scientific" focus on the structure and rules of ritual action is Frits Staal. *Rules without Meaning: Ritual, Mantras, and the Human Sciences* (1989) is a series of essays that echo the theoretical assumptions of his earlier article, "The Meaninglessness of Ritual" (1979). Ritual, Staal argues, must first be released from the contexts of religion and from its associations with symbol, communication, and function before it can be studied properly as "a system of acts and sounds" related to "rules without reference to meaning."

Eugene G. d'Aquili et al. analyzes human ceremonial ritual from a neurological perspective in *The Spectrum of Ritual: A Biogenetic Structural Analysis* (1979). Based on data and examples from neuroanthropology and ethology, these articles explore the connection between cognitive activity and the social environment by offering explanations for the psychological and biological bases of ritual and trance. Another theoretical perspective on cognition and ritual is E. Thomas Lawson and Robert N. McCauley's *Rethinking Religion: Connecting Cognition and Culture* (1990), which upholds the symbolist study of ritual. Their concept of "representation of action" in religious ritual distinguishes between "interpretation" and "explanation." Lawson and McCauley posit semantics and linguistics as a way to study the "internal structure" of religious ritual and ritual meaning. (Also, see Charles Laughlin's chapter and "Ritual and Current Studies of Ritual: Overview" in this volume.)

THE DIVERSITY OF SOURCES: AN EXAMPLE

Even a cursory bibliographic search on a particular topic reveals both the types of sources available to scholars and the theoretical concerns that currently dominate the study of ritual in the United States. This section will illustrate the variety of books available on any given topic. If one looked, for example, under the heading of "Ritual and Judaism in America," one would find historical and anthropological case studies of Jewish groups and communities, handbooks or guides to Jewish ritual practice, and collections of essays discussing the modern Jewish "religious experience." A search for sources on this topic should begin with Barbara Myerhoff's *Number Our Days* (1978). This work is a methodologically innovative, nuanced case study of an elderly Jewish community in Venice, California. In four years of participant observation fieldwork as both insider and outsider (i.e., a "secular" Jew), Myerhoff explored ritual's role in the creation and maintenance of this community and the role of ritual performance and participation (for both scholar and practitioner) in the construction of meaning. Her discovery that even newly created rituals function as sources for order and continuity is a startling corrective to the view that only traditional, time-honored rituals can accomplish this feat. A film of the same title produced by Myerhoff and Lynne Litman won a 1977 Academy Award for Best Documentary. Myerhoff later produced another film, *In Her Own Time*, a poignant study of her ritual interaction with a Los Angeles Hasidic community filmed in the final months of her struggle with terminal cancer.

Other case studies of Jewish life followed Myerhoff's work. Lis Harris, a journalist-turned-fieldworker, presents a year in the traditional, communitarian life of Lubavitchers in *Holy Days: The World of a Hasidic Family* (1985). While the book is a compelling and descriptive account of Hasidic ritual life, it has little methodological or theoretical self-consciousness beyond subtly presenting various points of view on orthodox practices and lifestyles. On the other hand, Jack Kugelmass's *The Miracle of Intervale Avenue: The Story of a Jewish Congregation in the South Bronx* (1986) is as much a story of place as it is a sketch of community. This study shows how members of this inner-city Orthodox synagogue use the traditions of Torah to mediate urban transition and change. Ranging beyond its subject, it serves as a model for future examinations of popular religion in urban contexts. Riv-Ellen Prell's *Prayer and Community: The Havurah in American Judaism* (1989) also uses a group study to suggest new directions for studying innovation and tradition in American religious ritual. Prell finds that her subjects, a group of highly educated young adults, use the traditional Jewish *havurot*, or "prayer group," both to critique the strictures of denominational Judaism and to affirm religious commitment and its spiritual relevance. Prell sees the ritual intention of prayer as a balance between personal choice (aesthetics and noetic meaning) and context (commitment to *halakha* and tradition).

Scholarly overviews of Judaism in America tend to dwell on the historical context of Jewish life and often omit the descriptive accounts of religious practices that may be found in denominational manuals or ritual handbooks. Among the best is Leo Trepp's *The Complete Book of Jewish Observance: A Practical Manual for the Modern Jew* (1980). Arlene Rossen Cardozo combines ritual description and personal testimony in her *Jewish Family Celebrations, the Sabbath, Festivals, and Ceremonies* (1982). In telling the collective history of Jewish festivals and embellishing her account with family songs, recipes, and stories, she demonstrates ritual's vitality in modern American Jewish life. The authors of essays in Elizabeth Koltun's *The Jewish Woman: New Perspectives* (1976) discuss traditional Jewish laws and customs in order to promote rituals that celebrate and support Jewish womanhood. These essays echo the approach employed by similar "ritual revisionist" works produced by feminists in a variety of other religious traditions.

THE CASE STUDY AS SHOWCASE FOR
METHODOLOGICAL INNOVATION

Many scholars of ritual in the United States use a case study of a particular community to showcase their innovative methods for fieldwork observation and ritual interpretation. A field observer's perspective and data are used to test and challenge current theoretical approaches to ritual and to offer alternative explanations for the religious meaning and social context of ritual in American life.

Robert A. Orsi's *The Madonna of 115th Street: Faith and Community in Italian Harlem, 1880–1950* (1985) highlights the summer communal *festa* of the Madonna of Mount Carmel. As the whole neighborhood prepares for this event, cleaning, decorating, reminiscing, and displaying religious articles and selling food, Orsi shows that the *festa* is more than just the climactic procession through the streets of Harlem. Orsi's findings demonstrate the indivisibility of the sacred and secular. The conflicts, tensions, and interactions of family life, or *"domus,"* of Italian American immigrant Catholicism both reflect and influence the form and expression of ritual and spirituality. The end result of Orsi's judicious use of historical records and interviews is an interpretation that is faithful to this community's own articulation of what constitutes the significant and the sacred.

In Karen McCarthy Brown's *Mama Lola: A Vodou Priestess in Brooklyn* (1991), the author becomes initiate, and the barriers between informant and observer-scholar shatter. Based on over ten years of participant observation fieldwork, McCarthy Brown's changes in methodological approach parallel her own shifting perspective as she details the limits to knowing as others know and the process of initiation as a means of coming to know. In her innovative intertwining of biography and autobiography, McCarthy Brown uses her own "recollections" and her informants' "memories" to recount the shaping of many women's lives in this Haitian immigrant community. *Mama Lola* retains the appeal engendered by earlier accounts of voodoo possession and initiation that challenge the insider/outsider dichotomy: Maya Deren's *Divine Horsemen: Voodoo Gods of Haiti* (1970) and Zora Neale Hurston's *Mules and Men* (1935/ 1990).

Salvation on Sand Mountain: Snake Handling and Redemption in Southern Appalachia (Covington 1995) is an English professor's foray into the world of ritual serpent handling in a northeastern Alabama church. Dennis Covington's fieldwork becomes a personal odyssey as he becomes increasingly devoted to the worship, teachings, and spirituality of snake handlers. After two years of research, he finally takes up serpents himself and is riveted by the realization that the spiritual power and victory in snake handling is a foretaste of what some have called paradise, an experience of limbo, a suspension, a profound loss of self in a strong, silent white light. To gain personal access to the mystery of this ritual practice, Covington chooses to become, at least temporarily, a practicing member of the community he studies.

Another work that self-consciously attempts to balance "observation and participation, scholarship and experience" is Joseph M. Murphy's *Santeria: An African Religion in America* (1988). Murphy argues that the religious experience of both scholar and practitioner is not properly examined in scholarly accounts of ritual, even though subjective experience is crucial to discovering what makes religious practice "real" and understandable. Murphy's study also challenges the way scholars categorize ritual practice in America: Santeria does not belong to the margins of American culture but must be seen as a diasporic expression of a living African religion. By placing Santeria within its larger historical context and explicating its ritual practices, Murphy suggests that Santeria is more akin to "world religion" than sect or cult. In *Working the Spirit: Ceremonies of the African Diaspora* (Murphy 1994), Murphy continues to study Santeria in America but expands his analysis to include the African diaspora in the Caribbean, South America, and the Black Church in America. Here he most often assumes the position of an "outsider." Murphy shows that the "links" or reciprocal relationship of spirit(s), ancestors, and human beings are recreated, maintained, and discovered within the performance of community rituals and ceremonies.

A community study dealing with the impact of modernity on ritual practice is John D. Loftin's *Religion and Hopi Life in the Twentieth Century* (1991). Loftin uses field data and information from Hopi "consultants" to present a portrayal of modern Hopi life challenging the "romantic notion" that the Hopi are "living fossils" of an earlier, traditional time. Change is natural to this culture, he argues, yet some "forced" changes from the Euro-American dominant culture have been difficult to assimilate into the Hopi mythic "orientation to the world." Loftin uses a study of Hopi religious acts to demonstrate the interconnection between the practical and the spiritual and to examine the relationship between Hopi "work" (*tumala*) and "ritual" (*wiimi*).

Addressing the lack of resources on southern regional religion, Ruel W. Tyson, Jr., and James. L. Peacock collaborated on *Pilgrims of Paradox: Calvinism and Experience among the Primitive Baptists of the Blue Ridge* (Peacock and Tyson 1989). Here they use a case study to demonstrate the seemingly elusive role that "ambiguity and paradox" play in religious expression and belief, by examining Primitive Baptists in light of the theories and paradigms of Weber and Durkheim. Peacock and Tyson also worked with Daniel W. Patterson to collect fieldwork-based essays on a variety of local religious communities. *Diversities of Gifts: Field Studies in Southern Religion* (Tyson, Peacock, and Patterson 1988) includes case studies of a variety of ethnically and doctrinally diverse groups, including Primitive Baptist, Quaker, Holiness, and African Methodist Episcopal Zion. The editors attempt to organize these descriptive studies under the rubric of examining "ritual gesture." Instead of focusing on theological categories, they suggest that the study of ritual gesture provides better access to the beliefs and feelings engendered and expressed within these religious communities. While many of the essays do not employ this methodological approach, this book and other similar projects like *American Congregations: Portraits of Twelve Religious Communities* (Vol. 1) and *New Perspectives in the Study of Congregations* (Vol. 2) (Wind and Lewis 1994, 1995) testify to the value scholars continue to place on the case study's potential in elucidating the role and function of ritual in American life.

Aesthetic anthropology is John Forrest's method of choice in *Lord I'm Coming Home: Everyday Aesthetics in Tidewater, North Carolina* (1988). In an endeavor to reproduce the "local view" of church, home, work, and leisure, Forrest as fieldworker "sifts out the aesthetic experiences," which he then documents as "live, affecting, subjectively real entities." While he considers the subjectivity of experience worthy of and possible to study, Forrest is only concerned with one's day-to-day *encounter* of aesthetics. He does not explore how aesthetics plays a role in constructing and transmitting ritual forms and meanings.

HISTORICAL AND SOCIOCULTURAL STUDIES

Many anthropologists and historians study a particular type of religious ritual as a social phenomenon providing clues and insights into a society, community, culture, or region. These works differ from a case study in point of emphasis; the focus here is not on how or why a group practices specific rituals. Instead, ritual is studied for what it reveals about the community's attendant culture. Since many historical treatments preclude fieldwork analysis, the ritual is necessarily placed in its historic, rather than communal, context.

Gwen Kennedy Neville's *Kinship and Pilgrimage: Rituals of Reunion in American Protestant Culture* (1987) builds on Turnerian theories of pilgrimage to examine a traditional ritual pattern enacted in a modern complex society. "Pilgrimage" here is less an ethnographic description of ritual practice than a way to frame and explain a variety of southern rural Protestant rituals of reunion, such as family homecomings, and gatherings at denominational conference centers. In a historical sketch, Neville contrasts Catholic and Protestant manifestations or varieties of pilgrimage. Yet her theoretical analysis rests on the ritual's sociopolitical goal and purpose, rather than upon pilgrimage rituals as a form of religious experience.

Mark C. Carnes focuses on the initiation rituals of freemasonry in his *Secret Ritual and Manhood in Victorian America* (1989). Elaborate, secret initiation rituals are integral to freemasonry's appeal and effectiveness. These rituals are important not only for their esoteric allure, nor only for their function in gaining entrance to a fraternal society, but because they offered a countercultural way for males to make the transition from "boyhood to manhood" in nineteenth-century America.

In an ambitious transatlantic study, Leigh Eric Schmidt connects "commun-

ion season'' rituals of penitence, preaching, and sacrament to the rise and development of the camp meeting and American revivalism. While *Holy Fairs:
Scottish Communions and American Revivals in the Early Modern Period* (1990)
seeks to explain the roots of revivalism, Schmidt carefully frames the religious
and experiential dimensions of the variety of ritual activities he describes.

Several works focus on rituals of ''devotion'' to examine the social life of a
particular religious group. Charles E. Hambrick-Stowe's *The Practice of Piety:
Puritan Devotional Disciplines in Seventeenth-Century New England* (1982)
claims that New England colonial Puritanism itself can be seen as a ''devotional
movement''—and that common devotional techniques, worship rites, vocabulary, and ideas pervade both the elite and popular culture of seventeenth-century
Puritanism. Hambrick-Stowe uses ritual to describe and illuminate Puritan
''spirituality,'' which in turn reveals the Puritan character to be both activist
and contemplative. Ann Taves's *The Household of Faith: Roman Catholic Devotions in Mid-Nineteenth-Century America* (1986) also looks at popular devotional publications and local parish ritual practices. As she recreates the
spiritual life of Catholic laity, Taves uncovers a familial piety that includes Jesus
and Mary in the family circle. This ''household of faith'' contributed to the
creation and maintenance of a unique Catholic subculture and distinct version
of the cult of domesticity.

In *The Christian Home in Victorian America, 1840–1900* (1986), Colleen
McDannell also studies ''rituals of the hearth,'' but she analyzes the material
culture: domestic architecture and artifacts (journals, calendars, paintings,
crosses, rosaries, musical instruments, printed materials, family Bibles, etc.) of
both Protestants and Catholics to contextualize the devotional life of Victorian
Americans. McDannell illustrates how the various ritual practices affirm the
religious centrality of ''home'' within a wider domestic ideology.

Dining rituals are the subject of Patricia Curran's *Grace before Meals: Food
Ritual and Body Discipline in Convent Culture* (1989). Curran compares and
contrasts various food rituals and how they relate to the spiritual development
and penance activity of two generations of nuns in the Dominican Sisters of
Mission San Jose and the Sisters of Notre Dame de Namur. Alongside interviews
with nuns and detailed description of dining practices, Curran uses historical
data to place the rituals in their general Christian context (see chapter 3, ''Christian Food Beliefs''). Curran uses food rituals as a way to contrast Jesuit and
Dominican convent culture generally and to discuss post–Vatican II amelioration
and change in convent life.

Many historians find ritual practices omnipresent yet underrated and largely
unexplored in cultural life. David D. Hall's *Worlds of Wonder, Days of Judgment: Popular Religious Belief in Early New England* (1989) examines the popular religion in colonial New England and finds there a ''mentality of the
supernatural.'' This culture's ''ritual enclosing'' of sickness, death, and moral
disobedience is replete with magic and ritual, and these rituals directly refer to
both the maintenance of and desire for a sense of community. Hall refuses to

separate the "churchly" from the popular and examines the various "uses of ritual"—from meetinghouse to sick bed to scaffold—as one interconnected and interrelated fabric of religious and ritual sensibility. In *The Devil's Dominion: Magic and Religion in Early New England* (1992), Richard Godbeer also studies magic in seventeenth-century New England. Witchcraft cases are replete with references to countermagic, "malific" or harmful magic, and rituals of healing and divination. Godbeer sees the ways in which magic might both complement and challenge Puritan theology and thus contribute to the tensions that produced the witchcraft outbreaks. Steven M. Stowe's *Intimacy and Power in the Old South: Ritual in the Lives of the Planters* (1987) examines courtship, duelling, and life passage rituals in the experience of selected planter families to illustrate how ritual shaped the values and lifestyles of antebellum planters. Stowe finds that rituals defined gender roles that maintained the elitism, hierarchy, and ethos of planter culture.

PUBLIC RITUALS: FESTIVAL, CEREMONY, AND POWER

Works on festival and ceremony highlight ritual's role in the construction of private and public identities. They often note the complexity of public ritual— its varied functions, forms, and goals. For theory on "festival" generally, con- sult Alessandro Falassi's introduction to his collection *Time Out of Time: Essays on the Festival* (1987). Here Falassi discusses the types of rituals present within a festival. The transition into and out of "festival time" is made by way of "framing rituals" such as parades, and the festival itself is a series of elaborate rituals of purification, passage, reversal, display, consumption, and competition.

In *All Around the Year: Holidays and Celebrations in American Life* (1995), Jack Santino uses an interdisciplinary approach to analyze how Americans cre- ate, adapt, and celebrate private and public holidays, festivals, and life cycle rituals. Pamela R. Frese edited a collection of essays, *Celebrations of Identity: Multiple Voices in American Ritual Performance* (1993), that documents how culturally and geographically diverse groups of Americans use ritual celebrations to both "validate and reinvent" their ethnic, racial, national, and religious iden- tities and how such research helps to define and refine the concept of a collec- tive, pluralistic "American" identity.

Other works on public ritual choose to compare one festival cross-culturally. Two American manifestations of the Mardi Gras festival are the subject of Sam- uel Kinser's *Carnival, American Style: Mardi Gras at New Orleans and Mobile* (1990). Kinser combines a historical study with firsthand descriptions of the modern carnival. He details the dynamics of gender, race, class, and ethnicity enacted and challenged in both Mardi Gras celebrations. Kinser notes the com- mon ground of Carnival's political, staged ceremoniousness as well as its spon- taneous, infectious creativity. Ronald L. Grimes focuses on the role of public pageantry in the creation, maintenance, and merging of ethnic, religious, and civic identities in Santa Fe, New Mexico. In *Symbol and Conquest: Public Ritual and Drama in Santa Fe* (Grimes 1976/1992), he shows how public procession and festival mark and display the city's heritage of interracial and interreligious commingling. Specific festal symbols and personages manifest the complexity of the residents' multiple public identities.

David I. Kertzer's *Ritual, Politics, and Power* (1988) outlines ritual's role in political solidarity and identity formation. Although his supporting examples range from KKK (Ku Klux Klan) cross burnings to medieval European coronation ceremonies, he includes an abundance of illustrations from America's political life. Kertzer emphasizes the potentiality inherent in ritual, noting the multiplicity of meanings possible in political symbols and the ability of ritual to both display and undermine power. For more on the appropriation of power through ritual, see the *Journal of Ritual Studies'* "Ritual and Power" issue ("Ritual and Power" 1990). Christopher Vecsey's collection *Handbook of American Indian Religious Freedom* (1991) also addresses the interplay of power and ritual. Here scholars and lawyers discuss the 1978 American Indian Religious Freedom Act and cases of land, fishing, and peyote rights currently challenged in the courts. This book is a fascinating glimpse of how the U.S. government can restrict ritual: Legal definitional boundaries for religion cause many traditional indigenous rituals to fall outside the canon of verifiable, acceptable, and viable religious practices.

MUSIC, DRAMA, DANCE, AND RITUAL LANGUAGE

Sources directly addressing the ritual dimensions of musical or artistic performance vary in both style and content. Some texts on this topic are generated by art exhibitions and museum displays, such as *Ritual and Myth: A Survey of African-American Art* (1982) and the Smithsonian Office of Folklife Program's *Celebration: A World of Art and Ritual* (1982). Monographs and essays on Native American religion and culture often include the ritual context of art, music, and dance. See Reginald and Gladys Laubin's *Indian Dances of North America, Their Importance to Indian Life* (1977/1989) for historical descriptions, photographs, and illustrations of dances organized by type (i.e., Sun Dance, War Dance, Corn Dance, etc.) and geographical region. Volume 1 of *Kiowa Voices* by Maurice Boyd (1981) is devoted to "Ceremonial Dance, Ritual, and Song." This source highlights traditional Indian and Christian Kiowa songs and dances as part of a multivolume anthology produced by Kiowas in conjunction with Texas Christian University. Another analysis of ritual and the arts is *Dance as Religious Studies*, edited by Doug Adams and Diane Apostolos-Cappadona (1990). This collection contains articles on topics ranging from the form and content of Christian liturgical dance to a psychological study of how dance conveys religious meaning. Distinctions between religious and secular ritual are blurred in *Old Hollywood/New Hollywood: Ritual, Art and Industry* by Thomas G. Schatz (1983), a work highlighting the role of art and cinema in the creation and marketing of modern myths.

Works that focus primarily on the ritual and music of a specific community, such as Edward Deming Andrews's classic collection of Shaker music *The Gift to Be Simple: Songs, Dances, and Rituals of the American Shakers* (1940/1967), are generally detailed and instructive. Andrews not only provides the actual Shaker musical scores and text but describes the gestures, choreography, and ritual context of these songs. A similar resource on antebellum Protestants is by musicologist Ellen Jane Lorenz, *Glory, Hallelujah!: The Story of the Camp-meeting Spiritual* (1980). Lorenz intersperses musical scores and lyrics with reminiscences of camp meeting life and descriptions of the song sequences. Then she discusses their impact on other American musical forms and worship styles. A very different treatment of music and ritual is Neil Leonard's *Jazz, Myth, and Religion* (1987), which considers jazz music *as* ritual. According to Leonard, jazz rituals are "prescribed, repeated practice and patterns" relating to musical performance, language, and style.

In addition to historical, anthropological, and musicological monographs, students of ritual and music should not overlook the variety of sound recordings available. The Library of Congress collection *Folk Music of the United States* is a large archive of American folk song (Frances Densmore's early twentieth-century "Songs of the Sioux" recordings are one example from this collection). *Folkways Ethnic Library* is another series that provides musical recordings and accompanying descriptive pamphlets. These records are currently distributed by the Smithsonian Institution and are usually available at city public libraries; the Library of Congress collection offers many titles through mail order. Also, a wide variety of Christian, Jewish, and Mormon denominational groups regularly produce sacred or worship music recordings for public purchase.

Works exploring African-American worship, music, and preaching include Gerald L. Davis's *I Got the Word in Me and I Can Sing It, You Know: A Study of the Performed African-American Sermon* (1985). Davis profiles the sermon as a "ritual genre" that provides a paradigm for other African-American public performances: political speeches, toasts, raps, and jokes. His examination of the sermon's verbal modality highlights the spontaneous and formulaic generation of sound in sermonic style, as well as the antiphonal resonance of black preaching. In *Old Ship of Zion: The Afro-Baptist Ritual in the African Diaspora* (1993), Walter F. Pitts, a linguistic anthropologist and musician, recounts his participation in five years of Baptist worship services in rural Texas. He finds striking similarities between the "binary structure" of both African and African-American worship styles and outlines parallels between American Afro-Baptist rituals and African-derived religious rituals of the Caribbean, the U.S. Sea Islands, and Brazil, as well as rituals indigenous to West and central Africa.

Another work featuring the ritualized format and emotive power of preaching is Elaine J. Lawless's *Handmaidens of the Lord: Pentecostal Women Preachers and Traditional Religion* (1988). Using interviews and tapes of white female Pentecostal preachers in rural Missouri, Lawless provides detailed descriptions and reproductions of the actual sermon texts. She studies the religious roles these women occupy and the sermon texts they preach in order to illuminate the construction and negotiation of gender roles in these communities.

The role of language and song in healing is addressed by William K. Powers in *Sacred Language: The Nature of Supernatural Discourse in Lakota* (1986). In chapter 3, Powers discusses over twenty songs used in the Lakota Yuwipi curing ceremony. He translates each song's symbolic and metaphoric content, copies the Lakota- and English-language text, and locates the music's ceremonial function by telling how the song is actually performed during the healing rite. Meredith B. McGuire looks at nonmedical healing techniques in suburban, middle-class New Jersey in the 1980s. In *Ritual Healing in Suburban America* (1988), she shows how ritual language promotes the efficacy and appeal of these healing practices. Chapter 9 focuses on practices from five types of healing groups, including neo-Pentecostal, Christian Science, Eckanar, and Transcendental Meditation. A unique look at the ritual language and practice of medicine is Robbie E. Davis-Floyd's *Birth as an American Rite of Passage* (1992). She outlines how the stylized technological model of a modern hospital birth constitutes a ritual sequence that demonstrates American's need to culturally contain and control what should be a natural and transformative process of the "birthing" of woman into mother.

Many theorists assume that religious action is necessarily "performative" or dramatic in nature. Sam Gill's *Native American Religious Action: A Performance Approach to Religion* (1987) employs field study data from Navajo and Hopi cultures to view rituals like prayer as more than simply "text." Prayer is a performative ritual that evokes a "network of images related to sense experience, moods, emotion, and values" and must be observed in context as a performed, pragmatic, and poetic medium. Richard Schechner's work elucidates the performance aspects of ritual in general. In *Between Theater & Anthropology* (Schechner 1985), *Performance Theory* (Schechner 1988), and his edited collection with Willa Appel, *By Means of Performance: Intercultural Studies of Theatre and Ritual* (Schechner and Appel 1990), Schechner offers new ways to scrutinize both the boundaries of ritual action (i.e., when a ritual actually begins and ends) and the aesthetics and meanings engendered by the dramatic elements or staged performance of ritual.

INVENTING AND REINVENTING RITES: POPULAR RELIGION

Scholars and religious practitioners have worked to document American "popular" religion in terms of ritual's day-to-day context and meaning among mainline Christian communities as well as in groups ranging outside mainstream religious institutions. A general introduction to "what usually gets left out" of courses and bibliographies is *Being Religious, American Style: A History of Popular Religiosity in the United States* (Lippy 1994). Charles H. Lippy takes a chronological look at the meaning of "popular religiosity" as the inventive, personal, open-ended way individuals often blend an eclectic mix of practices and beliefs. Lippy chooses a chronological and geographical framework upon which to organize his inherently "disorganized" topic: the unofficial, dynamic religious expressions of ordinary people who are constantly "creating and maintaining personal worlds of meaning." He argues that since America is a society that shares many core values of religious symbols and beliefs, he is able to examine the sources and documents of popular culture (novels, media, oral transmission, music, diaries, guides, and handbooks) and discern those unique religious rituals, practices, and ideas that people choose to integrate into their daily lives, regardless of formal religious structures and institutions. As an alternative to such broad, historical surveys, many writers prefer to profile specific American subgroups, often employing methods of field observation, interviews, and biography. In one of the first surveys of burgeoning neopagan religions in the United States, Margot Adler's *Drawing Down the Moon: Witches, Druids, Goddess-Worshippers, and Other Pagans in America Today* (1986) evaluates and accounts for the reappearance, recovery, and increasing popularity of long-held, nonauthoritarian pagan magic and Wiccan traditions and ritual.

Scholar/practioners of alternative or "new religious movements" are also increasingly producing handbooks or guides for ritual practice and performance. These books are indispensable resource manuals for both the academic and popular markets. The collection by Louise Carus Mahdi and coauthors, *Betwixt and Between: Patterns of Masculine and Feminine Initiation* (Mahdi, Foster, and Little 1987) builds on the theoretical insights of van Gennep, Turner, and Jung to offer a variety of ways to mark and explore initiations into life stages and states of being. While it does not imply that modern life is devoid of ritual, many of these essays attempt to show how one might construct more effective and meaningful rituals of initiation by borrowing and adapting ritual forms from other cultures or by becoming more self-conscious of one's "ritual intent." The book's creative, multidisciplinary suggestions for constructing rituals, plus its useful film list and bibliography, make this collection of essays and "pieces" on ritual an important resource on popular interpretations and practices of initiation ritual.

Many books that endorse ritual renewal in U.S. society endeavor to reclaim forgotten traditional rites. Here the boundaries between ancient rites and modern creations are intentionally blurred; innovation and creativity help to adapt and translate ancient ritual forms to modern lifestyles. In *King Warrior Magician Lover: Rediscovering the Archetypes of the Mature Masculine* (Moore and Gillette 1990), Robert Moore and Douglas Gillette bemoan the loss of masculine initiation rituals and the absence of the "father" in many American homes. They blame the post-Enlightenment-Protestant ethos for systematically eliminating culture-sustaining rituals for men. Sam Keen's *Fire in the Belly: On Being a Man* (1991) also claims that this "crisis" of masculine identity can only be redressed through revitalized initiation rites. Invocations, exercises, and magic are the subject of Starhawk's (Miriam Simos) *The Spiral*

Dance: A Rebirth of the Ancient Religion of the Great Goddess (Starhawk/Simos 1979/1989), a book fast becoming a classic of the genre. Diane Stein's collections of rituals are also worth noting, such as *Casting the Circle: A Women's Book of Ritual* (1990) and especially *The Goddess Celebrates: An Anthology of Women's Rituals* (1991), which includes photos and biographical sketches of the women leaders central to Goddess-centered ritual and spirituality. For feminist writers more explicit about the political and countercultural implications of alternative ritual practices, see Charlene Spretnak's *The Politics of Women's Spirituality* (1982) and Barbara G. Walker's *Women's Rituals: A Sourcebook* (1990).

The creation and adaptation of life transition rituals has long fascinated scholars and theologians. Some works focus on a specific rite, while others broach the topic of life passage rituals generally. Two of the many intriguing historical treatments of the evolution of death rituals in American culture include James Farrell's *Inventing the American Way of Death, 1830–1920* (1980) and Margaret Coffin's *Death in Early America: The History and Folklore of Early Medicine, Funerals, Burials and Mourning* (1976). Jack Riemer's collection of essays *Jewish Reflections on Death* (1974) provides a compelling glimpse into modern Jewish death rites by augmenting a discussion of mourning laws and customs with personal narratives from Jews of varying backgrounds, attesting to the meaning and significance of this ritual cycle. Ronald L. Grimes's autobiographical *Marrying and Burying: Rites of Passage in a Man's Life* (1995) also uses life story to discuss the processes of death, marriage, and birth enacted in rites both individual and communal. He weaves personal story, fiction, and ritual theory into a testament to the "extraordinary ordinariness" of the piecemeal, patchwork spirituality of effective life passage rites. Liturgical renewal in Christian communities has also inspired a variety of theological studies of baptism, confirmation, marriage, death, and divorce. These works typically reassess and restate the goals and style of modern Christian ritual practice both in light of either early Church antecedents or by using models taken from preindustrial tribal societies. William O. Roberts, Jr.'s *Initiation to Adulthood: An Ancient Rite of Passage in Contemporary Form* (1982) chronicles how Roberts and other youth leaders in his congregation successfully recast tribal forms of initiation for use as a two-year ritual of initiation for a high school Confirmation class. Aidan Kavanagh's *The Shape of Baptism: The Rite of Christian Initiation* (1978/1991) is a more theologically nuanced, historically sensitive look at this sacrament as a Christian initiation practice. For the various concerns expressed by Christian liturgical renewal, ranging from aesthetic form to theological content, see Kavanagh's *Elements of Rite: A Handbook of Liturgical Style* (1982), Marjorie Procter-Smith's *In Her Own Rite: Constructing Feminist Liturgical Tradition* (1990), and *Women-Church: Theology and Practice of Feminist Liturgical Communities* (1985) by Rosemary Radford Ruether.

SELECTED ACADEMIC JOURNALS

Clearly, the study of ritual in America requires the use of many different types of source materials. Equally important to research, but beyond the scope of this chapter, is the information contained in articles published by academic journals. Such articles typically describe and interpret ritual practices, explicate rituals in texts and literature, and present and critique fieldwork methodologies and theoretical approaches. Many journals also include reviews and bibliographies pertinent to this field.

Below is a list of academic journals that regularly feature articles and book reviews on various aspects of ritual in American life.

American Anthropologist

American Ethnologist

American Historical Review

American Indian Quarterly

American Indian Religions: An Interdisciplinary Journal

Anthropologica

Anthropological Quarterly

Anthropology and Humanism Quarterly

Ethnomusicology

Journal for the Scientific Study of Religion

Journal of the American Academy of Religion

Journal of American History

Journal of Religion

Journal of Ritual Studies

Numen

Religion and American Culture: A Journal of Interpretation

Semiotica

Soundings

Syzygy: Journal of Alternative Religion and Culture

Theory & Method in the Study of Religion

Western Folklore

Zygon

REFERENCES

Adams, Doug, and Diane Apostolos-Cappadona, editors. 1990. *Dance as Religious Studies*. New York: Crossroad Publishing Company.

Adler, Margot. 1979. *Drawing Down the Moon: Witches Druids, Goddess-Worshippers and Other Pagans in America Today*. New York: Viking Press.

Andrews, Edward Deming. 1940/1967. *The Gift to Be Simple: Songs, Dances, and Rituals of the American Shakers*. New York: Dover Publications.

Bell, Catherine. 1992. *Ritual Theory, Ritual Practice*. New York: Oxford University Press.

Boyd, Maurice. 1981. *Kiowa Voices*. Vol. 1. Fort Worth: Texas Christian University Press.

Brown, Karen McCarthy. 1991. *Mama Lola: A Vodou Priestess in Brooklyn*. Berkeley: University of California Press.

Cardozo, Arlene Rossen. 1982. *Jewish Family Celebrations, the Sabbath, Festivals, and Ceremonies*. New York: St. Martin's Press.

Carnes, Mark C. 1989. *Secret Ritual and Manhood in Victorian America*. New Haven: Yale University Press.

Celebration, a World of Art and Ritual. 1982. Washington, D.C.: Smithsonian Institution Press.

Coffin, Margaret. 1976. *Death in Early America: The History and Folklore of Early Medicine, Funerals, Burials and Mourning*. Nashville: Thomas Nelson.

Covington, Dennis. 1995. *Salvation on Sand Mountain: Snake Handling and Redemption in Southern Appalachia*. Redding, MA: Addison-Wesley.

Curran, Patricia. 1989. *Grace before Meals: Food Ritual and Body Discipline in Covent Culture*. Urbana: University of Illinois Press.

d'Aquili, Eugene G.; Charles D. Loughlin; John McManus, and Tom Burns. 1979. *The Spectrum of Ritual: A Biogenetic Structural Analysis*. New York: Columbia University Press.

Davis, Gerald L. 1985. *I Got the Word in Me and I Can Sing It, You Know: A Study of the Performed African-American Sermon*. Philadelphia: University of Pennsylvania Press.

Davis-Floyd, Robbie E. 1992. *Birth as an American Rite of Passage*. Berkeley: University of California Press.

Densmore, Frances. 1951. *Songs of the Sioux*. Recording from the Folk Music of the United States Archive of the Library of Congress.

Deren, Maya. 1970. *Divine Horsemen: Voodoo Gods of Haiti*. New York: Chelsea House.

Doty, William G. 1986. *Mythography: The Study of Myths and Rituals*. AL: University of Alabama Press.

Driver, Tom F. 1991. *The Magic of Ritual: Our Need for Liberating Rites that Transform Our Lives and Our Communities*. San Francisco: Harper San Francisco.

Falassi, Alessandro. 1987. *Time Out of Time: Essays on the Festival*. Albuquerque: University of New Mexico Press.

Farrell, James. 1980. *Inventing the American Way of Death, 1830–1920*. Philadelphia: Temple University Press.

Forrest, John. 1988. *Lord I'm Coming Home: Everyday Aesthetics in Tidewater, North Carolina*. Ithaca: Cornell University Press.

Frese, Pamela R., editor. 1993. *Celebrations of Identity: Multiple Voices in American Ritual Performance*. Westport, CT: Bergin & Garvey.

Gill, Sam D. 1987. *Native American Religious Action: A Performance Approach to Religion*. Columbia: University of South Carolina Press.

Godbeer, Richard. 1992. *The Devil's Dominion: Magic and Religion in Early New England*. New York: Cambridge University Press.

Grimes, Ronald L. 1976/1992. *Symbol and Conquest: Public Ritual and Drama in Santa Fe*. Albuquerque: University of New Mexico Press.

Grimes, Ronald L. 1982/1995. *Beginnings in Ritual Studies*. Revised edition. Columbia: University of South Carolina Press.

Grimes, Ronald L. 1985. *Research in Ritual Studies: A Programmatic Essay and Bibliography*. Metuchen, NJ: Scarecrow Press and the American Theological Library Association.

Grimes, Ronald L. 1990. *Ritual Criticism: Case Studies in Its Practice, Essays on Its Theory*. Columbia: University of South Carolina Press.

Grimes, Ronald L. 1995. *Marrying and Burying: Rites of Passage in a Man's Life*. Boulder: Westview Press.

Hall, David D. 1989. *Worlds of Wonder, Days of Judgment: Popular Religious Belief in Early New England*. New York: Alfred A. Knopf.

Hambrick-Stowe, Charles E. 1982. *The Practice of Piety: Puritan Devotional Disciplines in Seventeenth-Century New England*. Chapel Hill: University of North Carolina Press.

Harris, Lis. 1985. *Holy Days: The World of a Hasidic Family*. New York: Summit Books.

Hurston, Zora Neale. 1935/1990. *Mules and Men*. New York: Perennial Library.

Kavanagh, Aidan. 1978/1991. *The Shape of Baptism: The Rite of Christian Initiation*. Collegeville, MN: Liturgical Press.

Kavanagh, Aidan. 1982. *Elements of Rite: A Handbook of Liturgical Style*. New York: Pueblo Publishing Company.

Keen, Sam. 1991. *Fire in the Belly: On Being a Man*. New York: Bantam Books.

Kertzer, David I. 1988. *Ritual, Politics, and Power*. New Haven: Yale University Press.

Kinser, Samuel. 1990. *Carnival, American Style: Mardi Gras at New Orleans and Mobile*. Chicago: University of Chicago Press.

Koltun, Elizabeth, editor. 1976. *The Jewish Woman: New Perspectives*. New York: Schocken Books.

Kugelmass, Jack. 1986. *The Miracle of Intervale Avenue: The Story of a Jewish Congregation in the South Bronx*. New York: Schocken Books.

Laubin, Reginald and Gladys Laubin. 1977/1989. *Indian Dances of North America, Their Importance to Indian Life*. Norman: University of Oklahoma Press.

Lawless, Elain J. 1988. *Handmaidens of the Lord: Pentecostal Women Preachers and Traditional Religion*. Philadelphia: University of Pennsylvania Press.

Lawson, E. Thomas, and Robert N. McCauley. 1990. *Rethinking Religion: Connecting Cognition and Culture*. Cambridge: Cambridge University Press.

Leonard, Neil. 1987. *Jazz, Myth, and Religion*. New York: Oxford University Press.

Lippy, Charles H. 1994. *Being Religious, American Style: A History of Popular Religiosity in the United States*. Westport, CT: Greenwood Press.

Loftin, John D. 1991. *Religion and Hopi Life in the Twentieth Century*. Bloomington: Indiana University Press.

Lorenz, Ellen Jame. 1980. *Glory, Hallelujah!: The Story of the Campmeeting Spiritual*. Nashville: Abingdon Press.

McDannell, Colleen. 1986. *The Christian Home in Victorian America, 1840–1900*. Bloomington: Indiana University Press.

McGuire, Meredith B. 1988. *Ritual Healing in Suburban America*. New Brunswick: Rutgers University Press.

Mahdi, Louise Carus; Steven Foster; and Meredith Little, editors. 1987. *Betwixt and Between: Patterns of Masculine and Feminine Initiation*. La Salle, IL: Open Court.

Moore, Robert and Douglas Gillette. 1990. *King Warrior Magician Lover: Rediscovering the Archetypes of the Mature Masculine*. San Francisco: Harper San Francisco.

Murphy, Joseph M. 1988. *Santeria: An African Religion in America*. Boston: Beacon Press.

Murphy, Joseph M. 1994. *Working the Spirit: Ceremonies of the African Diaspora*. Boston: Beacon Press.

Myerhoff, Barbara G. 1978. *Number Our Days*. New York: Simon & Schuster.

Neville, Gwen Kennedy. 1987. *Kinship and Pilgrimage: Rituals of Reunion in American Protestant Culture*. New York: Oxford University Press.

Orsi, Robert A. 1985. *The Madonna of 115th Street: Faith and Community in Italian Harlem, 1880–1950*. New Haven: Yale University Press.

Peacock, James L., and Ruel W. Tyson, Jr. 1989. *Pilgrims of Paradox: Calvinism and Experience among the Primitive Baptists of the Blue Ridge*. Washington, D.C.: Smithsonian Institution Press.

Pitts, Walter F. 1993. *Old Ship of Zion: The Afro-Baptist Ritual in the African Diaspora*. New York: Oxford University Press.

Powers, William K. 1986. *Sacred Language: The Nature of Supernatural Discourse in Lakota*. Norman: University of Oklahoma Press.

Prell, Riv-Ellen. 1989. *Prayer and Community: The Havurah in American Judaism*. Detroit: Wayne State University Press.

Proctor-Smith, Marjorie. 1990. *In Her Own Rite: Constructing Feminist Liturgical Tradition*. Nashville: Abingdon Press.

Rappaport, Roy A. 1979. *Ecology, Meaning, and Religion*. Richmond, CA: North Atlantic Books.

Riemer, Jack, editor. 1974. *Jewish Reflections on Death*. New York: Schocken Books.

Ritual and Myth: A Survey of African-American Art. 1982. New York: Studio Museum in Harlem.

"Ritual and Power." 1990. *Journal of Ritual Studies*, vol. 4 (2) (summer).

Roberts, William O., Jr. 1982. *Initiation to Adulthood: An Ancient Rite of Passage in Contemporary Form*. New York: Pilgrim Press.

Ruether, Rosemary Radford. 1985. *Women-Church: Theology and Practice of Feminist Liturgical Communities*. San Francisco: Harper & Row.

Santino, Jack. 1995. *All Around the Year: Holidays and Celebrations in American Life*. Champaign: University of Illinois Press.

Schatz, Thomas G. 1983. *Old Hollywood/New Hollywood: Ritual, Art and Industry*. Ann Arbor: UMI Research Press.

Schechner, Richard. 1985. *Between Theater & Anthropology*. Philadelphia: University of Philadelphia Press.

Schechner, Richard. 1988. *Performance Theory*. Revised edition. New York: Routledge.

Schechner, Richard, and Willa Appel, editors. 1990. *By Means of Performance: Intercultural Studies of Theatre and Ritual*. Cambridge: Cambridge University Press.

Schmidt, Leigh Eric. 1990. *Holy Fairs: Scottish Communions and American Revivals in the Early Modern Period*. Princeton: Princeton University Press.

Smith, Jonathan Z. 1982. *Imagining Religion: From Babylon to Jonestown*. Chicago: University of Chicago Press.

Smith, Jonathan Z. 1987. *To Take Place: Toward Theory in Ritual*. Chicago: University of Chicago Press.

Spretnak, Charlene, editor. 1982. *The Politics of Women's Spirituality: Essays on the Rise of Spiritual Power within the Feminist Movement*. Garden City, NY: Anchor Books.

Staal, Frits. 1979. "The Meaninglessness of Ritual." *Numen* 26 (2): 2–22.

Staal, Frits. 1989. *Rules without Meaning: Ritual, Mantras, and the Human Sciences*. New York: Peter Lang.

Starhawk (Miriam Simos). 1979/1989. *The Spiral Dance: A Rebirth of the Ancient Religion of the Great Goddess*. San Francisco: Harper & Row.

Stein, Diane. 1990. *Casting the Circle: A Women's Book of Ritual*. Freedom, CA: Crossing Press.

Stein, Diane. 1991. *The Goddess Celebrates: An Anthology of Women's Rituals*. Freedom, CA: Crossing Press.

Stowe, Steven M. 1987. *Intimacy and Power in the Old South: Ritual in the Lives of the Planters*. Baltimore: Johns Hopkins University Press.

Taves, Ann. 1986. *The Household of Faith: Roman Catholic Devotions in Mid-Nineteenth-Century America*. Notre Dame: University of Notre Dame Press.

Trepp, Leo. 1980. *The Complete Book of Jewish Observance: A Practical Manual for the Modern Jew*. New York: Summit Books.

Tyson, Ruel W., Jr.; James L. Peacock; and Daniel W. Patterson, editors. 1988. *Diversities of Gifts: Field Studies in Southern Religion*. Urbana: University of Illinois Press.

Vecsey, Christopher, editor. 1991. *Handbook of American Indian Religious Freedom*. New York: Crossroad.

Walker, Barbara G. 1990. *Women's Rituals: A Sourcebook*. San Francisco: Harper & Row.

Wind, James P., and James W. Lewis, editors. 1994. *American Congregations*. Vol. 1, *Portraits of Twelve Religious Communities*. Chicago: University of Chicago Press.

Wind, James P., and James W. Lewis, editors. 1995. *American Congregations*. Vol. 2, *New Perspectives in the Study of Congregations*. Chicago: University of Chicago Press.

Part III

LITTLE AND GREAT TRADITIONS

11

THE ANTHROPOLOGY OF ISLAM

Gregory Starrett

"Of course the radio says that everything comes directly from God. But just as the king has his ministers, God has his [saints]. If you need a paper from the government office, which is better? Do you go straight to the official and ask for it? You might wait a long time and never receive it. Or do you go to someone who knows you and also knows the official? Of course, you go to the friend, who presents the case to the official. Same thing with *baraka* [blessing]."

Moroccan Barber (Eickelman 1976: 161–162)

"My son now is telling me about the true Islam; they have to fight a holy war and if necessary get killed. I tell him there is no holy war in the absence of the Last Imam. He shouts at me saying I do not understand a thing. These young ones are like unfledged birds. When they try to fly, they fall from the tree and a cat eats them. They cannot discern the right road. I tell him to stay out of everything, to mind his own business, to do his studies; it's not the right time. But he won't listen."

Rural Iranian, 1980 (Loeffler 1988: 237)

[T]here is no discipline, no structure of knowledge, no institution or epistemology that can or has ever stood free of the various sociocultural, historical, and political formations that give epochs their peculiar individuality.

Edward Said (1989: 211)

In late September 1989, just a week before I was set to end my fieldwork in Cairo, I stood on a balcony facing the inside courtyard of a large, private Islamic school in the city's western suburbs, talking to the head of the English Department, Mme. Layla. She was wearing a long dress with an enormous scarf that covered her hair, neck, and arms, an outfit called *khimar*, midway between the colorful and attractive costumes that many of Egypt's young women call "modest dress" and the more conservative (and extremely rare) sort of garb in which even the face and hands are covered entirely. She had first donned this type of clothing seven years previously as part of her self-described rediscovery of Islam and had joined the staff at the school some years later out of the desire to teach young people about being good Muslims.

I had been attempting for several weeks to arrange for permission to do research at the school on a future trip, permission that never came because of their suspicion that I might write something unflattering to Islam based on my experiences or that I might be a spy (just the week before, two Egyptian physicians had been arrested for spying on some of Egypt's Islamic radical groups and passing information to an American editor at the English-language magazine *Cairo Today*, who turned out to be an employee of the American Central Intelligence Agency [CIA]. School officials were rightly wary of strangers.)

During a short lull in our conversation, Mme. Layla faced me suddenly and said, "I'm worried about you." We had been talking about what and why I wanted to study about Islam, and I had been trying to explain how anthropologists view the study of religion. We didn't study religion with a mind to converting, I said, but with a mind to finding out how religions and social systems interacted with one another. If I studied the Navajo Indians, I said, I couldn't very well convert to their religion, then come to Egypt and convert to Islam, then to something else later on. I'm not studying Islam to *become* a Muslim, I concluded, but to *understand* it.

She shook her head sharply. "You cannot continue merely to approach Islam with a scientific perspective," she replied, "or you will be in a great deal of trouble. You can't ignore it like you are. *To understand Islam means to understand the truth of its revelation.*"

I had no quick reply. And I still have none. Her remark caught me short and still gives me pause today. It is, of course, true. Only a Muslim can understand entirely what it is like to be a Muslim, to believe the truth of God's revelation. Of course each individual only understands fully what it is like to be themselves, a particular kind of person with a specific sex, a specific age, a specific point of origin, occupation, language (Geertz 1973: 53). But framing "understanding" as "commitment" undermines entirely the possibility of an anthropological study of religion. Even if understanding "Islam" is a different thing from understanding "*islam*," personal submission to the will of God (and it may be), the point was still clear that my very presence there was an unsolved problem, another example of the uncertain relationship of anthropologists to their (in both senses) societies.

Writing about Islam has been made more difficult, and also more important, by the publication of Edward Said's *Orientalism* (1978), which propelled the metascholarship of the Middle East and Islam into the forefront of anthropological concern. Arguing that scholars do not merely confront bare reality but confront realities shaped by histories of scholarly tradition and discourse, Said pointed out that

geographical sectors such as "Orient" and "Occident" are man-made. Therefore as much as the West itself, the Orient is an idea that has a history and a tradition of thought, imagery, and vocabulary that have given it reality and presence in and for the West. The two geographical entities thus support and to an extent reflect each other. (1978: 5)

Detailing the coevolution of area scholarship and political confrontation, Said concluded that there can be no possible theoretical understanding of the Middle East—or of Islamic practice, by extension—independent of the historical development of international power structures. This sort of argument is obviously apposite of any anthropological field context, but with respect to Islamic cultures, it has not only longer historical roots but a far sharper economic and political edge. The geopolitical security concerns surrounding the conflict between two nationalisms in Palestine/Israel, a possibly nuclear arms race between India and Pakistan, the burgeoning economic power of the Organization of Petroleum Exporting Countries (OPEC), the 1978–1979 Iranian Revolution, the succeeding decade of devastating war in the Gulf, the Salman Rushdie affair and anti-Muslim violence in Europe, the collapse of the Soviet Union, and the fear of continued political fragmentation and shifting global power balances all make the academic study of Muslim societies sensitive and contentious. From the other direction, Muslims understand, in the words of one of Lila Abu-Lughod's Bedouin hosts, that "knowledge is power. . . . The Americans and the British . . . want to know everything about people, about us. Then if they come to a country, or come to rule it, they know what people need and they know how to rule" (L. Abu-Lughod 1989: 267).

Popular "Western" understandings of Muslim societies flow from a three-part identity in Euroamerican folk sociology: (1) between geographical nomenclature and religious tradition, the Middle East and Islam appearing to "belong" exclusively to each other; (2) between that religious tradition and the behavior of its adherents, such that any and all activity by Muslims is credited to Islam as a motivational system; and (3) between Islam as it is practiced on the ground and Islam as it exists as a conceptual system. This last identity is not a feature merely of folk sociology but of the traditional orientation of some area scholars as well. According to Said, Orientalism "saw Islam . . . as a 'cultural synthesis' . . . that could be studied apart from the economics, sociology, and politics of the Islamic peoples" (1978: 105), with the term *Islam* coming "to signify all at once a society, a religion, a prototype [of closed traditional societies], and an actuality" (299).

Anthropology has obviously not been immune to the overvaluation of religion as a factor creating the social topography of Muslim societies. Dated as it is, Raphael Patai's (1952: 19) notion that "[r]eligion is the fundamental motivating force in most phases and aspects of [Middle Eastern] culture and has its say in practically every act and moment in life" (see also Patai 1976) is still vaguely seductive because of the potential breadth of the anthropological concept of culture. "All custom and tradition is basically religious. . . . Thus the entire field of custom—wide and infinitely ramified in its permeation of everyday life—cannot be divorced from religion either in theory or in practice" (Patai 1952: 19). A more sophisticated reading of either culture or religion will, of course, serve easily to divorce the two notions in the anthropological mind. People do have other beliefs, concepts, motivations, and activities than religious ones.

But the complicating factor is that this view of the intimate connection between Islam and normative social life is shared by Muslims. Islam for educated Muslims resembles nothing more than the sort of "high culture" Orientalist framework favored by many Western scholars:

Islam is the blueprint of a social order. It holds that a set of rules exists, eternal, divinely ordained, and independent of the will of men, which defines the proper ordering of society. The model is available in writing; it is equally and symmetrically available to all literate men, and to all those willing to heed literate men. These rules are to be implemented throughout social life. (Gellner 1981: 1)

Like any "high" tradition, the normative system is held by Muslims to exist independently of local conditions. But in fact, local differences in the practice and understanding of even "universal" features of the religion like the attestation of faith, prayer, fasting, alms giving, and pilgrimage (see Munson 1984: 28) are quite variable (Bowen 1984, 1989, 1992b; Woodward 1988).

The complexity of understanding local manifestations of the Islamic heritage stems in part from the geographic extent of the Islamic world. While Mecca is the center of Islam's sacred geography, the center of its billion-strong total population lies between Iran and Pakistan, with nearly as many Muslims in Indonesia alone as in all of the Arab states of the Middle East (Eickelman 1989: 10). Muslims form the majority confession in over twenty states, from Southeast Asia (Indonesia and Malaysia) through Bangladesh, nearly the whole of Southwest Asia (Afghanistan, Pakistan, Iran, the Arabian Peninsula, Turkey, and the Arab states of the eastern Mediterranean), North and Sahelian Africa (from Somalia, Sudan, and Egypt westward to Morocco, Mauritania, and Guinea), and much of former Soviet Central Asia. Muslims form a significant minority in the Philippines, India, and Nigeria, among others. There are major Muslim populations in North America and Europe (with 3 million each in France and the United States, for example) and smaller Muslim communities in nearly every other country in the world (Eickelman 1989: 10; for central Asia, see Eickelman and Pasha 1991; for the United States, see Haddad and Lummis 1987; Haddad 1991).

Unfortunately—but understandably, given the investment necessary to master the literature on even a single complex society—there is relatively little explicitly comparative ethnographic work on different Muslim societies. Geertz's (1968) classic comparison of the role and symbolism of saints in Morocco and Indonesia remains the most noteworthy, both for its concise elegance and for its theoretical contribution to the study of religious systems in general. Gilsenan (1982) studied manifestations of Islam in Yemen, Egypt, Lebanon, Algeria, and elsewhere, with a fine eye for the constant changes wrought by class and colonial penetration. Munson (1988) discusses the Islamic revival in the Arab world in the light of the Iranian Revolution, one of the only anthropological attempts to come to terms with the contemporary political role of Islam in the Middle East. Antoun (1987) compares religious leadership in Jordan and Iran, while Bowen (1992b) addresses the differential logic of sacrifice in Morocco and Sumatra, and Meeker (1979) investigates the relationship between pastoralism and literate urban society in Arabia and North Africa. With the exception of Geertz and Bowen, all of these works are confined to the Middle East. As a partial remedy to the theoretical (and logistical) problems of comparing Muslim societies in space and time, the Social Science Research Council formed during the 1980s, an interdisciplinary Committee for the Comparative Study of Muslim Societies.

HISTORY

In Muslim theory, Islam originated with the patriarch Abraham's willing submission to God's command that he sacrifice his son Isma'il (*islam* in Arabic is a verbal noun based on a root that can generate words with a number of meanings related to the idea of safety, security, protection, submission, peacemaking, and surrender. It indicates committing oneself fully to the will of God). It was Abraham who built the Ka'ba at Mecca, the focus of the annual Muslim pilgrimage.

It is more usual for secular scholars to date Islam's origin from the beginning of the revelation of the Qur'an (Arabic "recitation") by the angel Gabriel to Muhammad ibn Abdallah, a forty-year-old Meccan merchant, in C.E. 610. The Qur'an is the literal and uncreated speech of God, His final revelation to humankind. It is identical to the revelations given earlier to other Semitic prophets, such as Moses and Jesus, but subsequently distorted by the Jewish and Christian communities. Ideally committed to memory and recited by Muslims in the original Arabic (Nelson 1985), the Qur'an is the primary source of the subsequent elaboration of Islamic theology and law, along with the *sunna*, or traditional behavior of the Prophet Muhammad and his early companions (for a highly readable summary of Muslim sacred history and an overview of religious institutions, see Esposito 1988).

But different still is the dating of the Muslim lunar calendar, which is based neither on the submission of Abraham nor on the commencement of the revelation of the Qur'an but on the flight of Muhammad and his supporters in C.E. 622 from persecution by the Meccan trading establishment and their foundation of the first Muslim polity at Yathrib, an oasis town north of Mecca that was subsequently known simply as Medina (for "Medinat al-Nabi," "City of the Prophet"). The fact that the Muslim sacred calendar is based not on the date of first revelation but on the date of the founding of a political community is one of the reasons both Muslim and non-Muslim scholars cite to underline the importance of political and social concerns in Islamic thought. Unlike Christianity, Islam has resisted the establishment of formal churchlike hierarchies, and although various religious specialists can act as shamans, saints, teachers, judges, and political leaders, there is explicitly no priestly role. Religious leadership is secured through descent from the family of the Prophet, through personal charisma and the reputation for supernatural power, or from a reputation for learning.

The energy and organization of the early Islamic community allowed it to expand rapidly into the territories of the exhausted Byzantine and Sassanian empires after uniting the tribes of the Arabian peninsula in the seventh century. Continuing westward, Muslim armies reached Morocco only four decades after the death of the Prophet Muhammad, continuing northward into Spain. In the east, Muslim armies expanded their empires into northern India by the sixteenth century. Muslims followed trade routes southward across the Sahara and eastward into the Indian Ocean and Southeast Asia, gaining strength in the indigenous kingdoms of West Africa by the tenth century, and in Java by the fourteenth century, linking the world together in an immense web of commerce and culture (J. Abu-Lughod 1989).

The enormous volume of historical literature on the origin and spread of Islam is easily entered through Hourani's (1988) history of the Arab peoples, along with Hodgson's (1974) immense and remarkable interpretation of worldwide Islamic civilization (though for Africa, see Clarke 1982), and Rodinson's (1971) controversial psychobiography of Muhammad. Wolf (1951) and Combs-Schilling (1989) have usefully and briefly analyzed the origins of Islamic civilization from materialist and symbolic/historical perspectives, respectively, but neither comes close in theoretical sophistication to Muhammad Bamyeh's (1990) application of current European social theory to reinterpret the origins of Islam.

SOCIETY

Islam has become the religious orientation of societies with patrilineal (Combs-Schilling 1989; Delaney 1991), matrilineal (Rasmussen 1989, 1991, 1993), and bilateral kinship (Ong 1990); of pastoralists (Evans-Pritchard 1949; Lewis 1961, 1986; Ahmed and Hart 1984), peasants (Bowen 1991; Delaney 1991), and urbanites (Gilsenan 1973; Fischer and Abedi 1990). It provides central concepts and symbols for societies with entirely divergent systems of authority and ethos (Geertz 1968), and within particular societies, for different classes (Bujra 1971; Kessler 1978), groups with varying degrees of access to education (Horvatich 1992, 1993; Loeffler 1988; Eickelman 1992), different political views (Fischer and Abedi 1990), and for both males and females (Macleod 1991; Tapper and Tapper 1987). It can provide a source of law, custom, and ethnicity (Ewing 1988) and also the foundation for powerful military resistance (Shahrani 1984).

Muslim scholars, recognizing the importance—and connection between—different social structures and the processes of historical change, produced as early as the fourteenth century important works of historical sociology analyzing the rise and fall of kingdoms and empires (Ibn Khaldun 1967 [1377]). By contrast, early Western anthropological scholarship on Islam tended to take the form of detailed descriptive monographs that lack the rigor of Ibn Khaldun but that are still valuable sources for (sometimes extinct) social practices and folklore. Edward Lane (1963 [1860]) detailed the dress, material culture, and customs of nineteenth-century Cairo. His descriptions of magical practices, talismans, and religious festivals, for example, are still peerless, aided by his long residency in Egypt and fluency in Arabic. The same is true for Edward Westermarck's (1911, 1914, 1926) work on belief, ritual, and folklore in Morocco, and Sir Richard F. Burton's (1964 [1855]) chronicle of his disguised pilgrimage to Mecca. The latter contains invaluable contemporary folklore about the pilgrimage and the holy precincts of the city, including the sort of curious information students always ask about but upon which modern, theoretically oriented scholarship is entirely silent (for example, what's *inside* the Ka'ba?).

Specifically anthropological studies of Muslim societies were rare before the late 1960s. The notable exceptions are, of course, Evans-Pritchard's (1949) social history of the Sanusi, an intertribal religious brotherhood in Libya during the nineteenth century, and Greenberg's (1941, 1946, 1947) important and detailed analyses of the effects of the contact and interpenetration of Islam with the traditional religious and social organization of the Hausa of northern Nigeria. Skinner (1958) addressed similar processes in the Ivory Coast.

THEORY

As indicated above, the question of how "Islam" is to be studied comparatively has been an important concern. The best starting point is, of course, Geertz's (1968) *Islam Observed*, which contrasts the mystical styles of Moroccan and Indonesian Islam, a contrast between active personal charisma, on the one hand, and serene psychic balance, on the other. As well as addressing in general terms the role of Islam in the political development of the two countries, *Islam Observed* also sets forth one of Geertz's most detailed discussions of the place of religion in human life and the anthropological difficulties in gaining access to the phenomenological aspects of faith. The book's lasting influence flows from a holistic orientation that carefully considers the contributions of social structure, history, and textual resources to Islamization, a dual effort "to adapt a universal, in theory standardized and essentially unchangeable . . . system of ritual and belief to the realities of local, even individual, moral and metaphysical perception," while at the same time "struggl[ing] to maintain

... the identity of Islam ... as the particular directives communicated by God to mankind through the preemptory prophecies of Muhammad'' (14).

The central tension in this process is the same for anthropology as for theology: how to apply a sacred model to profane existence.

> What a given religion is—its specific content—is embodied in the images and metaphors its adherents use to characterize reality; it makes ... a great deal of difference whether you call life a dream, a pilgrimage, a labyrinth, or a carnival. But such a religion's career—its historical course—rests in turn upon the institutions which render these images and metaphors available to those who thus employ them. (2–3)

Other scholars have continued to work along these lines, charting the historical transformation of Islamic practices in different parts of the world (Bowen 1991; Eickelman 1976; Woodward 1989), while others have dealt more narrowly with the political (Bujra 1971; Kessler 1978), psychological (Crapanzano 1973, 1980; Ewing 1990), and gender differentiation of Muslim experience (L. Abu-Lughod 1986, 1993b; Boddy 1989; Delaney 1991; Holy 1988, 1991; Tapper and Tapper 1987).

There are already some excellent, though inevitably dated, reviews of the anthropological literature on Islam, addressing precisely the question raised by Geertz of what our analytical object should be. What, for anthropological purposes, is Islam? A text? An institution? A set of rituals? A devotional style? A social system? Four of these should be consulted for their perceptive discussions of the major issues involved in the study of Muslim societies. Eickelman (1982), Asad (1986), and Lila Abu-Lughod (1989) each recognize that

> the main challenge for the study of Islam in local contexts is to describe and analyze how the universalistic principles of Islam have been realized in various social and historical contexts without representing Islam as a seamless essence on the one hand or as a plastic congeries of beliefs and practices on the other. (Eickelman 1982: 1–2)

El-Zein (1974), on the other hand, argues for the primacy of local experience, noting that if "native" models of Islam are the starting point of analysis, "the system can be entered and explored in depth from any point. ... [T]here are no autonomous entities and ... there can be no fixed and wholly isolable function of meaning attributed to any basic unit of analysis, be it symbol, institution, or process, which does not impose an artificial order on the system from outside" (251–252). This sort of reading results not in an anthropology of Islam but in an anthropology of *islams* in which "there are no inherent differences in the content of either folk or formal theology to suggest that one is more objective, reflective, or systematic than the other. ... They differ only as modes of expression: one exists as an institution, and the other as literature" (249; see also Woodward 1989: 63). While elites sometimes distinguish between "real" Islam and "degraded" local variants that partake of pre-Islamic custom or modern innovation (Antoun 1989; Bowen 1984, 1989; Horvatich 1993; Woodward 1988, 1989), it is equally the case that nonelites will distinguish between "government Islam" and that of the people, reversing quite explicitly the elite valuation of local understandings and practices (Loeffler 1988; Eickelman 1982).

Asad's (1986) dismissal of el-Zein's and of Gellner's (1981) competing view that Islam is a distinct social blueprint allows him to formulate an alternative view that has recently been elaborated by a number of other scholars. According to Asad, if we are to avoid the twin problems of either essentializing or dissolving "Islam" as an object of study, we need to recognize that "Islam is neither a distinctive social structure nor a heterogeneous collection of beliefs, artifacts, customs, and morals. It is a tradition" (14) that links together past, present, and future in specific ways. Summarizing this view, L. Abu-Lughod (1989) imagines the study of this three-way linkage as a focus on "the interplay between . . . everyday practices and discourses and the religious texts they invoke, the histories of which they are a part, and the political enterprises of which they partake" (297).

The effort to apply these theoretical concerns to living societies has been prosecuted by a number of scholars, most notably Bowen (1984, 1987, 1989, 1991, 1992a, 1992b), who has studied "processes of narrative selection and elaboration, . . . tacking between broad cultural traditions (Gayo, Indonesian, Islamic) and microlevel processes" (1992a: 495). He notes with respect to Sumatra a common process throughout the Muslim world:

The shift between Islamic and local perspectives characterizes not only my own interpretive strategy but Gayo Muslim consciousness as well. Gayo make reference to scripture, to religious writings of Middle Eastern origin and to tales of the prophets for the light they shed on Gayo funds of knowledge, and *vice versa*. To teach me in matters religious and social, Gayo men and women would at times elucidate an Arabic text (or its translation) with a Gayo proverb, or compare the power exercised by Moses with that wielded by a local ancestor spirit. As in Jewish, Christian and Muslim communities elsewhere, Gayo have drawn from scripture-based repertoires to shape, through narrative, multivalent social worlds: worlds that are distinctive and yet also part of larger, religiously defined communities. (496)

Muslims use the Islamic heritage as only one of the sources from which they draw their understanding and practice. Along with Fischer and Abedi (1990), Lambek (1990), Launay (1990, 1992), Messick (1986, 1993), and Woodward (1988, 1989), Bowen has helped direct the study of Islam in local contexts toward understanding how specific texts are actually used by Muslims in specific contexts. Woodward (1989: 49) reminds us that "the analysis of texts should proceed in the same manner as that of myth, ritual, social behavior, and other cultural materials. . . . The meaning of a text or a body of texts can be determined only within the context of the body of cultural knowledge to which it or they refer." Studying the "political economy of meaning" (Roff 1987) is vital since Islam can be understood "as an essentially unbounded complex of symbols and principles which on most any issue offer a wide range of possible, even opposing conceptions, meanings, attitudes, and modes of thought" (Loeffler 1988: 246–247).

The notion that anthropologists study shared culture must be dismissed as a myth. Rather, what anthropologists actually present in their descriptions are composite pictures, systems meticulously pieced together from the most explicit, elaborate, and plausible accounts available on any given subject. The problem with this approach is that it gives the impression that everything is common knowledge, whereas, in fact, virtuosi and anthropologists were collaborating as high priests in creating the authentic text. (248)

KNOWLEDGE

Distributions of "correct" knowledge mirror distributions of power. Regardless of how a Muslim society is organized, the definition of what is and is not "Islamic" is likely not to be about how closely society mirrors a known textual blueprint as about how and by whom specific texts are used to underwrite specific practices and general notions of authority. Orthodoxy, writes Asad, "is not a mere body of opinion but a distinctive relationship—a relationship of power. Wherever Muslims have the power to regulate, uphold, require or adjust *correct* practices, and to condemn, exclude, undermine, or replace *incorrect* ones, there is the domain of orthodoxy" (Asad 1986: 15). Antoun (1989), Messick (1986), and Woodward (1989: 63) show how the second- and third-order constructions of reality produced by indigenous intellectuals and religious professionals are produced and how they are embedded in personal and institutional networks of power, traditions of scriptural interpretation, and understandings of the commonsense world of social transactions.

The interpretation of the Islamic corpus is given social reality through both traditional and innovative channels of communication and cultural practice. One of the most important means of spreading the Ayatollah Khomeini's antiestablishment message through Iran in the 1970s was through the medium of cassette tapes of his sermons made in exile, first in Iraq and then in Paris. Technology has had similar effects in other parts of the Muslim world, a development that has been remarked upon by many scholars but addressed systematically by none. Messick (1986), Fischer (1980), Fischer and Abedi (1990), and especially Antoun (1989) and Gaffney (1987a, 1987b, 1991) have studied the way that religious scholars and preachers construct and communicate specialized and "authoritative" knowledge about Islam through the historically well-established channels of the legal opinion, the Friday sermon, and the mosque-based afternoon study circle.

Prior to the dissemination of knowledge to various publics is the production of Islamic scholars and scholarship through the traditional mosque-based educational system. The organization of indigenous learning has been well described

by Fischer (1980), Fischer and Abedi (1990), and Mottahedeh (1985); by Eickelman (1978, 1985), Messick (1993), and Wagner and his colleagues (1980,
1983, 1987b) (for elementary education.) While the content of traditional education in Iran, Yemen, and Morocco was based on the memorization of a set
corpus, the style of learning and the attitude toward scholarly authority could
differ quite radically from one place to another, ranging from the Iranian *mad-
rasa*'s lively Talmudic-style interchanges between scholar and teacher to the
actual discouragement of questioning in Morocco. These studies of the reproduction of knowledge and authority through preaching, pedagogy, and legal
practice—but most especially, studies of how these systems are changing—are
currently among the most important developments in the anthropological scholarship on Islam, promising to illuminate processes of cultural invention, reproduction, transmission, and transformation in other literate traditions.

The creation of orthodoxy and political order by groups claiming descent from
the Prophet Muhammad (Bujra 1971), by groups and individuals claiming special power to intercede with God (Eickelman 1976; Gellner 1969; Gilsenan
1973), by groups enjoying special training as Muslim scholars (Eickelman 1978,
1985; Fischer 1980; Fischer and Abedi 1990; Mottahedeh 1985; Messick 1974,
1986, 1993), and by groups controlling modern political and educational appa-
ratuses (Eickelman 1986, 1992; Starrett 1991) has been an important focus of
study in recent anthropology. But it is significant, and in fact one of the central
features of modernity in the Muslim world, that one need not have special
training as a religious scholar or special claim to auspicious descent to have
potential access to religious knowledge. The growth of publishing and higher
education (Eickelman 1992), the spread of literacy through mass elementary and
secondary schooling (Starrett 1991), and the dissemination of electronic media
(L. Abu-Lughod 1993a) are having enormous effects on the structure of religious
authority in the Muslim world, as

socially recognized carriers of religious learning are no longer confined to those who
have studied accepted texts in circumstances equivalent to those of the mosque-
universities, with their bias toward favoring members of the elite. . . . The carriers of
religious knowledge will increasingly be anyone who can claim a strong Islamic commitment, as is the case among many of the educated urban youth. Freed from mnemonic
domination, religious knowledge can be delineated and interpreted in a more abstract and
flexible fashion. A long apprenticeship under an established man of learning is no longer
a necessary prerequisite to legitimizing one's own religious knowledge. Printed and mim-
eographed tracts and the clandestine dissemination of ''lessons'' on cassettes have begun
to replace the mosque as the center for disseminating visions of Islam that challenge
those offered by the state. (Eickelman 1985: 168)

Such an opening up of previously ''restricted'' literacies (Messick 1974; Niezen 1991; Street 1984; Wagner and Lotfi 1980, 1983; Wagner and Spratt 1987a,
1987b) has triggered widespread dissatisfaction with incumbent power structures

both political and religious. In Indonesia (Bowen 1984; Nagata 1982), Malaysia (Banks 1990; Nagata 1987), the Philippines (Horvatich 1992, 1993), Morocco (Munson 1986; Eickelman 1992), Iran and the United States (Fischer and Abedi 1990), Egypt (Starrett 1991), and elsewhere, the young beneficiaries of secular education and increased mobility are asserting religious authority through their newfound access to information and secular resources.

Depending on social and political contexts, this authority may be exerted over practitioners of long-standing indigenous Islamic forms, creating a division between "old" and "young" (Woodward 1989: 79), "traditional" and "modern," or "Ahmadi" (adherents of a modernist reform movement) and "orthodox" factions (Horvatich 1994). Alternately, dissatisfaction may be expressed against state institutions that monopolize legitimate interpretation of scripture (Goldberg 1991).

POWER

For Gellner (1981), this "egalitarian scripturalism" is a natural feature of the Islamic blueprint for social order, so that,

though not the source of modernity, Islam may yet turn out to be its beneficiary. The fact that its central, official, "pure" variant was egalitarian and scholarly, whilst hierarchy and ecstasy pertained to its expendable, eventually disavowed, peripheral forms, greatly aids its adaptation to the modern world. In an age of aspiration to universal literacy, the open class of scholars can expand towards embracing the entire community, and thus the "protestant" ideal of equal access for all believers can be implemented. Modern egalitarianism is satisfied. . . . [T]he reawakened Muslim potential for egalitarian scripturalism can actually *fuse* with nationalism, so that one can hardly tell which one of the two is of most benefit to the other. (5)

What sounds like an effortless transition from hierarchy to equality has in fact been a difficult struggle between incumbent power structures and groups aspiring to power. The relationship between hierarchy and scripture is entirely different in Iran than in Egypt, in Egypt than Algeria. In the twentieth century this conflict over religious and political authority has sometimes taken the form of violent confrontations between authorities and popular movements lumped together under the labels "fundamentalism," "radical" or "militant Islam," "the Islamic revival" or "resurgence," and so on. Historically, Islamic reformist movements based on the notion of "purifying" local Islamic practices of contamination from pre-Islamic or foreign sources have been common not only in the Middle East but elsewhere (for Indonesia and Malaysia, see Peacock 1978; Nagata 1984). Such movements are comparable to other social movements (Burke and Lapidus 1988) that seek to push political structures or social practices toward a given religious or political ideal. In West Africa and Southeast Asia, reformist movements have often been triggered by the return of local scholars or workers from employment or pilgrimage to Saudi Arabia, bearing new knowledge about a more "legitimate" form of Islam than that practiced at home, or by diffusion of written material from the central Islamic lands of the Middle East (for a specific example of the desire for behavior reform by returning workers, see Boddy 1989: 51–52).

Because Western industrial interests are focused on ensuring the easy availability of Middle Eastern oil, religious and political movements in the region have provoked a great deal of anxious publicity, particularly following the Iranian Revolution. An entire publishing industry has grown up around titles like "Islam and Politics," "Islam and Revolution," and so on. Unfortunately, much of this literature is of poor quality, and little has been written by anthropologists. There is good historical and interpretive material by Keddie (1981, 1983, 1986) and Fischer (1980) on Iran, and Kepel (1984) and (with some reservation) Sivan (1985) on Egypt. Journalist Edward Mortimer (1982) summarizes the history of Islamic reform in the Middle East and, along with Munson (1988) and Stowasser (1987), provides some of the best analysis of the relationship between Islam and popular movements in the contemporary Middle East as a whole. Piscatori (1991) discusses the effect of the 1991 Gulf War on Muslim political movements.

Rare ethnographic perspectives on revolutionary change are provided by Fischer (1980), Beeman (1983), and Hegland (1983a, 1983b, 1987), who were conducting fieldwork in Iran at the time of the Revolution. All deal in various ways with the manner in which popular religious symbols were mobilized and transformed for revolutionary purposes. Fischer and Abedi (1990), in addition to discussing the ideologies of Khomeini and Shariati, analyze revolutionary art and imagery and provide a marvelous essay on the multilayered symbolism of the flag of the Islamic Republic, showing how its form combines seamlessly and simultaneously imagery from both specifically Iranian and generically Islamic cultural sources and how its semiotics are in turn used and transformed in popular practice.

GENDER

One of the most striking, and consequently stereotypical, manifestations of the Islamic "resurgence" is the so-called return to the veil among Muslim women, a trend that is in fact not a return to any sort of traditional clothing style but a reinterpretation of what it means to be a woman in contemporary Muslim societies and a reassertion of identity using quite novel means. El-Guindi's (1981) excellent early work on veiling in Egypt has recently been supplemented by longer studies from Zuhur (1992) and Macleod (1991), who argues that modest dress is simultaneously an accommodation to male-centered power structures and a movement of resistance against those structures, a protest against the declining status of women relative to men in contemporary Egypt.

The Egyptian case should be compared with Fischer's (1980) description of the very different protest symbolism of the *chador* for Iranian revolutionaries.

These special cases of the symbolism of female covering have counterparts in the excellent work of Lila Abu-Lughod (1986), Boddy (1989), and Delaney (1991), each of whom analyzes in great detail the practical ideologies of female covering and enclosure in rural Egypt, the Sudan, and Turkey, respectively. Abu-Lughod particularly shows that the meaning of covering and enclosure is radically different among "traditional" Bedouins than for urban Egyptians, indicating some interesting discontinuities between notions of modesty, which are linked to bounded networks of honor/shame relationships, and notions of Islamic identity, which are absolute and entirely different in their emotional and cognitive significance.

Like Judaism and Christianity, Islam is the heir to a long tradition of Mediterranean patriarchy, reflected in scripture, law, and custom throughout much of the Muslim world. Delaney (1991) and Combs-Schilling (1989) both locate the pervasive disability of Middle Eastern females in the essential structure of Islam and related folk beliefs (see also Delaney 1986). Combs-Schilling analyzes the creation of a habitus of male authority through the historical manipulation of rituals of kingship, first marriage, and sacrifice during the annual pilgrimage season. Beginning in the sixteenth century with the shift in relative economic and political power from Morocco to Europe, the Moroccan monarchy seized on the powerful visceral symbolism of blood and intercourse to underwrite royal authority, compensating for its lack of practical hegemony by binding male heads of household to the political center in the same manner that females and junior males were bound to the authority of senior males. "The Qur'anic myth of Ibrahim and Muhammad's sacrificial enactment helped establish patrilineality and patriarchy at the center of the cultural matrix of Islam . . . powerfully undergird[ing] the rightful domination of father over son, of senior men over junior men, of all males over females and children" (Combs-Schilling 1989: 57).

Bowen's (1992b) critique of this essentialist notion that there is a uniquely "Islamic" view of gender and authority is based on evidence from Indonesia where a very different sort of social structure results in a different reading of sacrifice and of the significance of male and female. As Eickelman (1989) indicates, scholars like Mernissi (1987) or Bouhdiba (1985) who imply that Muslims share a single, well-defined understanding of gender roles or sexuality are overgeneralizing either from evidence from a single society or from uncontextualized bodies of literature. Collections like those of Fernea (1985) and Fernea and Bezirgan (1977) are useful antidotes to stereotyped portrayals of Muslim women.

Lila Abu-Lughod (1993b, 1993c), Boddy (1989), Delaney (1991), Holy (1988, 1991), Nancy Tapper (1990), Tapper and Tapper (1987), and Rasmussen (1991) discuss the gendered division of religious labor in a number of Muslim societies. In their influential article, Tapper and Tapper (1987) stress the importance of analyses linking gender and religion in opening the possibility for comparative studies of different Muslim communities. Summarizing their conclusions from a study of how males and females approach differently a single type of ritual event (the recitation of poems commemorating the birth of the Prophet, often on the occasion of a death or other life crisis), they

do not suggest that women and men necessarily have discreet systems of belief and practice ... but that different aspects of a religious system may be the province of one sex or the other, and an understanding of any particular Islamic tradition depends on examining *both*. . . . We maintain on the one hand that men's day-to-day observance of apparent "orthodoxy" is far from unproblematic, and on the other that it is wrong to assume *a priori* that women's religious "work" is less important than or peripheral to that of men. Not only do women too practice the central, day-to-day rites of Islam, but in their performances they may carry a religious load often of greater transcendental importance to the community than that borne by men. (72)

Holy's analysis of the social importance of women's rituals in the Sudan, Boddy's on spirit possession, and Abu-Lughod's on mourning rituals concur that the division of ritual labor between men and women can forge an interdependence in which women's rituals express important aspects of the psychological and social order for which Islamic symbols are inadequate or overly restrictive, even though this may result in a lowering of women's status relative to a growing hegemonic set of "Islamic" concerns (L. Abu-Lughod 1993b, 1993c). Friedl (1980) and Ong (1990) expand on the relationship between Islamic ideology and practice, on the one hand, and women's relationships to the encompassing political order, on the other. Ong in particular examines how religious ideologies are used to intensify gender inequalities and underwrite male authority over the family in the context of rapid economic and political changes.

RITUAL

Ironically, studies of Islamic ritual form by far the smallest subset of anthropological research on Islam. It has long been noted that the scholarly study of Islamic ritual is relatively impoverished (Martin 1985). Not until recently have anthropologists found ways to deal productively with Islamic rituals, linking them theoretically with gender, notions of authority, political contests between factions representing "old" and "new" cultural orientations, or with their contribution to the establishment of general practical orientations (Bourdieu 1977; L. Abu-Lughod 1989).

In addition to the above-mentioned research by Antoun and Gaffney on Friday prayer services, Bowen (1989), Horvatich (1992), Rasmussen (1991), and Starrett (1993) have dealt with the different meanings given to the Muslim requirement of formal communal worship. Abu-Zahra (1988) explicates a special category of traditional prayer, the rain prayer.

The importance of pilgrimage and travel has recently received quite a bit of attention as well (Eickelman and Piscatori 1990), particularly from the perspective of its gender symbolism (Delaney 1990, 1991; Young 1993) and the creation of competing visions of the pilgrimage's social and political significance (Fischer and Abedi 1990). Sacrifice and ritual meals are analyzed by Bowen (1992b), Woodward (1988), and Combs-Schilling (1989). (For the fascinating discussion of sacrifice that informed Freud's theories in *Totem and Taboo*, see William Robertson Smith 1956).

Finally, rituals of the life cycle are discussed by Starrett (1991) and Peacock (1978), while rituals and beliefs surrounding death, burial, and mourning are addressed by L. Abu-Lughod (1993b), Ahmed (1986), Antoun (1989), Bowen (1984), and from a textual perspective, Haddad and Smith (1981). Fischer and Abedi (1990) provide a description of the special Shi'ite rituals surrounding the mourning of Husayn.

REFERENCES

Abu-Lughod, Janet. 1989. *Before European Hegemony: The World System* A.D. *1250–1350*. New York: Oxford University Press.

Abu-Lughod, Lila. 1986. *Veiled Sentiments: Honor and Poetry in a Bedouin Society*. Berkeley: University of California Press.

Abu-Lughod, Lila. 1989. "Zones of Theory in the Anthropology of the Arab World." *Annual Review of Anthropology* 18: 267–306.

Abu-Lughod, Lila. 1993a. "Islam and Public Culture: The Politics of Egyptian Television Serials." *Middle East Report* 23 (1): 25–30.

Abu-Lughod, Lila. 1993b. "Islam and the Gendered Discourses of Death." *International Journal of Middle East Studies* 25 (2): 187–205.

Abu-Lughod, Lila. 1993c. *Writing Women's Worlds: Bedouin Stories*. Berkeley: University of California Press.

Abu-Zahra, Nadia. 1988. "The Rain Rituals as Rites of Spiritual Passage." *International Journal of Middle East Studies* 20 (4): 507–529.

Ahmed, Akbar S. 1976. *Millenium and Charisma among Pathans*. Boston: Routledge & Kegan Paul.

Ahmed, Akbar S. 1983. *Religion and Politics in Muslim Society: Order and Conflict in Pakistan*. New York: Cambridge University Press.

Ahmed, Akbar S. 1986. "Death in Islam: The Hawkes Bay Case." *Man*, n.s., 21: 120–134.

Ahmed, Akbar S. 1992. *Postmodernism and Islam: Predicament and Promise*. London and New York: Routledge.

Ahmed, Akbar S., and David M. Hart, editors. 1984. *Islam in Tribal Societies*. London: Routledge & Kegan Paul.

Antoun, Richard T. 1987. "Key Variables Affecting Muslim Local-Level Religious Leadership in Iran and Jordan." *The Islamic Impulse*. Barbara Freyer editor. Washington, D.C.: Center for Contemporary Arab Studies. 175–183.

Antoun, Richard T. 1989. *Muslim Preacher in the Modern World: A Jordanian Case Study in Comparative Perspective*. Princeton, NJ: Princeton University Press.

Antoun, Richard T., and Mary Elaine Hegland, editors. 1987. *Religious Resurgence:*

Contemporary Cases in Islam, Christianity, and Judaism. Syracuse: Syracuse University Press.

Asad, Talal. 1986. "The Idea of an Anthropology of Islam." Center for Contemporary Arab Studies, Georgetown University, Occasional Paper Series.

Badran, Margot. 1994. "Gender Activism: Feminists and Islamists in Egypt." *Identity Politics and Women: Culture Reassertions and Feminisms in International Perspective*. Valentine M. Moghadam, editor. Boulder, CO: Westview Press. 202–227.

Baffoun, Alya. 1994. "Feminism and Muslim Fundamentalism: The Tunisian and Algerian Cases." *Identity Politics and Women: Cultural Reassertions and Feminisms in International Perspective*. Valentine M. Moghadam, editor. Boulder, CO: Westview Press. 167–182.

Bamyeh, Muhammad. 1990. "The Origins of Islam: A Study in Historical Sociology." Ph.D. dissertation, Department of Sociology, University of Wisconsin at Madison.

Banks, David J. 1990. "Resurgent Islam and Malay Rural Culture: Malay Novelists and the Invention of Culture." *American Ethnologist* 17 (3): 531–548.

Beeman, William O. 1983. "Images of the Great Satan: Representations of the United States in the Iranian Revolution." *Religion and Politics in Iran*. Nikki R. Keddie, editor. New Haven: Yale University Press. 191–217.

Bernal, Victoria. 1994. "Gender, Culture and Capitalism: Women and the Remaking of Islamic 'Tradition' in a Sudanese Village." *Comparative Studies in Society and History* 36 (1): 36–67.

Boddy, Janice. 1989. *Wombs and Alien Spirits: Women, Men and the Zar Cult in Northern Sudan*. Madison: University of Wisconsin Press.

Bouatta, Cherifa, and Doria Cherifati-Merabtine. 1994. "The Social Representation of Women in Algeria's Islamist Movement." *Identity Politics and Women: Cultural Reassertions and Feminisms in International Perspective*. Valentine M. Moghadam, editor. Boulder, CO: Westview Press. 183–201.

Bouhdiba, Abdelwahab. 1985. *Sexuality in Islam*. Translated by Alan Sheridan. London: Routledge & Kegan Paul.

Bourdieu, Pierre. 1977. *Outline of a Theory of Practice*. Cambridge: Cambridge University Press.

Bowen, John. 1984. "Death and the History of Islam in Highland Aceh." *Indonesia* 38: 21–38.

Bowen, John. 1987. "Islamic Transformations: From Sufi Doctrine to Ritual Practice in Gayo Culture." *Indonesian Religions in Transition*. Rita Smith Kipp and Susan Rodgers, editors. Tuscon: University of Arizona Press. 113–135.

Bowen, John. 1988. "The Transformation of an Indonesian Property System: *Adat*, Islam and Social Change in the Gayo Highlands." *American Ethnologist* 15 (2): 274–293.

Bowen, John. 1989. "*Salat* in Indonesia: The Social Meanings of an Islamic Ritual." *Man*, n.s., 24 (4): 600–619.

Bowen, John. 1991. *Sumatran Politics and Poetics: Gayo History 1900–1989*. New Haven: Yale University Press.

Bowen, John. 1992a. "Elaborating Scriptures: Cain and Abel in Gayo Society." *Man*, n.s., 27 (3): 495–516.

Bowen, John. 1992b. "On Scriptural Essentialism and Ritual Variation: Muslim Sacrifice in Sumatra and Morocco." *American Ethnologist* 19 (4): 656–671.

Bowen, John. 1993. *Muslims through Discourse: Religion and Ritual in Gayo Society.* Princeton: Princeton University Press.

Bujra, A. S. 1971. *The Politics of Stratification: A Study of Political Change in a South Arabian Town.* Oxford: Clarendon Press.

Burke III, Edmund, and Ira M. Lapidus, editors. 1988. *Islam, Politics, and Social Movements.* Berkeley: University of California Press.

Burton, Sir Richard Francis. 1964. *Personal Narrative of a Pilgrimage to al-Madinah and Meccah.* 2 vols. New York: Dover. (Originally published 1855)

Clarke, Peter B. 1982. *West Africa and Islam.* London: Edward Arnold.

Combs-Schilling, M. E. 1984. ''Islam, Power, and Change: Variation in North African Independence Movements.'' *Opportunity, Constraint and Change: Essays in Honor of Elizabeth Colson.* Jack Glazier, editor. Kroeber Anthropological Society Papers, no. 63–64, 59–74.

Combs-Schilling, M. E. 1989. *Sacred Performances: Islam, Sexuality and Sacrifice.* New York: Columbia University Press.

Crapanzano, Vincent. 1973. *The Hamadsha: A Study in Moroccan Ethnopsychiatry.* Berkeley: University of California Press.

Crapanzano, Vincent. 1980. *Tuhami: Portrait of a Moroccan.* Chicago: University of Chicago Press.

Delaney, Carol. 1986. ''The Meaning of Paternity and the Virgin Birth Debate.'' *Man,* n.s., 21: 494–513.

Delaney, Carol. 1990. ''The Hajj: Sacred and Secular.'' *American Ethnologist* 17 (3): 513–530.

Delaney, Carol. 1991. *The Seed and the Soil: Gender and Cosmology in Turkish Village Society.* Berkeley: University of California Press.

Eickelman, Dale F. 1976. *Moroccan Islam: Tradition and Society in a Pilgrimage Center.* Austin: University of Texas Press.

Eickelman, Dale F. 1978. ''The Art of Memory: Islamic Education and Its Social Reproduction.'' *Comparative Studies in Society and History* 20 (4): 485–516.

Eickelman, Dale F. 1982. ''The Study of Islam in Local Contexts.'' *Contributions to Asian Studies* 17: 1–16.

Eickelman, Dale F. 1985. *Knowledge and Power in Morocco: The Education of a Twentieth-Century Notable.* Princeton: Princeton University Press.

Eickelman, Dale F. 1986. ''Royal Authority and Religious Legitimacy: Morocco's Elections, 1960–84.'' *The Frailty of Authority.* Myron Aronoff, editor. New Brunswick, NJ: Transaction Books. 181–205.

Eickelman, Dale F. 1987. ''Changing Interpretations of Islamic Movements.'' *Islam and the Political Economy of Meaning: Comparative Studies of Muslim Discourse.* William R. Roff, editor. Berkeley: University of California Press. 13–30.

Eickelman, Dale F. 1989. *The Middle East: An Anthropological Approach.* 2nd edition. Englewood Cliffs, NJ: Prentice-Hall.

Eickelman, Dale F. 1992. ''Mass Higher Education and the Religious Imagination in Contemporary Arab Societies.'' *American Ethnologist* 19 (4): 643–655.

Eickelman, Dale F., and Kamran Pasha. 1991. ''Muslim Societies and Politics: Soviet and U.S. Approaches—A Conference Report.'' *Middle East Journal* 45 (4): 630–647.

Eickelman, Dale F., and James Piscatori, editors. 1990. *Muslim Travellers: Pilgrimage,*

Migration and the Religious Imagination. Berkeley: University of California Press.

el-Guindi, Fadwa. 1981. "Veiling *Infitah* with Muslim Ethic: Egypt's Contemporary Islamic Movement." *Social Problems* 28: 465–485.

el-Zein, Abdul Hamid. 1974. *The Sacred Meadows: A Structural Analysis of Religious Symbolism in an East African Town*. Evanston: Northwestern University Press.

el-Zein, Abdul Hamid. 1977. "Beyond Ideology and Theology: The Search for the Anthropology of Islam." *Annual Review of Anthropology* 6: 227–254.

Esposito, John. 1988. *Islam: The Straight Path*. New York: Oxford University Press.

Evans-Pritchard, E. E. 1949. *The Sanusi of Cyrenaica*. Oxford: Oxford University Press.

Ewing, Katherine P. 1988. *Shari'at and Ambiguity in South Asian Islam*. Berkeley: University of California Press.

Ewing, Katherine P. 1990. "The Dream of Spiritual Initiation and the Organization of Self Representations among Pakistani Sufis." *American Ethnologist* 17 (1): 56–74.

Fernea, Elizabeth W. 1985. *Women and the Family in the Middle East: New Voices of Change*. Austin: University of Texas Press.

Fernea, Elizabeth, and Basima Qattan Bezirgan, editors. 1977. *Middle Eastern Muslim Women Speak*. Austin: University of Texas Press.

Fischer, Michael M. J. 1980. *Iran: From Religious Dispute to Revolution*. Cambridge: Harvard University Press.

Fischer, Michael M. J. 1982. "Islam and the Revolt of the Petit Bourgeoise." *Daedalus* 3 (1): 101–125.

Fischer, Michael M. J., and Mehdi Abedi. 1990. *Debating Muslims: Cultural Dialogues in Postmodernity and Tradition*. Madison: University of Wisconsin Press.

Friedl, Erika. 1980. "Islam and Tribal Women in a Village in Iran." *Unspoken Worlds: Women's Religious Lives in Non-Western Cultures*. Nancy A. Falk and Rita M. Gross, editors. San Francisco: Harper & Row. 159–173.

Gaffney, Patrick D. 1987a. "Authority and the Mosque in Upper Egypt: The Islamic Preacher as Image and Actor." *Islam and the Political Economy of Meaning: Comparative Studies of Muslim Discourse*. William R. Roff, editor. Berkeley: University of California Press. 199–225.

Gaffney, Patrick D. 1987b. "The Local Preacher and Islamic Resurgence in Upper Egypt." *Religious Resurgence: Contemporary Cases in Islam, Christianity, and Judaism*. Richard T. Antoun and Mary Elaine Hegland, editors. Syracuse: Syracuse University Press. 35–63.

Gaffney, Patrick D. 1991. "The Changing Voices of Islam: The Emergence of Professional Preachers in Contemporary Egypt." *Muslim World* 81 (1): 27–47.

Geertz, Clifford. 1960. *The Religion of Java*. New York: Free Press.

Geertz, Clifford. 1968. *Islam Observed: Religious Development in Morocco and Indonesia*. Chicago: University of Chicago Press.

Geertz, Clifford. 1973. *The Interpretation of Cultures; Selected Essays*. New York: Basic Books.

Gellner, Ernest. 1969. *Saints of the Atlas*. Chicago: University of Chicago Press.

Gellner, Ernest. 1981. *Muslim Society*. Cambridge: Cambridge University Press.

Gellner, Ernest. 1992. *Postmodernism, Reason and Religion*. London and New York: Routledge.

Gerami, Shahin. 1994. "The Role, Place, and Power of Middle-Class Women in the

Islamic Republic." *Identity Politics and Women: Cultural Reassertions and Feminisms in International Perspective*. Valentine M. Moghadam, editor. Boulden, CO: Westview Press. 329–348.

Gilsenan, Michael. 1973. *Saint and Sufi in Modern Egypt: An Essay in the Sociology of Religion*. Oxford: Oxford University Press.

Gilsenan, Michael. 1982. *Recognizing Islam: Religion and Society in the Modern Arab World*. New York: Pantheon.

Goldberg, Ellis. 1991. "Smashing Idols and the State: The Protestant Ethic and Egyptian Sunni Radicalism." *Comparative Studies in Society and History* 33: 3–35.

Greenberg, Joseph H. 1941. "Some Aspects of Negro-Mohammedan Culture-Contact among the Hausa." *American Anthropologist* 43 (1): 51–61.

Greenberg, Joseph H. 1946. *The Influence of Islam on a Sudanese Religion*. New York: J. J. Augustin.

Greenberg, Joseph H. 1947. "Islam and Clan Organization among the Hausa." *Southwestern Journal of Anthropology* 3 (3): 193–211.

Gursoy-Tezcan, Akile. 1991. "Mosque or Health Centre? A Dispute in Gecekondu." *Islam in Modern Turkey: Religion, Politics and Literature in a Secular State*. Richard Tapper, editor. London and New York: I. B. Tauris & Co. Ltd. 84–101.

Haddad, Yvonne Y., editor. 1991. *The Muslims of America*. New York: Oxford University Press.

Haddad, Yvonne Yazbeck, and Adair T. Lummis. 1987. *Islamic Values in the United States: A Comparative Study*. New York: Oxford University Press.

Haddad, Yvonne Y., and Jane I. Smith. 1981. *The Islamic Understanding of Death and Resurrection*. Albany: State University of New York Press.

Hale, Sondra. 1994. "Gender, Religious Identity, and Political Mobilization in Sudan." *Identity Politics and Women: Cultural Reassertions and Feminisms in International Perspective*. Valentine M. Moghadam, editor. Boulder, CO: Westview Press. 145–166.

Hefner, Robert W. 1985. *Hindu Javanese: Tengger Tradition and Islam*. Princeton: Princeton University Press.

Hefner, Robert W. 1987a. "Islamizing Java? Religion and Politics in Rural East Java." *Journal of Asian Studies* 46 (3): 533–553.

Hefner, Robert W. 1987b. "The Political Economy of Islamic Conversion in Modern East Java." *Islam and the Political Economy of Meaning: Comparative Studies of Muslim Discourse*. William R. Roff, editor. Berkeley: University of California Press. 53–78.

Hegland, Mary. 1983a. "Ritual and Revolution in Iran." *Political Anthropology*. Vol. 2. Myron Aronoff, editor. New York: Transaction Books.

Hegland, Mary. 1983b. "Two Images of Husain: Accommodation and Revolution in an Iranian Village." *Religion and Politics in Iran*. Nikki R. Keddie, editor. New Haven: Yale University Press. 218–236.

Hegland, Mary. 1987. "Islamic Revival or Political and Cultural Revolution?" *Religious Resurgence: Comtemporary Cases in Islam, Christianity, and Judaism*. Richard T. Antoun and Mary Elaine Hegland, editors. Syracuse: Syracuse University Press. 194–219.

Helie-Lucas, Marie-Aimee. 1994. "The Preferential Symbol for Islamic Identity: Women in Muslim Personal Laws." *Identity Politics and Women: Cultural Reassertions and Feminisms in International Perspective.* Valentine M. Moghadam, editor. Boulder, CO: Westview Press. 391–407.

Hodgson, Marshall G. S. 1974. *The Venture of Islam: Conscience and History in a World Civilization.* 3 vols. Chicago: University of Chicago Press.

Holy, Ladislav. 1988. "Gender and Ritual in an Islamic Society: The Berti of Darfur." *Man,* n.s., 23 (3): 469–487.

Holy, Ladislav. 1991. *Religion and Custom in a Muslim Society: The Berti of Sudan.* Cambridge: Cambridge University Press.

Horvatich, Patricia. 1992. "Mosques and Misunderstandings: Muslim Discourses in Tawi-Tawi, Philippines." Ph.D. dissertation, Department of Anthropology, Stanford University.

Horvatich, Patricia. 1994. "Ways of Knowing Islam." *American Ethnologist* 21 (4): 811–826.

Hourani, Albert, editor. 1988. *The Cambridge Encyclopedia of the Middle East and North Africa.* New York: Cambridge University Press.

Houtsonen, Jarmo. 1994. "Traditional Qur'anic Education in a Southern Moroccan Village." *International Journal of Middle East Studies* 26 (3): 489–500.

Ibn Khaldun. 1967. *The Muqaddimah: An Introduction to History.* Translated by Franz Rosenthal. Edited by N. J. Dawood. Princeton: Princeton University Press. (Originally published 1377)

Imam, Ayesha M. 1994. "Politics, Islam and Women in Kano, Northern Nigeria." *Identity Politics and Women: Cultural Reassertions and Feminisms in International Perspective.* Valentine M. Moghadam, editor. Boulder, CO: Westview Press. 123–144.

Keddie, Nikki R. 1981. *Roots of Revolution: An Interpretive History of Modern Iran.* New Haven: Yale University Press.

Keddie, Nikki R., editor. 1983. *Religion and Politics in Iran.* New Haven: Yale University Press.

Keddie, Nikki R., and Juan R. I. Cole, editors. 1986. *Shi'ism and Social Protest.* New Haven: Yale University Press.

Kepel, Gilles. 1984. *Muslim Extremism in Egypt.* Berkeley: University of California Press.

Kessler, Clive S. 1978. *Islam and Politics in a Malay State: Kelantan 1838–1969.* Ithaca: Cornell University Press.

Kipp, Rita Smith, and Susan Rodgers, editors. 1987. *Indonesian Religions in Transition.* Tucson: University of Arizona Press.

Lambek, Michael. 1990. "Certain Knowledge, Contestable Authority: Power and Practice on the Islamic Periphery." *American Ethnologist* 17 (1): 23–40.

Lane, Edward. 1963. *Manners and Customs of the Modern Egyptians.* New York: Dutton. (Originally published 1860)

Launay, Robert. 1990. "Pedigrees and Paradigms: Scholarly Credentials among the Dyula of the Northern Ivory Coast." *Muslim Travellers: Pilgrimage, Migration and the Religious Imagination.* Dale F. Eickelman and James Piscatori, editors. Berkeley: University of California Press. 175–199.

Launay, Robert. 1992. *Beyond the Stream: Islam and Society in a West African Town.* Berkeley: University of California Press.

Lewis, I. M. 1961. *A Pastoral Democracy: A Study of Pastoralism and Politics among the Northern Somali of the Horn of Africa.* London: Oxford University Press.

Lewis, I. M. 1964. *Islam in Tropical Africa.* Bloomington: International African Institute.

Lewis, I. M. 1986. *Religion in Context: Cults and Charisma*. Cambridge: Cambridge University Press.

Loeffler, Reinhold. 1988. *Islam in Practice: Religious Beliefs in a Persian Village*. Albany: State University of New York Press.

Macleod, Arlene Elowe. 1991. *Accommodating Protest: Working Women, the New Veiling, and Change in Cairo*. New York: Columbia University Press.

Marcus, Michael A. 1985. " 'The Saint Has Been Stolen': Sanctity and Social Change in a Tribe of Eastern Morocco." *American Ethnologist* 12 (3): 455–467.

Martin, Richard C., editor. 1985. *Approaches to Islam in Religious Studies*. Tucson: University of Arizona Press.

Meeker, Michael E. 1979. *Literature & Violence in North Arabia*. Cambridge: Cambridge University Press.

Mernissi, Fatima. 1987. *Beyond the Veil: Male-Female Dynamics in a Modern Muslim Society*. Bloomington: Indiana University Press.

Messick, Brinkley. 1974. "Legal Documents and the Concept of 'Restricted Literacy' in a Traditional Society." *International Journal of the Sociology of Language* 42: 41–52.

Messick, Brinkley. 1986. "The Mufti, the Text and the World: Legal Interpretation in Yemen." *Man*, n.s., 21: 102–119.

Messick, Brinkley. 1993. *The Calligraphic State: Textual Domination and History in a Muslim Society*. Berkeley: University of California Press.

Moghadam, Valentine M. 1994. *Identity Politics and Women: Cultural Reassertions and Feminisms in International Perspective*. Boulder, CO: Westview Press.

Mortimer, Edward. 1982. *Faith and Power: The Politics of Islam*. New York: Vintage.

Mottahedeh, Roy. 1985. *The Mantle of the Prophet: Religion and Politics in Iran*. New York: Simon and Schuster.

Mumtaz, Khawar. 1994. "Identity Politics and Women: 'Fundamentalism' and Women in Pakistan." *Identity Politics and Women: Cultural Reassertions and Feminisms in International Perspective*. Valentine M. Moghadam, editor. Boulder, CO: Westview Press. 228–242.

Munson, Henry, Jr. 1984. *The House of Si Abd Allah: The Oral History of a Moroccan Family*. New Haven: Yale University Press.

Munson, Henry, Jr. 1986. "The Social Base of Islamic Militancy in Morocco." *Middle East Journal* 40 (2): 267–284.

Munson, Henry, Jr. 1988. *Islam and Revolution in the Middle East*. New Haven: Yale University Press.

Munson, Henry, Jr. 1993. *Religion and Power in Morocco*. New Haven: Yale University Press.

Nagata, Judith. 1982. "Islamic Revival and the Problem of Legitimacy among Rural Religious Elites in Malaysia." *Man*, n.s., 17 (1): 42–57.

Nagata, Judith. 1984. *The Reflowering of Malaysian Islam: Modern Religious Radicals and Their Roots*. Vancouver: University of British Columbia Press.

Nagata, Judith. 1987. "Indices of the Islamic Resurgence in Malaysia." *Religious Resurgence: Contemporary Cases in Islam, Christianity, and Judaism*. Richard T. Antoun and Mary Elaine Hegland, editors. Syracuse: Syracuse University Press. 108–124.

Nelson, Cynthia. 1974. "Religious Experience, Sacred Symbols, and Social Reality." *Humaniora Islamica* 2: 253–266.

Nelson, Kristina. 1985. *The Art of Reciting the Qur'an.* Austin: University of Texas Press.

Niezen, R. W. 1991. "Hot Literacy in Cold Societies: A Comparative Study of the Sacred Value of Writing." *Comparative Studies in Society and History* 33: 225–254.

Ong, Aihwa. 1990. "States versus Islam: Malay Families, Women's Bodies, and the Body Politic in Malaysia." *American Ethnologist* 17 (2): 258–276.

Patai, Raphael. 1952. "The Middle East as a Culture Area." *Middle East Journal* 6 (1): 1–21.

Patai, Raphael. 1976. *The Arab Mind.* New York: Charles Scribner's Sons.

Peacock, James. 1978. *Muslim Puritans: Reformist Psychology in Southeast Asian Islam.* Berkeley: University of California Press.

Peletz, Michael G. 1993. "Sacred Texts and Dangerous Words: The Politics of Law and Cultural Rationalization in Malaysia." *Comparative Studies in Society and History* 35 (1): 66–109.

Peters, Emrys. 1984. "The Paucity of Ritual among Middle Eastern Pastoralists." *Islam in Tribal Societies.* Akbar S. Ahmed and David M. Hart, editors. London: Routledge & Kegan Paul. 187–219.

Piscatori, James, editor. 1991. *Islamic Fundamentalisms and the Gulf Crisis.* Chicago: Fundamentalism Project of the American Academy of Arts and Sciences.

Rasmussen, Susan J. 1989. "Accounting for Belief: Causation, Evil and Misfortune in Tuareg Systems of Thought." *Man,* n.s., 24: 124–144.

Rasmussen, Susan J. 1991. "Lack of Prayer: Ritual Restrictions, Social Experience, and the Anthropology of Menstruation among the Tuareg." *American Ethnologist* 18 (4): 751–769.

Rasmussen, Susan J. 1993. "Ritual Specialists, Ambiguity and Power in Tuareg Society." *Man,* n.s., 27 (3): 105–128.

Rodinson, Maxime. 1971. *Muhammad.* Translated by Anne Carter. New York: Pantheon.

Roff, William R., editor. 1987. *Islam and the Political Economy of Meaning: Comparative Studies of Muslim Discourse.* Berkeley: University of California Press.

Rosen, Lawrence. 1984. *Bargaining for Reality: The Construction of Social Relations in a Muslim Community.* Chicago: University of Chicago Press.

Rugh, Andrea B. 1984. *Family in Contemporary Egypt.* Syracuse: Syracuse University Press.

Said, Edward. 1978. *Orientalism.* New York: Vintage.

Said, Edward. 1989. "Representing the Colonized: Anthropology's Interlocutors." *Critical Inquiry* 15: 205–252.

Shahrani, M. Nazif. 1984. "Introduction: Marxist 'Revolution' and Islamic Resistance in Afghanistan." *Revolutions & Rebellions in Afghanistan: Anthropological Perspectives.* M. Nazif Shaharani and Robert L. Canfield, editors. Berkeley: Institute of International Studies. 3–57.

Shaharani, M. Nazif, and Robert L. Canfield, editors. 1984. *Revolutions & Rebellions in Afghanistan: Anthropological Perspectives.* Berkeley: Institute of International Studies.

Simmons, William S. 1979. "Islamic Conversion and Social Change in a Senegalese Village." *Ethnology* 18 (4): 303–323.

Sivan, Emmanuel. 1985. *Radical Islam: Medieval Theology and Modern Politics.* New Haven: Yale University Press.

Skinner, Elliot. 1958. "Christianity and Islam among the Mossi." *American Anthropologist* 60 (6): 1102–1119.

Smith, William Robertson. 1956. *The Religion of the Semites*. New York: Meridian. (Originally published 1889)

Starrett, Gregory. 1991. "Our Children and Our Youth: Religious Education and Political Authority in Mubarak's Egypt." Ph.D. dissertation, Department of Anthropology, Stanford University.

Starrett, Gregory. 1993. "The Hexis of Interpretation: Islam and the Body in the Egyptian Popular School." *American Ethnologist* 22 (4): 953–969.

Starrett, Gregory. 1995. "The Political Economy of Religious Commodities in Cairo." *American Anthropologist* 97 (1): 51–68.

Stowasser, Barbara Freyer. 1987. *The Islamic Impulse*. Washington, D.C.: Center for Contemporary Arab Studies.

Street, Brian. 1984. *Literacy in Theory and Practice*. Cambridge: Cambridge University Press.

Tapper, Nancy. 1990. "*Ziyaret*: Gender, Movement, and Exchange in a Turkish Community." *Muslim Travellers: Pilgrimage, Migration and the Religious Imagination*. Dale F. Eickelman and James Piscatori, editors. Berkeley: University of California Press. 236–255.

Tapper, Nancy, and Richard Tapper. 1987. "The Birth of the Prophet: Ritual and Gender in Turkish Islam." *Man*, n.s., 22 (1): 69–92.

Tapper, Richard, editor. 1991. *Islam in Modern Turkey: Religion, Politics and Literature in a Secular State*. London and New York: I. B. Tauris & Co. Ltd.

Toprak, Binnaz. 1994. "Women and Fundamentalism: The Case of Turkey." *Identity Politics and Women: Cultural Reassertions and Feminisms in International Perspective*. Valentine M. Moghadam, editor. Boulder, CO: Westview Press. 293–306.

Wagner, Daniel, and Abdelhamid Lotfi. 1980. "Traditional Islamic Education in Morocco: Sociohistorical and Psychological Perspectives." *Comparative Education Review* 24: 238–251.

Wagner, Daniel, and Abdelhamid Lotfi. 1983. "Learning to Read by 'Rote.' " *International Journal of the Sociology of Language* 42: 111–121.

Wagner, Daniel, and Jennifer E. Spratt. 1987a. "Cognitive Consequences of Contrasting Pedagogies: The Effects of Quranic Preschooling in Morocco." *Child Development* 58: 1207–1219.

Wagner, Daniel, and Jennifer E. Spratt. 1987b. "Reading Acquisition in Morocco." *Growth and Progress in Cross-Cultural Psychology*. C. Kagitcibase, editor. Lisse: Swets & Zeitlinger B.V. 346–355.

Westermarck, Edward. 1911. "The Popular Ritual of the Great Feast in Morocco." *Folk-Lore*, 22.

Westermarck, Edward. 1914. *Marriage Ceremonies in Morocco*. London: Macmillan.

Westermarck, Edward. 1926. *Ritual and Belief in Morocco*. 2 vols. London: Macmillan.

Wolf, Eric. 1951. "The Social Organization of Mecca and the Origins of Islam." *Southwestern Journal of Anthropology* 7: 329–356.

Woodward, Mark R. 1988. "The *Slametan*: Textual Knowledge and Ritual Performance in Central Javanese Islam." *History of Religions* 28 (1): 54–89.

Woodward, Mark R. 1989. *Islam in Java: Normative Piety and Mysticism in the Sultanate of Yogyakarta*. Tucson: University of Arizona Press.

Young, William C. 1993. ''The Ka'ba, Gender, and the Rites of Pilgrimage.'' *International Journal of Middle East Studies* 25 (2): 285–300.

Zuhur, Sherifa. 1992. *Revealing Reveiling: Islamist Gender Ideology in Contemporary Egypt*. Albany: State University of New York Press.

12

Hinduism in Context: Approaching a Religious Tradition through External Sources

Cynthia Keppley Mahmood

Anthropologists of late have been rethinking their discipline. One key aspect of this rethinking is a rejection of the "cultures-as-entities" style of research and writing that characterized the field throughout most of its history. Instead, new theorists proclaim the need to recognize the constructedness of the classic notion of "cultures," bringing out the interactive and polyvocal character of cultural relations in our work. Artificially constraining this complexity in a "cookie-cutter" model of cultural units with the ethnographer as the privileged voice was, it is asserted, a rhetorical device with important repercussions for anthropology's claims to "objectivity." It was also inextricably tied to issues of who represents whom—and hence to the politics of domination and repression. (For initial expositions see Marcus and Fischer [1986] and Clifford and Marcus [1986].)

Much experimental ethnographic writing has been inspired by the new critiques, some of it directly challenging the reality of "cultures" as we used to think about them (e.g., Handler 1988; McDonald 1989). Less impact has been felt in the sphere of religion. But issues surrounding the anthropological study of religion are similar. What does it mean to talk about "Hinduism" as a tradition, or to talk about "Hindus" as if they were a definable social group? Does conceptualizing Hinduism as a single phenomenon, despite what we know about the immense diversity of belief and ritual conducted in vaguely Hindu contexts, compromise our academic and political integrity?

Much questioning that might be occasioned by a thoughtful critique of anthropological treatments of religion, has been precluded by the way in which anthropologists of religion are typically educated. This holds especially for those who focus on literate or text-based religions. Students of Judaism, Christianity, Islam, Hinduism, Buddhism, and so on, generally have been kept busy mastering relevant classical texts, philosophical or theological perspectives, basic history, and the range of popular belief and ritual of their chosen tradition. Combine this with a general training in ethnography and anthropological theory, and there is little time left for serious comparative study of two or more of the literate religious systems. Yet this kind of comparative context is just what is necessary to provide the kind of foundation for skeptical criticism that led, in the area of ethnography, to the current challenging innovations.

The case of Hinduism is particularly informative in this light. Hinduism evolved in continual dialogue with other literate religious traditions, particularly Jainism and Buddhism in ancient times and Sikhism and Islam later on. In fact, though India is today a Hindu majority state (of about 83 percent), other ''heterodox'' or non-Hindu faiths played key roles in the shaping of Indian history and in the shaping of Hinduism itself. So when scholars attempt to understand Hindu India by focusing their study on the Hindu tradition alone, as defined primarily by modern Hindus, they risk missing out on important components of the society's history. More important, they fail to acquire the very different perspective on the Hindu tradition provided by those who either rejected it or were rejected by it. This complementary perspective, which is skeptical of many of the claims of both the classic Hindu texts and many contemporary Hindus, gives a radically different reading of Indian civilization as a whole.

In this chapter I will look at Buddhist interpretations of Hinduism in particular, arguing that the study of Hinduism can benefit dramatically from attention to this key heterodox tradition. In addition, by calling into question some of the traditional Hindu assumptions about Hindu history, alternative readings from Buddhism bring us to a better understanding of the dialectical interplay among various communities that provides much of the dynamism of Indian religious thought. Along the lines of postmodernist critiques of cookie-cutter cultures, it is necessary to transcend the boundaries of what is traditionally considered Hinduism, looking at India in terms of interacting circles of discourse instead of monolithic and relatively separable traditions. This shift of emphasis provides different political insights as well.

THE "ENIGMA" OF BUDDHISM'S DECLINE

While imprisoned by the British, Jawaharlal Nehru wrote an essay about his personal discovery of India and Indian history. In *Discovery of India* (1945), Nehru describes an incident in which Andre Malraux asked him what ever happened to Buddhism in India. Why should a religion enormously popular in every country it touched in Asia have all but disappeared in the land of its birth? (India is no more than 1 to 2 percent Buddhist today, many of them recent converts.) Nehru found himself unable to answer Malraux's query, and most

contemporary Indians are likewise perplexed when this question is put to them. The reason why the conversation with Malraux was something of an epiphany to Nehru, prompting the intellectual search that led to *Discovery of India*, was because Indian Buddhism's decline cannot but be seen as paradoxical or enigmatic within the received historiography. To resolve the puzzle, one has to go outside of the dominant Hindu framework and look at Indian history from another
angle.

The common Hindu response to questions regarding the decline of Buddhism (which Nehru, to his credit, did not take at face value) is that Buddhism was essentially a reform movement from within Hinduism that faded as the reform succeeded and Hinduism itself was transformed. The former president of India, Sarvapeli Radhakrishnan, expresses this oft-heard point of view clearly when he writes:

The Buddha was born, grew up, and died a Hindu. He was restating with a new emphasis the ancient ideals of the Indo-Aryan civilization. . . .

Buddhism did not start as a new and independent religion. It was an offshoot of the more ancient faith of the Hindus; perhaps a schism or a heresy. . . .

The Buddha utilized the Hindu inheritance to correct some of its expressions. He came to fulfill, not to destroy. For us, in this country, the Buddha is an outstanding representative of our religious tradition. (Radhakrishnan 1956: ix–xv)

The idea of Buddhism as a Hindu reform movement (which then treats Buddhism's decline as a measure of the actual success of the movement) is so common today that many anthropologists have picked it up as well and thereby influenced a generation of Indologists (e.g., Cohn 1971). But we would do well to rethink this acceptance of contemporary ideology as historical truth. The use of the word *Hindu* in the above quote should, first of all, alert us to the lack of historical acumen on the part of the writer. Since the term *Hindu* had no religious meaning until about a thousand years after the time of the Buddha, talking about "Hinduism" as a kind of stock from which Buddhism arose is entirely inappropriate. Religious scholars know that Hinduism as we observe it today is a highly syncretic tradition drawing heavily on Buddhism itself, and the ancestral religion that Radhakrishnan is actually referring to is better termed "Vedicism" or "Brahminism." The fact that Radhakrishnan uses the term *Hindu*, however, should be a flag that draws our attention to the nationalist aims of the author; the quotes above are part of an apologetic genre of writing that took shape in the anticolonial struggle and continues to exalt Hinduism as nearly equivalent to Indianness itself. (They were published by the Indian government in a volume celebrating the 2,500th anniversary of Buddhism.)

More important than this quirk of terminology (okay, then can we say that Buddhism was a reform of Vedicism/Brahminism?) is the fact that paradigms placing Buddhism within some larger Indian religious tradition, which it reformed and then lost its independent raison d'être, receive little support from

Buddhist sources themselves. Not only is there intriguing evidence that much of Buddhism may be related to pre-Aryan tradition, antedating the system from which it is supposed to have sprung, but according to the Buddhist sources, it is clear that not all the "Hindus" shared Radhakrishnan's fervent admiration for the Buddhist tradition. If we attend to what these exogenous sources offer (while recognizing their own biases and inaccuracies), light is shed not only on what Buddhism was or wasn't but also on the dynamics of Hinduism's response to heterodoxy—and hence on Hinduism itself.

The most shocking thing about the Buddhist texts is the reporting of extensive persecution meted out by the Brahminic establishment. These reports contradict everything most Hindus believe about the tolerance of their tradition and are virtually ignored in most readings of Indian history. Yuan Chwang (Hiuen Tsang), for example, visited India in the seventh century and reported that King Mihirakula usurped the throne of Kashmir from a Buddhist ruler, destroying Buddhist pagodas and monasteries totaling "one thousand six hundred foundations." Mihirakula is also reported as having killed many thousands of lay followers of Buddhism, threatening "the utter extermination of the Buddhist church throughout the domain" (Watters 1904: 1: 288–289). This account is repeated in the so-called "Chronicle of Kashmir," the *Rajatarangini* by the Kashmir historian Kalhana, who compared Mihirakula with Yama, the god of death, for his atrocities. Remarking that "one's tongue would become polluted if one attempted to record his cruelties and evil deeds in detail," Kalhana reports that Mihirakula killed 300,000 lay Buddhists (I. 304–310). Further evidence for the oppressiveness of Mihirakula's regime comes from the Greek voyager Cosmas Indicopleustes, who as a non-Buddhist could be more easily cleared of the accusation of bias in his observations (Winstedt 1909).

Yuan Chwang also describes the persecution of Buddhists in the region of Kusinagara by Sasanka, who according to this traveler killed monks and broke up existing communities of Buddhists (Watters 1904: 2: 111). Most dramatically, Sasanka is reported to have thrown into the Ganges a stone bearing the footprints of the Buddha at Pataliputra (now Patna) and to have cut down the *bodhi* tree under which the Buddha attained Enlightenment (2: 115). At the holy site of Bodh Gaya, he replaced a statue of the Buddha with one of the Hindu god Siva, still worshiped there today (2: 92). Again, we have a corroboration of this account in the *Manjusrimulakalpa*, which states that "Somakya [Sasanka] of wicked intellect, will destroy the beautiful image of the Buddha; . . . then, that angry and greedy evil-doer of false notions and bad opinion, will bring down all the monasteries gardens and caityas [pagodas]" (LIII. 715–718).

Sankara, today considered one of the great sages of Hinduism, is reported in the *Samara-Digvijaya* to have destroyed Buddhists "from the Himalayas to Cape Cormorin" (I. 93), and the *Visvabharati Annals* from Tibet state that at Sankara's approach "the Buddhist monasteries began to tremble" (VI). The scholar-saint Sankara himself, in clear disagreement with President Radhakrishnan, called the Buddha "an enemy of the people" in the *Brahmasutra* (2. 2. 32).

Other Hindu texts also in fact convey a clear image of Hindu-Buddhist emnity. The *Brihadaradiya Purana* declares that it is a sin for a Brahmin to enter the house of a Buddhist, even in times of peril (XIV). The *Vayu Purana* says in a clear reference to the noncaste Buddhists, "with white teeth, eyes brought under control, head shaved and red clothes, the Sudras will perform religious deeds" (LXXVIII. 58–59), and the *Visnu Purana* sees Buddha as "the deluder," who came into the world to make the people give up the true religion (III. 17–18). (He is later destroyed by wrathful gods in this text.) The famous epic tale beloved by all Hindus, the *Rāmāyana*, denounces the Buddha as an atheist (CIX. 34).

One could go on and on with this sort of evidence, and the above is just a sampling of some of the material coming out of classic texts that gives a very different picture from that of the Buddha as "an outstanding representative of our religious tradition" upheld by Radhakrishnan and many Hindus today. The fact of persecution of Buddhists by Hindus is simply ignored in most accounts, clashing as it does with the idea of the Buddha as a welcomed reformer and of tolerance as a key characteristic of the Hindu tradition. But recognition of the antagonism between Hindus and Buddhists, with power concentrating in the hands of the former, relieves a great deal of the burden improperly placed on the "enigmatic" quality of Buddhism's decline. The decline of Buddhism is enigmatic only within a system that misrepresents Indian history, privileging one voice over all discordant others.

REDEFINING BUDDHISM

Awareness of the hostility between the Hindu and Buddhist traditions, as brought to light by study of the classical sources, leads to a further rethinking of each of these two religious systems. One has to ask seriously what it was about Buddhism that prompted the vehement reaction against it, and then also ask what it was about Hinduism that demanded such a response. We can then see whether these reconceptualizations of Buddhism and Hinduism offer any insights into the later development of these traditions and into their current identities.

Despite the fact that religious life in India today is obviously highly politicized, many Western scholars continue to exhibit a certain resistance to thinking about Buddhist-Hindu relations in political terms. This is of course a long-standing Orientalist tradition (problematically congruent with the traditions of the Indian upper castes) of overmysticizing Eastern religions. Max Weber's *Religion of India: The Sociology of Hinduism and Buddhism* (1958) is a key example of this genre. Though Weber is known for his concern with the social context and implications of religion, his approach to Buddhism was virtually devoid of sociology. Writing that Buddhism is "a specifically unpolitical and anti-political status religion'' (206) that ''has had no influence whatsoever upon the lay economy'' (218), Weber states outright that Buddhism ''had no tie with any sort of 'social' movement, nor did it run parallel with such and it has established no 'socio-political' goal'' (226). Weber runs into trouble with this completely asocial definition of Buddhism when he considers the fact that Buddhism became one of the great missionary religions, takings its message across an entire continent. It is worth quoting Weber's comments on this in full, as they are quite instructive as we look at ''enigmas'':

Buddhism became one of the greatest missionary religions on earth. That must seem baffling. Viewed rationally, there is no motive to be discovered which should have destined Buddhism for this. What could cause a monk who was seeking only his own salvation and therefore was utterly self-dependent to trouble himself with saving the souls of others and engaging in missionary work? . . .

First, presumably, in that psychological circumstance which is not rationally further explainable (perhaps physiologically conditioned circumstance) which we know to be peculiar to the great virtuosi of mystic piety. For the most part there is a compassionate acosmic love which almost always goes with the psychological form of mystical holy state, the peculiar euphoria of god-possessed tranquility. This drove the majority of them . . . on the road toward saving souls. (228–229)

Because of the way in which he defined Buddhism, as an inward-looking cult with no social aspirations, Weber was forced to explain an important part of the way Buddhism has functioned historically through an appeal to ''not rationally further explainable'' circumstances. If we revise our way of thinking about what early Buddhism was, however, both its missionary impulse and the ire it evoked in Vedic/Brahminic/Hindu circles can be readily explained.

That Buddhism was from the beginning, in fact, a social movement is apparent as soon as one examines its central vocabulary. First, the Western neologism ''Buddhism'' has traditionally had no corresponding term in the Buddhist vocabulary itself, which has more often defined itself by the term *sangha*, community. The word *bikkhu*, most often translated ''monk'' in Western scholarship, in fact carries the truer connotation of ''priest''—a word with very different social implications. Furthermore, the fact that the central vehicle of religious practice in early Buddhism was the *sutta (sutra)* or public sermon, spoken in popular dialects, and that the Buddhist religious communities were located near population centers rather than in isolated habitats all speak clearly to the very social nature of the early Buddhist movement. That Buddhism should be regarded as inner-directed and ''mystical'' by many Westerners comes as a shock to practicing Asian Buddhists, for whom it is entirely intertwined with everyday social life. (The work of Trevor Ling [e.g., 1968, 1980] looks at South Asian religious history from a more pragmatic standpoint and is a useful antidote to the overly philosophical reading often given. The Indian Marxist R. S. Sharma is another interesting, native source [1983].)

Weber, however, also said of Buddhism that "the concept of neighborly love, at least in the sense of the great Christian virtuosi of brotherliness, is unknown" (Weber 1958: 208), revealing his own ignorance of the concept of *metta*, or compassion (sometimes translated "loving kindness"), which is at the heart of the doctrine. More important than this is his failure to recognize the egalitarian message of early Buddhism, which was probably the key irritant to the power holders of caste-based Hindu society. One of the more famous statements against caste is found in the *Suttānipāta*, which denies the heritability of inequality by saying, "No brahmin is such by his birth. No outcaste is such by his birth. An outcaste is such by his deeds. A brahman is such by his deeds" (136). The *Majjhima Nikaya* takes this theme further in a sequence of questions and answers regarding caste divisions. Can a Brahmin go to a river and wash away dust, but no other man? No. Is the Brahmin capable of developing a mind without hate, but no other man? No. Does the Brahmin's fire of sandalwood burn higher or brighter than the common man's fire of common wood? No. This dialogue concludes with the Buddha saying to his interlocutor, "Finally you have come round to my way of thinking, that all four classes are equally pure!" (II.147). The most polemic work against caste prerogative is probably the *Vajrasuci* by Asvaghosa, dated at about the first or second century C.E.

Though it would certainly be going too far to say that Buddhism was a revolutionary movement aimed at the virtual overthrow of caste hierarchy (as claimed by some recent Buddhist political thinkers), it is clear that the neglect of caste distinctions in the Buddhist communities presented a direct challenge to Brahminic hierarchy. The idea of a *dhamma*, or law, that would apply indiscriminately to all individuals, as propagated during the famous reign of the Buddhist emperor Ashoka, was likewise threatening to the more particularistic conception of *varna-asrama-dharma*, laws or duties applying to particular caste levels and particular stages of life. Renouncing warfare and coercion as tools of statecraft (*ahimsa*) and looking at political rulers merely as turners of the wheel of cosmic law rather than as its sources or initiators were other ideals of the Ashokan state that, though undoubtedly exaggerated in Buddhist hindsight, nevertheless represented really revolutionary changes.

The last emperor of this dynasty was finally assassinated by his Brahmin commander in chief, ushering in the period of Hindu revitalization now thought of as India's "Golden Age." But it was also a period of crackdown on heterodoxy. The *Divyavadana*, a text of about the second to third century A.D., describes the founder of the new Brahminic dynastry, Pushyamitra Shunga, as marching at the head of an army that destroyed *stupas*, burned monasteries, and killed monks. That Hindu revitalization should be accompanied by mobilization against non-Hindus resonates out of history to the present day, in which newfound Hindu pride moves hand in hand with agitation against the major challengers today, the Muslims (cf. Mahmood 1994).

REDEFINING HINDUISM

We might also ask, however, in looking critically at the notion of Buddhism as "a Hindu reform movement," to what extent the syncretic Hinduism that evolved in the centuries after Buddhism's disappearance actually did reflect Buddhist influences. In fact, although the Buddha was incorporated as an *avatara*, or incarnation, of Vishnu in the *Matsya Purana* (28.5–7), the *Varah Purana* (IV.2), the *Bhagavad Purana* (I.3.24; X.40.22), and the *Vishnu Purana* (III.17–18), the major social aims of the religion (e.g., its rejection of caste) were incorporated into Hinduism not at all. Here is the very clear statement authorizing caste distinctions from the *Bhagavad Gita*, regarded by most Hindus today as an exemplary religious text:

Prescribed duties must never be renounced. If, by illusion, one gives up his prescribed duties, such renunciation is said to be in the mode of ignorance. . . . *Brahmanas, kshatriyas, vaishyas,* and *shudras* are distinguished by their qualities of work . . . in accord with the modes of nature. . . . It is better to be engaged in one's own occupation, even if one performs it imperfectly, than to accept another's occupation and perform it perfectly. (18.7–27)

Perhaps inspired by Buddhism, religious texts started to be composed in popular languages (the above-mentioned *Puranas* and the *Bhagavad Gītā*, for example), but the "revealed" and hence sacred texts in Sanskrit remained the prerogative of the Brahmins. Sankara, the Hindu scholar-saint who "destroyed Buddhists from the Himalayas to Cape Cormorin" (above), did bring some elements of Buddhist philosophy into syncretic Hinduism and even copied its pattern of community retreats (*mathas*) but completely acquiesced in the notion of caste divisions in which some were more and some less capable of striving for *nirvana* (Buddhist *nibbana*). While nonviolence, or *ahimsa*, was absorbed into Hinduism in the form of vegetarianism (for the upper castes), as a tool of statecraft it never made much headway. (Hindu legal writings like the *Gautama Dharmasūtra* [XII.1–15] that recommended pouring molten tin into the ears of a Sudra who overheard the reading of the sacred texts, whether actually put into practice or not, can hardly be read as being in the spirit of *ahimsa*.)

Karma (Buddhist *kamma*), the endless chain of causes and effects that points to an ethical stance of nonattachment or disinterestedness (attention to process rather than outcome), in some Hindu texts took the odd form of being an additional buttress for caste. The *Bhagavad Gita*'s most famous episode is a case in point. When Arjuna hesitates at the thought of killing on the battlefield, he is told by his charioteer Krishna:

Considering your specific duty as a *kshatriya*, you should know that there is no better engagement for you than fighting on religious principles. . . . If, however, you do not fight this religious war, then you will certainly incur sin for neglecting your duties and thus lose your reputation as a fighter. . . . Do thou fight for the sake of fighting, without considering happiness or distress . . . and, by so doing, you shall never incur sin. (2.33–38)

Though this passage is interpreted metaphorically by more thoughtful Hindus, the overt message is clearly very different from that of Buddhism in its encouragement of the performance of duty without noisome second thoughts. And when one is told that "he who dwells in the body is eternal and can never be slain. Therefore you need not grieve for any creature" (*Bhagavad Gita* 2.30), this is about as far from the position of loving kindness toward all that one can imagine.

The mass conversion of several million Untouchables to Buddhism in the recent past should be a strong hint that the picture of the Buddha as an incarnation of Visnu, sent down to reform Hinduism from within, is one that does not resonate with the lived reality of lower-caste and noncaste individuals in Indian society (cf. Contussi 1989). Combine this with the very interesting historical pattern in which the same regions that were once predominately Buddhist are the ones that later went over to other heterodoxies such as Islam, and you get the distinct feeling that what we are seeing is a continuing concert of rebellions against Hindu orthodoxy. (Another recent episode of the mass conversion of Untouchables away from Hinduism was to Islam, in many ways even more threatening than the rejection in favor of Buddhism [Majahid 1989].) Hinduism claims to be the umbrella category that absorbs and incorporates diverse movements, but their ongoing appeal in peripheral regions and to lower castes indicates that the incorporation is not definitive. As David Mandelbaum (1970) notes, "[I]t seems almost to be a property of this social system that such movements well up periodically, develop through the cycle, and then devolve back into the system" (525). To me this is too apolitical a vision. Buddhism did not simply "fall back" into Hinduism because of some kind of structural property of "the system"; its message was consciously appropriated into Hindu texts as part of a reassertion of prerogative by a privileged group.

To understand the Hindu/Buddhist encounter in Indian history, which I believe serves as a kind of template for Hindu/Other interactions up to the present, one has to get beyond Hindu informants and Hindu texts. Hindus are the winners in Indian history; they now dominate India not only numerically but also culturally and politically. To see what this domination means one has to listen to the losers, too. Anthropologists should know this, but sometimes lack of historical depth in their research ends up blurring the key distinction between hegemony and consensus.

WHAT DIFFERENCE DOES IT MAKE?

To show how the altered conceptualization of Hinduism prompted by looking seriously at non-Hindu perspectives can subvert the received understanding of Indian civilization today, I will look at some current issues in light of the orthodoxy/heterodoxy dynamic of ancient times. I will conclude by considering how such subversion can contribute to the solution of social problems through providing alternative frames of discourse through which issues can be discussed.

The Sauria Paharia of Bihar are one of India's "Scheduled Tribes," accorded special benefits and slated for development under the 6th Schedule of the Indian Constitution. In the spring of 1992 I visited five Sauria Paharia villages as part of an assessment of development needs in cooperation with Dr. Sachindra Narayan of the A. N. Sinha Institute in Patna, the Sauria Paharia's main ethnographer thus far (Narayan 1986a, 1986b, 1988).

Among many interesting things about this expedition was the religious status of the Sauria Paharia. Though they were until recently isolated foragers in the hilltop forests of Santal Parganas district (one of the remoter areas of India and still requiring special permits to visit), the Sauria Paharia are classed as "Hindus" by Narayan. Interviews with Sauria Paharia as well as Narayan's own published work revealed that the Sauria Paharia are essentially animists, venerating a range of nature spirits whom they placate and appeal to through offerings and rituals. Though they have come to look down upon the Mal Paharia and Santals, other tribal groups with whom they are in contact, the Sauria Paharia exhibit no caste or castelike divisions within their own society. The consumption of native alcoholic beverages, anathema to Hindus, forms a central part of their social life. Despite these indications, however, and despite the absence of key Hindu deities like Shiva, Vishnu, and so on, Narayan calls them "Hindus."

I pursued this issue with Sachindra Narayan because I think the labeling of the Sauria Paharia as "Hindus" is instructive for our understanding of just what is meant when Indians assert that their nation is 83 percent Hindu. When pressed, Narayan ventured that since the Sauria Paharia venerate nature, and since the Hindus venerate nature, the Sauria Paharia are Hindus. I inquired as to whether, then, Native American groups that venerate nature could be called Hindus as well. At this suggestion, clearly ludicrous except perhaps to the most diehard mystics of the Hindu tradition, Narayan changed his argument and claimed that since the Sauria Paharia had not converted to Islam or Christianity, they must be Hindus. Hinduism, that is, is seen by him as a kind of default category for people of the subcontinent. Whether the Sauria Paharia themselves, if asked, would identify themselves as Hindus is a moot point for Narayan.

This encounter is an instructive one in light of the "Buddhism as a kind of Hinduism" conception discussed above. The long-standing tendency of the Hindu tradition is to embrace others within its rhetorical fold. While most Hindus view this embrace as a positive part of the tolerant inclusiveness of the religion, many non-Hindus view it as a particularly intolerant attempt at spiritual hegemony. Coupled with the equation of Hinduism with Indianness generally (the "default category" idea), this leads to a vision in which refusal to acquiesce to the Hindu embrace can be read as a nearly treasonous posture (cf. Embree 1990).

This is, in fact, exactly how the assertiveness of India's Muslim minority is interpreted by extreme Hindu nationalist groups today. Rejecting the secular state model developed by Nehru, Hindu nationalists hope to define India as a Hindu nation—leaving room, however, for the inclusion of Muslims and others as special kinds of Hindus. If the Muslims are truly loyal to India, they should take Hindu names, celebrate Hindu festivals, and so on. The refusal to do these things, and the corresponding refusal to construe Islam as just one path among many equally viable paths to spiritual truth, is taken as a slap in the face by militant Hindus. Despite the fact that the bulk of India's Muslim population comes from people who converted away from Hinduism, the Muslims are often perceived as a foreign element "contaminating" the Indian (Hindu) nation. So the drive to replace a mosque at Ayodhya with a Hindu temple (Van der Veer 1985, 1994) has the ring of nationalist fervor to it, and the most extreme rhetoric envisions those Muslims insistent on a separate (non-Hindu) identity thrown out of India altogether. Insofar as they continue to maintain a religious identity distinct from Hinduism, the Muslims are not quite trustworthy as Indians, in this perspective. As an anthropologist delving into the question of whether the Sauria Paharia actually want to be considered as Hindus, I was also personally perceived as politically questionable, a perception made especially problematic by my (Muslim origin) last name.

Though it would be seriously misrepresenting the state of affairs in India today to overemphasize the degree of support for so-called Hindu fundamentalism, it is nevertheless clear that a renascent Hindu pride is on the rise and that this revitalization is moving in parallel with increasing discrimination against non-Hindu minorities. The current respectability of the Bharatīya Janata Party (BJP) and its successes at the polls is accompanied by a widespread tolerance for communalist rhetoric in the public domain that would have been greeted with outrage a mere decade ago (Malik and Vajpeyi 1989; Duara 1991; Gold 1991). Even more intriguing is the continuing presence and influence of the Rashtriya Swayamsevak Sangh (RSS), a militant brotherhood of Hindu extremists whose organization, training, activities, and public pronouncements make it, as Nehru is reputed to have said, "the Indian version of fascism" (cf. Andersen and Damle 1987). The oceans of orange-robed Hindus photographed at Ayodhya, shouting anti-Muslim slogans with raised fists and angry faces, strikes most Westerners as paradoxical, given the image of Hinduism as all tolerant that we have learned from upper-caste interpretations of Hindu texts. But these phenomena are only enigmatic in the way that Buddhism's decline in India is also enigmatic—through the distorted lens of Brahmin historiography. Looking at the Hindu traditions from other perspectives makes the periodic

appearances of fundamentalist retrenchments quite understandable and even predictable.

Although some recent analyses of Hindu revitalization have emphasized the
recency of this phenomenon (e.g., Hawley 1991), even a cursory examination
of the Vedic texts shows an us-them distinction extending far back into antiquity.
The early contrast between pure and impure (*arya* and *anarya*) is the most
obvious assertion of exclusivism, with the latter category most frequently associated with *mleccha*, or barbarians (cf. Thapar 1989). Combine this vocabulary
with such traditions as the restriction of sacred knowledge to the priestly circle,
the closure of Hindu temples to any but "twice-born" Hindus, and the impos-
sibility or difficulty of converting to Hinduism, and a picture emerges of a highly
exclusive, rather than inclusive, religious tradition.

The situation involving the Sikhs of Punjab is another that appears problematic in light of the received history of India and the received image of Hinduism.
Hindus have long considered Sikhism as a sect or branch, or even a caste, within
the Hindu tradition. While it is true that there are key elements of Hinduism in
the Sikh faith (and that they are historically intertwined), many aspects of Sikhism involve the outright rejection of Hindu tradition. Two of the especially
definitive rejections involve multiple deities (Sikhism is firmly monotheistic)
and caste hierarchy (it is ideally at least committed to equality). Yet Sikhs have
at one time or another felt compelled to write essays called *We Are Not Hindu*,
to demand from a heavily armed encampment at the Golden Temple in Amritsar
that Sikhism be recognized as a separate faith, and eventually to launch a guer-
rilla insurgency partly based on the theme of religious sovereignty (cf. Mahmood
1996). Has any group attempting to split away from Catholicism, Protestantism,
or any other religious system experienced such difficulty in seceding?

We are into shaky ground here, and the labyrinthine morass of modern Indian
politics shouldn't be simplified as crassly as I have just done. But my point here
is to simply point to the connections between the study of ancient religious
history and modern ethnographic understanding of India. It should be clear that
the skepticism toward Hindu claims provoked by looking at classic Buddhist
texts opens up new interpretations of contemporary Hindu interactions with non-
Hindus. The fact that these interactions have serious political implications that
should give pause to those who are tempted to take modern Hindu ideology—
which glosses over the actual religious pluralism of India—at face value. Recent
scholarship focused on the deconstruction of ideologies (e.g., Breckenridge and
van der Veer 1993; Chatterjee 1993; Ludden 1996) is radically changing the
face of academic Indology, but its repercussions have yet to be fully felt in
politics.

India cannot be understood by a focus on Hinduism alone. Even the understanding of Hinduism is not best served by a focus on Hinduism alone. Buddhism, Jainism, Zoroastrianism, Sikhism, Christianity, Islam, and tribal beliefs
are all components of Indian civilization and its dominant religious system. They
are all players in the forum in which India's very serious problems and conflicts

must be resolved. In addition, the mosaic of Indian religion with its shifting identities and counteridentities offers a most fertile ground for explorations of theoretical frameworks that do not rest on primordial assumptions but on the constructedness and dynamism of social categories. In the study of religions in India, a broader holism is methodologically mandated, theoretically promising, and politically responsible.

REFERENCES

Andersen, Walter K., and Shridhar D. Damle. 1987. *The Brotherhood in Saffron*. Boulder, CO: Westview.

Breckenridge, Carol, and Peter van der Veer, editors. 1993. *Orientalism and the Postcolonial Predicament: Perspectives on South Asia*. Philadelphia: University of Pennsylvania Press.

Chatterjee, Partha. 1993. *The Nation and Its Fragments: Colonial and Post-Colonial Histories*. Princeton, NJ: Princeton University Press.

Clifford, James, and George Marcus, editors. 1986. *Writing Culture: The Poetics and Politics of Ethnography*. Berkeley: University of California Press.

Cohn, Bernard S. 1971. *India: The Social Anthropology of a Civilization*. Englewood Cliffs, NJ: Prentice-Hall.

Contusrsi, Janet A. 1989. "Militant Hinduism and the Buddhist Dalits." *American Ethnologist* 16 (3): 441–457.

Duara, Prasenjit. 1991. "The New Politics of Hinduism." *Wilson Quarterly* 15: 42–45. (summer).

Embree, Ainslie. 1990. *Utopias in Conflict: Religion and Nationalism in Modern India*. Berkeley: University of California Press.

Gold, Daniel. 1991. "Organized Hinduisms: From Vedic Tradition to Hindu Nation." *Fundamentalisms Observed*. M. E. Marty and R. S. Appleby, editors. Chicago: University of Chicago Press. 531–593.

Handler, Richard. 1988. *Nationalism and the Politics of Culture in Quebec*. Madison: University of Wisconsin Press.

Hawley, John Stratton. 1991. "Naming Hinduism." *Wilson Quarterly* (summer).

Kalhana. 1979. *Rajatarangini*. Translated by M. A. Stein. Delhi: Montilal Banarsidass.

Ling, Trevor. 1968. *A History of Religion East and West*. New York: Torchbook Library.

Ling, Trevor. 1980. *Karl Marx and Religion in Europe and India*. New York: Harper and Row.

Ludden, David, editor. 1996. *Contesting the Nation: Religion, Community, and the Politics of Democracy in India*. Philadelphia: University of Pennsylvania Press.

McDonald, Maryon. 1989. *"We Are Not French!" Language, Culture and Identity in Brittany*. London: Routledge.

Mahmood, Cynthia Keppley. 1994. "Ayodhya and the Hindu Resurgence." *Religion* 24: 73–80.

Mahmood, Cynthia Keppley. 1996. *Fighting for Faith and Nation: Dialogues with Sikh Militants*. Philadelphia: University of Pennsylvania Press.

Majahid, Abdul Malik. 1989. *Conversion to Islam: Untouchables' Strategy for Protest in India*. Chambersburg: Anima Press.

Malik, Yogendra, and Dhirendra Vajpeyi. 1989. "The Rise of Hindu Militancy: India's Secular Democracy at Risk." *Asian Survey* 29 (3): 308–325.

Mandelbaum, David G. 1970. *Society in India: Change and Continuity*. Vols. 1–2. Berkeley: University of California Press.

Marcus, George and Michael M. J. Fischer. 1986. *Anthropology as Cultural Critique: An Experimental Moment in the Human Sciences*. Chicago: University of Chicago Press.

Narayan, Sachindra. 1986a. *Dimensions of Development in Tribal Bihar*. Delhi: Inter-India Publications.

Narayan, Sachindra. 1986b. *Tribe in Transition*. Delhi: Inter-India Publications.

Narayan, Sachindra. 1988. *A Dwindling Hill Tribe of Bihar*. Calcutta: Naya Prakash.

Nehru, Jawaharlal. 1945. *Discovery of India*. New York: John Day Company.

Radhakrishnan, S. 1956. Foreword to *2500 Years of Buddhism*. Edited. By P. V. Bapat. Delhi: Indian Ministry of Information.

Sharma, R. S. 1983. *Material Culture and Social Formations in Ancient India*. New Delhi: Macmillan.

Thapar, Romila. 1989. "Imagined Religious Communities? Ancient History and the Modern Search for a Hindu Identity." *Modern Asian Studies* 23 (2): 209–231.

Van der Veer, Peter. 1985. "God Must Be Liberated! A Hindu Liberation Movement in Ayodhya." *Modern Asian Studies* 21 (2): 283–301.

Van der Veer, Peter. 1994. *Religious Nationalism: Hindus and Muslims in India*. Berkeley: University of California Press.

Watters, Thomas, editor. 1904. *On Yuan Chwang's Travels in India*. Vols. 1–2. London: Royal Asiatic Society.

Weber, Max. 1958. *The Religion of India: The Sociology of Hinduism and Buddhism*. Translated by H. Gerth and D. Martindale. New York: Macmillan, Free Press.

Winstedt, E. O., editor. 1909. *The Christian Topography of Cosmas Indicopleustes*. Cambridge: Cambridge University Press.

13

Buddhist Communities: Historical Precedents and Ethnographic Paradigms

Todd T. Lewis

Buddhism has been transplanted to diverse ecological, linguistic, and cultural contexts across Asia and, in recent centuries, globally. Inclusive and practical, and guided by a missionary ethos, renunciant and lay traditions have been effectively adapted to settings as diverse as settled farming villages, pastoral grasslands, and urban communities. Among missionary religions, Buddhist tradition (śāsana) is distinctive in its accommodation of myriad texts, doctrinal formulations, spiritual disciplines, and devotional practices, yet still (where vibrant) retaining a strong monastic center that asserts Buddhism's primacy over indigenous ancestral religions and other world faiths. Since exchange is the basis of social life (Murphy 1971; Harris 1989), anthropological studies of Buddhist communities can account for the tradition's maintenance, specifying how institutions and cultural performances have secured the survival of fundamental relationships.

The presence of a textual canon and devotional art is a universal feature of Buddhist contexts, although contents vary among Buddhist culture regions.[1] Lack of grounding in the textual tradition, especially the oft-neglected ritual and popular discourses, has been a weakness in anthropological studies of Buddhism: Future research should be informed by an understanding of the textual-historical precedents for modern practice (Buswell 1990: 1; Strong 1992). Given the vast textual corpus and the lack of any overarching panregional institutional authority that ever dictated (or enforced) doctrinal orthodoxy, command over the historical sources and precedents for modern practices is a complicated assignment. This chapter, in part, is addressed to this desideratum.[2]

Section I provides an introduction to the classical precepts that defined early

Indic traditions of practice. It presents the key principles that informed the missionary transplantation of the faith across northern, southern, and eastern Asia, including those that defined the normative existence of the monastic order (*saṃgha*) and monasteries (*vihāra*)[3] and the nature of proper householder support for monks and nuns who centered the tradition in these institutions. Buddhist civilization was sustained by the exchanges between householders and renunciants, as orchestrated through ritual. Many formulations of proper Buddhist practice, from simple to advanced (leading to *nirvāṇa* ["a state of blissful illumination, cessation of karma generation, ending rebirth"]), were made in the course of early Buddhist history to guide the faithful among alternatives. The traditional triad of meditation (*dhyāna*), moral practice (*śīla*), and meritorious donations (*dāna*) is an early, enduring formulation that defines central organizing points for practice and so the anthropological study of all Buddhist communities.

Section II discusses, in pan-Asian and comparative terms, patterns in Buddhism's local domestications. A key concept throughout this chapter, "domestication" is the dialectical process by which a religious tradition is adapted to a region's or ethnic group's socioeconomic and cultural life (Wright 1959; Strenski 1983; Kitagawa 1965; Ramble 1990). This refers to every dimension of Buddhist praxis, including text transmission, doctrinal interpretation, monastic customs, spiritual instruction, institution building, and so on. The anthropological study of Buddhist communities can demonstrate the underlying reasons for selectivity as the tradition has evolved according to the "logic of the locality." Section III notes transcultural issues that need to be addressed through research on both past and contemporary communities. Future desiderata for interdisciplinary inquiry in Buddhist studies are also cited.

SECTION I: ENVISIONING BUDDHISM AND SOCIETY

The Ideal of Buddhist Civilization

Buddhist monasticism arose to provide refuge and support for renunciants seeking enlightenment, but the tradition survived by building multifaceted relationships with lay patron communities that provided for the monks' subsistence. Solidifying the loyalty of a cross section of society's economic classes, Buddhism evolved to espouse the basic foundations of spiritually and morally centered civilization. Buddhism adapted to myriad local traditions, yet still, when vital, its community focused on the *triratna* ("Three Jewels" or "Three Refuges")—Buddha, *dharma* ("teachings"), and *saṃgha* ("monastic community")—while living amidst the vicissitudes of *saṃsāra* ("the world of rebirth, suffering, impermanence"). Over the first millennium, the *saṃgha*'s central role developed as monks taught a variety of audiences, provided ritual assistance, and participated in a yearly festival agenda.

The norm of Buddhist pluralism is a striking feature in the tradition's sociohistorical profile (Holt 1991: 18), as its traditions encompassed a broad range of intellectual discourse and ritual performance. The monastic rule books (*vinayas*) all show an early sensitivity to the greatly varying ecological, social, and cultural contexts that monks entered. Recognizing this legitimate "malleability to contextual circumstances" helps explain the great differences in praxis seen even in the early sources. Gregory Schopen has begun to articulate this central historical variable in antiquity, noting how the *saṃgha* must have adapted variously amidst varying populations as diverse as tribal rain forest dwellers, highland nomadic herders, or highly Brahmanical urban settings.[4] The need for such adaptability is an emic Buddhist perception: The *Vinaya*s make a distinction between situations in central places where the rules must be strictly observed (*madhyadeśa*, "middle country," i.e., the Buddhist homeland) and the far-off areas where less strict standards were to be tolerated (*pratyantajanapada*, "frontier principalities") (Lamotte 1988:8).[5]

The general ideals of Buddhist civilization are well outlined in the monastic literature. Monks and nuns served the world through their example of renunciation and meditation (Wijayaratna 1990), by performing rituals (Gombrich 1971: 201ff; Lewis 1994d), and by providing medical service (Zysk 1991). As preservers, transmitters, and exemplars of the *dharma*, the *saṃgha*'s duty was to attract the Buddhist lay community's merit-making donations by being spiritually worthy (Lamotte 1984); complementing this, *saṃgha* members were explicitly taught to seek out *prasāditas* ("dedicated sympathizers") and *dānapatis* ("generous donors") (Lamotte 1988: 78) so as to ensure the Buddhist *śāsana*'s existence.[6]

Buddhism shows an array of evolutionary trajectories sharing common traits: *stūpas* ("shrines"; see discussion below) as centers of community ritual (Lewis 1993a); *vihāras* as refuges for meditation, study, and material resources; and *saṃgha* members who assume leadership of the community's spiritual instruction and ritual life. Buddhism in practice so encompassed the elaboration of myriad distinctive lifestyles and cultures that even by the Chinese pilgrim's Fa-Hsien's time (400 C.E.) there was already seemingly indescribable diversity in India: "Practices of the *śramanas* ("monks") are so various and have increased so that they cannot be recorded" (Beal 1970: 1:xxx). The succeeding 1,500 years have only further multiplied the diversity of Buddhism's successful domestications across Asia.

Just as the culture hearth itself evolved effulgently, then declined precipitously after 1200 C.E., so, too, did the peripheries variously absorb, adopt, and adapt the *triratna*.[7] David Snellgrove has noted the seeming paradox of how a decentralized, pluralistic faith has still evolved to observe common traditions over large areas:

Buddhism was clearly incorporating all the time notions which the earliest *śrāvaka*s [monks] might have considered unnecessary, if not altogether erroneous. Nevertheless

the general stream of Buddhist tradition . . . was sufficiently strong to absorb and transform these new notions, enriching itself in the process. There is of course nothing strange
in this process, for the same thing happened in Christianity, but whereas in this case a
fairly effective control was maintained for at least 15 centuries, *the only check in the
history of Buddhism was the living tradition itself.* It is perhaps surprising that its power
has proved to be so strong in the event. (1959: 211–212; emphasis added)

The anthropological study of any Buddhist community can be defined simply
as seeking comprehension of how the Buddha, the *dharma*, and the *saṃgha*
have been domesticated into local institutions, vernacular and classical texts,
sermons, as expressed in icons and architecture, temporally incorporated through
daily, yearly, and life cycle rituals, and as reported by individual monks and
laity. Manning Nash has noted the breadth of the anthropological research undertaking in Buddhist cultural zones: "Buddhism is not a separate compartment
of belief and practice, but a system of symbols, psychological attitudes, and
ritual behavior forming the warp against which the wool of daily life is woven"
(1965: 104).

The Spiritual Foundations of Buddhist Practice

Early European interpreters sought in early Buddhism a purely rational, athe-
istic doctrine that rejected "popular" practices, and their scholarship has long
suggested that its rituals represented a degradation of primitive Buddhism's purity, a concession to the masses. (This is a view many early anthropologists
accepted.)[8] It is now clear that numerous other early textual discourses present
rationales for "popular devotional activities" that make positive, meritorious
contributions to the tradition. These authoritative sources express a broad vision
of the Buddhist community and of proper Buddhist practice: The *Dīghanikāya*
speaks of the devout layman's (*upāsaka's*) duty to "[h]elp others in increasing
faith, moral virtues, knowledge, charity" (N. Dutt 1945b: 169); the Pali *Sigo-
lavada Sutta* specifically enjoins the layman to "maintain . . . the traditions of
family and lineage; make himself worthy of his heritage; and he should make
offerings to the spirits of the departed" (de Bary 1972: 43). There are also
certain short texts (called *mantra* and *paritta*, later *dhāraṇī*) given by Śākyamuni
that could be effective, when repeated, in repelling negative influences in any
environment; in the influential Pali *Milindapañha*, the laity is instructed to listen
to the *dharma* and to make efforts to resist its decline (N. Dutt 1945b: 175).
Still other voices (quoted below) speak about the merit of spiritual celebrations
in the presence of the Buddha's relics. Thus, a sound working definition of a
"good Buddhist" is simple: one who takes the three refuges and practices.

Puṇya and Dāna: The Fundamental Buddhist Exchange. The early formulation called "the graded teaching" (*anupūrvīkathā*) established *puṇya/dāna*
("merit"/"gift giving") as the foundation for Buddhist practice while also

legitimating a Buddhist community's diverse cultural activities. The *anupūrvī-katha* are:

1. *Dāna/punya*
2. *Śīla/svarga* (morality/heaven)
3. Evils of *pāpa/kāma* (immoral acts/pleasure seeking)
4. Value of renunciation
5. Four Noble Truths (Lamotte 1988: 77)

This hierarchy of legitimate, progressive practices defines a "syllabus" for advancing in spiritual attainment. As *punya* has provided the chief orientation point and goal in the Buddhist layman's worldview and ethos, *dāna* ("giving," "charity," "generosity") has always been the starting practice for accumulating *punya*, the lifelong measure of spiritual advancement.

Merit making remained the universal, integrating transaction in Buddhist settings (Dargyay 1986: 180), regardless of the respective intellectual elite's orientation toward competing Theravāda, Mahāyāna, or Vajrayāna doctrinal formulations or spiritual disciplines.[9] The wish for merit leading to rebirth in heaven was—and is, in practice—the most popular and pan-Buddhist aspiration; indeed, from the Pali Canon onward (100 C.E.), monks are instructed to "show the layfolk the way to heaven." *Punya* is needed to reach heaven, although Buddhist doctrine holds that this is a temporary state and that *nirvāa* realization entails the final, eternal cessation of both merit and bad karma. Thus, merit making has both soteriological as well as practical, worldly consequences (G. Obeyesekere 1968). *Punya* leads one closer to release, while having impact on worldly destiny in both this lifetime and across future lifetimes. Buddhists likewise seek *punya* to change their karma "account" to affect this life and their future rebirth destiny (Hanks 1962).

To maximize *punya* and so the course of spiritual advancement, early texts urge all disciples, monastic and lay, to cultivate the Five Cardinal Precepts (*śiksādāni*):

1. *Śraddhā* (faith)
2. *Śīla* (moral observances)
3. *Tyāga* (generosity)
4. *Śruti* (listening)
5. *Prajñā* (insight) (Lamotte 1988: 70)

The Indic sources thus implicitly authorized many practices through which Buddhists could accomplish the Cardinal Precepts: venerating images (*śiksādāni* 1), taking precepts and fasting (2), organizing compassionate actions and charitable institutions (2 and 3), arranging public recitations of the texts (4), and encouraging meditation (5) (Conze 1967: 47–55; Warder 1970: 191; Welch 1967: 377–382). How Buddhist communities domesticate the Five Cardinal Precepts can be a fruitful, emically informed avenue for anthropological inquiry.

The most universal expression of lay Buddhist faith and *puṇya* seeking has been through *dāna* (*śikṣādāni* 3). *Dāna*'s "investment" is described and celebrated in the vast *jātaka* and *avadāna* literature and in the great Mahāyāna *sūtras* (Strong 1979). *Dāna* is the foundation for householder practice. Generosity to all beings is applauded, although the best "*puṇya* return" accrues to gifts made to the Buddhas, *bodhisattvas* ("Buddhas-to-be"), and the *saṃgha*. Passages in the Mahāyāna *sūtras* articulate the value of *dāna* to the individual as an expression of compassion (*kāruṇa*) and for its value as renunciatory practice (Dayal 1932: 165–193).

Buddhist Monasticism. Points of *saṃgha* discipline, not doctrine, were the first areas of sectarian discord and schism in Buddhist history (S. Dutt 1962). The books with rules and regulations for the different *saṃgha*s have a remarkable consistency and enduring importance in Buddhist monastic history (Prebish 1975b; Wijayaratna 1990), with the Mahāyāna simply adding the *bodhisattva* vow to the earlier formulations (Robinson 1966). The specific rules of residence in each *vihāra* were copied and consulted regularly in China (Welch 1967: 105ff), indicating the centrality of rules in communal societies of each *saṃgha*.

One prominent division within the *saṃgha*s was that between the village monk versus the forest monk: The latter's practice was ideally dedicated to meditation, the former's to service and study. These were the two ideal poles of the monastic orientation, but monks have always moved between them, both in geography and practice. Theravāda Buddhists in Sri Lanka even debated as to whether the most important monks' pursuit was that of meditation or learning. (Citing the danger of the faith's decline, it was decided that the latter was more important.) Later Buddhists have also venerated solitary meditating hermits and wandering saints (*siddhas*) in both Theravāda (Carrithers 1983; Tambiah 1984) and Mahāyāna contexts (Ray 1994; Snellgrove 1987; Welch 1967: 318ff).

An early six-fold division of monastic specialization gives a clear definition of the *saṃgha*'s early engaged, multiple orientations to society:

Instructors (*dharmakathika*)

Meditators (*dhyayin*)

Folklorists (*tiraścakathika*)

Sūtra specialists (*sūtradhara*)

Vinaya specialists (*vinayadhara*)

Catecheticists (*Mātṛkādhara*) (Lamotte 1988: 149)

Another specific designation often mentioned in inscriptions is the reciter (*bhāṇaka*), which also suggests popular service. By 400 C.E., Indic monks had "patron saints" among the classical disciples of Śākyamuni, depending on their focus. (See discussion on this topic below.)

It is particularly important to note the difference between *samgha* and *vihāra:* A *samgha* is the association of monks (*bhiksus*) or (separately) nuns (*bhiksunīs*)[10] living communally under *Vinaya* rules and participating together in the fortnightly *uposatha* ritual; the *vihāra*, by contrast, refers to dwellings and institutions designed for the *samgha*'s upkeep under the *Vinaya*, the founding and maintenance of which is usually arranged for by the lay community.

A *vihāra* can be of humble construction or built to imperial, aristocratic standards. Each *vihāra* must have a place for the monks to sleep and a site, marked with boundary stones (*sīmā*), for them to gather for the *uposatha*; a *stūpa*, "*bodhi* tree" (*ficus religiousa*, the fig tree under which Śākyamuni was enlightened), meditation hall, image hall, and memorial shrines for deceased monks are other fixtures of typical monastery compounds (e.g., Dutt 1962; Swearer 1976; Bunnag 1973; Spiro 1982; Evers 1972).

The subsistence of the monks from classical times was dependent upon the donations of food and shelter by the lay community. Food was gathered in morning begging rounds, and the day's solid food had to be eaten by noon. Over the centuries, however, the community developed more routinized methods: In some places the laity worked out systems of their coming to the monastery with food donations; in others, monks came to cook their own foods. (In the modern Buddhist world, the begging round is rarely practiced daily.) In most of east Asia, the *vihāra*s were given landholdings, and in some schools, monks of certain schools worked in the fields (Welch 1967; Gernet 1995). It was in the Mahāyāna East, too, that monastery rules specified vegetarianism as a requirement, but in later centuries, others did not enforce the restriction against alcohol. Other issues pertinent to the institutional role of Buddhist monastics are treated in subsequent sections.

Meditation Practices. It was not sublime philosophical exegesis nor meditative rapture but ritual acts directed to making *punya* for heavenly rebirth that inspired the practice of most Buddhists throughout history. Nonetheless, as the last stretch of the final path to *nirvāna*, meditation practice by the few certifies Buddhism's continuing spiritual vitality, inspiring layfolk to respect and take refuge with the *samgha*. Until modern times, it was almost entirely monks and nuns who practiced meditation.

Buddhism inherited and extended the spiritual experiments of ancient India. The practice of trance (*samādhi*) was accepted, even encouraged, but the states achieved were not given priority, as they were regarded as a diversion from *nirvāna* realization. The key salvific practice was mindfulness meditation (*vipaśyāna*): a careful attending to the three characteristics of existential reality— suffering (*duhkha*), impermanence (*anitya*), and no-soul (*anātman*). Attention to, and comprehension of, these facts in direct personal experience has critical twofold effect: It develops nonattachment (*virāga*) that stills desire (*trsna*), and it cultivates spiritual insight (*prajñā*) that dispells ignorance (*avidyā*). The development of both eliminates bad karma (*pāp*) and creates good (*puṇya*), but their perfection eventually leads to the fullness of *prajñā* in the breakthrough, transformative experience (Jap. *satori*) of an enlightened mind (*bodhi*) that eliminates all karma, making future rebirth impossible. Modern Theravāda meditation (P. *vipassana*) still follows this early formulation closely (Thera 1970).

Mahāyāna meditations elaborated upon these precedents. (Chi.) Ch'an (Jap. Zen) mindfulness practice is similar to the Theravāda practice, although the doctrine of all beings possessing the Buddha nature (*tathāgatagarba*) shifted the notions underlying practice (Williams 1989). In Japan, the ideal was extended: Since all reality, including persons, possessed the Buddha nature, then all activities practiced with mindfulness could become meditation: tea ceremony, martial arts, flower arranging, and so on.

The Pure Land schools, directing hope for *nirvāṇa* attainment to an otherworldly paradise (*Sukhāvatī*), encouraged devotees to visualize the Pure Land as revealed in textual descriptions. These practices were especially important as death neared, for if individuals could visualize this realm, they were promised painless passage into Pure Land rebirth.

Other Mahāyāna schools, especially those influenced by esoteric Vajrayāna innovations, developed *sādhana* ("communion with enlightened deity") meditations. The exact procedures and instructions were passed from teacher to student, with an initiation (*abhiṣeka*) necessary for entering the practice. Such *sādhana* practices utilize visualizations of enlightened beings (*bodhisattva*s) along with *mantra* recitations to awaken the mind's powers and foster disciplined spiritual development (Beyer 1973). By controlling the appearance of mental images, one sees the empty nature (*śūnyā*) of all existence, including one's own ego. Related to this is the esoteric or tantric Buddhist path: Its traditions of *sādhana* found the Buddha nature in the extreme domains of human experience, using sexual sensation (Kvaerne 1977: 61–64)—real or as merely visualized—and gender symbolisms to bring the mind past attachments and toward a clear, balanced seeing (*prajñā*) of reality (Snellgrove 1987). Only the tantric teacher (*ācārya*) could discern those whose karmic inheritance required such unusual practices.

Buddhist Ritualism. It was for regularizing needed *dāna* presentations and valued *puṇya* making that monks and laity doubtless developed standard ritual procedures (*pūjā*) and calendrical norms. There is some evidence that monastic rituals and *dāna* "events" sponsored by notable individuals likely set precedents for later traditions (Beal 1970: 1:xxxvii). Orthoprax rituals evolved that complemented meditation and study; employing medical terms, specific rituals were seen as compassionate action (Pye 1978: 58–59, 98; Stablein 1973, 1978) that could achieve specific results for suffering humanity. For the Mahāyāna devotee, *pūjā* was quintessentially an expression of *upāya*, a disciplined act that aids the spiritual destiny of all beings, self, and others.

Buddhist rituals link spoken words with simple deeds. The *paritta* texts of the Pali Canon are one early manifestation (Skilling 1992) as monks chant while

their senior pours water, symbolizing the blessing's dispersal. The earliest Mahāyāna ritual is an elaboration of the *bodhisattva*'s ritual service, emphasizing
mastery of word chains known for their spiritual powers: *mantra*s and (if longer)
*dhāraṇī*s (Bharati 1965: 101–165; Dayal 1932: 267–269). These can be spoken
to protect both the speaker, the *saṃgha*, and entire settlements. Resort to these
formulas was one of the divisions in early Buddhist medicine (Zysk 1991: 66).
This ritual chanting, which eventually included entire texts, was thought to further the foundations of spiritual practice and provide infusions of good karma
and radiant auspiciousness for towns and domiciles and at moments of life cycle
passage or crisis (Welch 1967: 179ff).

Ritual service came to dominate Mahāyāna Buddhism in its missionary program. This is clear in early east Asian Buddhist history, where cummulative
dhāraṇī traditions were instrumental in the successful missionization of China
(Strickmann 1990). Myriad other Buddhist householder rituals evolved to ensure
the regular performance of such *mantra* recitations that both expressed and,
through recitation, orchestrated the attempt to actualize the spiritual ideals.

Conforming to the desiderata of the Five Cardinal Precepts (above), the Mahāyāna *Bhadracarīpranidhāna* developed the 7–Fold Worship as a guideline for
practice:

1. Honor the Buddha
2. Serve the Buddha
3. Confession of misdeeds
4. Delight in good actions of beings
5. Invitation of Buddhas to preach the *dharma*
6. Arouse the thought of enlightenment
7. Dedication of merit to all beings (Lamotte 1988: 433)

Mahāyāna ritual traditions were crafted to serve the devout's seeking both practical blessings and final salvation (cf. Dargyay 1986: 179–180). The Mahāyāna
developed much more elaborated ritual traditions, and its practitioners felt free
to freelance innovations.[11]

Buddhist Festival Traditions

We now turn to the specific observances that defined early Buddhism in practice. While the South Asian hearth provided many traditional precedents for
modern observances, it should be noted that the Buddhist ethos of adapting the
triratna to specific sociocultural environments did not compel missionary monks
to adopt every tradition, either.

Like other great world religions, Buddhist cultures ordered and shaped time
through regular monthly and yearly festivals. Some festivals orchestrated the
reliving of classical Buddhist events *in illo tempore* (Eliade 1959: 70): Celebra-

tions of the Buddha's birth, enlightenment, and *parinirvāṇa* are universal, although differing as to season (Swearer 1987); other more regional sacred events
likewise mark the year (Gombrich 1986), as different communities were free to
assign their own definitions for these "auspicious days." These include Śākyamuni's ascent/descent from Tuṣita heaven to preach to his mother, or events
marking a key point in a *bodhisattva*'s life, be it Vessantara (Cone and Gombrich 1977), the Mahāyāna figure Avalokiteśvara, or the death anniversary of a
local saint (Tambiah 1984; Strong 1992). Across Asia, local communities have
domesticated stories of visits by Buddhas or *bodhisattvas*, often explaining the
ordering of the local pantheon and sacred geography through conquest and conversion.

The Indic *Uposatha* and the Monthly Calendar

Each fortnight on the new and full moon days, Indic *saṃgha* members had
to recite the *Pratimokṣa*, a summary of the community's *Vinaya* regulations.
This recitation came after any transgressions were confessed (*ālocanā*) in private
to the monk's superior. *Uposatha* became the regular occasions to review, correct, and certify the proper standards of monastery discipline (Prebish 1975b;
Wijayaratna 1990). (Based upon the Indic lunar calendar [Das 1928], *uposatha*
includes the overnight of the full- and no-moon period; hence, each can span
two solar days each month [Lamotte 1988: 70].)

Emphasizing the fundamental interdependence between *saṃgha* and lay community, householders were encouraged to visit their *vihāra*s on the *uposatha*
days to make offerings (*dāna*). On these days, devout layfolk (*upasākas*) could
take the opportunity to observe eight of the ten monastic rules while residing
continuously on the *vihāra* grounds. (The frequent lay observance of fasting
after midday (until the next morning) led to their being commonly referred to
as "fasting days" [Beal 1970:1:1xxiv].) In many places across India, *upāsakas*
donned white robes while living under their extended vows (Dutt 1945a: 176).
Another common *uposatha* custom was for layfolk to remain in the *vihāra* to
hear monks preach the *dharma*. Thus, the lunar fortnight rhythm clearly dominated the early Buddhist festival year: Each year's passing has had the absolutely
regular succession of *uposatha*s.

The Indic Buddhist calendar also utilized the eighth lunar day (*aṣṭamī*) of
each fortnight as another auspicious time for pious actions and vow taking. In
the Pali Canon (*Mahāvagga* II: 1), as in I-Tsing's time, *aṣṭamī* was also called
a "fasting day" and seems to have been the common day chosen for the early
festivals outside the *vihāra*s: *Aṣṭamī* of Jyeṣṭha is also mentioned by Fa-Hsien
as the day when a great Buddhist chariot festival was celebrated in Pāṭaliputra
(Legge 1965: 79; N. Dutt 1977: 39). Hsuan Tsang also records that there were
three months each year—Phālguna, Āṣādha, Kārtika—when Buddhists observed
"long fasts" (Beal 1970:1:180).

Monastic Rain Retreat: Varṣāvāsa

Meshed with the lunar month system, the most prominent yearly Indic Buddhist observance was the monsoon rain retreat called *varṣāvāsa* (Pali: *vassa* or *vassāvāsa* [S. Dutt 1962: 54]). Dating from pre-Buddhist *śramaṇas* and adopted by Śākyamuni, the rain retreat practice, as required by the *Vinaya*, curtailed monks' mobility outside the monastery and encouraged meditation and study for its three-month duration (Wijayaratna 1990). It was likewise a time for intensive lay devotional exertions, as it is until today in Burma, Sri Lanka, and Thailand (Tambiah 1970: 155).[12]

Varṣāvāsa ceremonies mark the beginning, formal ending (*pavāraṇā*), and new robe donations (*kaṭhina*) to monks who completed the retreat. The *pavāraṇā* ceremony is much like the biweekly *uposatha* for the *saṃgha*, but for the lay community the emphasis is on a grander scale of merit making, as the texts specify that *dāna* made on this day would be more fruitful than at other times (N. Dutt 1945b: 249). The post-*varṣā* presentation of new robes by the laity—some traditions also evolved to have the laity sew them in special ways—likewise garners special karmic rewards. *Pavāraṇā*, the day marking the completion of the rain retreat, became the year's merit-making landmark for the early community (Beal 1970:1: xxxix), a tradition that endures across South and Southeast Asia (Tambiah 1970: 154–160).

Special ceremonies were developed by the community around the monastic initiations for novices (P. *pabbajjā*) and full monks (*upasampadā*). The custom of adolescent, premarital short-term monasticism evolved in Theravādin Burma (Spiro 1986), Thailand (Tambiah 1970), and modern Mahāyāna Nepal (Gellner 1992).

It is striking to note here, as in the east Asian adaptations of Buddhism generally, that Mahāyāna monastic traditions did not follow Indic precedents literally or rigorously. As Holmes Welch notes:

In China, however, the summer retreat was generally ignored. Monks were aware that it was supposed to run from the 15th of the fourth month to the 15th of the seventh and some might choose to observe it as individuals, but in most institutions life continued as usual.... On the other hand, at many monasteries during the period it was customary to expound the *sūtras*. The abbot, or perhaps some eminent dharma master called in from outside, would lecture for a couple of hours a day.... It was still a time for study. ... At most Chinese monasteries there were no *uposatha* days.... The only liturgical change on the 1st and 15th of the month was the addition of certain items to morning and evening devotions. (1967: 110)

Welch does note several Chinese monasteries that did follow the Indic norm exactingly. Descriptions of modern rain retreat practices and the history of transformations await future research.

Pious Constructions: Stūpas. For all Buddhist schools, the *stūpa* (or *caitya*)[13] became a focal point and the singular landmark denoting the tradition's spiritual presence on the landscape (Dallapiccola 1980; Harvey 1984; Snodgrass 1985). Early texts and the archaeological record link *stūpa* worship with Śākyamuni Buddha's life and especially the key venues in his religious career. The tradition eventually recognized a standard "Eight Great *Caityas*" for pilgrimage and veneration (Tucci 1988). *Stūpa* or *caitya* worship thus became the chief focus of Buddhist ritual activity linking veneration of the Buddha's "sacred traces" (Falk 1977) to an individual's attention to managing karma destiny and mundane well-being. The Chinese pilgrim I-Tsing around 690 C.E. noted a variety of forms and traditions:

The priests and laymen in India make *caitya*s or images with earth, or impress the Buddha's image on silk or paper, and worship it with offerings wherever they go. Sometimes they build *stūpa*s of the Buddha by making a pile and surrounding it with bricks. . . . This is the reason why the *sūtra*s praise in parables the merit of making images or *caitya*s as unspeakable . . . as limitless as the seven seas, and good rewards will last as long as the coming four births. The detailed account of this matter is found in the separate *sūtra*s. (Takakusu 1982: 150–151)

Throughout history, Buddhist writers have advanced many levels of understanding to explain *stūpa* veneration. First, a *stūpa* is a site marking supernatural celestial events associated with a Buddha and for remembering him through joyful devotional celebration. The classical account in the Pali *Mahāparinibbāna Sutta* describes the origins of the first veneration directed to Śākyamuni's relics:

And when the body of the Exalted One had been burnt up, there came down streams of water from the sky and extinguished the funeral pyre . . . and there burst forth streams of water from the storehouse of waters [beneath the earth], and extinguished the funeral pyre. . . . The Mallas of Kushinara also brought water scented with all kinds of perfumes . . . surrounded the bones of the Exalted One in their council hall with a lattice work of spears, and with a rampart of bows; and there for seven days they paid honor, and reverence, and respect, and homage to them with dance, and song, and music, and with garlands and perfumes. (T. Rhys-Davids 1969: 130–131)

Another prominent Pali text, the *Milindapañha* (IV,8,51), asserts that celestial wonders are visible at *caitya*s:

Some woman or some man of believing heart, able, intelligent, wise, endowed with insight, may deliberately take perfumes, or a garland, or a cloth, and place it on a *caitya*, making the resolve: "May such and such a wonder take place!" Thus is it that wonders take place at the *caitya* of one entirely set free. (T. Rhys-Davids 1963: II, 175)

The subsequent elaborations on *stūpa* ritual in Buddhist history are extensive: a "power place" tapping the Buddha's (or saint's) relic presence (Schopen

1987: 196) and its healing potency; a site to earn merit through veneration (Lamotte 1988: 415); a monument marking the conversion and control of *nāga*s and *yakṣa*s (Bloss 1973: 48–49). Only the Theravāda *Vinaya* omits instructions to monks on how to construct and make offerings at *stūpa*s (Bareau 1962; cf. Schopen 1989), and the archaeological record shows that *stūpa*s were frequently built in the center of *vihāra* courtyards (Seckel 1964: 132–134), often by monks themselves (Snellgrove 1973: 410), especially those with particular monastic specializations.[14] I-Tsing's account illustrates the monastic focus on *stūpa* in the *saṃgha*'s communal life.

In India priests perform the worship of a *caitya* and ordinary service late in the afternoon or at the evening twilight. All the assembled priests come out of the gate of their monastery, and walk three times around a *stūpa*, offering incense and flowers. They all kneel down, and one of them who sings well begins to chant hymns describing the virtues of the Great Teacher . . . [and] in succession returns to the place in the monastery where they usually assemble. (Takakusu 1982: 152)

In the Mahāyāna schools, the *stūpa* came to symbolize other ideas: of Buddhahood's omnipresence (Snellgrove and Skorupski 1977: 13); a center of *sūtra* revelation (Schopen 1975); a worship center guaranteeing rebirth in Amitabha Buddha's paradise, Sukhāvatī (Williams 1989); and a form showing the unity of the five elements with Buddha nature (Rimpoche 1990; Seckel 1964). A passage from the *Pañcarakṣākathā* states that those worshipping relic *caitya*s and chanting *dhāraṇī*s will make themselves immune from diseases of all kinds (Lewis 1998). Later Buddhists identified *stūpa*s as the physical representations of the eternal teachings (the *dharmakāya* in the Mahāyāna *trikāya* ["three bodies of the Buddha" doctrinal schema]) and expanded the possible *sacra* deposited to include his words in textual form (*sūtra, dhāraṇī, mantra*) (Seckel 1964: 103) and the remains of exemplary human *bodhisattva*s (Mumford 1989).

One final and recently noted dimension to *stūpa* veneration was a votive/mortuary aspect (Schopen 1987): Certain Buddhists, and especially monks (Schopen 1989), apparently had their own ashes deposited in small votive *caitya*s, often arranged close to a Buddha relic *stūpa* (Schopen 1991b, 1991c, 1992a). These structures established a means for perpetual *puṇya* generation for the deceased. The surviving *caitya*-making customs for laity in Nepal (Lewis 1994a) and in Tibet utilize cremation ash and bone.[15]

The passage of the *Mahāparinibbaāna Sutta* (above) describes the first veneration of Śākyamuni's relics as a time for communal ritual; making joyful Buddhist devotional processions accompanied by musicians had a strong precedent. Despite the many understandings Buddhists of every level of sophistication advanced regarding *stūpa*s, in practice all could nonetheless converge to mark events associated with the Tathāgata(s) ("Buddhas") or saints. *Stūpa*s thus became the natural sites for Buddhist festivals of remembrance and veneration.

Great Regional Stūpa*s: Centers of Tradition*. Great regional *stūpa*s were pivotal in the history of Buddhism: These monuments became magnets attracting *vihāra* building and votive construction, for local *pūjā* and regional pilgrimage. The symbiotic economics of Buddhist devotionalism at these centers generated income for local *saṃgha*s, artisans, and merchants (Liu 1988), an alliance basic to Buddhism throughout its history (Dehejia 1972; Lewis 1993a). At these geographical centers arrayed around the symbolic monument, diverse devotional exertions, textual/doctrinal studies, and devotees' mercantile pursuits could all prosper in synergistic style. The regional *Mahācaitya* ("Great Shrine") complexes, with their interlinked components—*vihāra*s with land endowments, votive/pilgrimage centers, markets, state support, and soon—represent central fixtures in Asian Buddhist civilizations. For local communities, such *stūpa*s were also focal points in the yearly festival round, drawing Buddhists toward the sacred precincts. Empowered votive artifacts dispensed by monasteries and/or bought by the pilgrims at key sites were used to establish *vihāra*s, *caitya*s, and Buddha images in the diaspora of the faith to distant settlements.

Pious Constructions: Vihāra *Building*. Some texts make quite specific recommendations to the laity on the best *puṇya* investments. The Sanskrit *Puṇyakriyāvastu*, for example, arranges the following hierarchy of donations, tying securely the wish for individual good karma accounting with donations that establish the *saṃgha*'s material existence:

1. Donating land to the *saṃgha*

2. Building a *vihāra* on it

3. Furnishing it

4. Allocating revenue for it

5. Assisting strangers

6. Tending the sick

7. In cold weather or famine, giving food to the *saṃgha* (Lamotte 1988: 72)

All Buddhist lineages applaud the great *puṇya* accruing to those who build *vihāra*s. Modern studies also suggest that this has remained among the greatest acts of *dāna* (Spiro 1986: 458; Tambiah 1970: 147ff; Welch 1967: 210ff).

There are indications that ancient yearly festivals were established locally to celebrate each shrine's anniversary of dedication, and these became thereby its yearly "birthday" when donor families should refurbish, clean, and ritually renew it (Beal 1970:1:xxxix).

Buddha Image Veneration. The making of Buddha shrines and images (for *vihāra*s or homes) entailed rituals of proper construction, consecration, and upkeep (Dehejia 1989; Lancaster 1974). The Chinese pilgrim I-Tsing describes the role of images in Buddhist practice:

There is no more reverent worship than that of the Three Jewels, and there is no higher road to perfect understanding than meditation on the Four Noble Truths. But the meaning of the Truths is so profound that it is a matter beyond the comprehension of vulgar minds, while the ablution of the Holy Image is practicable to all. Though the Great Teacher has entered Nirvana, yet his image exists, and we should worship it with zeal as though in his very presence. Those who constantly offer incense and flowers to it are enabled to purify their thoughts, and also those who perpetually bathe his image are enabled to overcome their sins . . . receive rewards, and those who advise others to perform it are doing good to themselves as well as to others. (Takakusu 1982: 147)

Such were the sentiments that by 700 C.E. legitimated the elaboration of Indic Buddhist ritual and festival traditions, and this historical observation is matched by texts such as the Mahāyāna *Bodhicaryāvatāra* that laud precisely these activities. Image *pūjā* ("ritual") was practiced by entire *vihāra*s in conjunction with the lay community and by individual monks with their private icons. The Chinese accounts mention detailed procedures, including image-bathing rites with annointed water, repainting, polishing; accompanied by music, the icon would then be reinstated in the temple, with offerings of incense and flowers. The water used for this ritual is likewise described as medicinal (Takakusu 1982: 147). The documentation of rites of consecration can yield valuable insight into wider questions of belief (e.g., Gombrich 1966).

An Indic "Bathing the Buddha Image" *pūjā* commemorated Śākyamuni's birthday in the month *Vaiśākha*. As described in the Kashmiri *Nilamatapurāṇa* (800 C.E.): "In the bright fortnight, the image of the Buddha is to be bathed with water containing all herbs, jewels, and scents and by uttering the words of the Buddha. The place is to be carefully besmeared with honey; the temple and *stūpa* must have frescoes, and there should be dancing and amusements" (N. Dutt 1977: 14). This practice seems to have spread across all of Buddhist Asia (Lessing 1976).

I-Tsing underlines the immense *puṇya* earned by Buddha *pūjā*s: "The washing of the holy image is a meritorious deed which leads to a meeting with the Buddha in every birth, and the offering of incense and flowers is a cause of riches and joy in every life to come. Do it yourself, and teach others to do the same, then you will gain immeasurable blessings" (Takakusu 1982: 151–152). A popular Khotanese Mahāyāna text concurs, stating that to make a Buddha image is to guarantee rebirth in future Buddha Maitreya's era (Emmerick 1968: 321); in another passage, worshipping an image is said to be equal in merit to worshipping the Buddha himself: "Whoever in my presence should perform *pūjā*, or whoever should produce faith equally before an image, equal will be his many, innumerable, great merits. There is really no difference between them" (201). Thus, many Mahāyāna *sūtra*s, in agreement with the *Parinibbāna Sutta*, laud as especially meritorious offerings of incense and flowers to images, encouraging the presentation with musical accompaniment.

Indic Mahāyāna Vratas. Still surviving in the Himalayan region, *vrata*s (Tib.

nyungne) are special Mahāyāna forms of *saṃgha*-led, lay-sponsored practice that focuses on basic doctrines amidst devotional attention to a particular Buddha or *bodhisattva* (Ortner 1978: 35ff; Locke 1987; Lewis 1989a). Doubtless originating in the lay wish to spend *uposatha* or *aṣṭamī* days in stricter devotionalism, *vrata*s were the means by which groups of individuals could devote one or more days to fasting, making *dāna* offerings, meditating, hearing stories, and maintaining a high state of ritual purity. Tradition specifies a series of boons for each type of *vrata*, and all add appreciably to one's stock of *puṇya*. By so doing, Newar and Tibetan *vrata*s, like Hindu *vrata*s (Wadley 1983), are performed to improve the devotee's mundane and supramundane destiny.[16]

Text Festivals. Another Mahāyāna festival focused on the "cult of the book" (Schopen 1975). According to the early *Prajñāpāramitā* texts, veneration of the Buddha's *dharma* was vastly superior to worshipping his bodily relics. (This custom still endures in modern Nepal [Lewis 1993b].) A section of the *Saddharmapuṇḍarīka* describes the superior ritual in which a Mahāyāna text is venerated (Kern 1884: 96) (and in the Chinese version is carried on the devotees' heads [Hurvitz 1976: 82]).

Ratha Yātrās. The most extraordinary Indic form of Buddha image veneration noted in numerous locations was the *ratha yātrā* ("chariot festival"). The Chinese pilgrim Fa-Hsien noted that in ancient Pataliputra there were images of Buddhas and *bodhisattva*s placed on twenty-four-wheeled, five-story *ratha*s made of wood and bamboo. Beginning on an *aṣṭamī* day and continuing for two nights, the local *vaiśya*s are said to have made vast donations from specially erected dwellings along the path; in Khotan, too, there was a fourteen-day event that was attended by the entire city, for which each monastery constructed a different four-wheeled *ratha* (Legge 1965: 18–19). Nepal's surviving *ratha yātrā*s dedicated to Avalokiteśvara in Nepal are now well documented (Locke 1980; Owens 1989).

Pilgrimage. Travel to venerate the *stūpa*s and *caitya*s marking important events in the Buddha's life also defined early Buddhist pilgrimage (Lamotte 1988: 665; Gokhale 1980). This meritorious veneration of the Buddha's "sacred traces" (Falk 1977) was organized into extended processional rituals. The development of pilgrimage traditions shaped the early composition of site-coordinated biographies of Śākyamuni (Lamotte 1988: 669; Foucher 1949) and likely did so for some of the *jātaka* and *avadāna* compilations. Such texts also promise the laity vast improvements in their karma destiny as well as mundane benefits as rewards for undertaking pilgrimage.[17] Khotanese sources assert that sites identified with *bodhisattva*s were also centers of Mahāyāna pilgrimage: "Whatever Bodhisattvas for the sake of *bodhi* have performed difficult tasks such as giving, this place I worship" (Emmerick 1968: 163).

It is noteworthy how each missionized region of Asia developed its own Buddhist overlay of pilgrimage involving mountains, sites for saint veneration, with monasteries built to "colonize" the sacred venue. Much recent work has focused upon these regional complexes in Tibet, China, Japan, and Burma.[18]

Because it is an avenue of cultural diffusion, local domestication, and lucrative income for both Buddhist monasteries and merchants involved, Buddhist pilgrimage should be studied further.

Buddhist Polity: Lay Associations (Goṣṭhī). Just as the *vihāra* was the institution that has ordered and sustained the *saṃgha*'s communal life, so, too, were there institutions organized by lay patrons to advance their religious interests. Some Indic inscriptions indicate the coordinated pious activities of craft guilds (*śreṇī*s); more common are the *goṣṭhī*—"assemblies, associations, fellowships" (Monier-Williams 1956: 367)—that coordinate large donations or regular rituals. These institutions are ancient, as the Pali *jātaka*s cite subscription plans among *upāsaka*s (C. Rhys-Davids 1901: 886). Such groups were often formed to complete *caitya*s or *vihāra* caves or for renovation projects (Dehejia 1972; Kosambi 1965: 182). These patron societies were common in China (Chen 1964: 290ff; Zurcher 1972: 97) and integral to Buddhist community activities:

[T]hese religious societies enjoyed close relations with the monasteries. The latter furnished leadership in matters pertaining to the religious life of the members, and also provided economic support for many of their activities. For their part, the society members assisted the monasteries in every way possible. They helped in the fund-raising campaigns, the missionary endeavors, the festivals and celebrations conducted by the monastery during the course of the year. By working hard for the welfare of the monastery they shared in its glory. (Chen 1964: 292)

In Nepal, there are still *goṣṭhī* traditions that organize regular rituals, pilgrimage, restorations, even shrine cleanings (Toffin 1984; Lewis 1984: 179–182). In Nepalese practice, the *goṣṭhī*s also hold collective properties, including money; most include some provision for increasing the group treasury by lending these funds at interest serially through the membership. Thus, *goṣṭhī*s not only underwrote pious Buddhist practice: Such institutions became important sources of community investment capital, and such merchant shrine/monastery relations were universal across the urban Buddhist diaspora (Lewis 1993a, 1994b). Few studies have documented other modern lay groups (Welch 1965–1966).

Buddhist Polity: Monks, Royalty, Pañcavārsika. For most of its history, the Buddhist *saṃgha* has existed in polities ruled by kings or emperors (Gokhale 1966). As a result, the tradition developed an exchange rapproachement: The *saṃgha* adopted no rules to break state law; it also certified the monarch's moral standing by accepting his patronage and bestowed prestigious titles (*bodhisattva*, *dharmarājā* ["just king"], *mahādānapati* ["lord of great generosity"], *cakravartin* ["wheel-turning spiritual leader"]) to those who were most exemplary (Tambiah 1976; Wright 1959: 51). Monastic Buddhism served to promote social stability, accommodating itself to local traditions. In China,

[t]hose who revere the Buddhist teaching but remain in their homes are subjects who are obedient to the transforming power of the temporal rulers. Their inclination is not to

alter prevailing custom, and their conduct accords with secular norms. In them there are the affections of natural kinship and the proprieties of respect for authority. . . . The retribution of evil karma is regarded as punishment; it makes people fearful and this circumspect. The halls of heaven are regarded as a reward; this makes them think of the pleasures of heaven and act accordingly. . . . Therefore, they who rejoice in the way of Sākya [the Buddha] invariably first serve their parents and respect their lords. (From a fourth-century text, quoted in Wright 1959: 50)

The Chinese monks also performed long-life rituals for the rulers, a custom continued in modern Thailand and in Nepal (even for the Hindu king).

The just king is the first among laymen, with the legendary King Asoka (250 B.C.E.) the paradigm for later rulers (Strong 1983; Tambiah 1976; Reynolds 1972c). The early texts also mention an extraordinary quinquennial festival that Asoka performed and that expresses the fundamental exchanges within the Buddhist polity: "*pañcavārsika.*"[19] It was a time for vast royal donations to the *samgha*, other deserving ascetics, Brahmanas, and the destitute; it was also a time for displaying extraordinary images or renowned relics during festivities organized by kings and merchants, while witnessed by a huge social gathering.

The Buddhist community also looks to the sovereign as responsible for the *samgha*'s living by its *Vinaya*, and there are many instances of Asian kings "purifying the *samgha*" by chastising certain monastic lineages or starting entirely new lines of ordination (Mendelson 1975; Coedes 1971: 197ff).

The special role of the king creates a three-part division in the socioreligious organization of Buddhist polities. The replication of the royal system into the macro- and micro- "galactic" order (Tambiah 1977; see discussion in Part II) of the polity—scaled to governor, district chief, village headman—underlines the importance of network analysis of Buddhist polities as monastic and political organization tend toward similar patterns of expansion.

SECTION II: ISSUES IN THE ANTHROPOLOGY OF BUDDHISM

> Hence, side by side with the Buddha's shrine stand the nat or spirit shrine, the good-luck symbol, the astrologer's stall and the sacred trees.
>
> Winston King (1964b: 72)

Interdisciplinary Methodologies

Anthropologists working in Buddhist societies must be aware of the limitations of designing research in terms of a two-tier, Great-little, elite-masses division that has been employed in some modern scholarship. The chief problem with this division—between the true followers and everyone else—is that it really does not find expression in institutional networks or cultural performances that crosscut any presumed "folk-urban continuum." There is also no emic terminology that corresponds to them or divides the *śāsana* into "Great-little" compartments. The paradigm is also undermined decisively by the texts describing the *śāsana*, with progressive practices articulating no such emic categories; it is also refuted in the biographies of Theravāda Arhats, Mahāyāna dialecticians, and Vajrayāna adepts that all show that these philosopher-saints did not eschew their ancestral traditions, avoid all "folk religion," or withdraw from popular devotional practices.[20] The two-tier image of Buddhist tradition is simplistic for portraying the typical biography of a Buddhist monk or for comprehending the history of Buddhism's doctrinal or institutional evolution. As Tambiah (1984) has stated:

> Development in Buddhism over time . . . was informed by both continuities and transformations, the latter being not merely the gross handiwork of the masses but wrought by all parties, elite monks and ordinary monks, kings and court circles, urban merchants and traders, and peasant farmers and artisans, all responsive to their existential conditions and aspirations.

The following sections offer possible avenues of anthropological study in Buddhist contexts that resonate with emerging historical processes. The overall dearth of studies on Mahāyāna-centered communities still obviates thoroughgoing comparative analyses (Gellner 1990).

Patterns of Buddhist "Conversion": Buddhism as Missionary Religion

The sense of history that usually arises from textual-philosophical representations of Buddhism is that on the basis of doctrine this tradition triumphed over contending ideas of other faiths (e.g., Gombrich 1988: 151). Yet a recognition of the many facets of tradition and the usual marginality of philosophers in shaping world events casts doubt upon texts and doctrine being of central importance. An ecological and ethnic awareness is essential for understanding Buddhism's ability to convert populations to its religious orientation.

In South and Southeast Asia, the Buddhist *saṃgha* competed with Hinduism for the conversion of frontier regions, contending for patronage with Brahmanas at court and their kin-based ritualist (*purohita*) diaspora to the Indic hinterlands (Tambiah 1985). This expansion process followed with state formation and was based upon ecological transformations of the land that moved polities up river valleys, with the cutting of forests followed by the concentrated cultivation of grains, especially rice, and the utilization of bovine husbandry. Since the time before Śākyamuni Buddha up to today, the intensive rice-growing Indicized polities have inexorably pushed against their tribal frontiers, where tribal-state (or ethnic-state) relations remain ongoing processes, often violently contested, across the modern Buddhist states inheriting these long-standing confrontations.

Built on such ecological possibilities were galactic networks of economic, political, and religious organization that linked village peoples to regional and core centers (Tambiah 1976, 1977). These interlocking networks also define Buddhist history's gridwork and the avenues of cultural diffusion through which peoples from, or allied with, core centers have impinged on and transformed the periphery.

Buddhist institution building by forest monks has often meshed with state formation and is fundamental to understanding the frontier dynamism of Buddhist polities of the Himalayas (B. Miller 1960) and Southeast Asia (Lewis 1994b). As Tambiah states:

> Starting as little-endowed fraternities, and locating themselves on forest edges on the frontiers of advancing settlements, the forest monks could act as elite carriers of literate civilization and could serve as foci for the collective religious activities and moral sentiments of frontier settlements. It is an alliance of this sort, a paired relationship between founding kings . . . with expansionist ambitions and the ascetically vigorous forest monks at the moving edge of human habitation . . . that domesticated the local cults and incorporated them within a Buddhist hierarchy and cosmos. (1984: 69)

Vihāras in certain places served as caravan stops, and the lay stewards lent monastic funds at interest to individual traders, a feature symbiotic with the process of Indic expansion (R. Miller 1962; Schopen 1994, 1996).

The Buddhist conquest of eastern Asia is in certain respects quite different—though no less successful—from the śāsana's expansion into south and Southeast Asia. This is because monks entering the civilizations in the Sinic culture zone—China, Korea, Japan—had to contend with equally ancient and textual religions (Confucianism and Taoism) long integrated within expansive empires and local cultures.[21] All these show distinctive histories of assimilation but with common patterns of domestication: the initial conversion of aristocracy and this class's expansive promotion of the faith; entry first into urban centers; and the saṃgha securing its presence via land grants and monk-literati preachers promulgating ideas of superiority over indigenous deities, sacred sites (especially mountains [e.g., Collcutt 1988]), and religious systems. The Mahāyāna proved especially attractive as it "handled what seemed to be similar concepts while placing them in a new perspective, giving them another and deeper significance and surrounding them with the halo of supramundane revelation" (Zurcher 1972: 73).

In all venues, it was by forging alliances with royalty at centers of the polity, converting local saints and deities, integrating the teachings with ancestor ritualism, garnering patronage donations that made the vihāras landowners (Clark 1991: 141–145; Evers 1967b; Gunawardana 1979) that the saṃgha adapted to the expansion of many Asian polities, tied to the soil and attracting ethnic groups into its fold.

Buddhist Expansion and Ethnic Boundary Maintenance. Successful monasteries expanded. The pattern was to send out monks who would proceed to establish satellite institutions of that lineage. This network of "Mother-daughter'' monasteries (B. Miller 1960; R. Miller 1962) created all sorts of alliances, religious and otherwise, providing the pattern of institution building found from Ladakh to Bali, Bangkok to Los Angeles, Dharamsala to New York.

The logic of the Buddhist galactic system led to similiar patterns of historical adaptation across these frontier zones: close ties with aristocratic/dominant caste families who at times controlled the local *vihāra*s or favored one monastic line-age (Evers 1967b). This pattern of ethnic group dominance is still visible in Buddhist Tibet, the Kathmandu Valley, and upland Sri Lanka.[22]

When Buddhist monasticism spread across Asia, it introduced independent, corporate institutions that had thoroughgoing transformative potential in local societies and regional polities. Buddhist *vihāra*s have, at times, functioned to break down ethnic and class boundaries, blurring divisions between peoples (Zurcher 1972: 9). The anthropology of missionizing religions finds a common comparative theme here: Newly introduced religious institutions can fundamentally alter previous alignments of kinship, ethnicity, and political power.

But the large celibate monastery was *not* the Buddhist *saṃgha*'s only institutional form. There was another noncelibate, small-scale model, in places justified by the ''decadent age'' Mahāyāna doctrine (Nattier 1991), that sustained ''householder Mahāyāna *saṃgha*s'' in Tibet, Nepal (Gellner 1987, 1988, 1989), and Japan. The Newar Buddhist diaspora across the hills of Nepal (Lewis and Shakya 1988), like the Nyingmapa diffusion over Tibet (Snellgrove and Richardson 1980: 170–172), has been built on the logic of lineages whose acquaintance with the celibate *saṃgha* norm usually consists merely of short-term monastic initiation (Mumford 1989; Holmberg 1989; Ortner 1989; Locke 1975; Gellner 1992) followed by marriage and lifelong ritual service.[23]

In areas dominated by celibate-monastic lineages, the *vihāra* institutions accumulated wealth and resources that could easily exceed those of individual families, and monastic expansion could follow different evolutionary trajectories. Once established, separate Buddhist monasteries (or schools) might contend for dominance with local elites, or in some localities, single ethnic groups might come to control local *saṃgha*s as part of their larger political dominance. Competing economic factions were at times patrons of different monastic lineages, creating a healthy diversity of lineages and practices.

At other times, inter-Buddhist competition existed between monastic lineages. As Robert Miller has pointed out:

The creation of daughter monasteries may be seen as an effort to stabilize and stretch out the local resources of support and to tap sources further afield. . . .
   There will inevitably be a point at which competition between different monasteries becomes acute. The larger monasteries . . . could reach out beyond the immediate locality to attract rich patrons, and could draw laymen into trade on their behalf. But competition from large, expanding monasteries sometimes led to the collapse of a local *saṃgha*. (1962: 437)

In yet other historical instances of south and Southeast Asia (Cambodia, Java), factions have supported either the Buddhist *vihāra* or the Hindu temple in their competitions for power. Buddhism's strength through concentrating wealth and human resources was also its historical weakness: *Vihāra*s were vulnerable to the vagaries of corruption, state patronage, and royal protection.[24]

Popular Dissemination of the Dharma. While the philosophers continued to compose new tracts and doctrinal formulations, the *jātaka*s and *avadāna*s endured throughout Buddhist history as the most popular paradigms for the faithful. The *avadāna* and *jātaka* collections, in a multitude of compilations, contain hundreds of exemplary tales. Drawing upon a story or incident from a previous lifetime of Śākyamuni, other Buddhas, or saints (*bodhisattva*s or *arhat*s), the narrative is turned to show any number of positive Buddhist observances: moral behavior, renunciation, selfless service, the utility of a ritual, mundane wisdom, faith in the enlightened.

These story texts formed in close relationship with the early lay communities, a dialectical evolution providing a Buddhist example of what A. K. Ramanujan (1990: 12) so aptly describes as "the way texts do not simply go from one written form to another but get reworked through oral cycles that surround the written word." Recalling the "folklorists" of the ancient Indic *saṃgha* cited above, anthropologists need to track exactly where the narratives do reside in Buddhist communities and how the written words and ideas pass into the wider society.

Other attendant themes in this area concern the fact of literacy: Buddhism promoted this transformative change in all societies (Gough 1968; Tambiah 1968b).

Another research topic that has been touched on in China and in the Himalayan region is the practice of public storytelling as a means of doctrinal transmission from text to society (Hrdlickova 1958; Lewis 1984).

Texts in Domestication. While the doctrinal texts may supply a clear spiritual direction to followers who are close to the charismatic founders, including norms of orthodox adaptation and missionizing, religious traditions' long-term historical survival are related—often paradoxically—to their texts also being "multivocalic" so that later devotees have a large spectrum of doctrine, situational instructions, and examplary folktales to draw upon. The study of "religious text domestication" in Buddhist studies must demonstrate the underlying reasons for selectivity from the whole as the tradition evolves in specific places and times to the "logic of the locality."

Popular story narrative collections exist in every Buddhist locality, and the researcher should know their contents and discover their local origins and uses. The most popular, domesticated stories of a locality engender the community's familiarity such that "retelling the myths takes on the function of communion rather than communication. People listen to the stories not merely to learn something new (communication) but to relive, together, the stories that they already know, stories about themselves (communion)" (O'Flaherty 1989:). Our task in studying literary domestication can thus be defined in anthropological terms: Among the hundreds of *avadāna*s and *jātaka*s available, why were only a small number—over all others—adopted for special import, with special traditions of shrine worship, pilgrimage, frequent public recitation? The few studies of this phenomenon provide useful bibliographies in this field (see Lewis 1993a, 1994a; Keyes 1975).

Votive Amulets. A neglected field in historical and anthropological studies has been Buddhist traditions of amulet resort. Tambiah's (1984) study of modern Thai practices has been of signal importance in pointing to the continuity of Buddhists using empowered symbols to obtain spiritual and worldly blessings. The most common has been the votive *stūpa*.

Molded miniature *stūpa*s were also made as empowered souvenirs for pilgrims who visited great *stūpa*s. Such votive traditions are evident in studies of central Asia (Taddei 1970), Tibet (Tucci 1988), Nepal (Lewis 1993b), India (Desai 1986), Burma, Thailand (Griswold 1965), and Śrīvijaya (O'Connor 1974, 1975). The modern Thai enthusiasm for amulets is a survival of this tradition, as are those in modern Japan (e.g., McFarland 1987). Further research is needed in both historical and modern periods.

Merchants and Buddhism. Wealthy merchants are both extolled and cultivated as exemplary donors in all early Buddhist literatures. One measure of the early *saṃgha* itself suggests that about 30 percent were *vaiśyas* (Gokhale 1965), and inscriptions at early monastic centers suggest that individual merchants and artisans, as well as their collective communities (*goṣṭhī*) or guilds (*śrenī*), vied with kings to act as principal supporters. This relationship spanned the earliest sectarian divisions within the greater Buddhist community, with strong evidence from both Hīnayāna and Mahāyāna literatures as well as in the epigraphic sources.

The tradition supported merchants in a multitude of areas. In India, there were natural doctrinal affinities: Buddhist teachings undermined the ideology of birth-determined sociospiritual privilege of Brahmanas and *kṣatriyas*, for whom the *vaiśya*s were inferiors. We have noted that in all Asian venues the duty of giving (*dāna*) to the *saṃgha* is presented as the best investment for maximum *puṇya*. Early texts instructed devout layfolk (*upāsaka*s) to avoid trade in weapons, animals, meat, wine, and poison. A Pali *jātaka* also lists ''the four honest trades: tillage, trade, lending, and gleaning.'' Such declarations by the Buddha surely encouraged followers to move into these occupations, a tendency (and similar preference) especially pronounced in the history of Jainism. In addition to encouraging nonviolent occupations, early Mahāyāna texts also emphasize mercantile honesty (standing by quoted prices and measuring accurately), sobriety, and disciplined investment. Little anthropological attention has been devoted to class-nuanced portraits of Buddhist communities.

Faith, Wealth, Buddhist Practice. Wealth, though not the *summum bonum*, is ubiquitously held up as the reward for moral uprightness and pious generosity (Strong 1990). Wealth acquired dishonestly is said to lead to later torments in hells. Many texts clearly promise worldly blessings to the laity in return for adhering to the Buddhist norm (Falk 1990). This meshes with textual descriptions of an ideal Buddhist kingdom: Among traits listed in the *Mahāvastu* is "thriving in wealth." Note that "rightly acquired wealth," if donated as *dāna*, will beget even greater future wealth, encouraging the merchants to redistribute their riches back into society: Material wealth cannot be "taken with you"; but turned into *puṇya* through *dāna*, one can seek to reacquire the circumstances of wealth beyond this life.

Mahāyāna texts explicitly promise success in overseas trade as a reward for proper service to one's parents. Another area of the tradition designated certain Buddhas, *bodhisattvas*, and allied *devas* as protectors of merchants. Buddhist merchants across the maritime communities of medieval south and Southeast Asia worshipped former Buddha Dīpankara as "Calmer of Waters." There is also panregional evidence for special Buddhist "world protector deities" (*lokapāla*) that give assistance to devotees seeking wealth and trade: Pañcika and Pāṇḍuka seemed to have enjoyed popularity in ancient Gandhara (Northwest India) and Khotan, Jambhala in Tibet and Java, and Bhimsena in Nepal.

Economics of Buddhism: Tradition as Commodity. A recent historical study of Chinese and Kushan merchants has demonstrated that the spread of Buddhist tradition itself motivated transregional trade and that the material culture of later Buddhist decoration and devotion—silks, gems, metalwork, amulets—itself created a commodity market, as monks and merchants crossed the lands synergistically while cultivating, respectively, converts and new markets (Liu 1988). The alliances and wealth generated by devotional establishments affected the entire Indo-Sinic region. Across the trade routes leaving south Asia—northward on the international silk route, across the Himalayas, via Tibet and Yunnan, and eastward via maritime trade to Southeast Asia, coastal China, Japan—the network of marts, ports, and oases defined a web of Buddhist monasticism. Thus, the logic of Buddhism's diasporas, domestications, and historical survivals conformed, in part, to the exigencies of trade and the patronage of merchants.

The practice of teachers requiring payment for their bestowing initiations—a system that developed in the tantric lineages from Indic times and continues in Tibet and Nepal—is another area for "commodity" analysis.

Class, Caste, and Buddhism. The juxtaposition of wealth and advanced spiritual progress is one of the great paradoxes of Buddhist tradition, embodied in the life of Śākyamuni in his last and former lives. Early scholarly debates took opposing sides as to whether the Buddha was for or against the caste system (Thomas 1951: 84ff). Textual analysis has shown that the preponderance of famous early monks come from high-caste families (Gokhale 1965) and that in many story narratives the future Buddha is most frequently born in the top two Indic castes (Brahman or *kṣatrīya*). In fact, Buddhism existed throughout its history in India, Nepal, Sri Lanka, and even Tibet (Gombo 1982) in a caste-ordered society.

The Buddhist "ideology of merit" has always been used to explain life's disparities and legitimate those with social, material, intellectual, or political standing (Tambiah 1968a).

Deities, Ghosts, Demons, and Their Control. Another venerable armchair characterization of Buddhism in the West has been its alleged "atheism," a debate that continues. This has been a curious phenomenon, since from the earliest texts onward, Buddhist doctrine has recognized the realm of rebirth as having six paths (*gatis*): human (the best and only realm of *nirvāṇa*), deities (*deva*), demons (*daitya* or *yakṣa*), hungry ghosts (*preta*, P. *peta*), animals, and hell-dwellers. Thus, Buddhists have always believed in the existence of these beings—although salvation could not be sought through their aid—and early texts instruct the laity to perform rituals to assist or propitiate each (Mendelson 1963; Lehman 1971).

In almost every Buddhist region, devotees set out offerings before or after meals to feed/appease the *preta*s and to share merit to help those in any of the hot or cold hells. Likewise, the indigenous deities of localities—beings acknowledged to be born divine through their good karma—can also be respected with offerings since they possess supermundane powers that can affect the local environment (fertility, climate) and individuals living within "their" territories. A "good Buddhist" layman can believe in and worship deities for mundane results: To do so is simply common sense.

Buddhist texts describe the ideal of "converting" local divinities to be protectors (*lokapāla*) of the *triratna*, and this conversion is often enacted in festivals or ad hoc curing rituals. The biographical narratives of Śākyamuni's conversion of the *nāgas*—"snake deities" who own the subterranean regions and control the rains—became archetypal throughout Asia for the conversion of autochthonous deities (Chi. *lung* ["dragon"], Jap. *kami*, Burmese *nat*, etc.) and the modified continuation of their cults. The domestication of indigenous pantheons has been an area of both historical and anthropological investigation.[25]

Across Asia, premodern etiologies identified demonic possession as one common cause of illness. Out of compassion to suffering humanity, the early texts describe rituals to exorcise these beings: Many of the Pali *paritta*s and Sanskrit *rakṣā* formuli are dedicated to restoring the individual's health by infusing the environment with the Buddha's words (*dharma*) and making utterances that scare off all spirits. But in the effort to expel specific demons, Buddhist traditions across Asia have developed most varyingly in using the "religious resources" in interaction with indigenous pre- or non-Buddhist practices. In modern Theravādin zones, monks do not exorcise, although Buddhist doctrine and saints "back up the transaction" (e.g., Kapferer 1983; Ames 1968; Yalman 1964; G. Obeyesekere 1964, 1969). In modern Mahāyāna-Vajrayāna zones, monks perform these rites (e.g., Mumford 1989; Nebesky-Wojkowitz 1956; Stablein 1976; Samuel 1993).

This same pattern of extra- or intra-*saṃgha* differentiation can also be noted for astrology. Although rejected in some *Vinaya*s as an art monks could not practice, some have still done so (e.g., Shukla 1975). Buddhists have tended to see astrology providing a "reading" on karma, and many consult specialists and almanacs for useful guidance in acting (individually, as family, or communally) in accordance with karmic tendencies.

Karma and Causality. One can make the case from textual sources that karma doctrine is not fatalistic since one can always make new *puṇya* or *pāp* to change the ongoing calculus of karmic destiny. This is not to deny that Buddhist philosophy stresses certain strong karma effects as setting off mechanistic causal connections between past and future; but it is also so that karma, like all phenomena, changes every instant.

It is quite important for anthropologists to note that Buddhist causality doctrine holds that not all contingencies in life are karma dependent: a *Milinda-pañha* passage[26] explaining why the enlightened Buddha still was subject to suffering identifies eight casual contingencies in the world:

> It is not all suffering that has its root in Karma. There are eight causes by which sufferings arise ... superabundance of wind, bile, and phlegm, the union of these humours;[27] variations in temperature; the avoiding of dissimilarities; external agency; and karma. ... So what arises as the fruit of karma is much less than that which arises from other causes. ... No one without a Buddha's insight [*prajñā*] can fix the extent of the action of karma. (Rhys-Davids 1963: 190–191)

Since only enlightened Buddhas can ascertain whether karma or other contingencies are at work in ongoing life, individuals are faced with uncertainty as to its momentary status. What is clear is the *ex post facto* "reading" from birth station and biography and that good rebirth is never certain. But for the future, the logic of the doctrine motivates seeking guidance through astrology and clearly compels Buddhists to keep making *puṇya*.

The question still remains as to how individual Buddhists and Buddhist communities have emphasized the fate or free will factors in the equation. This issue has quite great significance for assessing Buddhist history, making historical comparisons with other religions, and for theories of religious modernization.

Death Ritualism

In all Buddhist countries, death ritual is the purview of the *saṃgha* and a key time when monks both expound core teachings and receive *dāna*. Although with many regional differences, mourners in Buddhist death rituals carefully dispose of the corpse due to the danger of the dead becoming a *preta* or *yakṣa*, and they seek to avert bad destiny for the deceased by making *puṇya* in her name.

Buddhist tradition plays to both sides of the ancient Indic question of whether one's destiny is based strictly upon the individual's own karma from past and present lifetimes or whether rituals can overrule this and manipulate rebirth destiny (Edgerton 1927). Since Buddhism is conceptually centered on the doctrine that the cosmos is governed by karmic law, ritual traditions naturally surround death, as it is the critical time when such causal mechanisms operate. Both Theravāda monks and—more effulgently—Mahāyāna ritualists applied ritual expertise to this time.[28]

In almost all regions, including the Indic hearthland (Schopen 1984), Buddhism has entered societies that have various traditions of kin-organized ancestor veneration (Teiser 1988). Buddhist domestication with these practices has generally sought not to challenge the practices but to reinterpret the meaning, that is, ritual as a means of *punya* transfer. This may seem a striking transformation: If the philosophical texts deny the existence of the soul,[29] how to explain the existence of abbot ancestor graves in Japan or the Buddhist *śraddhā piṇḍa dāna* of Nepal (Toffin 1984; Lewis 1994d)?

Whatever the answer, the tradition's evolution is certain: Dependence on after-death ritual service for *saṃgha* donations is evident in all modern traditions, where such rituals are the predominant area where Buddhist tradition endures (Kitagawa 1966: 296; Holmberg 1989; Martinez 1990; Lewis 1994d).

The Question of Syncretism

In its expansion throughout Asia (and now, globally), Buddhism has been transposed into every kind of cultural environment, and where its community has flourished, it has been necessary to shape coexistence in many dimensions. Domestication has entailed the literal translation of texts and ideas into non-Indic languages to advance the *dharma* against competing ideological systems. From high philosophy to manners to medicine, Buddhist responses to competing systems evolved dialectically. From "within," the Buddha and *bodhisattva*s were superior to all beings, the *dharma* provided standards to measure all truth statements, the "Six Rebirth Stations" (above) reordered local pantheons, and the *saṃgha* lifestyle is the most respected and effective spiritual refuge. Thus, the Buddhist intellectual tradition provided ideal standards to assess and establish Buddhist hierarchy; it did so, in almost all known cases, without violence,[30] often refitting local culture into a larger Buddhist framework. The tradition's missionary success has certainly proven the power of this "loosely structured" ideological system, at least in premodern times.

The question of how each Buddhist community came to understand and domesticate the *triratna* amidst competing indigenous systems is one that is still poorly understood, and anthropologists will likely confront the issue of syncretism in their fieldwork. This is very difficult territory, and it is precisely here that clarity about the textual tradition (local venacular and classical) can help pose questions soundly. Studies of syncretism in Buddhist communities include those by Gombrich (1971),[31] Pye (1971), Berling (1980), and Bechert (1968, 1978). Research on the actual opinions of individual Buddhists is a rare but sorely needed area of study.

SECTION III: TOWARD A TRANSCULTURAL
HISTORIOGRAPHY OF BUDDHISM

For cultivating mutual insight benefiting both disciplines, scholars interested in Buddhism need to foster new dialogues between textual and anthropological research. There are many rich yet still underexplored avenues for comparative and collaborative inquiry. Centering analysis on the full range of tradition, the anthropological approach can provide alternative conceptual frameworks to philologically defined representations of Buddhism as religious tradition. For generalizing about a particular aspect of tradition (textual or praxis) or a spiritual lineage amidst the vicissitudes of a given historical context, there is the need for modern ethnographies to shed light on pertinent historical issues, suggest paradigms for comparative inquiry, and illuminate enduring, fundamental features of practice to cipher the Buddhist past. The field's goal, in technical terminology, should now be to develop a transcultural historiography of Buddhist civilizations. Tambiah's summary of anthropology's contributions define this task decisively:

The virtue of a synchronic structural account of contemporary religion is . . . the construction of a total field. And the structural relations of hierarchy, opposition, complementarity and linkage between Buddhism and the spirit cults arranged in one single field in contemporary life can therefore give insights into the historical processes by which Buddhism came to terms with indigenous religions in its march outward from India. (1970: 377)

From the textual side of the dialogue, scholars can highlight documents bearing on social aspects of tradition, develop a history of ritual practices and their sources, uncover the doctrinal underpinnings or debates that authorize important practices, and clarify the relationships between popular portions of the canon and more philosophical lineages (e.g., Snellgrove 1966). The following headings indicate subjects that can illuminate the understanding of Buddhist history, past and present.

*Bodhisattva*s, *Arhat*s, Intellectuals

Using as sample the polemic textual sources on the *bodhisattva* and *arhat* in Buddhist societies predisposes text-based analysts to describe sharp contrasts between those societies devoted to the Mahāyāna or Hīnayāna traditions. Local practice across Asia, however, shows a great degree of both intellectual and ritual overlap. To what extent did philosophical beliefs ever really divide the Buddhist community?

Texts, Art, and Practice

Just as texts are present as part of the doctrinal culture within local Buddhist societies, artistic traditions must also be reckoned as important elements in anthropological study. Often it is the choice of images made and displayed in public, in monasteries, in homes, that provide decisive clues about the nature of local tradition. What relationships exist between the material culture (of icons, texts, etc.)[32] and practices in a locality? Is there a local amulet tradition? Perhaps the most fruitful area of collaborative research in Buddhist studies would be to synthesize these academically separated dominions, unifying the data of written word, iconic symbols, and ritual studies in successive epochs.

Buddhist Ethics

Little attention to ethical injunctions and their effects in individual or community activities has been visible in anthropological studies. Recent works in the field have been limited mostly to theoretical, textual-doctrinal exegesis (e.g., King 1964b; Sizemore and Swearer 1990) and to linking Buddhist views to statements of global utopianism, with Western devotees joining in the latter discourse (e.g., Fu and Wawrytko 1991; Sivaraksa 1992). The question of abortion in Japan has gotten recent treatment (Smith 1992; LaFleur 1993), as have the issues of prostitution (Kabilsingh 1991) and "ethical choice" in Thailand (Keyes 1990).

Buddhist Community Belief Patterns

> The Buddhism of Nondwin is the most general framework for the interpretation of the world, the explanatory device for understanding the flow of events, the symbolic system for the attribution of ultimate meaning to life and death, and the standard and guide for moral action.
>
> Manning Nash (1965: 104)

As refuge of intellectual freedom, Buddhism nurtured and enriched the civilizations of Asia. Buddhist teachers articulated alternative traditions of remembrance and analysis regarding the Buddha's *dharma*. Surveying the belief patterns of a Buddhist community challenges an anthropologist both with the sheer diversity of doctrinal expression and with the complexities of extracting systematic thought from a tradition that held the ultimate to be beyond conception and recounted stories of the Buddha expressing dismay over those who would overintellectualize the *śāsana*. Systematic statement nonetheless had its place in Buddhist history: Right views are included in the eightfold path, doctrinal formulas abound, and royal court patronage debates required the mastery of doctrinal elucidation and argumentation. What remains uncertain is how the great majority of nonintellectual Buddhists adhered to the teachings. It is surprising that few studies of belief patterns have been done in communities in the manner that sociology has probed the Judeo-Christian believing community and that life history cases of individual Buddhists have been so rarely reported (e.g., Snellgrove 1967; Richardson 1986; Lewis 1996).

Colonialism and Modernity

In a sense, all anthropological studies must take account of the modern transformations that have reshaped almost every aspect of global life. The legacy of the past 300 years has been the acceleration of change and the expansion of choices in every sphere of life. Few areas of Asian Buddhism have been removed from the effects of these events and trends, including scientific thought and technology derived from the European enlightenment that challenged traditional doctrines, cosmologies, and medical theories; the impact of European colonialism on Asian societies that forced (to varying degress) economic transformations that undermined traditional rulers and patronage; the (not-always-detached) ideologies of Christian missionary triumphalism and racism that forced dissonance with indigenous ethnocentrisms; and the (sometimes) competing ideologies toward democracy that challenged indigenous elites. Fundamental shifts in the political, socioeconomic, and intellectual spheres have inevitably changed individuals and caused Buddhist traditions to confront a changed world. To chart the cummulative, interactive impact of these variables almost defies analytical possibility.[33]

Modern state formation caused fixed boundary lines and national laws to be drawn over former ethnic regions and small-scale spheres of influence, as the legacy of colonialism and later independence movements have been strong forces shaping modern human geography (Bechert 1973; Keyes 1971; Tambiah 1973b; Reynolds 1977). In some areas, adherance to Buddhism was a powerful force of anticolonial struggle; this has in places led to reform movements within the *samgha* that introduced state supervision or weakened the older institutional lineages (e.g., Bechert 1974; Kemper 1984; Mendelson 1975; Tambiah 1978). Buddhist monks have been called upon to serve as leaders in development projects (e.g., Swearer 1981; Suksamran 1977; Reynolds 1977). In China and Outer Mongolia, Buddhism was identified by revolutionary regimes with the old feudal order and fiercely disestablished (Welch 1972), and in both the Tibetan and Inner Mongolian regions, the policy of the People's Republic of China (1949–), especially during the Cultural Revolution (1976–1986), was to destroy Buddhist architecture, monasticism, and public expressions of devotion.

In other regions, once nationalistic Buddhist movements won independence, they turned their efforts inward: By seeking to legislate "purer Buddhist states," they ushered in activist political monks and unprecedented ethnic conflicts with minorities long established in their polities (Tambiah 1986, 1992; Kapferer 1988; Gombrich and Obeyesekere 1988). Buddhist universalism and the ideology of compassion have not resisted modern attempts at "ethnic cleansing" in Sri Lanka, Burma, and Bhutan. Studies of institutional change in given polities are needed, including in local monastery and village contexts, to understand this pattern development more fully.

The impact of missionary Christianity has been rather minimal in terms of converts but quite significant in what Buddhists have learned of modern missionary practices (Malalgoda 1976). Buddhists have learned about the power of media, from the printing press to radio, cassette players, and television; they have recognized the need to reinterpret the *dharma* in light of modern science to keep the growing segment of their urban middle classes interested. The emergence of the laity as key actors in these movements is unprecedented (Swearer 1970; Malalgoda 1972), with lay meditation an important emphasis. Westerners in Asia and Asian teachers in the West have accelerated the global process of transformation (e.g., Malalgoda 1976; Houtman 1990).

The question of Buddhism's impact on economic modernization has been discussed from Max Weber's time onward (Spiro 1966; Sarkisyanz 1970; Tambiah 1973a) and we have described the unambiguous lay ethos of "good Buddhists" attaining worldly success. To summarize our discussions, Buddhism has tended to promote sober, compassionate, medically advanced, disciplined, mercantile, and literate polities. That these can have a positive effect on modernization in the state capitalism mode seems clear, as modern Thailand and Japan surely attest. Only by fashioning more finely articulated studies of the faith's exact domestication in specific contexts can anthropologists effectively insert Buddhism into the data on modernity studies.

Like other great world religions, Buddhism has shown that its definition of the human condition and its solutions to finite existence have enduring value to those undergoing modern change. It will remain the challenging task for anthropologists to discern how and why a tradition originating 2,500 years ago can remain so compelling in Asia and beyond.

NOTES

The author would like to thank his anthropologist mentors for their guidance and encouragement, particularly Morton Klass, Marvin Harris, the late Margaret Mead, and Stanley Tambiah. The technical vocabulary is Sanskrit (Skt.) unless indicated as from Pali (P.), Tibetan (Tib.), Chinese (Chi.), Japanese (Jap.), or Newari (New.).

1. Useful overviews on Buddhist canonical literature are found in Thomas (1951: 261–287), Mizuno (1982), Akira (1987), and Reynolds (1981). Lewis Lancaster's (1979) discussion of the concept of canon in Buddhist contexts is particularly important, as is Tambiah's (1968b) exploration of Buddhism's association with literacy. For a fine discussion of the problem of scriptural authority in Indic Buddhism, see Ron Davidson (1990). Reginald Ray's (1990) discussion of the relationship between text and practice is also germane for anthropological studies, as is Frank Hoffman's article (1992) concerning the orality of the Pali Canon.

The Pali Canon of Theravāda or southern Buddhism, roughly four times the size of the Bible, is universally accepted and entirely translated into English. Extant Mahāyāna literature is more diverse and less translated, knows no universal canon, and remains variously extant in Sanskrit, Tibetan, Chinese, Mongolian, and Japanese. In some respects, the evolution of Mahāyāna tradition lineages in east Asia occurred around different texts recognized by each as the Buddha's "highest teaching." The *Lotus Sūtra* (Skt. *Saddharma Puṇḍarīka*) was by far the most influential, universally respected text. Paul Williams (1989) provides a useful recent summation of these trends.

2. A particularly useful sociologically informed historical account of Buddhism is Peter Pardue's *Buddhism* (1971), although it has long been out of print. A recent survey of Buddhism that devotes considerable attention to devotional practices, festivals, and institutions in relation to doctrine is by Peter Harvey (1990). Alex Wayman's (1971) overview of the tradition provides useful information, as does Luis Gomez's (1987) more recent encyclopedia article. Pardue's statement on Buddhism's unique historical configuration bears repetition:

Buddhism has evidenced from the very beginning a deep commitment to the exploration of the mystery and meaning of the self amid the finite conditions of human life and the transience of worldly forms to which man has compulsively attributed ultimate worth. The paradoxa of illusion and reality, or anxious human striving in the world and the longing for withdrawal from it, of dogmatic ethical imperatives and their merely provisional conditions—all these have been richly elaborated within a prognostic framework. (1971: xxiv)

His book discusses the study of Buddhism and society comprehensively, although given the multivariance of texts and precedents, each world region really requires much more specific and detailed attention, including bibliographic annotation. This article indicates a sampling of important sources; he does not assume the historical priority of either Theravāda or Mahāyāna lineages, seeing both as authentic transmissions of Śākyamuni Buddha's (c. 560–480 B.C.E.) spiritual legacy.

3. The term *vihāra* is used here to refer to monasteries generally because it became the most universal by the classical Gupta period in India (400 C.E.). Early terms included *āvāsa* ("shelter"), *ārāma* ("grove"), and *lena* ("private dwelling house"). The key source for the history of Indic monasticism is Sukumar Dutt (1962).

4. Gregory Schopen's studies have challenged many of the old assumptions about early Buddhism; his publications address a host of issues that should inform fruitful anthropological inquiries. See the references.

5. This difference finds dramatic articulation in the fifth century C.E. Chinese pilgrim Fa-Hsien's journal where he describes the devout reasons for his Chinese monk companion's decision to forsake return to China. What could motivate a Chinese pilgrim to stay in India in C.E. 400? The spiritual integrity of Buddhist monasticism and the quality of the early Indic communities' devotion: Wishing to live in the strict discipline found in the Gangetic *vihāras*, he vows, "May I never be born again in a frontier country" (Beal 1970: 1: lxxi).

Anthropologists should consult the records of Chinese pilgrims to India to explore the possible ancient Indic precedents for modern practices. The sources for Fa-Hsien (c. 400 C.E.) and Hsuan Tsang (c. 630 C.E.) are Beal (1970); for I-Tsing (c. 680 C.E.), see Takakusu (1982). Later narratives from other regions and times, as well as monk biographies (Tib. *namthar*), constitute valuable but hardly utilized sources.

6. The specific benefits of being a generous Buddhist donor are extolled in a Pali text: appreciation by everyone, loved by worthy individuals, renowned everywhere, fearless in any company, and rebirth in a heavenly realm (Lamotte 1988: 415). The literatures of all schools in all periods extoll the great worth and rewards for *dāna*.

7. Scholarly discourse in Buddhist studies should adopt the "culture area" concept

and cease using "Indian" as a scientific label for premodern phenomena. "Indic" (and "Indicized") is preferred. Projecting the modern state boundaries backwards falsifies historical representation since Buddhism endures continuously in South Asia outside the culture hearth zone up to the present: in the north in the Kathmandu Valley and Himalayas; in the far south, in Sri Lanka; and to the east in Burma, Thailand, and points along the Indian Ocean. Although it was eclipsed by the Muslim invasions and rule across the Gangetic plain by 1200, the tradition was also preserved far past the twelfth century in small communities lying in inner frontiers: Orissa (Das Gupta 1969) and in port town communities (Tucci 1931). The more heuristic geographical representation is that Buddhism did survive on the Indic frontiers of the original core zone. To say that "Indian Buddhism was extinguished" is poor methodology and, in literal point of geographical fact, false.

8. The classical rejections of this paradigm came in Stanley Tambiah's *Buddhism and the Spirit Cults of Northeast Thailand* (1970) and Richard Gombrich's *Precept and Practice* (1971). See Schopen (1991d) and Gombrich (1988: 172–197) for a good discussion of how Protestantism informed the modern revival of Buddhism and the Western construction of its "normative" core tradition.

9. The persistence of the *punya* orientation is likewise mirrored in Vajrayāna texts. In the *Sarvarahasyatantra*, full Buddhist praxis—which leads one to become "best among gods and humans"—is defined by amassing the "Two Collections": the *punya* collection and the *jñāna* ("spiritual knowledge" developed via *prajñā* cultivation) collection (Wayman 1984: 525).

10. Discussion on the history of the *bhikṣuṇī saṃgha* and of women in Buddhism is found in recent works by Falk (1980), Paul (1985), Willis (1985), Kabilsingh (1991), and Sponberg (1992).

11. One Mahāyāna rationale for later Buddhism's luxuriant ritualism is succinctly expressed in the *guru maṇḍala pūjā*, which orchestrates the repetition of the Three Refuges, Six *Pāramitā*s ["*bodhisattva* perfections"], the *bodhisattva* vow (to help all beings reach *nirvāṇa* before enjoying it for oneself), and the Eightfold Path (Gellner 1991). This trend toward ritual service continued in great elaboration with the Vajrayāna (Skilling 1992; Lewis 1994d).

It also was the competing Brahman priesthood and the distinctive caste-ordered societies of south (and Southeast) Asia that shaped Mahāyāna-Vajrayāna ritualism. The later Indic Buddhist adaptation of pollution-purity norms, formal life cycle rites (*saṃskāra*s), royal ritualism, procedures for image veneration, and calendarical organization all represent, within the early faith, the domestication of Buddhist lay praxis amidst Hindu polities and cultural norms (Mus 1964; Tambiah 1985).

12. Hsuan Tsang notes that the time for retreat in India could be either Āṣāḍha, 15 → Āśvina, 15 or Śrāvaṇa, 15 → Kārtika, 15 (Beal 1970: 1: 72–73), a variation allowed in the Pali *Vinaya* (Warren 1922: 412). His account also suggests that monks could alter the time for retreat to suit local conditions: In Bāluka (central Asia) monks retreated during the winter-spring rainy season (Beal 1970: 1: 38).

13. From antiquity, *stūpa* and *caitya* were used in Buddhist inscriptions and literature as synonyms. Poussin (1937: 284) has noted that a Dharmagupta *Vinaya* commentary suggested the existence of a technical distinction between shrines with relics (*stūpa*) and shrines without (*caitya*). I-Tsing indicates another Buddhist definition: "Again, when the people make images and *caitya*s which consist of gold, silver, copper, iron, earth, laquer, bricks, and stone, or when they heap up the snowy sand, they put into the images or *caitya*s two kinds of *sarīra*s: 1. The relics of the Great Teacher; 2. The *Gāthā* [verse]

of the chain of causation.'' The *Gāthā* is: *"Ye dharmā hetuprabhavā hetuṃ teṣāṃ tath-āgato hy avadat Teṣāṃ ca yo nirodha evaṃ vādī mahāśramaṇaḥ"* (The Buddha, the great truthful ascetic, revealed the cause of things having their beginning from a cause, and their cessation).

14. Hsuan Tsang, the Chinese monk-pilgrim in seventh-century South Asia, noted that monks and nuns performed rituals at individual *stūpa*s depending upon which early saints had associations with the individual's "school" or specialization. The specific list (Beal 1970: 1: 180–181) for this is:

Specialization	*Pūjā to*
Abhidharma	Śāriputra
Meditation	Mudgalaputra
Sūtras	Purnamaitrāyaṇiputra
Vinaya	Upali
*Bhikṣuni*s	Ānanda
Śrāmaneras	Rāhula
Mahāyāna	*Bodhisattvas*

15. Eva Dargyay's study of popular Buddhist practices in Zanskar (western Tibet) includes the construction of a small *stūpa* using cremation ashes and bones; this and other typical lay rituals after death (image making and text copying) have a threefold purpose: "to let the previously deceased attain to the path of liberation; to purge the defilements of the living ones; and to ensure the future prosperity and power of one's dynasty" (Dargyay 1986: 87). Other Tibetan areas also preserve this cultic use of monks' and layfolks' cremation remains (Schopen 1992b).

16. In the Newar Buddhist *vrata*s, there is a standard structural order: Led by a *vajrācārya* priest (who is often assisted by several *vajrācārya* assistants), laymen worship a *guru-maṇḍala* that includes all major deities of the Mahāyāna Buddhist cosmos (Gellner 1991). They then participate in a *kalaśa pūjā* to the special *vrata* deity, take refuge in the *triratna-maṇḍala*s (Buddha, *dharma, saṃgha*), and finally make offerings to the *vrata* deity, again on a *maṇḍala*. Most texts specify that the *vajrācārya* should explain the *maṇḍala* symbolism(s) and tell the story (*kathā*) (or stories) associated with the particular *vrata*. As the latter is done, all participants hold a special thread (New. *bartakā*; Skt. *vratasūtra*) unwound from the *kalaśa*. This symbolic act links the deity to each individual and binds the circle of devotees in worship. Broken up and tied around the neck, this thread is a special *prasād* laymen take away from all *vrata* ceremonies. Specific boons, good fortune, heaven, or even supernormal powers and the possibility of enlightenment itself are mentioned in the stories read (*vratakathā*).

17. The traditional designation of Buddhist sites specified first four, then eight centers marked by monuments (Bagchi 1941; Chandra 1988). By the time of the *Aśokāvadāna*'s composition, thirty-two pilgrimage centers existed in the Gangetic basin visited by devotees (Strong 1983: 119ff). There was also a circuit in northwest India (Lamotte 1988: 335). Such religious travel had important economic effects, and vibrant microeconomies developed around the great *caitya*s. By C.E. 400, the world of Mahāyāna Buddhist pilgrimage had long transcended the Gangetic culture hearth to include *stūpa* sites in Khotan, Śrī Lanka, Śrīvijāya, ancient Funan, and China. Monks, pilgrims, and traders traveled the same routes (Takakusu 1982; Birnbaum 1989–1990: 115–120).

18. See Susan Naquin and Chun-fang Yu's *Pilgrims and Sacred Sites in China* (1992)

for a recent collection of studies, past and present, that is also invaluable for its extensive bibliography.

19. For literary references, see Strong (1979: 91–97; 1990). Although there is no clear consensus as to its origins (e.g., Lamotte 1988: 66; Edgerton 1953), *pañcavārsika* was clearly a time for royal-*saṃgha* exchange. The Chinese accounts and the *avadāna* citations point to the custom of a king giving all material goods he owned to the *saṃgha*, followed by his ministers buying it all back with gold from the treasury. (There are a number of these celebrations mentioned in accounts of ancient central Asia and south Asia, several during the autumnal equinox. *Pañcavārsika* seems to have been celebrated by Emperor Wu [502–541 C.E.] of northern China [Wright 1959: 51], and it may survive in Nepal, too [Lewis 1992, 1994e].)

20. The attempt to utilize Robert Redfield's paradigm led to many ill-fated efforts to force Buddhist communities into the "Great-little" framework, example, G. Obeyesekere (1964) and Spiro (1982). Important criticisms are found in Bechert (1968), Tambiah (1970), Jayawardena (1970), Reynolds (1972a), and Lehman (1971).

21. The indispensable sources for the domestication of Buddhism in China, both written with sociocultural analyses, are Chen (1973), Zurcher (1972), and Gernet (1995).

22. Entrance into the Newar *saṃgha* is now based upon birth into only a few high-caste lineages (Allen 1971; Gellner 1992); in Sri Lanka, the dominant Siyama Nikaya is open only to Goyigama caste members (Gombrich 1971; Evers 1967a). The Buddhist *śākyas* and *vajrācāryas* of Nepal, like the Nyingmapa of Tibet, conform to the "Buddhist Brahmana" pattern, where adherence to Buddhist tradition is an important and durable principle of ethnic/caste boundary maintenance and group replication (Gellner 1992). See Clarke (1983, 1990) and Holmberg (1984, 1989) for other Tibeto-Burman case studies in the midmontane Himalayan region.

23. This works exactly like the lineage "Brahmana-frontier" model articulated by John Hitchcock (1974). Perhaps the householder *saṃgha*s of Nepal, Tibet, and Japan indicate a Mahāyāna-Vajrayāna Buddhist pattern of frontier adaptation: expansion of the religious elite confined within ethnic group and lineage boundaries, justified by the *bodhisattva* doctrine (e.g., Shukla 1975).

24. An example of this can be cited from twelfth-century sources in Fuzhou province of southeastern coastal China: "Formerly the ursurping kings [of Min] one by one actually seized the rich lands of the common people and gave them to the Buddhists. Since the establishment of our dynasty nothing has changed. Consequently, the Buddhists do absolutely no labor, yet they do not lack for food and they even have excess clothing" (Clark 1991: 144).

25. Examples of recent studies are Ames (1964), G. Obeyesekere (1984), Locke (1980), Owens (1989), and Hardacre (1988). John Holt (1991) has shown how the Mahāyāna divinity Avalokiteśvara has been transformed in Sri Lanka over the centuries to "demotion" as a Hindu world protector.

26. Every anthropologist working in Theravāda regions should read this entire passage to "textualize" the Buddhist attitude toward "the religious field."

27. This refers to the *tridoṣa* system of Indic medical analysis (Zysk 1991).

28. The general attitude of all Buddhist schools is to face death calmly, recollecting the *triratna*. The Mahāyāna schools added their distinctive emphases: The Pure Land devotee is to direct consciousness to Pure Land visualization; the *Tibetan Book of the Dead* (Freemantle and Trungpa 1987) includes instruction in experiencing the interme-

diate state consciousness and coaching in how to will release—or at least better rebirth—through this afterlife journey.

29. But the philosophers debate the issue throughout history: How can a karma law operate without a *vehicle* for transmigration? Given the host of diverse, complex, and conflicting answers given over the centuries by the Buddhist intelligentsia, it is understandable that the *saṃgha* did not veto terms in popular use such as the Thai "butterfly soul" to explain rebirth. In China, Buddhist doctrine was defended for its *teaching* of the soul's immortality (Zurcher 1972: 11).

30. An account of the Tibetan state's first contact with the Lepchas of northern Sikkim provides a dramatic exception:

> Later the sons of *zo khe bu* and their families [central Tibetan nobility] came down to Sikkim with their followers, invaded and conquered the country. . . . At that time Lamaism had nearly reached its peak in Tibet, and the second son . . . introduced it into Sikkim. They collected all the Lepcha manuscripts and books containing the historical records, mythology, legends, laws, literature, etc. of the Lepchas and burned them. They took the ashes to the high hills and blew them into the air and built Lamaist monasteries on the hills from which they had scattered the ashes . . . and forced the Lepcha scribes to translate the Lamaist scriptures . . . and venerate them. (Siiger 1967: 28)

31. Richard Gombrich (1971) has suggested that the distinction "cognitive" versus "affective" belief be used to explain the attitudes underlying Buddhist image veneration. This has led to a spirited debate (Gellner 1990).

32. For a sample of the material culture of a Japanese tradition, an overview of Pure Land practice (Matsunami 1976: 168–176) lists the following as "Buddhist Objects of Worship": Gautama Buddha image, Amida Buddha image, Honen image, family Buddhist altar, family memorial tablet, rosary, candle, metal gong, incense, flowers, wooden gong, robe, relic shrines (body and textual), *sūtras*, monasteries, temples, wheel of the law, *swastika* symbol, and Buddhist flag. "Buddhist Forms of Worship" are enumerated as well: Offerings (incense, flowers, rice, sweets, candles, water, money), greeting, meditation (cited twice), *sūtra* chanting, uttering *nembutsu*, singing, and dancing. (Terms used as given in the English text.)

33. An extensive, if uneven, literature exists on Buddhism and modernity in specific contexts. Valuable recent anthologies (and their bibliographies) include those edited by Prebish (1975a), Bechert and Gombrich (1984), Dumoulin (1976), and Queen and King (1996). The conversion to Buddhism by low castes in Maharastra state in India deserves special mention (Zelliot 1966, 1992). Donald Swearer has made numerous contributions (1990, 1995), as has Charles F. Keyes (1989). The "New Religions" of Japan also represent a unique modern development in their reworking of Buddhism traditions with other religious systems (e.g., McFarland 1967; Hardacre 1988; Reader 1991).

REFERENCES

Akira, Hirakawa. 1987. "Buddhist Literature: Survey of Texts." *Encyclopaedia of Religion* 2: 509–529.

Allen, Michael. 1971. "Buddhism without Monks: The Vajrayāna Religion of the Newars of the Kathmandu Valley." *South Asia* 3: 1–14.

Ames, Michael M. 1964. "Buddha and the Dancing Goblins: A Theory of Magic and Religion." *American Anthropologist* 66: 75–82.

Ames, Michael M. 1968. "Ritual Pretestations and the Structure of the Sinhalese Pantheon.'' *Theravāda Buddhism: Anthropological Studies*. Manning Nash, editor. New Haven: Yale University Press. 27–50.

Aronson, Harvey B. 1980. "Motivations to Social Action in Theravāda Buddhism: Uses and Misuses of Traditional Doctrines." *Studies in the History of Buddhism*. A. K. Narain, editor. New Delhi: B. R. Publishing. 1–12.

Ashkenazi, Michael. 1993. *Matsuri: Festivals of the Japanese Town*. Honolulu: University of Hawaii Press.

Aung, Maung Htin. 1960. *Folk Elements in Burmese Buddhism*. Rangoon: Religious Affairs Department Press.

Aung-Thwin, Michael. 1985. *Pagan: The Origins of Modern Burma*. Honolulu: University of Hawaii Press.

Bagchi, P. C. 1941. "The Eight Great Caityas and Their Cult." *Indian Historical Quarterly* 17: 223–235.

Bareau, Andres. 1962. "La Construction et le culte des stupa d'apre les Vinayapitaka." *Bulletin de l'École française d'Extreme-Orient* 50: 229–274.

Beal, Samuel. 1970. *Si-Yu-Ki: Buddhist Records of the Western World*. 2 vols. New York: Paragon Book Reprint Corporation.

Bechert, Heinz. 1968. "Einige Fragen der Religionssoziologie und Struktur des sudasiatischen Buddhismus." *Internationales Jährbuch für Religionssoziologie* 4: 251–295.

Bechert, Heinz. 1973. "Sangha, State, Society, 'Nation': The Persistence of Traditions in 'Post-Traditional' Buddhist Societies." *Daedalus* 102(1): 85–95.

Bechert, Heinz. 1974. "Buddhism as a Factor of Political Modernization: The Case of Sri Lanka." *Religion and Development in Asian Societies*. Donald E. Smith, editor. Columbo: Marga Publications. 1–11.

Bechert, Heinz, editor. 1978. *Buddhism in Ceylon and Studies on Religious Syncretism in Buddhist Countries*. Gottingen: Vandenhoeck and Ruprecht.

Bechert, Heinz, and Richard Gombrich, editors. 1984. *The World of Buddhism*. New York: Thames and Hudson.

Berling, Judith A. 1980. *The Syncretic Religion of Lin Chao-en*. New York: Columbia University Press.

Beyer, Stephan. 1973. *The Cult of Tara*. Berkeley: University of California Press.

Bharati, Agehananda. 1965. *The Tantric Tradition*. London: Rider and Company.

Birnbaum, Raoul. 1989–1990. "Secret Halls of the Mountain Lords: The Caves of Wu-T'ai Shan." *Cahiers d'Extreme-Asie* 5: 115–140.

Bloss, Lowell W. 1973. "The Buddha and the Nāga: A Study in Buddhist Folk Religiosity." *History of Religions* 13 (1): 36–53.

Brokow, Cynthia J. 1991. *The Ledgers of Merit and Demerit: Social Change and Moral Order in Late Imperial China*. Princeton: Princeton University Press.

Bunnag, Jane. 1973. *Buddhist Monk, Buddhist Layman: A Study of Urban Monastic Organization in Central Thailand*. Cambridge: Cambridge University Press.

Buswell, Robert E., editor. 1990. *Chinese Buddhist Apocrypha*. Honolulu: University of Hawaii Press.

Buswell, Robert E. 1992. *The Zen Monastic Experience: Buddhist Practice in Contemporary Korea*. Princeton: Princeton University Press.

Carrithers, Michael. 1983. *The Forest Monks of Sri Lanka: An Anthropological and Historical Study*. Delhi: Oxford University Press.

Chandra, Lokesh. 1988. Introduction to *The Stūpa: Art, Architectonics and Symbolism*

(Indo-Tibetica I), by Guissepe Tucci. English translation in *Sata-Pitaka Series* #347. Lokesh Chandra, editor. New Delhi: Aditya Prakashan. v–xxxvi.

Chen, Kenneth. 1964. *Buddhism in China: A Historical Survey*. Princeton: Princeton University Press.

Chen, Kenneth. 1973. *The Chinese Transformation of Buddhism*. Princeton: Princeton University Press.

Clark, Hugh R. 1991. *Community, Trade, and Networks: Southern Fujian Province from the Third to the Thirteenth Century*. Cambridge: Cambridge University Press.

Clarke, Graham E. 1983. "The Great and Little Traditions in the Study of Yolmo, Nepal." *Wiener Studies zur Tibetologie and Buddhismuskunde* 10: 21–37.

Clarke, Graham E. 1990. "The Ideas of Merit (*Bsod-nams*), Virtue (*Dge-ba*), Blessing (*Byin-rlabs*) and Material Prosperity (*Rten-'brel*) in Highland Nepal." *Journal of the Anthropological Society of Oxford* 21(2): 165–184.

Cleary, J. C. 1993. "Buddhism and Popular Religion in Medieval Vietnam." *Journal of the American Academy of Religion* 59 (1): 93–118.

Coedes, G. 1971. *The Indianized States of Southeast Asia*. Honolulu: University of Hawaii Press.

Cohen, Alvin P. 1987. "Chinese Religion: Popular Religion." *The Encyclopaedia of Religion*. Vol. 3. Mircea Eliade, editor. New York: Macmillan. 298–296.

Collcutt, Martin. 1988. "Mt. Fuji as the Realm of Miroku." *Maitreya, the Future Buddha*. Alan Sponberg and Helen Hardacre, editors. Cambridge: Cambridge University Press. 248–269.

Cone, Margaret and Richard F. Gombrich. 1977. *The Perfect Generosity of Prince Vessantara*. Oxford: Clarendon Press.

Conze, Edward. 1967. *Buddhist Thought in India*. Ann Arbor: University of Michigan Press.

Dallapiccola, Anna, editor. 1980. *The* Stūpa: *Its Religious, Historical, and Architectural Significance*. Wiesbaden: Franz Steiner Verlag. 112–126.

Dargyay, Eva K. 1986. "Merit-Making and Ritual Aspects in the Religious Life of Zanskar (West Tibet)." *Karma and Rebirth*. Ronald W. Neufeldt, editor. Albany, NY: SUNY Press. 179–189.

Das, Sukumar Ranjan. 1928. "Hindu Calendar." *Indian Historical Quarterly* 4: 483–511.

Das Gupta, Shashibhusan. 1969. *Obscure Religious Cults*. Calcutta: Firma K. L. Mukhopadhyay.

Davidson, Ronald M. 1990. "An Introduction to the Standards of Scriptural Authenticity in Indian Buddhism." *Chinese Buddhist Apocrypha*. Robert A. Buswell, editor. Honolulu: University of Hawaii Press. 291–325.

Dayal, Har. 1932. *The Bodhisattva Doctrine in Buddhist Sanskrit Literature*. London: K. Paul. Trench, Trubner.

de Bary, William Theodore. 1972. *The Buddhist Tradition*. New York: Vintage.

Dehejia, Vidya. 1972. *Early Buddhist Rock Temples: A Chronology*. Ithaca: Cornell University Press.

Dehejia, Vidya. 1989. "*Stūpa*s and Sculptures in Early Buddhism." *Asian Art* 11(3): 7–31.

Desai, Devangana. 1986. "The Social Milieu of Indian Terracottas 600 B.C–600 A.D." *From Indian Earth* Amy Poster, editor. New York: Brooklyn Museum. 29–42.

Dumoulin, Heinrich, editor. 1976. *Buddhism in the Modern World*. New York: Macmillan.

Dutt, Nalinaksha. 1945a. "The Place of Laity in Early Buddhism." *Indian Historical Quarterly* 21 (3): 163–183.

Dutt, Nalinaksha. 1945b. "Popular Buddhism." *Indian Historical Quarterly* 21 (4): 245–270.

Dutt, Nalinaksha. 1977. *Mahāyāna Buddhism*. Delhi: Motilal Banarsidass.

Dutt, Sukumar. 1962. *Buddhist Monks and Monasteries of India*. London: Allen and Unwin.

Edgerton, Franklin. 1927. "The Hour of Death." *Bhandarkar Institute Annals* 7–8: 219–249.

Edgerton, Franklin. 1953. *Buddhist Hybrid Sanskrit Dictionary*. New Haven: Yale University Press.

Eliade, Mircea. 1959. *The Sacred and the Profane*. New York: Harcourt, Brace.

Emmerick, R. E. 1968. *The Book of Zambasta: A Khotanese Poem on Buddhism*. London: Oxford University Press.

Evers, Hans-Dieter. 1967a. "Buddha and the Seven Gods." *Journal of Asian Studies* 27: 541–550.

Evers, Hans-Dieter. 1967b. "Kinship and Property Rights in a Buddhist Monastery in Central Ceylon." *American Anthropologist* 69: 703–710.

Evers, Hans-Dieter. 1969. "Monastic Landlordism in Ceylon." *Journal of Asian Studies* 28 (4): 20–35.

Evers, Hans-Dieter. 1972. *Monks, Priests, and Peasants: A Study of Buddhism and Social Structure in Central Ceylon*. Leiden: E. J. Brill.

Falk, Nancy. 1977. "To Gaze on the Sacred Traces." *History of Religions* 16: 281–293.

Falk, Nancy. 1980. "The Case of the Vanishing Nuns: The Fruits of Ambivalence in Ancient Indian Buddhism." *Upspoken Worlds: Women's Religious Lives in Non-Western Cultures*. Nancy Auer Falk and Rita M. Gross, editors. New York: Harper and Row. 207–224.

Falk, Nancy. 1990. "Exemplary Donors of the Pali Canon." *Ethics, Wealth, and Salvation: A Study in Buddhist Social Ethics*. Russell F. Sizemore and Donald K. Swearer, editors. Columbia: University of South Carolina Press. 124–143.

Foucher, Alfred. 1949. *La vie du Bouddha d'apres les textes et les monuments de l'Inde*. Paris: A. Maisonneuve.

Foucher, Alfred. 1972. *The Life of the Buddha, according to the ancient texts and monuments of India*. Simon Brangier Boas, translator. Westport, CT: Greenwood.

Freemantle, Francesca, and Chogyam Trungpa. 1987. *The Tibetan Book of the Dead*. Boston: Shambala Press.

Fu, Charles We-hsun, and Sandra A. Wawrytko, editors. 1991. *Buddhist Ethics and Modern Society*. Westport, CT: Greenwood Press.

Gellner, David N. Monk. 1987. "The Newar Buddhist Monastery: An Anthropological and Historical Typology." *The Heritage of the Kathmandu Valley*. N. Gutschow and A. Michaels, editors. Sankt Augustin: VGH Wissenschaftsverlag. 364–414.

Gellner, David N. Monk. 1988. "Monastic Initiation in Newar Buddhism." *Oxford University Papers on India* 2 (1): 42–112. R. F. Gombrich, editor.

Gellner, David N. Monk. 1989. "Monkhood and Priesthood in Newar Buddhism." *Purushārtha* 12: 165–191.

Gellner, David N. Monk. 1990. "Introduction: What Is the Anthropology of Buddhism About?" *Journal of the Anthropological Society of Oxford* 21 (2): 95–112.

Gellner, David N. Monk. 1991. "Ritualized Devotion, Altruism, and Meditation: The Offering of the *Guru Mandala* in Newar Buddhism." *Indo-Iranian Journal* 34: 161–197.

Gellner, David N. Monk. 1992. *Householder and Tantric Priest: Newar Buddhism and Its Hierarchy of Ritual.* New York: Cambridge University Press.

Gernet, Jacques. 1995. *Buddhism in Chinese Society.* New York: Columbia University Press.

Gokhale, Balkrishna Govind. 1965. "The Early Buddhist Elite." *Journal of Indian History* 43: 391–402.

Gokhale, Balkrishna Govind. 1966. "Early Buddhist Kingship." *Journal of Asian Studies* 26 (1): 15–22.

Gokhale, Balkrishna Govind. 1980. "Bhakti in Early Buddhism." *Journal of Asian and African Studies* 15 (1–2): 16–27.

Gombo, Ugen. 1982. "Cultural Expressions of Social Stratification in Traditional Tibet: Caste and Casteism in Traditional Tibetan Society." *Anthropology* 7 (1): 43–72.

Gombrich, Richard F. 1966. "The Consecration of the Buddhist Image." *Journal of Asian Studies* 26 (1): 23–36.

Gombrich, Richard F. 1971. *Precept and Practice: Traditional Buddhism in the Rural Highlands of Ceylon.* Oxford: Clarendon Press.

Gombrich, Richard F. 1986. "Buddhist Festivals." *Festivals in World Religions.* Allan Brown, editor. London: Longman. 31–59.

Gombrich, Richard F. 1988. *Theravada Buddhism: A Social History from Ancient Benares to Modern Colombo.* New York: Routledge and Kegan Paul.

Gombrich, Richard F. and Gananath Obeyesekere. 1988. *Buddhism Transformed: Religious Change in Sri Lanka.* Princeton: Princeton University Press.

Gomez, Luis O. 1987. "Buddhism in India." *The Encyclopaedia of Religion.* M. Eliade, editor. New York: Macmillan. 2: 351–385.

Gough, Kathleen. 1968. "Implications of Literacy in Traditional China and India." *Literacy in Traditional Societies.* J. Goody, editor. London: Cambridge University Press. 70–84.

Greenblatt, Kristin Yu. 1975. "Chu-hung and Lay Buddhism in the Late Ming." *The Unfolding of Neo-Confucianism.* William Theodore DeBarry, editor. New York: Columbia University Press. 93–140.

Griswold, A. B. 1965. "The Holy Land Transported: Replicas of the Mahābodhi Shrine in Siam and Elsewhere." In *Paranavitana Felicitation Volume.* Colombo: M.D. Gunasena. 173–221.

Gunawardana, R. A. L. H. 1979. *Robe and Plough: Monasticism and Economic Interest in Early Medieval Sri Lanka.* Tucson: Association for Asian Studies.

Hall, Kenneth R. 1985. "Temples as Economic Centers in Early Cambodia." *Maritime Trade and State Development in Early Southeast Asia.* Kenneth R. Hall, editor. Honolulu: University of Hawaii Press. 136–168.

Hanks, L. M. 1962. "Merit and Power in the Thai Social Order." *American Anthropologist* 64: 1247–1261.

Hardacre, Helen. 1984. *Lay Buddhism in Contemporary Japan: Reikukai Kyodan.* Princeton: Princeton University Press, 1984.

Hardacre, Helen. 1988. "Maitreya in Modern Japan." *Maitreya, the Future Buddha.* Alan

Sponberg and Helen Hardacre, editors. Cambridge: Cambridge University Press. 270–284.

Harvey, Peter. 1984. "The Symbolism of the Early Stupa." *Journal of the International Association of Buddhist Studies* 7: 67–93.

Harvey, Peter. 1990. *An Introduction to Buddhism: Teachings, History and Practices.* New York: Cambridge University Press.

Harris, Marvin. 1989. *Our Kind.* New York: Harper and Row.

Hitchcock, John. 1974. "Himalayan Ecology and Family Religious Variations." *The Family in India: A Regional View.* G. Kurian, editor. The Hague: Mouton.

Hoffman, Frank J. 1992. "Evam Me Sutam: Oral Tradition in Nikāya Buddhism." *Texts in Context.* Jeffrey R. Timm, editor. New York: State University of New York Press. 195–218.

Holmberg, David H. 1984. "Ritual Paradoxes in Nepal: Comparative Perspectives on Tamang Religion." *Journal of Asian Studies* 43: 697–722.

Holmberg, David H. 1989. *Order in Paradox: Myth, Ritual, and Exchange among Nepal's Tamang.* Ithaca: Cornell University Press.

Holt, John Clifford. 1991. *Buddha in the Crown: Avalokiteśvara in the Buddhist Traditions of Sri Lanka.* New York: Oxford University Press.

Houtman, Gustaaf. 1990. "How Foreigner Invented 'Buddendom' in Burmese: From tha-tha-na to bok-da' ba-tha." *Journal of the Anthropological Society of Oxford* 21 (2): 113–128.

Hrdlickova, V. 1958. "The First Translations of Buddhist *Sūtras* in Chinese Literature and Their Place in the Development of Storytelling." *Archiv Orientalni* 26: 114–144.

Hurvitz, Leon. 1976. *The Lotus Blossom of the True Law.* New York: Columbia University Press.

Jaini, Padmanabh. 1991. "Is There a Popular Jainism?" *The Assembly of Listeners: Jains in Society.* Michael Carrithers and Caroline Humphrey, editors. New York: Cambridge University Press. 187–199.

Jayawardena, Chandra. 1970. "The Psychology of Burmese Supernaturalism: A Review Article." *Oceania* 41: 12–19.

Kabilsingh, Catsumarn. 1991. *Thai Women in Buddhism.* Berkeley: Parallax Press.

Kapferer, Bruce. 1983. *A Celebration of Demons: Exorcism and the Aesthetics of Healing in Sri Lanka.* Bloomington: Indiana University Press.

Kapferer, Bruce. 1988. *Legends of People, Myths of State.* Washington, D.C.: Smithsonian University Press.

Kemper, Steven. 1984. "The Buddhist Monkhood, the Law, and the State in Colonial Sri Lanka." *Comparative Studies in Society and History* 26: 401–427.

Kern, H. 1884. *Saddharma-Pundarika or Lotus of the True Law.* Oxford: Clarendon Press.

Keyes, Charles F. 1971. "Buddhism and National Integration." *Journal of Asian Studies* 30: 551–568.

Keyes, Charles F. 1975. "Buddhist Pilgrimage Centers and the Twelve-Year Cycle: Northern Thai Moral Orders in Space and Time." *History of Religions* 15: 71–89.

Keyes, Charles F. 1989. "Buddhist Politics and Their Revolutionary Origins in Thailand." *International Political Science Review* 10 (2): 121–142.

Keyes, Charles F. 1990. "Buddhist Practical Morality in a Changing Agrarian World: A Case from Northeastern Thailand." *Ethics, Wealth, and Salvation: A Study in Buddhist Social Ethics.* Russell F. Sizemore and Donald K. Swearer, editors. Columbia: University of South Carolina Press. 170–189.

King, Winston L. 1964a. *In the Hope of Nibbana: The Ethics of Theravāda Buddhism.* Lasalle: Open Court.

King, Winston L. 1964b. *A Thousand Lives Away: Buddhism in Contemporary Burma.* Oxford: Bruno Cassirer.

Kitagawa, Joseph M. 1965. "The Buddhist Transformation in Japan." *History of Religions* 4: 319–336.

Kitagawa, Joseph M. 1966. *Religion in Japanese History.* New York: Columbia University Press.

Klein, Julie Thompson. 1990. *Interdisciplinarity: History, Theory, and Practice.* Detroit: Wayne State University Press.

Kosambi, D. D. 1965. *Ancient India: A History of Its Culture and Civilization.* New York: Meridian.

Krishnan, Y. 1986. "Buddhism and the Caste System." *Journal of the International Association of Buddhist Studies* 9 (1): 71–83.

Kvaerne, Per. 1977. *An Anthology of Buddhist Tantric Songs: A Study of the Caryāgīti.* Oslo: Norwegian Academy of Science and Letters.

LaFleur, William R. 1993. *Liquid Life: Abortion and Buddhism in Japan.* Princeton: Princeton University Press.

Lamotte, Etienne. 1984. "The Buddha, His Teachings, and His Sangha." *The World of Buddhism.* Heinz Bechert and Richard Gombrich, editors. New York: Facts on File. 41–58.

Lamotte, Etienne. 1988. *History of Indian Buddhism: From the Origins to the Saka Era.* (Translation by Sara Webb-Boin of *Histoire du Bouddhisme Indien, des origines a l'ere Śaka*, 1958.) Louvain: Institut Orientaliste.

Lancaster, Lewis R. 1974. "An Early Mahāyāna Sermon about the Body of the Buddha and the Making of Images." *Artibus Asiae* 36 (4): 287–291.

Lancaster, Lewis R. 1979. "Buddhist Literature: Its Canons, Scribes, and Editors." *The Critical Study of Sacred Texts.* Wendy Doniger O'Flaherty, editor. Berkeley: Berkeley Religious Studies Series. 215–230.

Legge, James. 1965. *A Record of Buddhist Kingdoms.* New York: Dover.

Lehman, F. K. 1971. "Doctrine, Practice, and Belief in Theravāda Buddhism." *Journal of Asian Studies* 31: 372–380.

Lessing, Ferdinand D. 1976. "Structure and Meaning of the Rite Called Bath of the Buddha According to Tibetan and Chinese Sources." In *Collected Essays on Lemaism and Chinese Symbolism.* Taipei: Shihlin. 45–57.

Lester, Robert. 1987. *Buddhism.* San Francisco: Harper and Row.

Lewis, Todd T. 1984. *The Tulādhars of Kathmandu: A Study of Buddhist Tradition in a Newar Merchant Community.* Ann Arbor: University Microfilms International.

Lewis, Todd T. 1989a. "Mahāyāna *Vratas* in Newar Buddhism." *Journal of the International Association of Buddhist Studies* 12 (1): 109–138.

Lewis, Todd T. 1989b. "Newars and Tibetans in the Kathmandu Valley: Ethnic Boundaries and Religious History." *Journal of Asian and African Studies* 38: 31–57.

Lewis, Todd T. 1992. *The Samyaka Festival of 1980.* Film (38 minutes).

Lewis, Todd T. 1993a. "Newar-Tibetan Trade and the Domestication of the Simhalasārthabāhu *Avadāna.*" *History of Religions* 33 (2).

Lewis, Todd T. 1993b. "Contributions to the Study of Popular Buddhism: The Newar Buddhist Festival of Gumla Dharma." *Journal of the International Association of Buddhist Studies* 16 (2): 7–52.

Lewis, Todd T. 1993c. "Himalayan Frontier Trade: Newar Diaspora Merchants and Buddhism." *Anthropology of Tibet and the Himalayas*. Martin Brauen, editor. Zurich: Volkerkundemuseum. 165–178.

Lewis, Todd T. 1994a. "Contributions to the History of Buddhist Ritualism: A Mahāyāna *Avadāna* on *Stūpa* Veneration from the Kathmandu Valley." *Journal of Asian History* 28 (1): 1–38.

Lewis, Todd T. 1994b. "The Himalayan Frontier in Comparative Perspective: Considerations regarding Buddhism and Hinduism in Diaspora." *Himalayan Research Bulletin* 14 (1–2): 25–46.

Lewis, Todd T. 1994c. "Mahāyāna Protection Rituals: The *Pañcarakṣā Kathāsāra*."

Lewis, Todd T. 1994d. "The Nepāl Jana Jīvan Kriyā Paddhati, a Modern Newar Guide for Vajrayāna Life-Cycle Rites." *Indo-Iranian Journal* 37: 135–181.

Lewis, Todd T. 1995. "Buddhist Merchants in Kathmandu: The Asan Tol Market and Uray Social Organization." *Contested Hierarchies: A Collaborative Ethnography of Caste among the Newars of the Kathmandu Valley, Nepal*. Gellner and Quigley, editors. Oxford: Oxford University Press.

Lewis, Todd T. 1996. "Patterns of Religious Belief in a Buddhist Merchant Community, Nepal." *Asian Folklore Studies* 55 (2).

Lewis, Todd T. 1998. *Mahayana Buddhist Texts from Nepal: Narratives and Rituals of Newar Buddhism*. Albany: State University of New York Press.

Lewis, Todd T., and D. R. Shakya. 1988. "Contributions to the History of Nepal; Eastern Newar Diaspora Settlements." *Contributions to Nepalese Studies* 15 (1): 25–65.

Liu, Hsin-ju. 1988. *Ancient India and Ancient China*. Delhi: Oxford University Press.

Locke, John K. 1975. "Newar Buddhist Initiation Rites." *Contributions to Nepalese Studies* 2: 1–23.

Locke, John K. 1980. *Karunamaya*. Kathmandu: Sahiyogi.

Locke, John K. 1985. *Buddhist Monasteries of Nepal*. Kathmandu: Sahiyogi.

Locke, John K. 1987. "Uposadha Vrata of Amoghapasa Lokesvara in Nepal." *l'Ethnographie* 83 (100–101): 159–189.

Lowe, H. Y. 1983. *The Adventures of Wu: The Life Cycle of a Peking Man*. Princeton: Princeton University Press. (Originally published 1940)

McFarland, H. Neill. 1967. *The Rush Hour of the Gods*. New York: Macmillan.

McFarland, H. Neill. 1987. *Daruma: The Founder of Zen in Japanese Art and Popular Culture*. New York: Kodansha.

Malalgoda, Kirsiri. 1972. "Sinhalese Buddhism: Orthodox and Syncretistic, Traditional and Modern." *Ceylon Journal of Historical and Social Studies*, n.s., 2 (2): 156–169.

Malalgoda, Kirsiri. 1976. *Buddhism in Sinhalese Society 1750–1900*. Berkeley: University of California Press.

Martinez, D. P. 1990. "The Dead: Shinto Aspects of a Buddhist Ritual." *Journal of the Anthropological Society of Oxford* 21 (2): 199–209.

Matics, Marion L. 1970. *Entering the Path of Enlightenment*. New York: Macmillan.

Matsunami, Kodo. 1976. *Introducing Buddhism*. Rutland, VT: Charles Tuttle.

Mendelson, E. Michael. 1963. "The Uses of Religious Scepticism in Modern Burma." *Diogenes* 41: 94–116.

Mendelson, E. Michael. 1975. *Sangha and State in Burma: A Study of Monastic Sectarianism and Leadership*. Ithaca: Cornell University Press.

Miller, Beatrice D. 1960. "The Web of Tibetan Monasticism." *Journal of Asian Studies* 20 (2): 197–204.

Miller, Robert J. 1962. "The Buddhist Monastic Economy: The Jisa Mechanism." *Comparative Studies in Society and History* 3: 427–438.

Mizuno, Kogen. 1982. *Buddhist Sūtras: Origin, Development, Transmission*. Tokyo: Kosei Publishing.

Moerman, Michael. 1966. "Ban Ping's Temple: The Center of a 'Loosely Structured' Society." *Theravāda Buddhism: Anthropological Studies*. Manning Nash, editor. New Haven: Yale Southeast Asia Studies. 138–174.

Monier-Williams, Sir Monier. 1956. *A Sanskrit-English Dictionary*. 2nd edition. London: Oxford University Press.

Mumford, Stan R. 1989. *Himalayan Dialogue*. Madison: University of Wisconsin Press.

Murphy, Robert F. 1971. *The Dialectics of Social Life: Alarms and Excursions in Anthropological Theory*. New York: Basic Books.

Mus, Paul. 1964. "Thousand-Armed Kannon: A Mystery or a Problem?" *Indogaka Bakkyogaku Kenkyo* 12 (1): 407–438.

Naquin, Susan and Chun-fang Yu. 1992. *Pilgrims and Sacred Sites in China*. Berkeley: University of California Press.

Nash, Manning. 1965. *The Golden Road to Modernity: Village Life in Contemporary Burma*. Chicago: University of Chicago Press.

Nattier, Jan. 1991. *Once Upon a Future Time: Studies in a Buddhist Prophecy of Decline*. Berkeley: Asian Humanities.

Nebesky-Wojkowitz, Rene. 1956. *Oracles and Demons of Tibet*. The Hague: Mouton.

Norman, K. R. 1991. "The Role of the Layman according to the Jain Canon." *The Assembly of Listeners: Jains in Society*. Michael Carrithers and Caroline Humphrey, editors. New York: Cambridge University Press. 31–49.

Obeyesekere, Gananath. 1963. "The Great Tradition and Little in the Perspective of Sinhalese Buddhism." *Journal of Asian Studies* 22 (2): 139–153.

Obeyesekere, Gananath. 1964. "The Buddhist Pantheon in Ceylon and Its Extensions." *Theravāda Buddhism: Anthropological Studies*. Manning Nash, editor. New Haven: Yale University Press. 1–26.

Obeyesekere, Gananath. 1968. "Theodicy, Sin, and Salvation in a Sociology of Buddhism." *Dialectic in Practical Religion*. Edmund Leach, editor. Cambridge: Cambridge University Papers in Anthropology 5. 7–40.

Obeyesekere, Gananath. 1969. "The Ritual Drama of the *Sanni* Demons: Collective Representations of Disease in Ceylon." *Comparative Studies in Society and History* 11: 174–216.

Obeyesekere, Gananath. 1972. "Religious Symbolism and Political Change in Ceylon." *The Two Wheels of Dharma*. Bardwell Smith, editor. Missoula: American Academy of Religion. 58–78.

Obeyesekere, Gananath. 1984. *The Cult of the Goddess Pattini*. Chicago: University of Chicago Press.

Obeyesekere, Ranjini. 1991. *Jewels of the Doctrine: Stories of the Saddharma Ratnavaliya*. Albany: State University Press of New York.

O'Connor, Stanley J. 1974. "Buddhist Votive Tablets and Caves in Penninsular Thailand." *Art and Archaeology in Thailand*. M. C. Subhadradis Diskul, editor. Bangkok: Fine Arts Department. 67–84.

O'Connor, Stanley J. 1975. "A Metal Mould for the Manufacture of Clay Buddhist Votive *Stūpa*s." *Journal of the Malaysia Branch of the Royal Asiatic Society* 48 (2): 60–63.

O'Flaherty, Wendy Doniger. 1989. "Impermanence and Eternity in Indian Art and Myth." *Contemporary Indian Tradition*. Carla M. Borden, editor. Washington, D.C.: Smithsonian Institution Press.

Ortner, Sherry B. 1978. *Sherpas through Their Rituals*. New York: Cambridge University Press.

Ortner, Sherry B. 1989. *High Religion: A Cultural and Political History of Sherpa Buddhism*. Princeton: Princeton University Press.

Overmyer, Daniel L. 1976. *Folk Buddhist Religion: Dissenting Sects in Late Traditional China*. Cambridge: Harvard University Press.

Owens, Bruce. 1989. "The Politics of Divinity in the Kathmandu Valley: The Festival of Bunga Dya/Rato Matsyendranath." Ph.D. dissertation, Columbia University.

Pardue, Peter A. 1971. *Buddhism*. New York: Macmillan.

Paul, Diane Y. 1985. *Women in Buddhism: Images of the Feminine in the Mahāyāna Tradition*. Berkeley: University of California Press.

Piker, Steven, editor. 1975. *The Psychological Study of Theravāda Societies*. Leiden: E. J. Brill.

Poussin, Louis de La Vallee. 1937. "Staupikam." *Harvard Journal of Asiatic Studies* 2: 276–289.

Prebish, Charles S., editor. 1975a. *Buddhism: A Modern Perspective*. University Park: Pennsylvania State University Press.

Prebish, Charles S. 1975b. *Buddhist Monastic Discipline: The Sanskrit Pratimoksa Sūtras of the Mahasamghikas and Mulasarvastivadins*. University Park: Pennsylvania State University Press.

Pye, Michael. 1971. "Syncretism and Ambiguity." *Numen* 18 (2): 83–93.

Pye, Michael. 1978. *Skillful Means: A Concept in Mahāyāna Buddhism*. London: Duckworth.

Queen, Christopher S., and King, Sallie B., editors. *Engaged Buddhism: Buddhist Liberation Movements in Asia*. Albany: State University of New York Press.

Ramanujan, A. K. 1990. "Who Needs Folklore? The Relevance of Oral Traditions to South Asian Studies." South Asia occasional papers, no. 1, University of Hawaii, 1–32.

Ramble, Charles. 1990. "How Buddhist Are Buddhist Communities? The Construction of Tradition in Two Lamaist Villages." *Journal of the Anthropological Society of Oxford* 21 (2): 185–197.

Ray, Reginald A. 1990. "Buddhism: Sacred Text Written and Realized." *The Holy Book in Comparative Perspective*. Frederick M. Denny and Rodney L. Taylor, editors. Columbia: University of South Carolina Press.

Ray, Reginald A. 1994. *Buddhist Saints in India*. New York: Oxford University Press.

Reader, Ian. 1991. *Religion in Contemporary Japan*. Honolulu: University of Hawaii Press.

Reynolds, F. 1972a. "Buddhism and the Anthropologists: Some Comments concerning Recent Works on Southeast Asia." *History of Religions* 12: 303–314.

Reynolds, F. 1972b. "From Philology to Anthropology: A Bibliographical Essay on Works Related to Early, Theravāda, and Sinhalese Buddhism." *The Two Wheels of Dharma*. Bardwell Smith, editor. Missoula: American Academy of Religion. 107–121.

Reynolds, F. 1972c. "The Two Wheels of Dharma: A Study of Early Buddhism." *The Two Wheels of Dharma: Essays on the Theravāda Tradition in India and Ceylon*.

Bardwell L. Smith, editor. Chambersburg, PA: American Academy of Religion.

Reynolds, F. 1973. "Sacral Kingship and National Development: The Case of Thailand." *Contributions to Asian Studies* 4: 40–50.

Reynolds, F. 1977. "Civil Religion and National Community in Thailand." *Journal of Asian Studies* 36 (2): 267–282.

Reynolds, F. 1981. *Guide to the Buddhist Religion*. Boston: G. K. Hall.

Rhys-Davids, Caroline F. 1901. "Notes on the Early Economic Conditions in Northern India." *Journal of the Royal Asiatic Society* 53: 859–888.

Rhys-Davids, Thomas W. 1963. *The Questions of King Milinda*. New York: Dover.

Rhys-Davids, Thomas W. 1969. *Buddhist Suttas*. New York: Dover.

Richardson, Hugh, editor. 1986. *Adventures of a Tibetan Fighting Monk*. Bangkok: Tamarind Press.

Rimpoche, Tenga. 1990. "The Benefits of Building a *Stūpa*." *Vajradhatu Sun* (fall): 23–25.

Robinson, Richard H. 1966. "The Ethic of the Householder Bodhisattva." *Bharati* 9 (2): 25–26.

Samuel, Geoffrey. 1994. *Civilized Shamans: Buddhism in Tibetan Societies*. Washington, DC: Smithsonian Institution Press.

Sangharakshita, Bhikshu. 1959. "Ordination and Initiation in the Three Yanas." *The Middle Way* 34 (3): 94–104.

Sarksiyanz, Manuel. 1970. "The Social Ethics of Buddhism and Socio-Economic Development in Southeast Asia." *Asian and African Studies* 6: 7–21.

Schopen, Gregory. 1975. "The Phrase 'sa prthivīpradeśaṣ caityabhūto bhavet' in the *Vajracchedikā*: Notes on the Cult of the Book in Mahāyāna." *Indo-Iranian Journal* 17: 147–181.

Schopen, Gregory. 1984. "Filial Piety and the Monk in the Practice of Indian Buddhism: A Question of 'Sinicization' Viewed from the Other Side." *T'oung Pao* 70: 110–126.

Schopen, Gregory. 1987. "Burial 'ad sanctos' and the Physical Presence of the Buddha in Early Indian Buddhism: A Study in the Archaeology of Relations." *Religion* 17: 193–225.

Schopen, Gregory. 1989. "The *Stūpa* Cult and the Extant Pali *Vinaya*." *Journal of the Pali Text Society* 13: 83–100.

Schopen, Gregory. 1991a. "Monks and the Relic Cult in the Mahaparinibbanasutta: An Old Misunderstanding in Regard to Monastic Buddhism." *From Benares to Beijing: Essays on Buddhism and Chinese Religion in Honor of Jan Yun-hua*. G. Schopen and K. Shinohara, editors. Oakville, Ont.: Mosaic Press. 187–201.

Schopen, Gregory. 1991b. "An Old Inscription from Amaravati and the Cult of the Local Monastic Dead in Indian Buddhist Monasteries." *Journal of the International Association of Buddhist Studies* 14 (2): 281–329.

Schopen, Gregory. 1991c. "The Ritual Obligations and Donor Roles of Monks in the Pali *Vinaya*." *Journal of the Pali Text Society* 16: 1–21.

Schopen, Gregory. 1991d. "Archaeology and Protestant Assumptions in the Study of Indian Buddhism." *History of Religions* 31 (1): 1–23.

Schopen, Gregory. 1992a. "On Avoiding Ghosts and Social Censure: Monastic Funerals in the *Mulasarvastivada-Vinaya*." *Journal of Indian Philosophy* 20: 1–39.

Schopen, Gregory. 1992b. "*Stūpa* and *Tirtha*: Tibetan Mortuary Practices and an Unrecognized Form of Burial ad Sanctos at Buddhist Sites in India," in press.

Schopen, Gregory. 1994. "Doing Business for the Lord: Lending on Interest and Written Contracts in the Mulasarvastivadin Vinaya." *Journal of the American Oriental Society* 114: 527–554.

Schopen, Gregory. 1996. "The Lay Ownership of Monasteries and the Role of the Monk in Mulasarvastivadin Monasticism." *Journal of the International Association of Buddhist Studies* 19 (1): 81–126.

Seckel, Dietrich. 1964. *The Art of Buddhism*. New York: Crown.

Shukla, N. S. 1975. "The Qualities of an Ācārya on the Basis of the Ācāryakriyasamuccaya of Jagaddarpana." *Buddhist Studies in India*. R. C. Pandeva, editor. New Delhi: Monohar. 126–129.

Siiger, Halfdan. 1967. *The Lepchas: Culture and Religion of a Himalayan People*. Copenhagen: National Museum of Denmark.

Sivaraksa, Sulak. 1992. *Seeds of Peace, a Buddhist Vision for Renewing Society*. Berkeley: Parallax Press.

Sizemore, Russell F., and Donald K. Swearer. 1990. *Ethics, Wealth, and Salvation: A Study in Buddhist Social Ethics*. Columbia: University of South Carolina Press.

Skilling, Peter. 1992. "The Rakṣā Literature of the Śrāvakayāna." *Journal of the Pali Text Society* 16: 109–182.

Smith, Bardwell L. 1964. "Toward a Buddhist Anthropology: The Problem of the Secular." *Journal of the American Academy of Religion* 32: 203–216.

Smith, Bardwell L., editor. 1972. *The Two Wheels of Dharma*. Missoula: American Academy of Religion.

Smith, Bardwell. 1992. "Buddhism and the Abortion in Contemporary Japan: *Mizuko Kuyo* and the Confrontation with Death." *Buddhism, Sexuality, Gender*. José Ignacio Cabezon, editor. Albany: State University Press of New York. 65–89.

Snellgrove, David S. 1957. *Buddhist Himalaya*. Oxford: Cassirer.

Snellgrove, David S. 1959. "The Notion of Divine Kingship in Tantric Buddhism." *Studies in the History of Religions* 4: 204–218.

Snellgrove, David S. 1966. "For a Sociology of Tibetan Speaking Regions." *Central Asiatic Journal* 11 (3): 199–219.

Snellgrove, David S. 1967. *Four Lamas of Dolpo*. Oxford: Cassirer.

Snellgrove, David S. 1973. "The Śākyamuni's Final Nirvāna." *Bulletin of the School of Oriental and African Studies* 36: 399–411.

Snellgrove, David S. 1987. *Indo-Tibetan Buddhism*. Boulder: Shambala Press.

Snellgrove, David and Hugh Richardson. 1980. *A Cultural History of Tibet*. Boulder: Prajna Press.

Snellgrove, David L. and Tadeusz Skorupski. 1977. *The Cultural Heritage of Ladakh, Volume 1*. New Delhi: Vikas.

Snodgrass, A. 1985. *The Symbolism of the Stūpa*. New York: Cornell University Press.

Spencer, Robert F. 1966. "Ethical Expressions in a Burmese *Jātaka*." *Journal of American Folklore* 79: 278–301.

Spiro, Melford E. 1966. "Buddhism and Economic Action in Burma." *American Anthropologist* 68: 1163–1173.

Spiro, Melford E. 1982. *Buddhism and Society*. 2nd edition. Berkeley: University of California Press.

Sponberg, A. 1992. "Attitudes toward Woman and the Feminine in Early Buddhism." *Buddhism, Sexuality, Gender*. José Ignacio Cabezon, editor. Albany: State University Press of New York. 3–36.

Stablein, William. 1973. "A Medical-Cultural System among the Tibetan and Newar Buddhists: Ceremonial Medicine." *Kailash* 1 (3): 193–203.

Stablein, William. 1976. "Mahakala the Neo-Shaman: Master of the Ritual." *Spirit Possession in the Nepal Himalayas*. John Hitchcock and Rex L. Jones, editors. Warminster, Eng.: Aris and Phillips Ltd. 316–325.

Stablein, William. 1976. "A Descriptive Analysis of the Content of Nepalese Buddhist *Pūjās* as a Medical-Cultural System, with References to Tibetan Parallels." *The Realm of the Extrahuman: Ideas and Actions*. Agehananda Bharati, editor. The Hague: Mouton. 403–411.

Strenski, Ivan. 1983. "On Generalized Exchange and the Domestication of the *Saṅgha*." *Man*, n.s., 18: 463–477.

Strickmann, Michel. 1990. "The Consecration *Sūtra*: A Buddhist Book of Spells." *Chinese Buddhist Apocrypha*. Robert Buswell, Jr., editor. Honolulu: University of Hawaii Press. 75–118.

Strong, John S. 1979. "The Transforming Gift: An Analysis of Devotional Acts of Offering in Buddhist *Avadāna* Literature." *History of Religions* 18 (3): 221–237.

Strong, John S. 1983. *The Legend of King Aśoka*. Princeton: Princeton University Press.

Strong, John S. 1990. "Rich Man, Poor Man, Bhikkhu, King: Aśoka's Great Quinquennial Festival and the Nature of *Dāna*." *Ethics, Wealth, and Salvation: A Study in Buddhist Social Ethics*. Russell F. Sizemore and Donald K. Swearer, editors. Columbia: University of South Carolina Press. 107–123.

Strong, John S. 1992. *The Legend and Cult of Upagupta: Sanskrit Buddhism in North India and Southeast Asia*. Princeton: Princeton University Press.

Suksamran, Somboon. 1977. *Political Buddhism in Southeast Asia*. London: C. Hurst.

Swearer, Donald K. 1970. "Lay Buddhism and the Buddhist Revival in Ceylon." *Journal of the American Academy of Religion* 28 (3): 255–275.

Swearer, Donald K. 1976. *Wat Haripuñjaya*. Missoula: Scholars Press.

Swearer, Donald K. 1987. "Buddhist Religious Year." *The Encyclopedia of Religion*. Mircea Eliade, editor. 2: 547–554.

Swearer, Donald K. 1990. "Fundamentalistic Movements in Theravada Buddhism." *Fundamentalisms Observed*. Martin E. Marty and R. Scott Appleby, editors. Chicago, IL: University of Chicago Press. 628–690.

Swearer, Donald K. 1995. *The Buddhist World of Southeast Asia*. Albany: State University of New York Press.

Taddei, Maurizio. 1970. "Inscribed Clay Tablets and Miniature *Stūpas* from Gazni." *East and West* 20: 70–84.

Takakusu, J. 1982. *A Record of the Buddhist Religion*. Ann Arbor, MI: University Microfilms International. (Originally published 1896)

Tambiah, Stanley J. 1968a. "The Ideology of Merit and the Social Correlates of Buddhism in a Thai Village." *Dialectic in Practical Religion*. E. Leach, editor. Cambridge Papers in Social Anthropology 5. London: Cambridge University Press.

Tambiah, Stanley J. 1968b. "Literacy in a Buddhist Village in Northeast Thailand." *Literacy in Traditional Societies*. J. Goody, editor. New York: Cambridge University Press. 86–131.

Tambiah, Stanley J. 1970. *Buddhism and the Spirit Cults of Northeast Thailand*. London: Cambridge University Press.

Tambiah, Stanley J. 1973a. "Buddhism and This-Worldly Activity." *Modern Asian Studies* 7 (1): 1–20.

Tambiah, Stanley J. 1973b. "The Persistence and Transformation of Tradition in Southeast Asia, with Special Reference to Thailand." *Daedalus* 102 (1): 55–84.

Tambiah, Stanley J. 1976. *World Conqueror and World Renouncer: A Study of Buddhism and Polity in Thailand against a Historical Background.* New York: Cambridge University Press.

Tambiah, Stanley J. 1977. "The Galactic Polity: The Structure of Traditional Kingdoms in Southeast Asia." *Annals of the New York Academy of Sciences* 293: 67–97.

Tambiah, Stanley J. 1978. "Saṅgha and Polity in Modern Thailand: An Overview." *Religion and Legitimation of Power in Thailand, Laos and Burma.* Bardwell Smith, editor. Chambersburg, PA: Anima Books. 111–133.

Tambiah, Stanley J. 1984. *Buddhist Saints of the Forest and the Cult of Amulets.* New York: Cambridge University Press.

Tambiah, Stanley J. 1985. "Purity and Auspiciousness at the Edges of the Hindu Context—In Theravāda Buddhist Societies." *Purity and Auspiciousness in Indian Society.* John B. Carman and Frederique A. Marglin, editors. Leiden: E. J. Brill. 94–108.

Tambiah, Stanley J. 1986. *Sri Lanka: Ethnic Fratricide and the Dismantling of Democracy.* Chicago: University of Chicago Press.

Tambiah, Stanley J. 1992. *Buddhism Betrayed? Religion, Politics, and Violence in Sri Lanka.* Chicago: University of Chicago Press.

Teiser, Stephen F. 1988. *The Ghost Festival in Medieval China.* Princeton: Princeton University Press.

Thera, Nyanaponika. 1970. *The Heart of Buddhist Meditation.* New York: Samuel Weiser.

Thomas, Edward J. 1951. *The History of Buddhist Thought.* London: Routledge and Kegan Paul.

Toffin, Gerard. 1984. *Societe et religion chez les Newar du Nepal.* Paris: CNRS.

Tucci, Guiseppe. 1931. "The Sea and Land Routes of a Buddhist Sadhu in the Sixteenth Century." *Indian Historical Quarterly* 7 (4): 683–702.

Tucci, Guiseppe. 1988. *Stūpa: Art, Architectonics and Symbolism (Indo-Tibetica I).* English translation in *Sata-Pitaka Series* #347. Lokesh Chandra, editor. New Delhi: Aditya Prakashan.

Wadley, Susan S. 1983. "*Vrats*: Transformers of Destiny." *Karma: An Anthropological Inquiry.* Charles F. Keyes and E. Valentine Daniel, editors. Berkeley: University of California Press. 147–162.

Warder, A. K. 1970. *Indian Buddhism.* New Delhi: Motilal Barnassidass.

Warren, Henry Clarke. 1922. *Buddhism in Translations.* Cambridge: Harvard University Press.

Wayman, Alex. 1971. "Buddhism." *Historia Religionum* 2: 372–464.

Wayman, Alex. 1984. "The Sarvarahasyatantra." *Acta Indologica* 6: 521–569.

Welch, Holmes. 1965–1966. "Buddhist Organizations in Hong Kong." *Journal of the Hong Kong Branch of the Royal Asiatic Society* 1: 98–114.

Welch, Holmes. 1967. *The Practice of Chinese Buddhism: 1900–1950.* Cambridge: Harvard University Press.

Welch, Holmes. 1972. *Buddhism under Mao.* Cambridge: Harvard University Press.

Wijayaratna, Mohan. 1990. *Buddhist Monastic Life.* New York: Cambridge University Press.

Williams, Paul. 1989. *Mahāyāna Buddhism: The Doctrinal Foundations.* New York: Routledge.

Willis, Janice D. 1985. "Nuns and Benefactresses: The Role of Women in the Development of Buddhism." *Religion and Social Change.* Yvonne Haddad and Ellison Findly, editors. Albany: State University of New York Press.

Wright, Arthur F. 1959. *Buddhism in Chinese History.* Stanford: Stanford University Press.

Yalman, Nur. 1964. "The Structure of Sinhalese Healing Rituals." *Religion in South Asia.* Edward Harper, editor. Seattle: University of Washington Press. 115–150.

Zelliot, Eleanor. 1966. "Buddhism and Politics in Maharastra." *South Asian Politics and Religion.* Donald E. Smith, editor. Princeton: Princeton University Press.

Zelliot, Eleanor. 1992. "Buddhist Women of the Contemporary Maharashtrian Conversion Movement." *Buddhism, Sexuality, Gender.* José Ignacio Cabezon, editor. Albany: State University Press of New York. 91–107.

Zurcher, Erik. 1972. *The Buddhist Conquest of China.* Leiden: E. J. Brill.

Zurcher, Erik. 1987. "Buddhism in China." *The Encyclopedia of Religion.* Mircea Eliade, editor. New York: Macmillan. 2: 414–421.

Zysk, Keneth G. 1991. *Asceticism and Healing in Ancient India: Medicine in the Buddhist Monastery.* New York: Oxford University Press.

14

THE PILGRIMAGE TO MAGDALENA

Mary I. O'Connor

Until quite recently, anthropologists have not regarded pilgrimages as objects of research despite clear indications of their importance, historically and in the present, in both simple and complex societies (Bowman, in Jha 1985: 1–3; Morinis 1984: 3–4). This lack of interest stemmed at least in part from the post-Boasian emphasis on economic and political elements as the independent variables controlling belief systems in general and religion in particular (O'Connor 1989a: 34; Bowman, in Jha 1985: 2–3).

The study of pilgrimages has also suffered from the constraints of ordinary academic life, which tend to influence dramatically the scope of scholarly research (Bourdieu 1981). By their very nature as transitory, if regularly occurring, cultural phenomena, pilgrimages are difficult to study extensively in the one- or two-year period that characterizes the bulk of anthropological field research. Because pilgrimages tend to be short in duration, it is not possible to study them intensively over a long stretch of time. The necessity to observe a pilgrimage several times over a period of years makes it almost impossible to study within the ordinary academic frame of reference.

The result of these forces at work has been that anthropologists study aspects of pilgrimages but never a pilgrimage in its entirety. The number and variety of pilgrimage traditions, each with its own religious, social, political, and economic contexts, make anything approaching cross-cultural analysis hazardous at best. The process of sorting out the global whole is just beginning (Morinis 1992). The pilgrimage to Magdalena provides a basis for analyzing existing theoretical and methodological constructs. This analysis also contributes to the growing store of case studies.

BACKGROUND

The shrine at Magdalena, Sonora, Mexico, is the center of a regional cult as defined by Werbner (1977: xi–xvii) and is comparable to that described by Sallnow (1987). It is distinct from community-based religious shrines in that it draws pilgrims from a variety of different communities. It is unlike more important shrines such as that of the Virgin of Guadalupe, near Mexico City, in that the pilgrims to Magdalena come from a well-defined and fairly circumscribed geographical area, the Sonoran Desert. This has been the case since the earliest reported pilgrimages (Bartlett 1854: 425; Dobyns 1960: 159–163).

Earlier observers of the Magdalena fiesta have noted that Yaqui and Papago Indians[1] are visible minorities among the pilgrims (Dobyns 1960; Griffith 1967; Nabhan 1982). There were members of these two Native American groups, as well as Mayos, present at the fiestas I have observed. It is now also possible to distinguish between Mexican and Mexican-American pilgrims. Thus, the Magdalena pilgrimage has been and remains a multiethnic event in which people of substantially different cultural traditions come together to honor a religious symbol they all venerate.

The tradition of pilgrimages to Magdalena was clearly established by 1851 (Bartlett 1854: 424) and may well date from earlier times. Dobyns's 1960 dissertation on Magdalena provides a baseline for comparison with contemporary pilgrimages to the site. By way of explication of the festival, Dobyns proposes a functional analysis that, though useful as an organizational tool, is not really an explanation.[2] James Griffith has been an observer of the Magdalena pilgrimage for many years. His most recent work (1992) provides excellent descriptions of the origin myths about the saint and of the variety of beliefs about his spiritual power. These contemporary myths and beliefs are in many respects identical to those reported by Bartlett (1854: 424, 427) on his 1851 visit to Magdalena. The similarity of such folk beliefs over time, given the lack of any texts to support them, demonstrates a remarkable continuity. Like Dobyns's work, Griffith's provides a basis for comparison with my own research, and this makes Magdalena unusual: Few pilgrimage sites have been studied so extensively in the past, and the additional time depth made possible by these authors helps to overcome, at least in part, the limitations imposed by the temporary nature of the festival.

THE MAGDALENA FIESTA

The pilgrimage to Magdalena is centered upon the life-size plaster statue of the Catholic saint Francis Xavier; this statue is located in the church in the center of the town of Magdalena (population: approximately 40,000). The original church, a small chapel subordinate to the larger mission at San Ignacio, was founded in 1687 by Eusebio Kino, a Jesuit missionary who converted many of the indigenous peoples of present-day Sonora and Arizona (Bolton 1984: 262). The church fell into ruins after 1767, when the Jesuits were expelled from

Spanish territory, and was rebuilt during the nineteenth century by the Franciscans, who replaced the Jesuits (Dobyns, in Crumrine and Morinis 1991: 60; Murphy 1966: 93; Griffith 1992: 37). Kino's body was discovered buried near the church during a construction project in 1966 (Murphy 1966: 89); it is now enshrined in situ and has also become an object of veneration (Griffith 1992: 38).

The fact that there are two important St. Francises in the Catholic belief system and the presence of Kino's shrine at the site make for a certain amount of ambiguity, or multivocality, of the central symbols of the festival. St. Francis Xavier was a forceful Jesuit missionary who traveled all over the world converting native peoples, while St. Francis of Assisi was a pacifist monk. The confusion, or combination, of traits of these two saints at Magdalena is discussed at length by Griffith (1992: 35–43). Reproductions of the statue are sold at stands near the church; both Franciscan and Jesuit versions are available. In addition, although the official position of the Church is that the saint is St. Francis Xavier, the festival is held on the feast day of St. Francis of Assisi, October 4. When queried during my fieldwork, most pilgrims replied that the saint is Francis Xavier; however, other observers report that pilgrims variously believe the saint to be Francis Xavier, Francis of Assisi, or Father Kino. Some are said to believe that Kino and Xavier are one and the same (Nabhan 1982: 114; Williamson 1950: 4–5; Griffith 1992: 38–39).

This variety of beliefs about the saint is an example of folk Catholicism and is frowned on by the orthodox Catholic clergy. When I interviewed the pastor of the Magdalena church, who had been appointed in 1982,[3] he emphasized that the Church position is that St. Francis Xavier is the saint and that the behavior of the pilgrims was not derived from any formal teachings of the Catholic Church. He professed to be mystified at the importance of physical pain and hardship that characterizes many of the vows made and completed by pilgrims. He could not understand why they did not do something more "positive," such as getting married by a priest or going to Mass and communion regularly. In other words, he saw no value in the folk behavior and wished that people would be more orthodox. He also said that he was trying to change the day of the fiesta from October 4 (the day of St. Francis of Assisi) to the correct day, that of St. Francis Xavier, on December 3. The priest said that he had nothing to do with the rituals of the pilgrims and that his role during the fiesta was to officiate at the Masses and other ceremonies of the formal Church. The schedule for these ceremonies is the same as for any other day, and currently no special rituals are performed by the clergy in honor of the festival.

This disdain for folk Catholicism can be found in the communities of origin of the pilgrims as well: The Papago woman whose journey is described by Nabhan (1982: 115) reported that the parish priest in her home community discouraged her pilgrimage, saying it was not necessary. His opinion was clearly not as important as the folk belief that calamity will befall the person who does not repay the saint for services rendered (Griffith 1992: 39–40).

Although Brown (1981) and Morinis (1984: 242; 263–267) have both criticized the notion of "little" and "great" religious traditions formulated by Redfield (1956: 50–59), both Dobyns (1960: 4, 88) and Sallnow (1987: 5–6) have
demonstrated its usefulness in comprehending Catholicism in Latin America.
My description of folk Catholic beliefs versus orthodox beliefs at Magdalena is
an example of the linkage between the little and great traditions. The apparent
gulf between orthodox and folk beliefs at Magdalena is closed by the fact that
both the orthodox and the folk versions of events recognize the saint as a powerful spiritual being. An attitude of mutual tolerance here, as in many other
religious contexts throughout Mexico, makes possible the simultaneous occurrence of events that are accepted and interpreted in different ways by a variety
of believers.

The religious behaviors associated with the veneration of the saint are as
varied as the beliefs of the people. These behaviors range from merely touching
the statue, to placing near or on the saint a small metal object (a *milagro*, or
ex-voto) representing some desired thing or event, to walking from the U.S.–
Mexico border, sixty miles north of the town, or from the city of Hermosillo,
approximately one hundred miles to the south. Between these extremes of ease
and difficulty of the task of pilgrimage is a vast array of acts. These include the
wearing of *hábitos*, brown or black garments, during the fiesta, the passing of
objects over the saint or under his head to make them holy, and the hiring of a
mariachi band to play "Las Mañanitas" (the Spanish equivalent of "Happy
Birthday") to the saint at dawn on October 4, the saint's "birthday."

The behavior that most resembles that of the classic pilgrimage, the trip on
foot, takes several days and includes visits to shrines along the road. One pilgrim's account of the journey from the border describes a trip of five days,
during which the group of three received free food from several people and
camped along the road at night (Laguna 1950). Griffith (1992: personal communication) knows a woman who provides food and drink to such pilgrims
every year.

Most of this behavior represents a payment to the saint for favors done for
the pilgrim or a relative of the pilgrim. Many pilgrims make specific vows to
the saint in return for the curing of illness. For example, among the pilgrims I
interviewed, 49 percent gave as the reason for their pilgrimage the healing of
some illness. Tooker (1950: 9) reports the belief among pilgrims that touching
the saint and then an afflicted area of the pilgrim's body brings relief. Touching
the saint with an afflicted limb can also bring about a cure.

Regardless of their specific reasons for going on the pilgrimage, all the pilgrims touch the saint, lifting the head of the saint and sometimes kissing the
face. Many people believe that by lifting the head they prove that they "believe
in the saints" and that an inability to lift the head proves that they are not
believers. In my observation of hundreds of pilgrims, I have never seen one
who was unable to lift the head. Nevertheless, Griffith reports myths in which

strong men have wept because they could not lift the saint's head (Griffith 1992: personal communication).

Dobyns (1960: 134–136) estimates that 20,000 people attended the 1957 festival. This is twice the number of inhabitants of the town at that time, and although residents do participate in the fiesta, I have found that they comprise a tiny minority of the total number of participants. My estimates of attendance, based on the size of the crowd in the central plaza at various times during the festival, show considerable variation from year to year. In 1982, I estimated 10,000 pilgrims. In 1983, this number was cut at least in half by devastating floods in Arizona and Sonora. In 1984, the crowd was larger than in 1983 but smaller than in 1982. Because the saint's day was on a weekend in 1987, the crowd that year was larger than during any of the previous years I was present— approximately 15,000 people.

I expected the crowd size in 1992 to be similar to that in 1987, because in both years the saint's day was on a weekend. In 1992, however, I estimated the size of the crowd at peak hours to be between 4,000 and 5,000—less than half the number in 1987. My preliminary explanation for this is the economic recession plaguing both sides of the border at the time. The number of people selling goods and services did not change so dramatically—there were simply fewer people buying. In any event, crowd size can be said to fluctuate considerably from year to year. Even in years when the crowd is relatively small, however, the festival literally takes over the town, making ordinary activities difficult, if not impossible, for the residents.

THEORETICAL PERSPECTIVES

In his wide-ranging and seminal article "Pilgrimages as Social Processes" (1974), Turner discusses several social phenomena he believes to be generally characteristic of pilgrimages in complex societies. Voluntary participation, rather than the socially imposed participation that characterizes most religious behavior, is one of these. Another is the temporary nature of the pilgrim's journey. Although it is true that some pilgrimages in history and literature appear to last a lifetime, the supposition at the outset is that the pilgrim will at some point return to his or her home community. Pilgrims leave the normal daily life of the home and go into the unknown and unpredictable world outside, on a journey to a sacred place. In most instances, the journey itself takes on a sacred quality.

This combination of unpredictability and the sacred, according to Turner, makes the pilgrimage experience one of liminality, or antistructure. Liminality is characterized by a lack of socially structured relationships, by role reversals, by a norm of equality that replaces the hierarchy of everyday experience, and by a sense of mystery in the unpredictable nature of the individual's experience. In the case of pilgrimages, Turner sees liminality expressed in the form of *communitas*, a feeling of shared identity among people who in most ordinary situations would be strangers to each other. Specifically, *communitas* on pilgrimages "liberates the individual from the obligatory everyday constraints of status and role, defines him as an integral human being with a capacity for free choice, and . . . presents for him a living model of human brotherhood and sisterhood" (1974: 207).

A final characteristic Turner identifies in pilgrimages is the existence of catchment areas that help to define shrines as local, regional, national, and international. A local shrine's catchment area is limited to the local community. Regional shrines attract pilgrims from several or many local communities, while national and international pilgrimages have much larger catchment areas. Turner also suggests that there is a tendency for religious shrines to be perceived as ranked in order of importance in such societies and that the size of the area from which pilgrims are drawn to a shrine is an indication of the locality's place in such a hierarchy.

The notion of typologies from simplest to most complex can also be found in the work of Bhardwaj (1973) and others. If nothing else, this idea is helpful in understanding levels of social complexity as revealed by religious behavior. As Morinis (1984: 234–238) aptly points out, however, most pilgrimage traditions are too multifaceted to be fitted neatly into typologies based on social or religious complexity.[4]

While typologies featuring national or international levels of pilgrimage suffer from oversimplification, it may be appropriate to establish a distinction between local and regional shrines. Werbner's edited volume (1977) has several examples of this distinction and demonstrates the importance of regional shrines in Africa. Magdalena aptly fits the category of regional shrine: Although the beliefs and behaviors of the pilgrims are quite varied, they are comprehensible in ways that traditions encompassing larger areas are not. Shrines such as Lourdes and Mecca draw pilgrims from around the world, and the varieties of traditions associated with them are too complex to be easily understood within a single frame of reference such as a geographical or, as in this case, a cultural as well as geographical catchment area. Sallnow has demonstrated the usefulness of the concept of regional shrines in his analysis of Andean pilgrimage. He agrees with Werbner that regional cults "should be accorded full analytic autonomy, to enable us to attend to their proper, internal relations and processes" (1987: 9).

Morinis (1984: 260–263) dismisses Turner's idea that *communitas* is a universal aspect of the pilgrimage experience and cites numerous examples of divisions within pilgrims' ranks to support his position. Indeed, it might appear from existing literature that *communitas* is *never* to be found in pilgrimages; however, this is perhaps too hasty a conclusion.

As in the case of other aspects of pilgrimage, the question of *communitas* may be more fruitfully studied in the context of the regional shrine. Sallnow, for example, finds that pilgrims from a local community become "brothers and sisters to one another" (Sallnow 1987: 3), thus eliminating the everyday divisions among community members. This equality, in turn, is contrasted with the opposition that develops among local groups in the larger arena of the regional shrine, demonstrating an "equality of opposition rather than the equality of brotherhood" (203). The concept of opposition as an element that reinforces identity is also found in other pilgrimage studies (Pfaffenberger 1979; Bhardwaj 1973; Messerschmidt and Sharma 1981).

In Sallnow's study, this opposition takes the form of ethnic expression (Sallnow 1987: 204–205). The pilgrimage reinforces ethnic boundaries by bringing together into one ritual context people who perceive themselves as ethnically distinct from each other. This is also true of the Magdalena pilgrimage.

Without delving too deeply into the vast literature on ethnic identity, it is possible to state that whether one sees ethnicity as a matter of primordial ties (e.g., Stack 1986) or as a response to external reinforcements (e.g., Roosens 1989), opposition between social groups is a major mechanism for reinforcing ethnic identity. Pilgrimages, then, can provide the context for an expression of ethnicity that may not occur in ethnically homogeneous local communities. At the same time, the pilgrimage site also includes the means to mediate ethnic oppositions: Every pilgrim, regardless of ethnic allegiance, believes in the power of the shrine. The multivocality of the religious symbol serves to include all pilgrims, even those of different religious as well as ethnic identities (cf. Pfaffenberger 1979).

At Magdalena, a combination of this multivocality, the voluntary nature of the pilgrimage, and the lack of either texts or shrine-based social organizations to enforce specific behavior makes for a wide range of individual interpretations of the pilgrimage.

Morinis (1984: 249–255) points out that it is the behavior of individuals that actually brings about the pilgrimage: "The personal motives of the pilgrims themselves are of a wide variety of types—some emotional, many otherwise. . . . The motives and behavior of the participants . . . are the key to understanding the aspects of the religious system which are expressed in pilgrimage" (253). In this context, Turner's point that pilgrimages are voluntary is important. I have commented elsewhere (O'Connor, in press) on the remarkable continuity of the folk Catholic Mayo religious system, given the fact that it is based entirely on vows made voluntarily to specific saints or to God. The Yaqui system is similarly based on individual decisions to participate (Spicer 1980: 202; Moisés 1977: 52–53). The shamanic traditions of the O'odham (Underhill 1938; Nabhan 1982) and the independence of their folk Catholicism from the formal structure of the Church (Dobyns, in Crumrine and Morinis 1991: 56–57) are likewise suited to the voluntary nature of their veneration of Magdalena's regional shrine. Mestizo pilgrims also participate in this folk Catholicism. Indeed, it is the overlap of their beliefs that brings members of the various ethnic categories to Magdalena at the same time every year.

The absence of official documents about the saint or the shrine helps to foster the individual and voluntary aspects of the pilgrimage: There is no "great" pilgrimage tradition associated with the shrine, and so the views of individuals and families, as communicated through the generations, are the paramount authority on the matter. This makes for a variety of beliefs based on many "little" traditions, themselves at least in part distinguishable by ethnic category.

Within these little traditions, individuals make commitments to certain particular behaviors that, cumulatively, carry on and reinforce the belief in and efficacy of the tradition itself. Thus, it is in the dialectic, the interaction between individuals and cultural meanings as they understand them, that we find the explanation for culture, as well as culture change or cultural continuity. This perspective, based on voluntary individual beliefs and actions carried out in a context of mutually agreed upon religious concepts and beliefs about the power of religious beings, is perhaps the only one broad enough to encompass all the variations of pilgrimage. It is, at least, very well suited to the regional shrine at Magdalena.

METHODS

Because of the temporary nature of pilgrimages, it is almost impossible to create the face-to-face relationships that have traditionally characterized long-term fieldwork. The field researcher is therefore confronted with the necessity of going up to strangers and asking them personal questions. The drawbacks inherent in this are obvious: One must expect rejection in various forms as well as the possibility that informants are not telling the truth or are giving only superficial, truncated accounts of their beliefs and behaviors. These limitations demand a certain shallowness in the questions to be put, because people are more likely to give correct and complete answers to such questions as, Where do you come from? than, for example, Why are you here? On the other hand, the fact that the pilgrims are in a strange place where anything may happen, unlike the predictable nature of day-to-day life, may make them more willing to speak candidly with a stranger, who is unlikely to recount the details of the response to other members of their home communities.

Griffith (1992) has demonstrated one solution to these methodological problems. He has maintained contact over many years with people who regularly go on pilgrimages to Magdalena. He has accompanied pilgrims on their journeys and has developed with them the kind of rapport that can only come from such intensive interaction. His work is richly contextualized, and his descriptions of the myths surrounding the saint are superb. His work also suggests some of the limitations of this kind of research. His informants are all from one ethnic group, and he would undoubtedly be uncomfortable in generalizing about other ethnic categories. In addition, he does not address the theoretical issues that are important to me and to other researchers on the topic.

At the other methodological extreme from participant observations such as Griffith's are statistical analyses. These also suffer from limitations on validity and reliability, with the added problem of a lack of cultural context. The conditions for reliability and validity (Cohen and Eames 1982: 28–30) in large surveys can rarely be met in the selection of a population at a pilgrimage site.

The lack of cultural contexts inherent in statistical studies makes it difficult to give meaning to the sometimes impressive quantities of data that are generated by such studies.

These matters are addressed briefly by Bhardwaj (1973: 229–230). He concedes that a random sample of pilgrims was not possible in his study. The question of the validity of his data is not discussed, however. Likewise, Morinis provides a copy of his questionnaire and a brief description of how it was administered, but he does not discuss the methods used to select the informants or the limitations of data gathered in this manner at a pilgrimage site (Morinis 1984: 10).

More recently, Kendall (in Crumrine and Morinis 1991: 139–156) does discuss the limitations inherent in statistical surveys at pilgrimage sites. By carefully choosing his questions and by noting the contextual meanings of his answers, he shows the usefulness of such surveys when properly executed.

Of course, the problems encountered by the naive field researcher at a pilgrimage pale by comparison with the methodological quagmire that some recent writers have created in anthropology. Among the proponents of postmodernism, for example, the matter of the relative appropriateness of participant observation or statistical methods has almost entirely disappeared, replaced by calls for a radical reevaluation of what anthropology is, the nature of reality and its relationship to ethnography, what a field observer should observe, and virtually every aspect of the discipline (see Clifford, in Clifford and Marcus 1986: 1–26; Collin 1985: i–xx).

Geertz's call for a rethinking of anthropological methods (1973), although not the first, was among the most noticed. The plethora of subsequent recommendations on how this should be done (e.g., Pool 1991; Rabinow and Sullivan 1987; Ulin 1991; Fox 1991) can perhaps best be understood in terms of what they oppose: science. Science is a Western construct; by imposing the scientific method on other cultures, we are allowing our own culture to interfere with perception, and the results cannot be true. The role of the ethnographer must at the very least be much more prominently displayed in the ethnography itself. The personal experiences of the fieldworker necessarily affect the product and thus must be described in much more detail than is generally found in ethnographic accounts (Clifford, in Clifford and Marcus 1986: 13). Relexivity, the back-and-forth relationship between observer and observed, must be recognized and included as an essential part of the ethnography (Fox 1991: 75–80).

These views represent a movement away from the materialism and positivism that dominated anthropology in the 1960s, 1970s, and to some extent, the 1980s. In this, postmodernism and other elements of the interpretive approach present a useful critique of anthropological methods. The focus on the role of the ethnographer in the work, the emphasis on cultural context, and the rejection of materialist reductionism all constitute a necessary methodological tonic.

Much of this "antiscience" view can be more accurately seen as anti*scientism*—an objection to the veneer of complete validity and to the absolute "reality'' that scientists often construct. This veneer hides the struggle to define reality that goes on even in the ''hard'' sciences. As the biologist Evelyn Keller notes, language is the ultimate means of categorizing any experience if it is to be conveyed to others (Keller 1992: 305). This applies to physics as much as to anthropology.

Looked at in this light, proponents of the new methods can be seen as asking anthropologists to be good ethnographers instead of bad ones. We are asked to be more forthcoming with the details of everyday life we find in the field. We must let the culture speak in its many voices so that a rich tapestry, rather than a stark model or diagram, is the result of our work. A deeper understanding will come from the presentation of many different perspectives within a given cultural milieu.

Sallnow (1987), Eade and Sallnow (1991: 1–27), and others (Gold 1988; Dahlberg, in Eade and Sallnow 1991) have responded to some of the criticisms raised by proponents of interpretive studies. In the process, they have taken major steps toward creating a methodology for pilgrimage studies.

Gold (1988: 3–22) clearly defines her methods in the description of her fieldwork. She also goes into considerable detail on the personal aspects of her research and how they affected it. Only after she has immersed herself in the cultural meanings of local pilgrimage journeys does she draw back in order to develop her anthropological analysis, rooted in the cultural context of her study.

Like Gold, Sallnow (1987) reveals his own field experiences and how they affected his work. He clearly bases his description of the pilgrimage he studied on the points of view of the villagers whom he accompanied. He uses native categories to describe the Andean religious landscape; this in itself represents a major change in Andean studies. Also like Gold, Sallnow presents an analytical view of the experiences of the people with whom he worked.

These authors discuss in detail their methods, and all of them feature intensive participant observation, including accompanying pilgrims on their journeys, as a major means of documenting the pilgrimage process. Dahlberg (in Eade and Sallnow 1991) breaks new ground by accompanying three separate sets of pilgrims to Lourdes, France. Her research shows that the pilgrimage experience is influenced by the diocesan structure of the Catholic Church in Europe as well as by the self-selection process leading to different pilgrim cohorts. Unlike earlier studies, Dahlberg's work demonstrates the variety of experiences of different groups of pilgrims to the same site, based on their beliefs and expectations, which are in turn shaped by their earlier experiences as pilgrims.

In my own work, I have tried to counterbalance the various strengths and weaknesses inherent in any field research strategy. I have not accompanied pilgrims on their journey. Likewise, I have not conducted fieldwork on the role of the Magdalena pilgrimage in the religious beliefs and behaviors of people in the communities from which pilgrims come, although I have done extensive research in one region of the catchment area (O'Connor 1989a). My five visits to Magdalena have, nonetheless, given me a broader overview than is to be gained from a single visit, even one in which the ethnographer accompanies pilgrims to the site. I have also done considerable archival research on Magdalena and the pilgrimage.

I am acutely aware of my outsider status at Magdalena: I am almost always the only Anglo-American at the fiesta; I am a lone woman; I am not a religious pilgrim. These factors make me an anomaly. I believe that the pilgrimage context itself helps to downplay the importance of my anomalous presence, however. The sense of freedom and adventure that characterizes the pilgrimage experience to some extent allows me to ask questions that would not be acceptable if asked in the context of the local communities where the pilgrims live. Another aspect of my field experiences in Magdalena is my own sense of bewilderment at the complexity of the festival. The ethnic and economic elements of that experience have been my focus so far; even these fairly narrow subjects are part of a whole that almost certainly no single visitor to the festival can analyze without many visits.

On each of my trips, I have noticed things that I had not seen before. For example, the more times I go, the more clear the ethnic markers become. Each time, I am more able to predict certain events and am therefore open to noticing others. Familiarity with one aspect of the fiesta, such as the economic activities in the front of the church, leaves room for awareness of other aspects, such as the activities behind the church. Each year that I am in Magdalena, I find more things that I need to know more about. I suspect that this may become a lifetime effort, as Griffith's seems to be.

I conducted the field research that forms the basis of this chapter in October 1982, 1983, 1984, 1987 and 1992. During these five periods, I observed social interaction among pilgrims and between pilgrims and merchants; I also observed the religious behavior of pilgrims.

In addition to this participant observation, I conducted short, closed-ended interviews with 166 pilgrims. This task was made simple by the fact that during the two days prior to the saint's day there are long lines of pilgrims waiting to visit the shrine. I interviewed every fifth adult pilgrim standing in line at various times of the day on the days when there were pilgrims in line. While this by no means resulted in a random sample, the purposiveness has, I believe, given me a fairly representative group. Still, the superficiality of the questions limits the validity of the information in the answers, which would in themselves be unintelligible without an in-depth understanding of the fiesta as a whole.

In addition to these pilgrim interviews, I conducted closed-ended interviews with thirty-four merchants. The selection of interviewees for these was somewhat haphazard. The goal was to interview purveyors of all the different kinds of goods and services available, rather than a representative sample. The results provide a rough idea of where merchants come from, what they sell, and their views of the pilgrimage.

Finally, I interviewed thirty-two individuals representing four ethnic categories; these interviews were open-ended and lasted from fifteen to forty-five minutes. The interviewees included knowledgeable pilgrims who attend the fiesta yearly, as well as less experienced individuals; I also interviewed merchants. The pastor of the church and his assistant were also interviewed in open-ended sessions.

ETHNIC ASPECTS OF THE FESTIVAL

Observers of the Magdalena pilgrimage have noted that several different ethnic groups are represented at the fiesta, but I have not seen an account of how members of these groups were discerned in the field. I had some difficulty in assigning ethnic identity to individuals at first, and only after interviewing Yaquis and O'odham in their respective camping areas was I able to identify members of these groups in the larger milieu.

Distinct camping areas provide the clearest ethnic markers; they also are the contexts for representing opposition between ethnic groups at the fiesta. The Yaquis charter a train and travel as a cohesive group with a named leader. They camp in and near the train, on the outskirts of town, and in general they remain aloof from other participants in the pilgrimage. Each year there are also thirty to fifty Mayos attending the fiesta. They tend to camp with or near the Yaquis, who are culturally and linguistically similar to them. The O'odham also camp in a distinct area, but they are not such a well-defined group as the Yaquis. They arrive in extended family groups, in pickup campers, which they park in established lots along one street in the town. Most of these lots are enclosed and quite private. O'odham do not have a named leader, and their camping area is very near the center of activity.

The camping areas of the two Indian groups were the key to my estimates of their numbers at the site. Yaqui attendance has varied from approximately 3,000 in 1983, 1984, and 1987 to only about 200 in 1992. The only explanation offered for this precipitous decline in Yaqui attendance was a general lack of money: "No hay billetes." O'odham numbers have remained fairly steady at about 500 to 800, with the exception of 1983, when rains prevented many from making the journey. Only members of these two ethnic groups maintain distinct camping areas at the festival.

Outside of these camping areas, identity markers are subtle, with a few exceptions. One of the clearest of these is language use. O'odham as a rule speak only O'odham and English; Yaquis, though bilingual in Yaqui and Spanish, generally speak Yaqui among themselves. My knowledge of Mayo, which is very similar to Yaqui, enables me to distinguish Yaqui from O'odham. By listening attentively to conversations among pilgrims in line and by standing unobtrusively near people making purchases at the food and game booths, I am able to identify members of these groups in the larger milieu of the fiesta.

From interviews, both closed- and open-ended, emerge certain differences in behavior between O'odham and Yaquis. The principal goal of the Yaquis is visiting the saint, to complete a vow or merely to greet him. Beyond this, Yaquis said that they go to Magdalena to see Yaquis from Arizona, who also go to the fiesta. Two Yaqui informants stated that the various Yaqui communities in Sonora and Arizona were brought together at Magdalena. Several commented that they saw their in-laws at the fiesta only, indicating that bonds of friendship strong enough to lead to bonds of marriage are also forged among the Yaquis during this period. Another reason Yaquis give for going is to buy medicinal herbs, which have been an important product for sale in the past. Entertainment, dancing, and drinking at the fiesta are discouraged.

For O'odham, the main goal is to get their saints blessed and to get a year's supply of holy water. Many O'odham have small statues of Catholic saints; others have images that are specifically made by a few artisans in Magdalena. These are photographs of St. Francis and other saints that are decorated and incorporated into tin frames. Only O'odham buy these images. The saints must be blessed every year; this is done by touching them to the statue of the saint in the church. Holy water, which is used to bless O'odham children and houses every night, is obtained from the church's supply. One O'odham woman gave as her reason for going to Magdalena: "To bless ourselves, to ask the saint to bless us and bless our family—so our home will be more blessed." Thus, O'odham religious behavior is quite different from that of the other pilgrims in that O'odham rarely make vows to the saint.

Unlike the Yaquis, O'odham also go specifically to have a good time. There are several temporary bars set up by merchants along the street where O'odham camp. Itinerant musicians are often found in the bars, in the camping areas, and in the makeshift dining areas on this street. Here, O'odham from different communities meet and greet each other amid a general air of festivity. Although the O'odham camping areas are near the central plaza, this proximity is mainly for their convenience rather than a symbol of togetherness with non-O'odham. The ethnic boundary here is maintained primarily by language: O'odham and English predominate.

The remaining pilgrims, who form the majority by far, do not evince ethnic distinctions among themselves—all speak Spanish and camp near the church or stay in hotels. I characterize these pilgrims as "Mestizos—Mexicans without Indian identities," and "Latinos—Mexicans and Mexican Americans who live in the United States." The word *Mestizo* is problematic. Some people find it pejorative[5] and prefer to be known as Mexicanos—Mexicans. This is the term used by Griffith (1992), but the Indians who live in Sonora consider themselves Mexicanos, too. As there is no term satisfactory to all, I use Mestizo as an etic category for purposes of identifying people who are not clearly Indian. In my survey of pilgrims, I classified 72 percent of the interviewees as Mexican Mestizos.

The main reason Mestizos give for going to Magdalena is to pay a "manda"—a vow to the saint. As one interviewee said, "Si no le pagamos, él nos cobra" (If we don't pay him, he will charge us). The implication is that the saint will bring misfortune to the person who defaults on a vow. In this, Mestizo

beliefs are similar to those of the Yaquis. Some Mestizos, especially those who
live in communities near Magdalena, go only to greet the saint briefly and to
participate in the secular entertainment at the fiesta. This includes special foods
at the numerous stands, as well as dances at night featuring bands from all over
Sonora.

These are the behaviors of the vast majority of the people who go to the
fiesta. They do not perceive themselves as distinct from anyone, and they do
not display ethnic symbols such as those of the Yaquis and the O'odham. Within
this population, Latinos are nearly impossible to recognize. A few words of
English mixed in with Spanish; expensive camping gear; a slight accent in Spanish—these are the kinds of ephemeral indicators of residence in the United
States. In my survey of pilgrims, 3 percent were Latinos. Rather than setting
themselves apart, Latinos blend in with the overall majority; evidently, they do
not wish to stand out.

It is the Native American minorities who set themselves apart. Whether or
not Yaquis and O'odham intentionally create ethnic boundaries is a difficult
question to answer. Intentionality, like *communitas*, may be a construct created
by anthropologists to explain behavior that is not actually purposive (cf. Keller
1992: 299–305). In any event, the result of individual Yaqui and O'odham
decisions is clearly recognizable ethnic distinctions between themselves and the
Mestizo majority. Such boundaries are not nearly so clearly evinced by the
Mestizos. Whatever the intentions of any of these pilgrims, an opposition exists
between each of the two minority populations and the rest of the pilgrims. This
opposition is created and enforced by the Indians rather than the Mestizos.

As for *communitas*, it is difficult to observe and even more so to elicit, especially in a fluid context such as the Magdalena fiesta. I have not observed any
of the indications of *communitas* described by Turner (1974: 168–172). I believe
that a closer rapport with pilgrims in their communities of origin is necessary
to an informed discussion of *communitas* at Magdalena.

ECONOMIC ASPECTS OF THE FESTIVAL

While most people visit the festival for religious purposes, the pilgrims also
provide a market for the merchants who go to Magdalena primarily to sell their
wares. Merely feeding such a population requires numerous food stands, but the
merchants do not limit their offerings to the necessities of life. Religious articles
are of course important. The *milagros, hábitos*, candles, and other articles promised to the saint as part of the vows pilgrims make are all available at the
permanent shops near the church. These shops, which also have the usual complement of religious articles, are run exclusively by Magdalena residents.

Until quite recently, medicinal herbs were an important product sold at Magdalena. Many medicinal herbs are part of folk Catholic traditions, as religious
healing rituals often include the use of herbs. *Yerberas*, women who collect and
sell herbs and who know the medicinal uses for them, as recently as 1987 took

up one whole side of the plaza in front of the church. Here, Yaquis, O'odham, and Latinos were able to buy herbs not readily available in their home areas. In 1992, there was only one *yerbera*. This is consistent with the overall drop in attendance in 1992, the causes of which are not clear. Certainly, the general economic gloom has had some impact on the fiesta.

Immediately in front of the church, along the sidewalks and the lawn of the plaza, and along the streets bordering the plaza, an immense variety of nonreligious goods are to be found in the temporary stands set up for the event. Food, trinkets, balloons, clothing, blankets, pots and pans, and saddles are just a few examples of the items offered for sale. In addition, there are many games of chance and skill, carnival rides, makeshift bars, and wandering musicians who charge by the song.

A less formal arrangement of booths is found in the area behind the church. Here, the products of the local harvests are sold. These include strings of garlic and chiles, honey, pumpkins and squashes, apples, guavas, and a variety of other fruits of the season. Some people also sell cooked corn on the cob, shrimp from the nearby Bahía de Kino, and other ready-to-eat local foods. Unlike the other stands, these have no electricity or gas for cooking, and they are made of locally available materials rather than the sturdier booths of the merchants in the plaza. In some cases, pickup trucks and horse-drawn wagons filled with produce are simply backed into line with the ramshackle booths. In these cases, the local farmers and fisherfolk are taking advantage of a market conveniently available at harvest time.

The merchants who sell in front of the church make more money than the local sellers because they are much more visible. It is in these more well-constructed stalls that products from beyond the Magdalena region are sold. The vendors here are for the most part full-time merchants who go from one festival to another throughout the year.

DISCUSSION

If religious and social aspects of the fiesta help to reinforce ethnic distinctions for certain participants, it is in the marketplace that behaviors tend to be less clearly ethnic in nature. The merchants are all Mestizo, and the Spanish language predominates, although merchants try to oblige O'odham who do not speak Spanish. The O'odham and the Yaquis tend to eat at specific stands near their camping areas, but they seek out other goods that are of universal use at stands also frequented by Mestizos and Latinos. For example, medicinal herbs are in high demand by members of all ethnic categories; likewise, clothing and blankets. Although the Yaquis, when interviewed, stated that they did not visit games or bars, it is possible to see Yaqui men at such entertainments. O'odham freely state that they enjoy the games and bars, and indeed many O'odham are to be found in the pursuit of such pleasures at the fiesta, over and above those taken into their camping area.

It would appear, then, that the economic sphere is where the greatest mixing occurs among people who otherwise remain separate from the general populace of pilgrims. It is in the market area that Yaquis, O'odham, Mestizos, and Latinos can be found seeking the same items for the same reasons—their need for certain goods and the availability of these goods.

In symbolic and religious terms, Magdalena can be categorized as a regional shrine, for it draws pilgrims from a quite well-defined area. Of the pilgrims I interviewed, 95 percent came from Sonora or the states bordering it in Mexico. The remaining 5 percent came from Arizona and New Mexico. These figures accord with Dobyns's report of the 1957 fiesta (Dobyns 1960). The fact that only 4 percent of the pilgrims in my sample were actually from Magdalena demonstrates that this is truly a regional rather than a local shrine.

The merchants, on the other hand, come from a nationwide economic sphere. Of the merchants I interviewed, 42 percent were from areas beyond the region defined by the religious pilgrims. The proveniences of these merchants included places as far as 1,500 miles from Magdalena. Clearly, knowledge of the existence of the market extends beyond the appeal of the religious symbols.

It is the marketplace that provides goods from areas outside the region of the religious pilgrim's provenience. This is especially true of medicinal herbs and other goods not readily available in the larger international market in which all festival-goers participate, to some extent, in their everyday lives. Thus, while the religious symbols call forth pilgrims from a circumscribed region, these same pilgrims provide the market for a much larger economic "catchment area."

CONCLUSION

Many travelers have passed through or near Magdalena without realizing the historic and contemporary religious importance of this place, which appears to be no different from all the other dusty towns along the highway. For the religious pilgrims, however, Magdalena is the home of the powerful San Francisco who grants favors in return for specific ritual payment or who blesses their homes and their children. Belief in the saint's power results in the continuation of the pilgrimage tradition. This tradition has lasted for over one hundred years despite the absence of any formal documents or organizations to promulgate it and despite the lack of Church-sponsored religious rituals conducted expressly in honor of the saint. For many of the merchants who go to sell their wares, Magdalena is one fiesta in an annual round that covers the republic; for others, it is a yearly harvest festival. In the conjunction of these diverse views of the event, the anthropologist finds a rich cultural loam.

Here is a seemingly ephemeral occurrence that is temporary but ongoing. Every year, thousands of people from a well-defined geographical and cultural area participate voluntarily in a ritual drama made up of thousands of individual decisions to perform specific acts. These decisions are made and carried out under the broad religious umbrella of folk Catholicism, which in turn endures precisely by means of these individual acts.

The coming together of so large and ethnically diverse a population is facilitated by the multivocalic character of the shrine. The saint represents a variety of folk beliefs as well as the orthodox mythology of the Catholic Church. Because each individual's particular beliefs about the saint and each act expressing these beliefs is potentially unique, it is the symbol itself that must mediate and incorporate all of these views into a powerful religious whole.

This symbolic unity does not extend to interethnic relations, however. Through clearly demarcated camping areas and language use, Yaquis and O'odham express the ethnic distinctions that separate them from each other and from the Mestizo majority. These distinctions, in turn, are downplayed in the market context, where common economic needs and desires are expressed and filled. Whether *communitas* is characteristic of relations within ethnic or community groups can only be discovered through research based in these groups themselves.

In "Thick Description," Geertz calls for an interpretive approach to ethnography. At the same time (1973: 14–15), he states that anthropology is "a developing system of scientific analysis." This scientific aspect of our field has become buried of late by a blizzard of exhortations to immerse ourselves in discourse, text, and context. In "Deep Play," without abandoning his scientific roots, Geertz writes that "societies, like lives, contain their own interpretations. One has only to learn how to gain access to them" (Rabinow and Sullivan 1987: 240). I believe, along with Geertz, that these interpretations must be scientific if they are to be anthropological. My research on Magdalena has, I believe, resulted in such an interpretation: Only by repeated observations of the pilgrimage have I been able to ascertain and to some extent comprehend the many strands of culture at Magdalena. I cannot foresee, in my lifetime, an end to my study of this fascinating and perplexing subject.

NOTES

1. The people who for many years have been identified as Papagos by anthropologists and others have recently made public their wish to be called Tohon O'odham, or O'odham. The name *Papago* will be used here in referring to publications that use it; otherwise, I will use the name *O'odham*.

2. For a more thorough discussion of Dobyns's study, see Sallnow 1987: 4–6.

3. This priest's name, ironically, is Francisco; however, in true orthodox fashion, he is certain that he is named after St. Francis Xavier.

4. For a more thorough critique of Turner's work, see Morinis (1984: 255–262).

5. See O'Connor (1989b: 107) for a discussion of ethnic terms in Sonora.

REFERENCES

Abu-Lughod, Lila. 1986. *Veiled Sentiments: Honor and Poetry in a Boudouin Society.* Berkeley and Los Angeles: University of California Press.

Bancroft, Hubert Howe. 1886. *History of the North Mexican States and Texas.* Vol. 15 of *The Works of Hubert Howe Bancroft.* San Francisco: History Company.

Barth, Fredrik. 1969. *Ethnic Groups and Boundaries*. Boston: Little, Brown and Company.

Bartlett, John R. 1854. *Personal Narrative of Explorations and Incidents in Texas, New Mexico, California, Sonora, and Chihuahua, Connected with the United States and Mexican Boundary Commission, during the Years 1850, '51, '52, and '53*. Vol. 1. Chicago: Rio Grande Press.

Bhardwaj, Surinder M. 1973. *Hindu Places of Pilgrimage in India; a Study in Cultural Geography*. Berkeley: University of California Press.

Bloch, Maurice. 1989. *Ritual, History and Power: Selected Papers in Anthropology*. London and Atlantic Highlands, NJ: Athlone Press.

Bolton, Herbert. 1984. *Rim of Christendom: A Biography of Eusebio Francisco Kino*. Tucson: University of Arizona Press.

Bourdieu, Pierre. 1981. "The Specificity of the Scientific Field." *French Sociology: Rupture and Revewal since 1968*. Charles C. Lemert, editor. New York: Columbia University Press. 257–292.

Box, Michael James. 1869. *Adventures and Explorations in New and Old Mexico, Being the Record of Ten Years of Travel and Research by Capt. Michael James Box, of the Texas Rangers*. New York: J. Miller.

Brown, Peter. 1981. *The Cult of the Saints: Its Rise and Function in Latin Christianity*. Chicago: University of Chicago Press.

Cámara Barbachando, Fernando, and Teófilo Reyes Couturier. 1972. "Los santuarios y las peregrinaciones, una expresión de relaciones sociales en una sociedad compelja: el caso de México." *Boletín Bibliográfico de Antropología* 35/2 (44): 29–45.

Clifford, James, and George E. Marcus, editors. 1986. *Writing Culture: The Poetics and Politics of Ethnography*. Berkeley: University of California Press.

Cohen, Erik. 1992. "Pilgrimage Centers Concentric and Excentric." *Annals of Tourism Research* 19: 33–50.

Cohen, Eugene N., and Edwin Eames 1982. *Cultural Anthropology*. Boston and Toronto: Little, Brown and Company.

Collin, Fin. 1985. *Theory and Understanding: A Critique of Interpretive Social Science*. Oxford and New York: Basic Blackwell Ltd.

Crumrine, N. Ross. 1978. "The Peruvian Pilgrimage: A Ritual Drama." *Americas* (Washington, D.C.) 30 (8): 28–34.

Crumrine, N. Ross, and Alan Morinis, editors. 1991. *Pilgrimage in Latin America*. Westport, CT: Greenwood Press.

Davies, Horton. 1982. *Holy Days and Holidays, The Medieval Pilgrimage to Compostela*. Lewisburg, PA: Bucknell University Press.

Dobyns, Henry F. 1950. "Papago Pilgrims on the Town." *The Kiva* 16: 27–32.

Dobyns, Henry F. 1960. "The Religious Festival." Ph.D. dissertation, Cornell University.

Dobyns, Henry F. 1972. *The Papago People*. Phoenix: Indian Tribal Series.

Eade, John, and Michael Sallnow, editors. 1991. *Contesting the Sacred: The Anthropology of Christian Pilgrimage*. New York: Routledge.

Engelhardt, Zephyrin. 1899. *The Franciscans in Arizona*. Harbor Springs, MI.

Fox, Richard G., editor. 1991. *Recapturing Anthropology: Working in the Present*. Santa Fe, NM: School of American Research Press.

Geertz, Clifford. 1973. "Thick Description: Toward an Interpretive Theory of Culture."
    In *The Interpretation of Cultures*, by Clifford Geertz. New York: Basic Books.
    3–30.

Geertz, Clifford. 1983. *Local Knowledge: Further Essays in Interpretive Anthropology.*
    New York: Basic Books.

Geiger, Maynard. 1939. *The Kingdom of Saint Francis in Arizona.* Santa Barbara, CA:
    Mission Archives.

Gold, Ann Grodzins. 1988. *Fruitful Journeys: The Ways of Rajasthani Pilgrims.* Berke-
    ley: University of California Press.

Griffith, James. 1967. "Magdalena Revisited: The Growth of a Fiesta." *The Kiva* 33:
    82–86.

Griffith, James. 1988. *Legends and Religious Arts of Magdalena de Kina.* Tucson: South-
    west Folklore Center, University of Arizona.

Griffith, James. 1992. *Beliefs and Holy Places: A Spiritual Geography of the Pimería
    Alta.* Tucson: University of Arizona Press.

Gross, Daniel R. 1971. "Ritual and Conformity: A Religious Pilgrimage to Northeastern
    Brazil." *Ethnology* 10: 129–148.

Hill, Vera. 1966. *The Great Pilgrimage of the Middle Ages: The Road to St. James of
    Compostella.* New York: C. N. Potter.

Jha, Makhan, editor. 1985. *Dimensions of Pilgrimage: An Anthropological Appraisal
    Based on the Transactions of a World Symposium on Pilgrimage.* New Delhi:
    Inter-India Publications.

Keller, Evelyn Fox. 1992. "Between Language and Science: The Question of Directed
    Mutation in Molecular Genetics." *Perspectives in Biology and Medicine* 35: 292–
    306.

Kessel, John. 1976. *Friars, Soldiers and Reformers: Hispanic Arizona and the Sonora
    Mission Frontier, 1767–1856.* Tucson: University of Arizona Press.

King, William S. 1954. "The Folk Catholicism of the Tucson Papagos." Master's thesis,
    University of Arizona.

Laguna, Angel. 1950. "My Pilgrimage to Magdalena." *The Kiva* 16: 14–18.

Leach, Edmund. 1972. "Melchisedech and the Emperor: Icons of Subversion and Or-
    thodoxy." *Proceedings of the Royal Anthropological Institute* 1972: 5–14.

Marino Ferro, Xosé Ramón. 1987. *Las romerías: Peregrinaciones y sus símbolos.* Vigo:
    Ediciones Xerais de Galicia.

Messerschmidt, Donald A., and Jyoti Sharma. 1981. "Hindu Pilgrimage in the Nepal
    Himalayas." *Current Anthropology* 22: 571–572.

Moisés, Rosalio. 1977. *A Yaqui Life.* Lincoln: University of Nebraska Press.

Moore, Robert L., and Franch E. Reynolds, editors. 1984. *Anthropology and the Study
    of Religion.* Chicago: Center for the Scientific Study of Religion.

Morinis, E. Alan. 1984. *Pilgrimage in the Hindu Tradition: A Case Study of Western
    Bengal.* Oxford University South Asian Series. Delhi: Oxford University Press.

Morinis, E. Alan, editor. 1992. *Sacred Journeys: The Anthropology of Pilgrimage.* West-
    port, CT: Greenwood Press.

Murphy, James M. 1966. "The Discovery of Kino's Grave." *Journal of Arizona History*
    8: 89.

Nabhan, Gary. 1982. *The Desert Smells Like Rain.* San Francisco: North Point Press.

Nentwig, Juan. 1980. *Rudo Ensayo: A Description of Sonora and Arizona in 1764.*

Translated, clarified, and annotated by Alberto Francisco Pradeau and Robert R. Rasmussesn. Tucson: University of Arizona Press.

O'Connor, Mary I. "Lenten Ceremonials in Two Villages of the Mayo Valley." *Easter Ceremonies in Northwest Mexico*. N. Ross Crumrine and Rosamond B. Spicer, editors. Lanham, MD: University of America Press, in press.

O'Connor, Mary I. 1989a. *Descendants of Totoliguoqui: Ethnicity and Economics in the Mayo Valley*. Berkeley: University of California Press.

O'Connor, Mary I. 1989b. "The Virgin of Guadalupe and the Economics of Symbolic Behaviour." *Journal for the Scientific Study of Religion* 18: 105–119.

Officer, James E. 1987. *Hispanic Arizona, 1536–1856*. Tucson: University of Arizona Press.

Orsi, R. A. 1989. "The Cult of the Saints and the Reimagination of the Space and Time of Sickness in 20th-Century American Catholicism." *Literature and Medicine* 8: 63–77.

Ostierrieth, Anne. 1989. "Medieval Pilgrimage—Society and Individual Quest." *Social Compass* 36: 145–157.

Pace, E. 1989. "Pilgrimage as Spiritual Journey—An Analysis of Pilgrimage Using the Theory of V. Turner and the Resource Mobilization Approach." *Social Compass* 36: 229–244.

Pfaffenberger, Bryan. 1979. "The Karagama Pilgrimage: Hindu-Buddhist Interaction and Its Significance in Sri Lanka's Polyethnic Social System." *Journal of Asian Studies* 38: 253–270.

Poltzer, Charles. 1976. *Rules and Precepts of the Jesuit Missions of Northwestern New Spain*. Tucson: University of Arizona Press.

Pool, Robert. 1991. "Postmodern Ethnography." *Critique of Anthropology* 11: 309–331.

Rabinow, Paul, and William M. Sullivan, editors. 1987. *Interpretive Social Science: A Second Look*. Berkeley: University of California Press.

Redfield, Robert. 1956. *Peasant Society and Culture: An Anthropological Approach to Civilization*. Chicago: University of Chicago Press.

Remi, J. 1989. "Pilgrimage and Modernity." *Social Compass* 36: 139–143.

Ricard, Robert. 1966. *The Spiritual Conquest of Mexico*. Translated by Lesley Byrd Simpson. Berkeley: University of California Press.

Romano, V. Octavio Ignacio. 1965. "Charismatic Medicine, Folk-Healing, and Folk-Sainthood." *American Anthropologist* 67: 1151–1173.

Roosens, Eugene E. 1989. *Creating Ethnicity: The Process of Ethnogenesis*. Frontiers of Anthropology, vol. 5. Newbury Park: Sage Publications.

Sahagún, F. Bernardino. 1982. *Historia general de las cosas de Nueva Espana*. Mexico, D.F.: Editorial Porrúa, S.A.

Sallnow, Michael J. 1987. *Pilgrims of the Andes: Regional Cults in Cusco*. Washington, D.C.: Smithsonian Institution.

Sax, William. 1990a. The Ramnagar Ramlilia—Text, Performance, Pilgrimage." *History of Religions* 30: 129–153.

Sax, William. 1990b. "Village Daughter, Village Goddess: Residence, Gender, and Politics in a Himalayan Pilgrimage." *American Ethnologist* 17: 491–512.

Slater, Candace. 1986. *Trail of Miracles: Stories from a Pilgrimage in Northeast Brazil*. Berkeley: University of California Press.

Spicer, Edward H. 1980. *The Yaquis: A Culture History*. Tucson: University of Arizona Press.

Stack, John F., editor. 1986. *The Primordial Challenge: Ethnicity in the Contemporary World*. Westport, CT: Greenwood Press.

Tooker, Elisabeth. 1950. "The Pilgrims in Church." *The Kiva* 16: 9–13.

Turner, Victor. 1974. "Pilgrimages as Social Processes." *Dramas, Fields and Metaphors*. Victor Turner editor. Ithaca: Cornell University Press.

Ulin, Robert C. 1991. "Critical Anthropology Twenty Years Later: Modernism and Postmodernism in Anthropology." *Critique of Anthropology* 11: 63–89.

Underhill, Ruth. 1938. *Singing for Power: The Song Magic of the Papago Indians of Southern Arizona*. Berkeley: University of California Press.

Webster's Third New International Dictionary of the English Language. Unabridged. 1967. Springfield, MA: G. & C. Merriam Co.

Werbner, Richard P., editor. 1977. *Regional Cults*. Association of Social Anthropologists Monograph no. 16. London: Academic Press.

Williamson, George H. 1950. "Why the Pilgrims Come." *The Kiva* 16: 19–26.

Part IV

SHAMANISM AND RELIGIOUS CONSCIOUSNESS

15

Altered States of Consciousness and Religious Behavior

Michael Winkelman

Altered states of consciousness (ASC) in religious behavior is widely reported, perhaps a universal of human societies. Bourguignon (1968) found approximately 90 percent of the societies she studied had institutionalized forms of ASC. Winkelman's cross-cultural studies (1986b, 1992) reported all societies have ASC associated with healing, indicating ASC-based healing is a universal phenomenon.[1] This universal distribution of ASC suggests a biological basis for this aspect of religious behavior. This chapter addresses evidence for the universality of altered states of consciousness as an origin for religious experience and as a foundation for some manifestations of religious behavior.

In this chapter the role of ASC in religious behavior is addressed from cross-cultural, physiological, and cognitive perspectives. The universality of the shaman, the original progenitor of ecstatic (ASC) religious behavior, is examined in cross-cultural perspective. The worldwide distribution of shaman in hunting and gathering societies raises questions about the source of such universal behavior. The universal features of shaman are shown to be structured by biologically based potentials of ASC. A psychobiological model of ASC and the functional aspects of ASC in shamanic activities provides a basis for explicating the role of ASC in the ontogenesis of religious experience. A psychophysiological model of ASC is presented, illustrating the diverse procedures that evoke common changes in brain physiology. Physiological evidence indicates consciousness is systematically altered in similar ways by diverse ASC induction procedures, providing the basis for a common alteration of experience as manifested in transpersonal modes of consciousness. These changes involve a state of parasympathetic dominance in which the frontal cortex is dominated by slow wave patterns originating in the limbic system and related projections into the frontal parts of the brain. This pattern reflects the activation of a biologically based mode of consciousness with adaptive functions. This biological basis provides the substrate for shamanism and other ASC traditions, where the adaptive potentials of ASC are utilized. The functional bases of ASC as therapies are addressed in terms of general ASC effects and in terms of specific induction procedures. Phenomenological differences of ASC are addressed with specific consideration given to soul flight, possession, and mystical states. The different labels associated with ASC are shown to be related to social, physiological, and psychocognitive variables. The relationship of ASC types to societal conditions, the commonalities in mystical experiences, and the continuing role of ASC in contemporary societies are briefly considered.

THE SHAMAN AND ASC

The most widely recognized institutionalized use of ASC is the shaman. The seminal cross-cultural perspective was provided by Eliade, who summarized the classic core of shamanism as involving the use of "techniques of ecstasy" (altered states of consciousness) in interaction with the spirit world on behalf of the community, particularly in healing, divination, protection, and finding game animals. The shaman's ecstatic states were not possession but characterized as "a trance during which his soul is believed to leave his body and ascend to the sky or descend to the underworld" (Eliade 1969: 5). Eliade suggested that selection for the role of the shaman derived from a crisis, a period of illness or insanity characterized as a spirit affliction and sickness, in which a divine being chooses the individual for the role and gives him new rules for life. This initiation crisis typically involved an experience of suffering, followed by death, dismemberment, and rebirth, and ascent to the sky and descent to the underworld, and conversations with spirits and souls.

Subsequent research also suggested the shaman was a worldwide phenomenon and that practitioners in diverse parts of the world shared some common characteristics and functions (e.g., Eliade 1972; Hultkrantz 1973, 1978; Halifax 1979; cf. Siikala 1978 for review). Nonetheless, disagreements persist. While the trend has been to consider the shaman a universal phenomenon, some argue that the term *shaman* should be reserved exclusively for Siberian, Eurasian, or sub-Arctic practitioners. Others have extended the label shaman to other practitioners, for instance, any practitioners who interact with the spirit world through ASC.

The problems of definitional approaches to determining what a shaman is have been addressed by an empirical cross-cultural research project on magico-religious practitioners and shamanistic healers (Winkelman 1984, 1986a, 1990, 1992; Winkelman and White 1987). This study avoided some of the *a priori* and definitional problems of other studies by utilizing the formal analysis of descriptive cross-cultural data. This permits an empirical determination of whether there exist cross-culturally practitioners who conform to the classic description of the shaman and how these shaman and their characteristics relate to other types of magico-religious practitioners and healers utilizing ASC in their activities.

An empirically determined typology of different types of shamanistic healers and magico-religious practitioners was derived, based upon formal mathematical analysis of the characteristics and activities of the magico-religious practitioners found in a cross-cultural sample. The different types of empirically determined magico-religious practitioners and shamanistic healers have been labeled utilizing terms frequently employed by anthropologists: *shaman, shaman/healer, healer, medium, priest*, and *sorcerer/witch* (see Winkelman 1986a, 1990, 1992). The practitioners labeled *shaman, shaman/healers, healers*, and *mediums* shared major characteristics in common, including the core characteristics of shamanism suggested by Eliade: the use of ASC for their communities and in interaction with spiritual entities. These practitioners represent the institutionalization of universally distributed practices of using ASC as the basis for healing and divination. However, these shamanistic healers differed not only with respect to socioeconomic characteristics of their respective societies but also with respect to their socioeconomic and political status, their selection and training procedures, the specific characteristics of their ASC, the sources of their power, and additional magico-religious activities. This cross-cultural analysis found that practitioners from distinct areas (e.g., Africa, Asia, the Americas) share more characteristics in common across regions than they do with other healers in their own cultures and geographic regions. In some cases, practitioners that the ethnographers had called shaman were empirically grouped with the practitioner types labeled here as mediums or healers. The empirical similarity is more relevant than *a priori* definitions or geographical location. This suggests that the term *shaman* be restricted to those practitioners empirically sharing similar characteristics, which are reviewed next.

The Cross-Cultural Characteristics of Shaman

The formal cross-cultural research indicates an empirical group labeled as shaman, which closely conform to many of the general characterizations found in the classic descriptions of shamanism. Shaman are the charismatic political leaders in hunting and gathering societies where political integration or leadership is limited to the level of the local community. Their involvement with political power was generally informal, indicated by high social status or involvement in leadership in war or raiding parties, organization of communal hunts, and deciding group movement. Shamans engaged in activities on behalf of a client group or the community, most frequently in the form of healing and divination activities; however, they all also engaged in malevolent magical acts designed to harm others. They utilize ASC activities as the basis for their service to individuals and the community. The shamans are selected and trained through a variety of auguries and procedures. These include having had involuntary visions; receiving signs from spirits; having experienced serious illness; deliberately undertaking vision quests; and the induction of ASC through a variety of agents and procedures including hallucinogens, fasting and water deprivation, exposure to temperature extremes, extensive exercise such as dancing and long-distance running, various austerities, sleep deprivation, auditory stimuli (such as drumming and chanting), and social and sensory deprivation. Their ASC states are generally labeled as involving soul flight, journeys to the underworld, and/ or transformation into animals. Also typical of the shaman are death and rebirth experiences; control of spirits, particularly animal spirits; the provision of hunting magic; and the capacity to fly (Winkelman 1992).

These interrelated findings about the shaman require explanation, specifically: (1) the worldwide distribution of the shaman in hunting and gathering societies; (2) the fundamental role of ASC in shamanistic practices; and (3) the universality of ASC and their use in healing and divination.

Since the status of the shaman, with a similar complex of characteristics, roles, activities, and beliefs, is found in widely separated societies, the question is raised as to whether this resulted from diffusion of a single tradition or from the independent invention of essentially the same institution. While shamanism apparently was a part of the culture of the Paleolithic hunting and gathering groups that migrated from Asia to populate the Americas (Furst 1976; La Barre 1970), explanation of the distribution of shaman through the processes of diffusion is rejected by autocorrelation analysis (Winkelman 1986a). The absence of shaman in some regions of the sample is related to the absence of nomadic hunting and gathering societies without political integration, so other factors must be considered crucial to the worldwide distribution of shamanism.

Hultkrantz (1966) suggests that shamanism corresponds to an ecologically and socially determined "type of religion," modeled on the corresponding notion suggested by Steward (1955) with respect to "types of culture." This notion of a "type of religion" suggests that shamanism originates from sources associated with the psychological makeup of humans, while taking its specific form from adaptation to environmental conditions. A type of religion "contains those religious patterns and features which belong to or are intimately associated with the cultural core and therefore arise out of environmental adaptations" (Hultkrantz 1966: 146). As Hultkrantz points out, while shamanistic phenomena spring from "religious sentiment," sources associated with the psychological makeup of humans, these psychological bases are shaped by ecological conditions. Hultkrantz's religious sentiment corresponds to the biologically based ASC (see below). Shamanic practices have substantial similarities cross-culturally as a result of the interaction between the innate structure of the brain and certain ecological and social conditions. To substantiate this explanation of the universals of shamanism and other ASC traditions, I will first illustrate the common psychobiological basis for diverse ASC.

THE PHYSIOLOGICAL BASES OF ASC

The cultural roles of altered states of consciousness have been of concern to many anthropologists.[2] However, only a few (e.g., Lex 1976, 1979; Prince 1982a, 1982b; Winkelman 1986b, 1991a; Laughlin, McManus, and d'Aquili 1990) have addressed the psychophysiological basis of ASC. Most investigators have implicitly or explicitly assumed that psychophysical aspects of ASC of different shamanistic practitioners and in different societies are similar or identical without explication of the grounds for such assumptions. This section presents a psychophysiological model of the basic structure, physiology, and function of the brain as they relate to ASC. Evidence is presented that illustrates that ASC reflect normal brain functioning. A wide variety of ASC induction techniques lead to a similar alteration in the biology of consciousness, characterized by a state of parasympathetic dominance in which the frontal cortex is dominated by slow wave patterns originating in the limbic system and related projections into the frontal parts of the brain.

A wide range of ASC share basic physiological characteristics including cortical synchronization and a dominant trophotropic (parasympathetic) state. A physiological mechanism for explaining these regularities was outlined by Mandell (1980), who suggested "transcendent states" are based in a common underlying neurobiochemical pathway involving a biogenic amine-temporal lobe interaction.[3] This is manifested in high-voltage slow wave EEG (electroencephalogram) activity (alpha, delta, and theta, especially 3 to 6 cps [cycles per second]) that originates in the hippocampal-septal area and imposes a synchronous slow wave pattern on the frontal lobes. Agents and procedures that invoke this pattern include hallucinogens, amphetamines, cocaine, marijuana, polypeptide opiates, long-distance running, hunger, thirst, sleep loss, drumming and chanting, sensory deprivation, dream states, meditation, and a variety of psychophysiological imbalances or sensitivities resulting from injury, trauma, disease, or hereditarily transmitted nervous system labilities or sensitivities (Winkelman 1986b).

The central focus of brain activity in ASC is the hippocampal-septal region, a central aspect of the limbic system that serves as the gateway between the limbic system and the neocortex (Winson 1977, 1985). The limbic system is the central processor of the brain, integrating emotion and memory, and interoceptive and exteroceptive information (MacLean 1990). The hippocampal-septal region receives the terminal projections from the somatic and autonomic nervous systems, forming part of an extensive system of innervation linking the frontal cortex with the limbic system.

The hippocampal-septal system and amygdala receive input from and exert control over the hypothalamus. The hypothalamus has direct control over a wide range of neural transmitter substances, including those similar to hallucinogens and opiates. It also releases substances that act upon the reticular activating system and regulate the sleeping and waking cycles. The hypothalamus is considered to be the control center of the autonomic nervous system. It regulates the balance between the sympathetic and parasympathetic divisions of the autonomic nervous system, maintaining body functions in an interactive balance of activation and deactivation, respectively. The sympathetic nervous system is the activating system, responsible for the stimulation of the adrenal medulla and the release of hormones. Activation of the sympathetic nervous system results in diffuse cortical excitation, desynchronization of the EEG, and increased skeletal tone, as manifested in the orienting response and the waking mode of consciousness. Activation of the parasympathetic system leads to decreased cortical excitation and an increase in hemispheric synchronization. The parasympathetic nervous system is evoked by a number of chemical, hormonal, temperature, and other influences, including direct stimulation in the 3 to 8 cps range. An increase in parasympathetic dominance leads to the relaxation response and ultimately sleep, coma, and death. ASC generally involve phases with a parasympathetic dominant state as evidenced in collapse and unconsciousness, which normally occur only during sleep.

The normal state of balance within the autonomic nervous system breaks down under intense stimulation of the sympathetic system, leading to a collapse into a state of parasympathetic dominance. This pattern of parasympathetic rebound or collapse is a fundamental mechanism used by shamanistic healers to induce an altered state of consciousness. Gellhorn (1969) has shown that a wide variety of conditions will evoke this sequence of excitation and collapse. In the following section, some of the procedures that evoke this normal biologically based pattern of consciousness are reviewed. Original sources of this information are available in previous publications (Winkelman 1986b, 1991a, 1991b, 1992). The following material illustrates that diverse ASC induction procedures induce a state of parasympathetic dominance in which the frontal cortex is dominated by slow wave discharge patterns originating in the lower centers of the brain.

The Physiology of ASC Induction Procedures

Auditory Driving. Rhythmic auditory stimulation imposes a pattern upon the brain that is distinct from the normal asynchronous pattern. This is referred to as "driving," since the stimulus imposes a pattern on the listener's brain waves that can be measured with the electroencephalograph, normally involving entrainment of both alpha and theta waves. Activities such as drumming, chanting, and music are capable of producing this driving response. While Neher's (1961, 1962) original research has been questioned methodologically, more recent studies confirm predominant activation of the EEG in the theta range (Maxfield 1990; Rogers and Walters 1981; cf. Wright 1991 for review).

Extensive Motor Behavior. Extensive motor behavior and prolonged repetition of motor behavior cause slow wave activity (2 to 3 cps) and hallucinatory experience (Prince 1968; Leukel 1972). Dancing and similar extensive exercise and stimulation of the extremities also induce the release of endogenous opiates

(Thoren et al. 1990; Rahkila et al. 1987; Sforzo 1989; Mougin et al. 1987), which also produce this basic ASC pattern (see below). Exercise can overwhelm temperature regulation mechanisms with heat stroke, which causes increases in endogenous opioids (Appenzeller 1987).

Fasting and Nutritional Deficits. Fasting increases susceptibility to driving influences upon the EEG (Strauss, Ostow, and Greenstein 1952). Food and water deprivation have a direct effect upon the hypothalamus and hippocampal-septal systems. Nutritional deficiencies can also contribute to the induction of ASC states. Gussler (1973) reviews a range of dietary and malnutrition factors that affect serotonin synthesis and result in emotional disturbances, hallucinations, changes in cognitive and emotional functioning, and in some cases, production of symptoms such as convulsions that are frequently interpreted as possession.

Sensory Deprivation and Stimulation. Social isolation and reduction of motor behavior tend to lead to an increase in cortical synchronization, a greater sensitivity to parasympathetic stimulation, and a slowing of the alpha band with the emergence of delta waves. Mandell (1980) reviews research indicating reduction of sensory stimuli can lead to a loss of serotonin inhibition similar to the interference of hallucinogens in serotonin synthesis and release (see below). Extreme levels of sensory stimulation can lead to the same effects as sensory deprivation. Sensory stimulation of a distressing nature, both physical and psychological, can result in the induction of an ASC (Gellhorn 1969). A variety of stimuli (burns, extreme cold, pain, injury, and toxic substances) all lead to hypertropic activity of the adrenal cortex and the secretion of ACTH (adrenocorticotropic hormone); while such reactions are sympathetic rather than parasympathetic, stimulation of the sympathetic system to collapse then results in a parasympathetic-dominant state and the emergence of synchronized slow wave potentials in the EEG (Gellhorn and Loofbourrow 1963; Leukel 1972). Exposure to extreme cold, heat, or other physical or emotional stressors will elicit both opioid and nonopioid forms of analgesia (Kiefel, Paul, and Bodnar 1989), which have ASC induction properties discussed below.

Sleep and Dream States. The deliberate induction of sleep or dream states as a part of shamanistic ritual is widespread. Sleep is not only the basic pattern of shift to parasympathetic dominance, it shares basic characteristics with other well-recognized ASC procedures. There are substantial parallels of REM (rapid eye movement) sleeping and dreaming with yoga ecstasy in terms of cortical and visceral arousal, inhibition of skeletal muscle tone, loss of distinctiveness in sense of time, vivid perceptual imagery, and parasympathetic (trophotropic) dominance (Gellhorn and Kiely 1972). REM sleep evokes a pattern very similar to hallucinogens, producing not only visual imagery but the pattern of hippocampal-septal slow waves (Mandell 1980).

Meditation. There are fundamental physiological similarities across many different meditative practices and techniques even though the psychophysiological concomitants are to some extent subject to the intents of the practitioner. The overall changes in brain and bodily functioning involve a shift toward parasympathetic dominance (e.g., reduced cortical arousal, muscle tension, skin conductance, cardiac function, and respiration rate) (Gellhorn and Kiely 1972). In general, the EEG during meditation shows an overall decrease in frequency of the brain wave pattern to alpha and theta ranges and an increase in alpha and theta amplitude and regularity in the frontal and central regions of the brain (Wallace and Benson 1972; Davidson 1976; Kasamatsu and Hirai 1966). Stroebel and Glueck (1980) speculate that passive meditation leads to a reduction of affective outflow from the limbic structures and enhanced interhemispheric transmission of signals. A range of studies indicate an increase of coherence, a "synchronization and spreading out of spindling within the thalamic structures, thus causing an increased similarity of spectral frequencies in different cortical areas" (Fenwick 1987: 109).

Sexual Restrictions. Sexual restrictions may facilitate ASC induction. Vogel et al. (1974) report that testosterone and estrogen reduce EEG response to driving stimuli, suggesting that abstinence from sexual activity may be designed to reduce testosterone production and its effect upon driving response. Sexual activity culminating in orgasm generally results in a collapse of the skeletal musculature and a state of parasympathetic dominance. Prohibitions on sex may prevent a collapse until the appropriate ritual period or until a sufficient tension is achieved in the sympathetic system.

Endogenous Opiates. Opiates directly affect the hypothalamus, producing slow wave activity involving a rapid increase in delta/theta brain waves and a reduction of fast wave frequencies. Many typical shamanic ASC induction procedures result in the release of endogenous opiates or endorphins, including nighttime activities, prolonged rhythmic and exhaustive exercise and motor behavior, physical austerities, and temperature extremes (cf. Thoren et al. 1990; Rahkila et al. 1987; Sforzo 1989; Mougin et al. 1987).

Hallucinogens. The term *hallucinogen* is used to refer to thousands of substances that produce visual distortions and visionary experiences. While hallucinogens differ in their chemical structure and specific modes of action, they share some common physiological effects (Aghajanian 1982; Mandell 1985). Common effects include an overall synchronization of the cortex through producing a state of slow wave, high-voltage synchronous activity in the hippocampus and, ultimately, a parasympathetic-dominant state (Aghajanian 1982; Hoffmeister and Stille 1982; cf. Winkelman 1991b, 1996). The major hallucinogens (e.g., mescaline, peyote, psilocybin mushrooms, LSD [lysergic acid diethylamide]) contain phenylalkylamine and indole alkaloids similar in chemical structure to the neural transmitter serotonin. These hallucinogens affect serotonin uptake and directly or indirectly inhibit the firing of the serotonergic systems. The resulting loss of the inhibitory effect upon the mesolimbic temporal lobe structures causes synchronous discharges in the temporal lobe limbic structures (Mandell 1980, 1985). The hallucinogen's effects upon the serotonin mechanism leads to inhibition of the raphe cells' regulation of the visual cortex, hyperactivity of the visual regions, and the experience of an ongoing visual panorama.

Winkelman (1996) reviews research illustrating how the interactions of these "psychointegrators" in the serotonergic system produce information integration along the neuraxis of the brain, creating coherence among the activities of the brain stem, limbic system, and frontal cortex.

Alcohol. Alcohol also induces a slowing of the alpha frequencies, the emergence of theta, and synchronization of the cortical discharges. This has been interpreted as a reflection of ethanol action upon the amygdala and hippocampus and the transformation of the alcohol into endogenous morphinelike alkaloids.

Community Rituals. The community rituals fundamental to shamanistic healing practices have a role in the induction of ASC. Shamanistic healing practices involve neurobiologically mediated forms of attachment that serve to release endogenous opiates through a variety of mechanisms (Frecska and Kulcsar 1989). Research indicates that brain opioid systems provide neurochemical mediation of social bonding (see Frecska and Kulcsar 1989 for review). Frecska and Kulcsar suggest that "the social connotations and activation of the endogenous opioid system become cross-conditioned during early ontogenesis, so that later in life whenever the opioid system is activated by stress and pain, social connotations could arise together. . . . [R]egression promotes endogenous opioid mediation while endogenous opioids mediate affiliation, and help depersonalization by loss of ego boundaries. . . . [R]itually induced endogenous opioid activity supports social activity," and vice versa (1989: 79).

The Temporal Lobe Syndrome and ASC. The association of shamanistic ASC with pathological states has been frequently noted. There is abundant evidence to substantiate that shamans are not pathological from their own culture's point of view. Nonetheless, several anthropologists have recognized the presence of symptomology reflecting some nervous system lability in shamanistic practitioners while at the same time explicitly rejecting a pathological interpretation (Noll 1983; Ackerknecht 1943; Siikala 1978; Hultkrantz 1978). The reason for this association is illustrated by Mandell (1980), who shows that the physiological changes that result from certain kinds of central nervous system disinhibitions associated with epilepsy involve the same basic psychophysiological changes as ASC. Temporal lobe discharges and other central nervous system conditions associated with epilepsy, trauma, toxicity, and related seizure and disinhibition conditions involve the same basic pattern of brain changes outlined above in the model of an ASC. Epileptic symptoms share underlying conditions of discharges resulting in the dominance of synchronized slow wave patterns in the EEG. Epilepsy may result from genetic factors or be acquired as a result of injury or disease (electrical or chemical stimulation, hypoxia at birth, fevers in infancy, a wide range of diseases, injuries, or other nervous system disorders or stimulations [e.g., metabolic imbalances, hypocalcemia and hypoglycemia, endocrine disorders] [see Forster and Booker 1975; Adams and Victor 1977]). The importance of illness or other trauma lies in the occurrence of "kindling," a permanently reduced threshold for neural excitability as a result of previous excitation. Once convulsions or other major excitation occurs, there is a change in central nervous system "tuning" that makes the individual more susceptible to reestablishment of the central nervous system conditions (Gellhorn 1969).

This suggests that the association of ASC with pathological conditions lies in the increased facility for entering ASC that the physiological conditions provide. The relation of epileptic syndromes to deliberately induced ASC is illustrated in the hot water bath used in India as part of ritual (Subrahmanyam 1972; Mani et al. 1968; Mani et al. 1972). Hot water, or hot water rapidly alternated with cold water, is poured over the individual's head, resulting in a variety of temporal lobe symptoms, including generalized seizures, even in those without neurological or mental disorder (cf. Neppe 1981, 1983).

Summary. The variety of ASC induction techniques and conditions reviewed illustrates the ubiquitous response of the human brain to a variety of stimulations. A wide range of procedures and agents will evoke a brain response characterized by limbic system slow wave discharges that synchronize and dominate the frontal cortex. While not all conditions labeled as ASC evoke this pattern (e.g., hypnosis is a notable exception), the common response from widely divergent stimulation indicates that this is a biologically based mode of human consciousness. These are widely referred to as transcendent, transpersonal, and mystical states of consciousness. While ASC have been viewed as pathological in IndoEuropean cultures, a wide variety of evidence indicates that they are not primitive mental states. Not only are associated limbic system activation and hippocampal slow wave states optimal brain conditions for learning, memory, and attention, but they also provide mechanisms responsible for self-realization and the feelings of conviction and authenticity used to substantiate our mental concepts and theories (MacLean 1990). ASC are not primitive mental conditions but represent further development of human capacities within the transpersonal mode of consciousness.

The ASC Origins of Shamanism

Since shamans share the utilization of ASC in training and healing, and since the ASC that they utilize induce a common alteration in the psychophysiology of consciousness, the altered state appears to be the basis of shamanism and related practices. This perspective is supported by the functional relationship of the ASC training procedures to the magico-religious and shamanistic activities. When practitioners have ASC induction as a part of their training, they also engage in healing and divination as a part of their role. These and other commonalities underlying these different types of healing practitioners are directly tied to this use of ASC and their psychobiological effects. Previous research has suggested numerous reasons for a functional relationship between the ASC and healing and divination abilities (see Winkelman 1982, 1984, 1986b, 1991a, 1991b; Finkler 1985; Blacker 1981; cf. below). The universal presence of ASC and their functional relationships with healing and divination suggest that shamanistic practices are psychobiologically based. This indicates that the worldwide similarity in the shaman results in part from the similar ecological conditions associated with the hunting and gathering societies and in part from the biologically based ASC, the importance of which is reflected in its universal distribution and relationship to healing and divination.

Since ASC are central to the classic description and activities of the shaman, the practitioners utilizing ASC in training and healing are referred to as "shamanistic healers." The origins of shamanism lie in cultural adaptations to the biological potentials of ASC. Shaman form the original basis in hunting and gathering societies for the universal distribution of healing practitioners who utilize ASC for healing and divination. Evidence that shaman derive from an ecological adaptation to biologically based potentials includes: the universal distribution of similarly characterized shamans in hunting and gathering societies; the lack of evidence of diffusion; the biological basis of the ASC; and the functional characteristics of ASC.

Shamanistic traditions have substantial similarities cross-culturally since they have arisen as a result of the interaction between the innate structure of the brain and certain ecological conditions and social demands. This is possible since the ASC basic to selection, training, and therapeutic activities of the shamanic healers can occur under a wide variety of circumstances. These experiences can occur spontaneously, as a result of chance processes (e.g., injury, extreme fatigue, near starvation, or accidental ingestion of hallucinogens), or as a consequence of a wide variety of procedures that induce these states. Shamanism was apparently reinvented or rediscovered in diverse cultures and geographical regions as a result of those experiences. Since the ASC of shamanism have powerful effects upon experience and provide important adaptive capabilities, they were apparently institutionalized and reinduced once discovered.

The universality of basic experiences related to shamanism is substantiated by divergent research, including cross-cultural distribution of experiences that share a common structure of experience related to the shamanic soul flight or journey: the out-of-the-body experience (Shields 1978); near death or clinical death experiences (e.g., Moody 1975; Ring 1981); and "astral projection" or out-of-the-body experiences (e.g., Green 1968; McIntosh 1980; Blackmore 1982). These homologies suggest the shamanic experience is an archetypal and psychophysiological structure and that shamanism originated from that basis.

Summary. The psychophysiological basis of shamanism and the transpersonal mode of consciousness lie in the potentials provided by a particular pattern of biologically based organismic operation. This involves a state of parasympathetic dominance in which the frontal cortex is dominated and synchronized by slow wave patterns originating in the limbic system and related projections into the frontal parts of the brain. The diverse conditions and procedures that evoke this state indicate not only that it is a natural state of the human organism but that the independent discovery and rediscovery of this state and its potentials have given rise to shamanism and related magicoreligious practices. The adaptive potential of these states is examined next.

FUNCTIONS OF ASC

There appears to be a cultural resistance to ASC experiences in Western/Indo-European cultures. However, we should not let cultural biases nor ratiocentric perspectives blind us to the fundamental role of these aspects of brain system activation in higher mental processes. Western psychology and culture have tended to consider shamanic and mystical experiences to be pathological or infantile (Noll 1983; cf. Wilber 1977, 1979 for discussion and critique). Evidence from contemplative traditions indicates that ASC can provide the basis for a more objective perception of the external world. Rather than being bound up in subjectivity, the transpersonal mode of consciousness is viewed as a means of recognizing the illusions and constructed nature of ordinary perception. Many reports from these traditions indicate that these transpersonal states of consciousness provide the basis for a more objective perception of reality, which are examined below.

Although ASC, or the transpersonal mode of consciousness, are characterized by the dominance of activity from evolutionarily earlier parts of the brain, these states are neither primitive nor inferior to what is identified as rational thought. However, insofar as ASC are associated with the comparatively greater predominance of brain activity from the right hemisphere and nonfrontal parts of the brain, these states contrast with the ordinary waking state of awareness, which is dominated by left hemisphere's rational, linear, verbal modes of experience and the activation of the sympathetic nervous system. In contrast to these perspectives that depreciate the importance of ASC, Mandell (1980) reviews research that indicates that the associated hippocampal slow wave states are an optimal level of brain activity for energy, orienting, learning, memory, and attention. In spite of a perceived association of higher mental processes with the left hemisphere and fast wave EEG, there is a positive association of slow wave EEG and alpha with efficient cognitive performance under conditions of mental effort (Vogel, Boverman, and Klaiber 1974). The limbic system plays a vital role in subjective apperception in both protomentation and emotional mentation, as well as in rational thought (MacLean 1990).

The hippocampal formation influences the hypothalamus and other brain structures responsible for self-preservation, procreation activities, and family-related behavior (MacLean 1990). The hippocampus integrates information from neurovegetative, somatovisceral, and emotional functions relevant to feelings of individuality, aspects of memorization, and a sense of personal identity (MacLean 1990). The limbic system and its activities are responsible for an integrated sense of self, which provides a locus for memory and the generation of feelings of conviction, and a sense of authenticity, which we use to substantiate our mental ideas, concepts, beliefs, and theories (MacLean 1990).

Therapeutic Aspects of ASC

Previous research has suggested numerous reasons for a functional relationship of ASC to healing and divination abilities (see Winkelman 1982, 1984, 1986b, 1991a, 1991b; Finkler 1985; Blacker 1981). The physiological changes of ASC facilitate the typical shamanic tasks of healing and divination in improving psychological and physiological well-being in a number of ways, including: physiological relaxation; facilitating self-regulation of physiological processes; reducing tension, anxiety, and phobic reactions; inducing and eliminating psychosomatic effects; facilitating extrasensory perception and psychokinesis; bypassing normal cognitive processes in accessing unconscious information; interhemispheric fusion and synchronized coherence; cognitive-emotional integration; and social bonding and affiliation. The universal presence of ASC associated with magicoreligious healing practices, coupled with functional relationships of ASC with the abilities of healing and divination, suggests that this is psychobiologically based, derived from characteristics of ASC. The psychophysiology of ASC induction procedures indicates that a wide variety of ASC states share common psychophysiological features, including cortical synchronization, interhemispheric integration, and a parasympathetic-dominant state. These psychophysiological changes associated with a wide range of ASC induction conditions and procedures have inherent therapeutic properties.

General Therapeutic Aspects of ASC

Assessment of the therapeutic role of ASC requires recognition of the implications of the fact that a wide variety of procedures, both drug and nondrug, are used interchangeably to induce ASC. The differences in drug and nondrug ASC must be subsumed within a broader model that examines their commonality. The common psychophysiological changes of ASC—parasympathetic dominance, interhemispheric integration, and limbic-frontal synchronization—can be seen as having therapeutic effects *sui generis*. The parasympathetic-dominant state, synchronization of the frontal cortex, and interhemispheric integration are associated with conditions of physiological integration and coordination (limbic-frontal and left-right hemisphere) that have inherent benefits for the functioning of the human system. The parasympathetic-dominant state reflects a basic relaxation response characterized by an integrated hypothalamic response and a generalized decrease in the activation of the sympathetic nervous system. This is the basic body response to counteract the overreactivity of the sympathetic nervous system. The relaxation response has preventive and therapeutic value in diseases characterized by increased sympathetic nervous system activity. Benson and colleagues (Benson, Beary, and Carol 1974; Benson et al. 1979) suggest its therapeutic usefulness in lowering of blood pressure, in control of hypertension, in ischemic heart disease, and in reduction of premature ventricular contractions.

Parasympathetic-dominant states induce relaxation with therapeutic effectiveness against a range of stress-induced and-exacerbated maladies. Lehrer, Woolfolk, and Goldman (1984) review the application of progressive relaxation techniques, showing that the modification of troublesome emotions and other maladaptive mental processes can be achieved by changing the use of the skeletal muscles. Progressive relaxation therapy also decreases psychophysiological reactivity and produces lasting somatic changes in anxiety neurotics, indicating potential for treatment of hypertension. Further effects of relaxation responses are discussed below in conjunction with the therapeutic effects of meditation.

Therapeutic effects may be achieved by a parasympathetic collapse that can lead to erasure of previously conditioned responses, changes of beliefs, loss of memories, and increased suggestibility (Sargent 1974). The induction of a total parasympathetic collapse from stress and emotional excitement has a variety of effects upon previous learning. These include the complete abolition of conditioned reflexes and the ultraparadoxical phase in which the conditioned behavior and responses are reversed (Sargent 1974). Increases in suggestibility combined with critical screening by the left hemisphere facilitate psychoemotional reprogramming with the chants, songs, myths, psychodrama, and direct suggestion provided by the shaman. Increases in suggestibility may also increase placebo or other psychosomatic effects, resulting in physiological improvement for the patient.

ASC activate the unconscious aspects of the brain/mind interface and permit conscious control and regulation of what are typically unconscious bodily processes or repressed memories and complexes. Abreaction and conscious-unconscious integration permit the resolution of conflicts. Many personal(ity) conflicts can be seen as a result of the failure of the conscious mind to understand and know about the unconscious mind. The unconscious mind, whose functioning is more represented by limbic system and right hemisphere processing, is likely to be repressed by the dominant frontal hemispheres. These right hemisphere tendencies or scripts nonetheless persist and affect behavior, emotions, and physiology. These repressions can be curtailed by reducing critical screening by the left hemisphere through ASC that move cortical arousal outside of the normal range. This then permits expression of the normally repressed side of the brain, as well as reprogramming at these unconscious nonverbal levels (Budzynski 1986). The cross-cultural literature on healing suggests that giving expression to these repressed aspects of the self is achieved through ASC healing rituals, which reduce critical screening, elicit emotional events, and present a new message.

Therapeutic Effects of Hallucinogens

In spite of predominant Western perspectives that hallucinogens are dangerous drugs, there is ample evidence that hallucinogens or psychedelic substances have therapeutic applications. A wide range of ethnographic data on hallucinogen use in non-Western societies provides data on positive cultural beliefs and therapeutic uses associated with these substances. Corroborative evidence of therapeutic effectiveness in found in Western clinical medicine's studies on the effects of LSD. Laboratory studies of physiological, sensory, emotional, behavioral, and cognitive effects of hallucinogens illuminate the general psychophysiological effects of hallucinogens, their consciousness-altering properties, and their therapeutic mechanisms. The therapeutic effects of hallucinogens derive from both the general aspects of altered states of consciousness induction and the associated psychophysiological effects and benefits, as well as from specific mechanisms related to the physiological effects of the hallucinogens (Winkelman 1991b).

Clinical Studies of Hallucinogens. A wide range of studies on hallucinogens and their therapeutic effects upon humans were carried out prior to legal prohibitions that halted research (see Grof 1975, 1980; Lukoff, Zanger, and Lu 1990; Bliss 1988; Yensen 1985; Aaronson and Osmond 1970; Cohen 1968; Abramson 1967; and Bravo and Grob 1989 for reviews). Clinical study of LSD in psychotherapy has provided the basis for three models or perspectives on the mechanisms underlying the clinical effects of hallucinogens: the psychotomimetic, psycholytic, and psychedelic approaches (Yensen 1985; Bravo and Grob 1989).

While early research viewed hallucinogens as mimicking psychosis (psychotomimetic model), the positive aspects of the LSD experience led to the development of the psycholytic approach. Early studies illustrated the ability of LSD to ease memory blocks, to promote catharsis, and to shorten the course of therapy. This approach emerged as a result of recognition that LSD was an effective aid to psychotherapy, especially with chronically withdrawn patients unable to express their repressed conflicts. The psycholytic approach employed a series of low doses of LSD as a part of a longer series of regular therapeutic sessions. The term *psycholytic* means "mind dissolving." Psycholytic therapy reflected the notion that a dissolution of tensions and conflicts occurred in the course of these therapeutic sessions (Bliss 1988). The psycholytic approach used LSD as a means of altering the relationship between the conscious and unconscious in a way that facilitated psychoanalytic psychology. This facilitation was frequently manifested in the initial LSD sessions, where the patients would literally or symbolically express key aspects of the psychodynamics underlying their illness.

A number of psychological mechanisms were found to be frequently manifested under the experiences of LSD, including identification, projection, and fantasizing (Bliss 1988). Psychedelic drugs were thought to weaken psychological defenses, heighten emotional responsiveness, and release unconscious material. The ability to relive early life memories and to retain the memories in post-LSD sessions proved to be highly useful in the course of psychotherapy. Among those patients for whom psycholytic therapy has been recommended are those with psychosomatic problems and psychic rigidity; isolated individuals and those fixated at egocentric levels; concentration camp survivors with rigid defenses; patients with whom classic psychoanalysis has been unsuccessful; disorders rarely healed by psychotherapy such as severe chronic compulsions and severe alcoholism; and severe character neuroses, depression, and compulsion (Zanger 1989).

The subsequent model of LSD therapy is referred to as psychedelic therapy, referring to the "mind manifesting" properties of the substances. The psychedelic model derived from studies on the effects of large doses of LSD, particularly on alcoholics (Osmond et al. 1967). These studies indicated those who benefited most from the therapies had reported mystical experiences followed by profound personality changes, suggesting that the mystical insights were responsible for the therapeutic outcomes (Kurland 1985). The psychedelic approach employed a single large dose of LSD, using it to facilitate peak and mystical experiences that would bring about major personality changes. The therapeutic effects were thought to derive from the LSD-induced "peak experiences," which provide a profound sense of interconnectedness, unity, and meaningfulness. The dramatic effect of LSD in psychotherapy lies in that it promoted a resolution of psychosocial conflicts and provided access to a sense of a higher self. These experiences gave the patient a greater sense of self-control and the opportunity to make use of these insights for life changes. LSD and similar agents activate repressed memories, producing catharsis and abreaction and leading to an awareness and sense of freedom (Kurland 1985). The psychedelic paradigm "recast the psychiatrist as a modern day shaman" (Bravo and Grob 1989), who utilized altered states of consciousness as therapeutic tools.

It has been suggested that hallucinogens do not in themselves effect a cure but rather play the role of a medicinal aid in the total context of psychotherapy (Schultes and Hofmann 1979). While recognizing that set and setting factors will necessarily affect the outcome of the experience, there are physiological properties that tend to promote therapeutic processes when not subjected to negative set and setting influences. Langner (1967) also noted that LSD patients had less need for the therapist since they were able to directly access the deeply embedded traumas, emotions, and conflicts relevant to their problems. The hallucinogens' effects upon ego lead to an alteration of or dissolution of the typical sense of self, breaking up the habitual experiences of the world. This release from egocentric fixations and other modifications in the relationship between the conscious and unconscious make the patient more open to multiple interpretations and integration of new awarenesses outside of habitual interpretations. Hallucinogens also produce a depatterning influence, increasing the individual's suggestibility and susceptibility to reprogramming. These substances also stimulate memories, bringing them to consciousness where they can be addressed (see Winkelman 1991b for brief discussion of physiological mechanisms). Mandell's (1985) suggestion that hallucinogens cause interhemispheric integration of thought and feeling also points to inherent therapeutic effects. Winkelman (1996) discusses the neurophysiological basis for the psychointegrative effects of these substances.

Therapeutic Aspects of Meditation

The therapeutic efficacy of meditation is widely reported (see Shapiro 1980, 1990; Walsh 1979, 1980, 1983, 1988 for reviews). Meditative practices improve individual psychological and physiological well-being and appear to be particularly applicable for psychosomatic disorders (Walsh 1983). Studies show successful outcomes in dealing with fears, phobias, personal integration and control, stress and tension management, and a range of physical changes, including lowering blood pressure (Shapiro 1980). Meditation serves as a self-regulation strategy and as a clinical intervention technique affecting several stress-related dependent variables (Shapiro 1980, 1990). Meditation is also used as an ego regression technique that prompts the manifestation of unconscious material. It has been used as a means of assisting individuals in gaining a sense of inner directedness and increased self-responsibility, as well as a means of stress management.

However, critical reviews of the research literature indicate that meditation is no more effective than are other self-control strategies (e.g., progressive relaxation, hypnosis, and biofeedback) (Shapiro 1990; Pagano and Warrenburg 1983). The cause of meditation's therapeutic effects may be a part of the general relaxation produced by the state of parasympathetic dominance. The beneficial effects of meditation in treatment of psychosomatic tension states, anxiety, and phobic reactions might be generally expected of parasympathetic-dominant states. It is, however, important to recognize that these assessments generally are not dealing with the goals or essence of meditation, nor with highly developed practitioners. The intents of meditation disciplines differ from those of Western health sciences, with goals that are quite different (e.g., dissolution of the ego and disattachment rather than ego strengthening). Furthermore, these studies apply meditation to medical symptoms, frequently with novice meditators. Such clinical perspectives provide but scant coverage of the nature of meditative effects.

We nonetheless find evidence of the psychotherapeutic effects of meditation (see Shapiro 1980, 1990; Walsh 1983, 1988; Shapiro and Walsh 1984; West 1987c). Delmonte (1987b) reviews evidence showing meditators with significantly lower levels of depression than dropouts. Meditation also improves self-actualization and reduces anxiety, particularly for those relatively healthy individuals who adopt meditation practices. Carrington (1987) cites clinical evidence that indicates that meditation leads to greater psychological differentiation, with a clearer understanding of one's own psychological needs and attributes. Carrington suggests that positive consequences of meditation may include increased self-acceptance, increased self-esteem, enhanced self-control and confidence, increased empathy, and greater self-actualization (cf., West 1987a). West (1987a) suggests meditative experiences will necessarily lead the individual to an increase in private self-conscious as a consequence of attention paid to the self. Walsh (1983) cites research findings indicating that the physical and psychosomatic benefits of meditation are found in the treatment of myocardial infarction, bronchial asthma, insomnia, reduction of blood cholesterol levels, and high blood pressure. Meditation has also been found to improve responsiveness to medication for a range of stress-related illnesses; other studies have shown reductions in addictive drug use, mood elevation, and improvements in affect. Practices such as insight meditation that focus upon the arising perceptions, memories, thoughts, sensations, and emotions provide primary material for psychodynamic processing. As this material is processed and resolved, it provides the opportunity for further examination of and insight into the nature of psychological processes (Walsh 1983).

The healthful quality of mediatative and mystical experiences is widely recognized in the context of "transcendent experience." Walsh (1980) reviews evidence that indicates that these experiences occur most frequently among those who are psychologically the most healthy. Transcendent experiences are most likely during advanced stages of psychotherapy, among those who are most self-actualized, who are better educated and economically more successful, who are less racist, and who test at higher levels of psychological well-being. Not only do transcendent experiences occur among the most healthy, but they are also recognized as being responsible for long-term beneficial changes.

NEUROPHENOMENOLOGICAL DIFFERENCES IN ASC

There are many manifestations of ASC, with not only different labels (e.g., soul flight, out-of-body experiences, possession, obsession, vision quests, enlightenment, samadhi, and others), but also with phenomenologically different experiences (e.g., flight, dream body, amnesia, external domination, void, etc.). This section addresses the patterns within this variation, identifying types of ASC and assessing the physiological and social concomitants of the different types of ASC.

Several lines of evidence indicate phenomenological and physiological differences in ASC. Although the ASC conditions discussed above support the hypothesis of a common mode of consciousness being utilized by shamanistic healers, this does not preclude there being differences within the ASC. Not all types of induction procedures and conditions cooccur; that is, although ASC induction procedures induce common physiological changes, this does not preclude patterns in terms of the association of ASC induction procedures and characteristics. Winkelman (1986b) found three main entailment chains in the ASC data, all of which have exclusion relationships with the others. The first entailment chain indicates the association of excessive motor behavior (e.g., dancing), sleep states, and unconscious, interpreted as a soul flight. The second entailment chain shows the empirical association of amnesia, convulsions, and spontaneous seizures with the phenomena of possession. The third entailment chain has the association of sleep deprivation, auditory driving, fasting, social isolation, and austerities. These three entailment chains correspond to three major types of ASC traditions. The first chain corresponds to the soul flight of the shamanic tradition. The second chain corresponds to a mediumistic or possession trance tradition. The third chain represents a yogic or meditative tradition. The social and physiological relationships to ASC labels illustrate further reasons for differentiating among ASC.

The Soul Flight or Shamanic Journey

The shamanic soul flight (or soul journey) can be defined as an ASC in which some aspect of the experient—soul, spirit, or perceptual capacities—is thought to travel to or be projected to another place, generally a spirit world. The availability of these experiences is widely attested to in contemporary culture by individuals who seek out the shamanic path (e.g., see Harner 1982). The typical shamanic procedures for inducing the soul journey illustrate some basic behavioral commonalities that permit inference about the physiological concomitants underlying and presumably giving rise to their phenomenological experience. The extensive dancing and percussive activity lead to exhaustion, collapse, unconscious, and a state of parasympathetic dominance. The shaman appears unconscious, but the visionary experience illustrates that the shaman is still aware.

The universality of the basic experiences of shamanism is substantiated by divergent research that illustrates a cross-cultural distribution of experiences that share a common structure of experience related to the shamanic soul flight or journey—the out-of-the-body experiences, "astral projection," and near death or clinical death experiences. These homologies show that this shamanic experience is an integrated psychophysiological and archetypal structure. Laughlin, McManus, and d'Aquili (1990) suggest that the ergoptrophic-trophotrophic (sympathetic-parasympathetic) system activation and manipulation are responsible for these and other invariant features of shamanic and mystical experience, which result from the consistent entrainment and organization of neurognostic structures of humans. The universal availability of soul flight experiences reflects its symbolization of the transformative experiences and the homeomorphogenetic transformations that take place in the internal structures of consciousness.

Soul flight is not a central feature of the meditative traditions, but soul flight or out-of-body experiences are widely reported and can be developed as *siddhis* (Eliade 1964). Shields's (1978) cross-cultural study of the out-of-the-body experience, the core element of the shamanic soul flight, found it to be nearly universal. Contemporary research indicates that phenomena that share many fundamental experiential similarities with shamanistic soul journey occur both spontaneously and deliberately among modern populations (Green 1968; McIntosh 1980; Blackmore 1982). Experiences such as those revealed in the studies of near death or clinical death experiences (e.g., Moody 1975; Sabom 1982; Schoonmaker 1979; Ring 1981, 1986; Blackmore 1991) reflect similar patterns. These individuals report experiences similar to shamans, traveling/flying through diverse worlds, interacting with spirit beings, and acquiring information about both the ordinary and spiritual worlds. Given both the predominant association of soul flight with the shaman of hunting and gathering societies, and the availability of such experiences to moderns, we must determine why the cross-cultural data indicate a shift to the predominance of other types of ASC.

Possession

Goodman (1988a, 1988b) illustrates that possession and exorcism are not merely folklore beliefs of the past but also vital and dynamic parts of the modern world. Her material points out strong cross-cultural similarities that suggest a common basis for the possession experiences. However, a closer examination of the phenomena grouped under the guise of possession illustrates variation and ultimately problems in assuming a unitary phenomenon. In the anthropological and other literature, the term *possession* has been used to refer to a wide variety of phenomena—ASC, trance, dissociation, hysteria, spirit domination, displacement of personality, obsession, mental illness, and a variety of other conditions. Such variation in the phenomena and imprecision in the use of the term confuse discussion about the putative phenomena. In order to address possession phenomena with greater rigor and clarity, I have followed Bourguignon's (1968, 1976a, 1976b) precedent in using the term *possession* in a more restricted way.

Bourguignon (1968, 1976a, 1976b) distinguishes possession trances (ASC) and their incidence from other types of spirit relationships established during ASC. Bourguignon defines possession trances as involving "alterations or discontinuity in consciousness, awareness or personality or other aspects of psychological functioning" that are accounted for by possession. Possession is defined as a belief that a "person is changed in some way through the presence in or on him of a spirit entity or power, other than his own personality, soul [or] self" (1976a: 8). Bourguignon has also defined possession trances in what can be characterized as a stronger sense as cases "in which the altered state is explained as due to a take over (possession) of the body by a spirit entity" (Bourguignon and Evascu 1977: 198). In Bourguignon's research, ASC not explained by reference to possession beliefs were grouped together as nonpossession trances. In nonpossession trances "the predominant explanation concerns soul absence, and . . . is frequently linked to types of hallucinations or visions" (Bourguignon and Evascu 1977: 198). Bourguignon's distinction of nonpossession ASC encompasses (but is not exhausted by) the ASC referred to as soul journey or soul flight. While Bourguignon's research has shown the importance of distinguishing possession from other forms of ASC, some researchers have subordinated the differences between possession and soul flight to their commonality as ASC. While their point of view would appear well taken in light of the psychophysiological modal ASC, there are nonetheless good grounds for distinguishing the ASC labeled possession from other ASC.

One argument of Peters and Price-Williams (1980) for abandoning the classic distinction between shamanic flight and spirit possession is the lack of a precise association with nonamnesic and amnesic states, respectively, which had been used as one of the justifications for the distinction. They point out that memory does occur in some situations of possession. However, their own data show amnesia does not occur with soul flight; all of the cases of amnesia are associated with possession, and there is a significant association between possession and amnesia (tau = .43; p < .001). My studies also show possession is significantly associated with variables reflecting the temporal lobe syndrome (amnesia, spontaneous seizures, rapid onset of illness, tremors or convulsions, and compulsive motor behavior). Variables assessing compulsive motor behavior and tremors/convulsions provided the strongest prediction, an independently significant contribution, accounting for 58 percent of the variance in the incidence of possession (F = 17.6; 2,65 df; p < .000). This establishes that temporal lobe discharges are strongly and significantly related to the labeling of ASC and confirms that temporal lobe conditions contribute to the phenomena of possession.

Possession ASC and Societal Complexity. Societal differences in labeling of ASC were investigated by Bourguignon (1976b; Bourguignon and Evascu 1977), who has presented analyses from her cross-cultural study that indicate that possession trances occur in more complex societies. The study reported significant positive relationships of possession ASC with stratification, jurisdictional hierarchy, and variables measuring food production and agriculture, as well as significant evidence of diffusion. Winkelman (1986b, 1992) also found that the societal incidence of possession in the training of shamanistic healers was correlated positively with all of the social complexity variables from Murdock and Provost (1973), and significantly with most of them. The strongest correlations were with political integration, population density, and social stratification (tau = .60, .45, and .35, respectively; all p < .001). However, only political integration has significant predictive power beyond the main effects and interactions. These results refine Bourguignon's findings of the association of possession with social complexity, indicating the societal factors leading to possession beliefs are specifically associated with political integration. In order to control for the possibility that the relationship between the possession variables and political integration was a result of the diffusion of traits, the autocorrelation method developed by Dow et al. (1984) was employed. There were no significant diffusion effects under either model of relatedness and a very strong correlation with the political integration variable (Possession r = .62; p < .001). This indicates that the relationship between political integration and possession beliefs is affected by social conditions and is not a result of diffusion.

Possession Ontology: Psychophysiological and Societal Causation. In order to assess the relationship between physiological effects (temporal lobe syndrome) and the social effects with respect to the possession, both types of variables were included in analysis of variance. The two temporal lobe variables with the strongest prediction of possession (compulsive motor behavior and tremors/convulsions) were combined into a single variable, referred to here as the temporal lobe discharge (TLD) variable. If a society had a magico-religious practitioner present who had either of the conditions present, it was coded for the presence of the TLD variable. The TLD and political integration variables were regressed on the societal possession variable. Each accounted for significant variance beyond the main and interaction effects, with the TLD variable accounting for substantially more variance than the political integration variable (58 percent versus 40 percent). Together they account for 75 percent of the variance in the possession variable ($F = 41.1$; 3,41 df; $p < .000$).

The analyses indicate that both physiological variables related to temporal lobe disinhibition and social variables related to political integration have a strong predictive value in explaining the incidence of possession ASC. The substantially stronger prediction by the temporal lobe variables suggests that psychophysiological factors are central to the bases that motivate the development of beliefs in possession. However, we must also recognize that societal conditions and institutional practices can contribute to the incidence of temporal lobe symptoms. Possession ASC traditions that are associated with temporal lobe symptomology occur in the lower classes of stratified societies, indicating that their deprived status and resultant experiences may contribute directly to the physiological conditions. The predominance of women in possession ASC cults corresponds to areas in which women are restricted from adequate nutrition by cultural rules. This may be a consequence of dietary and nutritional deficiencies that can cause behavioral symptoms similar to the temporal lobe syndrome (e.g., tremors) (Kehoe and Giletti 1981). Dietary deficiencies can contribute to changes in the central nervous system resulting in emotional disturbances, changes in cognitive and emotional functioning, and in some cases, the production of symptoms interpreted as possession (Gussler 1973). Epilepsy and other temporal lobe syndromes may be acquired as a result of metabolic imbalances such as hypocalcemia and hypoglycemia (Forster and Booker 1975; Adams and Victor 1977).

Active ASC Induction and Temporal Lobe Control. The nature of shamanistic traditions and training may also affect the manifestation of different types of ASC and in particular the manifestation of temporal lobe discharge phenomena. These differences are seen in a contrast of the shaman and mediums identified in my cross-cultural studies (Winkelman 1986a, 1986b, 1992). While the shaman were generally characterized by a deliberate seeking of their ASC, mediums were invariably characterized by having illness and seizures overwhelm them before they sought training. Shaman induce ASC deliberately and at early ages (childhood or puberty). Mediums wait until late adolescence or early adulthood when spontaneous phenomena associated with the temporal lobe syndromes induce ASC and lead them to begin to deliberately induce ASC. Shaman deliberately sought training for their positions at significantly younger ages than the age at which mediums experienced their calling through possession.

The differences in the means of acquiring ASC—being actively sought in childhood by the shaman as opposed to the mediums' illness episodes later in adolescence and early adulthood (medium)—are related to the manifestation of seizure phenomena and possession interpretations. This active versus passive approach affects the differences in ASC characteristics in that active ASC induction apparently prevents involuntary induction of the physiologically triggered states by developing conscious or ritual control of these psychophysiological discharges. The shaman, like the mediums, may also have psychophysiological conditions and personality configurations disposing them to ASC experiences. Shaman also have involuntary visions and dreams as indications of their selection for their positions, phenomena that are also associated with the temporal lobe syndrome. Similar to the mediums who apparently control temporal lobe discharges through their involvement in ASC training, the shaman may have avoided such conditions by their early ASC training. This notion that active ASC induction leads to control is supported by the finding that although mediums were selected on the basis of spontaneous seizure experiences, their professional possession ASC were always deliberately induced, not spontaneous or unplanned.

Meditative and Mystical Traditions

The meditative, yogic, and mystical traditions are associated with religious traditions of Asia (Hinduism, Buddhism, Taoism). Recent perspectives suggest that they be conceived of as consciousness traditions, psychologies, or contemplative traditions (Walsh 1983, 1988; Laughlin, McManus, and d'Aquili 1990), emphasizing their empirical character in addressing the nature of human psychology and consciousness. These traditions have focused upon observation of internal subjective experience and reporting on its nature and processes. They therefore provide a more substantial and valid basis for understanding human consciousness than does Western psychology that has historically rejected consciousness as a topic of study and introspection as a valid methodology.

Studies of meditation have provided a plethora of definitions (e.g., see West 1987a; Goleman 1977; Shapiro 1990). Walsh (1983) offers a summary definition: ''The term 'meditation' refers to a family of practices that train attention in order to heighten awareness and bring mental processes under greater voluntary control. The ultimate aims of these practices are the development of deep insight into the nature of mental processes, consciousness, identity and reality, and the development of optimal states of psychological well-being and consciousness. However, they can also be used for a variety of intermediate aims, such as psychotherapeutic and psychophysiological benefits'' (19). Investigators of diverse meditation traditions have concluded that beneath the cultural forms and traditions there are common objectives, practices, and principles of meditation (West 1987b; Walsh 1988; Goleman 1977; Wilber 1977). The commonalties to be reviewed below include their perception of the organization of the different levels of consciousness and its characteristics; the nature of perceptual and attentional processes and how they are developed; the nature of human identity; and the development of the self and consciousness.

Consciousness and Reality. The meditative traditions recognize a broad range or spectrum of states or levels of consciousness. The levels and development of consciousness involve a progression from a state of disillusion and illusion to a greater understanding and awareness of the characteristics and nature of self, god, and the ultimate ground of reality. The meditative traditions concur in seeing our usual state of awareness as suboptimal, a kind of culturally induced hypnosis in which we habitually identify with our ego, thoughts, and behaviors (Walsh 1983). The Asian psychologies identify additional states that are considered to be "higher" than the ordinary state of awareness in that they provide additional capacities and potentials. In this sense of higher consciousness, development is seen as "a progressive heightening of awareness of, and disidentification from, mental content" (Walsh 1983: 26). This development provides for an awakening, liberation, or enlightenment.

Attention and Perception. The meditative traditions include a retraining of attention as a means of inducing an ASC and leading to greater awareness. A common emphasis among these traditions is that most human behavior is mindless and unconscious, lacking all but the most rudimentary control of attentional processes. These traditions focus upon the internal training and intentional manipulation of attention in order to develop a greater control of the mind and attention. This results in an increased awareness of unconscious mental processes and insight into the nature and process of mental operations.

Claxton (1987) provides a psychological gloss of the doctrines of Buddhism with respect to the central role of meditation. Rather than accepting perception as given, its analysis and understanding are seen as essential to understanding the human condition. Similar to the constructivist view, Buddhists postulate a mental model that subserves and provides our experiences and actions. The conclusion derived from the examination of the construction of experience is that "mostly unexamined and unconscious assumptions that constitute the very foundation of our perception are inaccurate, and that therefore the entire range of experience to which they contribute is ill-founded and misguided" (25–26). This leads to the conclusion that the world is not a collection of things but rather a perception of interdependent characteristics that we have come to label as a thing. Such analysis is extended to the concept of the self and individual identity, where a separate identity and autonomous and unchanging existence are denied.

Self and Identity. Another common point of the meditative disciplines is their emphasis on the mindless and unconscious automatic information processing characteristic of most human behavior and thought. Unlearning this conditioning of thought and behavior, and the automatic identification with these contents, is fundamental to realization of another commonality of the Asian psychologies— the notion of the self and individual identity as distorted and illusory. This illusory belief in self and individual identity is maintained by a lack of awareness of the unconscious processes that serve to construct the perception of continuity of identity (Walsh 1988). One of the ways in which meditation practices bring about a greater awareness of unconscious processes is through deautomatization, unlearning this habitual conditioning of thought and behavior. The development of greater attention and awareness, and a dehabituation from our habitual identifications and reactions, permits the development of perspectives on the self that are less tied to mental contents and processes. Such development leads the individuals to the experience of self as pure awareness or an observer.

Divided Consciousness and Enlightenment. Castillo (1991) analyzes the experiences and development of Hindu Yogis in relationship to consciousness of self, which is seen as having an inherently dual nature. He suggests that Yogi development leads to the creating of coconscious selves, a divided consciousness. One participates in the world, which he calls the personal self; the other is an uninvolved observing self, the transpersonal self (Castillo 1991). One self, *jiva*, participating consciousness, is "physical, impermanent, and engaged with the world . . . , performs actions in accordance with social norms" (1). "The *jiva* is comprised of the personal mind, thoughts, emotions, sensations, and memories" (2). Another self, *atman* or *purusha*, observing consciousness, is "nonphysical, permanent (immortal), an uninvolved witness of the physical self and the world . . . and experiences those actions as if they were performed by someone else" (1).

The conquering of self and senses that is characteristic of Yogic development refers to this transcendence of the ordinary self. While "both aspects of consciousness exist simultaneously, observing consciousness (*atman*) is only experienced as a separate entity when participating consciousness (*jiva*) is restrained" (1). The goals of Yoga are the separation of these two aspects of self and consciousness so that the *atman* may be experienced separately. Castillo suggests that the ultimate goal of Yoga meditation is this separation of the observing self or true self (*atman*) from the participating self or false self (*jiva*), where it has been assimilated. In the Yoga traditions, the achievement of this separation is referred to as *moksha*, meaning liberation. This liberation refers to the fact that since the transpersonal consciousness in only witnessing events and not participating in them, it is freed from the pain and suffering that comes from an identification with the personal self and its external world.

Meditative Cognition and the Brain. Because meditation emphasizes a receptive mode, early investigators suggested that meditation was a right hemisphere experience, in contrast to the active, logical, analytical, and verbal aspects of left hemisphere mentation. However, the hypothesis of meditation as a right hemisphere phenomenon has not been supported by the research data (Pagano and Warrenburg 1983). "During the advanced stages of meditation, however, cognitive functions associated with each hemisphere are either automatised or inhibited, leading to a reduction of cortical activity or diminished cortical participation in the generation of mental phenomena" (Delmonte 1987b). Advanced meditators are no longer concerned with the cognitive processes associated with the left hemisphere and frontal lobes. Rather, they are concerned with the processes of attention that are dependent upon the activities of the lower centers of the brain. It is precisely these deeply automatized activities that the meditators attempt to reelevate to conscious control.

The EEG data also support the position that while meditation may lead to an increased activation of the right hemisphere versus the habitual left hemisphere activation, the overall pattern is one of interhemispheric integration and synchronization. While the EEG correlates of meditative states are to some extent subject to the intents of the practitioner, as well as to phases within meditation, there are some fundamental EEG similarities across many different practices. In general, the EEG during meditation shows an overall decrease in frequency of the brain wave pattern to alpha and theta ranges and an increase in alpha and theta amplitude and regularity in the frontal and central regions of the brain (Wallace and Benson 1972; Davidson 1976; Kasamatsu and Hirai 1966; Stroebel and Glueck 1980). The increased low-frequency theta activity as a function of meditation and meditator's competence is perhaps the most important result found in meditation research, since the sustained production of low-amplitude theta is associated with sustained attention. A range of studies also indicates an increase of coherence, a synchronization within the thalamic structures, and a greater coherence across different cortical areas (Fenwick 1987). While the long-term alteration of cerebral rhythms by meditation has been established, the specificity of these changes to meditation, as opposed to collateral effects (e.g., relaxation) or lifestyle changes, has not been established. However, the similar effects of hallucinogens (Mandell 1985) suggests that increased interhemispheric coherence is a property *sui generis* of the transpersonal modes of consciousness.

Neurophenomenological Perspectives on Contemplative Traditions. Laughlin, McManus, and d'Aquili (1990) suggest that meditative and mystical practices and their higher phases of consciousness represent a stage in neurocognitive development they call *contemplation.* "Transcendence is a process of extraordinary neural development . . . which produces a fundamental reorganization of the nervous system. . . . [This] results from the application of awareness to the very processes that produce . . . the entire cognized environment. The ego is the maturation of adaptation, mature contemplation is the maturation of reflection. Both are mediated by the same neurobiological processes" (336). These phases of consciousness represent advanced individuation and development of neurophysiological structural features. It is increasingly evident that these traditions and their realizations reflect an evolution or development of human thought that surpasses the formal operational and logical thought characteristic of Piaget's highest stages. The examination of the transcendent unity of these traditions indicates that their realization of cultural relativism constitutes one of these recognitions.

Summary. This section has introduced some of the variation found cross-culturally in the phenomena of ASC. While there have been good reasons to see a commonality underlying the transpersonal ASC, there are also important reasons for distinguishing between different states within that mode. One of the classic concerns about different ASC within anthropology has been the distinction between soul flight and possession. Such differences have not only social distinctions in terms of what types of societies in which they are most likely manifested but also differences in terms of associated physiological conditions. Differences in the manifestations of different types of transpersonal states apparently reflect not only social and physiological factors but also the intentionality of actors. The contemplative traditions illustrate that deliberately cultivated attention provides the basis for further development of the potentials of human consciousness.

SOCIETAL CONDITIONS AND ASC INDUCTION

Dobkin De Rios and Smith (1977) have pointed out that as societies grow in structural complexity, there is a change in the use of and access to plant hallucinogens. The case studies indicate that as societies change from egalitarian to hierarchical, drugs are eliminated from widespread use and are usurped by the elite segments. Previous research (Winkelman 1992) has found that extent of use of ASC induction procedures significantly declines from the shaman of hunting and gathering societies to the healers of the politically integrated and socially stratified societies. Jorgensen (1980) found that as sodalities increased, the use of vision quests by shaman and the access to vision quests by the general populace declined. This suggests that there are societal differences in the use of ASC induction procedures.

The incidence of different types of drug and nondrug ASC induction procedures in training of magico-religious practitioners was examined at the societal level through comparing the data set of Winkelman (Winkelman and White 1987) with the social complexity variables coded by Murdock and Provost (1973). The relationship of social conditions to hallucinogenic drug use, alcohol use, hallucinogenic drug and alcohol use, and non-drug ASC are individually examined and then assessed in a general model of evolutionary transformation of ASC induction practices.

Based upon these distinctions between different types of drug-induced ASC and the different types of nondrug ASC, the following variable and values were created to represent different types of societies in terms of ASC induction procedures:

Drug/Nondrug ASC Variable

1. Hallucinogenic shamanic ASC

2. Nondrug shamanic ASC

3. Hallucinogen and alcohol ASC

4. Alcohol only ASC

5. Nondrug mediumistic ASC

This drug/nondrug ASC variable represents a hypothesized evolutionary model assessing the assumption that shamanic altered states of consciousness originate in hallucinogens and eventually transform into alcohol-induced ASC and nondrug mediumistic ASC as a function of increases in social complexity.

All of the social complexity variables were positively correlated with this drug/nondrug ASC variable, with the strongest correlations with political integration ($r = .50$; $p < .0003$) and social stratification ($r = .41$; $p < .003$). All of the social complexity variables reported by Murdock and Provost (1973) were entered as predictor variables in multiple linear regression to predict the drug/nondrug ASC variable. Three variables were significant: political integration, writing and records, and social stratification (multiple $r = .69$; $r = .47$; $F = 12.1$; 3,41 df; $p < .0000$), indicating that substantial amounts of variance in ASC induction types are accounted for by social factors. The temporal lobe discharge variable did not add significantly to prediction of the drug/nondrug ASC variable. These correlations support an evolutionary model with political integration as a principal cause of change; however, other social or cultural variables must be responsible for explanation of the remaining variance in the ASC induction practices.

The decline in ASC as a function of increasing social complexity is partially called into question by the universal incidence of ASC training associated with shamanistic practitioners, which indicates that the institutionalized use of ASC is also present in the more complex societies. Although the more complex societies do have priest and healers, which have a significantly lower incidence of ASC induction procedures and tend to utilize deliberate ASC induction techniques less frequently, the hypothesis of a decline in the intensity of ASC in more complex societies does not appear to be substantiated. Using the overall number of ASC induction techniques and procedures as a rough indication of intensity of ASC induction, it appears that the importance of ASC does not decrease with increases in social complexity. This is because the mediums, which are present in the most complex societies, have an overall incidence of ASC induction procedures and characteristics that are as high as the shaman, which are present in the simplest societies. However, the nature of the ASC do change as a function of social complexity, and there is a reduction or delay in the *deliberate* seeking of ASC in the more complex societies, as reflected in a comparison of the shaman and mediums. In summary, while ASC as a basis for training shamanistic healers is universal, the specific characteristics of the ASC and the induction procedures do vary as a function of the complexity of the society (Winkelman 1986b).

CONCLUSIONS

While cross-cultural research does not substantiate a decline in religious ASC, examination of our own society suggest changes. While religious sects and cults (e.g., fundamentalist, Eastern cults) do permit ecstatic or ASC experiences and behavior, they do not constitute the primary religious activities of the society at large. Are such ASC behaviors no longer necessary?

The biological model of ASC is further supported by Siegel's (1989) work entitled *Intoxication*. Siegel points to evidence that humans have an innate drive to seek ASC. Such evidence suggests that religion has been an institutionalized base for meeting this human for ASC. What are the consequences for a society that views such behavior as aberrant, atavistic, and pathological?

Since these ASC behaviors represent fundamental human drives, the failure of legitimated religious organizations to address these needs means that other institutionalized forms of behavior will be developed to address the needs. In the context of U.S. society, several alternate behavioral patterns appear to address this biologically based need for ASC. One is the "bar scene" and alcohol consumption, combining the physiological induction of ASC with the provision of community relations found in traditional shamanic practices. A second related ASC feature of modern societies is the illegal drug use considered to be a rampant problem in our country. Such drug-induced ASC can be seen as an alternate to transcendence. And finally, the increase of Eastern religions and associated meditative practices constitute another set of practices for inducing ASC. These phenomena suggest that societal failure to create legitimate modes for the alteration of consciousness will result in the emergence of other traditions that may be at odds with other aspects of society.

The use of these ASC procedures in other societies is explicitly in the context of healing, which means "to make whole." The physiological properties of ASC are a "wholing" of the individual, an interaction of different aspects of brain function. The common roots of *heal, whole,* and *holy* suggest that these conjunctions of healing and religious experience represent a fundamental adaptation of human societies to the manipulation of consciousness for health.

NOTES

1. This universal generalization is apparently true in spite of the fact that a few societies lack institutionalized shamanistic healers. Those few societies without specialized shamanistic healers statuses present have ASC induction techniques involved in performance of their nonprofessional community healing activities (Winkelman 1990, 1992).

2. For example, see Bourguignon 1968, 1976a, 1976b; Peters and Price-Williams 1980; Prince 1982a, 1982b; Jilek 1982; Heinze 1983; Noll 1983; Kelly and Locke 1981; Locke and Kelly 1985; Winkelman 1986b, 1991b, 1992.

3. Mandell (1980, 1985) suggests that there are two bases for transcendent states in the temporal lobe hypersynchronous activities: the hippocampal-septal system and the amygdala. Spontaneous discharges originating in the hippocampal-septal system are referred to as interictal attacks. Spontaneous synchronous discharges originating in the amygdala are more common and are generally labeled as temporal lobe epilepsy or, mistakenly, schizophrenia. Mandell's model for transcendent states of consciousness involves the loss of serotonin inhibition to the hippocampal CA3 cells, which results in an increase in their activity and manifestation of hippocampal-septal slow waves. This ac-

tivity may manifest a range from the slowing of the EEG, as in a relaxed state, to the strongly driven hypersynchronous hippocampal-septal seizures.

REFERENCES

Aaronson, B., and H. Osmond, editors. 1970. *Psychedelics—The Uses and Implications of Hallucinogenic Drugs*. New York: Doubleday.

Abramson, H., editor. 1967. *The Use of LSD in Psychotherapy and Alcoholism*. New York: Bobbs-Merrill.

Ackerknecht, E. 1943. "Psychopathology, Primitive Medicine and Primitive Culture." Reprinted from *Bulletin of the History of Medicine* 14: 30–67.

Adams, R., and M. Victor. 1977. "Epilepsy and Convulsive States." In *Principles of Neurology*. New York: McGraw-Hill. 211–231.

Aghajanian, G. 1982. "Neurophysiologic Properties of Psychotomimetics." *Psychotropic Agents III*. F. Hoffmeister and G. Stille, editors. New York: Springer-Verlag. 89–109.

Andritzky, W. 1989. "Sociopsychotherapeutic Functions of Ayahuasca Healing in Amazonia." *Journal of Psychoactive Drugs* 21 (1):77–89.

Appenzeller, O. 1987. "The Autonomic Nervous System and Fatigue." *Functional Neurology* 2 (4): 473–485.

Benson, H. J. Beary, and M. Carol. 1974. "The Relaxation Response." *Psychiatry* 37: 37–46.

Benson, H.; J. Kotch; K. Crassweller; and M. Greenwood. 1979. "The Relaxation Response." *Consciousness: The Brain, States of Awareness, and Alternate Realities*. D. Goleman and R. Davidson, editors. New York: Irvington.

Blacker, C. 1981. "Japan." *Divination and Oracles*. M. Loewe and C. Blacker, editors. London: George Allen and Unwin.

Blackmore, S. 1982. *Beyond the Body: An Investigation of Out-of-the-Body Experiences*. London: Society for Psychical Research.

Blackmore, S. 1991. "Near-Death Experiences: In or Out of the Body." *Skeptical Inquirer* 16:34–45.

Bliss, K. 1988. "LSD and Psychotherapy." *Contemporary Drug Problems* (winter): 519–563.

Bourguignon, E. 1968. *Cross-cultural Study of Dissociational States*. Columbus: Ohio State University Press.

Bourguignon, E. 1976a. *Possession*. San Francisco: Chandler and Sharp.

Bourguignon, E. 1976b. "Spirit Possession Beliefs and Social Structure." *The Realm of the Extra-Human Ideas and Actions*. A. Bhardati, editor. The Hague: Mouton. 17–26.

Bourguignon, E., and T. Evascu. 1977. "Altered States of Consciousness within a General Evolutionary Perspective: A Holocultural Analysis." *Behavior Science Research* 12 (3): 197–216.

Bravo, G., and C. Grob. 1989. "Shamans, Sacraments and Psychiatrists." *Journal of Psychoactive Drugs* 21 (1): 123–128.

Budzynski, T. 1986. "Clinical Applications of Non-Drug Induced States." *Handbook of States of Consciousness*. B. Wolman and M. Ullman, editors. New York: Van Nostrand Reinhold. 428–460.

Carrington, P. 1987. "Managing Meditation in Clinical Practice." *The Psychology of Meditation*. M. West, editor. Oxford: Clarendon Press. 150–172.

Castillo, R. 1991. "Divided Consciousness and Enlightenment in Hindu Yogis." *Anthropology of Consciousness* 2 (304): 1–6.

Claxton, G. 1987. "Meditation in Buddhist Psychology." *The Psychology of Meditation*. M. West, editor. Oxford: Clarendon Press. 23–38.

Cohen, S. 1968. "A Quarter Century of Research with LSD." *The Problem and Prospects of LSD*. J. Ungerleide, editor. Springfield: Charles C. Thomas.

Davidson, J. 1976. "The Physiology of Meditation and Mystical States of Consciousness." *Perspectives in Biology and Medicine* (spring): 345–379.

Delmonte, M. 1987a. "Meditation: Contemporary Theoretical Approaches." *The Psychology of Meditation*. M. West, editor. Oxford: Clarendon Press. 39–53.

Delmonte, M. 1987b. "Personality and Meditation." *The Psychology of Meditation*. M. West, editor. Oxford: Clarendon Press. 118–132.

Dobkin De Rios, M., and D. Smith. 1977. "Drug Use and Abuse in Cross-cultural Perspective." *Human Organization* 36 (1): 14–21.

Dow, M.; M. Burton; D. White; and K. Reitz. 1984. "Galton's Problem as Network Autocorrelation." *American Ethnologist* 11: 4.

Eliade, M. 1964. *Shamanism: Archaic Techniques of Ecstasy*. Princeton: Princeton University Press.

Fenwick, P. 1987. "Meditation and the EEG." *The Psychology of Meditation*. M. West, editor. Oxford: Clarendon Press. 104–117.

Finkler, K. 1985. *Spiritualist Healers in Mexico*. South Hadley, MA: Bergin and Garvey.

Forster, F. M., and H. E. Booker. 1975. "The Epilepsies and Convulsive Disorders." *Clinical Neurology*. A. B. Baker and L. H. Baker, editors. Philadelphia: Harper and Row Publishers.

Frecska, E., and Z. Kulcsar. 1989. "Social Bonding in the Modulation of the Physiology of Ritual Trance." *Ethos* 17 (1): 70–87.

Furst, Peter. 1976. *Hallucinations and Culture*. San Francisco: Chandler and Sharp.

Gellhorn, E. 1969. "Further Studies on the Physiology and Pathophysiology of Tuning of the Central Nervous System." *Psychosomatics* 10: 94–103.

Gellhorn, E., and W. F. Kiely. 1972. "Mystical States of Consciousness: Neurophysiological and Clinical Aspects." *Journal of Nervous and Mental Disease* 154 (6): 399–405.

Gellhorn, E., and G. Loofbourrow. 1963. *Emotions and Emotional Disorders. A Neurophysiological Study*. New York: Harper and Row.

Goleman, D. 1977. *The Varieties of Meditative Experience*. New York: Dutton.

Goodman, Felicitas D. 1988a. *How about Demons? Possession and Exorcism in the Modern World*. Bloomington: Indiana University Press.

Goodman, Felicitas D. 1988b. *Ecstasy, Ritual and Alternate Reality: Religion in a Pluralistic World*. Bloomington: Indiana University Press.

Green, C. 1968. *Out-of-the-Body Experiences*. New York: Ballatine Books.

Grof, S. 1975. *Realms of the Unconscious: Observations from LSD Research*. New York: Viking Press.

Grof, S. 1980. *LSD Psychotherapy*. Pomona, CA: Hunter House.

Gussler, J. 1973. "Social Change, Ecology, and Spirit Possession among the South African Nguni." *Religion, Altered States of Consciousness and Social Change*. E. Bourguignon, editor. Columbus: Ohio State University Press.

Halifax, J. 1979. *Shamanic Voices*. New York: E. P. Dutton.

Harner, M. 1982. *The Way of the Shaman*. New York: Bantam.

Heinze, R-I. 1983. "Shamans or Medium." *Phoenix* 6 (1–2): 25–44.

Hoffmeister, F., and G. Stille, editors. 1982. *Psychotropic Agents III*. New York: Springer-Verlag.

Hultkrantz, A. 1966. "An Ecological Approach to Religion." *Ethos* 31: 131–150.

Hultkrantz, A. 1973. "A Definition of Shamanism." *Temenos* 9: 25–37.

Hultkrantz, A. 1978. "Ecological and Phenomenological Aspects of Shamanism." *Shamanism in Siberia*. V. Dioszegi and M. Hoppal, editors. Budapest: Akademiai Kiado.

Jilek, W. 1982. "Altered States of Consciousness in North American Indian Ceremonials." *Ethos* 10 (4): 326–343.

Jorgensen, J. 1980. *Western Indians: Comparative Environments, Languages, and Cultures of 172 Western American Indian Tribes*. San Francisco: W. H. Freeman.

Kasamatsu, A., and T. Hirai. 1966. "An Electroencephalographic Study on the Zen Meditation." *Japanese Journal of Psychiatry and Neurology* 20: 315–336.

Kehoe, A., and Dody H. Giletti. 1981. "Women's Preponderance in Possession Cults: The Calcium Deficiency Hypothesis Extended." *American Anthropologist* 83: 549–561.

Kelly, E., and R. Locke. 1981. *Altered States of Consciousness and Laboratory Psi Research: A Historical Survey and Research Prospectus*. New York: Parapsychology Foundation.

Kiefel, J.; D. Paul; and R. Bodnar. 1989. "Reduction of Opioid and Non-opioid Forms of Swim Analgesia by 5–HT2 Receptor Antagonists." *Brain Research* 500: 231–240.

Kurland, A. 1985. "LSD in the Supportive Care of the Terminally Ill Cancer Patient." *Journal of Psychoactive Drugs* 17 (4): 279–290.

La Barre, Weston. 1970. "Old and New World Narcotics: A Statistical Question and Ethnological Reply." *Economic Botany* 24: 368–373.

Langner, R. 1967. "Six Years' Experience with LSD Therapy." *The Use of LSD in Psychotherapy and Alcoholism*. H. Abramson, editor. New York: Bobbs-Merrill.

Laughlin, C.; J. McManus; and E. d'Aquili. 1990. *Brain, Symbol and Experience: Toward a Neurophenomenology of Consciousness*. Boston and Shaftesbury: Shambhala.

Lehrer, P.; R. Woolfolk; and N. Goldman. 1984. "Progressive Relaxation Then and Now: Does Change Always Mean Progress?" *Consciousness and Self Regulation: Advances in Research and Theory*. Vol. 4. G. Schwartz, D. Shapiro, and R. Davidson, editors. New York: Plenum Press. 183–216.

Leukel, F. 1972. *Introduction to Physiological Psychology*. Saint Louis: Mosley.

Lex, B. 1976. "Physiological Aspects of Ritual Trance." *Journal of Altered States of Consciousness* 2 (2): 109–122.

Lex, B. 1979. "The Neurobiology of Ritual Trance." *The Spectrum of Ritual: A Biogenetic Structural Analysis*. E. Aquili, C. Laughlin, and J. McManus, editors. New York: Columbia University Press.

Locke, R., and E. Kelly. 1985. "A Preliminary Model for the Cross-cultural Analysis of Altered States of Consciousness." *Ethos* 13: 3–55.

Lukoff, D., R. Zanger; and F. Lu. 1990. "Transpersonal Psychology Research Review:

Psychoactive Substances and Transpersonal States." *Journal of Transpersonal Psychology* 22 (2): 107–147.

McIntosh, A. 1980. "Beliefs about Out-of-the-Body Experiences among Elema, Gulf Kamea and Rigo Peoples of Papua, New Guinea." *Journal of the Society of Psychical Research* 50: 460–478.

MacLean, P. 1990. *The Triune Brain in Evolution.* New York: Plenum.

Mandell, A. 1980. "Toward a Psychobiology of Transcendence: God in the Brain." *The Psychobiology of Consciousness.* D. Davidson and R. Davidson, editors. New York: Plenum.

Mandell, A. 1985. "Interhemispheric Fusion." *Journal of Psychoactive Drugs* 17 (4): 257–266.

Mani, K.; P. Gopalakrishnan; J. Vyas; and M. Pillai. 1968. "Hot Water Epilepsy: A Peculiar Type of Reflex-Induced Epilepsy." *Neurology* (India) 16 (3): 107–110.

Mani, K.; A. J. Main; C. Ramesh; and G. Ahuja. 1972. Hot-Water Epilepsy—Clinical and Electroencephalographic Features—Study of 60 cases." *Neurology* (India) 20: 237–240.

Maxfield, M. 1990. "Effects of Rhythmic Drumming on EEG and Subjective Experience." Unpublished manuscript.

Moody, R. 1975. *Life after Life.* Atlanta: Mockingbird Books.

Mougin, C.; A. Baulay; M. Henriet; D. Haton; M. Jacquier; D. Turnhill; S. Berthelay; and R. Gaillard. 1987. "Assessment of Plasma Opioid Peptides, Beta-endorphin and Metenkephalin at the End of an International Nordic Ski Race." *European Journal of Applied Physiology* 56 (3): 281–286.

Murdock, G. P., and C. Provost. 1973. "Measurement of Cultural Complexity." *Ethnology* 12: 379–392.

Neher, A. 1961. "Auditory Driving Observed with Scalp Electrodes in Normal Subjects." *Electroencephalography and Clinical Neurophysiology* 13: 449–451.

Neher, A. 1962. "A Physiological Explanation of Unusual Behavior in Ceremonies involving Drums." *Human Biology* 34: 151–160.

Neppe, V. 1981. "Review Article: The Non-Epileptic Symptoms of Temporal Lobe Dysfunction." *South Africa Medical Journal* 60: 989–991.

Neppe, V. 1983. "Temporal Lobe Symptomatology in Subjective Paranormal Experiences." *Journal of the American Society of Psychical Research* 77: 1.

Noll, R. 1983. "Shamanism and Schizophrenia: A State-Specific Approach to the Schizophrenia Metaphor of Shamanic States." *American Ethnologist* 10 (3): 443–459.

Osmond, H. 1967. "Some Problems in the Use of LSD-25 in the Treatment of Alcoholism." *The Use of LSD in Psychotherapy and Alcoholism.* H. Abramson, editor. New York: Bobbs-Merrill.

Pagano, R., and S. Warrenburg. 1983. "Meditation: In Search of a Unique Effect." *Consciousness and Self-Regulation Advances in Research and Theory.* Vol. 3. R. Davidson, G. Schwartz, and D. Shapiro, editors. New York: Plenum Press. 153–210.

Peters, L., and D. Price-Williams. 1980. "Towards an Experiential Analysis of Shamanism." *American Ethnologist* 7: 397–418.

Prince, R. 1968. "Can the EEG Be Used in the Study of Possession States?" *Trance and Possession States.* R. Prince, editor. Montreal: McGill University Press.

Prince, R. 1982a. "The Endorphins: A Review of Psychological Anthropologists." *Ethos* 10 (4): 299–302.

Prince, R. 1982b. "Shamans and Endorphins." *Ethos* 10 (4): 409.

Rahkila, P.; E. Hakala; K. Salminen; and T. Laatikainen. 1987. "Response of Plasma Endorphins to Running Exercise in Male and Female Endurance Athletes." *Medicine and Science in Sports and Exercise* 19 (5): 451–455.

Ring, K. 1980. *Life at Death: A Scientific Investigation of the Near-Death Experience.* New York: Coward, McCann and Geoghegan.

Ring K. 1986. *Heading Toward Omega.* New York: Morrow.

Rogers, L. 1976. "Human EEG Response to Certain Rhythmic Pattern Stimuli, with Possible Relations to EEG Lateral Asymmetry Measures and EEG Correlates of Chanting." Ph.D. dissertation, Department of Physiology, University of California in Los Angeles.

Rogers, L., and D. Walters. 1981. "Methods of Finding Single Generators, with Applications to Auditory Driving of the Human EEG by Complex Stimuli." *Journal of Neuroscience Methods* 4: 257–265.

Sabom, M. 1982. *Recollections of Death.* New York: Harper and Row.

Sargent, W. 1974. *The Mind Possessed.* Philadelphia: Lippincott.

Schoonmaker, F. 1979. "Denver Cardiologist Discloses Findings after 18 Years of Near-Death Research." *Anabiosis* 1: 1–2. (Cited in Blackmore 1991)

Schultes, E., and A. Hofmann. 1979. *Plants of the Gods.* New York: McGraw-Hill.

Sforzo, G. 1989. "Opiods and Exercise: An Update." *Sports Medicine* 7 (2): 109–124.

Shapiro, Deane. 1980. *Meditation.* New York: Aldine.

Shapiro, Deane. 1990. "Meditation, Self-control, and Control by Benevolent Other: Issues of Content and Context." *Psychotherapy, Meditation and Health.* M. Kwee, editor. London: East-West Publications. 67–123.

Shapiro, D., and R. Walsh, editors. 1984. *Meditation: Classic and Contemporary Perspectives.* New York: Aldine.

Shields, D. 1978. "A Cross-cultural Study of Out-of-the-Body Experiences, Waking, and Sleeping." *Journal of the Society for Psychical Research* 49: 697–741.

Siegel, R. K. 1989. *Intoxication: Life in Pursuit of Artificial Paradise.* New York: Dutton.

Siikala, A. 1978. *The Rite Technique of Siberian Shaman.* Folklore Fellows Communications no. 220. Helsinki: Soumalainen Tiedeskaremia Academia.

Steward, Julian. 1955. *Theory of Cultural Change.* Urbana: University of Illinois.

Strauss, H.; M. Ostow; and L. Greenstein. 1952. *Diagnostic Electro-encephalography.* New York: Grune and Stratton.

Stroebel, C., and B. Glueck. 1980. "Passive Meditation: Subjective, Clinical and Electrographic Comparison with Feedback." *Consciousness and Self-Regulation Advances in Research and Theory.* Vol. 2. G. Schwartz and D. Shapiro, editors. New York: Plenum Press. 401–428.

Subrahmanyam, H. S. 1972. "Hot-Water Epilepsy." *Neurology* (India) 20: 240–243.

Szymusiak, R., and E. Satinoff. 1985. "Thermal Influences on Basal Forebrain Hypogenic Mechanisms." *Brain Mechanisms of Sleep.* D. McGinty, editors. New York: Raven Press. 301–319.

Thoren, P.; J. Floras; P. Hoffmann; and D. Seals. 1990. "Endorphins and Exercise: Physiological Mechanisms and Clinical Implications." *Medicine and Science in Sports and Exercise* 22 (4): 417–428.

Vogel, W.; D. Boverman; E. Klaiber; and Y. Kobayashi. 1974. "EEG Driving Responses as a Function of Monoamine Oxydase." *Electroencephalography in Clinical Neurophysiology* 36: 205.

Wallace, R., and H. Benson. 1972. "The Physiology of Meditation." *Scientific American* 226 (2): 84–90.

Walsh, R. 1979. "Meditation Research: An Introduction and Review." *Journal of Transpersonal Psychology* 11: 161–174.

Walsh, R. 1980. "The Consciousness Disciplines and the Behavioral Sciences." *American Journal of Psychiatry* 137: 663–673.

Walsh, R. 1983. "Meditation Practice and Research." *Journal of Humanistic Psychology* 23 (1): 18–50.

Walsh, R. 1988. "Two Asian Psychologies and Their Implications for Western Psychotherapists." *American Journal of Psychotherapy* 42 (4): 543–560.

Walsh, R. 1990. *The Spirit of Shamanism*. Los Angeles: Tarcher.

Ward, C., editor. 1989. *Altered States of Consciousness and Mental Health: A Cross-cultural Perspective*. Sage: Newbury Park.

West, M. 1987a. "Meditation: Magic, Myth and Mystery." *The Psychology of Meditation*. M. West, editor. Oxford: Clarendon Press. 192–210.

West, M., editor. 1987b. *The Psychology of Meditation*. Oxford: Clarendon Press.

West, M. 1987c. "Traditional Psychological Perspectives on Meditation." *The Psychology of Meditation*. M. West, editor. Oxford: Clarendon Press. 5–22.

Wilber, Ken. 1977. *The Spectrum of Consciousness*. Wheaton, IL: Theosophical Publishing.

Wilber, Ken. 1979. *No Boundary: Eastern and Western Approaches to Personal Growth*. Los Angeles: Zen Center Publications.

Winkelman, M. 1982. "Magic: A Theoretical Reassessment." *Current Anthropology* 23: 37–44, 59–66.

Winkelman, M. 1984. "A Cross-cultural Study of Magico-Religious Practitioners." Ph.D. dissertation, University of California at Irvine. Ann Arbor: University Microfilms.

Winkelman, M. 1986a. "Magico-Religious Practitioner Types and Socioeconomic Conditions." *Behavioral Science Research* 20 (1–4): 17–46.

Winkleman, M. 1986b. "Trance States: A Theoretical Model and Cross-Cultural Analysis." *Ethos* 14: 174–203.

Winkelman, M. 1990. "Shasmana and Other 'Magico-Religious' Healers: A Cross-cultural Study of Their Origins, Nature, and Social Transformations." *Ethos* 18: 308–352.

Winkelman, M. 1991a. "Physiological and Therapeutic Aspects of Shamanistic Healing." *Subtle Energies* 1: 1–18.

Winkelman, M. 1991b. "Therapeutic Effects of Hallucinogens." *Anthropology of Consciousness* 2 (3–4): 15–19.

Winkelman, M. 1992. "Shamans, Priests and Witches. A Cross-cultural Biosocial Study of Magico-Religious Practitioners." *Anthropological Research Papers* no. 44, Arizona State University.

Winkelman, M. 1996. "Psychointegrator Plants: Their Roles in Human Culture and Health." Introduction to *Sacred Plants, Consciousness and Healing: Cross-Cultural and Interdisciplinary Perspectives. Yearbook of Cross-Cultural Medicine and Psychotherapy Volume 6*. M. Winkelman and W. Andritzky, editors. Berlin: Springer-Verlag. 9–53.

Winkelman, M., and D. White. 1987. "A Cross-Cultural Study of Magico-Religious
    Practitioners and Trance States: Data Base." *Human Relations Area Files Re-
    search Series in Quantitative Cross-Cultural Data*. Vol. 3. D. Levinson and R.
    Wagner, editors. New Haven: HRAF Press.
Winson, J. 1977. *Brain and Psyche: The Biology of the Unconscious*. Garden City:
    Anchor Press/Doubleday.
Winson, J. 1990. "The Meaning of Dreams." *Scientific American* (November): 86–96.
Wright, P. 1989. "The Shamanic State of Consciousness." Theme Issue on: *Trance and
    Shamanism in the Cross-cultural Perspective*. M. Dobkin De Rios and M. Win-
    kelman, editors. *Journal of Psychoactive Drugs* 21 (1): 25–33.
Wright, P. 1991. "Rhythmic Drumming in Contemporary Shamanism and Its Relation-
    ship to Auditory Driving and Risk of Seizure Precipitation in Epileptics." *An-
    thropology of Consciousness* 2 (3–4): 7–14.
Yensen, R. 1985. "LSD and Psychotherapy." *Journal of Psychoactive Drugs* 17 (4):
    267–277.
Zanger, R. 1989. "Psycholytic Therapy in Europe." *Newsletter. The Albert Hoffman
    Foundation*, vol. 1, no. 2.

16

SHAMANISM

Joan B. Townsend

The shaman, who traffics in supernatural power and communes with spirits, has fascinated people for centuries. Thought of as a mystic, a hierophant, a healer, a devil, a psychotic, or a charlatan, he has been held in respect, awe, fear, or disgust or held up to ridicule. My goal is not to write the definitive study of shamanism but to provide an overview of *some* of the more significant aspects of shamanism and to point to some of the literature through which the reader may begin to pursue specific interests.

There is a plethora of material of varying quality on shamanism. Shamanism has been studied by both North Americans and Europeans (notably Russians, Hungarians, Scandinavians) for many years. Popov, in 1932, estimated that there were over 650 papers on the topic by Russian scholars (Rank 1967: 15). Like much Soviet anthropological research, shamanic studies were often couched in a Marxist evolutionary framework. Nevertheless, the ethnographic data are extensive and valuable. Western research concentrated primarily on the ecstatic states of shamanism and neglected the purely medical aspects of the practice (e.g., Rank 1967: 16,19). North Americans tended to concentrate on New World phenomena; the Europeans focused primarily on Siberian shamanism, which has come to be considered the "classical" form. Yakut, Tungus, Chukchi, and Buryat as well as Saami were heavily represented.[1] In recent years, scholars have begun to include south Asian, Japanese, and Korean studies.

In North America, particularly, interest shifted from the anthropological study of religion to other concerns for some forty years until about the early 1970s when a number of studies in religion again began to appear. The argument (discussed below) that shamans are psychologically abnormal contributed to the lack of interest in the topic as a significant social phenomenon. Shamanism was relegated to the realm of pathology or considered an epiphenomenon of past, more "primitive" cultures (cf. Kroeber 1952). Like religion, shamanism was expected to disappear to be replaced by psychologically oriented therapies and allopathic medicine, just as science was destined to replace religion (e.g., see Wallace 1966:265).

It is provocative to inquire whether the recent academic surge in interest stemmed in part from Castaneda's controversial studies (e.g., 1968) of the alleged Yaqui "Don Juan" and from other interests growing out of the rise in metaphysical consciousness following the 1960s. Psychological and psychoanalytic interpretations of shamanic trance, initiation, interaction with spirits, and so on, have become some of the major foci of recent research, and symbolism is of growing concern. In the 1970s a new facet of shamanism also developed within the overall New Religious movements genre: core and neoshamanism and the use of the concept of shamanism (however defined) as a metaphor for all sorts of beliefs and behaviors not strictly contained within "traditional" shamanism.[2]

Noll (1989: 49–50) pointed out that there are currently at least two explanatory metaphoric systems being developed to explore shamanism. One is materialistic, neurophysiological, or biochemical (e.g., Lex 1979; Winkelman 1986). Alternatively, the phenomenological school is directed toward studying subjective phenomenology of shamanic experiences, rather than arguing for a reductionist mechanistic perspective (e.g., Harner 1980; Noll 1983, 1985).

In spite of the extensive literature on shamanism, and Eliade's (1964) classic but somewhat uncritical survey of the topic, there is still confusion as to what, exactly, is shamanism and what is not (cf. Reinhard 1976: 12). There is no lack of attempts to define it, however. One cannot assume that because an author uses the term *shaman* for a religious or healing functionary that the individual conforms, even remotely, to any of the more common definitions of the term. It is necessary in every instance to examine the ethnographic data in detail to determine just what, specifically, the author is dealing with. If the parameters of shamanism can be clearly established, perhaps we can deal more fruitfully with particular manifestations of shamanism, aspects of trance, psychological makeup of shamans, and other issues.

DEFINITIONS OF SHAMANISM

Origins of the Term *Shamanism*

The term *shamanism*[3] has become fixed in anthropological and, more recently, popular literature. Usually it is said to be derived from a Tungus word (e.g., Hultkrantz 1973: 26). Nevertheless, others (e.g., Blacker 1975: 317–318, n. 4) suggest it is from the Vedic *śram*, meaning "to heat one's self or practice austerities." *Śramaṇā* derives from this and means "one who practices austerities, an ascetic.'' She references Professor Sir Harold Bailey, who argued that it entered central Asia from India ''through the north-west Prakrit used in the Shan-shan Kingdom about 300 A.D. as an administrative language, as ṣamaṇa'' (Blacker 1975: 318; see also Eliade 1964: 495–500). Shirokogoroff (1935: 268–270) found that although the term *saman* is used by Tungusic speakers to mean a person who has mastered spirits, it is of alien origin. Other ethnic groups in Siberia use other terms for this phenomenon (268–269). The term *shaman* entered the Western lexicon through Russian historians and travelers in the Tungus regions of Siberia in the seventeenth and later centuries. It was generalized, however, and came to mean simply ''pagan sorcerers'' (268).

A Definition

Most researchers feel that shamans are qualitatively distinct from others who traffic in healing and the supernatural such as medicine men/women, mediums, sorcerers, and spiritual healers. When all these are combined together under one label, it makes analysis virtually impossible and distorts any understanding we may have of shamanism.

Shamanism is not ''a religion'' in an organized or institutionalized sense (e.g., Hultkrantz 1978: 11; Reinhard 1976: 19; Shirokogoroff 1935: 276) but can be a part of a range of religious beliefs and practices. It is embedded within the whole social and religious fabric of a society. Neither is it manifest as a homogeneous phenomenon but varies with the culture throughout Siberia (cf. Siikala 1985: 455; Rank 1967) and other regions of the world. Hultkrantz (1973: 27) rightly notes that shamanism is not a *static* constellation of features; these can change through space and time. For these and other reasons, a simple yet workable definition of shamanism is exceedingly difficult to develop. Nevertheless, as Eliade, Harner, and others have argued, there is a fundamental and apparently universal nucleus of specific traits that must be present when shamanism is identified, and these may help segregate out shamans from other practitioners.

The entire raison d'être of shamanism is to interact with the spirit world for the benefit of those in the material world. All defining characteristics are related to that end. The most efficient method to implement this interaction is the employment of altered states of consciousness. Drawing from this basis, a working definition includes the following criteria:

Essential Criteria:

1. *Direct contact (communication) with spirits.* Spirits may be conceived of as forces of nature or *transcendent* energy as well as sentient beings, for example, animal or humanlike spirits. A corollary is the belief in the existence of spirits and/or transcendent ''energy'' and their ability to affect the material world. The shaman will have one or more special helping spirits for assistance and protection.

2. *Control of spirits.* As a "master of spirits," the shaman controls one or more spirits; they do not control him.

3. *Control of shamanic (altered) states of consciousness (SSC)* (Harner 1982: xvi, 20–30, 46–56). The SSC is the usual method through which spirits are dealt with (also called trance or ecstasy).

4. *A "this worldly" (or material world) focus.* The SSC is used for the benefit of individuals and the community, rather than for the shaman's personal enlightenment or progression of his soul.

5. *Soul flight (magical flight).* The shaman has the ability to separate the soul from the body while living and travel in the spirit world or to use a tutelary spirit or a "familiar" for that purpose.

Related Criteria

6. *Introduction of spirits into the shaman's body.* Spirits may speak through the shaman and/or

7. The shaman has the ability *to call in spirits to be present* at a séance or counsel him without necessarily possessing him.

8. *Memory.* The shaman remembers at least some aspects of the SSC.

9. *Healing.* The healing of physical, psychological, or emotional illnesses is a major focus.

This complex of criteria sets the phenomenon I define as "shamanism" apart from other similar phenomena that *may* have developed from or alongside of shamanism.

The criteria are based on a variety of sources[4] but differ slightly from any particular one of them. A number of writers (e.g., Gilberg 1984) argue that central to shamanism is an individual's ability to enter into a shamanic state of consciousness, to have his soul leave his body to travel in the spirit world, and to allow spirits to enter his body. Eliade's definition (1964: 5)—"a shaman specializes in a trance during which his soul is believed to leave his body and ascend to the sky or descend to the underworld"—isolates magical flight as *the* basic and distinctive characteristic of shamanism; "ecstasy" without soul journey is ignored. He specifically excludes (499) the "embodiment of spirits" (spirit possession). Nevertheless, Shirokogoroff (1935: 269) includes possession as a part of shamanism: people who have "mastered spirits, who at their will can introduce these spirits into themselves." Lewis (1971: 51) repeats Shirokogoroff's definition. Hultkrantz (1973: 28; 1985: 453) insists that the soul flight is not a primary trait of shamanism but that contact with spirits in an altered state of consciousness is. He stresses that spirits can be called and attend a séance without directly possessing the shaman. While I fully agree that spirits may be summoned and attend without speaking through a shaman, I am hesitant to use that as a complete definition and to delete the soul journey from the criteria; to do so without a number of other qualifiers would be to broaden the definition of shamanism to the extent that contemporary Western mediums and a range of others who deal with spirits would have to be included. I doubt that this would advance our understanding of shamanism.

Peters and Price-Williams (1980: 399) stress the primacy of mastery of "trance" (SSC) but not the mastery of spirits. I would argue, however, that the essential and primary "purpose" of shamanic activity is to interact with spirits and to be a bridge between the spirit world and the world of the living, rather than to experience an altered state per se. According to shamanic ideology, problems in this world are often caused by spirits, and they can be corrected by other spirits with the shaman acting as intermediary to bring about the solution. This is in agreement with the position of Firth (1973), Shirokogoroff (1935: 160ff), Eliade (1964), Siikala (1978: 319), and others.

The mastery or control of spirits is essential; unless the shaman maintains control, he cannot carry out his duties as a shaman. The issue is often more complex, however. The shaman must be able to exercise control over spirits that might appear or possess him and must be able to call them to assist him. Nevertheless, the command is sometimes more of an invitation or invocation than a demand. Spirits can also turn on a shaman or punish him if he breaches taboos or uses his powers in an inappropriate way. Finally, there are a variety of spirits that may be accessible to a shaman. These can range from deities, pure spirits, and spirits of the dead (ancestors, shamans, and so on) to normally malevolent spirits the shaman has managed to control, as well as animal, plant, and inanimate object spirits. These different categories of spirits may be dealt with in different ways.

Origins of Shamanism

It has been suggested by various authors (e.g., Furst 1977: 2, 21–22; Hult-krantz 1978: 27–28; Winkelman 1990) that shamanism has its roots in the Upper Paleolithic some 25,000 years ago. French cave paintings and other remains suggest that at least some aspects of shamanism may have been developed then. The fact that groups as far removed from each other as South American Indians (e.g., Amazonian Indians, Chilean Mapuche) and Siberian peoples share a num-ber of essential shamanic traits argues strongly for an explanation that shaman-ism was part of the cultural repertoire brought by the first migrants to the New World in the late Pleistocene and against suggestions that similarities are a result of simple diffusion or independent invention (e.g., Furst 1977: 6, 21–22). There were only hunters and gatherers in the Pleistocene; cultivation is only some 9,000 years old. For all these reasons and because shamanism often makes much of animal-human relationships, it also has been argued that shamanism is es-sentially a hunting and gathering method of dealing with the supernatural.

Siberian and Arctic shamanism is usually considered the "classic" form pre-sumably most closely reflective of "original" "Paleolithic" shamanism. This is in part because Siberians and other Arctic people, remote from centers of more extensive sociopolitical and economic change, have been hunter/gatherers or herders recently. Further, shamanism has been very common there in historic times, whereas it has disappeared or been immersed in other religious systems elsewhere. As a result, much research has been concentrated in the Siberian/ Arctic areas for the longest period of time, and classic shamanism, I suggest, perhaps has been defined on the Siberian/Arctic basis as a result of that research focus as much as from hard data.

There is a strong caveat against the use of contemporary and historic hunters and gatherers to determine what Paleolithic societies or especially their belief systems were like. Recent hunter/gatherers are not "pristine" but have had long contact with nonforaging peoples and used foraging as "a rational response to ecological, economic, and socio-political realities" (Stiles 1992: 14).

This raises the question of whether, in fact, Siberian/Arctic shamanism is the "pure" or "classic" form of shamanism, against which all other shamanic manifestations can be compared. As important is the question of whether Siberian/Arctic shamanism should be considered a holdover from Paleolithic foragers.

Shirokogoroff (1935: 276–286) and others (Eliade 1964: 495–507; compare Hultkrantz 1978: 29) argue that Buddhist Lamaism, which spread into northeast Asia in the early centuries of the Christian era, modified considerably Tungus and other north Asian shamanic traditions. Lamaism, in turn, had been heavily influenced by the earlier shamanic/Lamaistic Bon system of Tibet. Shirokogoroff (1935: 282) therefore considers that Tungus shamanism was "stimulated" by Buddhism. He argues, from the perspective of the Tungus and adjacent peoples, that "shamanism is not an initial complex in a chain of an 'evolving' process, but a complex of secondary formation. . . . [H]istoric evidence relating to shamanism in general and its elements fully support the result of our analysis, pointing to a secondary character of shamanism" (276). The Asian Tuva also merge shamanism and Lamaism (Eliade 1964: 498), as do at least some Nepalese shamanic systems. This does not require, however, that *all* shamanism ultimately "originated" from Tibetan sources. In a broader perspective, the search for "origins" of any ancient belief or behavioral system is problematic at least.

Rather than a Paleolithic fossil, shamanism in Siberia and the Arctic more likely evolved and changed there over the centuries, just as it has elsewhere in response to the vagaries of contacts, migrations, and inventions. The influence of the Tibetan Bon through Lamaism, however, cannot be underestimated, particularly in Asia. It must also be remembered that people invent, change, borrow, and "evolve" their traditions and, later, assume the evolved tradition represents the "timeless past" (e.g., Clifton 1990; Hobsbawm and Ranger 1983; Townsend 1991, concerning invented traditions). Researchers often make a similar mistake when we examine supposedly "classic" shamans. Nevertheless, common factors found in many shamanic traditions in widely separated areas of the world may give some insight into what early shamanism probably was like.

The Relation of Shamanism to Levels of Sociopolitical and Economic Integration

Some researchers hypothesize that shamans are causally associated with a subsistence strategy: that of small hunter/gatherer societies. Where more complex strategies occur, shamans change to other forms or cease to exist.

Gilberg (1984: 26) suggests that "shamanism is most widespread in crisis-prone societies," by which he means "hunters, collectors or nomads, who, unlike the calendar-based agriculture society, are more subject to sudden catastrophes or shifts in natural events." They are faced with unexpected, capricious situations and turn to the supernatural and its intermediary, the shaman, for help and protection. The shaman has the knowledge to prevent panic and return the society to normal. "Shamanism can thus be said to reflect concrete tension and environmentally or socially difficult adaptations in crisis situations" (26).

If this is the case, it becomes very difficult to explain not only the occurrence of well-developed shamanism among sophisticated marine hunters/fishermen who have evolved large village-based highly ranked societies (e.g., Northwest coast of North America including southern Alaska and the Aleutians: De Laguna 1972; Townsend 1980, 1981, 1983, 1985) but also their presence in stratified societies such as Nepal, Korea, and Japan. Of course, foragers and nomads do experience stresses and catastrophes that are unpredictable or beyond control. But this is true of all societies. Agrarians face starvation from crop failures due to flood, drought, insect, and other infestations and from disruptive raids and wars. Twentieth-century Western society is not immune. One has only to recall the two world wars or other recent wars and rumors of wars, economic crashes, homelessness, severe famines, and epidemics, notably the 1918 influenza pandemic and most recently AIDS (acquired immunodeficiency syndrome). Are the stresses faced by foragers and nomads any greater than these for individuals and sometimes whole societies? Some studies of foragers (e.g., Sahlins 1968; Lee 1968; Lee and DeVore 1968) indicate that they do not normally live in crisis conditions and continual uncertainty. By some values, they appear "better off" than many in industrial societies.

Similar to Gilberg, others (e.g., Hultkrantz 1966; Siikala 1978) have proposed evolutionary/typological schemes for shamans. Winkelman (1986, 1990), using the Standard Cross-cultural Sample (Murdock and White 1969), constructed a model of shamans, shaman/healers, healers, and mediums arguing that trance-based aspects of shamanism vary on the basis of social complexity and subsistence strategy. Shamans represent an ecological adaptation of hunting/gathering societies to psychobiologically based potentials for altered states of consciousness (Winkelman 1990: 308, 329). Political integration and agriculture change shamans into other types of healers. Shamans, then, are restricted to hunting/gathering societies, while shaman/healers occur in agrarian societies; mediums and healers are in complex societies.

As suggested above, two examples of contradictions to the hypothesis are Nepal, a highly stratified[5] society where village people are herders, traders, and agriculturalists, and the Northwest Pacific Rim from the Aleutians to at least British Columbia. There, people lived in permanent villages and were highly ranked (some approaching stratification), slave owning (averaging 10 percent slave per village),[6] and often clan structured, with economies based on marine hunting, salmon fishing, hunting, gathering, and trade. Shamans continue to exist in contemporary Nepal; they actively persisted in various parts of the Northwest Pacific Rim from precontact until at least the end of the nineteenth century. Shamans in both places employ shamanic states of consciousness ("trance"), perform divination, undertake journeys in the spirit world, bring spirits to séances, allow spirits to speak through them, "magically" fight with other shamans, fight witches, heal, and—on the Northwest Pacific Rim (e.g., Tanaina, Tlingit)—send spirits on missions for them and travel in material reality as their familiars. The association of the shaman with at least one of the helping spirits or the animal familiar is so close that if either is killed on a spirit mission, the shaman also dies in material reality (e.g., De Laguna 1972: 707; Townsend 1965: 309). Thus, at two complex sociopolitical levels, shamans manifest characteristics relegated to those only in small hunter/gatherer societies. One of these complex, sedentary societies is a state; the other is, "technically," a hunter/gatherer, but it certainly does not conform socially, economically, or politically to the generally accepted criteria for a small, egalitarian hunting/gathering society! I agree that shamanism does change in character and that the change, in many places, seems to proceed along the lines proposed by Winkelman, but I strongly question the strict association with merely a particular form of political complexity and subsistence base.

These hypotheses require considerable refinement. The causal factors are considerably more complex than these researchers have suggested, and I am not convinced that Murdock and White's Standard Cross-cultural Sample is fully adequate to provide an in-depth understanding of the dynamics. Shamanism is heavily represented in small foraging societies. Nevertheless, it has considerably more to recommend itself than simply a crisis-intervention method of people who lack continually inhabited villages, complex political structure, or domesticated plants and animals. It is not a unique phenomenon limited to one cultural setting.

SUMMARY ETHNOGRAPHY

Beliefs, Worldview—The World of the Shaman

Specific beliefs related to shamanic phenomena are grounded in the mythology and ideology of the society in which the shaman exists. Nevertheless, there is a considerable conformity in general beliefs that are for the most part central to it.[7]

Fundamental is a belief in the pervading sentience of the universe; for those who know how, this sentience can be used to benefit living people. There are two realities: material reality in which we live and alternate, or spiritual reality, which impinges on this reality.[8] What is done in spiritual reality can affect material reality. In the latter, unbridled power is pervasive. It is the abode of spirits: souls of the dead, deities, and other beings. While humans cannot enter this realm except by death (or as a shaman), spirits can move into material reality, often with impunity. This metaphysical paradigm is not unique to shamanism; it is found in part or whole in a variety of nonmaterialistic systems.

As the developing shaman progresses, he must become intimately familiar with a cognitive map of the spirit world so that he can anticipate and avoid dangers, as well as find his way to specific deities or spirits he may need to deal with. Without such intricate knowledge, disaster can befall him on his journeys. Some shamans are able to draw maps of these worlds in detail (Peters 1978; Townsend 1989, 1992).

The cosmos consists of three worlds. The middle world exists in two realities: the material universe inhabited by living beings and the spiritual aspect. The upper and lower worlds are further subdivided and are accessible only in spiritual reality. The upper world is the abode of deities and spirits, while the lower world is seen variously as merely another locale of spirits or a dark, negative place.

The three levels of the cosmos are connected by the *axis mundi*, which is represented, classically, by the "world tree." The exact type of connection varies, however, and may be conceptualized as a hollow tube or reed, a ladder, or a sacred mountain. Nevertheless, this central core is the means through which shamans and spirits traverse between levels.

Humans, animals, and often inanimate objects in nature have two aspects: material and spirit. It is possible, then, for the shaman to access the help of animal or stone spirits, for example, to assist in his tasks in spiritual reality. Humans have at least one soul and frequently several. These are essential to health and life itself. In some societies (e.g., Inuit, Yupik), the soul is thought to reside in the bones, that part of the body that endures the longest after death. Elsewhere (e.g., Chetri and Tamang of Nepal),[9] one soul is in the lower part of the body, a second around the heart, and the third and "highest" soul at the top of the head (or between the eyes). It is the two lower souls that most frequently become lost or stolen, resulting in illness (Peters 1982; Townsend 1989, 1992).

Two fundamental principles rule the cosmos: balance and reciprocity. Balance or harmony is the desired state but can be disrupted by the action, intentional or unintentional, of humans. When this occurs, the spirit world can retaliate with illness or disasters. It is part of the shaman's job to restore balance. The concept of reciprocity underlies many of the relationships of shamans with the spirits and with his fellow humans. A shaman may provide offerings to the spirits in return for which the spirits respond with what is requested. A shaman must give gifts to his earthly teacher in return for the knowledge provided him. People seeking the shaman's help for illness or other problems also must provide gifts for the shaman, and often the spirits, in return for that assistance.

The spirit world can also be demanding or malevolent without provocation. Again, it is the job of the shaman to placate these powers and prevent harm from befalling the people.

General Characteristics of Shamans

Shamans use a shamanic state of consciousness to facilitate contact with spirits, but it is undertaken in order to help and heal living people within their societies as well as to help and heal the dead. It contrasts markedly with meditation and trance as used by ascetics searching for "nirvana" or their own soul's perfection. Shamanism is a down-to-earth, practical method for the use of the supernatural to heal physical, psychological, and emotional illnesses, foretell the future, and improve the lot of the living.

Particularly in North America, the terms *medicine man* and *shaman* are often used interchangeably, which contributes appreciably to the confusion concerning the kinds of religious specialists that existed in Native American societies. I would suggest, as have others, that *shaman* be restricted to those who fulfill the working definition, while *medicine man* would apply to other healers, including herbalists and bone setters. In some instances, the term *medicine* also refers to spiritual power, but this does not necessarily infer shamanism. While virtually all shamans are, technically, also medicine men, certainly not all medicine men are shamans.

Gilberg (1984) and V. Turner (1972) reiterate Lessa and Vogt's (1958/1979) and Lowie's (1954) dichotomy between shamans and priests. Generally, they say that shamans are found in foraging societies, while priests appear in larger, agricultural ones. Shamans deal directly with the supernatural, while priests learn ritual from other priests. Shamanic rites are directed toward curing especially in the extended family unit, and priests tend to deal more with calendrical rites designed to benefit the whole community. Very generally, these distinctions provide a superficial rule-of-thumb validity, but, as von Fürer-Haimendorf (1970) points out, the roles often overlap; the distinction is not universal. For example, Rasmussen (1929) describes an Iglulik Inuit shaman's journey to the sea spirit to propitiate her and gain the release of the sea mammals. This was done for the village as a whole, although it was not a calendrical ritual. In Nepal and on the Northwest Pacific Coast, shamans conduct some rituals that might appear more in keeping with a priest's roles. The distinction must be made between the role and the individual. The roles of shamans, then, vary from society to society, and in addition, shamans may also perform some roles that are more priestly. Such dichotomies are useful analytically to highlight certain characteristics of a religious role but should not necessarily be taken as a reflection of the real world.

Shamans can be either male or female—although in a particular society, one or the other sex may be in the majority or hold the position exclusively. There seems to be a tendency for males to predominate as shamans in small societies, such as foraging, while in somewhat larger cultivating societies, both men and women are well represented. In large, stratified societies such as Korea and Japan, women mainly fulfill the role, although in Nepal, male shamans outnumber female shamans. The tendency for women more than men to be shamans in some large societies may be a reflection, in part, of the relegation of shamanism to the spiritual periphery when large, universalistic religions are present. Men, then, tend to gravitate toward the greater power and prestige positions of the dominant religion, leaving women to conserve the "folk" shamanic traditions as well as spiritual healing, mediumistic, and mystical practices. In some societies, women until menopause are at a disadvantage in becoming shamans because menstrual blood is considered polluting and offensive to spirits. One female Nepalese apprentice shaman felt she was prohibited from practicing during menstruation. Another full-fledged female shaman passed this off as unimportant; she merely recited a few purifying mantras and practiced as usual (Townsend 1992). Another apparent constraint on women is the problem they encounter in some societies because they are more restricted in their movement or their freedom to work closely with an unrelated male-shaman teacher. The fewer women in shamanism overall, then, may be merely an epiphenomenon of other cultural restrictions on women. On the other hand, lack of women represented in shamanism in some cultures historically might be partly a consequence of male researchers concentrating their studies on men and simply ignoring women or of women avoiding contact with male researchers because of cultural restrictions.

Many cultures have several grades or levels of shamans. Tanaina Athapaskans of southern Alaska have big (powerful) and little (little power) shamans, good and bad ones (Townsend 1965). Nepalese have several levels based on their abilities (Townsend 1989). Blacker (1975: 22) describes two types that have direct contact with spirits. The first is a medium (*miko*), who can be possessed by a spirit that speaks through her. (Blacker uses the pronoun *her*, implying that mediums are women.) The second and most powerful is the healer, whom she calls an ascetic. This individual undergoes the severe austerities typical of shamans and is able to journey to the other world. Blacker, here, makes a well-known distinction between the medium and the shaman: The spirits come to the medium; the shaman goes to the spirits. Some Siberian societies classify their shamans according to specialty or by whether they deal with spirits of the lower or upper world; others use criteria of comparative power of the shamans, and so on (e.g., Bäckman 1978; Rank 1967).

Shamans in the Northwest Pacific Rim societies were often feared and held in respect or wonder and might command high position. Their services were essential in warfare and all other important undertakings. They were not necessarily the primary political leaders, however, and did not necessarily become wealthy because of their abilities. Political authority was related primarily to lineage status derived from wealth, potlatch success, sheer numbers of the person's kin group, and age of the individual (e.g., De Laguna 1972: 670; Oberg 1973). In small, egalitarian societies, shamans may, as Winkelman (1990) contends, be leaders, but in most such egalitarian societies, leadership is often situation specific or ephemeral. Shamans may be held in awe and awarded high status (e.g., Siskin 1983: 66, 80) because of their ability to deal with supernatural power and may be consulted in matters of healing, game location, and so on. In contrast, however, shamans in some small societies are themselves in fear of others in their society who may level witchcraft accusations at them. This concern can be so great that, for example, when a young Nunivak Island boy (Yupik) began to dream and see spirits, his father warned him not to tell anyone (Lantis 1960: 127, 138).

Although séances are among the more notable of shamanic activities, most shamans are frequently involved with the supernatural in various other ways. Nepalese shamans conduct minor ceremonies almost every day. These might include activities such as blowing a mantra for protection or defending against the ever-present danger of attack. One may officiate, in a more priestly sense, at some village ceremonies several times a month. Séances directed primarily toward healing also occur several times a month (Skafte 1989–1993: personal communications).

Pilgrimages, either alone or in a group, to holy places are undertaken by shamans in Nepal, Japan, and Mexico (Huichol) (Blacker 1975: 100; Holmberg 1980; Myerhoff 1974; Skafte 1988). Isolation is practiced by some shamans (e.g., Northwest coast—De Laguna 1972; Japan—Blacker 1975: 98–99). All such practices are designed to honor the helping spirits, to create more intense contact with spirits, or to gain knowledge from them.

Special dreams may be an important means through which spirits communicate with a shaman both initially and throughout life. Although an apprentice will usually have a living teacher, spirits or a dead shaman may also instruct him through dreams. This method of gaining knowledge normally continues throughout the life of the shaman.

Heat and fire are powerful symbols in shamanism. Fire changes the person into spirit, and the shaman, by virtue of his work with fire, becomes the Master of Fire (Eliade 1964: 206). In order to deal with fire, he must learn to endure cold by creating internal mystical heat (e.g., Blacker 1975: 26, 93; Shirokogoroff 1935: 174, 353). Mastery of fire is further demonstrated by walking into a pit of burning wood, jumping into a heap of burning charcoal, walking on burning coals, holding coals in the hand or mouth for periods of time, putting hands in boiling oil, or placing flaming objects into the mouth (e.g., Bäckman 1978: 70; Blacker 1975: 250–251, 260–261; Hoffman 1891: 157; De Laguna 1972: 705; Shirokogoroff 1935: 174, 353; Siskin 1983: 64; Peters and Price-Williams 1980: 401; Townsend 1989, 1992).

The power of words and sounds is particularly important especially in Asian areas such as Japan (Blacker 1975: 93) and Nepal. Mantras (incantations) or magic spells accompany almost all ritual acts and are also used as protection or weapons against evil. Power can reside not only in specific words but also in a sequence of syllables that no longer have meaning (Blacker 1975: 95) or in the sound itself, for example "OM."

While blood sacrifice performed by shamans seems to have been absent in the New World (but note Chilean Mapuche), it is certainly widespread in the Asian shamanic tradition. The most common victims are horses, dogs, and reindeer as well as pigs, sheep, and oxen among Altaic societies, Tungus, Chukchi, and Koryak (Campbell 1988: 158, 175; Eliade 1964: 190ff and passim; Shirokogoroff 1935: 198–202, 370), and sheep, goats, chickens, and cattle in Nepal and other parts of south Asia. In most cases, sacrificial animals are domesticated, not wild. This is likely a reflection in part of availability in recent times. In addition to the broader analyses of sacrifice, animals are a valued possession and as such represent a real material loss; basic alliance and reciprocity themes are expressed when things of value are exchanged.[10] One rationale is that spirits must be fed with blood and meat as well as with vegetable foods such as rice. A second use of sacrifice is the transference of the evil or illness from the patient to the animal, which is then dispatched. Human sacrifice seems to have been exceedingly rare but not unknown. Blacker (1975: 120–121) notes that in time of catastrophe, such as a dam breaking, a person may be sacrificed by being buried alive. A deity might request a sacrifice through the *miko* (shaman medium); in one case, the *miko* was the selected victim. Blacker did not observe this, so she suggests that it might be symbolic. Among Chilean Mapuche, witches may sacrifice a human infant for revenge magic (Faron 1968: 86), and shamans may do so in time of disasters (Degarrod 1992).

Elements of other religious traditions have been incorporated into shamanism. For example, in Nepal, Hindu/Buddhist deities appear within the shamanic pantheon; many of the Tungus spirits are Buddhist; elsewhere, Christian deity and spirits can be called upon (Eliade 1964: 497; Shirokogoroff 1935: 278).

Two closely related issues need further exploration. One is the type of consciousness used in dealing with the spirit world and the other is what kind of possession is related to shamanism.

Shamanic States of Consciousness.[11] Most shamanic activities occur in the "nonordinary psychic state," and most agree that this state, usually called "ecstasy" or "trance," is an essential characteristic. Both terms pose problems (e.g., Reinhard 1976: 17, 20). *Ecstasy* (e.g., Eliade 1964) can be misleading because of its implications of rapture, frenzy, euphoria, or extremely strong emotion and may imply a condition where "rational thought and self-control are obliterated" (Morris 1981: 413). Some shamans indicate that they do experience euphoria, usually at the beginning of some shamanic states (Townsend 1992), but it is not the only kind of experience. *Trance* implies a hypnotic or dazed state that might be applicable in some but not all instances. The term *altered state of consciousness* (ASC) is now coming into vogue as a generic for a variety of nonordinary states. Perhaps better, Harner (1982: xvi, 20–30, 46–56) has suggested "shamanic state(s) of consciousness" (SSC) to set *shamanic* experiences apart from other alternate experiences that may or may not be the same.

The induction of a shamanic state of consciousness can be accomplished in a variety of ways including drumming, dancing, chanting, fasting, and meditation. In some societies, notably in Middle and South America and Siberia, hallucinogens may be used to induce the state, but this is by no means an essential or "worldwide" method (e.g., Bourguignon 1972; Elkin 1977; Furst 1972, 1976; Goodman 1990; Harner 1973a, 1973b, 1973c, 1982; Needham 1967). The state is, more correctly, "states"; there are various kinds and degrees of alternate consciousness available to shamans. The state can vary from a very light condition to the comatose in different cultures and occasionally within a culture (e.g., Harner 1982: 62; Hultkrantz 1978; Siikala 1985: 455; Wright 1989: 27). In a light level, the shaman alters his consciousness to interact with the spirit world and can undertake journeys there but at the same time is at least marginally aware of what is occurring around him in the material world. While on a journey to the upper world, for example, he might adjust the drum beat of his assistant when it is not being executed effectively. He may be able to avoid physical obstacles in his path while dancing and "traveling" in the spirit world. He may interact with the patient and audience and answer questions from the audience (Harner 1973b; Shirokogoroff 1935: 304ff; Townsend 1989, 1992). At the other end of the spectrum, the shaman is completely oblivious to the material world and may appear comatose (for example, Saami shamanism). Regardless of the depth, it is the shaman who consciously determines if and when he will enter a shamanic state and when he will leave it (see also Harner 1980; Hultkrantz 1973).

The experience of SSC is, minimally, pleasant. Nepalese shamans, similar to Tungus, described it as an initial feeling of physical lightness and floating upward (Townsend 1989, 1992). One Tungus shaman reported that when the spirits entered, he felt very hot and there was a loud noise in his ears so that he could not understand himself and couldn't remember what the spirits said. Shirokogoroff empirically verified the shaman's subjective impression; he observed that the shamans were much hotter during a performance but before their exertion from dancing (1935: 364).

One of the hallmarks of being a shaman is the ability to control shamanic states of consciousness (e.g., Shirokogoroff 1935: 362–366). Peters and Price-Williams (1980) stress the primacy of the *control* of SSC. While control is essential within the definition of shamanism, it cannot be the sole criterion. The belief system and the social context cannot be ignored. Shamanism still must be examined within the broader experience of the shaman and within the society in which it occurs.

In addition to control, the shaman must be able to clearly "see" spirits as well as other things in spiritual reality.[12] Noll has argued that part of the training of a shaman is the controlled, "deliberate, repeated induction of enhanced mental imagery'' (1985: 444; cf. Siikala 1978: 191). Learning to experience visions is a twofold process. Visions (at least among Nepal Tamang) develop from crude to clear visions.

External stimuli must be blocked so that vividness can be enhanced, and the ability to control and manipulate the visions developed (Noll 1985: 444–445; Peters 1982: 34). Researchers allude to shamanic visions as hallucinations or imagination. For the shaman (and for his audience), however, the spirit world and his visions are just as real as is the material world, and these are separate from himself. Nevertheless, the shaman clearly recognizes the difference between the two worlds (e.g., Handelman 1967; Harner 1973b, 1982; Noll 1985). Visions are seen with the ''mind's eye'' rather than with the physical eye (e.g., Peters 1982: 26; Siikala 1978: 184). To underline this point, séances are usually held at night (though not in pitch darkness); some shamans close their eyes or are blindfolded, or a dark cloth is hung in front of the eyes to ''see'' in the spirit world (e.g., Noll 1985: 447; Siikala 1978: 190; Siegel and Conquergood 1985). Nevertheless, at least some shamans are quite able to and do perform in the light of day or in a lighted area at night (Townsend 1989, 1992).

Although shamans seem to be able to recall their activities on soul journeys, they may or may not remember what is said by spirits speaking through them. When spirits speak, a shaman's assistant is usually available to talk to the spirit and to interpret what the spirit said, because the communications are often difficult or almost impossible to understand by the audience (Shirokogoroff 1935: 365; Townsend 1989, 1992).

The visual is only one part of the ''typical'' experience in a shamanic state of consciousness. Touch, smell, taste, hearing—all the senses can be involved (e.g., Harner 1982, 1985; Townsend 1989, 1992).

Possession. There are several possible variations of spirit possession of living humans by various kinds of spirits ranging from involuntary possession by a controlling spirit (as, for example, in voodoo) to the voluntary state of the shaman (e.g., Jones 1976; Lewis 1971; Bourguignon 1976).

Spirit possession in shamanism is a subset of the shamanic state of consciousness and normally occurs within a séance. The shaman enters a SSC before a possession takes place. Shamanic possession is also distinct in that it is the shaman who sets the time and place of the possession and determines if and when it will occur and when it will end. It is the shaman, ultimately, who controls the episode, not the spirits.[13]

Which spirit appears may or may not be decided by the shaman; once the ''door is open'' for spirits to enter, some may appear as a surprise and address the audience. In Korea, Japan, and Nepal, the shaman enters a shamanic state, and after a sometimes lengthy period of drumming, chanting, and often journeying to other worlds, spirits are allowed to enter the shaman's body and talk with those attending the ceremony. While the possessing spirit may diagnose and prescribe treatment for an illness, it may also enter into a discussion of behavior or wrongdoing of various people attending the ceremony. Past actions may be revealed; a future happening may be predicted. Possession séances may be held in daylight, but more commonly, they occur at night by firelight.

In some societies (e.g., North American Cree, Ojibwa, Arapaho) the spirit lodge or shaking tent was performed (for a summary, see Hultkrantz 1967). The shaman was bound up. Then while he was in a shamanic state of consciousness, alone in a completely darkened room or specially constructed tent, he brought in various spirits including ghosts of the dead. These might fly around the enclosure, causing it to shake, throw things, heal, and speak with the audience. This kind of spirit appearance and movement superficially resembles some contemporary Western spiritualist séances. After the spirits left, the shaman was found untied.

In a sense, possession can also go in the opposite direction, the shaman's spirit being the possessing one. His spirit may enter the material body of an animal (his familiar) and travel as that animal in material or spiritual reality to complete his own agenda. (See below for a more detailed description.) This form occurs outside the public séance.

The Call by Spirits, Initiation, and Preparation of the Candidate

Significantly, spirits determine who will become a shaman, not the individual, although there are various ways in which this selection is manifest. The spirits may be ancestors, deceased shamans, or pure spirits. Calls may be dramatic or subtle, and the individual may take an active or passive role at the inception.

In the North American Plains, many people actively searched for supernatural helpers through the vision quest (e.g., Eliade 1964: 297–300), but it was the spirits who determined whether or not a quester received a vision. Not all vision questers were candidates for becoming a shaman, however. A Plains shaman, where he existed, was distinguished by the intensity of his experiences, by his ability to go on magical journeys to the spirit world, and by his especially intense relationship with the supernaturals. An Iglulik (Inuit) man or woman may take gifts to a living shaman expressing a desire to become a shaman (Rasmussen 1929: 111). A Tlingit and also an Ammasalik (East Greenland Inuit) living shaman might be directed by spirits and his dreams in the selection of a candidate. When the Ammasalik shaman selected a candidate, the novice was sent to a lonely place where he repeatedly rubbed two stones together, sometimes throughout the summer, until the bear spirit attacked and he experienced mystical death and resurrection (Eliade 1964: 58–59). Tlingit shamanic powers were normally handed down the matrilineal line. When a shaman died, his body was not cremated because of its purity. Rather, it was laid in a grave house. The potential shaman, usually a nephew, would spend the night lying in the grave house with the body in order to take on the deceased's power (De Laguna 1972: 673–674; Kan 1989: 120). Another method observed by Harner (1973b: 118; 1973c; 1988: 13) is used by Ecuadorian Jívaro (Shuar). An individual who aspires to be a shaman may buy shamanic powers from a living shaman. Nevertheless, in all instances selection is ultimately in the hands of the spirits.

Most calls come unbidden. Dreams may be the medium through which spirits first inform a person of his selection to become a shaman, especially among Inuit and Yupik (e.g., Oswalt 1963, 1967; Birket-Smith 1953). A person may experience a series of illnesses or bad luck and discover that in order to rid himself of the problems, he must acquiesce to the spirits and become a shaman. A person may show a tendency to drum continually or to fall into trance; an ancestor or deceased shaman may appear to the person in dreams. The spirits may steal the soul of the individual, instruct him in shamanism, and later return him to the community. Regardless, if spirits call, the person must respond, or serious illnesses, disasters, or death will befall him and often his family and his village. (e.g., De Laguna 1972: 670, 673; Holmberg 1980).

Uncontrolled possession by a spirit, the identification of the possessing spirit, the acquisition of necessary ritual paraphernalia, tutelage by both a spiritual and a real-life teacher, and gradual control over the possessing spirits and SSC is the usual sequence in becoming a full shaman (e.g., Hitchcock 1976: 169). In an alternate sequence, the spirit takes the potential shaman's spirit away to his abode in the earth and instructs him there (Hitchcock 1976: 169; Skafte 1992; Townsend 1989, 1992). My Nepalese informants suggest that this latter may result in a more powerful form of shamanism.

Wright (1989: 29) provides a summary of the different paths leading to shamanism:

1. Recovery from an illness or injury
2. Physical signs
3. Dreams, visions
4. A slow change in personality, or erratic behavior
5. Inheritance
6. Strange happenings, such as being hit by lightning
7. Purchase or theft of power

To these I would add being kidnapped by a spirit for a period of time but without major trauma. The Nepalese Tamang woman who was captured at age seven, described below, is a case in point.

Following the call, the novice usually must become an apprentice to a full shaman, although the Conibo of eastern Peru learn primarily from a large tree (Harner 1988: 13). In some groups, such as those in Nepal, the novice may have to contact several before the teacher and student are found to be compatible. The two go into an SSC together. If both have the same experience, they are deemed suitable for a teacher-student relationship. A novice may have several teachers during his development, and they may not all be from his own culture or ethnic group. One teacher, however, will usually dominate the instruction. Throughout the shaman's life, he will also be instructed by the spirits and perhaps ancestors and deceased shamans. The learning from the spirits, deceased ancestors, or shamans is an essential and sometimes the primary or only kind of instruction a shaman may have.

In what is often considered the classic mystic initiation, the novice shaman travels upward where he is attacked by spirits who consume his flesh, reducing him to a skeleton. An Inuit (Rasmussen 1929: 114; compare, e.g., Eliade 1964; Spencer and Gillen 1899: 522–530) must see himself as a skeleton before he can attain full shamanic status. His old organs are replaced by new ones, sometimes of crystal, and he ascends to the top of the cosmos where he merges with the sun or a supreme being. He returns to the middle world reborn into a new body and a new status. The skeleton motif, frightening initiation, ascension, and merging with the supreme being are not found in all societies. Nevertheless, some kind of death-rebirth or major change symbolism usually will be found that moves the novice from his old status to a liminal, transitional position and finally to rebirth as a changed being (cf. Blacker 1975: 27; Hitchcock 1976: 167; Townsend 1989,1992).

Kortt's (1984: 292, 297–299) symbolic and social analysis of Samoyed and Dolgan Siberian shamanism stresses the social involvement of the community, especially the shaman's kin in his initiation and subsequent spirit journeys. During the chaos of "classic" initiatory dismemberment, the shaman and, in his person, the community undergo death and rebirth. Later, he may take living relatives' spirits with him on journeys or talk with the living while on a journey; wrong suggestions from them can result in the shaman's and the relatives' deaths. The costume worn is constructed by the community and seems to be symbolic of his matrilineal and patrilineal kin lines. As a consequence of the community contribution and its detailed skeletal symbolism, the shaman appears in the spirit world as the embodiment of the whole social group.

Four Nepalese shamans' stories of their calls by spirits can demonstrate the variety of calls even within one small region. In Nepal, most shamans initially experience an involuntary spirit possession during which they mentally or physically withdraw from society. Some try to run into the forest; others fall into a comatoselike trance. Finally, they are able to control the spirits and enter and exit the shamanic states of consciousness at will (Skafte 1992: 52). One shaman, born into the Chetri Hindu caste, received his call from his dead father who had also been a shaman. He was destined to become a shaman even before birth, and he began to tremble (part of the beginning of a shamanic state) at age six and to want to run away into the forest. By eleven years of age he had begun to use a drum for trance. He began to seek out a teacher and contacted several before he found the correct one. A Gurung shaman never had any intention of becoming a shaman until, as a youth, he began to see powerful spirits. Several years later, at sixteen, when herding cattle he fell asleep, and the thunder god appeared, calling him to be a shaman. He returned home and soon fell into trance for a week. The spirit taught him a mantra (incantation), and he came out of trance and began his apprenticeship. A Tamang woman said when she was seven she was in the forest herding cattle with her father and brother. One night she was captured by the powerful shaman spirit and taken to his cave. There he taught her to drum. She was returned to her family the next morning and didn't see the shaman spirit again until she was ten. Once more she was in the forest at night when the spirit again took her to his cave and taught her shamanic rituals, returning her in the morning. Two years later he appeared at a shamanic healing ritual and, as witnessed by the whole village, took her for the final time to his cave where she learned the mantras essential to being a shaman. That was her last encounter with the shaman spirit, but because of the power of her teacher, she never needed to study with a living shaman (Skafte 1992; Townsend 1989). Finally, the wife of a powerful Tamang shaman, a woman in her fifties, had been ill for almost ten years from attacks by a witch. When she was near death, the spirit of her husband's father, who had also been a shaman, appeared to her in her dreams and healed her with the proviso that she become a shaman. She is currently active in healing but has not yet completed her apprenticeship (Townsend 1992).

In multiethnic societies such as Nepal, one might expect each ethnic group to have its own shamans and fairly culturally specific shamanic characteristics. In fact, however, this is not necessarily the case. One Chetri shaman's main living teacher was a Chamling Rai, but he also studied with a Gurung, a Tamang, a low-caste street sweeper from India, and a Chetri. Because his main teacher was Rai, his rituals are primarily Rai, but he infused aspects of Tamang and Chetri ritual as well as segments of those languages into his rituals. Even after becoming a full shaman, one may apprentice one's self to another shaman in order to learn some specialty such as curing snakebite.

Difficulties and Austerities

Shamanic traumas do not end after the initiation to full status. A life of prescription and proscription, of spiritual dangers and of austerities, await him. In some societies, restrictions are also placed on the spouse and relatives by the spirits. The shaman must continue to acquire and maintain power or to intensify it: "[T]he acquisition of supernatural powers rendered [a shaman] more susceptible to disaster through his own neglect, and also exposed him to the attacks of jealous colleagues" (De Laguna 1972: 683).

The theme of purification through austerities in order to interact with the spirits pervades shamanism. Before a séance and at various other times, a Tlingit shaman had to fast and thirst for up to eight days, usually in isolation in the woods. Dietary taboos for himself and his spouse were extensive, and sexual abstinence was required at various times. He had to return to the forest to gain further power and visit precious amulets he kept hidden. This also demanded fasting, thirsting, and continence (De Laguna 1972: 680). In Japan (Blacker 1975: 85–103), severe food restrictions are sometimes endured to the point of starvation. The Manchus and Tungus had similar requirements of fasting and sexual abstinence, and a variety of taboos to restrict their freedom (Shirokogoroff 1935: 365, 378).

A shaman's person might also be imbued with power. Athapaskan and Tlingit shamans' hair was a repository of power and life; if the hair was cut, they died. It was worn in eight long, twisted locks that reached the ground and was said to have been able to move of its own volition. Further, neither the shaman nor the spouse could comb their hair, or power would be lost. Paring fingernails was also prohibited (De Laguna 1972: 684–685).

As noted above, most shamans must learn mastery of fire and must continue to prove this mastery throughout life by walking on coals, handling fire, and other dangerous feats. He may not always come through such ordeals unscathed.

The upper, middle, and lower worlds are dangerous places and not to be ventured into lightly. By sending his soul on a journey, the shaman risks death. (e.g., Shirokogoroff 1935: 365). Not only is there uncontrollable chaos in spiritual reality, but spirits are not all benign. Only a powerful shaman can create structure in this structureless arena, and only one with powerful helping spirits can withstand the onslaught of spirits that set upon him. A shaman may travel in the middle world as his animal familiar, which might appear to living people as a bear or deer. If the animal is killed while the shaman is traveling in that form, the shaman will also die. Such journeys are not taken lightly by shamans, and there is usually ritual preparation prior to undertaking a journey.

Shamanic contests to prove who has the most power are reported from Tanaina Athapaskans of Alaska (Townsend 1965), other northwestern North American areas (e.g., Tlingit: De Laguna 1972: 671, 706–708; Kwakiutl: Boas 1966: 145), Siberia (Jochelson 1926: 212–215; Shirokogoroff 1935: 371–373), and Asia. In Nepal, several shamans may go to a holy place to honor their teachers. When the public has assembled, they compete to show who is the most powerful. Each sends powerful spells at the other until one becomes unconscious. Porcupine quills, crystals, dirt, or stone axes may be used as magical implements to hurl at and enter the opponent. The victorious shaman then heals the other, either by sucking out the object magically sent into him or by merely chanting mantras over him. The defeated shaman then acknowledges the other as more powerful and sends him gifts (Skafte 1992; Townsend 1989). Tlingit shamanic battles may not end so civilly; the weaker might die, sometimes from a wasting away. The helping spirits of two shamans may fight; if one kills the other, the shaman related to it also dies (De Laguna 1972: 707; Siskin 1983: 63–65; for another example, see Harner 1973b: 164–165).

Shamans are also open to attacks by spirits in this reality. If a shaman inadvertently breaks a taboo or neglects a spirit in some way, he may be severely punished.

In Nepal and in many other shamanic traditions the shaman takes an oath to use his power only for good. If the oath is broken, the spirits will take revenge on the shaman or his family. A Gurung shaman in Nepal had invested some money with three friends, but they cheated him. In anger he sent his deadly mantra to them. In a few weeks, one died. He tried to undo the spell, but the other two also soon died, one of disease, one in an accident. Unfortunately, soon afterward his young son and daughter became ill and died (Skafte 1992: 50; Townsend 1989).

Shirokogoroff (1935: 378–381) outlined a number of material difficulties in being a shaman. Some animals normally used for food cannot be hunted by them because they may be familiars of other shamans. Duties of both male and female shamans often prevent them from pursuing the normal social and economic activities. The Tungus shaman receives gifts, but they are of no major economic importance; Manchus, however, were paid by nonkin. Peruvian Sharanahua shamans have respect as well as fear from others, but there is no practical reward (Siskind 1973: 165). The same was true of the Nepalese shamans I know who might receive some payment but, with one or two exceptions, could not rely on shamanism for their total livelihood. This is in contrast to some Tlingit shamans who did not become wealthy through shamanism; nevertheless, they fared better than the Tungus.

Witches. The cosmic drama of good and evil is played out between shamans and witches. Societies with shamans often believe also in witches; these are invariably prime adversaries who contend throughout their lives both to destroy each other and to gain control over the people. As Hitchcock observed for Nepal (1976:182; also, e.g., Townsend 1989, 1992) and De Laguna for Tlingit (1972: 728; also, e.g., Oberg 1973; Kan 1989), a major task of a shaman is to counteract the danger from witches; this function is perhaps second only to healing but relates to it because witches cause illness that shamans must cure. The good/ evil, shaman/witch duality can be found in such widely separated areas as Chile (Mapuche), Mesoamerica, North America, Japan, and Nepal, to name only a few. In some places (e.g., Kaska) children are thought to be witches (Honigmann 1970); elsewhere they may be kinsmen or strangers.

Witches are inherently evil; they are *born* witches. They have the inborn capacity to harm others even without intent, although they usually are intentionally malevolent. The witch is the epitome of evil power (Mayer 1970; Macfarlane 1970). In contrast, a sorcerer is born ''normal'' but intentionally *learns* magic techniques to inflict harm. Nevertheless, concepts of sorcerer and witch are often merged. Sometimes shamans are suspected of working witchcraft. Shamans as well as sorcerers and witches access the same kinds of supernatural power; the difference is the way in which that power is used and perhaps the kinds of spirits each may control. It may be feared, therefore, that a shaman will use his power for evil. This places the shaman in some degree of jeopardy (Eskimo: Lantis 1960; Washo: Siskin 1983; Siskind 1973: 165; see also Walker 1970) if there are unexplained, harmful occurrences. Jívaro use the concept of shaman (Harner 1973b: 117; 1973c) to include both bad or bewitching shamans and good or curing shamans. There, the same individual will cure or help if asked or bewitch if angered or paid to do so. While these roles may overlap in

some societies, I treat them as separate roles and individuals except where specifically noted.

Shaman's Responsibilities and Relationships with Others

The shaman acts to help maintain a suitable living environment for the people
by placating environmental (plants, animals, weather, earth) and other spirits,
ridding the community of evil forces, and assuring an abundance of food from
wild or domestic harvest. He may entice game to be caught, encourage the
growth of crops, and affect the weather.

There is also a personal relationship with clients. In small societies, a shaman
acts as a source of social control as well as a reservoir of traditional societal
lore. He is usually aware of the problems and conspiracies of his client and in
his society and can act to cajole, to correct, and to suggest proper responses for
the client.

Most shamans are adept at several tasks, although in a specific society one
function, such as divining, may be taken over by another person. The main
responsibilities include the following:

Healing. One of the most important functions of the shaman is healing physical, psychological, and emotional illness. Sometimes, at least in Nepal, helping
spirits are specialized in particular illnesses. As a consequence, a shaman who
has a "specialized" spirit may become a specialist in the healing of that particular illness.

In order to learn the cause of an illness, a variety of divination techniques
can be used that are influenced by the spirits. The shaman usually moves into
a light shamanic state to "see" the illness and may use quartz crystals or brass
mirrors to assist him (e.g., Harner 1980, 1982; Shirokogoroff 1935: 299–300;
Spencer and Gillen 1899: 481). A Nepalese Chetri shaman divines with the aid
of spirits by chanting mantras and arranging rice grains on a brass plate (Townsend 1989).

There are a number of causes of illness, all of which may have supernatural
implications:

Obvious causes. Broken limbs, wounds, and other injuries can be dealt with in a matter-
  of-fact way, and shamans are quite versed in these treatments. Some, especially in
  North America, may parcel these problems off to other herbal or bone-setting specialists. Nevertheless, the supernatural may be implicated. A witch or malevolent
  spirit could have caused the person to fall and break a leg. A Native American Zuñi,
  who was a Korean War veteran, was well aware of the germ theory of disease. He
  reasoned that germs were everywhere, but not everyone was infected. Therefore,
  those who got a disease were victims of witchcraft (Ellis 1970: 43).

Soul loss. A person's soul may temporarily leave the body, for example, during sleep.
  It may, however, become lost, and illness will ensue. Alternatively, it may be stolen
  by spirits or a witch. It is then the task of the shaman to go into spiritual reality

and search one or more worlds to locate it and bring it back. When the shaman returns with the soul, he may simply blow it into the sick individual or perhaps place it in water, which the patient then drinks.

Object intrusion. An object causing illness may be propelled magically into the victim's body by a witch or antagonistic shaman. The healing shaman must determine, in SSC, the cause and withdraw it from the victim, usually through sucking it out. It is this practice that is the target for skeptics who accuse the shaman of trickery, intentionally misleading his audience. It must be recognized that all things exist in two realities: material and spiritual. It is the spirit essence that enters the person, causing illness. In sucking, the shaman draws out the spirit that is causing the problem. But illness-causing spirit essences have a material reality, too. The shaman uses that material object, which is sometimes stored in his mouth, to "lure out" its spirit essence hiding in the body. It is this material object that is then shown the patient, who cannot see in spiritual reality, as proof that the spirit essence has been withdrawn (Harner 1973c: 24;1982: 22–23, 149–150). For the scientific materialist the pronouncement is patent nonsense. To the shaman and those who participate in his paradigm of two realities, it makes extremely good sense.

Witches. Witches and sorcerers attack people with intrusive objects or in other ways: stealing souls, harming crops and animals, and working all sorts of mischief. The shaman must work to counteract that mischief and often do battle with the witch.

Escorting the Dead. At a death, it is the responsibility of the shaman to escort the deceased's soul away from the living, usually across a barrier (bridge, river, etc.) to the land of the dead. Since the shaman is the only one who is capable of journeying to the land of the dead and returning, he is eminently qualified to assure the soul's safe departure. Occasionally, the soul is not willing to leave and must be driven out or bribed to leave. Officiating at death rituals seems to be one of the tasks that is usurped by priests or other religious functionaries when more organized religions are taken up by a society. In southern Alaska, the Russian Orthodox priests were quick to change the Tanaina death rituals from shamanic to Christian in the early 1800s (Townsend 1974). In Nepal, Buddhist lamas have taken over these rituals from the Tamang shamans, although the Rai still retain the shamanic rites (Townsend 1989).

Divination. Most shamans can discover past events, foretell and influence the future, find lost objects, or locate game. As noted above, he divines the cause of illness. As with other activities, a shamanic state of consciousness is normally employed.

Explanations of Shamanic Healing

A number of researchers have attempted to explain the healing success of shamanic, faith, or spiritual healers, relying primarily on psychophysiological explanations.

Moerman (1979) and later Dow (1986b) approach healing from the symbolic perspective. Dow accepts the unity of mind and body and argues that the nervous system/emotions then allow the flow of information to the body that triggers healing. He hypothesizes that both the healer and patient accept a cultural mythic world; the patient accepts the power of the healer to define the patient's problems in terms of the myth. The patient's emotions are then attached to the mythic symbols that the healer manipulates. The Cuna Indian shaman's chant has been used by Lévi-Strauss (1963) to demonstrate the effectiveness of symbols in assisting in difficult childbirth. (See also Siskind [1973:163] for an example of a shaman manipulating a vision.) Perhaps a better example is from the Navajo. A Navajo singer (not necessarily a shaman) creates one or more sand paintings that symbolize a cultural myth in which the hero has undergone and recovered from some of the problems the patient experiences. The patient sits in the center of the painting, and the singer, chanting aspects of the myth, makes direct analogies between the elements in the painting and the patient's body, so that the patient becomes one with the hero in the myth. As the hero was healed, so is the patient healed.

The patient's strong faith and belief in the shaman's (or other healer's) power to heal has also been offered as an explanation for successful outcomes (e.g., Kleinman 1979). I argue that the shaman (or other healer) must believe in his ability, but faith and belief on the part of the patient are not necessary requisites for healing.[14] Nevertheless, the patient should be open to the *possibility* of being healed; at least he should not be overtly negative toward the healer's attempts. The explanation ignores successful healings of infants, young children, and animals where belief is unlikely to be an issue.

Winkelman (1986), Prince (e.g., 1982), and others have examined what happens physiologically when a shaman is in a SSC and how such states affect analgesia and healing. In general, various altered states of consciousness, mock stress, auditory stimulation, and other mechanisms may trigger the release of endorphins that act as analgesics and at times promote healing. While this is an interesting and probably proper approach to healing, there are areas of concern with the hypothesis. In a séance, it is normally the shaman who goes into "trance." In some areas, the patient may also ingest a hallucinogenic compound or be brought into an altered state in other ways (e.g., Reichel-Dolmatoff 1975; Sharon 1978; Siskind 1973; Turner 1994: 94–95, n. 6). This is not the case with all healing, shamanic or otherwise. I have not observed patients of shamans in altered states. Much patient response was reverent and respectful and showed considerable interest but was often merely matter-of-fact. My observations with Western spiritual healing confirm this. Skafte (1989–1993: personal communications) said that during more than a decade of experience with shamans in Nepal the only time he had seen a patient go into an "altered state" was when the shaman was exorcising a witch who had taken over the person.

If one argues that an altered state is responsible for successful healing, it seems that the shaman would be the greatest beneficiary in a séance. The patient is subjected to auditory and visual stimuli of the shaman drumming and chanting to move himself into a shamanic state, and the dancing, firelight, perhaps incense, altar, and so on. As Prince (1982) notes, such stimuli can induce altered states. This, perhaps coupled with the long monotony of a séance and the positive attitudes around the patient assuring him that something is being done for him, might contribute to a mild state in which endorphins are released. The belief in the presence of spirits and other powerful forces around the patient might create a stressful situation in some instances that would stimulate endorphin release. I do not think, however, that this is adequate to bring about some of the recoveries of which I am aware.

I am not suggesting that the various explanations do not contribute to healing. Rather, none of these is a sufficient explanation; further exploration is required.

Shamanic Séance

The costume, and other ritual paraphernalia, for séance is highly symbolic of the spirits and the spirit world with which the shaman interacts while wearing it. A tree may be drawn on the shirt, symbolizing the world tree. Animal parts may be worn, which are the material manifestation of the spirits attached to the shaman. Wood, ivory, iron, or other types of spirit representations or stones or other objects with spirit power may be worn or incorporated within drum or rattle heads. Among other things, these act to help draw in spirits to the séance. Colors used in the costume may have special meaning: In Nepal, red may distinguish a shaman who conducts blood sacrifice, in contrast to others who do not; and rarely, black is used by shamans who have a close association with especially powerful and dangerous spirits. The complex symbolism of shamanic objects and costuming is specific to the particular society and cannot be dealt with efficiently here (see Kortt 1984: 297–298 for a discussion of the social significance of Siberian shaman costumes).

A Tamang or Chetri Nepalese séance begins when the audience and patient are assembled and can be held either indoors or outdoors, normally at night. An altar has been prepared with various sacred objects as well as offerings for the spirits. Some in the audience, in addition to the patient, may have placed coins on the altar in hopes that some of the spirits will answer their questions or address their illnesses. The shaman, in costume, sits in front of the altar and begins to drum and chant the names of the spirits. Finally, he begins to shake as the spirits enter. He then gets up and begins to dance, while continuing to chant. He may continue to drum or assistants might take it up. It is during this time that he is making his spirit world journeys. Eventually, one spirit may make his presence known and speak through the shaman. Assistants talk with the spirit, asking questions and prodding him on. It is usually at this time that the spirit helps the shaman understand the illness and other problems of the audience. Subsequently, the shaman resumes dancing and finally returns to the altar to tell the spirits goodbye as they leave.

It is argued that during a seance "the self-suggestion of the shaman on the one hand and the mass hypnosis of the audience on the other complement each other and make the whole séance fuse into a higher level, which causes the ecstasy'' (Gilberg 1984: 27). While this may be true in some societies, I have not witnessed any such ''mass hypnosis'' in séances I have attended. On the contrary, I have seen people watching intently with deep interest but not showing signs of hypnosis. Sometimes, a rather casual atmosphere prevails. Occasionally, private discussions are held with neighbors, someone will wander in or out, or children may play and perhaps cry.[15]

Shamanism as Performance and Role Playing

While shamans maintain that they do enter a shamanic state of consciousness, anthropologists have sometimes taken a different perspective. Hitchcock considers the state as no more than that of a good actor (1976: 168; see also 1977). Eliade (1964: 200), Shirokogoroff (1935: 362), Nadel (1946: 35), and Boas (1930: 1–41; 1966:121ff), for example, discuss instances in which the séance and ''trance'' were faked or ''role-played'' but argue that others are genuine. Boas (1966: 125) noted for the Kwakiutl that ''notwithstanding the knowledge of fraud, a deep-seated belief in the supernatural power of shamanism persists, even among the sophisticated.'' I recognize that some SSC fakery certainly does occur. Nevertheless, my research and study with shamans, Western healers, spiritualists, and neoshamans convince me that for the experiencer, shamanic and other altered states are very real and attempts at duplicity are not common. Regardless of whether the SSC is real or feigned, it can be exceptionally good theater (cf. Hitchcock 1977).

SHAMANS: NORMAL OR INSANE?

One theory of shamanism contends that shamans are mentally ill, severely neurotic, psychotic, or schizophrenic. This ''explains'' their use of shamanic (altered) states and their claims that they see spirits and journey into the spirit world. The theory has its roots in Western thought as early as the eighteenth century with explorations of Africa. ''Civilized'' religion and medicine were contrasted with ''primitive'' paganism and witch doctors (Torrey 1974: 331–332). In his work with Chukchi, Bogoras (1904–1909) reiterated the ''crazy shaman'' theory. More important, prolific twentieth-century anthropologists (e.g., Alfred Kroeber, Ralph Linton, George Devereux) became deeply involved with psychoanalysis and tended to see ''unusual'' shamanic beliefs and behaviors in those terms. In addition, any excesses in behavior in Western society, not to mention ''frenzied'' behavior associated with some shamanic activity, has been soundly condemned by ''sophisticated'' and educated people (Torrey 1974).

Wallace, a psychological anthropologist, adheres to this theory, asserting that ''the potential shaman is very often a sick human being, suffering from serious mental and physical disorders which spring from or involve profound identity conflict'' (1966: 145). He echoes Kroeber's 1940 (1952) thesis that ''primitive'' societies differ from ''developed'' ones in that primitive societies reward psychotics with the socially sanctioned role of, for example, healer. In the 1951 postscript, Kroeber (1952: 317–319) modified his earlier position slightly to argue that ''psychopathologies that get rewarded among primitives are only the mild or transient ones.'' Nevertheless, he persists in his overall thesis that (shamanic) experiences of spirits, trance, and so on, are ''neurotic symptoms of the hysteric type'' (318). He argues that primitives do recognize degrees and kinds of psychopathology and allocate tolerance and esteem to some of them. In fact, the whole lay public in such societies is involved in psychopathology when they entertain witchcraft belief. A real relation does exist, he says, between certain psychopathological symptoms in individuals and the degree of cultural advancement (318–319): ''Cultures that consistently maintain a resistive or regretful attitude toward all manifestations of psychopathology may be rated as having progressed beyond those that tend to induce certain kinds of psychopathology by rewarding them and thereby strengthening a vicious circle of cultural non-reality and individual abnormality'' (318). For Kroeber, shamanism remained relegated to a neurotic or psychopathological grab-bag and such societies to a less-progressed level of cultural development.

Shamans are considered mentally ill also by some scientific materialists/positivists because of the presumed ''delusion'' that they see and deal with spirits. By denying outright any possibility of mystical validity, any such contention is, then, by definition, absurd and is explained by psychological or pathological models. Noll (1989: 48) credits the mental illness label to the psychopathological model used by researchers who follow the three philosophical positions rampant in shamanic studies: scientism, psychoanalysis, and Marxism-Leninism. These three positions

base their legitimacy on a polemical devaluation of religion and religious experience. . . . [A]dherents to these world views often resort to psychiatric terminology as a powerful technique for the devaluation of such an important human experience. . . . [The schizophrenia model of shamanism] is in reality a Western (and Soviet) ethnocentric distortion based on the misapplication of psychiatric/medical schemata to experiences encountered in ASC. (48)

Silverman (1967), echoing Kroeber, diagnosed shamans as socially sanctioned schizophrenics. Noll (1983) tested the ''shamans as schizophrenics'' hypothesis by comparing shamanism with schizophrenia as defined in the diagnostic manual used in the United States and Canada: the *Diagnostic and Statistical Manual of Mental Disorders*, 1980 (DSM-III). He concluded that ''unless all shamans are suffering from a mysterious organic brain disease the symptoms of which they can willfully control, or until a better case can be made for a type of schizophrenia in primitive societies the symptoms of which are also willfully controlled over a lifetime, the schizophrenia metaphor for shamanism presents a false and misleading analogy'' (454).

The mentally ill argument has also been attacked by a number of other researchers, including Boyer (1964, 1969), Boyer et al. (1964), Eliade (1964), Handelman (1968), Murdock (1965), Murphy (1964), and Torrey (1974) (see also Kleinman 1979: 9). Elkin (1977) observed that Australian Aboriginal ''medicine men'' were respected, often outstanding men of ''high degree.''

Shamans I have known seem quintessential ''normal, average'' people when not engaged in shamanic activities. One was a carpenter, another a farmer, a third a school custodian; one woman was a mother who was a very active shaman, turning her abilities into a fairly substantial business in a large town. Another woman was a farm woman who had several children. Their personalities differ as much as those of any other people in their societies, but they demonstrate the range of normalcy, not the range of insanity.

Gilberg (1984: 26) points out that mentally disturbed people are burdens on others. Shamans are intelligent, balanced, and capable individuals who must move into dangerous conditions in spiritual reality—a feat that a neurotic person could not handle successfully. The shaman's society might consider him a strange or difficult person because he is an individualist and he traffics in a dangerous world. Handling the dangers of spiritual reality and dealing with emergencies and threats in his own society demand a competent, very sane individual (see also Lewis 1971: 182).

I do not deny that some people who are shamans also happen to have mental problems, although the vast majority are ''normal.'' What I question is the allegation of a functional relationship between shamanism and mental illness.

A better way of approaching the phenomena of shamanic beliefs, claimed experiences, and behaviors is through more social, symbolic, and phenomenological methods. Contacting spirits and experiencing an alternate, spiritual reality is a mystical experience not limited to shamans. The understanding of such experiences falls within an individual's personal epistemology and reality paradigm. The *manifestation* of this experience and epistemology within the societal context, however, is channeled through the belief system and expectations of the particular society in which the individual functions. Importantly, Handelman (1968: 354) argues that the social behavior of the shaman in, for example, SSC during a séance can be as much a product of cultural expectations as it is of any personal psychological condition.

THE ''IDEAL'' SHAMAN AS METAPHOR

I have discussed shaman/shamanism as a real phenomenon. Recently, others have transformed ''shaman'' into a metaphor for use in all sorts of analyses from contemporary Western dilemmas in social adjustment or medical problems to ways of approaching life. As a *constructed* concept, the shaman may be a metaphor for wild, untamed, chaos, disorganization, free, and unconstrained in contrast to the priest representing the civilized, order, organization, propriety, within the bounds of approved cultural behavior, controlled, proper. The shaman becomes a model of a "primitive," more noble, pure existence than is now found in modern corrupt industrial society. Alternatively, he is a holdover from the backward, "ignorant," "primitive" times that we have outgrown; he is a trafficker in evil or devil power.

A variety of presumed classic traits are delineated as shamanic and portrayed as characteristic of all shamans through all times and places. The call by spirits, the related illness, and initiation in which the shaman is attacked by spirits, consumed, given a new body, and merged with the "Great Spirit" are particularly popular motifs and become the template shaman. The shaman is viewed as the reservoir of all spiritual and traditional knowledge. He is larger than life.

Pandian (1991: 4) uses shaman and priest as metaphors of the sacred self in his study of the relation of self concepts to religion. His "shamanistic self" is a symbolic integration that manifests when resolutions of stress from illness, unpredictable events, life passages, and so on, are needed. It is expressed in divination, healing, and other ritual contexts. In contrast, the "priestly self" is symbolic coherence in everyday life thinking and behavior in which the social order and conventions are validated in terms of the sacred other.

The "wounded healer" archetype (e.g., Halifax's 1982 general psychosymbolic study) has become a psychoanalytic model of the person, severely physically or mentally ill, who by virtue of "healing" himself is now able to heal others. Illness "becomes a vehicle to a higher plane of consciousness" (Halifax 1979: 11). Achterberg (1985) has drawn analogies from shamanic SSC healing for use in imagery in modern medical healing and to some extent reflects Dow's (1986b) interest in symbolic healing.

Further afield, Bourguignon (1989) cites Judith Brown's (1986) comparison of a seventeenth-century Italian lesbian nun with shamans and Hutchinson's (1985) characterization of Walt Whitman's writings as a "literary shamanism." Horwatt (1988) equates Siberian shamans and Pentecostal preachers. Korp (1991) draws the analogy of shaman as artist and artist as shaman. In the nonprofessional arena, art persists as shamanic metaphor. Levy (1988) argues that artists have assumed the shamanic role as technicians of ecstasy. Finally, the shamanic "trance journey" becomes a metaphor for a psychological introspection journey within one's self to realize that "the universe was contained within me, that my consciousness had access to all other parts of consciousness" (O'Connell 1988: 123).

The shaman as metaphor is a creation by the West, for the West. It is not an attempt to understand the shaman as an individual who actually exists. The shaman "as shaman" provides the link between this world and the spirit world, between the people and the supernatural; the shaman as metaphor provides a link only between the individual and his own psychological "unconscious." We lose the immediateness of the spirit world. The supernatural is removed and replaced by a focus on individual consciousness.

No mere human can live up to the ideals portrayed by a metaphor. Unfortunately, modern shamans are sometimes compared to that metaphor and found wanting. They are people who contact spirits, but they are not all-wise hierophants who guard *all* the wisdom of the gods. To think so is to do a grave injustice to the real shamans who work so hard to help their people.

FIELD METHODS

One problem in studying shamanism is our own preconceptions of validity and reality. Many errors in the study of shamanism are the result of anthropological biases based on the researcher's theoretical and/or epistemological preconceptions of reality, of what is "true" and "valid" and what is the "proper" way to "analyze" a particular belief system. This is especially obvious in the debate on whether shamans are mentally ill. Apparently, religious phenomena are much more subject to these kinds of epistemological abuses than other sociocultural topics.

I am not arguing for or against the ontological existence of another reality, the existence of spirit beings, or the effectiveness of shamanic interventions. Nevertheless, I find it interesting that few researchers into shamanism entertain the possibility that shamans or other religious practitioners just *may* be correct regardless of our scientific materialist ability to "know better" (cf. Turner 1994: 71–72). I argue neither for "methodological atheism" (Fulton 1981: 2) nor for a "true believer." Berger (1969: 59) observed: that: "We may agree, say, that contemporary consciousness is incapable of conceiving of either angels or demons. We are still left with the question of whether, possibly, both angels and demons go on existing despite this incapacity of our contemporaries to conceive of them." Rather, it might be informative to suspend judgment, to bracket personal views as well as a scientific materialist stance, and for the period of fieldwork, to take things at face value. Later, we can apply the requisite psychological, sociological, anthropological, or other theoretical "reality" frameworks, if such are relevant.

Skafte (1989–1993: personal communications) and I agree that to study shamanism as a phenomenon the anthropological interpretive method has to be built upon an experiential background so that the researcher has something to interpret against. Constructing questions for the shaman-informant does not help much beyond forming general guidelines. To know the correct questions to ask, one must reconstruct not only the background of the sociocultural matrix but also the epistemological basis within which the shaman works. If the researcher has never experienced an alternate state of consciousness or attempted a "healing," he is in a compromised position when trying to comprehend what a shaman really means when he talks of experiences in SSC. It would be prudent for the field researcher to learn something of trance and healing methods prior to undertaking research. This can be acquired in the West through Spiritualist groups, and workshops, including some in Western core and neoshamanism. With this background, the researcher is better able to comprehend what the informant really means and experiences, and it greatly facilitates discourse. Nevertheless, the best way to learn about a particular shamanic system is to apprentice one's self to a shaman. Earlier trance training can facilitate and speed up the researcher's shamanic apprenticeship. The experiential method has been used by Harner (1973b, 1973c), Maquet (1975), Peters (1978), Staal (1975), Stoller (Stoller and Olkes 1987), Tart (1972), Wafer (1991), and others; appeals for this method include Stoller (1989: 68; compare Cohen 1992).[16]

This approach cannot be undertaken without trepidation, however, as witnessed by both my experiences and those of Karen Brown (1992). We both elected to participate intensively in the rituals and belief systems that we were studying. Brown chose to participate in voodoo for "a mix of professional and personal reasons. . . . The single clear feeling was a powerful need to understand what Voudou was about, what it had to offer those who turned to it in times of trouble" (1992: A56). I have participated in shamanism, spiritualism, and healing as well as core and neoshamanism. In both our cases, some colleagues questioned whether we had lost objectivity and had become biased in our analyses. No one presents an "objective" rendition of their subject. Bias is inherent in everything we do, including academic writing (compare Fulton 1981: 3). If those biases are made clear at the outset, that should be sufficient, whether we are speaking from an experiential perspective or from a psychoanalytic, Marxist, anthropological, or other point of view.

On a more mundane level, fieldwork with shamans can pose special problems including special vocabularies and concepts not known to the researcher or an interpreter. Shamans may be reluctant to discuss their beliefs either because of a hesitancy to reveal sacred information or because of fear of ridicule. This is not a new problem; similar situations were faced by Siberian researchers in the nineteenth century (Kortt 1984). Shamanism in most places has changed considerably over the last hundred years, particularly from Western influence and condemnation. It is important to distinguish a shamanic system that reflects more traditional ways from one that disappeared and is now being reconstituted from fragmented memories and input from a variety of extraneous sources, including New Age. These last may be believed by the modern practitioners to be the traditional way when, in fact, they are invented traditions (cf. Townsend 1991).

Dow's (1986a: 3) method of data recording is similar to mine and works well. He tape-recorded discussions to retain an accurate record and then made complete transcriptions. He permitted the shaman to shift from topic to topic, rather than trying to lead the conversation.

CONCLUSIONS

One major issue in the study of shamanism demands restating. That is the recognition of distinction between the shaman as an individual and as a performer of a socially defined role. As Handelman (1968: 354) pointed out, his personal philosophical premises may not be in complete accord with his socially defined behavior.

We need to recognize also the significance of sociocultural contact and change in regulating shamanic behavior (cf. Handelman 1968). Shamanism should not be seen simply as a "survival" from our foraging past but as a vibrant and ongoing system functioning in a variety of societies where it has not yet been usurped and destroyed by the more "institutionalized" approaches of allopathic medicine or the universalist religions and ideologies (e.g., Christianity, Islam, Buddhism, Hinduism, communism). Even there the shaman has shown a remarkable resilience and adaptive capacity by his syncretism of elements from the universalist religions both in his personal philosophy and in his performance. This is a major factor in the continual survival of shamanism. These adaptations and syncretisms also are one cause of the problem of defining shamanism.

It is provocative that for so long in human history throughout the world the presence of the spirit world—"the other"—has been part of the a priori assumptions. In the West following the Renaissance, and in other world areas as the Western "scientific materialism" swept upon them, the spirit world receded and could be disappearing in some places. It is just at this time that the West is rediscovering and sometimes reinventing the spiritual heritage. We might find that the gods may not be dead—only sleeping—and they seem to be awaking in the oddest places, for example, middle-class Western society. Will the incipient revitalization and attempted rediscovery of the sacred spread to other societies as materialism did and save the traditional spiritual cultures before they are irretrievably destroyed?[17] If nothing else, changes in Western attitudes, partly influenced by core and neoshamanism and some parts of New Age, may moderate the severe materialist approach being exported and might be one potential benefit of Western spiritual experimentation.

NOTES

I wish to acknowledge with sincere appreciation the University of Manitoba Social Sciences and Humanities Research Council Committee and the Foundation for Shamanic Studies for their generous support of my research. Peter Skafte provided invaluable help and insights into Nepalese shamanism. To the Nepalese shamans and interpreters who have given so generously of their knowledge and their time, I owe a debt of gratitude that can never be completely repaid. Edwin Anderson, Michael Harner, and John Matthiasson generously gave their time to read and critique the manuscript.

1. Societal names have changed in the literature in recent years. A few of those shifts are noted here:

Tungus:	Evenk
Lapp:	Saami
Eskimo:	Inuit—north and east of Norton Sound, Alaska; Yupik—south of Norton Sound, Alaska, the Bering Sea Islands, and Siberia

I use the older "Tungus" here because it is the most common in the literature, and Evenk is less familiar to researchers who are not specialists in northern regions.

2. For a complementary summary of shamanism, see Jane Monnig Atkinson's paper "Shamanisms Today" (1992). For discussions of core shamanism and neoshamanism in Western society, see Townsend (1988, 1991, forthcoming).

3. While it is politically correct to use both pronouns—she/he—I find it incredibly cumbersome to do so. Consequently, I have elected to retain the generic "he" to refer to both males and females. Where the reference is primarily to a woman, I will use the feminine; where it is primarily to a man, I will make that clear.

4. This definition of shamanism is based on a variety of sources including Eliade, Gilberg, Harner, Hultkrantz, Peters and Price-Williams, Shirokogoroff, and others, as well as my research.

5. For definitions of political organization, I use Fried (1967).

6. Slaveholdings in midnineteenth century Tlingit villages averaged about 10 percent of the population with a range from 2 percent to 22 percent. Northwest Pacific Rim slavery is considered true slavery, not merely the holding of captives (Petroff 1884; Tikhmenev 1978; Townsend 1983).

7. This section is a compilation from a variety of sources that include, but are not limited to, Blacker (1975), Eliade (1964), Harner (1982), Shirokogoroff (1935), and Townsend (1989, 1992).

8. Some would argue that there is only one reality, but we are inhibited from perceiving it in its totality. The shaman, however, is able to perceive it more fully.

9. Nepal has over thirty ethnic groups within two language families. Clearly, shamanism there is not homogeneous. In this chapter I am generalizing from my information derived from Tamang, Chetri, and Gurung shamans as well as from published materials from Peters, Hitchcock, and a number of other researchers.

10. Nepalese Gurung and some Tibetans do capture wild deer or yak for immediate ritual sacrifice (Mumford 1989: 64–65). Ainu sacrificed bears. The bear, however, was captured as a cub and raised in a family both as a deity and as a "grandchild" for almost two years (Ohnuki-Tierney 1974). Jochelson (1926: 210–211) describes a Yukaghir shaman obtaining the soul of an animal from the Owner of the Earth and giving it to a hunter who then finds and kills the living animal. This last is not quite the same as ritual sacrifice discussed here.

When animals are sacrificed, people normally eat the meat, except when the sacrifice is, for example, a dog or other animal not considered food. It is true that this may add needed protein to the diet; spirit demands can sometimes be used as an excuse to have a meal of meat. Demanding deities can, however, bankrupt a family by causing them to sacrifice all their animals and borrow from relatives for additional ones (e.g., Shirokogoroff 1935: 198–203).

11. There is an extensive literature on the psychophysiology of altered states of consciousness, but I will not address that material here.

12. Presumably, if a spirit enters a shaman to speak, the shaman does not "see" the spirit within himself.

13. There are some exceptions to the "rule" that the shaman controls the trance and the spirits. I witnessed one episode (Townsend 1989) in which a very adept shaman became involuntarily possessed. He had completed a séance and had decided to demonstrate some aspects of the ritual at the altar. He neglected to ask the permission of the spirits to do so; they became angry and possessed him, refusing to leave for five or ten minutes in spite of attempts by the shaman to free himself. He was visibly shaken by the experience.

14. I am preparing a paper on healing in which this will be discussed more fully.

15. Tangentially, I have not noticed any such mass hypnosis among spiritualist séances or healing ceremonies in Western society. The medium may enter deep trance, and the healer may be in a light altered state of consciousness, but in spite of inspiring music, singing, and so on, which is designed to set the mood and induce trance in the medium or healer, at least the overwhelming majority of the audience remains in this reality. In some Pentecostal Holiness or Charismatic meetings where the audience is expected to participate, enthusiastic dancing or trance may be entered, and speaking in tongues can occur.

16. Joseph Franz Thiel (1984: 14) argued that "those who have never personally experienced the religious, who have never grappled with it existentially, are not in a position to grasp the nature of religion; they must perforce be content with external appearances" (translated by Poewe 1994: 255; cf. Evans-Pritchard 1965: 121; Schmidt 1931: 6).

17. The Foundation for Shamanic Studies, created by Michael Harner, is dedicated to the preservation, study, and transmission of shamanic knowledge. To this end, the foundation sponsors basic research and, where invited by the indigenous people, assists them in their attempts to recover their shamanic traditions.

REFERENCES

Achterberg, Jeanne. 1985. *Imagery in Healing: Shamanism and Modern Medicine*. Boston: Shambhala.

Atkinson, Jane Monnig. 1992. "Shamanisms Today." *Annual Review of Anthropology* 21:307–330.

Bäckman, Louise. 1978. "Types of Shaman: Comparative Perspectives." *Studies in Lapp Shamanism*. Louise Bäckman and Åke Hultkrantz, editors. Acta Universitatis Stockholmiensis. Stockholm Studies in Comparative Religion. Stockholm: Almqvist & Wiksell. 62–90.

Berger, Peter L. 1969. *A Rumour of Angels: Modern Society and the Rediscovery of the Supernatural*. Baltimore: Penguin. (Paging for Penguin Pelican series, 1971)

Birket-Smith, Kaj. 1953. *The Chugach Eskimo*. Copenhagen: Nationalmuseets Publikationsfond.

Blacker, Carmen. 1975. *The Catalpa Bow: A Study of Shamanistic Practices in Japan*. London: George Allen & Unwin Ltd.

Boas, Franz. 1930. *Religion of the Kwakiutl Indians*. New York: Columbia University Press.

Boas, Franz. 1966. *Kwakiutl Ethnography*. Edited by Helen Codere. Chicago: University of Chicago Press.

Bogoras, Waldemar. 1904–1909. *The Chukchee*. Vol. 7. of *Publications of the Jessup North Pacific Expedition*. Edited by Franz Boas. Memoirs of the American Museum of Natural History. Vol. XI, Part 2, 3. Leiden: E. J. Brill.

Bourguignon, Erika. 1972. "Trance Dance." *The Highest State of Consciousness*. John White, editor. Garden City, NY: Doubleday and Co.

Bourguignon, Erika. 1976. *Possession*. San Francisco: Chandler & Sharp.

Bourguignon, Erika. 1989. "Trance and Shamanism: What's in a Name?" *Journal of Psychoactive Drugs* 21 (1): 9–15.

Boyer, L. Bruce. 1964. "Further Remarks Concerning Shamans and Shamanism." *Israel Annals of Psychiatry and Related Disciplines* 2:235–257.

Boyer, L. Bruce. 1969. "Shamans: To Set the Record Straight." *American Anthropologist* 71 (2): 307–309.

Boyer, L. Bryce; Bruno Klopfer; Florence B. Brawer; and Hayao Kawai. 1964. "Comparison of the Shamans and Pseudoshamans of the Apaches of the Mescalero Indian Reservation: A Rorschach Study." *Journal of Projective Techniques and Personality Assessment* 28:173–180.

Brown, Judith. 1986. *Immodest Acts*. New York: Oxford University Press.

Brown, Karen McCarthy. 1992. "Writing about 'the Other.' Point of View." *Chronicle of Higher Education* 38(34) (April): A56.

Campbell, Joseph. 1988. *Historical Atlas of World Mythology*. Volume 1: *The Way of the Animal Powers*. Part 2: *Mythologies of the Great Hunt*. New York: Harper and Row.

Castaneda, Carlos. 1968. *The Teachings of Don Juan: A Yaqui Way of Knowledge*. New York: Ballantine Books.

Clifton, James A., editor. 1990. *The Invented Indian: Cultural Fictions and Government Policies*. New Brunswick, NJ: Transaction Publishers.

Cohen, Anthony P. 1992. "Post-Fieldwork Fieldwork." *Journal of Anthropological Research* 48 (4): 339–354.

Degarrod, Lydia Nakashima. 1992. "Shamans as Political Leaders: The Sacred in the Construction of Ethnicity." Paper, Society for the Scientific Study of Religion, Washington, D.C., November.

De Laguna, Frederica. 1972. *Under Mount Saint Elias: The History and Culture of the Yakutat Tlingit*. Vol. 7 Smithsonian Contributions to Anthropology. Washington, D.C.: Smithsonian Institution Press.

Dow, James. 1986a. *The Shaman's Touch. Otomi Indian Symbolic Healing*. Salt Lake City: University of Utah Press.

Dow, James. 1986b. "Universal Aspects of Symbolic Healing: A Theoretical Synthesis." *American Anthropologist* 88:56–69.

Eliade, Mircea. 1964. *Shamanism: Archaic Techniques of Ecstasy*. Translated by Willard R. Trask. Bollingen Series LXXVI. Princeton: Princeton University Press.

Elkin, Adolphus Peter. 1977. *Aboriginal Men of High Degree*. New York: St. Martin's Press.

Ellis, Florence H. 1970. "Pueblo Witchcraft and Medicine." *Systems of North American Witchcraft and Sorcery*. Deward E. Walker, Jr., editor. Anthropological Monographs of the University of Idaho, no. 1. Moscow: University of Idaho. 37–72.

Evans-Pritchard, Edward E. 1965. *Theories of Primitive Religion*. Oxford: Clarendon Press.

Faron, Louis C. 1968. *The Mapuche Indians of Chile*. New York: Holt, Rinehart and Winston.

Firth, Raymond William. 1973. *Symbols: Public and Private*. Ithaca, NY: Cornell University Press.

Fried, Morton. 1967. *The Evolution of Political Society: An Essay in Political Anthropology*. New York: Random House.

Fulton, John. 1981. "Experience, Alienation and the Anthropological Condition of Religion." *Annual Review of the Social Sciences of Religion*. Amsterdam: Mouton Publishers. 1–32.

Furst, Peter T., editor. 1972. *Flesh of the Gods: The Ritual Use of Hallucinogens.* New York: Praeger.

Furst, Peter T. 1976. *Hallucinogens and Culture.* San Francisco: Chandler and Sharp.

Furst, Peter T. 1977. "The Roots and Continuities of Shamanism." *Stones, Bones, and Skin: Ritual and Shamanic Art.* A. T. Brodzky, R. Danesewich, N. Johnson, editors. Toronto: Society for Art Publications. 1–28.

Gilberg, R. 1984. "How to Recognize a Shaman among Other Religious Specialists." *Shamanism in Eurasia.* Part 1. Mihály Hoppál, editor. Gottingen: Herodot. 21–27.

Goodman, Felicita D. 1990. *Where the Spirits Ride the Wind: Trance Journeys and Other Ecstatic Experiences.* Bloomington: Indiana University Press.

Halifax, Joan, editor. 1979. *Shamanic Voices: A Survey of Visionary Narratives.* New York: E. P. Dutton.

Halifax, Joan. 1982. *Shaman, the Wounded Healer.* New York: Crossroad.

Handelman, D. 1967. "The Development of a Washo Shaman." *Ethnology* 6:444–464.

Handelman, D. 1968. "Shamanizing on an Empty Stomach." *American Anthropologist* 70 (2): 353–356.

Harner, Michael, editor. 1973a. *Hallucinogens and Shamanism.* New York: Oxford University Press.

Harner, Michael. 1973b. *The Jívaro: People of the Sacred Waterfall.* New York: Anchor.

Harner, Michael. 1973c. "The Sound of Rushing Water." *Hallucinogens and Shamanism.* Michael Harner, editor. New York: Oxford University Press. 15–27.

Harner, Michael. 1980. *The Way of the Shaman.* New York: Harper and Row.

Harner, Michael. 1982. *The Way of the Shaman: A Guide to Power and Healing.* 2nd edition. New York: Bantam Book.

Harner, Michael. 1985. "Comments on Richard Noll: Mental Imagery Cultivation as a Cultural Phenomenon: The Role of Visions in Shamanism." *Current Anthropology* 26 (4): 452.

Harner, Michael. 1988. "What Is a Shaman?" *Shaman's Path: Healing, Personal Growth and Empowerment.* Gary Doore, editor. Boston: Shambhala. 7–15.

Hitchcock, John T. 1976. "Aspects of Bhujel Shamanism." *Spirit Possession in the Nepal Himalayas.* John T. Hitchcock and Rex L. Jones, editors. New Delhi: Vikas Publishing House Pvt Ltd. 165–196.

Hitchcock, John T. 1977. "A Nepali Shaman's Performance as Theater." *Stones, Bones, and Skin: Ritual and Shamanic Art.* A. T. Brodzky, R. Danesewich, and N. Johnson, editors. Toronto: Society for Art Publications. 42–48.

Hobsbawm, Eric and Terence Ranger. 1983. *The Invention of Tradition.* Cambridge: Cambridge University Press.

Hoffman, Walter J. 1891. "The Midewiwin or 'Grand Medicine Society' of the Ojibwa." *Seventh Annual Report of the Bureau of American Ethnology for the Years 1885–1886.* Washington D.C.: Governemnt Printing Office. 149–300.

Holmberg, David H. 1980. "Lama, Shaman and Lambu in Tamang Religious Practice." Ph.D. dissertation, Cornell University. Ann Arbor: University Microfilms.

Honigmann, John J. 1970. "Witchcraft among the Kaska Indians." *Systems of North American Witchcraft and Sorcery.* Deward E. Walker, Jr., editor. Anthropological Monographs of the University of Idaho, no. 1. Occasional Series. Moscow: Department of Anthropology, University of Idaho.

Horwatt, K. 1988. "The Shamanistic Complex in the Pentecostal Church." *Ethos* 16: 128–145.

Hultkrantz, Åke. 1966. "An Ecological Approach to Religion." *Ethos* 31:131–150.

Hultkrantz, Åke. 1967. "Spirit Lodge: A North American Shamanistic Séance." *Studies in Shamanism*. Carl-Martin Edsman, editor. Stockholm: Almqvist and Wiksell. 32–68.

Hultkrantz, Åke. 1973. "A Definition of Shamanism." *Temenos* (Helsinki) 9:25–37.

Hultkrantz, Åke. 1978. "Ecological and Phenomenological Aspects of Shamanism." *Studies in Lapp Shamanism*. Louise Bäckman and Åke Hultkrantz, editors. Acta Universitatis Stockholmiensis. Stockholm Studies in Comparative Religion. Stockholm: Almqvist & Wiksell. 9–35. (Also published in *Shamanism in Siberia*. V. Diószegi and M. Hoppál, editors. Budapest: Akadémiai Kiadó. 1978. 27–58.)

Hultkrantz, Åke. 1985. "Comments on Richard Noll: Mental Imagery Cultivation as a Cultural Phenomenon: The Role of Visions in Shamanism." *Current Anthropology* 26 (4): 453.

Hultkrantz, Åke. 1992. *Shamanic Healing and Ritual Drama*. New York: Crossroad.

Hutchinson, G. B. 1985. *Ecstatic Walt Whitman: Literary Shamanism and the Crisis of the Union*. Columbus: Ohio State University Press.

Jochelson, Waldemar. 1926. *The Yukaghir and the Yukaghirized Tungus*. Franz Boas, editor. Vol. 9 of The Jesup North Pacific Expedition. Memoir of the American Museum of Natural History. Leiden: E. J. Brill, Ltd.

Jones, Rex L. 1976. "Spirit Possession and Society in Nepal." *Spirit Possession in the Nepal Himalayas*. John T. Hitchcock and Rex L. Jones, editors. New Delhi: Vikas Publishing House Pvt Ltd. 1–11.

Kan, Sergei. 1989. *Symbolic Immortality: The Tlingit Potlatch of the Nineteenth Century*. Washington, D.C.: Smithsonian Institution Press.

Kleinman, Arthur. 1979. "Why Do Indigenous Healers Successfully Heal?" *Social Science and Medicine* 13B:7–26.

Korp, Maureen Elizabeth. 1991. "Earthworks: Shamanism in Religious Experiences of Contemporary Artists in North America." Ph.D. dissertation, Religious Studies, University of Ottawa.

Kortt, I. R. 1984. "The Shaman as Social Representative in the World Beyond." *Shamanism in Eurasia*. Part 2. Mihály Hoppál, editor. Gottingen: Herodot. 289–306.

Kroeber, Alfred L. 1952. "Psychosis or Social Sanction." *The Nature of Culture*. Chicago: University of Chicago Press. 310–319.

Lantis, Margaret. 1960. *Eskimo Childhood and Interpersonal Relationships: Nunivak Biographies and Genealogies*. American Ethnological Society. Seattle: University of Washington Press.

Lee, Richard B. 1968. "What Hunters Do for a Living, or, How to Make Out on Scarce Resources." *Man the Hunter*. R. B. Lee and I. DeVore, editors. Chicago: Aldine. 30–48.

Lee, Richard B., and Irven DeVore, editors. 1968. *Man the Hunter*. Chicago: Aldine.

Lessa, William A., and Evon Z. Vogt. 1958. *Reader in Comparative Religion: An Anthropological Approach*. 1st edition. Evanston, IL: Row, Peterson and Co. (4th edition, 1979. New York: Harper & Row)

Levy, Mark. 1988. "Shamanism and Contemporary Art." *Proceedings of the Fourth International Conference on the Study of Shamanism and Alternate Models of Healing*. Ruth-Inge Heinze, editor. Madison: A-R Editions. 210–223.

Lévi-Strauss, Claude. 1963. *Structural Anthropology*. New York: Basic Books. (chapter 10 reprinted in *Reader in Comparative Religion: An Anthropological Approach*.

W. Lessa and E. Vogt, editors. 4th edition, 1979. New York: Harper & Row.
318–327)

Lewis, Ioan M. 1971. *Ecstatic Religion: An Anthropological Study of Spirit Possession and Shamanism.* Baltimore: Penguin.

Lex, B. 1979. "The Neurobiology of Ritual Trance." *The Spectrum of Ritual: A Biogenetic Structural Analysis.* E. G. d'Aquili, C. D. Laughlin, and J. McManus, editors. New York: Columbia University Press.

Lowie, Robert H. 1954. *Indians of the Plains.* American Museum of Natural History. New York: McGraw-Hill Book Company, Inc. (pp. 161–164 reprinted in W. Lessa and E. Vogt, editors. 1958. *Reader in Comparative Religion: An Anthropological Approach.* 1st edition. Evanston, IL: Row, Peterson and Co.)

Macfarlane, A. D. J. 1970. "Definitions of Witchcraft." *Witchcraft and Sorcery.* Max Marwick, editor. Penguin Modern Sociology Readings. Baltimore: Penguin. 41–44.

Maquet, Jacques. 1975. "Meditation in Contemporary Sri Lanka." *Journal of Transpersonal Psychology* 7:181–185.

Mayer, Philip. 1970. "Witches." *Witchcraft and Sorcery.* Max Marwick, editor. Penguin Modern Sociology Readings. Baltimore: Penguin. 45–64. (Originally published 1954)

Moerman, Daniel E. 1979. "Anthropology of Symbolic Healing." *Current Anthropology* 20 (1): 59–66.

Morris, William, editor. 1981. *The American Heritage Dictionary of the English Language.* Boston: Houghton Mifflin Co.

Mumford, Stan Royal. 1989. *Himalayan Dialogue: Tibetan Lamas and Gurung Shamans in Nepal.* Madison: University of Wisconsin Press.

Murdock, George Peter. 1965. "Tenino Shamanism." *Ethnology* 4:165–171.

Murdock, George Peter, and Douglas R. White. 1969. "Standard Cross-cultural Sample." *Ethnology* 8:329–369.

Murphy, Jane. 1964. "Psychotherapeutic Aspects of Shamanism on St. Lawrence Island, Alaska." *Magic, Faith, and Healing.* A. Kiev, editor. New York: Free Press.

Myerhoff, Barbara G. 1974. *Peyote Hunt: The Sacred Journey of the Huichol Indians.* Ithaca: Cornell University Press.

Nadel, S. F. 1946. "A Study of Shamanism in the Nuba Mountains." *Journal of the Royal Anthropological Institute of Great Britain and Ireland* 76 (part 1):25–37.

Needham, R. 1967. "Percussion and Transition." *Man,* n.s., 2:505–514.

Noll, Richard. 1983. "Shamanism and Schizophrenia: A State-specific Approach to the 'Schizophrenia Metaphor' of Shamanic States." *American Ethnologist* 10 (3): 443–459.

Noll, Richard. 1985. "Mental Imagery Cultivation as a Cultural Phenomenon: The Role of Visions in Shamanism." *Current Anthropology* 26 (4): 443–461.

Noll, Richard. 1989. "What Has Really Been Learned about Shamanism?" *Journal of Psychoactive Drugs* 21 (1): 47–50.

Oberg, Kalvero. 1973. *The Social Economy of the Tlingit Indians.* Seattle: Washington University Press.

O'Connell, Carol. 1988. "Urban Shamanism: My Integration of My Spiritual Path and Professional Career." *Proceedings of the Fourth International Conference on the Study of Shamanism and Alternate Models of Healing.* Ruth-Inge Heinze, editor. Madison: A-R Editions. 122–129.

Ohnuki-Tierney, Emiko. 1974. *The Ainu of the Northwest Coast of Southern Sakhalin.* Prospect Hills, IL: Waveland Press. (1984 printing)

Oswalt, Wendell H. 1963. *Mission of Change in Alaska: Eskimos and Moravians on the Kuskokwim.* San Marino, CA: Huntington Library.

Oswalt, Wendell H. 1967. *Alaskan Eskimos.* San Francisco: Chandler Publishing Co.

Pandian, Jacob. 1991. *Culture, Religion, and the Sacred Self: A Critical Introduction to the Anthropological Study of Religion.* Englewood Cliffs: Prentice-Hall.

Peters, Larry G. 1978. "Shamanism among the Tamang of Nepal: Folk Curing and Psychotherapy." Ph.D. dissertation, University of California at Los Angeles.

Peters, Larry G. 1982. "Trance, Initiation, and Psychotherapy in Tamang Shamanism." *American Ethnologist* 9:21–46.

Peters, Larry G., and Douglass Price-Williams. 1980. "Towards an Experiential Analysis of Shamanism." *American Ethnologist* 7 (3): 397–413.

Petroff, Ivan. 1884. *Report on the Population, Industries and Resources of Alaska.* Department of the Interior, Census Office. Washington, D.C.: U.S. Government Printing Office.

Poewe, Karla, editor. 1994. *Charismatic Christianity as a Global Culture.* Columbia: University of South Carolina Press.

Popov, A. 1932. *Materialy dlja bibliografi russkoj literaury po izuceniju samanstva.* Leningrad.

Prince, Raymond. 1982. "Shamans and Endorphins: Hypothesis for a Synthesis." *Ethos* 10 (4): 409–423.

Rank, Gustav. 1967. "Shamanism as a Research Subject: Some Methodological Viewpoints." *Studies in Shamanism.* Carl-Martin Edsman, editor. Stockholm: Almqvist & Wiksell. 15–22.

Rasmussen, Knud. 1929. *Intellectual Culture of the Iglulik Eskimos.* Report of the Fifth Thule Expedition 1921–1924. Vol 7, no 1. Copenhagen: Gyldendalske Boghandel.

Reichel-Dolmatoff, G. 1975. *The Shaman and the Jaguar.* Philadelphia: Temple University Press.

Reinhard, Johan. 1976. "Shamanism and Spirit Possession: The Definition Problem." *Spirit Possession in the Nepal Himalayas.* John T. Hitchcock and Rex L. Jones., editors. New Delhi: Vikas Publishing House Pvt Ltd. 12–20.

Sahlins, Marshall. 1968. "Notes on the Original Affluent Society." *Man the Hunter.* R. B. Lee and I. DeVore, editors. Chicago:Aldine. 85–89.

Schmidt, Wilhelm. 1931. *The Origin and Growth of Religion.* London: Methuen.

Sharon, Douglas. 1978. *Wizard of the Four Winds: A Shaman's Story.* New York: Free Press.

Shirokogoroff, Sergei Mikhailovich. 1935. *Psychomental Complex of the Tungus.* London: Kegan Paul, Trench, Trubner & Co., Ltd.

Siegel, Targatt, and Dwight Conquergood. 1985. *Between Two Worlds: Hmong Shaman in North America.* Los Angeles: Siegel Productions. Videocassette.

Siikala, Anna-Leena. 1978. *The Rite Technique of the Siberian Shaman.* Folklore Fellows Communications no. 220. Helsinki:Suomalainen Tiedeakatemia, Academia Scientiarum Fennica.

Siikala, Anna-Leena. 1985. "Comments on Richard Noll: Mental Imagery Cultivation as a Cultural Phenomenon: The Role of Visions in Shamanism." *Current Anthropology* 26 (4): 455.

Silverman, Julian. 1967. "Shamans and Acute Schizophrenia." *American Anthropologist* 69:21–31.

Siskin, Edgar E. 1983. *Washo Shamans and Peyotists: Religious Conflict in an American Indian Tribe*. Salt Lake City: University of Utah Press.

Siskind, Janet. 1973. *To Hunt in the Morning*. New York: Oxford University Press.

Skafte, Peter. 1988. "Following the Woman-Faced Deer: The Inner World of Nepalese Shamanism." *Shaman's Drum* 13 (summer):24–33.

Skafte, Peter. 1992. "Called by the Spirits: Three Accounts of Shamanic Initiation from Nepal." *Shaman's Drum* 27 (1): 46–52.

Spencer, Baldwin and F. J. Gillen. 1899. *The Native Tribes of Central Australia*. London: Macmillan and Co., Ltd. (Reprinted in 1968 by Dover)

Staal, Frits. 1975. *Exploring Mysticism*. Markham, Ontario: Penguin.

Stiles, Daniel. 1992. "The Hunter-Gatherer 'Revisionist' Debate." *Anthropology Today* 8 (2): 13–17.

Stoller, Paul. 1989. *The Taste of Ethnographic Things: The Senses in Anthropology*. Philadelphia: University of Pennsylvania Press

Stoller, Paul and Cheryl Olkes. 1987. *In Sorcery's Shadow: A Memoir of Apprenticeship among the Songhay of Niger*. Chicago: University of Chicago Press.

Tart, Charles. 1972. "State of Consciousness and State-Specific Sciences." *Science* 176: 1203–1210.

Thiel, Joseph Franz. 1984. *Religionsethnologie*. Berlin: Dietrich Reimer Verlag.

Tikhmenev, Petr Aleksandrovich. 1978. *A History of the Russian-American Company*. Translated by Richard A. Pierce and Alton S. Donnelly. Seattle: University of Washington Press. (Originally published 1861–1863)

Torrey, E. Fuller. 1974. "Spiritualists and Shamans as Psychotherapists: An Account of Original Anthropological Sin." *Religious Movements in Contemporary America*. Irving I. Zaretsky and Mark P. Leone, editors. Princeton: Princeton University Press. 330–337.

Townsend, Joan B. 1965. "Ethnohistory and Culture Change of the Iliamna Tanaina." Ph.D. dissertation, University of California at Los Angeles.

Townsend, Joan B. 1974. "Journals of Nineteenth Century Russian Priests to the Tanaina: Cook Inlet, Alaska (Edited Journals with an Introduction and Historical Summary)." *Arctic Anthropology* 11 (1): 1–30.

Townsend, Joan B. 1980. "Ranked Societies of the Alaskan Pacific Rim." *Alaskan Native Culture and History*. Y. Kotani and W. Workman, editors. Senri Ethnological Studies, no. 4. Osaka, Japan: National Museum of Ethnology (Japan). 123–156.

Townsend, Joan B. 1981. "Tanaina." *Sub-Arctic*. June Helm, editor. Vol. 6 of *Handbook of North American Indians*. Washington, D.C.: Smithsonian Institution. 623–640.

Townsend, Joan B. 1983. "Pre-Contact Political Organization and Slavery in Aleut Societies." *The Development of Political Organization in Native North America*. Elizabeth Tooker, editor. Washington, D.C.: American Ethnology Society. 120–132.

Townsend, Joan B. 1985. "The Autonomous Village and the Development of Chiefdoms." *Development and Decline: The Evolution of Sociopolitical Organization*. Henri J. M. Classen, Pieter van de Velde, and M. Estelle Smith, editors. South Hadley, MA: Bergin and Garvey. 141–155.

Townsend, Joan B. 1988. Neo-Shamanism and the Modern Mystical Movement." *Sha-*

man's Path: Healing, Personal Growth, and Empowerment. Gary Doore, editor. Boston: Shambhala. 73–83.

Townsend, Joan B. 1989. Field notes. Nepal.

Townsend, Joan B. 1991. "Neo-Shamanism: The Return of the Native." Paper, "The Empire Strikes Back" symposium, Society for the Scientific Study of Religion, Pittsburgh, November 10.

Townsend, Joan B. 1992. Field notes. Nepal.

Townsend, Joan B. Forthcoming. "Shamanic Spirituality: Core Shamanism and Neo-Shamanism in Contemporary Western Society." *Readings in Anthropology of Religion.* Stephen D. Glazier, editor. Westport, CT: Greenwood Press.

Turner, Edith. 1994. "A Visible Spirit Form in Zambia." *Being Changed: The Anthropology of Extraordinary Experience.* David E. Young and Jean-Guy Goulet, editors. Peterborough, Ontario: Broadview Press.

Turner, Victor. 1972. "Religious Specialists." *International Encyclopedia of the Social Sciences.* Vol. 13. David L. Sills, editor. New York: Crowell Collier and Macmillan. 437–444. (Reprinted in Lehmann, A. and J. Myers. 1993. *Magic, Witchcraft, and Religion.* 3rd edition. Palo Alto: Mayfield. 71–78.)

von Fürer-Haimendorf, Christoph. 1970. "Priests." *Man, Myth, and Magic.* Vol. 16. Richard Cavendish, editor. London: BPCC/Phoebus Publishing. 2248–2255. Reprinted in Lehmann, A. and J. Myers. 1993. *Magic, Witchcraft, and Religion.* 3rd edition. Palo Alto: Mayfield. 79–83.

Wafer, Jim. 1991. *The Taste of Blood: Spirit Possession in Brazilian Candomble.* Philadelphia: University of Pennsylvania Press.

Walker, Deward E., Jr., editor. 1970. *Systems of North American Witchcraft and Sorcery.* Anthropological Monographs of the University of Idaho, no. 1. Occasional Series. Moscow: Department of Anthropology, University of Idaho.

Wallace, Anthony F. C. 1966. *Religion, an Anthropological View.* New York: Random House.

Winkelman, Michael James. 1986. "Trance States: A Theoretical Model and Cross-cultural Analysis." *Ethos* 14:174–203.

Winkelman, Michael James. 1990. "Shamans and Other 'Magico-Religious' Healers: A Cross-cultural Study of Their Origins, Nature and Social Transformations." *Ethos* 18 (3): 308–352.

Wright, Peggy Ann. 1989. "The Nature of the Shamanic State of Consciousness: A Review." *Journal of Psychoactive Drugs* 21 (1): 25–33.

Young, David E., and Jean-Guy Goulet, editors. 1994. *Being Changed: The Anthropology of Extraordinary Experience.* Peterborough, Ontario: Broadview Press.

17

THE CYCLE OF MEANING: SOME METHODOLOGICAL IMPLICATIONS OF BIOGENETIC STRUCTURAL THEORY

Charles D. Laughlin

Over the years, a group of us have developed an entrainment theory of human consciousness we call *biogenetic structuralism*, a perspective we believe has methodological relevance for the anthropological study of religion. By *entrainment* we mean that each moment of consciousness and every attribute of consciousness are mediated by a distinct pattern of neuroendocrine organization. As the term metaphorically suggests, networks of cells carrying out specific physiological and psychological functions link up like the cars making up a train (hence, "en-train"). Consciousness and its component activities are produced by organizations of cells interacting in conditioned ways. This view of consciousness poses a number of methodological issues germane to the ethnological study of religion. Preeminent among these issues is the question of how the ethnographer can discover the structures that produce the behavior, symbolism, and experience that make up the stock in trade of the field. This is a distinct problem in the absence of the technology requisite for the direct measurement of internal brain states.

Much of our work has been carried out in various aspects of the study of religion, including the function of symbols and natural categories in the ritual evocation of experience (Laughlin 1988c, 1993; Laughlin et al. 1986; Laughlin, McManus, and Shearer 1983). We have shown that certain universal features of symbolism, spatial and temporal cognition, affect and energy states, alternative phases of consciousness, and the like, are due to the genetically predisposed organization of the human nervous system. We have argued that the invariant aspects of behavior, consciousness, and culture being discussed in the various structuralist theories of religion could be due to nothing other than inherent structures in the nervous system. Modern neuroscience can demonstrate that every thought, every image, and every feeling and action are demonstrably mediated by the human brain.

Yet we have remained wary of the tantalizing lure of physiological reductionism. Indeed, we have worked to develop a theoretical perspective that (1) is nondualistic in modeling the mind and body, (2) is at the same time not reductionistic in the positivist sense (i.e., that neurophysiology can give a complete account of all things mental and cultural), and (3) remains open to all reasonable sources of data about human experience, consciousness, and culture.

While it is true that—so far at least—few of us have had the opportunity to directly measure brain states in the field, considering consciousness in an evolutionary and developmental frame is still inescapable because (1) there exists considerable evidence of dramatic encephalization found in the hominid fossil record and (2) cultural variation seems to be the primary mode of human adaptation. It is my intention in this chapter to introduce a system of conceptual tools by which brain and consciousness may be considered in a unitary framework, despite the current lack in ethnography of direct measures of brain-consciousness interaction. Those readers wishing further information about these concepts and issues will be directed to relevant references.

NEUROGNOSIS AND THE COGNIZED ENVIRONMENT

Our first book (Laughlin and d'Aquili 1974) presented some general concepts that were later refined and used in other studies. One important concept was *neurognosis*, a term we coined to label the inherent, rudimentary knowledge available to cognition in the initial organization of the fetal and infant nervous system (83; see also Laughlin 1991). A human newborn and infant is a perceptually and cognitively competent being that takes its first conscious stance toward the world from the standpoint of a system of initial, genetically predisposed *neurognostic models* that come to mature in somatosensory interaction with the world (see Bower 1989; Spelke 1988a, 1988b; Laughlin 1991 on infant cognitive competence).

There is considerable evidence to show that most of the structures mediating consciousness at any given moment are located in the cortex of the brain (see Doty 1975). The principal function of the human nervous system at the level of the cerebral cortex is the construction of a vast network of these models. We call the totality of this network of neural models an individual's *cognized* environment and contrast this with the *operational* environment that includes both the real nature of that individual as an organism and the individual's external environment (see Laughlin and Brady 1978: 6; d'Aquili, Laughlin and McManus 1979: 12; Rubinstein, Laughlin, and McManus 1984: 21; Laughlin, McManus, and d'Aquili 1990: 82–90).[1] The cognized environment and its constituent models, being composed of living tissue, develop over a genetically predisposed course. Thus, not only is the initial organization of neural models neurognostic in their organization, so, too, is the course of development of those models and patterns of interaction and selection among models (see Changeux 1985; Edelman 1987; Varela 1979).

THE TRANSCENDENTAL AND THE ZONE OF UNCERTAINTY

One of our metaphysical assumptions is particularly pertinent to the anthropological study of religion. We assume that the operational environment is transcendental relative to the capacity of any individual or society to comprehend it. We do not mean by this that the operational environment is unknowable but, rather, that knowledge is always intentional, developing, incomplete, and limited by the capacities of the brain doing the knowing. The cognized environment is a system of points of view about the operational environment, and there is always more to know about the operational environment, or any aspect of it, than can be known. Of course, socially shared content of cognized environments is part of what we all mean by "culture."

The brain does not take passive snapshots of the world. The operational environment is modeled in an active and adaptively isomorphic[2] way. This means there must always exist a set of boundaries to knowledge, a *zone of uncertainty*[3] (d'Aquili, Laughlin, and McManus 1979: 40, 171), formed by the limits to spatial discernment and to the capacity of the individual or species to apprehend temporal and causal relations. The zone of uncertainty is the directly experienceable junction between the transcendental nature of the actual self and world, and the limits of an individual's or culture's understanding (see Elster 1984: chapter 4). It is often native ideas formulated about the zone of uncertainty that form much of the knowledge recognized as "religion" by ethnographers. Ideas about the meaning of death, the source of intuitive inspiration, the normally hidden forces behind perceived events, and the meaning of chance events, the source of the healing power of herbs and other medicines, and so on, are the very essence of religion in any society, whether or not the particular society has a concept equivalent to that of our English "religion."

NEUROGNOSIS AND MIND-BODY DUALISM

It is the concept of neurognosis that allows us to avoid the pitfalls of that most intractable of methodological problems, mind-body dualism. For the distinction between the cognized and operational environments is not suggested as a euphemism for mind versus body but rather emphasizes the fact that the structures that produce the cognized environment are themselves part of the operational environment. Consciousness and its structures are wholly of and within the body—and nowhere but the body. Or put another way, the cognized environment is how the operational environment models itself within organisms that have brains. Thus, in our writings the cognized environment is never intended either as an epiphenomenon of brain states or as only partially identical with brain activities. Moreover, neither mental nor physical accounts of consciousness and body are complete. The operational environment is not just the way we label the world as described by science. Scientific theories about, and descriptions of, the world are another kind of cognized environment. Both the cognized and the operational environments are aspects of a single transcendental mystery and thus cannot be reduced from one to the other. Biogenetic structuralism takes the view that because we are confronted with the profound mystery of the "mindbrain" (as Earl Count likes to call it), the widest possible scope of inquiry is appropriate for its study.

The trouble is that ethnographers tend to ignore neuroscientific questions— again, because they have no means of directly measuring brain states in the field. The unconscious result of ignoring the neurosciences has been to perpetuate mind-body dualism in ethnographic descriptions of symbolism and meaningful behavior. This constitutes a methodological error of the first moment. Just because the ethnographer cannot yet measure brain states does not mean they are not occurring. Moreover, there will come a time in the foreseeable future when the technology will be available for direct measures of brain states in the field, and unless ethnological methods and theories come into accord with what we already know about our neurophysiological nature, neuroscience could well supersede anthropology as the discipline of choice in explaining panhuman phenomena (see especially TenHouton 1991).

This criticism is particularly appropriate when ethnography comes intermittently under the influence of the kind of cultural relativistic "oddities and quiddities" approaches that theoretically ignore or deny panhuman universals in structure and culture. The knowledge composing much of culture is indeed "local" in the Geertzian sense (Geertz 1983), but it is also rife with universal patterns due to the fact that all knowledge is mediated by structures inherent to the human brain and that mature and develop in diverse settings. Thus, the ethnographer should be looking not only at the surface variance among peoples but also at the patterns of regularity and similarity across cultural boundaries. Ethnographers should be sensitized to both the variety and the structural commonalities in the religious symbolism and practices being studied.

RITUAL AND THE SYMBOLIC FUNCTION

The first book-length application of biogenetic structural theory was an account of the evolution and structure of ceremonial ritual. In *The Spectrum of Ritual* (d'Aquili, Laughlin, and McManus 1979), we generated a theory of ritual behavior as a mechanism by which intra- and interorganism entrainment of neurocognitive processes are evoked, thus making concerted action among social animals possible. It is methodologically crucial to understand that ritual always involves both internal communication within the organism and external communication between the organism and its conspecifics and world. In other words, ritual is activity that simultaneously constitutes external interactions among group members, or between the individual and its world (including the self)—what Wallace (1966: 218) called "allocommunication"—and internal relations among structures all the way up and down the functional hierarchy of the individual nervous system—what Wallace (220) called "autocommunication." Autocommunication may entail neural interactions ranging from those networks controlling the movement of muscle groups to those mediating the metabolic, emotional, imaginal, and cognitive processing (d'Aquili, Laughlin, and Mc-Manus 1979: 1–50).

We used the general theory in the first book to examine formalized behavior among animals generally, then specifically among mammals, primates, and humans, and finally looked at the various neurocognitive processes mediating arousal, affect, cognition, and so on. As it has turned out, ritual has been a major focus of our work (see also d'Aquili 1983; d'Aquili and Laughlin 1975; Laughlin and McManus 1982; Laughlin et al. 1986; Laughlin 1989) because of its ubiquitous nature and its role in controlling and transforming cognition and experience.

A related focus of biogenetic structural analysis has been the *symbolic function* (see Laughlin, McManus, and Stephens 1981; Laughlin and Stephens 1980; MacDonald et al. 1989; Young-Laughlin and Laughlin 1988). We have been particularly interested in how sensory stimuli as symbols are able to penetrate to and evoke those neurocognitive models mediating meaning and, in turn, how models express themselves via symbolic actions and artifacts. Among other things, we have developed a theory of the evolution of the symbolic function that proceeds from primordial symbols (e.g., the simple recognition of an object), through cognized symbols (e.g., metaphors, cosmograms, ritual procedures) to sign systems (e.g., natural language utterances), and finally to formal sign systems (e.g., symbolic logic, set theory), any or all of which may operate at any moment in adult human cognition (Laughlin, McManus, and Stephens 1981; Laughlin, McManus, and d'Aquili 1990: 172–187).

INTENTIONALITY AND PREFRONTAL-SENSORIAL POLARITY

The moment-by-moment organization of the cognized environment is essentially intentional (Searle 1983). This fact is very important to our understanding of the organization of consciousness. Intentionality means that neural networks organize themselves, both spatially and temporally, around an object of consciousness. The focal object (e.g., a percept, category, feeling, sensation, image, thought, etc.) is also mediated by a neural network and is, for the moment, the nexus of cognitive, affective, metabolic, and motor operations for the organism (Neisser 1976: 20; Biederman 1987).

Intentionality is the experienced result of a polar interaction between the prefrontal cortex and the sensory cortex of the human brain. This interaction is both neurognostic and ubiquitous to human consciousness, regardless of cultural background (Laughlin 1988b; Laughlin, McManus, and d'Aquili 1990: 105). Subsidiary structures entrained as a consequence of the dialogue between prefrontal and sensory cortical processes may be located over a wide expanse of cortical, subcortical, and endocrinal tissues. Intentionality is fundamental to understanding the mechanisms involved in religious practices such as meditation and dance that require intense concentration upon particularly salient objects. Under the proper conditions, the activity of virtually the entire nervous system and body may be reorganized around the object of focus. These conditions may be experienced as "absorption" or "ecstatic states."

EXPERIENCE AND INTENTIONALITY

Experience is produced by this intentional dialogue and consists of the construction of a meaningful, phenomenal world by the sensorium, the latter being a field of neural activity that arises and dissolves in temporally sequential epochs and that is coordinated with cognitive processes that associate meaning and form in a unitary frame (Laughlin 1988b; Laughlin, McManus, and d'Aquili 1990: 108–112). By *experience* we are referring to "that which arises before the subject" in consciousness (see Dilthey 1976; Husserl 1977). This includes perception, thought, imagination, intuition, affect, somasthesis, and sensation. A point to emphasize is that both the sensory and the cognitive-intentional aspects of experience are active products of neurological functioning and are exquisitely ordered in the service of abstract pattern recognition in experience (Gibson 1969).

It is well to remember that the natural motivation of the human brain is toward meaningful experience, rather than toward truth. The brain at every moment of consciousness imposes an order upon the experience it produces. Much of that order is an *interpretation of the relations* among objects and events—the very essence of meaning. Although experience usually occurs as a unitary field, maintaining a clear distinction between the interpretive and sensorial aspects of experience is methodologically useful. We can schematize this distinction as a kind of two hands clapping model of experience (see Figure 17.1).

The unity of experience arising each moment in our consciousness is mediated by a continuously changing field of neural entrainments that may include any particular neural network one moment and exclude it the next (Laughlin, McManus, and d'Aquili 1990: 94–95). This intentional field incorporates both interpretive cognitions and sensorial attributes or "quale." The quale (e.g., color, frequency of tone, texture, line, etc.) are more primitive and hence are more obviously universal. The products of the higher cognitive processes are

Figure 1
The Two Hands Clapping Model of Experience. Sensory and intentional-interpretive
processes rise to meet the sensorium in each moment of consciousness.

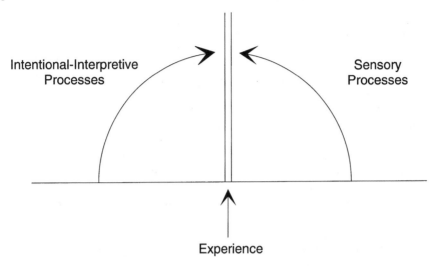

much more varied. This is why the interpretive aspects of experience tend to
diverge more dramatically from individual to individual, and from culture to
culture, than do the sensorial aspects. For example, while participating in native
rituals the ethnographer may experience numinous light phenomena, body "witness," feeling states, or lucid imagery similar to that described by the informants
but may come to interpret these perceptions according to views outside of the
worldview of the host culture. Indeed, overidentification with the host interpretation of such experiences may stifle a more complete scientific account of the
various processes and principles involved in the encounter. Overidentification
with the host worldview (the emic fallacy) may be just as detrimental to good
ethnological science as overidentification with current scientific views (the etic
fallacy).

CYCLES OF CONSCIOUSNESS

One of the salient characteristics of the cognized environment is that it is
experienced as a stream of recurring realities—what Alfred Schutz (1945) called
"multiple realities." The entrainments that mediate the cognized environment
tend to cycle in a circadian loop, regulated by internal oscillators located in the
thalamus of the diencephalon and the reticular activating system of the brain
stem in interaction with external "zeitgebers" (i.e., temporal cues in the environment, like night and day, alarm clock, cup of coffee, schedules, etc.). Each
moment of consciousness is a fresh reentrainment of the cognized environment,

a reentrainment that is constrained to the general limits of the organism's circadian cycle. Reentrainment may be experienced as anything from a continuity in the stream of consciousness to a radical transformation of experience.

PHASES AND WARPS OF CONSCIOUSNESS

Because the shifting entrainment of consciousness manifests recurrent temporal patterns, we may become aware of "chunks," or natural categories, of the cognized environment, that we recognize as distinct. The definitive characteristic of awareness is re-collection, re-membering, or re-cognition of patterns in experience, and therefore awareness tacitly presumes the role played by knowledge in the construction of experience.

Furthermore, since the recursive quality of experience displays discernible patterns, and may thus be recognized as such, reflexive knowledge about consciousness itself involves knowledge of experiential episodes. If an episode is perceived as a salient unit, then it may be cognized as distinct from other episodes and perhaps categorically labeled: for example, I am "awake," "stoned," "depressed," "dreaming," "angry," "out of my body," "playing," and so on. These cognized and labeled categories of experience, and their mediating neurocognitive entrainments, we call *phases* of consciousness. The points of experiential and neurophysiological transformation between phases we call *warps* of consciousness (Laughlin et al. 1986; Laughlin, McManus, and d'Aquili 1990: 140–145).

RITUAL AND WARP CONTROL

When a society wishes to exercise control over the recurrence and quality of a phase of consciousness, it will tend to ritualize the individual's activity during the warp preceding the phase (Laughlin et al. 1986). Warps are durations of neural transformation that are usually both short and efficacious. They also tend to occur unconsciously. For example, the hypnagogic warp before sleep lasts but a few seconds in most people in our society, yet its activity determines the quality of the dream phases that follow it. Tibetan dream Yogis learn to control the hypnagogic by practicing certain rituals and are able to exercise considerable control over the organization of experience during dreaming. For this reason, the ethnographer should learn to recognize shifts in states of consciousness in informants and ascertain what, if any, ritual activity has been positioned so as to mediate the change of their internal state.

Rituals are often symbolically rich events. Moreover, rituals incorporate a variety of *drivers* that may account in some measure for the rituals' efficacy. Drivers are ritual elements that evoke specific neurophysiological effects. They may be fairly gross in their form, such as drumming, dancing, ingestion of psychotropic drugs, sweat baths, ordeals, flickering lights, chanting, fasting, and special diets, or they may be relatively subtle in form, such as extraordinary concentration on the breath, on eidetic imagery, or on a question. Drivers are very often universal in essential form. That is, their most efficacious aspects are found in rituals of peoples all over the planet (e.g., long bouts of drumming or chanting).

The ethnographer should also be aware that while a ritual activity may be a necessary condition for an intended experience, and perhaps even include a profusion of drivers, it is unlikely to be a sufficient condition. A ritual is a totality that is itself an element in a greater play. There will be other ingredients required to evoke the intended experience. For example, one may repeat a meditation many times without reaching the intended goal, because perhaps one of the requisites for the intended experience may be a certain level of tranquillity. It is not uncommon (e.g., in the Sun Dance; see Jorgensen 1972) for practitioners to have to repeat a ritual activity numerous times, and perhaps for years, before the intended experience arises. In addition, because experience develops over the course of life, rituals may be repeated over the course of years with the experiences intended by the guide or teacher changing with the maturation of the practitioner. Just because the ethnographer has participated in a ritual and has had an experience recognized by the host culture does not mean that the ethnographer has exhausted the repertoire of possibly relevant experiences evoked by the practice in informants who have been at it for years. The fact that Napoleon Chagnon (1977) took the psychotropic drug used by Yanomamo shamans once does not mean that he experienced the many and varied subtleties of reality that a mature shaman might experience.

MONOPHASIC AND POLYPHASIC CULTURES

Mundane phases of consciousness naturally alternate between those phases that promote adaptation to the external operational environment (we lump these together and call them ''being awake'' in our culture) and those phases that promote mutual adaptation of tissues within the organism (we call these ''being asleep''; see McManus, Laughlin, and Shearer 1993). As a consequence, intentionality alternates between perceived objects and relations in the external operational environment, and imagined objects and relations representing internal processes of somatic activity. Many societies integrate knowledge gleaned from experiences encountered in all phases of consciousness within a single worldview. We call these *polyphasic* cultures.

By contrast, modern Euroamerican society typically gives credence only to experiences had in the ''normal'' waking phases—that is, in the phases of consciousness oriented primarily toward adaptation to the external operational environment. We thus live in a relatively *monophasic* culture. Monophasic cultures are often characterized by a marked concern for adaptation to the external world and have relatively less concern for inner growth and balance among phases of consciousness (Laughlin, McManus, and d'Aquili 1990: 155). Ethnographers who have been raised in monophasic cultures, and who find themselves working in polyphasic ones, may have to learn to access other phases of consciousness within their own experience that they may have heretofore ignored. Otherwise, they may miss precisely those experiences that enrich the worldview of their hosts. The ethnographer may be experientially out of accord with the host culture in two obvious situations: One is when the ethnographer is out of touch with his or her dream life and doing fieldwork among a society that routinely tracks their dream experiences and considers dreaming to be a substantial source of knowledge about themselves and their world. The other is when the polyphasic worldview of the host is enriched with experiences had while participating in rituals and drug-induced "trips" unavailable for whatever reason to the ethnographer.

CROSS-PHASE TRANSFERENCE

Phases of consciousness organized around the inner life of the individual are frequently ignored, repressed, negatively sanctioned, considered pathological, or otherwise derided by a monophasic culture. Experiences in alternative phases may be lost or compartmentalized in memory due to a failure of *cross-phase transference*. Memory of experiences in one phase of consciousness (dream, "trance") may be lost to another phase of consciousness ("awake") due to a radical transformation of intentionality during the warp between phases. Minimal reentrainment across warps is all that is required for integration of phases into some kind of continuity in memory. Fragmented phases of consciousness may arise in societies in which there are neither ritualized methods of cross-phase transference nor a culturally transmitted, multiple reality worldview.

THE CYCLE OF MEANING

The process of integrating knowledge, memory, and experience, especially within a polyphasic society, we call the *cycle of meaning*. According to this cycle, a society's cosmology is expressed in its mythopoeic symbolism (myth, ritual performance, drama, art, stories, etc.) in such a way that it evokes direct experiences in alternative phases of consciousness (see Figure 17.2). The experiences and memories that arise as a consequence of participation in the mythopoeic procedures are in turn interpreted in terms of the cosmology in such a way that they verify and vivify the cosmology. A living cycle of meaning would seem to be a delicate process—and one that requires change or "revitalization" (Wallace 1966) over time in order for meaningful dialogue to continue between worldview and experience. The social construction of knowledge and individual experience are indeed involved in a reciprocal feedback system, the properties of which may be changed by circumstances in such a way that the link between knowledge and experience may be hampered and even lost. In other words, a religious system may become moribund due, for some reason, to the failure of the dialogue between worldview and direct experience. Many polyphasic soci-

Figure 2
The Cycle of Meaning. The society's worldview is expressed symbolically in its mythopoeia, and especially its ritual, which leads to direct experiences that are interpreted in such a way that the worldview is vivified and verified. Shamans may interject their influence into the process by structuring the symbolic expression and again by helping to interpret experience.

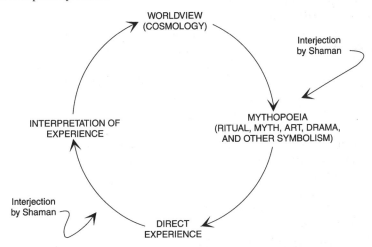

eties encourage their members to explore multiple phases of consciousness (through dreams, visions, meditation states, drug trips, trance states, etc.) and interpret experiences that arise according to culturally recognized systems of meaning (Winkelman 1986, 1990). This process of exploring experiences in multiple realities combined with social appropriation of the meaning of these experiences within a single cycle of meaning is definitive of polyphasic culture (see, e.g., Tonkinson [1978] and Poirier [1990] on the Australian Aborigines; Guedon [1984] on the Tsimshian in Canada; Laderman [1991] on Malay culture; Peters [1982] on Tamang shamanism). Many societies go so far as to compel alternative phases of consciousness by putting their members through initiation procedures, including ingesting psychotropic drugs and enforcing vision quests (see Bourguignon 1973; Naranjo 1987). The experiences encountered during these procedures in turn reify the society's multiple reality cosmology.

   The role of the shaman in both initiating practitioners into experiences and interpreting those experiences for the practitioner and the society at large may be important. In some societies the "shamanic" role may be diffused throughout the population of elders who have themselves undergone the requisite initiates. In other societies, control of initiation and interpretation may be in the hands of a secret society. In still other societies, particular individuals may be recognized as especially adept at leading others through healing and other initiatory experiences and interpreting experiences that arise in dreams and other phases of consciousness.

TRANSPERSONAL ANTHROPOLOGY

Competent ethnographic fieldwork among some religious systems requires nothing less than a trained transpersonal anthropologist. A transpersonal anthropologist is one that is capable of participating in transpersonal experience—that is, capable of both attaining whatever extraordinary experiences and phases of consciousness that enrich the religious system and relating these experiences to invariant patterns of symbolism, cognition, and practice found in religions and cosmologies all over the planet (see d'Aquili 1982; Laughlin 1988a, 1989; Laughlin et al. 1986; Laughlin, McManus, and Shearer 1983; Laughlin, McManus, and Webber 1984; MacDonald et al. 1989; Webber, Stephens, and Laughlin 1983). Our eventual goal is to understand (1) the maximum potential genetic and developmental limits to patterns of entrainment and therefore to human consciousness in any and all cultures, (2) the mechanisms by which societies condition patterns of entrainment so as to control (limit or extend) the range of human experience and the maturation of experience, (3) the mechanisms by which societies produce recurrent extraordinary experiences in some or all of their members so as to enliven their worldviews, and (4) by extrapolation, the possible future evolutionary possibilities of human consciousness (Laughlin and Richardson 1986).

Transpersonal anthropology is really just a natural extension of the grand tradition of "participant observation" that has made ethnology so unique among the social sciences. But it is an extension that requires the ethnographer to "suspend disbelief" in the native worldview to an extraordinary extent and to participate actively in those native procedures that guide one to the extraordinary experiences that give the worldview its spiritual grounding (see Young and Goulet 1994). The ethnographer may have to go to the extent of apprenticing to a shaman or becoming a member of a secret society in order to gain access to the teachings leading eventually to relevant transpersonal experiences. Transpersonal ethnography depends upon applying something like the process of spiritual exploration outlined by Ken Wilber in *A Sociable God* (1983: 133):

1. *Injunction.* This is always in the form, "If you want to know this, do this."

2. *Apprehension.* Cognitive apprehension and illumination of "object domain" addressed by the injunction.

3. *Communal confirmation.* Results are checked with those members of the host culture who have adequately completed the injunction and illuminative procedures.

To take an example from my own work among Tibetan Buddhist lamas, operationalizing the injunction was relatively straightforward. Lamas teach by a system of ritual initiations (*wang kur*) that dramatize the attributes of the focal deity. And the deity represents a state(s) of consciousness to be eventually realized by the initiate. The initiate participates rather passively in the drama but is given certain active meditation work to complete in the weeks and months following the initiation. In keeping with many esoteric religious systems, the lama knows the extent of the maturation of the meditation by the experiences reported to him by the initiate. The meditations incorporate such ritual drivers as chanting, percussion, visualization, intense concentration, special diet, fasting, breathing exercises, and body postures that all participate in incubating and eventually evoking transpersonal experiences that become the meaning of the symbolism for the initiate (Wilber's ''apprehension and illumination''). Confirmation is attained in dialogue with one's lama and with other meditators who have undergone the same or similar disciplines. It becomes clear in time that in order to comprehend the meaning of the symbolism one must do the work necessary to flesh out the experientially rich meaning. In a word, if the ethnographer has not undergone the apprehension phase, he or she cannot comprehend the real meaning the symbolism holds for the native.

To offer another example, Carol Laderman reports an experience she had of the *angin*, or ''Inner Wind,'' she had while working with a shaman named Pak Long during her fieldwork among the Malay:

I thought [Pak Long] wanted to do a short ritual for me, to release me from the dangers inherent in witnessing women give birth, a ritual he had often performed for my benefit at the close of Main Peteri. Instead, he proceeded to recite the story of Dewa Muda (which he had deduced was my primary Inner Wind), accompanied by the orchestra and his own rhythmic pounding on the floor. My trust in him was strong enough now to allay my fears, and I allowed my consciousness to shift into an altered state. At the height of my trance, I felt the Wind blowing inside my chest with the force of a hurricane. . . . When I later described the feelings I had while in trance to others who had been patients of Pak Long, they assured me that mine was a common experience. They also wondered at my surprise. One woman remarked, ''Why did you think we call them Winds?'' (1991: 75–76)

Following through with the commitment to participant observation in the transpersonal realm adds both to the richness of the descriptive literature on the ethnography of religion and to the depth of our understanding of how these systems work.

TRAINING IN PHENOMENOLOGY

One reason why anthropologists have so often neglected the transpersonal realm of experience is that the culture of science in our age is, and has been for many generations, anti-introspectionist in its positivistic bias. This is particularly noticeable today in some schools of cognitive science where introspective methods are considered anathema. What is needed in ethnology is some training in phenomenology, especially for those wishing to do cross-cultural research on religious systems. Phenomenology (à la Edmund Husserl, Maurice Merleau-

Ponty, Aron Gurwitsch, and others, as well as some shamanic and Eastern mystical traditions) is the study of the essential (invariant) processes of consciousness by way of mature contemplation.[4]

Phenomenological training directs the mind inward in a disciplined way. The student learns to direct concentration and inquiry toward his or her internal processes, be those processes dreaming, bodily functions (such as breathing, movement, etc.), eidetic imagery, feelings, thought processes, and the like. The training builds habit patterns that counter the Euroamerican conditioning toward ignoring or repressing internal processes and prepares the student for the kind of procedures used in the alien culture for incubating and attaining transpersonal experiences.

CONCLUSION

Disciplines such as humanistic and transpersonal psychology, ethnology, cognitive science, and the neurosciences have been profitably combined to produce a broader understanding of consciousness-related phenomena (e.g., LeDoux and Hirst 1986; see TenHouton 1991 on the ''ethnoneurologies''). Biogenetic structuralism is one such interdisciplinary dialogue in that we have attempted wherever possible to integrate transpersonal and phenomenological data into our avowed neuroanthropological analyses. In a word, we insist upon keeping the brain in mind—and the mind in brain. We feel the most profitable approach to the study of our species and its unique consciousness is one that casts the widest possible net—one that is open to, and that incorporates, data (1) that are derived from all relevant naturalistic (ethnographic), anatomical, clinical, and experimental sources; (2) that have the widest experiential and phenomenological grounding; and (3) that pertain to the total context of consciousness within which the particular phenomenon being studied is embedded.

Perhaps our most important message to ethnographers is that they should never lose sight of the relationship between experience and religious practice and institutions in non-Euroamerican societies. To treat ritual as merely exotic behavior, or even as meaningful behavior, without inquiring into the experiential realms associated with the behavior is to be satisfied with doing a half job. This is true even when the experience that may give core meaning to religious symbolism is for the most part invisible to the fieldworker. At least the fieldworker can give due credence to the native descriptions of experience, even though such experiences may elude the researcher (e.g., see Katz's 1982 description of his experiences with !Kung Bushman practices). The heuristic value of our model of the cycle of meaning is that it reminds us that the knowledge constituting much of culture derives its meaning in part via direct experience. And with respect to religious knowledge, the meaning in a living cosmology frequently derives from the extraordinary, even transpersonal experiences of the religion's practitioners. It is likely that few fieldworkers have accomplished these extraordinary experiences (but see Young and Goulet 1994), and as a consequence, the importance of such experiences has frequently been missed in the ethnographic accounts of religious systems. Biogenetic structuralism has developed a model of consciousness that requires an effort be made to describe both the external and internal activities of religious practitioners. Admittedly, this requirement poses a methodological challenge for the fieldworker. But it is not insurmountable, especially where the fieldworker is willing to participate in the activities designed to evoke the experiences that so enrich the religious aspects of the native worldview.

NOTES

The author wishes to thank Professor John Cove, Dr. Eugene d'Aquili, Dr. Robert Rubinstein, Jon Shearer, John McManus, and Susan Sample for sharing freely their many insights along the way. He also wishes to thank his teachers in the Tibetan Buddhist tradition, especially Namgyal Rimpoche, Chogay Trichen Rimpoche, and the late Kalu Rimpoche.

1. We borrowed these terms from Rappaport (1968) but have somewhat changed their meanings.

2. We have given a technical definition of *adaptive isomorphism* in d'Aquili, Laughlin, and McManus (1979: 17). The term implies that models are partially isomorphic to at least the extent required for survival. *Isomorphic* means that the elements and relations composing the neural model are not the same as those of the noumenon in the being or the world being modeled. And just as there is more to a real airplane than there is to a model airplane, so too is there "transcendentally" more to the noumenon than there is to the model—unless, of course, it is the neural network composing the model that is itself the noumenon.

3. Edmund Husserl's (1931) term for this is "horizon."

4. Several recent studies by the author exemplify this merging of contemplative anthropological and neuroscientific perspectives. Some of my own work has been directed at developing a "neurophenomenology"—that is, a phenomenology that is lodged in a neuroscientific and anthropological explanatory framework. One study discusses the essential intentionality of consciousness (noted by all phenomenologies) in terms of the dialogue between prefrontal cortex and sensorial cortex, as we discussed above (Laughlin 1988b). A second study suggests the relationship between invariant temporal patterns of perceptual sequencing and the neuropsychological literature available on "perceptual framing" (Laughlin 1992a). A third study pertains to the experimental foundations of the concept of causation (Laughlin 1993). And a fourth study looks at the fuzziness of natural categories in relation to transpersonal and contemplative experiences (Laughlin 1993).

REFERENCES

Biederman, I. 1987. "Recognition-by-Components: A Theory of Human Image Understanding." *Psychological Review* 94 (2): 115–147.

Bourguignon, E. 1973. *Religion, Altered States of Consciousness, and Social Change.* Columbus: Ohio State University Press.

Bower, T. G. 1989. *The Rational Infant: Learning in Infancy*. San Francisco: W. H. Freeman.

Chagnon, N. 1977. *Yanomamo: The Fierce People*. New York: Holt, Rinehart and Winston.

Changeux, J. P. 1985. *Neuronal Man: The Biology of Mind*. Oxford: Oxford University Press.

d'Aquili, E. G. 1982. "Senses of Reality in Science and Religion: A Neuroepistemological Perspective." *Zygon* 17 (4): 361–384.

d'Aquili, E. G. 1983. "The Myth-Ritual Complex: A Biogenetic Structural Analysis." *Zygon* 18 (3): 247–269.

d'Aquili, E. G. and C. D. Laughlin. 1975. "The Biopsychological Determinants of Religious Ritual Behavior." *Zygon* 10 (1): 32–58.

d'Aquili, E. G.; C. D. Laughlin; and J. McManus, editors. 1979. *The Spectrum of Ritual*. New York: Columbia University Press.

Dilthey, W. 1976. *Selected Writings* Edited by H. P. Richman. London: Cambridge University Press.

Doty, R. W. 1975. "Consciousness From Matter." *Acta neurobiologiae experimentalis*. 35: 791–804.

Edelman, G. M. 1987. *Neural Darwinism; The Theory of Neuronal Group Selection*. New York: Basic Books.

Elster, J. 1984. *Ulysses and the Sirens*. Cambridge: Cambridge University Press.

Geertz, C. 1983. *Local Knowledge*. New York: Basic Books.

Gibson, E. J. 1969. *Principles of Perceptual Learning and Development*. New York: Appleton-Century-Crofts.

Guedon, M. F. 1984. "An Introduction to Tsimshian Worldview and Its Practitioners." *The Tsimshian: Images of the Past*. M. Seguin, editor. Vancouver: University of British Columbia Press. 137–159.

Husserl, E. 1931. *Ideas: General Introduction to Pure Phenomenology*. New York: Macmillan Company.

Husserl, E. 1977. *Cartesian Meditations: An Introduction to Phenomenology*. The Hague: Martinus Nijhoff.

Jorgensen, J. G. 1972. *The Sun Dance Religion*. Chicago: University of Chicago Press.

Katz, R. 1982. *Boiling Energy: Community Healing among the Kalahari Kung*. Cambridge, MA: Harvard University Press.

Laderman, C. 1991. *Taming the Wind of Desire*. Berkeley: University of California Press.

Laughlin, C. D. 1988a. "On the Spirit of the Gift." *Anthropologica* 27 (1–2): 137–159. (Delayed 1985 issue)

Laughlin, C. D. 1988b. "The Prefrontosensorial Polarity Principle: Toward a Neurophenomenology of Intentionality." *Biological Forum* 81 (2): 245–262.

Laughlin, C. D. 1988c. "Transpersonal Anthropology: Some Methodological Issues." *Western Canadian Anthropologist* 5: 29–60.

Laughlin, C. D. 1989. "Ritual and the Symbolic Function: A Summary of Biogenetic Structural Theory." *Journal of Ritual Studies* 4 (1): 15–39.

Laughlin, C. D. 1991. "Pre- and Perinatal Brain Development and Enculturation: A Biogenetic Structural Approach." *Human Nature* 2 (3): 171–213.

Laughlin, C. D. 1992a. "Time, Intentionality, and a Neurophenomenology of the Dot." *Anthropology of Consciousness* 3 (3–4): 14–27.

Laughlin, C. D. 1992b. *Scientific Explanation and the Life-World: A Biogenetic Struc-*

tural Theory of Meaning and Causation. Sausalito, CA: Institute of Noetic Sciences.

Laughlin, C. D. 1993. "Fuzziness and Phenomenology in Ethnological Research." *Journal of Anthropological Research* 49: 17–37.

Laughlin, C. D. and I. A. Brady. 1978. *Extinction and Survival in Human Populations*. New York: Columbia University Press.

Laughlin, C. D. and E. G. d'Aquili. 1974. *Biogenetic Structuralism*. New York: Columbia University Press.

Laughlin, C. D. and J. McManus. 1982. "The Biopsychological Determinants of Play and Games." *Social Approaches to Sport*. R. M. Pankin, editor. Rutherford, NJ: Farleigh Dickinson University Press. 42–79.

Laughlin, C. D.; J. McManus; and E. G. d'Aquili. 1990. *Brain, Symbol and Experience: Toward a Neurophenomenology of Consciousness*. New York: Columbia University Press.

Laughlin, C. D.; J. McManus; R. A. Rubinstein; and J. Shearer. 1986. "The Ritual Transformation of Experience." *Studies in Symbolic Interaction (Part A)*. N. K. Denzin, editor. Greenwich, CT: JAI Press. 107–136.

Laughlin, C. D.; J. McManus; and J. Shearer. 1983. "Dreams, Trance and Visions: What a Transpersonal Anthropology Might Look Like." *Phoenix: The Journal of Transpersonal Anthropology* 7 (1–2): 141–159.

Laughlin, C. D.; J. McManus; and C. D. Stephens. 1981. "A Model of Brain and Symbol." *Semiotica* 33 (3–4): 211–236.

Laughlin, C. D.; J. McManus; and M. Webber. 1984. "Neurognosis, Individuation and Tibetan Arising Yoga Practice." *Phoenix: The Journal of Transpersonal Anthropology* 8 (1–2): 91–106.

Laughlin, C. D. and S. Richardson. 1986. "The Future of Human Consciousness." *Futures* (June): 401–419.

Laughlin, C. D. and C. D. Stephens. 1980. "Symbolism, Canalization and P-Structure." *Symbol as Sense*. M. L. Foster and S. Brandis, editors. New York: Academic Press. 323–363.

LeDoux, J. E. and W. Hirst. 1986. *Mind and Brain: Dialogues in Cognitive Neuroscience*. Cambridge: Cambridge University Press.

MacDonald, G. F.; J. Cove; C. D. Laughlin; and J. McManus. 1989. "Mirrors, Portals and Multiple Realities." *Zygon* 23 (4): 39–64.

McManus, J.; C. D. Laughlin; and J. Shearer. 1993. "The Function of Dreaming in the Cycles of Cognition." *The Functions of Dreaming*. A. Moffitt, M. Kramer, and R. Hoffman, editors. Albany, NY: SUNY Press.

Naranjo, C. 1987. "*Ayahuasca* Imagery and the Therapeutic Property of the Harmala Alkaloids." *Journal of Mental Imagery* 11 (2): 131–136.

Neisser, U. 1976. *Cognition and Reality: Principles and Implications of Cognitive Psychology*. San Francisco: Freeman.

Peters, L. G. 1982. "Trance, Initiation, and Psychotherapy in Tamang Shamanism." *American Ethnologist* 9 (1):21–46.

Poirier, S. 1990. "Flexibilite structurelle et creativite onirique chez les groupes aborigines du desert Occidental australien." Ph.D. dissertation, Laval University, Quebec, Canada.

Rappaport, R. A. 1968. *Pigs for the Ancestors*. New Haven: Yale University Press.

Rubinstein, R. A.; C. D. Laughlin; and J. McManus. 1984. *Science as Cognitive Process*. Philadelphia: University of Pennsylvania Press.

Schutz, A. 1945. "On Multiple Realities." *Philosophical and Phenomenological Research* 5:533–576.

Searle, J. R. 1983. *Intentionality: An Essay in the Philosophy of Mind*. Cambridge: Cambridge University Press.

Spelke, E. S. 1988a. "The Origins of Physical Knowledge." *Thought without Language*. L. Weiskrantz, editor. Oxford: Clarendon Press.

Spelke, E. S. 1988b. "Where Perceiving Ends and Thinking Begins: The Apprehension of Objects in Infancy." *Perceptual Development in Infancy*. A. Yonas, editor. Hillsdale, NJ: Erlbaum.

TenHouton, W. D. 1991. "Into the Wild Blue Yonder: On the Emergence of the Ethnoneurologies—The Social Science–Based Neurologies and the Philosophy-Based Neurologies." *Journal of Social and Biological Structures* 14 (4): 381–408.

Tonkinson, R. 1978. *The Mardudjara Aborigines*. New York: Holt, Rinehart and Winston.

Varela, F. J. 1979. *Principles of Biological Autonomy*. New York: Elsevier/North Holland.

Wallace, A. F. C. 1966. *Religion: An Anthropological View*. New York: Random House.

Webber, M.; C. D. Stephens; and C. D. Laughlin. 1983. "Masks: A Reexamination, or Masks? You Meant They Affect the brain?" *The Power of Symbols*. N. R. Crumrine and M. Halpin, editors. Vancouver: University of British Columbia Press. 204–218.

Wilber, Ken. 1983. *A Sociable God: Toward a New Understanding of Religion*. Boulder, CO: Shambhala New Science Library.

Winkelman, M. J. 1986. "Trance States: A Theoretical Model and Cross-cultural Analysis." *Ethos* 14: 174–203.

Winkelman, M. J. 1990. "Shamans and Other 'Magico-Religious' Healers: A Cross-cultural Study of Their Origins, Nature, and Social Transformations." *Ethos* 18: 308–352.

Young, D. E. and J. G. Goulet. 1994. Being Changed by Cross-Cultural Encounters Peterborough, Ont.: Broadview Press.

Young-Laughlin, J. and C. D. Laughlin. 1988. "How Masks Work, or Masks Work How?" *Journal of Ritual Studies* 2 (1): 59–86.

18

THE ORIGIN OF AN ILLUSION

Stewart Elliott Guthrie

> In order to explain a fact as general as [religion] by an illusion, it would
> be necessary that the illusion invoked . . . have causes of an equal generality.
>
> Émile Durkheim (1965)

I do, in fact, explain religion by an illusion. Moreover, the illusion invoked—anthropomorphism, the attribution of human characteristics to nonhuman things and events—has causes of an even greater generality than Durkheim requires. I suggest that these causes are our perceptual uncertainty and the gaming strategy with which we meet it[1] and that any "functions" that religion may have are inessential to its origin.[2]

That religion includes anthropomorphism is not news. The pre-Socratic Xenophanes already observed that people model their gods after themselves. Ever since, most scholars, even among religionists, have admitted that religion always is infused with anthropomorphism, and many say the two are inseparable.[3]

Even the more radical claim that religion *is* anthropomorphism has precedent. The claim occurs in Spinoza (1955) and Hume (1957) (at least concerning popular religion) and in Feuerbach (1957, 1967), Freud (1964), White (1949), Lévi-Strauss (1966), and Horton (1960, 1967), among others. Yet the assertion that anthropomorphism is the basis of religion still carries little weight in scholarly circles. Anthropologists, for example, mostly see anthropomorphism in religion as somehow beside the point and as incapable of fueling the virtually universal impulse to religious thought and action. That is because prevailing accounts of religion as anthropomorphism still lack a crucial element.

The missing element is an explanation of why anthropomorphism itself is so powerful, coupled with an affirmation that it pervades human thought and action and characterizes all religion. Without such an explanation, some scholars will not even admit anthropomorphism is universal in religion. With it, they must admit the ground under religion shifts. Indeed, as the systems we call religious seem to have little else in common,[4] a sufficient explanation of anthropomorphism looks very much like a sufficient explanation of religion.

CURRENT THEORIES: BELIEVERS

Present explanations of religion are, by consensus, inadequate. A quarter century or so after Geertz (1966) called the anthropological theory of religion "stagnant," writers in all disciplines concerned still say that no paradigm prevails and even that no strong theory exists (Wax 1984; Poole 1986; Preus 1987; Penner 1989).

Present theories may be considered as two broad camps, those of believers and those of nonbelievers. Explanations given by believers are unsatisfying because they either account only for their own religions or are incoherent. Most simply say how their own religious truths came to be known—usually by revelation or by discerning the works of gods in nature (for example, in the "design" of organisms). These accounts, addressing only particular religions, necessarily fall short of a general theory.

Other believers, such as Schleiermacher (1988), Otto (1950), and Eliade (1961), try for more abstract and thus more general accounts. They most frequently claim religion is neither belief nor practice but an experience, which they say is at once universal, unmediated, and ineffable. This claim avoids both the need to find something universal in belief or practice and any conflict with alternate systems such as natural science.

The claim also is vague, self-contradictory, or both. People who make it either can say nothing further or must ascribe some specific content to the experience. If they do attribute some content, this usually is an emotion, such as love, awe, or a sense of dependency. However, emotions do not exist in vacuums. Unlike sensations, for example, such as warmth or hunger, emotions are toward or about some object or state of affairs.[5] One does not simply love, fear, or feel dependent but loves, fears, or feels dependent on something or someone. Because an emotion assumes some state of affairs, it already is grounded in belief—that such a state of affairs obtains—and thus is neither direct nor unmediated.

CURRENT THEORIES: NONBELIEVERS

If accounts given by believers are unsatisfactory, nonbelievers fare little better. They must say not only what all religions have in common but also why systems of belief contrary to fact, as they see it, should arise and persist. For those who see beliefs as central features of religion, the latter task is especially burdensome. In addition, most nonbelievers tacitly accept a third task, which aggravates the second: They first assume religion provides some intrinsic benefit that accounts for its existence, then try to identify that benefit.

The resulting explanations are diverse but can be seen as belonging to one or more of three groups. The wishful-thinking group holds that religion serves to mitigate unpleasant feelings. The social-glue group holds that it serves to sustain a social order. The intellectualist or cognitive group, to which my approach belongs, maintains that religion is an attempt to explain and influence the world in general.

All three groups make plausible assertions, but all have problems. Members of the wishful-thinking group usually suggest that religion serves to reduce anxiety. This seems likely, at least insofar as *some* interpretation of the world appears more reassuring than no interpretation at all. But the claim that religions aim to comfort is contradicted by the fact that most also convey powerful threats, such as demons, hells, and wrathful or capricious gods. Perhaps interpretation as such is what comforts us; but then one would need to show how religious interpretations differ from, and are more comforting than, secular ones. If they differ by picturing the world as humanlike, that is not necessarily comforting. Humans may help but also may harm each other. Usually our most fearsome enemies are other humans. Hence, both real humans and their divine counterparts often are threatening.

Social-glue advocates, in contrast, can say readily why religions may threaten their followers and how religious interpretations differ from others. The purpose of religion, they say, is to promote respect for, and observance of, selected social relationships. To that end, religion may use stick as well as carrot. Religious interpretations of the world differ from others by symbolically supporting a code of ethics, by invoking the sacred, and by promoting social harmony.

But in fact religions may have little or no ethical content, as among egalitarian peoples such as the Inuit or San. They may lack a sacred/profane distinction, as in Buddhism and Shinto, and may result in social strife, not harmony, as in the religious wars of sixteenth-century Europe. They may even end in the virtual destruction of their adherents, as have many millennial movements from at least the peasant uprisings of late-medieval Germany to Jonestown in late-twentieth-century Guyana. Thus, the social-glue theorists are (though dominant in anthropology), like the wishful-thinking theorists, beset by contradictions.

Intellectualists avoid these particular problems by supposing that religion serves not emotional or social well-being but explanation. Its adherents may suffer anxiety or strife, as long as religion gives them a plausible account of the world. The chief intellectualist problem then is to say how and why religious explanations are plausible when, to many secular moderns, they seem mistaken, unbelievable, and even absurd.[6]

RELIGION AND FUNCTIONALISM

All three nonbelieving groups, while diverse, share the assumption that religion must be in some way intrinsically functional: It must have some human purpose or benefit that explains its existence. It must have arisen and evolved in a context of use. Despite the retreat of functionalism as a general approach in anthropology, this assumption persists in much of the study of religion.[7] But the assumption, questionable everywhere, is especially questionable here—not because religions cannot easily be shown to do something for someone but because that something varies so widely and because, as noted, contradictions abound.[8]

Wishful-thinking and social-glue approaches are contradicted mainly by frightening and divisive religions, which undercut any claims of universal purpose or benefit. Intellectualism, in addition, has a built-in paradox. Although intellectualists differ about *what* religion explains and why, they tend to agree *how* it does so, namely, by anthropomorphizing—that is, by populating the world with humanlike beings. Belief in such beings—gods or God—is central to religion. For most intellectualists, this belief exists to explain the world and otherwise requires no special scrutiny.

Yet not only the intellectualists but also most assenting scholars of religion see anthropomorphism as an error and (for differing reasons) an inevitable one. Many laypeople as well see anthropomorphism in general as a mistake. Thus, intellectualists identify religions primarily by a kind of belief that they and many others regard as mistaken. Hence, they are in the position of defining religion by its failure at its ostensible purpose: to provide plausible descriptions of the world.

Functionalism therefore is especially problematic as an approach to religion when combined with intellectualism. It must say how a mistaken worldview can be both central to religion and also inherently useful. The task is daunting but fortunately unnecessary, because the assumption that religion must be functional itself is unnecessary.

The underlying and crucial question is why functionalism, at least in its more subtle forms, has been so appealing in the first place. I suggest that (although political motivations may have played some role) it has appealed primarily because of our tendency to see the world as more humanlike than it is and because part of seeing it as humanlike is to see it as purposeful and designed.

The sense that the world (including society) shows design is widespread and probably universal. Certainly it is ancient. Xenophon, for example, wrote around 390 B.C.E. that the organs of animals are peculiarly well suited to them and quoted Socrates: "With such signs of forethought in these arrangements, can you doubt whether they are the work of chance or design?" (Gaskin 1984: 69).[9] The sense of design appears primitive as well. Piaget (1929), for instance, finds it in young children, who assume that the night is dark in order that we may sleep and who spontaneously ask, Who made the moon?

The observation that such perceptions of purpose and design in nature anthropomorphize also is old. Francis Bacon (1960) pointed out almost 500 years ago that people everywhere ascribe their own features to the world and hence see it as more humanlike (for example, more orderly) than it is. Spinoza (1955) added that we see the world as designed for our benefit, because we focus on those parts of it we use and because we know that our tools are purposefully made, not happenstance. Hume (1947: 154f) says that an apparently innate sense that the world is designed has a "force like that of sensation." He says the evidence supporting this feeling cannot account for its strength and remarks, "[A] Theory to solve this would be very acceptable."

RELIGION, DESIGN, AND ANTHROPOMORPHISM

My theory is that this feeling of design and religion itself are aspects of a mostly unconscious anthropomorphism. What is necessary, but hitherto lacking, for a credible theory of religion as anthropomorphism is a convincing description and explanation of that anthropomorphism. Although both anthropomorphism and the related phenomenon of animism are widely noted in religion and in other human thought and action, they are little explained. Both terms are used in several senses, yet neither is deeply examined.

Animism, a term brought to the forefront by Tylor, meant for him a belief in spirit beings: shadowy essences of ourselves that we conjure up to account for dreams and death. The term now mostly is used in two other senses. One, used by comparative religionists and the popular press, is closely related to Tylor's sense: Animism is any religion that credits a broad range of natural phenomena with spirits. The third sense, used mostly by psychologists but capable of including the first two, means attributing life to the lifeless.

The term *anthropomorphism* also is used in several ways, but two are salient. In the narrower sense, it means attributing human characteristics to God or gods. In the broader sense, it means attributing human characteristics to nonhuman things and events at large. As with the meanings of animism, the latter encompasses the former (and in fact now predominates, in part because a range of observers, beginning with Bacon, has pointed it out throughout human thought).

Humanlike characteristics attributed to nature and to gods vary widely. Christians, for example, may credit God with a body, a face, and even a long white beard, or with no body at all. Other religions may have gods in the forms of animals or, again, in no physical form whatever. However, although the attributes of gods vary greatly and may differ from those of humans in many respects, the crucial ones are not physical but behavioral or psychical. Most important, gods have the human capacity for symbolic interaction. For instance, they can hear prayer and respond to it. If they could not, potential adherents would have no way either of knowing of the ongoing presence of gods or of communicating worship. Symbolic interaction, then, is necessary for the relationship that constitutes religion.

Although widely seen as pervading both secular and religious experience, however, and although eliciting considerable admonition, neither animism nor anthropomorphism has received a good explanation. This discrepancy between widespread acknowledgment and scanty analysis persists largely because of the availability of two seemingly adequate commonsense explanations. These are variants of the wishful-thinking and intellectualist accounts also given for religion.

According to the first account, we see the world as like ourselves because we feel an affinity for whatever resembles us and, finding comfort in this illusion, nurture it. According to the other, what we want is explanation, and finding the nonhuman world incomprehensible but understanding ourselves easily, we use ourselves as an explanatory model. The two accounts sometimes are combined but have no intrinsic affinity. In fact, the ideal features of explanation—distinction, clarity, and order—are at odds with the conflation and confusion necessary for comforting illusion.

In any case, neither account is sound. According to the wishful-thinking version, as noted, we believe whatever we want to, and we want to think the world is humanlike. Freud, for example, says the nonhuman world, with its arbitrary storms, earthquakes, and disease and ultimately with our mortality, frightens us. We have no purchase on this strange and dangerous place. However, if only we can picture it as like ourselves, we can imagine we influence it by means of symbolic action such as prayer; and we leap at this possibility.

The chief trouble with this account is that although we may find other humans uniquely comforting, we also find them uniquely frightening. Much anthropomorphism—the shadowy shape of garbage sacks in an alley seen as a potential mugger, a wind-slammed door in the house heard as an intruder—is disturbing, not reassuring. When it is frightening, we can hardly call on wishful thinking to explain it. Another trouble is that human thought in general is not clearly controlled by wishful fantasy.

According to the other account (given by writers from Spinoza and Hume to White, Lévi-Strauss, and Horton), we face in nature an inscrutable world. This world operates on principles at which we can only guess and is full of apparent chance and accident. Trying to understand nature but failing, we are thrown back upon ourselves as models. Hume (1957: 28–29) writes: "We are placed in this world, as in a great theatre, where the true springs and causes of every event are entirely concealed from us; nor have we either sufficient wisdom to foresee, or power to prevent those ills, with which we are continually threatened." Uncertain and fearful, we have recourse to the model we know best: "There is an universal tendency among mankind to conceive all beings like themselves, and to transfer to every object, those qualities, with which they are familiarly acquainted, and of which they are intimately conscious."

As does the comfort account, this one has a little truth. Certainly we could not use ourselves as models if we were total strangers to ourselves. Again, however, it is flawed by contradictions. If easy and reliable explanation was our principal goal, we would draw on the most reliable sources. That in turn would require that we understand these sources well. But human self-understanding is notoriously uncertain. Although we know a good bit, the ratio of what we know to what we do not is low. The proportion of reliable knowledge we have of inanimate objects or of familiar nonhuman animals in our environments is at least as high as that which we have of ourselves. Yet we use ourselves as models for the world in remarkable disproportion.

Thus, the question remains, Why do we draw upon ourselves to construct humanlike but nonhuman others, from Mickey Mouse to Yaweh? The germ of a better answer exists, curiously, in Pascal's wager, an argument designed to persuade us to believe in God. In the face of perpetual uncertainty as to whether God exists, Pascal urges, we should try to believe He does. If we do and are right, we may win divine favor and eternal life, and if we are wrong, we do not lose very much.

Pascal's argument is a variant of game theory: The bets to cover first are the most important ones. We should bet that the most significant possibility is in fact the case, since winning such a bet carries a substantial reward (typically, preparation for some crucial situation), while losing usually costs relatively little.

This principle accounts not only for anthropomorphism but also for animism. Both stem from the same strategic fact: We gain more by correctly identifying things as alive or as humanlike than we lose by mistakenly so identifying them. This is because such identifications ready us for important contingencies and for appropriate responses. If we see something as alive, we can, for example, try to escape or capture it. If we see it as humanlike, we still can do these or try to form a social relationship. If we are mistaken in such identifications, the penalty typically is light. In consequence, our practice in the face of uncertainty is to guess at animacy over inanimacy and humanlikeness over its absence. Betting on these possibilities and often erring, we chronically animate and anthropomorphize the world.

Thus, we play it safe by betting high. It usually is safer, for instance, for a hiker to mistake a boulder for a bear, for a householder to mistake the wind slamming a door for an intruder, and for a soldier to mistake a cow for a foe than the reverse.

In this regard, we resemble other animals, which also animate the world: Predators may stalk inanimate but moving objects, and prey animals may shy away from them. Most pertinently, wild chimpanzees may direct threats against thunderstorms, which they dislike. According to Goodall (1975), males occasionally threaten storms by hooting, stamping, racing through the underbrush, and breaking limbs from small trees, much as they do when confronting competitors and predators.

Goodall says, if cautiously, that this "emotional" response to weather may parallel early religious experience in humans. I feel less hesitant. If religion is the attribution of human characteristics to the nonhuman world, then the nonhuman animal analogue is animism (or zoomorphism), the attribution of animal characteristics to the nonanimal world; and any assumption that thunderstorms can be threatened must at least be animistic.

PERCEPTUAL UNCERTAINTY, DECEPTION, AND ILLUSION

My claim that anthropomorphism results from betting high in the face of uncertainty underpins the claim that religion is a systematized form of anthropomorphism. The illusion underlying religion thus is grounded in a necessary strategy. Both claims gain strength from seeing that uncertainty and our resultant anthropomorphism alike permeate perception.

Though most perception in daily life seems unproblematic, its apparent certainty is illusory. In fact, although we remain mostly unaware of it, the data of perception are fundamentally ambiguous. They are ambiguous because any given sensation, from a tickling on our skin to a thin line on a printed page to a bright light in the evening sky, is susceptible to multiple interpretations. The tickling may be a spider or a loose thread, the line may be a hair or a pencil mark, and the bright light may be a UFO or a reflection in the windshield. Even the "line" itself is uncertain, since what our retinas receive really is just a collection of dots (from individual nerve endings) that we assemble into the most coherent and meaningful possibilities. The assemblage of lines into edges, edges into volumes, volumes into objects, and so on up, similarly is a process of interpretation. As Wittgenstein (1969) writes, we never just "see" but always "see as."[10]

The uncertainty of that process remains mostly unknown to us, kept from consciousness by a censorship that doubtless spares us much vacillation. However, because all sensations have multiple possible causes, every stage of perception and cognition—the two are continuous in this process—constitutes a guess at what model best construes the data.

In the face of this perceptual uncertainty, our strategy is to bet on the most important possibility. Living things are more important to us than nonliving things because they are concentrations of energy and organization and thus may be, for example, predators or prey. Humans are even more important than nonhumans because they are the most highly organized of all and therefore are the most potent actors and the greatest sources of information.

Necessarily and involuntarily, then, we scan our environments for what most concerns us and commonly bet first that something is humanlike or the result of human action. Perpetually though mostly unconsciously uncertain, we hear voices in the wind, find faces in clouds, and see design in the world at large. Since we look for them constantly, humanlike forms and results of humanlike activity appear to us everywhere.

We also continuously review our guesses and sometimes decide we have erred. We classify many errors into one of the two broad, residual categories of animism and anthropomorphism. We can make these designations, however, only after the fact, because the categorical errors they name are inherent in the perceptual process. No perceptual system can reliably distinguish the objects of its concern from the myriad phenomena that resemble them. Hence, all perceiving creatures are prone to occasional illusion. As two researchers in artificial intelligence (Fischler and Firschein 1987: 233) write, ''[E]ven good bets occasionally fail, so it is likely that all organisms experience illusion.''

In the case of animism, the inherent susceptibility to illusion is increased by natural deception. Virtually all animals and some plants are partly concealed from their enemies by camouflage. Forest-dwelling insects may resemble dead leaves or green stems, oceanic fishes may resemble sargasso weed or depthless blue sea, and temperate climate birds and mammals may change color with the seasons. A resultant primary illusion is that other animals mistake the camouflaged animal for its background. An inevitable secondary illusion[11] is to mistake background for animal. If an animal can be mistaken for something else, then that something else also can be, and often is, taken for the animal.

Similarly—though even more complexly—with humans. Whereas most other animals have a fixed supply of deceptive tricks, those humans use are endless. Clothing, face paint, foliage stuck on helmets, and other means may change our appearances radically. Some ruses keep us out of sight altogether. Hence, one must sometimes guess that humans are where none appear. Moreover, because the range of effects that humans can produce also is virtually limitless, no phenonemon can clearly be ruled out as an artifact of human activity. We often guess, in consequence, that humans are, or may be, behind the scenes. Sometimes we are right, but often we are mistaken. The mistake, seen in retrospect, is labeled anthropomorphism.

ANTHROPOMORPHISM AS PERVASIVE

Given that anthropomorphism results from a vital perceptual strategy, we might expect it to be more common in thought and action than is ordinarily acknowledged. And indeed, it is. Specialists in varied disciplines say we anthropomorphize comprehensively, from childhood through adulthood, in every sensory mode, and regarding phenomena of all sizes and levels of abstraction.

Developmental psychologists (Piaget 1929; Field 1985; Maurer 1985), for example, find a predisposition to see human forms already in the first months of life and find verbalizations of anthropomorphism in young children. Clinicians (Beck and Molish 1967; Beck 1968) report that people throughout life interpret Rorschach ink blots overwhelmingly as human forms, and folklorists (Thompson 1955) and ethnographers[12] discover anthropomorphism around the world. We anthropomorphize what we hear (a gurgle in the plumbing as a voice), touch (the unseen foot of a table as the foot of our tablemate), and see (a distant tree stump as a figure). We do so with things of all sizes, from subatomic ''charmed'' particles, to the Old Man of the Mountains, to the Earth as Gaia, to the universe as containing an ''anthropic principle.''[13]

Literary critics and art historians also report anthropomorphism throughout the arts, though they usually call it personification or the pathetic fallacy and find it baffling. Homer's spears are "hungry for flesh," Chinese painters depict mountains as monarchs (Sze 1963), and poets and painters everywhere make persons of such abstractions as old age, death, and time. Such artistic anthropomorphism often is elaborate and self-conscious but still springs initially from the same unconscious and involuntary strategy of perception as in daily life.

Even philosophers and natural scientists, the writers most wary of anthropomorphism, produce it in fair measure (Stack 1980; Guthrie 1993:152–176). Plato and Aristotle (Lloyd 1966) describe the cosmos both as an artifact and as alive, Darwin (Young 1985) depicts nature as actively shaping her creatures by selecting beneficial traits, and some modern geneticists (Dawkins 1978) describe genes as "selfish." In short, anthropomorphism—spontaneous or studied, customary or critical—runs throughout human thought and action.

ORIGIN: RELIGION AS ANTHROPOMORPHISM

Anthropomorphism may permeate secular systems, but it characterizes religious ones. Science, though not immune to anthropomorphism, at least in some measure roots it out. In contrast, religion is inseparable from it, as secular observers from Xenophanes to Feuerbach to Horton, and religious ones from Clement (Prestige 1952: 9) to Aquinas (Ferré 1980) to Buber (1952: 14–15), agree.

The testimony of Abrahamic religious philosophers and theologians (e.g., Ferré 1984; Werblowsky 1987) is most telling, for they are reluctant witnesses yet virtually univocal. A few demur, but these scholars find refuge largely in obscurity: Maimonides, for example, in the *via negativa*[14] and Tillich (1948: 63) in equally esoteric formulations. Most other scholars of religion find anthropomorphism inevitable. Indeed, most (e.g., Idowu 1973; Ferré 1984; Werblowsky 1987) say religion, unlike secular thought, cannot be extricated from anthropomorphism even in principle. If so, one must suspect that there is little in principle to extricate.[15]

That all religion is anthropomorphism does not, of course, mean all anthropomorphism is religion. In the systems of thought and action we call religious— that is, those with gods—discovery of humanity in the nonhuman world is central. It often is complex and subtle, born of genius and refined over generations. The discovery may or may not include physically human properties. Crucially, it does include the central human characteristic—a capacity for language and associated symbolic behavior—and the human mental and behavioral features that language and symbolism can disclose.

No clear line separates religion from nonreligion. Traditions such as Buddhism, Judaism, and Christianity also include philosophical subtraditions without gods, such as "demythologized" Christianity, secular Judaism, and much of the Buddhism now popular in the West. Religion is continuous, and interspersed, not only with philosophy but also with those systems we label science, magic, and common sense. All these labels represent categories created at particular times and in particular languages, for reasons that are historic and contingent. At other times and in other languages and cultures, those categories do not exist. Even within the modern West, they interact and intermingle. If the present approach provides no absolute criterion and if Buddhism, Christianity, and other traditions include both religious (that is, theistic) and nonreligious (for example, psychological and ethical) systems, that should be no surprise.

Like other distinctions between prominent categories—between the human and the nonhuman, animal and plant, living and nonliving—that between religious and secular domains has notably blurry edges. Most scholars and most believers, however, agree that religion includes something like prayer and that praying assumes the existence of something like gods or a God to hear it. Crucially humanlike features in the nonhuman world, then, appear as the common thread through religions, across cultures and time.

The view that religion *is* anthropomorphism depends, by definition, on a judgment that the humanlike beings and attributes that it claims to discover in the nonhuman world are illusory. Such a judgment, like judgments about other complex factual issues, cannot finally be shown right or wrong. It can only extrapolate from relevant precedents and offer relevant analysis. Here the precedent is the pervasive anthropomorphism elsewhere in our experience. The analysis is an account of the well-founded motivation from which anthropomorphism stems: to find actual humans and human artifacts wherever they are.

OUTCOME: RELIGION AS "EXAPTATION"

That religion is anthropomorphism means that it is a mistake. This flies in the face not only of functionalism as a persistent general assumption about religion but also of individual observations that religion sometimes does serve specific purposes. If religion is an illusion, are its persistence and especially its usefulness not paradoxical?

Three responses are relevant. The first is of the sort sometimes given to functionalist claims in other domains as well: that the uses of religion constitute mixed blessings. Although religion *may* serve to strengthen social bonds, sustain an environmental ethic, promote justice, and so on, it may also subvert such beneficial ends. That the benefits of an illusion are contingent at least diminishes any paradox.

Second, whether or not religion itself is useful, the strategy from which it stems—to search assiduously for any possible human presence—clearly is. Our powerful, pervasive, and inevitable first response to the perceptual world is to see it as humanlike. This is because we search first of all for anything that will fit our schemata, or models, of humans. These models of humans, on which religion ultimately is based, persist because they are vital: They enable us to discover real humans wherever and however they occur. To say that a strategy generally is useful, however, is not to say that *all* its results are good.

Third, even if the benefits of religion can be shown to outweigh its detriments, they do not explain why it arises. They still may be incidental, not intrinsic. An uncritical neo-Darwinism, abetted by our readiness to find design in nature, too readily assumes that features of organisms and societies are optimal and arise in order to serve some purpose. If they can be shown to serve some purpose, then we assume they exist *for* that purpose.

Recent thought in biology, however, as well as in anthropology, undercuts such assumptions. Features of organisms, like those of societies, may *not* be optimal even in stable environments. Francis Crick (1988), for example, says they never are optimal but always are arbitrarily constrained by the possibilities of past environments. The structure of the human lower back is a painfully obvious example.

Moreover, features of organisms and of societies often arise independent of any adaptive reason. Stephen Jay Gould (1991) points out that biological features frequently originate in one environment but are put to use in an entirely different one. Gould labels this process, by which useful characters appear for reasons unrelated to their usefulness, "exaptation." The tetrapod limb, for example, arose in the water but flourished on land, and delayed ossification of the skull arose in reptiles and birds but later enabled mammals to bear large-brained young through narrow birth canals. Features useful in a particular environment may even arise as side effects of other features, with no function at all in their original contexts, just as spandrels (spaces left over between structural elements of a building) in architecture may be used for important decorative purposes (54–55).

Despite the independence of origin and use, our strong tendency is, with Voltaire's Pangloss, to suppose that "everything is made for the best purpose" (Gould 1991: 46). That supposition is itself an aspect of anthropomorphism, assuming as it does that everything is "made" and indeed made for a purpose. The supposition is basic, though usually tacitly, to functionalism. As does other anthropomorphism, it misleads. Gould remarks that origin and utility in organic evolution are "distinct concepts and must never be conflated" (43).

Similarly, if we want to understand religion, we must look first to its origin and only afterward to its varied current uses. If we do, we can see better how an illusion still can be put to use. The fact of illusion goes to origin but not necessarily to outcome.

Simultaneously, we free ourselves from the impossible task of showing how religion could arise from its potential benefits. Once it has arisen, its uses *may* help perpetuate it; but such uses are neither necessary nor universal. Nor are they always beneficial, since religion may be harmful and even disastrous.

Most scholars now think any search for the origin of religion is a speculative if not impossible quest for ancient causes. However, the origin I have proposed is not so much historic and beyond reach as visible in the processes of contemporary perception. Equally important, this approach allows us to consider the origin of religion apart from any use. Acknowledging the independence of origin from function, we can better understand both.

NOTES

1. A slightly earlier and considerably more comprehensive discussion of this theory is in Guthrie (1993). I thank Phyllis Guthrie and Paul Kahn for their help with this chapter.

2. Although functionalism as a school has long been on the wane, functionalist assumptions persist in studies of religion (e.g., in Stark and Bainbridge 1987; Spickard 1991; Alexander 1991).

3. For example, Ferré (1984) and Werblowsky (1987). See also Guthrie (1993: chapter 7) for other sources and a discussion.

4. Preus (1987: 34), in his careful survey of theory, writes, for example, that "finding universal elements remains one of the key problems for defining religion."

5. Proudfoot (1985) makes this point persuasively regarding the emotions of religious experience, and Lazarus (1984) makes it regarding emotions in general. Lutz (1988), among others, argues that emotions are learned and culturally variable.

6. Evans-Pritchard (1965: 15), for example, writes that religion seems "absurd" to most anthropologists.

7. Penner (1989: 106) thinks functionalism underlies *all* twentieth-century theories of religion and asks how one can explain the "persistence of such a . . . seriously defective" approach.

8. Moreover, as Margolis (1987) notes of organisms, many different structures may serve the same "function." Douglas and Perry (1985: 416–417) write similarly that religion slips "between the meshes [of functional analysis because] many other beliefs perform these functions."

9. Gaskin (1984) notes that the design argument often is associated with Christianity but also appears elsewhere.

10. Friedrich Nietzsche (1966), William James (1890), and Alfred Schutz (1962) make the same observation.

11. Reported by ethologists including Mark Bekoff (personal communication), Hinton (1973), and Cheney and Seyfarth (1990).

12. For examples and a discussion, see Guthrie (1993: esp. chapter 5).

13. The "anthropic principle" (Earman 1987; Barrow and Tipler 1988; Wilson 1991) labels a medley of arguments, mostly by physicists, to the effect that human existence is somehow central to the universe.

14. That is, in denying any positive attributes to God.

15. This aspect of the argument needs considerable evidence, impossible in a short chapter but supplied elsewhere (Guthrie 1993).

REFERENCES

Alexander, Bobby C. 1991. "Correcting Misinterpretations of Turner's Theory: An African-American Pentecostal Example." *Journal for the Scientific Study of Religion* 30 (1): 26–44.

Bacon, Francis. 1960. *The New Organon and Related Writings*. Edited by Fulton H. Anderson. New York: Liberal Arts Press.

Barrow, John D. and Frank J. Tipler. 1988. *The Anthropic Cosmological Principle*. New York: Oxford University Press.

Beck, Samuel J. 1968. "Reality, Rorschach and Perceptual Theory." *Projective Techniques in Personality Assessment*. A. I. Rabin, editor. New York: Springer Publishing Company. 115–135.

Beck, Samuel J. and Herman B. Molish. 1967. *Rorschach's Test. Vol. 2: A Variety of Personality Pictures*. 2nd edition. New York: Grune and Stratton.

Buber, Martin. 1952. "Religion and Reality." In *Eclipse of God*, by Martin Buber. New York: Harper and Brothers.

Cheney, Dorothy L. and Robert M. Seyfarth. 1990. *How Monkeys See the World*. Chicago and London: University of Chicago Press.

Crick, Francis. 1988. "Lessons from Biology." *Natural History* 97 (11): 32–39.

Dawkins, Richard. 1978. *The Selfish Gene*. New York: Oxford University Press.

Douglas, Mary and Edmund Perry. 1985. "Anthropology and Comparative Religion." *Theology Today* 41 (4): 410–427.

Durkheim, Emile. 1965. *The Elementary Forms of the Religious Life*. New York: Free Press. (Originally published 1915)

Earman, John. 1987. "The SAP Also Rises: A Critical Examination of the Anthropic Principle." *American Philosophical Quarterly* 24 (4): 307–317.

Eliade, Mircea. 1961. *The Sacred and the Profane: The Nature of Religion*. Translated from the French by Willard R. Trask. New York: Harper and Row.

Evans-Pritchard, E. E. 1965. *Theories of Primitive Religion*. London: Oxford University Press.

Ferré, Frederick. 1980. "Theodicy and the Status of Animals." *American Philosophical Quarterly* 23: 23–34.

Ferré, Frederick. 1984. "In Praise of Anthropomorphism." *International Journal for Philosophy of Religion* 16 (3): 203–212.

Feuerbach, Ludwig. 1957. *The Essence of Christianity*. Translated by George Eliot. New York: Harper and Row. (Originally published 1873)

Feuerbach, Ludwig. 1967. *Lectures on the Essence of Religion*. Translated by Ralph Manheim. New York: Harper and Row.

Field, Tiffany M. 1985. "Neonatal Perception of People: Maturational and Individual Differences." *Social Perception in Infancy*. Tiffany M. Field and Nathan A. Fox, editors. Norwood, NJ: Ablex Publishing Corporation. 31–52.

Fischler, Martin A. and Oscar Firschein. 1987. *Intelligence: The Eye, the Brain, and the Computer*. Reading, MA: Addison-Wesley Publishing Company.

Freud, Sigmund. 1964. *The Future of an Illusion*. Garden City: Anchor Books. (Originally published 1927)

Gaskin, J. C. A. 1984. *The Quest for Eternity*. New York: Penguin Books.

Geertz, Clifford. 1966. "Religion as a Cultural System." *Anthropological Approaches to the Study of Religion*. Michael Banton, editor. London and New York: Tavistock Publications. 1–46.

Goodall, Jane. 1975. "The Chimpanzee." *The Quest for Man*. Vanne Goodall, editor. New York: Praeger. 131–170.

Gould, Stephen Jay. 1991. "Exaptation: A Crucial Tool for an Evolutionary Psychology." *Journal of Social Issues* 47 (3): 43–65.

Guthrie, Stewart Elliott. 1993. *Faces in the Clouds: A New Theory of Religion*. New York: Oxford University Press.

Hinton, H. E. 1973. "Natural Deception." *Illusion in Art and Nature*. Richard Gregory and Ernst Gombrich, editors. London: Gerald Duckworth and Company. 97–160.

Horton, Robin. 1960. "A Definition of Religion, and Its Uses." *Journal of the Royal Anthropological Institute* 90: 201–226.

Horton, Robin. 1967. "African Traditional Thought and Western Science." *Africa* 37: 50–71, 155–187.

Hume, David. 1947. *Dialogues concerning Natural Religion*. 2nd edition. Edited by N. Kemp Smith. New York: Library of Liberal Arts.

Hume, David. 1957. *The Natural History of Religion*. Edited by H. E. Root. Stanford: Stanford University Press. (Originally published 1757)

Idowu, E. Bolaji. 1973. *African Traditional Religion: A Definition*. London: SCM Press, Ltd.

James, William. 1890. *The Principles of Psychology*. New York: Henry Holt.

Lazarus, Richard S. 1984. "On the Primacy of Cognition." *American Psychologist* 39 (2): 124–129.

Lévi-Strauss, Claude. 1966. *The Savage Mind*. Chicago: University of Chicago Press.

Lloyd, G. E. R. 1966. *Polarity and Analogy: Two Types of Argumentation in Early Greek Thought*. Cambridge: Cambridge University Press.

Lutz, Catherine A. 1988. *Unnatural Emotions: Everyday Sentiments on a Micronesian Atoll and Their Challenge to Western Theory*. Chicago: University of Chicago Press.

Margolis, Howard. 1987. *Patterns, Thinking, and Cognition: A Theory of Judgment*. Chicago: University of Chicago Press.

Maurer, Daphne. 1985. "Infants' Perception of Facedness." *Social Perception in Infancy*. Tiffany M. Field and Nathan A. Fox, editors. Norwood, NJ: Ablex Publishing Corporation. 73–100.

Nietzsche, Friedrich. 1966. *Werke in Drei Bänder*. Vol. 3. Edited by Karl Schlechter. Munich: Carl Hanser.

Otto, Rudolf. 1950. *The Idea of the Holy*. 2nd edition. New York: Oxford University Press.

Penner, Hans H. 1989. *Impasse and Resolution: A Critique of the Study of Religion*. Toronto Studies in Religion. Vol. 8. Donald Wiebe, general editor. New York: Peter Lang.

Piaget, Jean. 1929. *The Child's Conception of the World*. London: Routledge and Kegan Paul.

Poole, Fitz John Porter. 1986. "Metaphors and Maps: Towards Comparison in the Anthropology of Religion." *Journal of the American Academy of Religion* 54 (3): 411–457.

Prestige, George Leonard. 1952. *God in Patristic Thought*. London: SPCK.

Preus, J. Samuel. 1987. *Explaining Religion: Criticism and Theory from Bodin to Freud*. New Haven: Yale University Press.

Proudfoot, Wayne. 1985. *Religious Experience*. Berkeley: University of California Press.

Schleiermacher, Friedrich. 1988. *On Religion*. New York: Cambridge University Press.

Schutz, Alfred. 1962. *Collected Papers 1. The Problem of Social Reality*. Edited by Maurice Natanson. The Hague: Martinus Nijhoff.

Spickard, James V. 1991. "A Revised Functionalism in the Sociology of Religion: Mary Douglas's Recent Work." *Religion* 21: 141–164.

Spinoza, Benedict de. 1955. *The Chief Works of Benedict de Spinoza: On the Improvement of the Understanding; The Ethics; Correspondence.* Translated from the Latin with an introduction by R. H. M. Elwes. New York: Dover Publications, Inc.

Stack, George J. 1980. "Nietzsche and Anthropomorphism." *Crítica: Revista Hispanoamericana de Filosofía* 12: 41–71.

Stark, Rodney, and William Sims Bainbridge. 1987. *A Theory of Religion.* Donald Wiebe, editor. Toronto Studies in Religion. Vol. 2. New York: Peter Lang.

Sze, Mai-mai. 1963. *The Tao of Painting: A Study of the Ritual Disposition of Chinese Painting.* With a translation of the *Chieh Tzu Yüan Hua Chuan* or *Mustard Seed Garden Manual of Painting 1679–1701.* Bollingen Series XLIX. New York: Pantheon Books.

Thompson, Stith. 1955. *Motif-Index of Folk-Literature.* Revised and enlarged edition. Bloomington: Indiana University Press.

Tillich, Paul. 1948. *The Shaking of the Foundations.* New York: Charles Scribner's Sons.

Tylor, Edward B. 1873. *Primitive Culture: Researches into the Development of Mythology, Philosophy, Religion, Language, Art, and Custom*: 2nd edition. 2 vol. London: John Murray.

Wax, Murray L. 1984. "Religion as Universal: Tribulations of an Anthropological Enterprise." *Zygon: Journal of Religion and Science* 19 (1): 5–20.

Werblowsky, R. J. Zwi. 1987. "Anthropomorphism." *The Encyclopedia of Religion.* Mircea Eliade, editor in chief. New York: Macmillan. 316–320.

White, Leslie. 1949. *The Science of Culture.* New York: Grove Press.

Wilson, Patrick A. 1991. "What Is the Explanandum of the Anthropic Principle?" *American Philosophical Quarterly* 28: 167–173.

Wittgenstein, Ludwig. 1969. *Blue and Brown Books.* 2nd edition. Oxford: Basil Blackwell.

Young, Robert M. 1985. *Darwin's Metaphor: Nature's Place in Victorian Culture.* Cambridge: Cambridge University Press.

19

The Sacred Integration of the Cultural Self: An Anthropological Approach to the Study of Religion

Jacob Pandian

The precariousness of the self is created not only by the discrepant roles in
which the person is involved but also by the perpetual threats of anomie
and marginality posed by the unresolved problem of human existence like
misfortune, evil, sickness, decay and, above all, death. These problems have
confronted man everywhere, in preindustrial and in industrial societies, past
and present. They are perennial problems, i.e., problems that are by their
very nature not given to rational explanation or solution. Almost everywhere
they have been explained in mystical terms and dealt with by patterns of
symbolic activities.

Cohen (1977: 124)

I suggest in this chapter that for an understanding of religious phenomena it is
crucial that we identify the cultural locus of the self and show how the formulations of sacred beings or powers provide coherence for the formulations of
the self. It is factually important and theoretically necessary to study how the
symbolic self is made coherent by certain religious formulations about human
suffering, death, and so on. It is also necessary to analyze how and why human
suffering and death are explained in different ways by different religious
traditions and to examine whether a correspondence between these explanations
and the formulations of the symbolic self exist. Religion does not eliminate
suffering or death, but it eliminates the contradictions between cultural formulations of suffering, death, and the symbolic self by constituting and maintaining

the symbolic self as sacred, rendering the symbolic self into a coherent, meaningful system of action despite the existence of "natural" inconsistencies and problems.

Anthropologists frequently use the term *supernaturalism* to identify religious phenomena. The term supernaturalism can refer either to phenomena that are conceptualized as superior to nature or to a reality that is conceptualized as apart from or beyond nature. I use the term *sacred other* to signify the existence of beliefs and practices or representations of entities that are conceptualized as superior to or apart from nature. In other words, beliefs in supernatural beings and powers can be identified or characterized as symbols of sacred others. The objective of this chapter is to formulate an anthropological approach to the study of religion that focuses on the study of the relationship between the cultural formulations of the self (symbolic self) and the cultural formulations of sacred others. I will examine the domains and processes that link cultural formulations of the self and the sacred other and will interpret the significance of such a linkage for the protection and integration of the symbolic self (which, in turn, provides protection and integration for particular cultural traditions).

THE CONCEPT OF SYMBOLIC (CULTURAL) SELF AND THE ANTHROPOLOGY OF RELIGION

In a recent book, Marsella, DeVos, and Hsu (1985: ix) point out that "self" has become an important anthropological concept for understanding culture and human behavior. I suggest that the self-concept can be fruitfully used for a cross-cultural, comparative study of religious phenomena, that is, in the study of beliefs and practices associated with supernatural beings and powers (sacred others). I offer below a brief discussion of the nature of the anthropological study of the self in order to illustrate the relevance of the self-concept for the study of religion.

Today's emphasis on the concept of the cultural or symbolic self is related to anthropology's concern with the study of symbol and meaning, and with the conceptualization of culture as a communication system, as evidenced in the writings of Claude Lévi-Strauss, Edmund Leach, Victor Turner, Clifford Geertz, and many other anthropologists. The anthropologists who have shown a theoretical interest in the study of the relationship between culture and the symbols of the self are not a uniform group. Semiotically oriented "symbolic" anthropologists as well as "psychological" and "social" anthropologists have contributed to the understanding of the relationship between culture and self. From an earlier interest in the study of the relationship between culture and personality (in American cultural anthropology) and between social structure and ideology (in British social anthropology), anthropologists have shifted in their interests to the study of the cultural communication and strategies of the self (Pandian

1985). The above approach to the study of the symbolic self is semiotic in terms of its focus on the interpretations of symbolic universes and the symbols of significance. There is convergence of interest among social scientists and humanists in the study of the self-symbol-culture relationship, and several sociologists, social-psychologists, historians, literary critics, philosophers, and semiotic anthropologists have contributed to the revived interest in the analysis of self-symbol-meaning (Geertz 1973).

Perhaps it is a truism to state that people who participate in different cultural universes differ in how they represent the self. Human beings acquire their self-conceptions by becoming symbols to themselves and others; they exist as subject and object, and as self and other, in an interactional relationship in a world of symbols, which involves taking the role of the other and organizing thoughts and feelings in a culturally coherent and appropriate manner. Cultural coherence and appropriateness are achieved by learning to deploy the structures of meaning embodied in the public symbols that constitute a culture or way of life. Cultures everywhere have symbols of the self that convey the meanings of being human; in other words, symbols that signify "who am I" or "what am I" are universal. However, a symbol's representation of an object, event, or person is an arbitrary association of meanings that is shared conventionally; an individual has to learn the meanings associated with human identities in specific cultural contexts or within the boundaries of the historical, cultural configurations of meaning.

From the ancient Greco-Roman times to the present, many scholars have correctly pointed out that religious beliefs (and practices) are representations that are based on, or modeled after, human experiences and that these formulations help human beings to deal or cope with unpredictable, uncertain, anxiety-provoking events of human life. Formulations of the existence of sacred beings or powers have been correctly explained as providing support for the maintenance and continuation of cultural traditions or social values that are constantly threatened (and face possible extinction) by the occurrences of human maturation processes, sickness, death, and various other calamities. Basic to anthropological theories of religion (even if not always explicitly stated) are certain valid assumptions and verifiable hypotheses: (1) Religious phenomena are "projective systems"; (2) such systems have personal/cultural functions; and (3) anthropomorphic, anthropopsychic, and anthroposocial characteristics are used in the construction of supernatural reality. Many anthropologists assumed that as scientific knowledge accumulated, the use of the projective models of sacred beings and powers would decline and that cultural traditions and social values could function rationally without emotional or "irrational" attachments to anthropomorphic gods and goddesses.

The "founders" of academic anthropology and sociology devoted considerable time and energy to explain the origin of beliefs in sacred beings and powers because it was believed that such as explanation would simultaneously explain the primitive or primordial stages in mental and cultural development. Gradually, anthropologists discarded the origin theories as unprovable and focused on the study of the formulations, functions, and meanings of beliefs and practices that were associated with sacred beings and powers. Implicit in such a study is the assumption that the origin of beliefs in sacred beings and powers is rooted in their function, just as the origin of economic or political institutions is rooted in their function. Thus, anthropologists have, in the recent past, accumulated descriptions pertaining to cultural formulations and practices associated with sacred beings and powers and have interpreted their significance and meaning for those who use them (Geertz 1973).

I suggest that descriptions of religious phenomena must include descriptions of how the symbolic self is constituted, maintained, evaluated, and dramatized. Methodologically, we could identify the cultural formulations of the sacred other and investigate how the symbols of the sacred other and the symbols of the self are related in myth and ritual. Such an analysis would show how the symbols of the sacred other and the symbols of the self are related dialectically and syntactically and would reveal how representations of the self are constituted, maintained, evaluated, and dramatized as sacred.

THE CREATION AND MAINTENANCE OF SHAMANISTIC AND PRIESTLY SYMBOLIC SELVES

Symbols of the self (the symbolic self) signify the characteristics and meanings of what it is to be human. Symbols of the sacred other signify the existence and characteristics of supernatural beings, entities, and powers; linkages between the symbolic self and the sacred other occur in different ways in different domains. "Religion" is a concept that we can use to identify cultural phenomena pertaining to the production and maintenance of the symbolic self as sacred or supernatural. The formulation or production of the symbols of the sacred self occurs in two modalities, with variations that result when these two modalities combine in different ways: (1) through contact, resulting in partial or complete union between the symbols of the sacred other and the self, and (2) through positive or negative identification with the symbols of the sacred other. The first modality constitutes what I characterize as the *shamanistic sacred self*; and the second type can be identified as the *priestly sacred self*. These are "ideal type" constructs that can be seen in the operation of shamanism and priesthood, as well as in the use of myth and ritual. The study of religious movements can reveal clearly the constitution, disintegration, and reconstitution of the sacred self and can shed light on the nature and significance of the different types of sacred selves (shamanistic and priestly) in different cultural contexts.

The shamanistic self is a type of symbolic sacred coherence and integration that manifests in cultural arenas in which a resolution of stress (arising from unpredictable events, sickness, life passages, etc.) occurs; thus, ritual contexts such as divination, healing, and initiation, and religious movements in their early stages, are "ideal" laboratories for the study of the nature and meaning of the shamanistic self. The priestly self is a type of symbolic sacred coherence that manifests in everyday life patterns of thought and behavior in which human beings validate social order and social conventions with reference to the symbols of the sacred other.

The following model is a brief illustration of the creation, maintenance, and dramatization of the shamanistic and priestly selves.

1. The symbolic self is a culturally created reality that is created and recreated in relation to empirical and nonempirical others.

2. The sacred others are projective (and anthropomorphic, anthropopsychic, anthroposocial) models or metaphors who (or which) serve as vehicles to symbolize the self as sacred; the symbolic self takes the role of, or interacts with, sacred others.

3. The construction of the symbolic self as sacred legitimizes the cultural order by providing sacred coherence for the symbolic self.

4. Basically, there are two kinds of sacred selves, namely, the priestly self and the shamanistic self, which are aligned with the human dimensions of social/political order and biological/psychological health.

5. The priestly self is constituted through the interaction with sacred others that signify social and political processes, and the shamanistic self is constituted through the interaction with sacred others that signify biological/psychological processes.

6. The priestly self occurs through positive or negative emulation of the sacred other and is linked with priesthood, social/political order, and myth; and the shamanistic self occurs through contact or union with the sacred other and is linked with shamanism, biological/psychological health, and ritual.

7. The priestly and shamanistic selves alternate and are manifested in different ways in different contexts.

8. The priestly and shamanistic selves are ideal types, and variations of different kinds occur in real action-orientations.

9. Both the priestly and shamanistic selves belong to the same category of the sacred self but provide different kinds of sacred coherence for the symbolic self.

10. The priestly self legitimizes the cultural order through making social and political conventions coherent.

11. The shamanistic self legitimizes the cultural order through making biological/psychological processes coherent.

12. The shamanistic self is adaptive in situations of individual or group crisis; to be in contact with or merged with the sacred other is the ultimate source of integration or coherence for the symbolic self.

Fundamental to the above model of religion and the sacred self (shamanistic and priestly) is the identification of the shaman and the priest as representing (prototypically) two contrasting types of sacredness: The shaman is the prototype for the representation of the biopsychological dimension or processes; the priest is the prototype for the representation of the sociopolitical dimension or processes. The shaman functions as the biopsychological therapist through his or her ability to manipulate the symbols of sacredness (gods, goddesses, spirits, and impersonal power) that represent the biopsychological dimensions and, in that process, may unite or merge with those symbols and manifest the shaman-istic sacred self. And as the shaman's role becomes important in situations of crisis, shamanism is associated with rituals of divination, witchcraft, and healing. The shaman has little or no significance in the sociopolitical or economic do-mains and is not a custodian of moral conventions or the social order. The lack of association between shamanism and politicoeconomic and moral order is one of the reasons for the recruitment of shamans from any segment of hierarchical societies and for not being associated with an exclusively male or heterosexual orientation.

The priest, on the other hand, legitimizes the sociopolitical and economic order through his ability to interpret the mythological tradition and the sacred lore of a society. As males have been traditionally associated with the socio-political and economic order, priesthood is often a male prerogative. The priest manipulates the symbols of the sacred other in ritualized forms but seldom merges or unites with such representations. He maintains a "respectful" ritual distance and acquires his authority from the mastery of the sacred knowledge. The priest usually embodies the moral and ethical values of the society (at least publically).

The anthropological distinction between the shaman and the priest as two contrasting types of religious practitioners is valid in terms of the shaman as one who communes *with* the supernatural reality and the priest as one who communicates *to* the supernatural reality: The shaman merges with the super-natural reality through his or her symbolic self becoming linked or united with the symbols of the sacred other; the priest emulates (or does not emulate through taboos) certain kinds of moral, ethical, and social conduct represented by the symbols of the sacred other. The shamanistic sacred self and the priestly sacred self are distinguishable clearly in the person of the shaman and priest as two modalities of achieving the sacredness of the symbolic self. The generally held view that shamans are part-time "magical" practitioners found in "primitive" societies and that priests are full-time "religious" practitioners found in "com-plex" societies is misleading because all societies have both types of religious practitioners who deal with different aspects of the human dimension. Members of a society may or may not seek to experience the shamanistic or priestly sacred selves, but they become aware of their existence in the ideal representations of the individuals who can be characterized as shamans or as priests.

Believers who use the symbols of the sacred other to represent the self as sacred differ in degree in their representation of either the shamanistic or priestly sacred self, and they may alternate between manifesting a shamanistic or a priestly orientation toward the symbols of the sacred other. The model that I have proposed has heuristic value for understanding the coexistence of shaman-ism and priesthood and is particularly useful to illustrate the structure and mean-ing of religious movements. By using the distinction that I have made between the representations of shamanistic and priestly selves, it is possible to illustrate how prophets of religious movements initially promote the shamanistic self in the construction of the sacred self, and how routinization or social organization of the movements may lead to the emergence of the priestly self. Shamanistic and priestly sacred selves are products of two types of symbolic interaction with the sacred other, each of which has particular or specific consequences for the integration of the symbolic self. The shamanistic sacred self provides protection at times of stress and anxiety, and the priestly sacred self provides protection for the continuation of social conventions. Prophets arise in situations of stress and anxiety and help restore the "disintegrated" symbolic self but are later replaced by priests or those who maintain the social order.

SHAMANISM AND THE DEIFICATION OF PSYCHOLOGY

As the sacred others who are used in shamanistic communication frequently represent or symbolize intrapsychic or psychological attributes of humankind, shamanism may be viewed as the deification or apotheosis of psychology. This fact concerning shamanism has led many early scholars to believe that it is a kind of magic or a primitive form of pseudoscience and to assert that it is an antisocial or amoral phenomenon. Émile Durkheim's well-known aphorism that religion is the deification or apotheosis of society would make shamanism, for the most part, into a nonreligious orientation because the basic premises of shamanism are not related to conventional morality or social processes but to the restoration of psychological and/or biological equilibrium.

Due to the close linkage between morality and Judeo-Christian religious orientations, it is difficult for many in the West to conceptualize religion as not having an intrinsic relationship with morality. Also, the concept of magic has been used in the Western tradition for a long time to designate pre-Christian "pagan" beliefs and practices as well as to identify what is believed to be satanic manifestations. But as students of Judeo-Christian religious orientations would attest, there have always been Judeo-Christian prophets, diviners, and healers (shamans) who have coexisted with the established Church priestly hierarchy, which is aligned with the political/social/moral order.

I suggest that shamanism can be analyzed as a kind of psychocultural, therapeutic system and as a kind of religious communication that has certain consequences for the maintenance of the integrity of the symbolic self and culture. When disintegration of the symbolic self and "cultural distortion" occur, shamanic communication with the sacred other takes on an added significance in society.

The shaman may have a clear understanding of the cultural categories of perception and cognition and may function as an effective diviner and healer because of such an understanding, but his or her legitimacy derives from the capacity to merge his or her symbolic self with the symbols of the sacred other. In other words, the shaman is the prototype for total or partial union between the symbols of the self and the symbols of supernatural beings and powers (the sacred other). Nonshamans differ in their capacity or inclination to attain such union, but in times of stress, sickness, and anxiety, and in the ritual context, direct contact and union with symbols of the sacred other are common.

The shaman and shamanistic orientation are universal; in many nonurban societies, the shaman and shamanism have significance beyond the healing and divining functions. Shamanism may operate with an elaborate system of symbolic classifications and may have an elaborate religious worldview, with beliefs in witchcraft and sorcery as components of this worldview. Although not constrained by social conventions, the shaman—as Kalweit (1988), Harner (1980), and others have noted—has a coherent religious worldview. Many urban societies have elaborate systems of shamanistic religious worldviews. *The Tibetan Book of the Dead* of Vajrayāna Buddhism, *Tao* of China, *Tantrism* of India, Islamic *Sufism*, and Jewish *Kabbala* are examples of shamanistic orientations that have focused on creating altered states of consciousness that enable the participants to transcend social categories and to merge their symbol-selves with the symbols of the sacred other.

Eliade (1964: 508–509) notes that shamanism and shamans have played an essential role in the defense of the psychic integrity of the community and that shamanism defends life, health, fertility, the world of 'light' against death, diseases, sterility, disaster, and the world of 'darkness.' The following quote illustrates the significance of shamanism as a system of knowledge about the supernatural reality and the shaman as one who is capable of undertaking ''mystical journeys'' to reveal the biopsychological mysteries of humanity and the universe.

It is as a further result of [the shaman's] ability to travel in the supernatural worlds and to see the superhuman beings (gods, demons, spirits of the dead, etc.) that the shaman has been able to contribute decisively to the knowledge of death. In all probability many features of ''funerary geography,'' as well as some themes of the mythology of death, are the result of the ecstatic experiences of shamans. The lands that the shaman sees and the personages that he meets during his ecstatic journeys in the beyond are minutely described by the shaman himself, during or after his trance. The unknown and terrifying world of death assumes form, is organized in accordance with particular patterns; finally it displays a structure and, in course of time, becomes familiar and acceptable. In turn, the supernatural inhabitants of the world of death become visible; they show a form, display a personality, even a biography. Little by little the world of the dead becomes knowable, and death itself is evaluated primarily as a rite of passage to a spiritual mode of being. In the last analysis, the accounts of the shamans' ecstatic journeys contribute to ''spiritualizing'' the world of the dead, at the same time that they enrich it with wondrous forms and figures. (Eliade 1964: 508–509)

La Barre, in his provocative book *The Ghost Dance: The Origins of Religion* (1970a), notes that ''the ancestor of god is the shaman himself, both historically and psychologically'' and argues that ''each religion is the ghost dance of a traumatized society." The shaman, in his view, is nonnormal and is preeminently suited to deal with nonnormal situations. Various other scholars such as Wallace (1966), Lewis (1971), and Bourguignon (1976) have theorized about the identity crisis of the shaman and about the crisis contexts in which shamanic performances occur.

In the various religious phenomena that we identify as divination, witchcraft, sorcery, healing, and ecstasy, the symbols of the self and the sacred other are united, and shamanistic religious practitioners often become identified with the symbols of the sacred other. As these activities are directly or indirectly connected with the health and sickness of an individual or group, the shamanistic self orientation may be delineated as ritual or religious therapy that occurs in contexts of individual and social stress; in initiation rituals as well as in other transition rituals and religious movements, we find people dramatizing their involvement with the symbols of the sacred other through contact or union with the sacred other.

We can see the operation of the shamanistic therapeutic orientation clearly in the context of religious movements. Religious movements arise when the health of individuals of a group is at stake. The messiah or religious leader of the group adopts the shamanistic orientation in forging a paradigm to bring the people back to health. The similarity between religious movements and rituals of various kinds has been noted by scholars such as Victor Turner (1969). In the liminal (middle) phase of rituals and in religious movements the priestly self is temporarily suspended. Religious movements in their initial beginning stages are seldom socially connected: The movements either reject the existing social forms or strive to change the social forms through a psychological understanding of human life, and as a result, the shamanistic self acquires great significance among the followers of religious movements.

The foregoing discussion of the difference between shamanistic and priestly selves may be summarized as follows: The shamanistic orientation gets greater emphasis in situations of crisis, be it an individual's health problems or transition or the group's cultural disintegration arising from famine, epidemic, or warfare. The priestly orientation gets greater emphasis in traditionally well-established social-political domains. The priest has traditional authority because people accept the tradition as "normal," and the symbols of the sacred other validate tradition through the priestly sacred self. The priest epitomizes the priestly sacred self, but even those who do not officiate as priests maintain the priestly sacred self to a lesser or greater degree because they uphold the tradition and the symbols of the sacred other, which validate the tradition, to a lesser or greater degree.

When social disruptions occur, the traditional authority structure crumbles along with questions about efficacy of the symbols of the sacred other. The symbols of the sacred other no longer represent the tradition, and the priestly sacred self has less or no significance. It is in such situations that prophets emerge, promoting the shamanistic sacred self through intense rituals that establish direct contact with new or modified symbols of the sacred other. People become ecstatic, experience a nonordinary reality, and it is not uncommon for them to engage in ritual self-immolation or ritual killings. Generally, the prophetic stage is followed by socially recognized new patterns of relationships, but occasionally prophets and/or their lieutenants perpetrate the shamanistic self and keep the followers from achieving symbolic sacred coherence through other means.

CONCLUSION

The anthropological approach to the study of religion, which focuses on the nature of the symbolic or cultural self, uses the insights and contributions of psychological, phenomenological, and hermeneutic/semiotic perspectives and analyzes how cultural/social integrity is maintained through the sacred or supernatural integration of the symbolic self. Also, such an approach to the study of religion explores the semantic significance of the emic categories of self and sacredness in terms of, and in relation to, intersubjective and syntactic intentionalities and motivations.

Until about 1900, a good deal of confusion in anthropological theorizing about religion occurred because of the prevalence of several fallacies: Scholars erroneously assumed that there was an intrinsic connection or link between religion and morality; scholars made a distinction between magic and religion for the wrong reasons, assuming that utopian-prophetic traditions such as Christianity and Islam were nonmagical, superior orientations as opposed to the beliefs and rituals of nonutopian and nonprophetic religious traditions as being magical and primitive; religion was erroneously conceptualized as an expression of inferior, underdeveloped rationality or as an irrational, prescientific mental manifestation of primitive people who had not climbed the ladder of progressive, rational civilization of the West; there was a misguided, nonscientific hope that sooner or later religion would be discarded and substituted by scientific knowledge of the world in humankind's progressive march toward greater enlightenment.

In general, there was a "positivistic muddle" in the effort to make science and scientific knowledge substitutes for religion and religious knowledge. There was little recognition of the fact that science and religion asked different kinds of questions and offered different premises, perspectives, and understandings of the world for achieving different kinds of results. Most scholars failed to realize that religious knowledge of the world was constituted for personal/cultural resolutions and meanings and to seek and attain (intersubjectively and syntactially) coherence of the world of human existence and experience. And most scholars disregarded the fact that the rationality that was used in the religious construction of the self and the world was the "mythological or expressive, non-Aristotelian rationality" of humankind and not an underdeveloped, analytic rationality of the "primitive" humankind.

There is still some confusion among scholars in not clearly conceptualizing differences between religion and science. In general, the confusion is more visible among scholars who pursue a psychological approach to the study of religion. Just as the nineteenth- and early twentieth-century evolutionary anthropologists (for example, Tylor, Frazer, and Freud) offered psychological theories of religion and foresaw the demise of religion, the contemporary American psychological anthropologist (who specializes in the study of religion) Anthony F. C. Wallace has predicted the eventual elimination of religion by science. And just as the social-symbolic anthropologists of the late nineteenth and early twentieth century (for example, Robertson-Smith, Durkheim, and Weber) theorized on the role of religion (in contrast to the role of science) in terms of personal and cultural integration and meaning, the contemporary American semiotic anthropologist (who specializes in the study of religion) Clifford Geertz has focused on the study of religious symbols that synthesize conceptions of order and experiences of disorder, functioning as paradigms for comprehending the world of human existence and human experience in a coherent and integrated manner. It is a fact worth noting that scholars who predict the death of religion may be believers or nonbelievers in supernatural beings, just as those who affirm the importance of religion may be either believers or nonbelievers in god. Both Wallace and Geertz have proclaimed their atheism but have arrived at different conclusions about the future of religion.

Perhaps it is also necessary to point out that predictions about the progressive elimination of religious "truths" in relation to progressive culmination of scientific "truths" reflect a kind of psychological reductionism (of religious beliefs and practices) against which Émile Durkheim initiated a successful debate at the turn of the century. The anthropological approach to the study of religion, which I have presented in this chapter, holds that religion or religious knowledge is a "fact" of culture that requires semiotic analysis, just as any other "fact" of culture. Although culture does not exist without the mental faculties of humankind, the study of culture cannot be reduced to psychology. Psychological reductionism of cultural phenomena is analogous to the view (if there is such a view) that the structure of language, which is a product of mental processes, should be studied by psychologists rather than by linguists. Had James Frazer recognized the nature and role of symbols in human life, he might not have presented (and labored over) his famous theory of magic as rooted in pseudo-scientific formulations of the laws of sympathy (hidden or mystical affinities between objects that look alike or objects that belonged to the same place), which, according to Frazer, characterized primitive, infantile, or neurotic thinking. Instead, Frazer might have theorized that the shaman or magician was adept at manipulating the symbolic representations of biopsychological processes to produce certain results—illness or healing. The shaman, Frazer might have concluded, dealt with the symbolic or cultural laws of disintegration and integration of the self rather than with the discovery of physical laws.

REFERENCES

Bourguignon, Erik. 1976. *Possession*. San Francisco: Chandler and Sharp.

Cohen, Abner. 1977. "Symbolic Action and the Structure of the Self." *Symbols and Sentiments: Cross-cultural Studies in Symbolism*. Ioan Lewis, editor. New York: Academic Press. 117–128.

Dow, James. 1986. "Universal Aspects of Symbolic Healing: A Theoretical Synthesis." *American Anthropologist* 88.

Durkheim, Émile. 1915. *The Elementary Forms of the Religious Life*. New York: George Allen and Unwin, Ltd.

Eliade, Mircea. 1964. *Shamanism: Archaic Techniques of Ecstasy*. Princeton: Princeton University Press.

Geertz, Clifford. 1973. *The Interpretation of Cultures*. New York: Basic Books.

Harner, Michael J., editor. 1973. *Hallucinogens and Shamanism*. New York: Oxford University Press.

Harner, Michael J. 1980. *The Way of the Shaman*. New York: Harper and Row.

Kalweit, Holger. 1988. *Dreamtime and Inner Space: The World of the Shaman*. Boston: Shambhala.

La Barre, Weston. 1970a. *The Ghost Dance: The Origins of Religion*. Garden City, NY: Doubleday.

La Barre, Weston. 1970b. *The Peyote Cult*. New York: Schocken Books.

Lewis, I. M. 1971. *Ecstatic Religion: An Anthropological Study of Spirit Possession and Shamanism*. London: Penguin Books.

Marsella, A. J., G. De Vos; and F. Hsu, editors. 1985. *Culture and Self: Asian and Western Perspectives*. New York: Tavistock Publications.

Moerman, Daniel E. 1979. "Anthropology of Symbolic Healing." *Current Anthropology* 20 (1): 59–80.

Pandian, Jacob. 1985. *Anthropology and the Western Tradition: Toward an Authentic Anthropology*. Prospect Heights: Waveland Press.

Pandian, Jacob. 1991. *Culture, Religion, and the Sacred Self: A Critical Introduction to the Anthropological Study of Religion*. Englewood Cliffs, NJ: Prentice-Hall.

Perinbanayagam, R. S. 1985. *Signifying Acts: Structure and Meaning in Everyday Life*. Carbondale: Southern Illinois University Press.

Reichel-Dolmatoff, G. 1975. *The Shaman and the Jaguar: A Study of Narcotic Drugs among the Indians of Columbia*. Philadelphia: Temple University Press.

Ritzer, George. 1983. *Contemporary Sociological Theory*. New York: Alfred A. Knopf.

Singer, Milton. 1980. "Signs of the Self: An Exploration in Semiotic Anthropology." *American Anthropologist* 82: 485–507.

Spiro, Melford. 1967. *Burmese Supernaturalism*. Englewood Cliffs, NJ: Prentice-Hall.

Turner, Victor W. 1968. "Religious Specialists: Anthropological Study." *International Encyclopedia of the Social Sciences* 13.

Turner, Victor W. 1969. *The Ritual Process: Structure and Anti-Structure*. Chicago: Aldine Publishing Co.

Tylor, Edward B. 1873. *Primitive Culture*. 2 vols. London: John Murray.

Wallace, Anthony F. C. 1966. *Religion: An Anthropological View*. New York: Random House.

SELECT TOPICAL BIBLIOGRAPHY

INTRODUCTORY TEXTBOOKS

Child, Alice B., and Irvin L. Child. 1993. *Religion and Magic in the Life of Traditional Peoples*. Englewood Cliffs, NJ: Prentice Hall.

de Waal Malefijt, Annemarie. 1968. *Religion and Culture: An Introduction to Anthropology of Religion*. New York: Macmillan.

Firth, Raymond. 1995. *Religion: A Humanist Interpretation*. New York: Routledge.

Gill, Sam D. 1982. *Beyond the Primitive: The Religion of Nonliterate Peoples*. Englewood Cliffs, NJ: Prentice-Hall.

Klass, Morton. 1995. *Ordered Universes: Approaches to the Anthropology of Religion*. Boulder, CO: Westview Press.

Lowie, Robert H. 1924. *Primitive Religion*. New York: Liveright.

Norbeck, Edward. 1961. *Religion in Primitive Society*. New York: Harper.

Norbeck, Edward. 1974. *Religion in Human Life: Anthropological Views*. New York: Holt, Rinehart and Winston.

Pandian, Jacob. 1991. *Culture, Religion, and the Sacred Self: A Critical Introduction to the Anthropological Study of Religion*. Englewood Cliffs, NJ: Prentice Hall.

Radian, Paul. 1937. *Primitive Religion: Its Nature and Origin*. New York: Viking.

Wallace, Anthony F. C. 1966. *Religion: An Anthropological View*. New York: Random House.

READERS IN ANTHROPOLOGY OF RELIGION

Lehmann, Arthur C., and James E. Myers, editors. 1985. *Magic, Witchcraft, and Religion: An Anthropological Study of the Supernatural*. Palo Alto: Mayfield.

Lehmann, Arthur C., and James E. Myers, editors. 1993. *Magic, Witchcraft, and Reli-*

gion: An Anthropological Approach to the Supernatural. 3rd edition. Mountain View: Mayfield.

Leslie, Charles M., editor. 1960. *Anthropology and Folk Religion.* New York: Vintage Books.

Lessa, William A., and Evon Z. Vogt. 1979. *Reader in Comparative Religion: An Anthropological Approach.* 4th edition. New York: Harper and Row.

Middleton, John J., editor. 1967a. *Magic, Witchcraft and Curing.* New York: The Natural History Press.

Middleton, John J., editor. 1967b. *Gods and Rituals: Readings in Religious Beliefs and Practices.* New York: Natural History Press.

Middleton, John J., editor. 1967c. *Myth and Cosmos: Readings in Mythology and Symbolism.* New York: Natural History Press.

REFERENCE WORKS

Eliade, Mircea, general editor. 1987. *The Encyclopedia of Religion.* New York: Free Press/Macmillan.

Honingmann, John J., editor. 1973. *Handbook of Social and Cultural Anthropology.* Chicago: Rand McNally.

Ingold, Tim. 1994. *Companion Encyclopedia of Anthropology: Humanity, Culture, and Social Life.* London: Routledge Reference.

Marty, Martin E., and R. Scott Appleby, editors. 1991. *Fundamentalisms Observed.* Chicago: University of Chicago Press.

Smith, Jonathan Z., and William Scott Green, editors. 1995. *The HarperCollins Dictionary of Religion.* San Francisco: HarperCollins.

Swatos, William H., Jr., editor. 1997. *Religion and the Social Sciences: An Encyclopedia.* New York: Garland.

Turner, Harold W. 1977–1992. *Bibliography of New Religious Movements in Primal Societies.* 6 vols. Boston: G. K. Hall.

Zaretsky, Irving I., and Cynthia Shambaugh, editors. 1978. *Spirit Possession and Spirit Mediumship in Africa and Afro-America: An Annotated Bibliography.* New York: Garland.

THEORETICAL CONTRIBUTIONS

Asad, Talal. 1993. *Genealogies of Religion: Discipline and Reasons of Power in Christianity and Islam.* Baltimore: The Johns Hopkins University Press.

Banton, Michael, editor. 1966. *Anthropological Approaches to the Study of Religion.* ASA # 3. London: Tavistock.

Bateson, Gregory, and Mary Catherine Bateson. 1987. *Angels Fear: Toward an Epistemology of the Sacred.* New York: Macmillan.

Boyer, Pascal. 1994. *The Naturalness of Religious Ideas: A Cognitive Theory of Religion.* Berkeley: University of California Press.

Boyer, Pascal, editor. 1993. *Cognitive Aspects of Religious Symbolism.* New York: Cambridge University Press.

Clarke, Peter B., and Peter Byrne. 1993. *Religion Defined and Explained.* New York: St Martin's Press.

Durkheim, Emile. 1912/1995. *The Elementary Forms of Religious Life*. A New Trans-
    lation by Karen E. Fields. New York: Free Press.
Eliade, Mircea. 1959. *The Sacred and the Profane: The Nature of Religion*. New York:
    Harcourt, Brace.
Evans-Pritchard, E. E. 1965. *Theories of Primitive Religion*. Oxford: Clarendon Press.
Guthrie, Stewart Elliott. 1993. *Faces in the Clouds: A New Theory of Religion*. New
    York: Oxford University Press.
Lawson, E. Thomas, and Robert M. McCauley. 1990. *Rethinking Religion: Connecting
    Cognition and Culture*. New York: Cambridge University Press.
Lett, James. 1987. *The Human Enterprise: A Critical Introduction to Anthropological
    Theory*. Boulder, CO: Westview Press.
Morris, Brian. 1987. *Anthropological Studies of Religion: An Introductory Text*. New
    York: Cambridge University Press.
Pals, Daniel L. 1996. *Seven Theories of Religion*. New York: Oxford University Press.
Saler, Benson. 1993. *Conceptualizing Religion: Immanent Anthropologists, Transcendent
    Natives, and Unbound Categories*. Leiden: E. J. Brill.
Smith, Jonathan Z. 1982. *Imagining Religion: From Babylon to Jonestown*. Chicago:
    University of Chicago Press.
Spiro, Melford E. 1994. *Culture and Human Nature*. New Edition edited by Benjamin
    Killborne and L. L. Langness. New Brunswick, NJ: Transaction Publishers.
Taylor, Mark Kline. 1986. *Beyond Explanation: Religious Dimensions in Cultural An-
    thropology*. Macon, GA: Mercer University Press.
Tylor, Edward B. 1873. *Primitive Culture*. 2 vols. London: John Murray
Weber, Max. 1963. *The Sociology of Religion*. Boston: Beacon Press.
Wilson, Bryan R., editor. 1970. *Rationality*. Oxford: Blackwell.

RITUAL

Alexander, Bobby C. 1991. *Victor Turner Revisited: Ritual and Social Change*. Atlanta:
    Scholars Press.
Bell, Catherine. 1992. *Ritual Theory, Ritual Practice*. New York: Oxford.
Driver, Tom. 1991. *The Magic of Ritual: Our Need for Liberating Rites That Transform
    Our Lives and Our Communities*. San Francisco: Harper.
Grimes, Ronald L. 1990. *Ritual Criticism: Case Studies in Its Practice, Essays on Its
    Theory*. Columbia: University of South Carolina Press.
Kertzer, David. 1988. *Ritual, Politics, and Power*. New Haven: Yale University Press.
Turner, Victor W. 1969. *The Ritual Process: Structure and Anti-Structure*. Chicago:
    Aldine Publishers.

MAGIC AND WITCHCRAFT

Brown, Michael Fobes. 1985. *Tsewa's Gift: Magic and Meaning in an Amazonian So-
    ciety*. Washington, D.C.: Smithsonian Institution Press.
Evans-Pritchard, E. E. 1937. *Witchcraft, Oracles and Magic among the Azande*. Oxford:
    Clarendon Press.
Frazer, Sir James. 1890/1935. *The Golden Bough: A Study of Magic and Religion*. New
    York: Macmillan.

Horton, Robin. 1993. *Patterns of Thought in Africa and the West*. New York: Cambridge University Press.
Malinowski, Bronislaw. 1935. *Coral Gardens and Their Magic*. 2 vols. New York: American Book Company.
Malinowski, Bronislaw. 1954. *Magic, Science and Religion and Other Essays*. Garden City, NY: Doubleday/Anchor.
Mauss, Marcel. 1972. *A General Theory of Magic*. Boston: Routledge and Kegan Paul.

SHAMANISM

Balzer, Marjorie M. 1996. "Flights of the Sacred: Symbolism and Theory in Siberian Shamanism." *American Anthropologist* 98 (2): 305–318.
Eliade, Mircea. 1964. *Shamanism: Archaic Techniques of Ecstasy*. Princeton: Princeton University Press.
Grim, John. 1983. *The Shaman: Patterns of Siberian and Ojibway Healing*. Norman: University of Oklahoma Press.
Harner, Michael J. 1980. *The Way of the Shaman*. San Francisco: Harper.
Rapinsky-Naxon, Michael. 1993. *The Nature of Shamanism: Substance and Function of a Religious Metaphor*. Albany: State University of New York Press.

TRANCE AND POSSESSION STATES

Boddy, Janice. 1994. "Spirit Possession Revisited: Beyond Instrumentality." *Annual Review of Anthropology* 23: 407–434.
Bourguignon, Erika. 1976. *Possession*. San Francisco: Chandler and Sharp.
Crapanzano, Vincent, and Vivian Garrison, editors. 1977. *Case Studies in Spirit Possession*. New York: John Wiley and Sons.
Furst, Peter. 1976. *Hallucinations and Culture*. San Francisco: Chandler and Sharp.
Goodman, Felicitas D. 1986. *Ecstasy, Ritual, and Alternate Reality: Religion in a Pluralistic World*. Bloomington, IN: Indiana University Press.
Laughlin, Charles D.; John McManus; and Eugene G. d'Aquili. 1993. *Brain, Symbol and Experience: Toward a Neurophenomenology of Human Consciousness*. New York: Columbia University Press.

LITTLE AND GREAT TRADITIONS

Eickelman, Dale F. 1989. *The Middle East: An Anthropological Approach*. Englewood Cliffs, NJ: Prentice-Hall.
Esposito, John. 1989. *Islam: The Straight Path*. New York: Oxford.
Geertz, Clifford. 1971. *Islam Observed: Religious Development in Morocco and Indonesia*. Chicago: University of Chicago Press.
Morinis, Alan, editor. 1992. *Sacred Journeys: the Anthropology of Pilgrimage*. Westport, CT: Greenwood Press.
Redfield, Robert. 1953. *The Primitive World and Its Transformations*. Chicago: University of Chicago Press.
Singer, Milton B. 1972. *When a Great Tradition Modernizes: An Anthropological Approach to Indian Civilization*. New York: Praeger.

Southwold, Martin. 1982. ''True Buddhism and Village Buddhism in Sri Lanka'' *Religious Organization and Religious Experience*. J. Davis, editor. New York: Academic Press.

Spiro, Melford E. 1978. *Burmese Supernaturalism*. Expanded edition. Philadelphia: Institute for the Study of Human Issues.

INDEX

About the Editor
and Contributors

BOBBY C. ALEXANDER is Lecturer in the School of Social Sciences at the University of Texas at Dallas and previously taught at Southern Methodist University. His Ph.D. in religion is from Columbia University (1985). Alexander is author of *Victor Turner Revisited: Ritual as Social Change* (1991) and *Televangelism Reconsidered: Ritual in the Search for Human Community* (1994).

JIM BIRCKHEAD teaches anthropology at Charles Sturt University, Albury, New South Wales, and is a member of the Johnstone Center of Parks, Recreation and Heritage, through which he conducts research and consults on indigenous land and cultural issues in Australia, Papua New Guinea, and Nepal. He earned his Ph.D. in anthropology from the University of Alberta in 1976.

MICHAEL F. BROWN is Professor of Anthropology at Williams College in Williamstown, Massachusetts. He earned his A.B. in anthropology from Princeton (1972) and his Ph.D. in anthropology from the University of Michigan (1981). Among his publications are *Tsewa's Gift: Magic and Meaning in an Amazonian Society* (1986); *War of Shadows: The Struggle for Utopia in the Peruvian Amazon* (1991); and *The Channeling Zone: American Spirituality in an Anxious Age* (1997).

PETER J. CLAUS teaches anthropology at California State University, Hayward. He earned his Ph.D. from Duke University in 1970. He is co-editor/author of *Folktales of India* (1987), *Indian Oral Epics* (1989), *Folkloristics and Indian*

Folklore (1991) and is currently working on *South Asian Folklore: An Encyclopedia* (forthcoming).

MADELINE DUNTLEY is Assistant Professor of Religious Studies at College of the Wooster, Wooster, Ohio, where she teaches courses in American religions and ritual studies. She received her B.A. from the University of Washington and her Ph.D. in religious studies from the University of Pittsburgh (1990). A charter editor of the *Journal of Ritual Studies* and recent Young Scholars in American Religion fellowship recipient, Duntley has published several articles on religion and ritual in American culture. Having completed her first book, *Rites of Conscience* (in press), she is currently engaged in research for a monograph on Asian-American Christians in inner-city Seattle, Washington.

STEPHEN D. GLAZIER is Professor of Anthropology and Graduate Faculty Fellow at the University of Nebraska. He is author of *Marchin' the Pilgrims Home: Leadership and Decision-Making in an Afro-Caribbean Faith* (Greenwood, 1983; Sheffield, 1991) and editor of *Caribbean Ethnicity Revisited* (1985) and *Perspectives on Pentecostalism: Case Studies from the Caribbean and Latin America* (1980). He studied anthropology of religion at Princeton University and at the University of Connecticut, from which he received his Ph.D. in 1981.

JOHN A. GRIM is Associate Professor in the History of Religions at Bucknell University. He is author of *The Shaman: Patterns of Siberian and Ojibway Healing* (1983) and editor, with Mary Evelyn Tucker, of *Worldviews and Ecology* (1994). He continues fieldwork among the Apsaaloke Crow peoples of Montana.

MATHIAS GUENTHER is Professor of Anthropology at Wilfred Laurier University in Waterloo, Ontario. He earned his Ph.D. in anthropology from the University of Toronto in 1973. His major area of interest is in the religious and expressive culture of the Bushmen of southern Africa.

STEWART ELLIOTT GUTHRIE is Professor of Anthropology at Fordham University's Lincoln Center Campus. He earned his Ph.D. in anthropology from Yale University in 1980. Guthrie is author of *Faces in the Clouds: A New Theory of Religion* (1993).

CHARLES D. LAUGHLIN is Professor of Anthropology at Carleton University, Ottawa, Canada. He is co-author of *Biogenetic Structuralism* (1974), *The Spectrum of Ritual* (1979), *Extinction and Survival in Human Populations* (1976), *Science as Cognitive Process* (1984), and *Brain, Symbol and Experience* (1990). Laughlin is a former editor of *Anthropology of Consciousness* and has conducted fieldwork among the So of northeastern Uganda, Tibetan lamas, and the Navaho of New Mexico.

JAMES LETT is Associate Professor and Chair of Anthropology at Indian River Community College. He is the author of *The Human Enterprise: A Critical Introduction to Anthropological Theory* (1987). Lett earned his Ph.D. in anthropology from the University of Florida in 1983.

TODD T. LEWIS is Associate Professor of Religious Studies at the College of the Holy Cross, Worcester, Massachusetts. His publications include the co-authored *The Himalayas: A Syllabus of the Region's History, Anthropology, and Religion* (1995) and the forthcoming *Mahayana Buddhist Texts from Nepal: Narratives and Rituals of Newar Buddhism.* Lewis earned his Ph.D. in religion from Columbia University in 1984.

CYNTHIA KEPPLEY MAHMOOD is Associate Professor of Anthropology at the University of Maine, Orono. She earned her Ph.D. in anthropology from Tulane in 1986, and is author of *Frisian and Free: A Study of an Ethnic Minority of the Netherlands* (1989) and *Fighting for Faith and Nation: Dialogues with Sikh Militants* (1996). She is editor of the series ''Ethnography of Political Violence'' for the University of Pennsylvania Press.

MARY I. O'CONNOR is a research anthropologist at the Community and Organizational Research Institute of the University of California, Santa Barbara. She is author of *Descendants of Totoliquoqui: Ethnicity and Economics in the Mayo Valley* (1989). O'Connor earned her Ph.D. in anthropology from UCSB in 1980.

JACOB PANDIAN is Professor and Chair of Anthropology at California State University, Fullerton. He is the author of *Culture, Religion, and the Sacred Self: A Critical Introduction to the Anthropological Study of Religion* (1991). Pandian earned his Ph.D. in anthropology from Rice University in 1972.

GREGORY STARRETT is Assistant Professor of Anthropology at the University of North Carolina at Charlotte. He earned his Ph.D. in anthropology from Stanford University in 1992.

JOAN B. TOWNSEND is Professor of Anthropology at the University of Manitoba. She has conducted research with Tanaina Athapskans in Alaska; Nepalese shamans; spiritualists; and people involved in new religious movements, including core and neo-shamanism. Her publications have appeared in numerous professional journals and edited volumes.

MARY EVELYN TUCKER teaches Asian religions at Bucknell University. She earned her Ph.D. in religion at Columbia University and is author of *Moral and Spiritual Cultivation in Japanese Neo-Confucianism* (1989).

MELINDA BOLLAR WAGNER is Professor of Anthropology at Radford University in Radford, Virginia. She is author of *God's Schools: Choice and Compromise in American Society* (1990) and *Metaphysics in Midwest America* (1983). Wagner earned her Ph.D. in anthropology from the University of Michigan in 1977.

MICHAEL WINKELMAN teaches at Arizona State University. A former president of the Society for the Anthropology of Consciousness, he earned his Ph.D. in anthropology from the University of California-Irvine (1984). Winkelman is author of *Shamans, Priests and Witches: A Cross-Cultural Study of Magico-Religious Practitioners* (1992).

ISBN 0-313-28351-6

90000>

EAN

9 780313 283512

HARDCOVER BAR CODE